Joachim Berendt has won many honours in his career as a writer on jazz and as publisher, musical director and producer of jazz shows, recordings, film and television programmes.

JOACHIM E. BERENDT

The Jazz Book

from New Orleans to Jazz Rock and Beyond

Translated by H. and B. Bredigkeit
with Dan Morgenstern

PALADIN
GRAFTON BOOKS
A Division of the Collins Publishing Group

LONDON GLASGOW
TORONTO SYDNEY AUCKLAND

Paladin
Grafton Books
A Division of the Collins Publishing Group
8 Grafton Street, London W1X 3LA

This revised edition published in Paladin Books 1984
Reprinted 1986, 1989

First published in Great Britain by
Granada Publishing 1983

ISBN 0-586-08474-6

Printed and bound in Great Britain by
Collins, Glasgow

Set in Baskerville

Table of Contents

Musical Examples and Tables

You've got to love to be able to play.

LOUIS ARMSTRONG

The idea is to extend the tradition.

ANTHONY DAVIS

There is something in music which is
more than melody and more than
harmony: music.

GIUSEPPE VERDI

Preface

It's been like this for twenty-three years now: what the publishers want is a revised edition of *The Jazz Book*, but what we end up with is basically a new book. We have seen with each new edition that it is not enough only to add the names of those who have entered the scene. Our understanding of past styles – of what is called roots and tradition, which today have become more important than ever – has deepened and changed. Above all, the point is not only to make an updated book, it is just as important to come up with a better book – or at least to attempt to do so.

Ever since 1953, when the first edition of *The Jazz Book* was published, there have been nine revised editions – in Europe, the United States, Japan, and Latin America. In the process, the size of the book has increased by about fifty per cent.

That is why I believe it is no exaggeration to say that almost thirty years of jazz history have left their mark on this book. Each edition was written in direct contact with the dominant styles of its time – and I think that this contact can still be felt today. In the chapters about bebop of the forties, cool jazz of the fifties, or free jazz of the sixties, you still can tell what was written in the particular decade under the impact of the newly developed style. On the other hand, wherever this impact seemed to have become unreflected, where more distance was necessary, I have rewritten passages and added new ones.

Some readers have asked me to make clear what has been added to this edition. Completely new are the following chapters and passages: 1970, 1980, Outlook, John McLaughlin, percussion instruments; almost totally rewritten are the chapters on the keyboards, the violin, and on miscellaneous instruments; finally, between one third and one half of all the instrumental chapters, as well as the sections on vocalists, big bands, and combos, are new.

Beyond that, there are changes, revisions, expansions, or reductions in each section and every chapter – in fact, on almost every page. Only 45 pages of the 1975 edition have remained entirely untouched.

II

Jazz, as Eric Dolphy put it, is 'human music'. Duke Ellington, too, often talked about 'humanity' when dealing with black music. And JoAnne Brackeen has said that jazz means 'making humanity spiritual'. I would be happy if some of that could be sensed through the pages of this book. The portraits in the section 'The Musicians of Jazz' were written mainly with this goal in mind: one outstanding musician for each style or each decade respectively (even though this principle could not be followed with total academic consistency). I have deliberately kept these musicians' portraits 'simple'. Some readers have felt this to be in contrast to the other sections of the book. This contrast is no accident – the portraits are also meant to be a possible point of entry into the book and its topic. The knowledgeable reader should consider that this book also has an introductory function; its earlier editions have opened the way to jazz – and thus also to more specialized and detailed books on jazz – for many people. If you find these chapters too 'simple' for your interests, please skip them. By the way, true humanity *is* 'simple', as much as this may seem contradicted by the alienated members of our modern industrialized societies.

Many readers of our earlier editions have found that the sections and chapters of this book do not necessarily have to be read in the order of their appearance. One could start with 'The Elements of Jazz'; or at the very end with the definition of jazz. If you are fond of jazz singing, why not start with the chapters dealing with the jazz vocalists; if you play an instrument, you could begin by reading the chapter about that one. If you encounter unexplained technical terms while reading 'across the chapters', their explanation can be found with the help of the index.

Very few record references are included in the body of the text, because there is too much fluctuation on the record market. That's why there is a discography at the end, compiled according to the following principle: Every musician of some importance mentioned in the book is represented with at least one record, while the outstanding jazz players appear with their most important albums, insofar as these are available.

Further details about the guiding principles of this book are included in the 'Postscript', which is recommended for those who really want to *work* with it (as well as for critics and jazz writers). That is also where I extend my gratitude to those who have helped me: critics, translators, colleagues – and, above all, the musicians.

III

I cannot claim to have avoided all errors. Nor can I expect that my personal interpretations will be accepted by everyone. I am not of the opinion that a music critic may be so presumptuous as to lay down 'final' judgements. But this book, with its numerous editions, has served so many readers, that I felt it a challenge and a duty to carry on the work, even though I said after the last edition, 'Never again!'

J.E.B.

Baden-Baden, January 1982

THE STYLES OF JAZZ

The Styles of Jazz

Jazz has always been the concern of a minority – always. Even in the age of Swing, the thirties, the jazz of creative black musicians was – except for very few recordings – recognized by only a few. Still, taking an active interest in jazz means working for a majority, because the popular music of our times feeds on jazz: All the music we hear in TV series and on top-forty radio, in hotel lobbies and on elevators, in commercials and in movies; all the music to which we dance, from Charleston to rock, funk and disco; all those sounds that daily engulf us – all that music comes from jazz (because beat came to Western music through jazz).

Taking an active interest in jazz means improving the quality of the 'sounds around us' – the level of musical quality, which implies, if there is any justification in talking about musical quality, the spiritual, intellectual, human quality – the level of our consciousness. In these times, when musical sounds accompany the takeoff of a plane as well as a detergent sales pitch, the 'sounds around us' directly influence our way of life, the quality of our lives. That is why we can say that taking an active interest in jazz means carrying some of the power, warmth, and intensity of jazz into our lives.

Because of this, there is a direct and concretely demonstrable connection between the different kinds, forms, and styles of jazz on the one hand and the periods and spaces of time of their creation on the other hand.

The most impressive thing about jazz – aside from its musical value – is in my opinion its stylistic development. The evolution of jazz shows the continuity, logic, unity, and inner necessity which characterize all true art. This development constitutes a whole – and those who single out one phase and view it as either uniquely valid or as an aberration, destroy this wholeness of conception. They distort that unity of large-scale evolution without which one can speak of fashions, but not of styles. It is my conviction that the styles of jazz are genuine, and reflect their own particular times in the same sense that classicism, baroque, romanticism, and impressionism reflect their respective periods in European concert music.

Let me suggest one way of getting an impression of the wealth and scope of the different jazz styles: After reading about the early styles, ragtime and New Orleans, skip a few chapters and jump into the one on free jazz, listening to some of the characteristic records as well (which can easily be found with the help of the discography at the end of the book)! What other art form has developed such contrasting, and yet clearly interrelated styles within a span of only fifty years?

It is important to be aware of the flowing, streamlike character of jazz history. It certainly is no coincidence that the word 'stream' has been used again and again by jazz critics and musicians in connection with different jazz styles – interestingly enough, as 'mainstream' first for Swing jazz, later for the main tendency of today's jazz, or as in 'third stream'. There is one mighty stream that flows from New Orleans right up to our contemporary music. Even breaks or revolutions in this history, such as the emergence of bebop or, later, free jazz, appear in retrospect as organic or even inevitable developments. The stream may flow over cataracts or form eddies or rapids from time to time – but it continues to flow on as ever the same stream.

Many great jazz musicians have felt the connection between their playing styles and the times in which they live. The untroubled joy of Dixieland corresponds to the days just prior to World War I. The restlessness of the 'roaring twenties' comes to life in Chicago style. Swing embodies the massive standardization of life before World War II; perhaps, to quote Marshall Stearns, Swing 'was the answer to the American – and very human – love of bigness.' Bebop captures the nervous restlessness of the forties. Cool jazz seems to reflect the resignation of men who live well, yet know that H-bombs are being stockpiled. Hard bop is full of protest, soon turned into conformity by the fashion for funk and soul music. This protest gains an uncompromising, often angry urgency in free jazz. After this, in the jazz of the seventies, there is a new phase of consolidation – not in the sense of resignation, but rather in the sense of painfully acquired wisdom, of wanting to accomplish the possible short of chaos and self-destruction. What has been said in such a generalized and simplified way here is even more applicable to the many different styles of individual musicians and bands.

Many jazz musicians have viewed attempts at reconstructing past jazz styles with scepticism. They know that historicism runs counter to the nature of jazz. Jazz stands and falls on being alive, and whatever lives, changes. When Count Basie's music become a world-wide success in the fifties, Lester Young, who had been one of the leading soloists of the old Basie band, was asked to participate in a recording with his old teammates for the purpose of reconstructing the Basie style of the thirties. 'I can't do it,' Lester said. 'I don't play that way any more. I play different; I live different. This is later. That was then. We change, move on.' Obviously, this is also true about contemporary reconstructions of historical jazz styles.

Around 1890: Ragtime

Jazz originated in New Orleans: a truism, with all that is true and false about such statements. It is true that New Orleans was the most important city in the genesis of jazz. It is false that it was the only one. Jazz – the music of a continent, a century, a civilization – was too much in the air to be reducible to the patented product of a single city. Similar ways of playing evolved in Memphis and St Louis, in Dallas and Kansas City, in other cities of the South and Midwest. And this, too, is the hallmark of a style: different people in different places making the same – or similar – artistic discoveries independently of each other.

It has become customary to speak of New Orleans style as the first style in jazz. But before New Orleans style developed, there was ragtime. Its capital was not New Orleans but Sedalia, Missouri, where Scott Joplin had settled. Joplin, born in Texas in 1868, was the leading ragtime composer and pianist – and thus we have made the decisive point about ragtime: It was composed, primarily pianistic music. Since it was composed, it lacks one essential characteristic of jazz – improvisation. Yet ragtime swings – at least in a rudimentary sense – and so it is considered part of jazz. And the practice of not only interpreting rags but also using them as themes for jazz improvisations began quite early.

Ragtime was written in the tradition of nineteenth-century piano music. It may adhere to the trio form of the classic minuet, or consist of several musical strophes in succession, connected in the fashion of a Strauss waltz. Pianistically, too, ragtime reflects the nineteenth century. Everything relevant to that time can be found in it – from Chopin and, most of all, Liszt, to marches and polkas – all recast in the black rhythmic conception and dynamic way of playing. And that was also how it was perceived – ragtime is, as the name suggests, ragged time.

Ragtime found an especially fertile field in the camps of the migrant labourers engaged in building railroads. Ragtime was heard everywhere – in Sedalia and Kansas City, in St Louis and Texas, Joplin's home state. The composers of rags hammered their pieces into player-piano rolls, which were distributed by the thousands.

That was way before the time of the phonograph and, for a long period, little was known about all this. Only in the fifties – sometimes quite accidentally in places like antique stores and junk shops – were substantial numbers of the old piano rolls rediscovered and transferred to records.

Aside from Joplin, there were many other ragtime pianists: Tom Turpin, a St Louis bar owner; James Scott, a theatre organist in Kansas City; Charles L. Johnson, Louis Chauvin, and Eubie Blake. Seventy years later, Blake – aged ninety – made a spectacular comeback at the great 1973 Newport–New York Festival; he even had his own Broadway show in the late seventies. Blake has made thousands of young people 'rag-conscious' once again.

There were several whites among the great rag pianists around the turn of the century, and it is significant that even experts were not able to detect differences in playing style between blacks and whites. Ragtime, as Orrin Keepnews once put it, is 'on the cool side'.

Scott Joplin was a master of melodic invention. He was amazingly productive, and his more than six hundred rags include such melodies as 'Maple Leaf Rag' and 'The Entertainer' (which became immensely popular in 1973, almost sixty years after Joplin's death, through the motion picture *The Sting*). In Joplin – as in ragtime per se – the old European tradition merged with the black rhythmic feeling. Ragtime, more than any other form of jazz, may be described as 'white music – played black'. How much Joplin was at home in the European tradition is apparent not only in the construction of his rags, but also in the fact that he composed two operas.

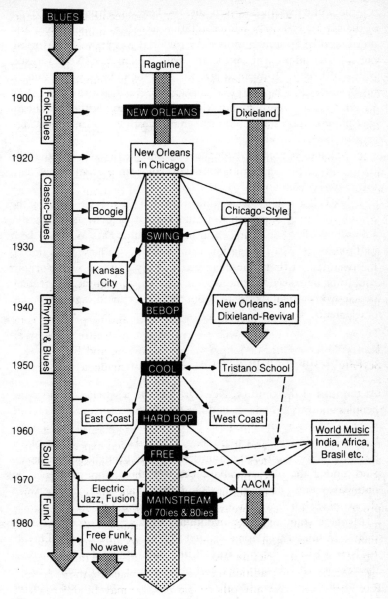

Table 1: The development of jazz (with the blues as backbone)

Among the first musicians to liberate themselves from the strictures of the composer-imposed interpretation of rags and take a freer and more jazzlike approach to melodic material was Jelly Roll Morton, one of the important musicians with whom the New Orleans tradition begins. 'I invented jazz in 1902,' he once claimed, and on his business card he described himself as 'creator of ragtime'. Both statements are hyperbole, but Morton is important as the first known jazz pianist who improvised on themes, mostly his own, which were rags or derived from ragtime music.

In Morton we recognize for the first time the decisive fact that the personality of the performing musician is more important in jazz than the material contributed by the composer.

Jelly Roll carried the ragtime tradition to the Chicago of the roaring twenties, and even to California. Other pianists – James P. Johnson, Willie 'The Lion' Smith, and young Fats Waller – kept ragtime, or at least the ragtime tradition, alive in New York during the twenties. At that time there was scarcely a pianist whose origins could not be traced, in one way or another, to ragtime. Even some boogie-woogie pianists (more about them later) used ragtime themes or elements.

Turn of the Century: New Orleans

At the turn of the century, New Orleans was a witches' cauldron of peoples and races. The city had been under Spanish and French rule prior to the Louisiana Purchase. Frenchmen and Spaniards, followed by Englishmen and Italians, and lastly joined by Germans and Slavs, faced the descendants of the countless Africans brought here as slaves. And among the black population as well there were differences in nationality and culture no less significant than those, say, between the whites from England and the whites from Spain.

All these voluntary and involuntary immigrants loved first of all their own music: what they wanted to keep alive as sounds of home. In New Orleans, people sang British folk songs, danced Spanish dances, played French dance and ballet music, and marched to the strains of brass bands based on Prussian or French models. In the many churches could be heard the hymns and chorales of Puritans and Catholics, Baptists and Methodists – and mingled with all these sounds were the 'shouts' of the black street vendors, and the black dances and rhythms. Deep into the eighteen eighties, blacks congregated periodically in Congo Square to perform voodoo rites – thus preserving a cult with origins in ancient, half-forgotten African traditions. Recent converts to Christianity, they celebrated the new god in song and dance much as they had honoured the deities of their native land. Old New Orleans must have been an incredibly musical city. We know of some thirty orchestras from the first decade of this century. To appreciate what that means, you have to know that the Delta City had little more than 200,000 inhabitants then. And in a city of that size, there were thirty orchestras, playing a vital, new kind of music.

All this created an atmosphere which made the New Orleans of those days a symbol of strange, exotic romanticism for travellers from all parts of the earth. It is certainly a myth that this city in the Mississippi delta was the sole birthplace of jazz, but New Orleans was indeed a point where many important aspects of the music first crystallized. New Orleans was a watershed – for the music of the countryside, such as the work songs of the black plantation labourers; for the spirituals which were sung during the religious services for which they gathered under open skies; and for the old 'primitive' blues-folk songs. All these things merged in the earliest forms of jazz.

W. C. Handy, the composer of blues, related that the music played in Memphis around 1905 was not very different from that of New Orleans. 'But we didn't discover until 1917 that New Orleans had such music too,' Handy said. 'Every circus band played this way.' The entire Mississippi delta was full of the new sounds – all rising independent of each other. 'The River and the City were equally important to jazz.'

New Orleans, in spite of this, held a special place. Well into the thirties more than half of the important jazz musicians came from there. Four reasons may have been decisive:

First, the old French–Spanish urban culture of the Delta City.

Second, the tensions and challenges arising from the fact that, as we shall see, two decidedly different black populations confronted each other here.

Third, the intense musical life of the city, in terms of European 'serious' and popular music, with which the blacks constantly came in touch.

And finally, the fact that all these varied elements came together in Storyville, the city's red-light district, without prejudice or class consciousness.

The two black populations of New Orleans were the Creoles and the 'American Negroes.' However, obviously, the Creoles – in the geographical sense – were just as 'American' as other Negroes – perhaps even more so. The Creoles of Louisiana emerged from the old French colonial culture. They were not – like other blacks – descendents of slaves who gained freedom at the end of the Civil War. Their ancestors had been free much longer. Many of them had been freed by rich French planters or merchants for reasons of distinguished service. The term 'Free Negro' was an important one in old New Orleans.

The Creole Negroes had made French culture their own. Many were wealthy businessmen. Their main language was not English but 'Creole,' a French patois with admixtures of Spanish and African words. Their names were French: Alphonse Picou, Sidney Bechet, Barney Bigard, Albert Nicholas, Buddy Petit, Freddie Keppard, Papa and Louis deLisle Nelson, Kid Ory, etc. It was an honour to be a Creole. Jelly Roll Morton took great pains to make clear that he was a Creole and that his real name was Ferdinand Joseph La Menthe.

Compared to the Creoles, the 'American Negroes' were more 'African.' Their masters were of Anglo-Saxon origin, and thus they were not exposed to the more liberal social attitudes of the French-Spanish orbit. The 'American Negroes' constituted the black proletariat of New Orleans. The Creoles looked down on them with a particular class- and colour-consciousness which 'at that time was even more prejudiced to other Negroes than the attitude of white people to the coloured generally was,' as guitarist Johnny St Cyr put it.

Consequently, there were two very different groups of New Orleans musicians, and the difference found expression in the music. The Creole group was more cultured; the American had more vitality. The main instrument of the French group was the clarinet, which has a great tradition in France. This old French woodwind tradition remained alive well into the thirties in the playing of the leading Swing clarinetists. In fact, Eric Dolphy, in the late fifties, was the first to drop it totally.

In New Orleans itself, the French influence can hardly be

overestimated. Many of the things which gave the city the fascinating atmosphere without which its jazz life would have been inconceivable stem from France. Thus, there is the famous Mardi Gras, which has become the expression of the city's lust for life. Even the funerals, during which a band escorts the deceased to the cemetery with sad music, and then leads the procession back home with joyful sounds, derive from a French custom; it prevails to this day in rural districts of Southern France.

In the mingling of the many ethnic and musical strains in New Orleans, which occurred almost automatically in the laissez-faire climate of Storyville, New Orleans style was born. It is characterized by a 'free counterpoint' played by the three melody instruments: cornet (or trumpet), trombone, and clarinet. The lead is taken by the brilliant sound of the cornet, effectively contrasted by the heavy, weighty trombone. The clarinet entwines the two brasses in an intricate pattern of melodic lines. This front line is supported by the rhythm section: string or brass bass, drums, banjo or guitar, and occasionally, piano.

The early New Orleans rhythm is still very close to European march rhythm: The peculiar 'floating' effect of jazz rhythm, stemming from the fact that 1 and 3 remain the strong beats, but 2 and 4 are accented, is as yet absent. The stress is still on 1 and 3, just as in a march.

The early New Orleans jazz bands resembled the marching and circus bands of the day in other respects, too, such as instrumentation and social function.

New Orleans style is the first example of 'hot' playing. *Hot* connotes the emotional warmth and intensity of the music, and has come to stand for the peculiar sound, phrasing, 'attack', and vibrato which characterize this style. From that point on, all this becomes individualized. The instrument is not so much played as made to 'talk' – to express the individual feelings of the musician.

The Teens: Dixieland

In New Orleans, playing jazz was not exclusively a privilege of the black man. There seem to have been white bands almost from the start. 'Papa' Jack Laine led bands in New Orleans from 1891 on. He is known as the 'father' of white jazz. Bands travelled through the city on carts – known as band wagons – or marched along the streets. When two bands met, a contest or 'battle' ensued. It sometimes happened that black and white bands became engaged in such contests, and when the white band was led by Papa Laine, it often 'blew out' its opponent.

From the earliest time, there was a white style of playing jazz: less expressive, but sometimes better versed technically. The melodies were smoother, the harmony 'purer', the sonorities not so unorthodox. There were fewer sliding notes, less expressive vibrato, less portamenti and glissandi. Whenever these effects were used, there was an element of self-consciousness involved, of knowing that one *could* also play 'legitimately'; and often the music approached the eccentric, even the downright comic. In contrast, the music of the black bands, whether joyful or blue, always contained the aspect of *having to be* that way.

All the successful early white bands stem from Papa Laine. And there is no doubt that the first successful groups in jazz were white: first and foremost the Original Dixieland Jazz Band, and then the New Orleans Rhythm Kings. The ODJB, as it has come to be known, with it punchy, collective style (there were almost no solos), made famous many early jazz standards. Among them were 'Tiger Rag' and 'Original Dixieland One-Step' (recorded in 1917) and 'At the Jazz Band Ball' (recorded in 1919). The New Orleans Rhythm Kings, with their two outstanding soloists, Leon Rappolo, clarinet, and Georg Brunis, trombone, devoted more room to solo improvisation. They first recorded in 1922, and became famous in the early twenties.

In 1917, the ODJB played at Reisenweber's Restaurant on Columbus Circle in New York and made a tremendous hit. From that time on, the word 'jazz' – at first usually spelled 'jass' – became known to the general public. Bandleader Tom Brown claims to have used the word publicly for the first time in Chicago in 1915. But it appears as early as 1913 in a San Francisco newspaper. Prior to that, 'jass' (and the earlier 'jasm' and 'gism') were in use as slang expressions for speed and energy in athletic pursuits – and in sexual contexts as well.

It has become customary to label all New Orleans white jazz 'Dixieland', thus separating it from essential New Orleans style, but the borderlines remain fluid. Especially in later years, with black musicians playing in white bands or vice versa, it no longer made any sense to argue about which style was being played.

With ragtime, New Orleans and Dixieland, the history of jazz begins. What was earlier belongs to what Marshall Stearns has called 'jazz prehistory.' Jazz does not belong to Africa, where it was unknown at its time of origin, and where until this day it is less understood than in most other parts of the world, albeit appreciated. The most often cited statement in this context is Barry Ulanov's: 'There is more of the sound of jazz in mid-European Gypsy fiddling than in a whole corps of African drummers.' To which Leonard Feather adds: 'In melodic and harmonic construction, the early jazz bears considerably more resemblance to such tunes of the 1850s as "Arkansas Traveler" and "Turkey in the Straw" than to any known African music.' When drummer Art Blakey returned from a trip to Africa, where he studied black music, he said: 'You can't mix what comes out of the African culture with what came out of our culture.' (We will return to this problem repeatedly in the course of this book.)

Jazz was born in the encounter between black and white. That is why it originated where this meeting took place in the most intensive fashion: the southern part of the United States. Until this day, jazz is conceivable only in terms of this interaction. It loses its fundamental rationale when one or the other element is overemphasized, or even given a status of exclusiveness, as has been done.

The contact between the races, which has been so important in the evolution and development of jazz, symbolizes that spirit of 'togetherness' per se which characterizes jazz in musical, national, international, social, sociological, political, expressive, aesthetic, ethical, and ethnological terms.

The Twenties: Chicago

We have chosen to divide the evolution of jazz into decades for the purpose of over-all perspective. To be sure, ragtime and New Orleans were alive at the beginning of our century, but both styles were still being played later – up to our time. On the other hand, what is decisive is not how long a style was cultivated, but when it originated and when it unfolded its greatest vitality and musical power. From this point of view, it is a fact that a new style has come into being roughly every ten years – and often at the beginning of a decade.

The essential things about jazz in the twenties are three: the great period of New Orleans music in Chicago, classic blues, and Chicago style.

The development of New Orleans jazz in Chicago is generally connected with the entry of the United States into World War I. This connection appears somewhat dubious, but may, along with other factors, have played a certain role. New Orleans became a war port. The Secretary of the Navy viewed the goings on in Storyville as a danger to the morale of his troops. Storyville was closed by official decree.

This decree deprived not only the ladies of Storyville but also many musicians of their daily bread. Many left town. Most of them went to Chicago. The 'Windy City' on Lake Michigan had previously been a source of fascination for many New Orleans musicians. Now came the great exodus of New Orleans musicians to Chicago, and it is clear that this was only a part of the general migration of blacks from South to North. It developed that the first jazz style, though called New Orleans, actually had its really great period in the Chicago of the twenties. It was in Chicago that the most famous New Orleans jazz recordings were made, as the phonograph became increasingly popular after World War I.

King Oliver was the leader of the most important New Orleans band in Chicago. It was here that Louis Armstrong formed his Hot Five and Hot Seven, Jelly Roll Morton his Red Hot Peppers, Johnny Dodds his New Orleans Wanderers, etc. What is known as New Orleans style today is not the archaic and barely recorded jazz which existed in New Orleans in the first two decades of this century, but the music made by New Orleans musicians in Chicago during the third decade.

The blues, too, had its great period in the Chicago of the twenties. Certainly blues songs existed long before there was jazz – at least from the middle of the nineteenth century. In those days, they were heard in the rural districts of the South, mostly without a steady jazz beat and often lacking the standard 12-bar pattern which characterizes the blues today. Itinerant blues singers travelled – as they still do today – from town to town, from plantation to plantation, with a banjo (or guitar) and a bundle containing all their wordly possessions, singing those songs with the drawn-out 'blue' notes known today as country or 'archaic' blues.

When the first marching bands began to play in New Orleans, there was a difference between their budding 'jazz' and the blues. But soon the rural blues began to flow into the mainstream of jazz, and from then on jazz and blues become so interwoven that, as Ernest Borneman has written, all of jazz is 'nothing but the application of the blues to European music, or vice versa.' Even the most modern and 'freest' jazz musician of today is indebted to the blues – in fact, blues consciousness is higher in today's jazz than in many previous styles.

The twenties are considered the period of 'classic' blues. Bessie Smith was its greatest singer. In later chapters, Bessie Smith herself and the harmony, melody, and form of the blues will be discussed. It is with good reason that the blues are treated in a special chapter as an 'element of jazz'. It was not only a certain 'style' of jazz in the early times, but has left its mark on all forms of jazz and on the whole history of the music. The intention here is to give a summary of the development of jazz in its entirety for easier orientation in the following chapters.

Around the great jazz instrumentalists from New Orleans and the famous blues singers there developed in Chicago a jazz life hardly less active than that of New Orleans in the Golden Age. Centred on the South Side, Chicago's black district, it lacked the happy exuberance of the old New Orleans days, but reflected the hectic pace of the metropolis and, increasingly, the problems of racial discrimination.

Stimulated by the jazz life of the South Side, young white high school and college students, amateur and professional musicians, began to develop what has been called Chicago style. They had become so inspired by the greats of New Orleans jazz that they wanted to emulate their style. As imitation their music was unsuccessful; instead they came up with something new: Chicago style. In it, the profusion of melodic lines, so typical of New Orleans style, is more or less absent. The voicings, if there is more than one line, are – in most cases – parallel. The individual has become the ruler. From this point on, the solo becomes increasingly important in jazz. Many Chicago-style recordings consist of hardly more than a sequence of solos or, in jazz terminology, 'choruses'.

Only now the saxophone, which to many laymen represents jazz incarnate, begins to gain importance. Chicago may be considered the second 'cool' style of jazz (the first being piano ragtime). Bix Beiderbecke is the foremost representative of this style. In the chapter about him, it will be discussed at greater length.

The Thirties: Swing

The older styles of jazz are grouped together under the heading 'two-beat jazz.' Towards the end of the twenties the two-beat styles seemed all but exhausted. In Harlem, and even more in Kansas City, a new way of playing developed around 1928-29. With the second great exodus in jazz history - the journey from Chicago to New York - Swing begins. Swing may be characterized as 'four-beat jazz', since it puts stress on all four beats of the bar. This is true in general, but as is so often the case in jazz, there are confusing exceptions. Louis Armstrong (and some Chicago-style players) were already conversant with four-beat style in the twenties. On the other hand, Jimmie Lunceford's big band at the height of the Swing era employed a beat that was simultaneously 2/4 and 4/4.

The word 'swing' is a key term in jazz, and it is used in two different senses. This may lead to a certain amount of confusion. First, swing connotes a rhythmic element from which jazz derives the tension classical music gets from its formal structure. This swing is present in all styles, phases, and periods of jazz. It is so essential that it has been said that if music does not swing, it is not jazz.

The other use of the term refers to the dominant jazz style of the thirties - the style through which jazz won its greatest commercial success before the emergence of fusion music. In the 'Swing era' Benny Goodman became the 'King of Swing'.

There is a difference between saying that a jazzpiece swings and that it *is* Swing. Any jazz tune which is Swing also swings - if it is any good. But, conversely, not all jazz that swings is necessarily Swing. In order to avoid confusion, I suggested in an earlier edition of this book that the *style* Swing should be capitalized, while lower-case swing should connote the rhythmic element. Many jazz scholars all over the world have adopted this practice. In the chapter on 'Rhythm' I will have more to say about the nature of swing (lower case).

One feature of the Swing era was the development of big bands. In

Kansas City – for instance, in the bands of Bennie Moten (and later Count Basie) – the 'riff' style developed. This was an application of the old, important call-and-response pattern (originating from Africa) to the sections of a large jazz band. These sections are trumpets, trombones, and saxes. Another contribution to big-band jazz was made by the white Chicago style: a more 'European' approach to the music. In Benny Goodman's band, the different styles flowed together: some New Orleans tradition, through Fletcher Henderson, who arranged for the band; the riff technique of Kansas City; and that white precision and training through which this brand of jazz somehow lost so much of its expressivity. On the other hand, the easy melodic quality and clean intonation of Goodman's band made it possible to 'sell' jazz to a mass audience.

It only seems to be a contradiction that the individual soloist gained in importance alongside of the development of big bands. Jazz has always been simultaneously collective and individualistic. That jazz, more than any other music, can be both at one and the same time, clarifies much about its nature. This is the 'sociological phenomenon' of jazz (we'll talk about it later), which mirrors the social situation of modern man.

Thus, the thirties also became the era of great soloists: the tenor saxists Coleman Hawkins and Chu Berry; the clarinetist Benny Goodman; the drummers Gene Krupa, Cozy Cole, and Sid Catlett; the pianists Fats Waller and Teddy Wilson; the alto saxists Benny Carter and Johnny Hodges; the trumpeters Roy Eldridge, Bunny Berigan, and Rex Stewart; and many, many more . . .

Often these two tendencies – the orchestral and the soloistic – merged. Benny Goodman's clarinet seemed all the more glamorous against the backdrop of his big band. Louis Armstrong's trumpet stood out in bold relief when accompanied by a big band. And the voluminous tone of Coleman Hawkins's or Chu Berry's tenor sax seemed to gain from the contrast to the 'hard' sound of Fletcher Henderson's big band.

The Forties: Bebop

Towards the end of the thirties, Swing had become a gigantic business enterprise. It has been called the 'greatest music business of all time' (which was true then, but the record sales of the thirties and forties were modest compared to the dimensions of today's music business). The word 'Swing' became a marketing device for all sorts of goods, from cigarettes to articles of female clothing, while the music, conforming to general commercial demands, often became a matter of endlessly repeated clichés.

As is so often the case in jazz when a style or way of playing becomes too commercialized, the evolution turned in the opposite direction. A group of musicians who had something new to say found each other in a healthy, although not in all cases deliberate, reaction against the general Swing fashion.

This new music developed – at first in spurts – originally in Kansas City and then, most of all, in the musicians' hangouts in Harlem (particularly in a place called Minton's Playhouse) and once again at the beginning of a decade. Contrary to what has been claimed, this new music did *not* develop when a group of musicians banded together to create something new, at whatever cost, because the old was no longer a draw. The old style drew very well – it was still the 'greatest music business of all time'. Nor is it true that the new jazz style was shaped as a conscious effort by an interrelated group of musicians. The new style was formed in the minds and instruments of different musicians in different places, independent of each other. But Minton's became a focal point – as New Orleans had been forty years earlier. And just as Jelly Roll Morton's claim to have 'invented' jazz was absurd, so would be the claim of any musician in the forties to have 'invented' modern jazz.

The new style was eventually named bebop, a word which seemed to mirror the vocalization of the then best-loved interval of the music: the flatted fifth. The term 'bebop' came into being spontaneously when someone attempted to 'sing' these melodic leaps. This is the explanation that trumpeter Dizzy Gillespie, one of the main exponents of the new style, gave for the origin of the term 'bebop'. There are as many theories about the origin of this word as there are about most jazz expressions.

The flatted fifth became the most important interval of bebop – or, as it was soon called, bop. Until then, this device would have been felt to be erroneous, or at least 'wrong' sounding, although it might have been used in passing chords, or for the special harmonic effects which Duke Ellington or pianist Willie 'The Lion' Smith liked to use as early as in the twenties. But now it characterized an entire style, as the narrow harmonic base of earlier jazz forms was constantly broadened. Within ten or twelve years (as we shall see) the flatted fifth was to become a 'blue note', as common as the undetermined thirds and sevenths familiar in traditional blues.

The most important musicians who gathered at Minton's were Thelonious Monk, piano; Kenny Clark, drums; Charlie Christian, guitar; trumpeter Dizzy Gillespie; and alto saxist Charlie Parker. The latter was to become the real genius of modern jazz as Louis Armstrong was the genius of traditional jazz.

One of these musicians – Christian – not only belongs among the founders of modern jazz but also among those who fashioned from Swing the foundations for its development. There is a whole group of such 'pioneers', at once the 'last' generation of Swing and the pathbreakers for bop. And almost every instrument had its own bebop pioneer; among trumpeters, it is Roy Eldridge; among pianists, Clyde Hart; among tenors, Lester Young; among bassists, Jimmy Blanton; among drummers, Jo Jones and Dave Tough; among guitarists, Charlie Christian.

To the listener of that time, the sounds characteristic of bebop seemed to be racing, nervous phrases which occasionally appeared as melodic fragments. Every unnecessary note was excluded. Everything was highly concentrated. As a bop musician once said: 'Everything that is obvious is excluded.' It is a kind of musical shorthand, and you have to listen to it in the same way you would read a stenographic transcript, establishing ordered relationships from a few hasty signs.

The improvisations are framed by the theme presented in unison at the beginning and the end of each piece, generally played by two horns, in most cases a trumpet and saxophone (Dizzy Gillespie and Charlie Parker are the archetypes). This unison alone – even before the musicians began to improvise – introduced a new sound and a new attitude. Music psychology knows: Unisons, wherever they appear – from Beethoven's 'Ode to Joy' (and even earlier in the Ninth Symphony, in the main motif of the first movement) to North African Bedouin music and to the choirs of the Arabic world – signal: listen, this is *our* statement. It is *we* who are talking. And you to whom we speak, you are different from us and probably our opponents.

Under the influence of the then avant-garde bop sound, many friends of jazz didn't know what to make of this new turn in the evolution of the music. With great determination, they oriented themselves backward, towards the basic forms of jazz. 'Simple' music was demanded. There was a New Orleans renaissance – or, as it was called, 'revival' – which spread all over the world.

This development began as a sound reconsideration of the roots of jazz – the tradition which to this day nourishes jazz in all its forms and phases. But soon the revival led to a simplified and cliché-ridden 'traditional' jazz from which black musicians turned away. (With the exception of the surviving New Orleans jazzmen, for whom traditional jazz was the logical form of expression, no important black musicians participated in the Dixieland revival – strange as this may sound to some.) Amateurs often worked against the commercialization of Dixieland, but regularly fell victims to it themselves as they attained professional status.

After World War II, the 'jazz boîtes' in Saint-German-des-Prés in Paris became the headquarters of the traditional movement, fortified with existentialist philosophy. But soon the young existentialists discovered that their philosophy was better suited to a music which did not reflect the happy, carefree attitudes of the early years of the century, but rather the unrest of their own times. They gravitated towards more contemporary jazz forms, and the centre of the movement shifted to England. In that country, Dixieland concerts were organized with the same commercial effort and success as presentations of rock 'n' roll singers.

In this section, bebop and the New Orleans revival have been contrasted in the same way that they appeared to be in contrast to each other to jazz fans at that time: as extremes of antagonistic opposition. Today – and actually since the genesis of free jazz in the sixties – these poles have approached each other, for today's young listener can no longer appreciate this contrast. To him, Charlie Parker is almost as much a part of the jazz tradition as Louis Armstrong.

In describing bebop, we have used terms like 'racing', 'nervous', 'melodic fragments', 'cypher', 'hasty'. But in the face of what is 'racing', 'nervous', 'fragmented', and 'hasty' in today's scene, most of the jazz of the forties seems of almost classic completeness to the young listener of our times. One can only hope that listeners and critics of today's jazz learn from this development and use greater caution in the application of extreme words and concepts. The critics who foresaw the 'end of jazz' or even the 'end of music' in reaction to the 'nervousness' of bop seem a bit ridiculous today, but there were a lot of them once. They are here today, too, in reaction to what seems 'nervous' and loud.

Today, thirty-five years later, we should pause and consider what has become of the great musicians who created bebop. Only one of them, Max Roach, is still creatively active in the vein of today's scene: with his contemporary percussion group, for instance, or with his duo concerts with musicians like Cecil Taylor, Anthony Braxton, Dollar Brand, or Archie Shepp. Another of the bop fathers, Dizzy Gillespie, is still creative in the bebop style. The others have either become artistically rigid or have died – most of them after psychological or physical illness, after heroin or alcohol addiction. And even though they died young – Charlie Parker, for example, was thirty-five – they were past the peak of their creativity at the time of their deaths, at an age when other artists often only begin to gain real stature.

Compare the bebop musicians with creative personalities of European art – figures like Stravinsky or Schoenberg, Picasso, Kandinsky, or Chagall. They lived to a ripe old age and remained creative and the whole world respects and admires them. For the creative musicians of bebop, however, early death was often the rule, and nobody is writing papers and essays about it. That seems to be the toll jazz artists in America have to pay to society – which accepts it without batting an eyelash.

But that is also the backdrop which make this music so powerful and impressive, and which makes the work of these soon rigidified or perished artists seem that much more admirable. And it is no accident that at the beginning of the eighties we are witnessing a bebop revival that none would have forecast some years ago. There is a whole generation of young people playing this music, most of them white, well-adjusted, and far from dying as heroin addicts. And all this twenty-five years after Charlie Parker's death, thirty-five years after the breakdown of Bud Powell, the 'father of bebop piano', and thirty years after bop trumpeter Fats Navarro died, right after his twenty-sixth birthday.

The Fifties: Cool, Hard Bop

Towards the end of the forties, the 'unrest and excitement of bop' were more and more replaced by a tendency towards calm and smoothness. This trend first became apparent in the playing of trumpeter Miles Davis. As an eighteen-year-old, he had played in Charlie Parker's Quintet of 1945 in the 'nervous' style of Dizzy Gillespie; not much later, however, he began to blow in a relaxed and 'cool' manner. The trend also showed up in the piano improvisations of John Lewis, an anthropology student from New Mexico who travelled with Dizzy Gillespie's big band to Paris in 1948 and only then decided to remain in music; and in the arrangements Tadd Dameron wrote in the second half of the forties for the same Gillespie big band and for various small combinations. Miles Davis's trumpet solos of 1947 with Charlie Parker, such as 'Chasin' the Bird', or John Lewis's piano solo in Dizzy Gillespie's 'Round Midnight', recorded at a concert in Paris in 1948 – these are the first 'cool' solos in jazz history . . . excepting Lester Young's tenor sax solos with Count Basie from the late thirties, in which he paved the way for the 'cool' conception even before the bebop era had begun.

With these three musicians – Miles Davis, John Lewis, and Tadd Dameron – the style known as 'cool jazz' begins.

The cool conception dominates all the jazz of the first half of the fifties, but it is notable that it found its most valid and representative expression at a moment almost coincidental with its origin: in the famed recordings of the Miles Davis Orchestra, which was formed for a brief engagement at New York's Royal Roost in 1948, and was recorded by the Capitol label in 1949 and 1950. In the chapter dealing with Davis, this group – of decisive importance to the ensemble sound and musical conception of the decade – will be discussed in detail.

Lennie Tristano (1919–1978) – a blind pianist from Chicago who came to New York in 1946 and founded his 'New School of Music' there in 1951 – gave a theoretical foundation to cool jazz through his music and thinking. The musicians of the Tristano school (notably altoist Lee Konitz, tenorman Warne Marsh, and guitarist Billy Bauer) were to a large extent responsible for the layman's idea of cool jazz as cold, intellectual, and emotionless music. However, there can be no doubt that Tristano and his musicians improvised with remarkable freedom, and that linear improvisation stood at the centre of their interests. Thus Tristano let himself be advertised as 'Lennie Tristano and his Intuitive Music'; he wanted to emphasize the intuitive character of his conception and ward off the lay opinion that his was an intellectually calculated music. Still, Tristano's music held for many listeners a coolness which often bordered on a chill. The evolution of modern jazz soon found less abstract, more sensuous and vital forms.

The problem was, as Stearns has said, 'to play cool without being cold.'

The influence of the Tristano school has remained traceable throughout all of modern jazz, however far removed from the 'tristanoite' mode of coolness. This is true harmonically, but most of all in a distinct preference for long, linear melodic lines.

After Tristano, the centre moved initially to the West Coast. Here evolved, directly connected to the Miles Davis Capitol Band, a 'West Coast jazz', often played by musicians who made their living in the Hollywood studio orchestras. Trumpeter Shorty Rogers, drummer Shelly Manne, and clarinetist–saxophonist Jimmy Giuffre became the style-setting musicians of the West Coast. Their music contained elements of the academic European musical tradition; direct and vital jazz content was often pushed into the background. The experts frequently pointed out that New York remained the true capital of jazz. This was where real and vital jazz was made: modern, yet rooted in jazz tradition. West Coast jazz was confronted with 'East Coast jazz'.

Since then, it has become apparent that both 'coasts' were not so much stylistic entities as advertising slogans promoted by record companies. The real tension in the evolution of jazz of the fifties was not between two coasts, but between a classicist direction and a group of young musicians, mostly black, who played a modern version of bebop, so-called hard bop.

The new jazz-classicism – as French critic André Hodeir has called it – found its 'classics' in the music Lester Young and Count Basie had played in the thirties, first in Kansas City and later in New York. Many musicians from either coast, white or black, were oriented towards this music: Al Cohn, Joe Newman, Ernie Wilkins, Manny Albam, Johnny Mandel, Chico Hamilton, Buddy Collette, Gerry Mulligan, Bob Brookmeyer, Shorty Rogers, Quincy Jones, Jimmy

Giuffre. In the fifties, a massive number of 'Count Basie tributes' were recorded. Basie's name stands for clarity, melodiousness, swing, and certainly that 'noble simplicity' of which Winckelmann, a German scholar of the eighteenth century, spoke in his famous definition of classicism. (It is amazing how often it is possible to employ, almost literally, the words of the German classicists of the Goethe period when speaking of modern jazz classicism. One needs only to substitute for the names and concepts from Greek art and mythology Count Basie and Lester Young, swing, beat, and blues.)

Confronting this classicism stood a generation of young musicians whose foremost representatives lived in New York, though few of them were born there. Most were from Detroit or Philadelphia. Their music was the purest bop, enriched by a greater knowledge of harmonic fundamentals and a greater degree of instrumental-technical perfection. This hard bop was the most dynamic jazz played in the second half of the fifties – by groups under the leadership of, among others, drummers Max Roach and Art Blakey and pianist Horace Silver; by musicians like trumpeters Clifford Brown, Lee Morgan, and Donald Byrd, and tenor men Sonny Rollins, Hank Mobley, and others – among them initially John Coltrane.

In hard bop, something new was created without sacrifice of vitality. All too often, the new in jazz can only be attained at the expense of vitality. Drummer Shelly Manne, for example, had to pay for the amazing musical refinement of his playing with some reduction in directness and vitality. His colleague Elvin Jones, on the other hand, managed to discover rhythms which simultaneously possess a complexity of structure *and* a vitality the likes of which, in such a relationship, was previously unheard-of in jazz. Horace Silver rediscovered new ways of combining the 32-bar song structure, which is the foundation for most jazz improvising, with other forms – combining them into 'groups' or 'blocks' of forms (as had been done in similar fashion by the ragtime pianists, Jelly Roll Morton, and other musicians of the early jazz period under the influence of the serial form of the Viennese waltz). Tenor saxophonist Sonny Rollins created through his improvisations grandiose structures, which at that time were considered 'polymetric', while striding across the given harmonic materials with a freedom and ease which not even the Tristano school could match.

Marshall Stearns has said: 'Indeed, modern jazz as played in New

York by Art Blakey and his Messengers, Jay and Kai, Max Roach and Clifford Brown, Art Farmer and Gigi Gryce, Gillespie, Davis, and others . . . has never lost its fire. The harmonies of cool jazz – and bop – were taken over, the posture of resignation disappeared, the light sound remained, but the music always has a biting sharpness. In a word: It has changed, but fundamentally it remained 'hot' and 'swinging' . . . The word 'cool' has lost its meaning – unless it is taken in a general sense of 'sensitive' and 'flexible'. The last sentence applies to both directions of the jazz of the fifties: classicism and new bop.

It is also true of both movements that they had found a new relationship to the blues. Pianist–composer Horace Silver – and with him a few others – broke through with a manner of playing known as 'funky': slow or medium blues, played hard on the beat, with all the feeling and expression characteristic of the old blues. And not only the blues, but also the gospel songs of black churches began to play a new, powerful role in jazz: in a playing style called 'soul', connected again with Horace Silver, but also with singer and pianist Ray Charles and vibraharpist Milt Jackson. Jazz musicians of all persuasions on both coasts threw themselves into 'funk' and 'soul' with notable enthusiasm. They did so in a manner which, since musical reasons are not readily apparent, leads one to conclude that extramusical influences were present. In a letter to the editor of *down beat* magazine (spring, 1958), a reader suggested that 'the cool musician, in his use of the funky-blues framework, may be thinking about the content which is hidden behind this framework . . . This content expresses a "warm" – as opposed to "cool" – relationship to life . . . Though the content of the real blues may be sad, it is not a hopeless sadness.' The letter continues with talk of a 'spiritual transformation' of the cool jazz musician. Novelist Jack Kerouac, who had a genuine relationship to jazz, suggests there might even be religious tendencies behind this phenomenon.

The tendency towards 'funk' and 'soul' expresses the wish to belong, and the desire for something offering a semblance of security in a world of cool realism. 'Soul', with its roots in the music of the gospel churches, experienced a large-scale success in popular music during the late sixties; 'funk', which comes from blues, did the same in the seventies. The important thing is to remember that both were born from jazz, or, more generally, from black tradition and feeling.

This tendency towards a feeling of security and belonging became even clearer a decade later, in free jazz. Albert Ayler, for example, transplanted circus, country, and marching music - clearly motifs from the safe and sane 'good old days' - into his free, atonal, ecstatic improvisations. Other free-jazz musicians overemphasized their hate for the white world and found a substitute realm of group acceptance and security in communion with those who shared this hate - a psychological reaction familiar to anyone conversant with psycho-analysis.

During the cool-jazz period, the contrapuntal and linear music of Johann Sebastian Bach fulfilled this need to belong in the Modern Jazz Quartet of pianist John Lewis. A whole tide of jazz fugues rose in the first half of the fifties; it subsided as power and vitality returned to the scene with hard bop.

The Sixties: Free Jazz

These are the innovations of the jazz of the sixties - of free jazz:

1. A breakthrough into the open space of 'free tonality'.
2. A new rhythmic conception, characterized by the disintegration of meter, beat, and symmetry.
3. The flow of 'world music' into jazz, which was suddenly open to all the great musical cultures - from India to Africa, from Japan to Arabia.
4. An emphasis on intensity unknown to earlier styles of jazz. Jazz had always been superior in intensity to other musical forms of the Western world, but never before had the accent been on intensity in such an ecstatic, orgiastic - sometimes even religious - sense as in free jazz. Many free-jazz musicians actually made a 'cult' of intensity.
5. An extension of musical sound into the realm of noise.

Around the early sixties, jazz music broke through into the realm of free tonality, or even atonality, as concert music had done forty or fifty years earlier. Jazz specialists had expected this development for some fifteen years; it was anticipated in Lennie Tristano's 'Intuition' and 'Digression' of 1949; some important musicians of the fifties - particularly George Russell and Charles Mingus - paved the way for it. A 'new music', a 'new jazz', was born - like many innovations in the arts, initially relying on shock value. The power and hardness of the new jazz, along with a revolutionary, partially extramusical pathos, affected the jazz scene of the sixties vehemently. This vehemence was even stronger because so many things had been bottled up in the fifties, when the breakthrough was imminent but was avoided with almost pathological anxiety. All these bottled-up things came down like an avalanche on a contented jazz public, which had accommodated itself to Oscar Peterson and the Modern Jazz Quartet.

For the younger generation of free-jazz musicians, the music preceding them had been depleted in terms of playing and procedural possibilities, harmonic structure, and metric symmetry. It had become rigid in its clichés and predictable formulas, similar to the situation twenty years earlier, when bebop was created. Everything seemed to run according to the same, unchangeable pattern in the same, unchanging way. All possibilities of traditional forms and conventional tonality seemed exhausted. That is why the young musicians searched for new ways of playing – and in the process, jazz again became what it had been in the twenties when the white public discovered it: a great, crazy, exciting, precarious adventure. At last, there was collective improvisation again, with lines rubbing against and crossing each other wildly and freely. That, too, is reminiscent of New Orleans – with modifications to be discussed later.

Don Heckmann, the critic and musician, once said: 'I think there's been a natural tendency towards this freeing of the improvisatory mind from harmonic restrictions throughout the history of jazz.'

In jazz, free tonality, however, is understood in a basically different way from that of European concert music. The free jazz of the New York avant-garde around 1965 featured – much more so than, say, the 'serial' European avant-garde music – so called 'tonal centres' (cf the chapter dealing with harmonics). This means that the music loosely partakes in the general gravitation from the dominant to the tonic, but has a wide range of freedom in all other aspects.

This development was so spontaneous and nonacademic that the European term 'atonality' cannot be used in an exclusively academic sense. Small wonder that many free-jazz musicians have expressed their explicit contempt for academic music and its vocabulary (Archie Shepp: 'Where my own dreams sufficed, I disregarded the western musical tradition altogether'). In the new jazz, 'atonality' –

or better, 'free tonality' – has a wide range of meaning: It includes all
steps, from the intimated 'tonal centres' to complete harmonic
freedom. However, in the face of radical atonality, the tendency to
realize that the harmonic system cannot simply be replaced by
'nothing' – by no system at all – has become stronger.

In spite of the brevity of its history, jazz has a much longer 'atonal
tradition' than European music. The 'shouts' and 'field hollers', the
archaic blues of the southern plantations, indeed, nearly all musical
forerunners of jazz – which also survived as elements of jazz – were
'free tonal', often enough simply because the singers didn't know
anything about European tonality. In the old days of New Orleans,
too, there were musicians unconcerned with harmonic laws. Certain
Louis Armstrong records from the twenties – 'Two Deuces' with Earl
Hines, for example – are among his most beautiful, though they
contain notes that are 'wrong' in terms of European academic
tonality.

Marshall Stearns, who pointed out all these things when they first
surfaced during the hard-bop era, foresaw: 'The knack for harmonic
liberties, which jazz musicians well knew how to take within the
system of perfect intonation of European music, moves steadily
towards a predictable goal: the freedom of the street cry and the field
holler.'

In other words, there is a tradition of atonality – or at least of
harmonic freedom – in the whole history of jazz, while atonality in
European music was first introduced by an avant-garde – the
'classical' avant-garde beginning with Schoenberg, Webern, and
Berg. Thus, jazz atonality has become the meeting ground for
tradition and avant-garde – a truly healthy and advantageous point
of departure rarely encountered in an art in flux!

There is no doubt: musicians like Ornette Coleman, Archie Shepp,
Pharoah Sanders, and Albert Ayler are closer to the 'concrete', folk
musiclike harmonic freedom of the 'field cry' and of the archaic folk
blues than to 'abstract', intellectual European atonality. Ornette
Coleman, for instance, didn't realize that there was also free tonality
in European music until he met John Lewis and Gunther Schuller in
1959–60. At that time he had already developed his own musical
concept.

For a number of years we were at a point where the freedom of free
jazz was often understood as freedom from any musical system

formed in Europe – with the emphasis on 'formed in Europe'. The formal and harmonic emancipation from the music of the 'white continent' was part of a greater racial, social, cultural, and political emancipation. 'Black music', as it was interpreted by many of these musicians and by LeRoi Jones (Amiri Baraka), one of their most eloquent spokesmen, became 'blacker' than ever before in this process of breaking its strongest link with the European tradition, the harmonic laws. (Cf the quotes by Jones and one of his associates in the chapter on Ornette Coleman and John Coltrane.)

There is a parallel between jazz and modern European concert music, but only insofar as both displayed a growing disgust with the mechanistic, machinelike character of the traditional system of functional harmonics. This system had become a roadblock in the development of the musics by increasingly substituting for individual decisions its own functional mechanics, and its abolition is a legitimate development familiar from many other arts, cultures, and traditions: When a structuring principle has been worn out and the creative artists become convinced that within its limits everything possible has been said, the principle must be abandoned. And after sixty years of modern concert music, nobody would seriously argue that this traditional principle is the *only* correct one.

The claim of exclusive validity for European harmonics is contradicted not only by artistic and physical considerations, but also by the many different principles and systems which have proven their value in other musical cultures of the world. Especially in view of today's political and cultural developments, the contention has become untenable that one system could have all the answers. On the other hand, it remains to be seen to what extent the free harmonic conception is the answer. It is not correct, however, to simply invalidate this conception as 'incomprehensible', since it is a fact that it was immediately understood without prior discussion by a minority of listeners and a majority of young jazz musicians all over the world.

Jazz should be seen as a spiritual and cultural phenomenon within the spiritual and cultural movements of this century. Parallels of a more than accidental nature can be found between the liberation of jazz from functional harmonics and similar developments in other contemporary arts. We have discussed concert music. The parallel with modern literature is just as obvious: The antigrammatical and antisyntactic tendencies of so many modern writers – Raymond

Queneau, Arno Schmidt, Helmut Heissenbüttel, Butor, William
Burroughs, and, first and foremost, James Joyce plus many others in
all important languages – in many respects correspond to the
antiharmonic tendencies of the free-jazz musicians. Increasingly, the
gravitation of syntax and grammar draws language into the same
functional and causal tunnel into which music moved under the
influence of functional harmonics. Each step derived directly and
necessarily from the preceding one, so that the creative artist finally
could do little more than choose from a catalogue determined by
syntax, grammar, and harmonics.

Modern philosophy, which moves further and further away from
closed systems, is another example of the same phenomenon: Once a
philosophical system was established, any further philosophizing
within that system showed the same characteristics of mechanically
answering grammatical or harmonic rules.

All new jazz styles have created new rhythmic concepts. Free jazz is
no exception. Two basic facts determine the different rhythmic
concepts in the history of jazz from New Orleans to hard bop: A fixed
meter, generally 2/4 or 4/4 (until the emergence of the waltz and
other uneven meters in the fifties), is carried out constantly. Secondly,
the jazz beat produces accents which do not necessarily correspond to
those a classically trained musician would place within that same
meter. Free jazz demolished the two pillars of conventional jazz
rhythm – meter and beat. The beat was replaced by the 'pulse' and
the meter, which was passed over by some free-jazz drummers as if it
did not exist, was replaced by wide arches of rhythmic tension, built
up with an incredible intensity. (More about this in the chapters on
rhythm and the drums.) Sunny Murray, one of the leading free-jazz
drummers, called traditional drum rhythm 'cliché beats' which are
'like slavery or poverty. Freedom drumming is an aspiration toward a
better condition.'

Just as important to jazz as harmonic and rhythmic innovation was
gaining access to world music. Jazz developed within a dialectic – the
meeting of black and white. In the first 60 years of jazz history, the
counterpart of jazz was European music. Interaction with the
European musical tradition was by no means a marginal activity.
Nearly all styles of jazz came into being in and through this dialectical
interaction.

In this process, the realm of what was meant by 'European music'

grew continually larger. To the ragtime pianists of the turn of the
century it meant the piano compositions of the nineteenth century.
To the New Orleans musicians it meant French opera, Spanish circus
music, and European marches. Bix Beiderbecke and his Chicago
colleagues of the twenties discovered Debussy . The Swing arrangers
learned orchestration skills from the late romantic symphonic
period . . . Finally, when the development had gone beyond cool
jazz, jazz musicians had incorporated almost all elements of
European music they could possibly use, from Baroque to Stockhausen.

Thus, the role of European music as the stimulating counterpart of
jazz – at least as its only counterpart – had run out. Aside from this
musical reason, there were extramusical ones – racial, social, and
political – as we have already mentioned. This is why jazz musicians
discovered new partners with growing fervour: the great non-
European musical cultures.

The Arabic and Indian cultures and musics have held a special
fascination. There have been Islamic tendencies among Afro-
Americans since the mid-forties; since the time, in other words, when
modern jazz originated. Dozens of jazz musicians converted to Islam,
and occasionally took Arabic names: For a couple of years, drummer
Art Blakey was known to his Muslim friends as Abdullah Ibn
Buhaina; in the forties, saxophonist Ed Gregory had already become
Sahib Shihab.

In this turning away from 'the white religion', the emancipation
from the white man is given particularly effective expression. James
Baldwin, the black writer, said: 'Whoever wishes to become a truly
moral human being must first divorce himself from all the
prohibitions, crimes and hypocrisies of the Christian church. The
idea of God is only valid and useful if it can make us greater, freer and
more capable of loving.' Millions of black Americans believe – 'after
two hundred years of vain attempts' – that the Christian God cannot
do that. For that reason, says Baldwin, 'it is time we got rid of Him.'

It was only a small step from religious conversion to Islam to a
growing interest in Islamic music. Musicians like Yusef Lateef,
Ornette Coleman, John Coltrane, Randy Weston, Herbie Mann, Art
Blakey, Roland Kirk, Sahib Shihab, and Don Cherry in the US; and,
among others, George Gruntz and Jean-Luc Ponty in Europe – many
of them not Muslims by faith – have expressed their fascination with

Arabic music in compositions and improvisations.

Even stronger than Arabic music was the interest in Indian music with its great classical tradition. What fascinates jazz musicians most about Indian music is, above all, its rhythmic wealth. The great classical music of India is based on talas and ragas.

Talas are rhythmic series and cycles of immense variety – from three to 108 beats. You have to be aware that Indian musicians and sophisticated listeners are able to appreciate even the longest tala – 108 beats – as a series and as a predetermined musical structure and to recall it as such.

Talas usually have a great wealth of rhythmical structuring possibilities. A tala consisting of ten beats, for example, can be conceived as a series of '2-3-2-3' or '3-3-4' or '3-4-3' beats.

Within the series, there is ample room for free improvisation; the improvising musicians can wander far away from each other. But the tension characteristic of Indian music is to a large extent founded on the fact that the individual lines of improvisation finally must meet again on the first beat, 'one' – the so-called 'sam'. After the widely diverging melodic movements, this meeting very often is felt like an almost orgiastic relief.

It is this rhythmic wealth of Indian music that particularly attracts modern jazz musicians. They want to liberate themselves from the 4/4 uniformity of the metrically conventional, constant jazz beat, while at the same time searching for rhythmic and metric structures which create a jazzlike intensity.

In contrast to the rhythmically well-defined tala, the raga is a melodic row in which many elements which have been categorized in numerous ways in European music come together: theme, key, mood, phrase, and the form determined by the melodic flow. A particular raga may require, for example, that a certain note can be used only after all other notes of the raga have been played. There are ragas which can be played only in the morning, at night, at full moon, or only with religious thoughts in mind. And, above all, ragas are 'modes', which makes them correspond ideally to the tendency towards modality in modern jazz (cf the chapter on harmonics).

A large number of jazz musicians have studied with the great masters of Indian classical music. The word 'classical', by the way, should be read with emphasis, because this is not folklore music. It is as 'classical' as the corresponding music in European culture. The openness with which dozens of jazz musicians of the fifties and sixties have approached the great exotic musical cultures goes far beyond comparable developments in modern European concert music. Overwhelming intensity and complexity are generated when Don Ellis derives big band compositions, such as '3-3-2-2-2-1-2-2-2' and 'New Nine', from Indian talas; when Miles Davis and Gil Evans transform Joaquin Rodrigo's 'Concierto de Aranjuez' into Flamenco jazz; when Yusef Lateef converts Japanese, Chinese, and Egyptian elements into blues on his record 'A flat, G flat and C'; and when Sahib Shihab, Jean-Luc Ponty, and George Gruntz play with Arab bedouins on the album 'Noon in Tunisia'. Compared to that, Debussy's, Messiaen's and Roussell's use of Indian and Balinese sounds and the influence of Chinese rhythms on the modern German composer Boris Blacher seem timid and marginal.

The new jazz musicians transform world music into swinging sounds. They do this with the liberating joy of the adventurer and discoverer, and with a fervour whose messianic, all-embracing gesture of love is manifest in many of their record album titles: in Albert Ayler's 'Spiritual Unity' and 'Holy Ghost'; Don Cherry's 'Complete Communion'; Carla Bley's 'Communication'; Schlippen-bach's 'Globe Unity'; Yusef Lateef's 'Try Love'; Ornette Coleman's 'Peace'; John Coltrane's 'Love', 'Love Supreme', 'Elation', and 'Ascension'; or in tunes such as 'Sun Song', 'Sun Myth', and 'Nebulae' from 'Heliocentric Worlds' by Sun Ra and his Solar Arkestra. The message of these titles can be felt when they are seen in a single context: '. . . from spiritual unity to complete communion and communication with the globe as a unity – and, through that, love and peace for everybody and salvation in pan-religious ecstasy . . . cosmic ascension and elation to mythological suns and nebulae and heliocentric worlds.'

It is important to note that the jazz musicians merely emphasize artistically and musically what the more aware members of the black community have been realizing extramusically. In March of 1967, for instance, teachers and students of a predominantly black New York high school boycotted all concerts of classical European music, not because they were not interested in European concert music – quite the contrary: musical activity at this school was above average – but because they felt it was wrong to be offered only concerts of European music, not jazz or Indian, Arabian, African, etc, music: 'This selection is arbitrary, based on European history, not ours.'

The opening of musical sounds into the realm of noise has to do with both world music and even more so with increased intensity. For centuries, there have been sounds in different exotic musical cultures, which may not necessarily seem 'musical' to a classically trained ear. Their explosive intensity has literally burst open the conventional sound barriers of the instruments of many free-jazz musicians: Saxophones sound like the intensified 'white noise' of electronic music, trombones like the noises of conveyor belts, trumpets like steel vessels bursting from atmospheric pressure, pianos like crackling wires, vibraphones like winds haunting metal branches; collectively improvising groups roar like mythical, howling primaeval creatures.

Indeed, the border between musical sound and noise, which seems so clear and natural to the average listener, is not physically definable; it is founded on traditional, tacit conventions. Fundamentally, music can use anything audible. In fact, this is its goal: the artistic utilization of what is audible. This goal cannot be reached when only some sounds are deemed suitable for music while all others are branded inappropriate.

Stockhausen says: 'Sounds previously classified as noise are now being incorporated into the vocabulary of our music . . . All sounds are music . . . music using all sounds is the music of today, not tomorrow, in our space age where the movement, direction, and speed of sounds are calculated elements of a composition. The object is to refresh and renew our known world of sounds with the available means of our time, just as every period of history has done.'

To be sure, Stockhausen says this essentially as a result of his experiences with electronic music. But it is true about every acoustic process generated by man: Pianos can be played not only on the keys, but also inside, on the strings; violins can be beaten; trumpets can be used (without mouthpiece) as blowpipes. People ridiculing these ways of playing instruments simply prove that to them, music is nothing but fulfilling conventional rules. An instrument exists to produce sounds. There are no laws governing the procedure of this production. On the contrary, it is the job of the musician to continually find new sounds. In doing so, he can use conventional instruments in new ways, or invent new instruments, or further develop conventional instruments. This job has become a major challenge for many musicians. For an edition of the avant-garde magazine *Microphone*, many modern British percussionists wrote detailed, page-long statements, but jazz drummer Tony Oxley simply wrote one sentence: 'The most important activity for me is the enlargement of my vocabulary.' This opinion is characteristic of many contemporary musicians.

We are living in an age which has created new sounds of unimaginable variety: jet planes and atomic explosions, the noises of oscillation and the ghostly crackling in the assembly buildings of precision industry. Big city dwellers are subject to a barrage of decibels which men of former times not only would have been unable to withstand physically, but which would have cast them into paroxysms of psychological confusion. Scientists have amplified the sounds of plant growth by millions of decibels so that they become a deafening roar. We now know that fish, deemed to be the quietest of all creatures by the romantics of the last century, exist in an environment of continual sounds. Every human being alive today is affected by this expansion of the realm of the audible. Are musicians, whose subject is sound, supposed to be the only ones unaffected?

Within a few years, free jazz became a richly varied means of expression, mastering the gamut of human emotions. We should free ourselves from the misconception that this music only voices anger, hate, and protest. This highly one-sided impression was created mainly by a small group of New York critics and musicians far from representative of all of free jazz. Besides the protest, there are the hymnlike religious fervour of John Coltrane, the joyous air of the folk musician in Albert Ayler, the intellectual, and yet humorous 'coolness' of Paul Bley or Ron Blake, the cosmic amplitude of Sun Ra, the sensibility of Carla Bley.

During the sixties, increasingly, young musicians and jazz fans all over the world were finding their way to the new sounds. While critics and unappreciative fans were still crying 'chaos', the new jazz was finding its audience – not only in the United States, but also in Europe, where an autonomous type of free music, European free jazz, evolved. There is hardly a country where as much free jazz is played as in Germany – first in West Germany, but since the end of the sixties also increasingly in East Germany. Today we have reason to suspect (with all the caution necessary in making such statements) that next to the Chicago-based AACM (cf the following chapter) there is no group of free-jazz musicians as homogeneous, musically as well as personally, as the German players of free music.

One claim keeps appearing in the countless critiques that this new style of music has spawned: the new freedom will ultimately end in chaos. However, after the understandable initial elation over the new freedom, the musicians began to emphasize that freedom was not the only point. Sunny Murray, the free-jazz drummer already mentioned, said: 'Complete freedom you could get from anyone who walks down the street. Give them $20, and they'll probably do something pretty free.' Similar statements have been made with increasing frequency since the end of the sixties. One reason for this is certainly that musicians became more aware that free jazz was developing its own clichés. And soon these free-jazz clichés – lacking a tradition – appeared even emptier than the clichés of conventional jazz which had just been so eagerly destroyed. In this way the majority of free-jazz musicians developed a new, dynamic interest in the jazz tradition. But there are other reasons why 'chaos' is an inappropriate concept. Let's take a look at the history of European music.

Three times in that history, a 'new music' appeared. First, there was *Ars Nova*, appearing around 1350; its most important composer was Guillaume de Machaut. Two and a half centuries later, around 1600, *Le Nuove Musiche* came into existence with the monodical music of the *Stilo Rappresentativo*, centring upon composers like Orazio Vecchi and Monteverdi. Both times, secular and religious musical authorities agreed that the new music meant the beginning of chaos in music. From this point on, that fear never vanished: Johann A. Hiller spoke 'with disgust' of Bach's 'crudities'. Copies of the first edition of Mozart's quartets were returned to him because the engraving was 'quite imperfect'. 'Many chords and dissonances were thought to be engraving faults.' (Franz Roh)

The reactions of critics contemporaneous with Beethoven are applicable to today: 'All neutral music specialists were in full accord that something as shrill, incoherent, and revolting to the ear was utterly without parallel in the history of music.' (This about the overture to 'Fidelio'!) Brahms, Bruckner, Wagner – at one time or another, they were all in the 'guild of chaotics'. Then came the third 'new music' – with all the well-documented scandals, misinterpretations, and misunderstandings. One need only recall the turbulence at the première of Stravinsky's 'Sacre du printemps' in Paris in 1913; the various Schoenberg scandals; or the première of Debussy's 'Pelléas et Mélisande' in 1902 (it was labelled 'brain music' and an example of 'nihilistic tendencies'). Today, all this music is considered 'classical', and the young avant-garde finds it 'old-fashioned'. Hollywood composers are using harmonies and sounds borrowed from it.

It was similar in jazz. At first, the 'new music' from New Orleans sounded 'chaotic' to the 'legitimate' ear: a wild, free departure to a confusing new land. However, by the turn of the fifties, New Orleans jazz had become party music for the young bourgeois.

When bebop appeared in 1943, the nearly universal opinion was that chaos had finally taken over, that jazz was nearing the end. Today, Dizzy Gillespie's trumpet and vocals sound as gay and familiar to us as 'When the Saints Go Marching In'.

The conclusion to be drawn from all this is that the word 'chaos' is merely a refrain that rhymes with 'history of music' – as simply as 'fun' and 'sun'. Free jazz also rhymes with it very well.

A bourgeois world which agrees on nothing as readily as on its need for security is first of all in need of awareness of the chaos surrounding it, if it wants to avoid totally despairing of consciously living. By bringing order to chaos, by giving it artistic expression, free jazz is one avenue for this consciousness. Ordering chaos, of course, is possible only by getting closer to it. This is where the 'sound of chaos' enters – first in classical European music, then, since the sixties, in jazz.

Free jazz wants to force us to cease understanding music as a means to self-affirmation. Man, who builds computers and sends satellites to Venus, has better means of self-affirmation. And the person whose racial problems and power politics are still in the style of the nineteenth century does not deserve self-affirmation, anyway.

By self-affirmation in music I mean the way all of us have been listening to music: always anticipating a few bars ahead – and when it comes out exactly (or at least nearly) as we expected we feel confirmed: we note with pride how right we have been. Music has had no other function than to cause such self-esteem. Everything has worked out perfectly – and the few places where things deviated have simply increased the fascination.

Free jazz must be listened to without this need for self-affirmation.

The music does not follow the listener anymore; the listener must follow the music – unconditionally – wherever it may lead. The members of a German avant-garde group, the Manfred Schoof Quintet, have spoken of the absolute 'emptiness', the 'tabula rasa' indispensable to that kind of musical experience. It was observed in the US that children could be enraptured by free jazz. They simply listen to what is happening – and a lot is! Wherever the sounds go, children follow. There is no place in their minds or sensory systems which, in the middle of each musical phrase, demands: This is the way it must continue; that is where it has to go; if it does anything else, it is 'wrong'. They demand nothing, and so get everything. The adults, however, for whom a piece of music – or a poem or picture – has almost no other function but to fulfil their demands, should not fool themselves: Except for guaranteed self-affirmation, they get nothing.

The Seventies

'The fusion has to happen inside you. Otherwise, it's not going to happen at all.' – John McLaughlin

Up to this point, we have been able to match each decade with a particular style – certainly at the cost of some fine distinctions, but with greater clarity as a result. With the beginning of the seventies, we have to drop this principle. This decade showed at least five distinct tendencies:

1. Fusion or jazz rock: the combination of jazz improvisation with rock rhythms and electronics.
2. A trend towards European romanticist chamber music, an 'aestheticization' of jazz, so to speak. Suddenly, large numbers of unaccompanied solos and duos appear on the scene, often without any rhythm section – no drums, no bass. Much that had been considered essential to jazz is dispensed with: explosive power, hardness, tremendous expressiveness, intensity, ecstasy, and no fear of 'ugliness' . . . As an American critic put it, jazz was being 'beautified' – or as we just put it, 'aestheticized'.
3. The new mainstream. Largely untouched by fads and trends,

the mainstream of jazz keeps on flowing. The mainstream musicians are heirs to the great jazz tradition from New Orleans and Louis Armstrong all the way to Miles Davis and John Coltrane. The times when 'mainstream' meant only Swing jazz, as in the fifties, are long gone. During the first half of the seventies, Miles Davis (see the chapter about him) was a sort of guiding star for many modern mainstream musicians; during the second half of the decade, John Coltrane (see the chapter on him and Ornette Coleman) assumed this function. A 'John Coltrane classicism' developed.

4. The music of the new free-jazz generation. When fusion music took over the scene in the early seventies, and immediately became a commercial success, many critics wrote: Free jazz is dead. But that was a rash judgement. Free music had only gone underground (and 'underground' back then also meant to Europe). The years 1973–74 marked the comeback of free playing, centred on the Chicago-based 'AACM', an association of musicians founded by pianist–composer Muhal Richard Abrams. In the course of the seventies, free-jazz musicians, spearheaded by the AACM players, became increasingly prominent. In 1979, *down beat* publisher Charles Suber wrote that the real surprise of the magazine's 1979 Critics Poll was that so many poll winners – individually or collectively – were identified with the AACM. And it only seems contradictory that free jazz of the seventies is more self-conscious on the one hand, while on the other (at least for the black players) it relates strongly and deliberately to the African roots of black music. The AACM musicians no longer call their music 'jazz', but – proudly – 'Great Black Music'. (More about the AACM in the chapter on jazz combos.)

Multi-instrumentalist and composer Anthony Braxton, also a product of the AACM, was the first free-jazz musician to achieve some commercial success in the United States in the seventies.

5. The gradual development of a new type of musician who transcends and integrates jazz, rock, and different musical cultures.

Among all these trends, there are countless overlaps and inter-conections. All of these playing styles developed through the interaction of free jazz with conventional tonality and musical structure, traditional jazz elements, modern European concert music, and elements of exotic musical cultures (India, above all), with European romanticism, blues, and rock. 'There's no longer just a free style of playing, it's all together,' said clarinetist Perry Robinson. Of course, the fundamentally new aspect is that the categorical nature of all these elements is dissolving. The elements no longer exist as distinct entities, as in earlier amalgams; they lose their singular nature and become pure music.

The jazz of the seventies is mainly cool, even where it seems hot. There is a similar kind of 'classicist' relation between the styles of the seventies and the sixties as there was between the cool jazz of the fifties and the bebop of the forties.

The freedom of free jazz did not simply mean caprice and chaos. Many free-jazz musicians knew and emphasized this from the beginning – but from the early seventies on, even outsiders have recognized it. The question of what goals the freedom of the sixties had set for itself found its answer in the music of the seventies. The musicians understood why freedom had been necessary: not so that everyone could do as he pleased, but rather to enable jazz musicians to freely make use of all the elements whose authoritarian and automatic characteristics they had overcome.

Harmonically, for example, jazz musicians did not abandon all harmony by learning to play with 'free tonality'. They merely liberated themselves from the automatic, machinelike functioning of conventional school harmony which, once a certain harmonic structure had been established, determined all harmonic progressions. The free-jazz musicians have broken through this 'authoritarian,' machinelike circularity of the harmonic process – and by doing so, are now that much better equipped to play aesthetically 'beautiful' harmonies.

Another example may be found in rhythm: Today we see that the regular meter of conventional jazz was not dissolved in order to destroy it, as it appeared to some fanatics in the initial phase of free jazz. Rather, it was dissolved because the automatic, mechanistic nature of the constant beat was in question. Indeed, an even, constant meter had become so taken for granted during the first sixty years of jazz history that personal artistic decisions in this realm were more or less impossible. Since the first half of the sixties, nothing in rhythm is taken for granted any longer. Now, all kinds of rhythm and meters, constant or not, can be used, with that much more freedom and independence.

Free jazz was a process of liberation. Only now can the jazz musician be really free – free to also play all the things that were strictly taboo for many creative musicians of the free-jazz period: thirds and triads, functional harmonic progressions, waltzes, songs and four-beat meters, discernible forms and structures, and romantic sounds.

The jazz of the seventies melodicizes and structuralizes the freedom of the jazz of the sixties.

To the nonspecialist, the seventies are primarily the decade of fusion music or, as it is often referred to in Europe, jazz–rock. But, as already mentioned, there were a lot of elements besides jazz and rock which were fusioned into this music.

The first signs of fusion could be seen in the late sixties – in groups like the Gary Burton Quartet, flutist Jeremy Steig's Jeremy and the Satyrs, the John Handy Quintet, pianist Mike Nock's Fourth Way, the Charles Lloyd Quartet, the Free Spirits of guitarist Larry Coryell, Tony Williams's first Lifetime group, and in various so-called compact big bands modelled after Blood, Sweat & Tears.

Interestingly enough, the fusion development was initially much stronger in Great Britain (beginning in 1963) – but it also came to an end much faster there (around 1969) – than in the US. With a bit of exaggeration one could say: In Great Britain, the sixties were already the decade of fusion music – in groups like the Graham Bond Organisation of organist Graham Bond; Colosseum and Cream; Soft Machine; and in musicians like guitarist John McLaughlin, bassist Jack Bruce, drummers Ginger Baker and Jon Hiseman, saxophonist Dick Heckstall-Smith.

And yet it was no doubt Miles Davis who made the breakthrough for fusion jazz with his album 'Bitches Brew', released in 1970. Miles was the first to reach a balanced and musically satisfactory integration of jazz and rock. He was the catalyst of jazz–rock – not only with his own records, but also because many of the decade's important players emerged from his groups.

The point in time when all this occurred is noteworthy. As we mentioned, 'Bitches Brew' was released in 1970, the time of the *Götterdämmerung* of the rock age: Jimi Hendrix, Janis Joplin, Brian Jones, Jim Morrison and Duane Allman died; the Beatles broke up. The worst disaster of the rock age occurred in Altamont, California, at a Rolling Stones concert: Four persons died, hundreds were wounded; all the wonderful goodwill of Woodstock was destroyed;

and Woodstock – the miracle of the 'Woodstock Nation', of a new, young society full of love, tolerance, and solidarity – showed its true business face. In New York and San Francisco, 'Fillmore East' and 'Fillmore West', centres of rock music, closed their doors for the last time. Suddenly the rock age had lost its drive, the age had lost its rock. No new groups or individual artists were appearing on the scene to tower above it. Towards the end of this period, Don McLean sang the sad, resigned refrain about the 'day when the music died', in his song 'American Pie', the closing hymn of the rock age. It was interpreted that way by the whole world. For weeks, the song was a top hit.

All that has been enumerated here happened between 1969 and 1972. The new jazz developed in exact parallel to these events, integrating rock and jazz. The year 1969 marked the release of Miles Davis's 'In a Silent Way', the album which paved the way for 'Bitches Brew'. In 1971, Weather Report and the Mahavishnu Orchestra were formed. From 1972 on, the new jazz is here, full-fledged, with all the groups to be introduced in the combo chapter. Anybody who 'integrates', who does not always focus on the one, rock *or* jazz, cannot help but conclude that this chronological parallel is not totally accidental. The rock age – or at least the best elements of it – flowed into the new jazz. The new jazz sensitized the rock music of the sixties, as the latter had similarly sensitized the rock 'n' roll of the fifties.

This point becomes clearer when one notes that there is a rock influence on jazz in four essential aspects: in the electronization of instruments, in rhythm, in a new attitude towards the solo, and – connected with that – in a stronger emphasis on composition and arrangement as well as on collective improvisation. In each of these aspects, the new jazz makes more sophisticated a characteristic of rock which rock musicians were unable to develop further.

In the area of electronics, the following instruments and accessories were added to the store of jazz instrumentation: electric pianos, organs, and other electronic keyboards: electronically amplified guitars and other instruments (among them saxophones, trumpets, and even drums), often used in connection with wah-wah and fuzz pedals, echolettes, phase shifters, ring modulators, and feedback units; varitones, multividers, etc (for octave duplication and automatic harmonization of melodic lines); two-board guitars (combining the possibilities of both six-string and twelve-string guitar or of guitar and bass); and synthesizers of various kinds, monophonic ones at the beginning of the decade, later also polyphonic.

Recording technology achieved similar importance. The modern recording studio has become so important that it has assumed the stature of an 'instrument' of equal value to those played by the musicians. A good recording engineer must have the same background knowledge and the same sensitivity as a musician – plus all the required technological expertise – because he 'plays' his controls and devices. The musicians, on the other hand, have acquired a level of technological know-how scarcely lower than that of many an engineer. Manipulating sound has become an art: with the aid of such devices as phasers, flangers, or chorus machines it is made to change, scintillate, 'migrate'. Some of these techniques are also used when recording conventional jazz, but of course much more discreetly than with jazz-rock or fusion.

At a superficial first glance, the tempting impression is that the jazz musicians simply took over all this equipment from rock and pop music; but on closer inspection, one discovers that the electric guitar, for example, was first featured by Charlie Christian in 1939 in Benny Goodman's sextet. And the electric organ first became popular in black rhythm & blues music, played by such musicians as Wild Bill Davis; it found its way into mass consciousness through the great success of jazz organist Jimmy Smith after 1956. The music world first became aware of the sparkling sound of the electric piano through Ray Charles's hit 'What'd I Say' in 1959. White rock music did not incorporate the instrument until Miles Davis recorded 'Filles de Kilimanjaro' with Herbie Hancock and Chick Corea on electric piano in 1968. The first experimentation with electronically amplified horns, varitones, and multividers was done by jazz musicians Sonny Stitt (1966) and Lee Konitz (1968). The synthesizer comes from concert music, where it had been developed and tested since 1957 by R. A. Moog in cooperation with Walter Carlos. Ring modulators, phase shifters, and feedback techniques were also first developed in the electronic studios of concert music.

The impression that all these sounds are sounds of rock is essentially the result of the gigantic publicity machine of the rock media and the record industry. Thus these sounds reached general mass consciousness. It must be seen, however, that the production of 'purely' electronic sounds first came from avant-garde concert music. The pioneer work in electrically amplifying and electronically manipulating conventional instruments was done by black musicians.

In this connection, it might be interesting to remember that it was a black singer in the thirties, Billie Holiday, who was the first to realize the potential of the microphone for a completely new use of the human singing voice. It has been said that Billie Holiday's style, which at the time was felt to be new and 'revolutionary', consisted mainly in 'microphonizing' the voice – in a way of singing unthinkable without the microphone. This 'microphone' style has become so commonplace for all kinds of popular music that hardly anyone can imagine how revolutionary it was when Billie Holiday created it.

Charles Keil and Marshal McLuhan point to the special talent of the Afro–American for making audible the new possibilities of electronics. Keil supposed that 'if McLuhan's thesis is correct, the electronic or post-literate age and its high-powered auditory forces that are now upon us ought to give Negro culture a big technological boost.'

In summary, we have shown that the electronization of the instruments was prepared by black musicians and that 'purely' electronic sounds were first developed in the studios of electronic concert music. The rock scene merely popularized these sounds. Jazz, rhythm & blues, electronic concert music, rock and pop all worked together. Such widespread cooperation, covering so many different areas of music, allows the conclusion that the introduction of electronics to music was a demand of the times. Not only the instruments but also the auditory needs of modern man are 'electronized' – of modern man from all social strata and classes, from the slums and ghettos to the music festivals of the intellectual world. Electronics, says American composer Steve Reich, have become 'ethnic'; electronics 'transport' the music which 'the people' want to hear – as animal hide and wood once transported the music in Africa. The music of an era is always 'transported' by that element which is the general determinant of life – and today that function is carried by electronics.

This is true especially for that segment of society which 'believes in electronics' – which believes that anything that can be done should be done, a way of thinking which today automatically implies electronics. Thus, this emphasis on electronics – and some of us would say: this overemphasis – signals a consensus with today's technologized world. The consensus stands in strange contradiction to the attitude of opposition with which many players of this music operate. It is obvious that the consensus is deeper than the opposition, because the consensus is expressed by the material and the sound of the music, the opposition merely by its gesture.

The question of loudness also belongs in this context. This point causes the outsider as many problems as did the constant beat of the basic meter thirty years ago. So many things have been said about loud volume. I have heard them all: that it is physiologically wrong, incommensurate with the potential of the human ear; that it therefore endangers the auditory faculties or eventually destroys them. There is always an otologist who can confirm this 'from daily experience' and the bourgeois press loves to print things like that. However, increased volume can also create sensibilities: Just a few years ago, nobody would have been able to discover as many subtleties as we can hear today in the gale-force range of sound waves generated by the Mahavishnu Orchestra or the group Weather Report, to name two. The new volume is a new challenge: he who meets that challenge will be capable of working with acoustic maxima that just yesterday seemed impossible for the ear to differentiate. In other words, loud volume widens human capacity and, thus, human consciousness – and therein lies its challenge. At a time when the sounds of our daily lives have reached decibels of unimagined dimensions, music cannot and must not remain fixed to the volume of yesterday or the day before. That would mean relinquishing the artistic breakthrough into the auditory ranges in which we live – in the sense which was sketched in the chapter on the jazz of the sixties in connection with the question of 'noise'.

So much for electronics. Let us consider rhythm next. The inadequacies of the jazz–rock combinations of the sixties were due mainly to the fact that the conventional rock rhythms of the popular groups were much too undifferentiated to be of interest to such a highly sensitized music as the jazz of today. Already in the early sixties, drummers like Elvin Jones, Tony Williams, or Sonny Murray were beating out rhythms without equal in Western music in their highly stratified complexity and intensity. In the face of this, the work of even the best rock drummers seems regressive. Interestingly, only jazz drummers have generally been successful in dealing with the extroverted, aggressive attitude of rock rhythms in such a way that structures corresponding to the high standards of jazz were produced. In the early seventies, the leading drummers in this field were Billy Cobham (of the first Mahavishnu Orchestra) and Alphonse Mouzon (of the first Weather Report). Both formed their own groups later.

The third aspect of the rock influence on jazz is the new approach to the solo. In all its periods, jazz always had its true culmination in the solo improvisations of outstanding individual artists. However, in the sixties – first in the US, then even more in Europe – an increasing number of free-jazz collectives came into being who began to doubt the validity of the conventional solo principle. Many of these jazz musicians – consciously or subconsciously – felt that the practice of individual improvisation, in which only the top individual performance counts, reflects all too faithfully the performance principle of the capitalist system. Parallel to the growing social and political criticism of this principle – in fact even a few years before its rise – a questioning of the value of the principle of individual improvisation had begun. The tendency to improvise collectively became stronger and stronger. The way for this was paved by bassist Charles Mingus, in whose groups there was a lot of free collective improvising as early as the late fifties. At the time it could not be foreseen that just a few years later such 'collectives' would be the hallmark of an entire musical development – in Europe even more so that in the US. Bands of the calibre of the Mahavishnu Orchestra showed such a high degree of complex interplay when improvising that one could barely tell which of the five musicians was leading at any given moment, not to speak of soloing in the traditional sense. Pianist Joe Zawinul said about his band, Weather Report: 'In this group, either nobody plays solo, or we all solo at the same time.'

From the start, record companies and producers played a bigger role in jazz-rock and fusion music than in any of the preceding jazz styles. They had a larger say about what was going to be recorded than the musicians themselves. And they made these decisions more with business than music in mind. Within a span of about five years, the musical impetus of fusion jazz got bogged down by this – in much the same way that, half a decade before, it got bogged down in Great Britain within five years.

As early as 1975, critic Robert Palmer wrote: 'Electric jazz/rock fusion music is a mutation that's beginning to show signs of adaptive strain . . . Fusion bands have found that it's a good idea to . . . stick with fairly simple chord voicings. Otherwise, the sound becomes muddy and overloaded. This means that the subtleties of jazz phrasing, the multilayered textures of jazz drumming and the music's rich harmonic language are being abandoned . . .'

The seventies produced an overwhelming inundation of jazz-rock records. Which will endure? At the highest quality level, certainly not much more than the two initial Miles Davis albums, all the records of the first Mahavishnu Orchestra (none by the other Mahavishnu formations!), a couple (and this is where the reservations start) by Chick Corea and Herbie Hancock and Weather Report, and four or five other albums: Not much, really, if you consider that during the peak of bebop – or during the Swing age before that – important, timeless recordings came out month after month; and today, after thirty or forty years, these are reissued because they have brilliantly stood the test of time. You can't help but wonder what will remain of rock-jazz and fusion music in thirty or forty years.

Many of the best rock-jazz musicians have felt a deficit in their music. Especially during the second half of the seventies, they increasingly returned to acoustic music in studio work or in concerts. ('Acoustic music' is the name for 'nonelectronic' sounds of conventional instruments – not a particularly fitting term, since of course all music is 'acoustic'.) When two of the most successful jazz-rock artists, Herbie Hancock and Chick Corea, went on their great duo tours, they dispensed with all the electronics they normally used and played only on the 'good old' concert grand piano. And the group VSOP brought musicians together on 'acoustic' instruments who had been particularly successful in 'electronic' jazz-rock, among them Herbie Hancock, Tony Williams, Freddie Hubbard, Wayne Shorter. It is striking how all these musicians really 'blossom out' when they 'finally' can play 'just music' again on 'normal' instruments without all the complicated electronics.

Only a few years ago, rock and free-jazz musicians represented two rather irreconcilable poles. Rock musicians considered free jazz esoteric and extremely hard to understand. On the other hand, free-jazz people felt that rock was primitive, simple-minded music, produced with an eye only to financial success. Certainly this popularity will continue to exist. But since the early seventies, more and more groups have emerged which are creating a new union from free jazz, rock, and all the other elements mentioned earlier.

One of the main reasons why rock elements could be integrated so smoothly into jazz is that, conversely, rock has drawn nearly all its elements from jazz – especially from blues, spirituals, gospel songs and the popular music of the black ghetto, rhythm & blues. Here the regular, steady rock beat, the gospel and soul phrases, the blues form and blues sound, the dominating sound of the electric guitar, etc, had all been in existence long before the appearance of rock. Drummer Shelly Manne once said: 'If jazz borrows from rock, it only borrows from itself.' A key figure in this development is blues guitarist B. B. King, who originated almost every element in the music of today's young rock and top-forty guitarists. Among these, one of the most successful is Eric Clapton, who was honest enough to admit: 'Some people talk about me like a revolutionary. That's nonsense – all I did was copy B. B. King . . .'

This is what vibraharpist Gary Burton meant when he said: 'There is no rock influence on us. We only have the same roots . . .'

We have talked about the way in which improvisation has become increasingly collective. You can hear this trend in the most diverse modern jazz styles, from free jazz to contemporary mainstream and on to fusion jazz. But as is almost always the case in jazz, it also has its countertrend, towards the solo unaccompanied by a conventional rhythm section, a trend initiated by vibraharpist Gary Burton. There have been many such unaccompanied solo or duo performances since the late sixties, from musicians such as pianists McCoy Tyner, Chick Corea, Keith Jarrett, Cecil Taylor, Oscar Peterson; saxophonists Archie Shepp, Anthony Braxton, Steve Lacy, and Roland Kirk; vibraharpist Karl Berger; trumpeter Leo Smith; trombonist George Lewis; guitarists John McLaughlin, Larry Coryell, Attila Zoller, John Abercrombie, Ralph Towner, and many others – and in Europe by Gunter Hampel, Martial Solal, Derek Bailey, Terje Rypdal, Albert Mangelsdorff, Alexander von Schlippenbach, John Surman; and in Japan by Masahiko Satoh and others.

Certainly, there had been earlier unaccompanied jazz solos. Coleman Hawkins recorded the first *a cappella* horn solo in 1947, 'Picasso'. Above all, unaccompanied playing was favoured by the great pianists, from the ragtime masters before and around the turn of the century to James P. Johnson and Fats Waller and on to Art Tatum and beyond.

As in almost all areas of jazz, Louis Armstrong was a forerunner in the field of the unaccompanied solo, too: in his duet with Earl Hines in 1928, 'Weather Bird', and in dozens of solo cadenzas and solo breaks.

However, these musicians merely paved the way for what has been, since the first half of the seventies, a clear tendency reflecting the social alienation, and the isolation of the jazz musician – and, in general, of modern man – the opposite of the collective spirit described above.

The trend towards the unaccompanied solo performance in the seventies was a romantic tendency, away from the loudness of electronic amplification and towards an intimate, extremely personalized, and sensitized form of expression, a symptom of a growing trend towards a new, objective, clear romanticism. And it is only fitting that in the history of this solo and duo movement – and also in the parallel movement towards an 'aestheticization' of jazz – Europe has played a special role. The first concerts in jazz history in which all the artists played without accompaniment took place at the jazz festival on the occasion of the Munich Olympic Games and at the Berlin Jazz Days in 1972 (both produced by this author). Among the artists appearing were Gary Burton, Chick Corea, Albert Mangelsdorff, Jean-Luc Ponty, John McLaughlin, Pierre Favre, Gunter Hampel, and ragtime pianist Eubie Blake. The Munich record company ECM has developed a concept and a sound which have become exemplary for this tendency towards the accent on aesthetics.

For the future, however, the gradual emergence of a new type of musician (which had already begun in free jazz, but is now becoming more of a world-wide tendency) promises to be more important than most of the trends described above. On the one hand, this new type of musician remains in touch with the jazz scene – but on the other hand he uses jazz only as a starting point, or even as merely one component among many others. These artists have integrated elements from a large number of musical cultures into their music – above all from India and Brazil, but also from Arabia, Bali, Japan, China, the various African cultures, and many others, and occasionally also from European concert music. They feel what McCoy Tyner put into these words: 'I see connections between all these different kinds of music. The music of the whole world is interrelated . . . What I see in music is something total . . .' And free-jazz trombonist Roswell Rudd, who was professor of music ethnology at the University of Maine, said: 'We're slowly starting to understand that there really is such a thing and that you can play it: world music . . . Today, we can listen to the musics of the whole world, from the Amazon jungles to the Malaysian highlands and to the recently discovered native people of the Philippines. All that music is now at our disposal . . . What's really important now is a new kind of hearing and seeing, right through these cultures.'

The prototype of this new breed of musician is Don Cherry, the former partner of Ornette Coleman. In the early sixties, we would still call him a free-jazz trumpeter. But what do we call him today? Cherry has become more deeply involved in the musics of the world than just about any other musician. And he has also learned to play instruments from different cultures, from Tibet, China, India, or Bali. His own answer to the question is: 'I'm a world musician.' And he calls his music 'primal music'.

The development towards this new type of musician was initiated by John Coltrane – even though he himself was not yet of that type. Clarinetist Tony Scott, who spent years in Asia and was one of the first to incorporate elements of many Asian music cultures, and flutist Paul Horn, who recorded a number of moving solos at the Taj Mahal in India, fit this description as early as the sixties. During the seventies, more and more of these 'world musicians' emerged, and this trend will continue. Among the younger generation of 'world musicians' are such artists as American sitar and tabla player Collin Walcott, Brazilian guitarist and composer Egberto Gismonti, the members of guitarist Ralph Towner's group Oregon, and Stephan Micus (who will be introduced at the end of the chapter on 'Miscellaneous Instruments').

In fact, there is even a music centre whose actual 'programme' includes world music: the Creative Music Studio of German vibraharpist Karl Berger in Woodstock, NY. Says Berger: 'When we started here in the early seventies, we may have called ourselves a "jazz school". But what actually interests us today, what we do and play and teach here, that's world music.'

The Eighties

As of the time of completion of this book, we can say only this about jazz in the eighties: The trends pointed to for the seventies continue to exist. Three further tendencies all had their beginnings in the last years of the seventies.

1. A remarkable return of Swing. All of a sudden, there is a whole generation of young musicians who look like rock or fusion players, but who play music reminiscent of the great masters of the Swing age: tenorists like Ben Webster or Coleman Hawkins, or trumpeters like Harry Edison or Buck Clayton. The most successful of these young musicians is tenor saxophonist Scott Hamilton from Providence, Rhode Island. Others are trumpeter Warren Vaché and guitarist Cal Collins.

There is even a record company specializing in the sound of the 'New Swing Age': the Concord Jazz label from California. But there are albums of this direction from other record companies, too; and reissues of classic Swing recordings have enjoyed amazing popularity.

2. An even more remarkable and wider comeback of bebop, initiated by the great tenor sax player Dexter Gordon. For years he had lived in relative seclusion in Europe, mostly in Copenhagen. Then, late in 1976, he came to New York for an appearance at the Village Vanguard. It was supposed to be a short engagement, but it became a triumphant comeback not only for Dexter Gordon (who has lived in the United States ever since), but also for bebop in general. At the beginning of the eighties, this bop revival had become so widespread that about 90 per cent of the New York clubs featured bebop music.

This is the third bebop wave in jazz history – after the original bop decade (the forties), and the hard bop of the late fifties. Just as hard bop incorporated the cool-jazz experience – above all, the longer melody phrases – the new bebop of the early eighties is incorporating all that has happened in the meantime. Two musicians seem to be omnipresent in the new bop wave though they are no longer living: Charles Mingus and John Coltrane. But there are also musicians who have incorporated their free-jazz experience into their bebop style, creating a sort of 'free bop'. This group includes musicians like drummer Barry Altschul and saxophonists Arthur Blythe, Oliver

Lake, Dewey Redman, and Julius Hemphill.

One of the amazing things is the musical perfection with which a whole generation of young American musicians is playing bebop again. Some of Charlie Parker's compositions are among the most difficult to play for a jazz musician. For decades there were only very few jazz musicians who could improvise over their complex harmonies – particularly because Parker loved to play them at a tempo bordering on the edge of human capability. But at the turn of the seventies to the eighties, dozens of Charlie Parker scores are being played and recorded by young musicians – and most of them at a tempo even exceeding Parker's original. One of Parker's most beautiful compositions, 'Donna Lee', which for decades had been all but forgotten, has become something of a trademark for contemporary young bebop musicians all over the world.

Of particular interest also is the 'classical' Max Roach–Clifford Brown Quintet, which initiated the development towards hard bop in the fifties. There are young players whose combo jazz clearly shows the influence of this group. Billy Harper, the tenor saxophonist, for example, has created a fascinating synthesis of the Parker tradition, Coltrane, Max Roach-Clifford Brown reminiscences, and gospel music. Young pianist Anthony Davis composed a 'Suite for Monk' in memory of Thelonious Monk's great music, and pianist and composer Heiner Stadler made a double-album tribute to Charlie Parker and Monk. And some record companies have specialized in bebop: Muse Records in New York, Bee Hive in Chicago, and the Danish-based Steeple Chase.

A number of bebop players have lived in obscurity for many years. It fits into the picture of the early eighties that many of them have returned to the New York scene, among them some of those great 'Americans in Europe' who left the United States – mainly in the early sixties – to carry the jazz message to the eastern shore of the Atlantic. Some of these players still reside in Europe but play in the US again quite regularly: one such is tenorist Johnny Griffin, from the Netherlands; others are trumpeter Art Farmer from Vienna, pianist Mal Waldron from Munich, bassist Red Mitchell from Stockholm. The two trombonists Jay Jay Johnson and Bob Brookmeyer – the former the actual creator of modern trombone playing in the forties; the latter a musician of West Coast jazz of the fifties – have given up their Californian seclusion and are featured on new records.

And trumpeter Woody Shaw, who had gone into 'inner exile' in San Francisco at the beginning of the seventies, is finally getting due recognition on the New York scene as the most creative contemporary bebop trumpeter.

3. With jazz–rock as a model, 'free funk' has come into being: a combination of free horn improvisations with rhythms and sounds from the funk, new wave (and even punk) scenes of popular music. The spokesman of 'free funk' – or as he likes to call it, 'no wave music' – is guitarist James Blood Ulmer, who had gained recognition in the early seventies as an Ornette Coleman sideman. In fact, there is still a lot of Coleman in his music. But there is also the simple directness – and the aggressiveness and the volume! – of new wave rock. Other groups heading in this direction are drummer Ronald Shannon Jackson's Decoding Society and altoist Luther Thomas's septet Dizzazz and trombonist Joe Bowie's Defunkt.

There will soon be more. Even old master Ornette Coleman has joined his former students in playing 'no wave'.

Outlook

It has become evident that most of today's more important jazz trends are conservative in nature. All of jazz history can be seen as a series of changes from hot to cool styles. New Orleans jazz was a hot style, while Chicago style had more cool aspects; Swing had both: cooler tendencies with white musicians like Benny Goodman or Artie Shaw and their bands, hotter ones with black musicians like those in the bands of Count Basie, Duke Ellington, Chick Webb, Jimmie Lunceford. Bebop, with its revolutionary attributes, of course was a hot style, followed by the mellowness of cool jazz. Then came another revolution, 'hot' free jazz – followed by the relatively cool seventies.

Consequently, the eighties ought to bring another revolution. And yet, it seems the eruption of a new hot style is unconsciously being delayed – in a way similar to what the hard-bop players did in the late fifties, who paved the way for and catalyzed the coming free jazz. It is possible that this is precisely what is happening at the moment, that exactly those musicians who embody the conservative elements of the jazz scene today are unconsciously helping to initiate a new style. Genuine revolutions – in jazz as in any other art form – are unthinkable without a vital awareness of what has gone before.

It is indisputable that jazz has gained a breadth that would have been unimaginable only a couple of years ago. In the last two chapters we have referred to eight trends influencing today's scene. In reality, there may be many more, if one considers marginal developments. This is in stark contrast to earlier decades, where one style generally was dominant and at most one or two more could be detected. Theodor W. Adorno, the German sociologist and philosopher of music, writing about Anton von Webern's adaptation of the 'Ricercar' from Bach's Musical Offering, coined the phrase '. . . break up what is mere style in it . . .' That's exactly what countless contemporary jazz musicians are doing. Webern's adaptation of Bach sounds late romantic, sometimes reminiscent of Richard Wagner or Schoenberg. All that, says Adorno, must already have been present in Bach's original work.

Something similar is true about jazz: the new bebop sounds contemporary. Its modern elements must have existed in Charlie Parker – or even further back, in New Orleans jazz. A whole generation of young contemporary jazz musicians has begun to break up styles – and will continue to do so even more decisively in years to come. That's why they often react so strongly when jazz critics or fans try to pin them to particular styles or ways of playing. They have created a new union of all the things which had been separated into different styles and ways of playing. In this union, the musical cliché has gained a new importance – previously felt, but never consciously realized.

Let me say something quite challenging: The jazz of the eighties and nineties will have to create new clichés. The general use by critics of the term 'cliché' as something exclusively negative has caused a lot of harm because vital, communicative music is impossible without clichés. Consider this: It is almost always the cliché that brings out emotions. A music without certain terms which we know from other contexts, familiar phrasings, structures realized many times in similar harmonies and sounds with which we (consciously or not) identify certain emotional processes – a music without all this can no longer be followed and empathized with.

We have to differentiate the concept 'cliché'. To be sure, there will always be clichés in the negative sense, and we will have to recognize them as such. Mere repetitions, all too self-evident, machinelike and obtrusively automatic features – as in the fusion clichés – will have to be avoided and attacked. But the fallacy of the jazz criticism and, more generally, jazz consciousness of the last twenty years was to consider everything that had been there before a cliché.

After twenty years of destroying clichés, all of a sudden we are realizing that we are faced with – I don't want to say 'nothing' – but very little. Says Herbie Hancock: 'It was as if you had to constantly talk with words never used before.' Anyone who does that consistently appears to be idiotic; or inconsiderate, inhumane, careless and loveless. I will take up this point later.

Make no mistake about it: If you criticize the beginning of a fairy tale because it starts with those words you've heard a thousand times before: 'Once upon a time . . .', you know nothing about fairy tales. Critics who cried 'Cliché!' at every blues cadence showed the same kind of ignorance, because the blues cadence is to jazz what 'Once upon a time' is to fairy tales. (I will return to this question, too, in connection with our attempt at a definition of jazz.)

Critics who characterize every festival by writing that 'once more, nothing new was presented', in the final analysis show only their own lack of maturity. He who is looking for novelty can no longer find the old, the warm, the human, and the communicative – which usually means that he can no longer find those things within himself, that he is alienated from himself.

The demand for something new at every festival, year after year, is an inhumane, cold, industrial, abstract demand. Art is love – and love is an act, something that only exists by doing. Anyone who says after this act that it was 'nothing new' robs himself of his own capacity for love. This is exactly what I see in that kind of critique: a lack of love. And that also characterizes the kind of music which wants to present something new at any cost: a lack of love. Jazz, however – perhaps more so than any other kind of music – is about loving, about recognizing, and doing it again.

THE MUSICIANS OF JAZZ

The Musicians of Jazz

'I play what I live,' said Sidney Bechet, one of the great men of old New Orleans. And Charlie Parker stated: 'Music is your own experience, your thoughts, your wisdom. If you don't live it, it won't come out on your horn.'

We shall see how the unmistakable sounds of the great jazz soloists, right down to technical elements, depend upon their personalities. The jazz musician's life is constantly transformed into music – without regard for 'beauty', 'form', and the many other concepts which mediate between music and life in the European tradition. That is why it is important to speak of the lives of the jazzmen. That is why the jazz enthusiast's desire to know the details of the lives of great musicians is legitimate. And it is also legitimate that such details make up a great part of the literature of jazz. They help us understand the music itself, and thus are quite a different story from the details fan magazines report about the lives of Hollywood stars.

'A person has to have lived to play great jazz, or else he'll be a copy,' says Milt Hinton, the bassist. Only a few musicians who exemplify this dictum could be selected for this book. But they are musicians in whom the history of a style is involved, with each one representing a specific period. Louis Armstrong stands for the great New Orleans period; Bessie Smith for the blues and jazz singing; Bix Beiderbecke for Chicago style; Duke Ellington for orchestra Swing; Coleman Hawkins and Lester Young for combo Swing; Charlie Parker for bebop, and modern jazz itself; Miles Davis for the whole development from cool jazz to the music of the seventies; Ornette Coleman and John Coltrane for the jazz revolution of the sixties; and John McLaughlin for the fusion music of the seventies.

Louis Armstrong

Until the rise of Dizzy Gillespie in the forties, there was no jazz trumpeter who did not stem from Louis Armstrong – or 'Satchmo', as he was called – and even after that, every player has been at least indirectly indebted to him.

The immense size of this debt became clear when impresario George Wein made the 1970 Newport Jazz Festival into one big birthday celebration for seventy-year-old Armstrong. World-famous jazz trumpeters competed for the most appropriate homage to Louis. Bobby Hackett called himself 'Louis Armstrong's Number One admirer', Joe Newman took exception: Not Hackett, but he himself should be called Louis's 'A-number one fan'; Jimmy Owens said that if he could not claim to be Armstrong's 'number one fan' or even 'A-one fan', he was at least his 'youngest fan'; and Dizzy Gillespie said: 'Louis Armstrong's station in the history of jazz . . . all I can say is UNIMPEACHABLE. If it weren't for him, there wouldn't be any of us. So I would like to take this moment to thank Louis Armstrong for my livelihood.'

Musicians other than trumpeters have also expressed their great debt to Armstrong. Frank Sinatra has pointed out that Armstrong made an art of singing popular music.

When Louis Armstrong died two days after his seventy-first birthday, on 6 July 1971, Duke Ellington said: 'If anyone was Mr Jazz, it was Louis Armstrong. He was the epitome of jazz and always will be. Every trumpet player who decided he wanted to lean towards the American idiom was influenced by him . . . he is what I call an American standard, an American original . . . I love him. God bless him.'

Louis Armstrong spent his youth in the turmoil of the great port on the Mississippi – in the old Creole quarter of New Orleans. The symbolic borders of this quarter were a jail, a church, a school for the poor, and a ballroom. His parents – his father was a factory worker, his mother a domestic – were separated when Louis barely had been born. Nobody paid much attention to him. Once or twice the authorities considered putting him in a reformatory, but nothing was done until, one New Year's Eve, Louis fired a pistol loaded with blanks in the streets. Then they put him in the reformatory. He became a member of the school choir which performed at funerals and at festivities. Louis received his first musical instruction on a battered old cornet from the leader of the reform school band.

One of the first bands in which Louis played was that of New Orleans' leading trombonist, Kid Ory. Little Louis happened to be passing by with his cornet as Ory's band was playing in the street. Somebody asked for whom he was carrying the instrument. 'Nobody. It's mine,' said Louis. Nobody would believe him. So Louis started to blow . . .

When during World War I the red-light district of Storyville was closed down by the Secretary of the Navy and the great exodus of musicians began, Louis was among those who remained. He did not go to Chicago until, in 1922, King Oliver sent for him to join his band, then playing at the Lincoln Gardens. Oliver's band – with the King himself and Louis on cornets, Honoré Dutrey on trombone, Johnny Dodds on clarinet, his brother Baby Dodds on drums, Bill Johnson on banjo, and Lil Hardin on piano – was then the most important jazz band. When Armstrong left it in 1924, it began to decline. To be sure, Oliver made several good recordings in later years – such as the 1926–27 series with his Savannah Syncopators – but by then other bands had become more important (Jelly Roll Morton's Red Hot Peppers, Fletcher Henderson, young Duke Ellington); and the end of Oliver's career presents the tragic spectacle of an impoverished man, without teeth, unable to play and earn money to live, a man who hides from his friends because he is ashamed and yet was once 'King of Jazz'. Here is an example of the tragedy of artistic existence – and there are many such tragedies in the annals of jazz. Louis Armstrong escaped this fate in an almost supernatural way. The ups and downs that characterize the lives of so many jazz musicians hardly ever affected him. For him there was only one direction: up.

It is a mark of Louis Armstrong's superiority that throughout his long career he had only two ensembles worthy of him . . . actually only one, because the first of these was a group organized for recording purposes only: Louis Armstrong's Hot Five (and later, Hot Seven) from 1925 to 1928. The other was the Louis Armstrong All Stars of the late forties – with trombonist Jack Teagarden, clarinetist Barney Bigard, and drummer Sid Catlett. With these 'All Stars' – and they really were – Armstrong won tremendous acclaim all over the world. With them he gave one of the most famous concerts of his career in Boston in 1947; it was later released on record.

The musicians who surrounded Satchmo in his Hot Five and Hot Seven are among the great personalities in traditional jazz. Johnny Dodds, the clarinetist, was there, as was trombonist Kid Ory, who many years earlier had given Louis a job in New Orleans. Later, pianist Earl Hines was added. He created a style of piano playing based on Louis's trumpet which became – and still is – a model for many pianists throughout the world.

There are few artists whose work and personality are as closely joined as Armstrong's. It is almost as if they had become interchangeable – and thus even the musically flawed Armstrong was made effective through his personality. In the liner notes to a record taken from Edward R. Murrow's film, *Satchmo the Great*, Armstrong says: 'When I pick up that horn . . . the world's behind me, and I don't concentrate on nothing but that horn . . . I mean, I don't feel no different about the horn now than I did when I was playing in New Orleans. No, that's my living and my life. I love them notes. That's why I try to make them right . . . That's why I married four times. The chicks didn't live with that horn . . . I mean, if I have an argument with my wife, that couldn't stop me from enjoying the show that I'm playing, I realize I could blow a horn after they pull away . . . I've expressed myself in the horn. I fell in love with it and it fell in love with me . . . What we play is life and a natural thing . . . If it's for laughs, for showmanship, it would be the same as if we were in a backyard practising or something. Everything that happens there is real . . . Yeah, I'm happy. Doing the right thing, playing for the highest people to the lowest . . . They come in Germany with them lorgnettes, and looking at you and everything, and by the time they get on the music, they done dropped the lorgnettes, and they're swinging, man! . . . When we played in Milano, after I finished my concert . . . I had to rush over to the La Scala and stand by those big cats like Verdi and Wagner . . . and take pictures, cause they figure our music's the same. We play them both from the heart.'

In such passages more is revealed about Armstrong's nature and music than from all the words a critic can say about them. The musical findings are, anyhow, as simple and immediate as the music itself: Louis Armstrong made jazz 'right'. He brought together emotional expression and musical technique. After Armstrong, it is no longer possible to make excuses for wrong notes with claims of vitality or authenticity. Since Armstrong, jazz has to be just as right as other music.

A brilliant article written on the occasion of Armstrong's death by critic Ralph Gleason has this to say: 'He took the tools of European musical organization – chords, notation, bars and the rest – and added to them the rhythms of the church and of New Orleans and (by definition) Africa, brought into the music the blue notes, the tricks of bending and twisting notes, and played it all with his unexcelled technique. He went as far with it as he could by using the blues and popular songs of the time as skeletons for his structural improvisations.'

Many of the young people who love to operate with the term 'revolution' have forgotten that Armstrong was the greatest of all jazz revolutionaries. They may be thinking of Charlie Parker or of Cecil Taylor and John Coltrane when they talk of musical revolutions. But the difference between the music before Armstrong and what he made of it is greater than the difference between the music before Parker or Taylor or Coltrane and what they made of it. So, the jazz revolution started by Armstrong is certainly the greater one.

A young fusion drummer, Bob Melton, was right when after Armstrong's death he wrote in a letter to the editor of *down beat* magazine: 'We've lost some great ones in the last five years . . . Today we lost the most daring innovator of all . . . I'm young, a "long-hair", a "jazz-rock" drummer . . . I've just played over and over about 20 times a 1947 Town Hall concert track of "Ain't Misbehavin' " with Pops . . . I've played it over that many times because in the last three years I've been filling my head with "free" tenor men and rock guitarists, and I've forgotten how audacious . . . is that the word? . . . I've forgotten how *outrageous* it *really was* . . . I mourn especially that so many of my generation . . . never heard Pops' message, and might not have listened if they had. You know that line of bull about not trusting anybody over thirty? Pops is one of the few people in this century I trusted!'

Between the Armstrong of the Hot Five and Hot Seven and the Armstrong of the All Stars of the forties and fifties stands the Armstrong of the big bands. This period began when Armstrong became a member of Fletcher Henderson's orchestra for a year, starting in 1924 and immediately following his departure from King Oliver. Armstrong brought so much stimulation to the rather commercial and mediocre Henderson aggregation of the time that one could say the year 1924 marks the real beginning of big-band jazz. There is a lot of significance and logic in the fact that Armstrong, the most important personality of the New Orleans jazz tradition, was co-founder of the jazz phase which years later replaced the great era of New Orleans: the Swing era of the thirties, with its big bands. Even with the recordings of his Hot Five and Hot Seven, however, Armstrong soon placed himself beyond the New Orleans form, with its three-voiced interweaving of trumpet, trombone, and clarinet. Armstrong is the man who, precisely with the most significant records of the Hot Five and Seven, dissolved this fabric . . . an achievement characteristic of many stylistic developments in jazz: Again and again, the important personalities within a style have paved the way for the next style when at the zenith of their own. Only the 'fans' demanded a standstill in one particular style. The musicians have always wanted to go on.

Armstrong's playing in Fletcher Henderson's band at the Roseland Ballroom in New York was a sensation among musicians. Armstrong himself found much inspiration in the – for that time – compact section sounds of the big band. Later he became convinced that his trumpet could unfold better against the backdrop of the big band than with a small ensemble – a feeling not shared by many jazz fans.

This feeling may be related to the fact that from the start Armstrong wanted to reach a larger audience – a wish which perhaps was the prime mover of his musical career. It might also account for the records through which the Armstrong of later years so often entered the realm of popular music. In fact, what is lost in simply saying that essentially all of Armstrong's music was meant to be 'popular' music – no matter how this might clash with the more or less naïve ideas of many a jazz fan?

'There is a definite implication that Louis has a primary interest in pleasing his audiences,' George Avakian has stated. Many jazz fans ignored Armstrong's success in the hit charts with 'Hello Dolly' with a determination that could give the impression that they were somewhat discomforted by his success. For Armstrong, however – and maybe even more so for his wife, Lucille – the real climax of his career came in 1964, when he took the top spot on the charts – the listings of the world's most popular records – away from the reigning Beatles, and held this spot for weeks with 'Hello Dolly'.

To Armstrong, singing was at least as important as trumpet playing – not just during his final years when, sometimes hardly able to blow his horn because of failing health, he remained a brilliant singer. During all phases of his career, he knew he could reach a larger audience as a singer than as an instrumentalist.

Rex Stewart, himself a trumpeter – in fact, one of the best – had to admit: 'Louis has bestowed so many gifts upon the world that it is almost impossible to assess in which area his definitive impact has been most felt. My vote would be for his tremendous talent of communication. As profoundly creative as his trumpet ability is, I would place this in a secondary position. He was revered mostly by other professionals, whereas his gravel-voiced singing has carried his message far and wide, to regions and places where not only was the music little known, the language foreign, but where there also was the further barrier of a political system having labelled jazz as decadent. But when Satchmo sang, the entire picture changed. People saw the truth.'

In a television programme produced on the occasion of the 1970 Newport Jazz Festival, Louis said: 'Well, people love me and my music and, you know, I love them and I have no problems at all with people. The minute I walk on the bandstand they know they're going to get something good and no jive and they know what they're there for and that's why they come . . . I'm the audience myself. I'm my own audience and I don't like to hear myself play bad or something, so I know it ain't no good for you . . . Some of the critics say I'm a clown, but a clown, that's something great. It's happiness to make people happy. Most of those critics don't know one note from the other . . . When I play, I just think of all my happy days . . . and the notes come by themselves. You've got to love to be able to play.'

During all of Armstrong's life, again and again, there was talk of the impending 'end of jazz music' or 'death of jazz' in papers and magazines, from the twenties right on up to the seventies. The communicative genius in Armstrong never believed such talk: 'I'd get me a record company and record nothing but what people said was finished – and we'd make a million dollars. You get those boys blowing out there – waitin' for that one gig, that one recording session, and we'd get together and set up, you know – we wouldn't go wrong. Everybody's looking for that top banana, but they're asleep on the good music that started all this,' he told Dan Morgenstern.

Louis Armstrong's success is, in a very important sense, the success of his personality. Anybody who knew him or worked with him can tell of an experience that illuminates the warmth and sincerity of Armstrong's personality. In 1962, I produced a television show in New York with the Armstrong All Stars. Only a short time before, Satchmo had been on camera sending regards to his German fans, asking them to have his *sauerkraut* and *wurst* ready for his upcoming tour. Then we were done; in a few minutes the studio had become dark and empty. I was next door, discussing the editing of the film. Satchmo, surrounded by a throng of fans, had left . . . About 45 minutes later, the elevator door opens and out comes Louis Armstrong, to tell me that he had already been sitting in a taxi when he realized he had not said goodbye to me. Somewhat in doubt, I suspected he had forgotten something. No, said Satchmo, he had just come back up to say goodbye. Which he did – and then he left. Jack Bradley, the jazz photographer, commented, 'Yes, that's the way he is.'

In the sixties, it became fashionable to call Armstrong an 'Uncle Tom' who had not shown any involvement in the black liberation struggle. However, in 1957 Satchmo said to a reporter of the Grand Forks (North Dakota) *Herald:* 'The way they are treating my people in the South – the Government can go to hell!' And then he cancelled a tour of the Soviet Union organized by the State Department, refusing to go abroad for a government led by such a President: 'The people over there ask me what's wrong with my country. What am I supposed to say? I have had a beautiful life in music, but I feel the situation the same as any other Negro . . .' His words resounded around the globe.

On a Scandinavian tour in 1965, as he was watching television coverage of the black protest in Selma, Alabama, he told a reporter: 'They would beat Jesus if he was black and marched.'

Louis Armstrong had human solidarity and human compassion, but he was not a political man. 'He loves people so much, he would even find good in a criminal. He is not capable of hate,' a British critic once wrote.

'Of how many American artists can it be said that they formed our century?' asks Martin Williams, and answers: 'I am not sure about our writers, painters, our concert composers. But I am certain Louis Armstrong has formed it.'

In a television programme on the occasion of Louis Armstrong's death in 1972, I said: 'There is no sound today on radio, television, or record which could not somehow be traced back to Armstrong. He must be compared with the other great innovators in the arts of this century – Stravinsky, Picasso, Schoenberg, James Joyce . . . He was the only native American among them. Without Armstrong, there would be no jazz – without jazz, there would be no modern popular music and no rock. All the sounds that surround us daily would be different without Satchmo; they would not exist without him. If it had not been for Armstrong, jazz would have remained the local folk music of New Orleans – as obscure as dozens of other bodies of folk music.'

'Folk music?' he once asked. 'Why, daddy, I don't know no other kind of music *but* folk music. I ain't never heard a horse sing a song.'

Soviet poet Yevgeny Yevtushenko wrote this poem in the days when the news of Louis Armstrong's death was going around the world:

> Do as you did in the past
> And play.
> Cheer up the state of the angels,
> And so the sinners won't get too
>   unhappy in Hell
> Make their lives a bit more hopeful
> Give to Armstrong a trumpet
> Angel Gabriel

Bessie Smith

> Papa, Papa, you're in a good man's way
> Papa, Papa, you're in a good man's way
> I can find one better than you any time of day.
>
> You ain't no good, so you'd better haul your freight
> You ain't no good, so you'd better haul your freight
> Mamma wants a live wire, Papa, you can take the gate.
>
> I'm a red hot woman, just full of flamin' youth
> I'm a red hot woman, just full of flamin' youth
> You can't cool me, daddy, you're no good, that's the truth.

'There was no pretence. It was the real thing: a woman cutting her

heart open with a knife until it was exposed for all to see . . .' as Carl
Van Vechten wrote.

Bessie Smith is the greatest of the many singers from the 'classical'
period of the blues, the twenties. She made 160 records, was featured
in a movie short, and was so successful at the peak of her career
during the early and mid-twenties that her record sales saved the old
Columbia Record Company from bankruptcy. Nearly ten million
Bessie Smith records were sold. Bessie 'is the Empress of the blues.'

Her personality had an awesome effect. She often elicited responses
from her listeners similar to religious experiences. They would shout
'amen' when she finished a blues – as they did after the spirituals or
gospel songs in the churches. At this time, nowhere else could one see
as clearly the relationship between spirituals and the blues.

Mahalia Jackson, the great singer of the modern spirituals, the
gospel songs, has said: 'Anybody that sings the blues is in a deep pit
yelling for help.' The blues tells of many things that have been lost:
lost love and lost happiness, lost freedom and lost human dignity.
Often the blues tells its story through a veil of irony. The coexistence
of sorrow and humour is characteristic of the blues. It is as if what one
is singing about becomes more bearable because it is not taken quite
seriously; even the most desperate situation may reveal something
amusing. At times, the comic element arises because one's misfortune
is so limitless that it cannot be presented in adequate words. And
always there is hope in the blues. As in 'Trouble in Mind': '. . . I
won't be blue always 'cause the sun will shine in my back door some
day.'

Bessie Smith sang like someone who hopes that the sun one day will
shine in her back door. And the sun did shine. Bessie earned a great
deal of money. But she lost it all. She spent it on drink, and on
whatever else she wanted; she gave it away to relatives and people
who seemed needy, or lost it to the men she was in love with.

Bessie Smith was born during the last decade of the nineteenth
century, in Tennessee. Nobody took care of her, but she started to
sing early. One day, blues singer Ma Rainey – 'the mother of the
blues' – came to town. Ma heard Bessie and took her in tow as a
member of her troupe.

Bessie sang in the circus and tent shows in the cities and towns of the
South. Frank Walker heard her, and signed her to a contract. In 1923

she made her first record: 'Downhearted Blues'. It was a sensation. It sold 800,000 copies – almost all bought by blacks. However, only one of her records was a real success among the white audience of those years, and that one for the wrong reason: her 'Empty Bed Blues', recorded in 1928 with trombonist Charlie Green, which was banned in Boston as obscene. 'But,' says George Hoefer, 'it's hard to believe that the Boston censor understood the words, not to speak of the music. The word "bed" alone did it.'

Aside from Bessie, there were many divas of the classic blues: Ma Rainey; Mamie Smith, who in 1920 made the first recording of a blues; Trixie Smith and Clara Smith, like Mamie, not related to Bessie; Ida Cox, who made 'Hard Times Blues' and was rediscovered and recorded in 1961, when she was past seventy; or Bertha 'Chippie' Hill, who recorded 'Trouble in Mind' with Louis Armstrong in 1926 and again with Lovie Austin's Blues Serenaders in 1946. But Bessie towers above them all.

It is hard to describe the magic of her voice. Maybe it is that its hardness and roughness seem to be edged with deep sorrow – even in the most frisky and humorous songs. Bessie sang as a representative of a people that had lived through centuries of slavery and, after Emancipation, often had to live through human situations that seemed worse than the darkest days of slavery. The fact that her sorrow found expression, without a trace of sentimentality, precisely in the rough hardness of her voice – this may be her secret.

On her recordings Bessie Smith often had first-rate accompanists – musicians like Louis Armstrong or James P. Johnson, Jack Teagarden, Chu Berry, Benny Goodman, Tommy Ladnier, Eddie Lang, Frankie Newton, Clarence Williams, and more of the best jazz musicians of the day. Fletcher Henderson – director of the then leading jazz orchestra – was responsible for her supporting combos for several years and placed his best men at her service.

No female singer in jazz is not influenced to some degree – directly or indirectly – by Bessie Smith. Louis Armstrong said of her: 'She used to thrill me at all times, the way she would phrase a note with a certain something in her voice no other blues singer could get. She had music in her soul and felt everything she did. Her sincerity with her music was an inspiration.'

Her decline began in the later twenties. By 1930, Bessie Smith, who five years earlier had been the most successful artist of her race (and one of the most successful in America), was in such dire straits that she had to accept bookings no longer in the great theatres of the North, but back where she had started from: rural travelling shows in the Deep South.

On 26 September 1937, Bessie Smith died after a highway collision near Clarksdale, Mississippi.

In an earlier edition of this book, a story of Bessie Smith's death was retold which reflected a belief still widespread in jazz circles: The singer died because the white hospital to which she was taken after the accident refused to treat a black patient; she bled to death 'on the steps' of this hospital.

While it must be granted that this story reflects the situation of the American Deep South at that time, it seems to have been proven (B. J. Skelton of the Clarksdale *Press Register* in the magazine *The Second Line* Vol 9, Nos 9 & 10, 1959) that the jazz world was misinformed in the case of Bessie Smith. She died in an ambulance en route to a black hospital in Clarksdale. It has also been ascertained that the wrong story originated in reports by members of the Chick Webb Band, which played Memphis shortly after the tragedy.

But the story of Bessie Smith's life and work does not end here. In 1971, Columbia Records rereleased the complete life work of Bessie Smith on five double albums. The 'Empress of the Blues' thus received an honour unprecedented in popular music: Thirty-four years after her death, she gained world-wide fame for the second time. Marketing analyses have shown that mainly young people bought the results of this 'most important and biggest single reissue project in history.' This shows that the words of Bessie Smith's great fan and rediscoverer, John Hammond, were understood: 'What Bessie sang in the twenties and thirties *is* the blues of today.'

This renaissance of the music and name of Bessie Smith was also the cause for the fact that her grave – a hardly identifiable hill in range 12, lot 20, section 10 of the Mount Lawn Cemetery in Sharon Hill, Pennsylvania – finally received a headstone. Black Philadelphia citizens and Janis Joplin, the white singer from Texas who had learned so much from Bessie, contributed towards the 500-dollar bill for the tombstone. The inscription reads: *The Greatest Blues Singer in the World Will Never Stop Singing* – Bessie Smith – 1895–1937.

Bix Beiderbecke

Bix Beiderbecke is among those musicians so well hidden by the myth which has evolved about them that it is difficult to discover the reality of the man. He was an inhibited person who never seemed satisfied with his achievements and always set unobtainable goals for himself: 'I think one of the reasons he drank so much was that he was a perfectionist and wanted to do more with music than any man possibly could. The frustration that resulted was a big factor,' says trumpeter Jimmy McPartland, who came particularly close to him musically.

And Paul Whiteman relates: 'Bix Beiderbecke, bless his soul, was crazy about the modern composers - Schoenberg, Stravinsky and Ravel . . . One evening I took him to the opera. It happened to be *Siegfried*. When he heard the bird calls in the third act, with those intervals that are modern today, when he began to realize that the *leitmotifs* of the opera were dressed, undressed, disguised, broken down, and built up again in every conceivable fashion, he decided that old man Wagner wasn't so corny after all and that Swing musicians didn't know such a helluva lot.'

Why Bix played in the dance orchestras of Whiteman and Jean Goldkette has often been misunderstood. The fans usually say he had to, because he could not make a living from jazz. But Bix was one of the most successful musicians during the second half of the twenties. He was in a position to play where he wanted, and always earn money enough. George Avakian has said: 'No one put a pistol in his back to make him join these bands.' Actually Bix joined Whiteman - the epitome of commercial music of the day - because he was fascinated by the fancy arrangements written for the band. Here he could at least hang on to a reflection of the colourful orchestral palettes of Ravel, Delius, Stravinsky, and Debussy.

And thus it was - later in the thirties and forties - that record collectors all over the world bought the old records of Paul Whiteman to listen over and over again to eight or sixteen bars of solo blown by Bix - and these recordings have repeatedly been reissued up to this day. (Indeed, no other musical form from the first half of the century has remained so alive on records as jazz. In opera, reissues of Caruso and a few other great stars are still an exception, for example. In jazz, on the other hand, the re-release of the most important records of the outstanding musicians from the first fifty years of jazz has become the rule.)

When Beiderbecke's work in Whiteman's orchestra is viewed from a contemporary perspective, the difference between it and the jazz records by Bix with his friends is really not too great. Few of the musicians with Bix on his own recording dates could shine his shoes. Not much lasts on them aside from Bix's cornet: the ensemble passages he leads and the solos he improvises.

Bix Beiderbecke is – more than any other musician – the essence of Chicago style. The following musicians – although some only stem from it and gained real importance in other styles – were part of Chicago style: saxophonist Frankie Trumbauer, trumpeters Muggsy Spanier and Jimmy McPartland; drummers Gene Krupa, George Wettling, and Dave Tough; the Dorsey Brothers (Jimmy on alto and clarinet, Tommy on trombone); tenor man Bud Freeman; violinist Joe Venuti, one of the few jazz violinists of those times; guitarists Eddie Lang and Eddie Condon; trombonists Glenn Miller and Jack Teagarden; clarinetists Pee Wee Russell, Frank Teschemacher, Benny Goodman, and Mezz Mezzrow; pianist Joe Sullivan; and a dozen or so others.

Their history is tragic in more ways than one. Rarely was so much enthusiasm for jazz concentrated in any single place as among them. Even so, most of their records from the period are unsatisfactory. The chief reason may be that there was no single band which, on a higher level, represented Chicago style per se. There is no ensemble like Louis Armstrong's Hot Seven or Jelly Roll Morton's Red Hot Peppers, which immediately comes to mind when New Orleans style is mentioned; or like the bands of Count Basie or Benny Goodman and the Teddy Wilson combos in Swing; or the Charlie Parker Quintet in bop. From an ensemble point of view – in the sense explicated in the combo chapter of this book – Chicago style failed to produce a single satisfying recording. Almost always, only solo passages are remarkable: the unmistakable clarinet sound of Frank Teschemacher, the tenor improvisations of Bud Freeman, the 'cool' alto lines of Frankie Trumbauer, and – most of all – Bix Beiderbecke's cornet.

It has been argued that Chicago style is not really a 'style'. Its best recordings, indeed, come so close to Dixieland or New Orleans that what is most typical of Chicago style seems to be only the unfinished quality of its few fine records. And yet, there are a few musical signposts – mainly the rather novel emphasis on solo contributions – which differentiate Chicago from New Orleans and Dixieland. Most of all, the *human* unity and rapport among the Chicagoans was so strong and was reflected in their music with such immediacy that one hesitates – even now – to tear them apart on theoretical and academic grounds.

Bix Beiderbecke came from Davenport, Iowa. He was born there in 1903, the son of a family of German immigrants. His ancestors had been clergymen and organists in Pomerania and Mecklenburg for generations. One of his father's given names was Bismarck and this name – shortened to Bix – was inherited by the son. As a boy, Bix sang in the chorus of the Lutheran church in Davenport. His grandfather led a German male glee club.

Bix was a musical prodigy. It is said that he first became acquainted with jazz through the riverboats which docked on the Mississippi; some of them had bands from New Orleans, and the music carried across the water.

Soon Bix became so absorbed in music that people began to think him a bit strange. He was expelled from school because he was interested only in music. The image of young Beiderbecke wandering the streets like a dreamer, his beat-up cornet wrapped in newspaper, became proverbial to all who knew him.

With Beiderbecke German romanticism – and the whole spectrum of feelings that belong to it – entered jazz. Perhaps it was this romantic heritage, fraught with yearning and melancholia, which created in Bix a state of mind similar to that which had come to black people through their American experience. What to the great New Orleans musician was the musical heritage of Africa, if preserved only subconsciously, was to Beiderbecke the 'Blue Flower' of German romanticism. He was a Novalis (a lyric poet of German romanticism [1772–1801]) of jazz, transported into the 'jazz age' of the roaring twenties with all the life-hungry characters of F. Scott Fitzgerald.

Beiderbecke was – aside from the old ragtime pianists – the first great 'cool' soloist of jazz history. From his cool conception a line leads straight to Miles Davis.

At eighteen, he began to play in public. In 1923, he was with the first real Chicago-style band, the Wolverines. In 1924, he met saxophonist Frank Trumbauer, with whom he made many of his finest records. There followed jobs with a variety of groups – with

Jean Goldkette, Hoagy Carmichael, and other bands, until, by the late twenties, Bix was one of the select musicians who gave the music of Paul Whiteman its jazz spice.

Around 1927 a lung complaint became noticeable. Bix paid no attention. He played and played, and when he wasn't playing, he drank or went to symphony concerts. He experimented in the harmonic world of Debussy, primarily at the piano. He wrote a few pieces in which – in astonishingly simple, naïve fashion – Impressionism was captured. The titles are revealing: 'In a Mist', 'In the Dark', 'Flashes'.

As a trumpeter he was mainly a jazz musician; at the piano he was rather more indebted to the European tradition.

Finally, Whiteman sent him to Davenport for a rest. (He kept him on salary.) But it was too late. Bix could not stay home long. A girl – one of the few in his life – persuaded him to move to Queens and got him an apartment.

Bix spent the last weeks of his life in the apartment of bassist George Kraslow. Here something occurred which is characteristic of the love which Bix inspired in everyone. He was in the habit of getting up around three or four in the morning to play his cornet. It is hard to imagine a jazz musician doing such a thing without bringing down upon himself the wrath of all the neighbours. Nothing of the sort happened. The neighbours told Kraslow: 'Please don't mention we said anything . . . we would hate for him to stop.'

In August, 1931, Beiderbecke died of pneumonia in Kraslow's apartment. In Germany – on the 'Lüneburger Heide' south of Hamburg – there are still Beiderbeckes. I asked them about Bix once. They had never heard of him.

Duke Ellington

Duke Ellington's Orchestra is a complex configuration of many spiritual and musical elements. To be sure, it was Duke Ellington's music which was created here; but it was just as much the music of each individual member of the band. Many Ellington pieces were genuine collective achievements, but it was Ellington who headed the collective. Attempts have been made to describe how Ellington recordings came into being – but the process was so subtle that verbalization appears crude. Duke, or his alter ego, the late Billy

Strayhorn, arranger and jazz composer, or one of the members of the band, would come to the studio with a theme. Ellington would play it on the piano. The rhythm section would fall in. One or another of the horn men would pick it up. Baritone saxophonist Harry Carney might improvise a solo on it. The brass would make up a suitable background for him, and Ellington would sit at the piano and listen, gently accenting the harmonies – and suddenly he'd know: This is how the piece should sound and no other way . . . later, when it was transcribed, the note paper only happened to retain what was – in the real meaning of the word – improvised into being.

The dynamic willpower with which Ellington stamped his ideas on his musicians, yet giving them the impression that he was only helping them to unfold and develop their hidden powers, was one of his many great gifts. Owing to this relationship between Duke and his musicians, which can barely be put into words, everything he had written seemed to be created for him and his orchestra – to such a degree that hardly anyone can copy it. Once, it is said, Paul Whiteman and Ferde Grofé, his arranger, went night after night to the club where Ellington was playing, because they wanted to assimilate some of Ellington's typical sounds. Finally they gave up: 'You can't steal from him.'

Duke Ellington has written countless popular melodies – melodies in the genre of Jerome Kern, Richard Rodgers, Cole Porter, or Irving Berlin. But even the most popular among them – 'Sophisticated Lady', 'Mood Indigo', 'Creole Love Call', 'Solitude', 'Caravan' – have seldom become big hits. No matter how memorable and melodic, they seem to lose too much of their essence when not played by Ellington himself.

When Ellington was eighteen, he wanted to become a painter. By becoming a musician he only seemed to have abandoned painting. He painted not in colours but in sounds. His compositions – with their many colours of timbre and harmony – are musical paintings. Sometimes this is revealed by the titles: 'The Flaming Sword', 'Beautiful Indians', 'Portrait of Bert Williams', 'Sepia Panorama', 'Country Girl', 'Dusk in the Desert', 'Mood Indigo', and so forth. Even as a conductor, Ellington remained the painter: in the grand manner in which he confronted the orchestra and, with a few sure movements of the hand, placed spots of colour on a canvas made of sounds.

It may be due to this that he perceived his music as 'the

transformation of memories into sounds.' The memories are pictures. Ellington said: 'The memory of things gone is important to a jazz musician. I remember I once wrote a sixty-four-bar piece about a memory of when I was a little boy in bed and heard a man whistling on the street outside, his footsteps echoing away.'

Again and again Ellington has expressed his pride in the colour of his skin. Many of his larger works took their themes from black history: 'Black, Brown, and Beige', the tone-painting of the American Negro who was 'black' when he came to the New World, became 'brown' in the days of slavery, and today is 'beige' – not only in his colour, but in his being as well; 'Liberian Suite' – a work in six movements commissioned by the small republic on the west coast of Africa for its centennial; 'Harlem', the work in which the atmosphere of New York's black city has been captured; 'Deep South Suite', which reminds us of the locale of the origins of jazz, or 'New World A-comin',' the work about a better world without racial discrimination.

'I want to create the music of the American Negro,' Ellington once said, placing the accent on 'American'. He was conscious of the fact that the American Negro had more in common with the world of the white man than with that of black Africa. To a man who once wrote him that he should take his jungle music and go back to Africa as soon as possible, he replied with extreme courtesy that this unfortunately was impossible, inasmuch as the blood of the American Negro in the course of generations had become so mixed with that of the letter writer that he would hardly be accepted there. But if it were all right with the writer, he would go to Europe. 'There we are accepted.'

Many critics have said that Ellington often comes too close to European music. They point to his concern with larger forms. But in this very concern is revealed an insufficiency in the moulding of these forms which is certainly not European: An astonishing, amiable naïveté. This naïveté was also present in those medleys – long series of his many successful tunes – with which the Duke again and again upset many of his more sophisticated fans at his concerts. Ellington simply failed to see why the idea of the hit medley should be alien to an artistic music.

In 1923 he joined a five-piece combo, which already included three of his later-to-be-famous instrumentalists: Otto Hardwicke, alto sax;

Sonny Greer, drums; Arthur Whetsol, trumpet. The combo took the name 'The Washingtonians' – from the capital, where Ellington was born in 1899, and where he spent a sheltered, carefree youth.

The Washingtonians went to New York where – as Duke told it – they sometimes had to split a hot dog five ways to keep from starving. After six months they gave up.

Three years later, Ellington tried again. This time it worked. Soon he was playing in Harlem's most expensive nightspot, the Cotton Club, located in Harlem but nevertheless catering to white tourists – to give them the feeling that they had 'really been to Harlem.' Ellington's first famous records were made: 'East St Louis Toodle-oo', 'Jubilee Stomp', 'Birmingham Breakdown', and 'Black and Tan Fantasy'.

The germ cell of his Cotton Club orchestra was preserved by Ellington well into the fifties. No other band leader has known so well how to keep an orchestra together. While other successful bands had personnel changes every few months, Ellington in twenty years only had six or seven significant alterations. Among the important soloists with Ellington at the Cotton Club were trumpeter Bubber Miley, trombonist Joe 'Tricky Sam' Nanton, and baritone saxophonist Harry Carney. Ellington created his 'jungle style' with Miley and Nanton. The expressive growl sounds of trumpet and trombone were reminiscent of voices moaning in a jungle night.

The 'jungle style' is one of the four styles identified with Duke Ellington. The other three are (in a somewhat simplistic, but also synoptically clear grouping): 'mood style', 'concerto style', and a 'standard style', which came rather directly from Fletcher Henderson, the most important band leader of the twenties, and initially did not contribute much that was new. What it did have to offer, though, was clothed in typically Ellington colours and sounds. In addition, of course, there is every imaginable mixture of these 'styles'.

The 'mood style' partakes of blues-feeling – even in pieces which are not really blues. 'Solitude', which says more in three minutes about the feeling its title describes than many a bulky book, is the most famous example of 'mood style'.

As far as the 'concerto style' is concerned, there are really two: real small concerti for different soloists in the Ellington orchestra – such as the famous 'Concerto for Cootie' for trumpeter Cootie Williams; and the aforementioned attempts to write jazz in larger forms.

The history of Duke Ellington is the history of the orchestra in jazz. No significant big band – and this includes commercial dance bands – has not been directly or indirectly influenced by the Duke. The list of innovations and techniques introduced by Ellington and subsequently picked up by other orchestras or players is unrivalled.

In 1927, he was the first to use the human voice as an instrument. The voice was Adelaide Hall's; the tune, 'Creole Love Call'. Later, he was to create similar effects with Kay Davis's coloratura soprano. Today, the expression 'voice as instrument' has become a household phrase.

With his 1937 recording, 'Caravan', a tune written with his Puerto Rican trombonist Juan Tizol, he paved the way for what has been called 'Cuban jazz' since the forties – and what is today called 'Latin jazz': the combination of Latin American rhythms with the melodies and harmonies of North American jazz.

Duke Ellington was first to use so-called echo chambers in recording. Today, echo chambers are taken for granted. In 1938, Johnny Hodges's solo on 'Empty Ballroom Blues' was the first solo ever to be recorded with echo chamber.

Towards the end of the twenties there is evidence of the 'flatted fifth', the interval so characteristic of bop, in more than one Ellington piece.

With his baritone saxophonist, Harry Carney, Ellington created a place for the baritone in jazz.

For years, the history of the jazz bass was so closely tied to the Ellington orchestra that it might be as appropriate to discuss it here as in the later chapter about the bass. There is a straight-line development from the first recording with amplified bass – 'Hot and Bothered' with bassist Wellman Braud in 1928 – to the playing of Oscar Pettiford and especially Jimmy Blanton, who as a member of the Ellington band around 1940 made the bass the instrument it is in jazz today.

Everything we mean when we speak of sound and instrumentation in jazz can almost without exception be traced to Duke Ellington.

And most significant: Duke Ellington anticipated by decades that strange and paradoxical creature called 'jazz composer'. He was the only one from 1925 to 1945 composing on the level on which jazz compositions were written later. Only then came all the others: John Lewis, Ralph Burns, Jimmy Giuffre, Bill Russo, George Russell, Gerry Mulligan, Charles Mingus, Carla Bley, Gil Evans, Oliver Nelson . . .

Incomparable, too, is the way in which Ellington dealt with the problem of the piano in jazz – about which we will hear later. The piano became an extension of his conducting hands. He played only what was most necessary, indicated harmonies, bridged gaps, and left everything else to his musicians. His piano breaks were like a drummer's. Duke often executed them without using the piano stool, but they are filled with admirable tension, and when he played one of his rare solos, one feels to this day his roots in the old, genuine ragtime.

Ellington's two most famous orchestras were that of the late twenties, with Bubber Miley and 'Tricky Sam' Nanton, and that of the early forties, with bassist Jimmy Blanton and tenor man Ben Webster. Modern big band jazz begins with the latter; 'Ko Ko' is its best-known piece. After that, there was occasional talk about the decline of Ellington. Some people advised him to disband his orchestra, or to keep it together for only a few months of the year and spend the rest of his time composing. But Duke needed his musicians: 'I want to have them around me,' Leonard Feather quoted him, 'to play my music. I'm not worried about creating music for posterity, I just want it to sound good right now!'

Besides, Duke Ellington himself put an end to the 'decline' of which hasty critics had spoken. This occurred at the Newport Festival in 1956. Duke Ellington was billed as just another of the many attractions. Nobody expected anything out of the ordinary, but his appearance proved to be the climax of the whole festival. Duke played his old (1937) 'Diminuendo and Crescendo in Blue', one of his first extended compositions; Paul Gonsalves blew twenty-seven choruses of stimulating tenor sax on it, and the band generated a vitality and drive the likes of which had not been heard from Ellington in a long time.

It was one of the great jazz nights of the fifties. And what had been forgotten for a few years again became apparent: Duke Ellington was still the 'grand old man' of big-band jazz. A string of new masterpieces came into being: first and foremost the Shakespeare suite 'Such Sweet Thunder', dedicated to the Shakespeare Festival at Stratford, Ontario. With its spirited glosses, persiflages, and caricatures of great Shakespearean characters, it is one of the most beautiful of the larger Ellington works.

In 1967, Billy Strayhorn died; in 1970, altoist Johnny Hodges. Since the death in 1932 of trumpeter Bubber Miley, who together with Ellington had formed the 'jungle style' with his 'growl play' between 1925 and 1929 (and who was replaced by another outstanding soloist, Cootie Williams), Ellington had not taken any personal loss so hard as the death of these two great musicians. The rich, sensuous solos of Johnny Hodges had reflected almost uninterruptedly since 1928 – for forty-two years! – the romantic, sensuous, impressionistic side of Ellington's character. Composer and arranger Billy Strayhorn had contributed many important pieces to the band's repertoire, such as 'Lush Life', 'Chelsea Bridge', and 'Take the A Train', the theme song of the Ellington orchestra. As an orchestrator, he 'tuned in' to Duke so perfectly that even specialists often were hard put to differentiate between what was written by Ellington and what by Billy 'Sweet Pea' Strayhorn.

But Strayhorn's loss unearthed once again a host of new creative powers in Ellington. During the sixties, he had increasingly left the main composing and arranging work to Strayhorn. Now he began – alone again – to take the initiative himself. A large number of important new great works were created: The 'Sacred Concert' and, following that, 'Second Sacred Concert'; Duke Ellington's '70th Birthday Concert' (chosen in 1969 as 'Jazz Record of the Year' all over the world); the 'Far East Suite' (in which Ellington reflects on a tour of Asia, sponsored by the Department of State, in a highly personal manner); and – above all – the 'New Orleans Suite', which became the 1970 'Record of the Year'. In the latter recording, Ellington salutes the New Orleans heritage of the jazz tradition, and transforms it into Ellingtonian music.

Jazz specialists have said that these years after Strayhorn's death comprise one of the richest and most fruitful periods in Ellington's fifty-year life work – in terms of composition, as well as in terms of the number of concerts and tours by the Ellington orchestra.

In 1970, the Ellington band went on one of the longest tours ever made by a jazz orchestra: the Soviet Union, Europe, Latin America – all without a break, for three months. And again and again, one had the impression that seventy-year-old Ellington was the youngest, most active, most dynamic man in this orchestra of his juniors. Often, when the other band members seemed to drift into sweet slumber behind their music stands, Ellington would fascinate his audience with his humour, spirit, and charm. And when his musicians would be exhausted towards the end of a concert, he would gather a small group of four or five soloists and create with them rare apexes of youthful vitality.

In 1969, we turned the Berlin Jazz Days into a grand birthday celebration for the seventy-year-old Ellington, and dozens of famous musicians – not only the older generation, but also personalities like Miles Davis and Cecil Taylor – paid tribute to the Duke. And a critic wrote that Ellington had been 'the youngest musician at the whole festival.'

Five years later, on 25 May 1974, Duke Ellington – the Great Orchestrator of Jazz – died of pneumonia in a New York hospital. Just a couple of weeks before, *down beat*, on the occasion of his seventy-fifth birthday, had dedicated to him a whole issue full of congratuations. From Leonard Bernstein to Miles Davis the music world paid homage to him. Drummer Louis Bellson, possibly, found the most moving words: 'You, the MAESTRO, have given me a beautiful education musically and have guided me to be a good human being. Your valued knowledge and friendship will be with me forever. You are the model citizen of the world. Your music is Peace, Love and Happiness.'

Duke Ellington's music will remain with us – not only in the Duke Ellington Orchestra, which was taken over by his son Mercer after his death, and which continues to play the compositions of the Grand Old Man. It is with an occasional tinge of disappointment that you hear this band now, but finally with the respect that is due the son of the great Duke Ellington.

First and foremost, though, Duke Ellington's music continues to live in the hundreds of musicians who learned from him and who, in turn, pass on their experiences and developments to their students and successors: a stream of 'Ellingtonia' that will continue to flow as long as there is jazz.

Coleman Hawkins and Lester Young

Until the late sixties, when the guitar and electronic instruments came into the foreground, the sound of modern jazz was – to use a favourite term of arranger Bill Russo – 'tenorized'. The man who tenorized it was Lester Young.

More important musicians play tenor saxophone than any other instrument. The sound of Miles Davis's 'Capitol' band has been described as the orchestration of Lester Young's tenor sound. The other important jazz sound of the fifties – the 'Four Brothers' sound of the Woody Herman band – is tenorized, too. The tenor men who played it, almost all other important tenorists, and even trumpeters, trombonists, pianists, alto and baritone saxists of the cool jazz of the fifties – all were influenced by Lester Young.

With Lester 'Pres' (from President) Young cool jazz, the jazz of the fifties, began long before there was bebop, the jazz of the forties. It began with the solos played by Lester in the old Count Basie band: 'Song of the Islands' and 'Clap Hands, Here Comes Charlie', recorded in 1939 – or 'Lady Be Good', recorded by a Count Basie combo in 1936 – or even earlier, when Lester Young became a member of Fletcher Henderson's band in 1934. 'The whole band was buzzing on me,' Lester reminisced, 'because I had taken Hawk's place. I didn't have the same kind of sound he had. I was rooming at the Hendersons' house, and Leora Henderson would wake me early in the morning and play Hawkins' records for me so I could play like he did. I wanted to play my own way, but I just listened. I didn't want to hurt her feelings.'

Coleman Hawkins and Lester Young – these two names designate two great eras of jazz. Since 'Bean' and 'Pres' both played tenor, and since each of them holds approximately the same position in the phase of jazz he represents, no two other personalities could show more clearly how wide the scale of being and meaning in jazz really is. At one end stands Coleman Hawkins – the extroverted rhapsodist with the voluminous tone. Hard and gripping on fast pieces, erotically expressive on slow numbers, always vitally communicative, never shying away from quantity in utterances or notes, he is a Rubens of jazz . . . And opposite him stands Lester Young – the introverted lyricist with the supple, soft tone, friendly and obliging on fast pieces, full of tender abandon on slow numbers, reserved in utterance, never stating a nuance more than is absolutely necessary. He is a Cézanne of jazz, as Marshall Stearns has called him – which not only indicates his artistic but also his historical position: As Cézanne paved the way for modern painting, so Young paved the way for modern jazz.

It would be an oversimplification, however, to assign one man to the jazz tradition and the other to modern jazz. Both stem from the tradition; both were 'modern'. Coleman Hawkins emerged from the Jazz Hounds, the group accompanying blues singer Mamie Smith; Lester Young was born near New Orleans and in his youth received the same impressions which affected the old New Orleans musicians: street parades, Mardi Gras, and New Orleans funerals. When the modern jazz of the forties sprang up, Coleman Hawkins was the first noted 'traditional' jazz musician to play with the young bebop revolutionaries. And in the second half of the fifties, the period just preceding the death of Young (who after years of almost constant indulgence in alcohol and marijuana was only a shadow of his former self), the man who preceded him - Coleman Hawkins - retained his old, indestructible vitality and power.

Hawkins is 'the father of the tenor saxophone.' To be sure, there were some tenor players before him, but the instrument was not an acknowledged jazz horn. It fell into the category of strange noise makers - like the euphonium, the sousaphone, or the bass sax.

Coleman Hawkins was twenty-one when he came to New York with Mamie Smith in 1923. He was playing blues and jazz in the style of that time - similar possibly to King Oliver and Louis Armstrong - and he was one of the few black musicians who played with the young Chicago-style jazzmen. That same year, he joined the first important big band - Fletcher Henderson's - and remained until 1934. He was the first real tenor saxophone soloist, in the sense of the great virtuosos of the Swing period. He was one of the first to make records with the young European musicians who were just then beginning to hear the jazz message: in 1934 with Jack Hylton in England, in 1935 with The Ramblers in Holland and with Django Reinhardt in Paris. And as modern jazz began - as we have mentioned - he was again one of the first to participate. Hawkins could always be found where alive and original jazz was being created.

His first famous solo record was the 1926 rendition of 'Stampede', with Fletcher Henderson. In 1929 came 'One Hour' with the Mound City Blue Blowers, who included some of the Chicago-style practitioners. And then, in 1934, again with Henderson, 'Talk of the Town' - probably the first great solo ballad interpretation in jazz history, the foundation for everything now meant by ballad playing in modern jazz. (Miles Davis said: 'When I heard Hawk, I learned to play ballads.') Then came the European recordings, such as 'I Wanna Go Back to Harlem' with the Dutch Ramblers, or 'Stardust' with Django

Reinhardt. When Hawkins returned to the United States in 1939, he almost immediately scored the greatest success of his career: 'Body and Soul', a jazz record which became a world-wide hit. Hawkins could not understand it: 'I've been playing like that all my life . . . it wasn't anything special.' In 1943 he blew a breathtaking solo on 'The Man I Love' with Oscar Pettiford's bass and Shelly Manne's drums, and then, in 1947, came 'Picasso' – a long improvisation for unaccompanied tenor saxophone, based on the harmonies of the piece identified with Hawkins – 'Body and Soul'. It is reminiscent in structure and delineation of Johann Sebastian Bach's Chaconne from the D-minor Partita for solo violin, and full of the same baroque vitality and linearity.

On all these records, and in almost everything he has ever played, Hawkins is the master of the chorus. A Hawkins solo, it has been said, is the classic example of how to develop a solo statement from a phrase. And almost every phrase Hawkins has blown could itself be used again as the theme for a jazz improvisation. There is only one musician who can be compared to him in this respect – the one who in almost every other respect is his opposite: Lester Young.

While everything about Hawkins, the human being, is simple and comprehensible, everything about Lester is strange and incomprehensible. A booking agent, Nat Hentoff relates, gave up working with Lester because he couldn't talk to him. 'I'd talk to him,' the agent said, 'and all he'd say was "Bells!" or "Ding Dong!" I finally decided I'd go to Bellevue if I wanted to talk to crazy people . . .'

He left the Count Basie band, from which he emerged and with which he was connected as Hawkins had been with Fletcher Henderson's band, because Basie had set a recording date for a Friday the thirteenth – and Lester refused to play on that day.

His jargon was almost a language in itself, which made it hard for people to understand him in conversation. No one has coined as many jazz expressions as he – right down to the word 'cool' – so that not only the style but also the expression stems from him. He called his colleagues 'lady' and addressed club owners as 'Pres'; he asked pianist Bobby Scott about his 'left people' when he wanted to tease Scott about the habit (shared by many modern pianists) of running hornlike lines with his right hand while the left hardly came into play. Norman Granz says that Lester for a time pretended to be speaking a foreign language: 'It was gibberish, but he did it with a straight face and with conviction.'

Lester had the sensibility of a Baudelaire or James Joyce. 'He lives in his own world,' an agent said about him. What was outside of this world, was, according to Pres's convictions, not in the world at all. But this world of his was a wonderful world, a world that was mild and friendly and lovely. 'Anything that hurts a human being hurts him,' said drummer Jo Jones.

Jones relates: 'Everyone playing an instrument in jazz expresses what's on his mind. Lester would play a lot of musical phrases that were actually words. He would literally talk on his horn. That's his conversation. I can tell what he's talking about in 85 per cent of what he'll play in a night. I could write his thoughts down on paper from what I hear from his horn. Benny Goodman even made a tune out of a phrase Lester would play on his horn – "I want some money".' Because Lester talked on his horn, he loved to listen to singers: 'Most of the time I spend in listening to records is listening to singers and getting the lyrics to different songs.'

When improvising on a melody, Lester Young attempted to convey the lyrics of this melody to the listener directly and without the aid of words. Thus, he recorded some of his most beautiful solos as accompanist to singer Billie Holiday, the greatest female singer since Bessie Smith – perhaps simply the greatest, and in any case the personification of Swing singing, as Bessie Smith was the personification of the classic blues. The way in which Pres backed 'Lady Day' – the name he gave her – set the standard for accompaniments to singing in jazz, with such pieces as 'Time on My Hands', 'Without Your Love', or 'Me, Myself and I'.

What Lester tells us when he improvises freely on his tenor sax might sound something like this: 'I was born near New Orleans, 27 August 1909. I stayed in New Orleans until I was ten. During the carnival season we all travelled with the minstrel show, through Kansas, Nebraska, South Dakota, all through there.

'I played drums from the time I was ten to about thirteen. Quit them because I got tired of packing them up. I'd take a look at the girls after the show, and before I'd get the drums packed, they'd be gone.

'For a good five or six years after that I played the alto, and then the baritone when I joined Art Bronson's band. Ran away from my father when I was about eighteen . . . I joined Art Bronson and his Bostonians. Played with him for three or four years . . . anyway, I was playing the baritone and it was weighing me down. I'm real lazy, you know. So when the tenor man left, I took over his instrument . . .

'Used to hear the Basie band all the time on the radio and figured they needed a tenor player. They were at the Reno Club in Kansas City. It was crazy, the whole band was gone, but just this tenor player. I figured it was about time, so I sent Basie a telegram . . .

'But Basie was like school. I used to fall asleep in school, because I had my lesson, and there was nothing else to do. The teacher would be teaching those who hadn't studied at home, but I had, so I'd go to sleep . . . you had to sit there and play it over and over again. Just sit in that chair.

'I joined Fletcher Henderson in Detroit in 1934. Basie was in Little Rock then, and Henderson offered me more money. Basie said I could go . . . was with Henderson only about six months. The band wasn't working very much . . . then back to Basie until 1944 and the army.'

The army broke Lester Young. Nat Hentoff has told of this. He was harassed, and his individuality and sensitivity were deadened, in the way armies all over the world deaden individuality and sensitivity. Through the army, hate came into his life; hate particularly for whites, or so Hentoff supposes. For a musician whose message was lyricism and tenderness and amiability there was not much left.

The other thing which oppressed him – subconsciously and sometimes consciously – was the fact that almost every tenor player was playing á la Pres . . . until during the last years of his life Sonny Rollins and the musicians of his school came up. The worst thing was that there was a man who often played a 'better' Lester Young than Lester himself: Paul Quinichette; Lester called him 'Lady Q'. Pres's manager tells of the time when both were playing at Birdland – the famous, now defunct jazz club in New York – and Lester came off the stand saying: 'I don't know whether to play like me or like Lady Q, because he's playing so much like me.'

It was a peculiar brand of irony: On the one hand, nothing underlined Lester's enormous artistic success more than that an entire generation of tenor men should play like him; on the other hand, as an uncompromising individualist he found it intolerable that they all should play like him – and he like them.

Most of the records Lester made in the fifties – such as the ones for Norman Granz's Verve label – were only a pale reflection of the great 'President'. But often there were sparks, and one could still feel something of the genius of this great musician – for instance, on the record 'Jazz Giants of 1956,' with Teddy Wilson, Roy Eldridge, Vic Dickenson, and other great Swing musicians.

For years Lester travelled with Norman Granz's concert unit, 'Jazz at the Philharmonic', all over the world. Night after night, he witnessed how Flip Phillips brought audiences to their feet with the exhibitionism of his tenor solos. He disliked this ecstatic way of playing tenor, but it reached the point where he himself often utilized it – and from this, too, he must have suffered. For years, Lester Young lived almost uninterruptedly in a state of intoxication, until, in March of 1959, he died after a tragic engagement at the Blue Note, a Paris jazz club. Ben Benjamin, the club owner, reports: 'Lester was very sick when he worked for me. He was almost apathetic. He wanted to go home because, as he said, he couldn't talk to the French doctors. He had ulcers, and I think he drank a little too much . . .'

Lester came back to New York in time to die. On the early morning of his arrival, he died in the Hotel Alvin, on the 'musician's crossroad', at 52nd Street and Broadway, where he lived during the last years of his life.

The only thing Lester retained throughout the crisis periods of his life, and down to his last days, was his sound – as Coleman Hawkins retained his. 'The only thing nobody can steal from you is your sound. Sound alone is important,' Hawkins once said.

Lester's sonority stems from Frankie Trumbauer and Bud Freeman, the Chicago-style musicians. 'Trumbauer was my idol . . . I imagine I can still play all those solos off the records. He played the C-melody saxophone. I tried to get the sound of a C-melody on a tenor. That's why I don't sound like other people . . . I did like Bud Freeman very much. Nobody played like him.' The line that leads from Chicago style via Lester Young to cool jazz is direct.

The name of Lester Young even stands at the beginning of bebop, Kenny Clarke tells about it: 'They began to talk about Bird [Charlie Parker] because he was playing like Pres on alto. People became concerned about what he was doing. We thought that was something phenomenal because Lester Young was the pace setter, the style setter at that time . . . We went to listen to Bird at Monroe's [a Harlem club] for no other reason except that he sounded like Pres . . . until we found out that he had something of his own to offer . . . something new.' And Parker himself said: 'I was crazy about

Lester. He played so clean and beautifully, but I wasn't influenced by
Lester. Our ideas ran on differently.'

Indeed, these were two different directions. It would be possible to
show that modern jazz as a whole – even up to free jazz – has
developed in the counterplay of the ideas of Lester Young and
Charlie Parker. Lester came first: then, when Parker arrived, *his*
influence became dominant – but then, in the fifties, Pres's hour
struck again, with a host of musicians playing 'cool' *à la* Lester
Young . . . until finally, with the coming of hard bop, Bird's influence
again assumed overwhelming importance. And with this Bird
influence, with the sonority of Sonny Rollins's tenor sax, we return –
and so the circle of this chapter closes – to Coleman Hawkins: His
hard, dramatic style now was in the right place – after Lester Young's
desire to make the world 'nice and cosy' had proven vain, although it
had been shared by all jazz musicians for so many years. Hawkins,
whose career preceded that of Lester Young by almost ten years, also
survived Lester by ten years. His health was as robust as his playing
(with the exception of the last years of his life), and only weeks before
his death – in June of 1969 – he appeared in concerts and on
television. The tenor saxophonists of free jazz who meanwhile had so
radically changed jazz – Archie Shepp, Pharoah Sanders, Albert
Ayler, and others – all agreed on who had given the first impulses to
those expanding inflections of tenor sound that were their main focus:
Coleman Hawkins. Archie Shepp said it clearly: 'I play Hawk today.'

For Coleman Hawkins, this whole rich era he had lived through –
from Mamie Smith in 1922 to the post-Coltrane period in 1969 – was
not as varied as it seems to us today. It was *one* style and *one* era. The
style was jazz, and from the beginning until today and beyond, it was
the era of jazz. Progress was a foreign word to Hawkins. He once said
to critic Stanley Dance: 'What Charlie Parker and Dizzy were doing
was "far out" to a lot of people, but it was just music to me.' And he
made recordings with the young bebop people only because 'they
needed help'. When Dance talked to him about Mamie Smith and
Fletcher Henderson and the good old days, Hawkins said: 'I don't
think I ever was a child.'

Charlie Parker and Dizzy Gillespie

'Just a week before his death,' Leonard Feather tells us, 'Parker ran into Gillespie at Basin Street. He was desperate, pitiful, pleading. "Let's get together again," he urged Dizzy. "I want to play with you again before it is too late." '

'Dizzy can't get over Bird saying that to him,' recalls Loraine, Dizzy's wife. 'His eyes get full of water even now when he thinks about it . . . '

Charlie Parker and Dizzy Gillespie are the Dioscuri of bebop.

Charlie Parker comes from Kansas City. He was born on 29 August 1920, but when he died in 1955, the doctors who performed the autopsy said that he might as well have been 55 as 35.

Dizzy Gillespie comes from South Carolina. He was born on 21 October 1917. In all phases of his life he has appeared to be five to eight years younger than he is.

Both grew up in the world of racial discrimination and from early youth they experienced the humiliations that are a part of it.

Nobody cared much about young Charlie. Throughout his youth, he lacked love and the warmth of the nest.

Dizzy had a sheltered youth and grew up in a well-ordered family environment.

No one was musical in Charlie Parker's family. At thirteen, he was playing baritone sax. A few years later, alto was added.

Dizzy Gillespie's father was an amateur musician. He taught his kids to play several instruments. At fourteen, Dizzy's chief horn was the trombone. A year later, trumpet was added.

It has always been a mystery why Charlie Parker became a musician. The alto-saxophonist Gigi Gryce – one of his best friends – says: 'Parker was a natural genius. If he had become a plumber, I

It seemed decided from the start that Dizzy would become a musician. He studied theory and harmony.

believe he would have become a
great one.'

At fifteen years of age – Charlie   . . . at the age at which Dizzy
was forced to earn his own keep.   completed the studies paid for by
'We had to play,' he said, 'from   his father . . .
nine in the evening to five in the
morning without a break. We
usually got $1 or $1.25 a night.'

In 1937 – at seventeen – Charlie   In the same year – 1937 – Dizzy
became a member of Jay Mc-   took over Roy Eldridge's chair in
Shann's band, a typical Kansas   Teddy Hill's band.
City riff and blues orchestra.
Parker said he was 'crazy about   Roy was Dizzy's great model. The
Lester Young,' but it is question-   Hill band had grown out of the
able whether he had a real model.   Luis Russell orchestra, and
It is probable that his colleagues at Russell himself had taken over the
first considered his style 'terrible' King Oliver band in 1929. Thus,
because he played 'different' from   the jazz genealogy from Dizzy
anybody else.   back to King Oliver and Louis
                                       Armstrong is surprisingly short.

Parker's real schooling and tradi-   Dizzy Gillespie, too, has roots in
tion was the blues. He heard it   the jazz tradition, but it is rather
constantly in Kansas City and   the happy tradition of New
played it night after night with   Orleans and Dixieland music.
Jay McShann.

   The titles of the first records made by both men are symbolic:

Charlie Parker recorded 'Confes-   Dizzy Gillespie recorded, in mid-
sin' the Blues' on 30 April 1941, in   1937, just after becoming a mem-
Dallas, Texas, with Jay Mc-   ber of Teddy Hill's band, Jelly
Shann's band (however, there are   Roll Morton's 'King Porter
earlier recordings – from 30   Stomp.'
November 1940, also with Jay
McShann, made for radio station
KFBI in Wichita, Kansas).

Charlie Parker at first did not get far from Kansas City. He lived a dreary, joyless life and became acquainted with narcotics almost simultaneously with music. It is believed that Parker had become a victim of 'the habit' by the time he was fifteen.

The inhibitions and complexes of his life began the moment he became a musician. Charlie Parker played with Jay McShann until 1941. There were a few interruptions. Once he landed in jail for twenty-two days when he refused to pay his cab fare. Then there was a fugitive journey to Chicago. He arrived there dirty and tattered as if he had 'just got off a freight car'. But he was playing 'like you never heard . . .'

For three months he was a dishwasher for $9 a week in a secondrate Harlem restaurant. Sometimes he didn't even have a horn to play on. 'I was always in a panic,' is one of his bestknown quotes. He slept in garages, became completely run down. 'Worst of all was that nobody understood my music.'

Dizzy went to Europe with Teddy Hill's band in the summer of 1937. Teddy Hill writes: 'Some of the guys threatened not to go if the frantic one went too. But it developed that youthful Dizzy, with all his eccentricities and practical jokes, was the most stable man of the group. He was able to save so much money that he encouraged the others to borrow from him so that he'd have an income in case things got rough back in the States.'

Dizzy Gillespie was successful from the moment he began to play. In Paris it was first noticed that his playing was different. A French drummer wrote at the time: 'There is in the band of Teddy Hill a very young trumpeter who promises much. It is a pity that he has no opportunity to make recordings here. He is - along with trombonist Dickie Wells - by far the most gifted musician in the band. His name is Dizzy Gillespie.'

Upon his return from Europe, Dizzy Gillespie became a successful musician, playing in different bands. In 1939, he became a member of Cab Calloway's orchestra.

When Parker once played in a jam session in Kansas City with members of the Basie band, and nobody liked what he was blowing, drummer Jo Jones 'as an expression of his feelings took his cymbal off and threw it almost the entire distance of the room. Bird just packed up his horn and went out.'

Parker tells: 'I'd been getting bored with the stereotyped changes that were being used all the time at the time, and I kept thinking there's bound to be something else. I could hear it sometimes, but I couldn't play it.'

'Well, that night I was working over "Cherokee," and, as I did, I found that by using the higher intervals of a chord as a melody line and backing them with appropriately related changes, I could play the thing I'd been hearing. I came alive.'

Cab Calloway didn't like the way Dizzy played. Nor did he care for Dizzy's penchant for practical jokes and, occasionally, also for quarrelling. During an engagement in Hartford, someone (not Dizzy) threw a spitball out on the stage, hitting the bandleader. After the curtain, Cab blamed Diz, 'and an argument ensued,' bassist Milt Hinton relates. 'Cab made a pass at Dizzy, and Dizzy came at him with a knife. I grabbed Diz's hand . . . but Cab was nicked in the scuffle. Cab hadn't realized he'd been cut until he was back in the dressing room.'

Dizzy tells: 'When I was growing up, all I wanted to play was Swing. Eldridge was my boy. All I ever did was try to play like him; but I never quite made it. I'd get all messed up because I couldn't get it. So I tried something else. That has developed into what became known as bop.'

One of the first records Dizzy made with Cab Calloway's band had the odd title, 'Chop, Chop, Charlie Chan'; that was on 8 March 1940. A dozen years later, Parker appeared on the last record made by Dizzy and Bird together under the pseudonym 'Charlie Chan.' (Chan was his wife's first name.)

When he was not playing with Jay McShann, Charlie Parker pulled through with menial jobs. He participated in every jam session he could find.

In 1941 he came to New York with the McShann band. They played at the Savoy Ballroom in Harlem.

Starting in 1939 Dizzy had begun to arrange. Successful bands like Woody Herman's, Jimmy Dorsey's and Ina Ray Hutton's bought his arrangements.

Dizzy Gillespie came by to sit in.

Bird and Dizzy had met in Kansas City in 1939, but it was most likely on this night that they really played together for the first time.

Soon, the McShann band left New York. Parker went along to Detroit. Then he no longer could stand the routine arrangements and left the band, without saying anything. He never cared much for big bands.

Dizzy Gillespie evolved more and more into a big-band musician. After the row with Calloway he worked in the big bands of Benny Carter, Charlie Barnet, Lucky Millinder, Earl Hines (1943), Duke Ellington, and Billy Eckstine (1944).

After he had left the McShann band, Charlie Parker went almost daily to Minton's in Harlem. A band consisting of pianist Thelonious Monk, guitarist Charlie Christian, trumpeter Joe Guy, bassist Nick Fenton, and drummer Kenny Clarke was playing there. 'Nobody,' Monk was to say later, 'was sitting there trying to make up something new on purpose. The job at Minton's was a job we were playing, that's all.' Yet Minton's became the point of crystallization for bop. There Charlie Parker and Dizzy Gillespie met again.

Monk relates that Charlie Parker's ability and authority were immediately accepted when he began to show up at Minton's. All could feel his creative productive genius.

A psychological point: Whenever you see Parker photographed with

Billy Eckstine relates: 'Now Diz is like a fox, you know. He's one of the smartest guys around. Musically, he knows what he is doing backwards and forwards. So what he hears – that you think maybe is going through – goes in and stays. Later, he'll go home and figure it all out just what it is.'

other musicians, he is always
standing further away from the
others than they are standing from
each other.

Charlie Parker and Dizzy Gillespie became inseparable. In 1943 they
played together in Earl Hine's band; in 1944 they were both with Billy
Eckstine. In the same year they co-led a combo on 52nd Street, which
became The Street of Bop. In 1944 they also made their first joint
recording.

Tony Scott relates: 'And Bird
came in one night and sat in with
Don Byas. He blew "Cherokee"
and everybody just flipped . . .
When Bird and Diz hit The Street
regularly a couple of years later,
everybody was astounded and
nobody could get near their way
of playing music. Finally, Bird
and Dizzy made records, and
then guys could imitate and go
from there. Everybody was
experimenting around 1942, but
nobody had set a style yet. Bird
provided the push.'

In Leonard Feather's words:
'. . . Dizzy's followers were aping
his goatee, beret and glasses, even
his gait.' Dizzy created then what
was to go around the world as
'bebop-fashion'. Fan magazines
advertised 'bebop ties'.

Charlie Parker had found, in the
quintet format of bebop, the
instrumentation most congenial
to him: sax, trumpet, and three
rhythm. The Charlie Parker
Quintet became as significant to
modern jazz as Louis Armstrong's
Hot Five had been to traditional.

Deep inside, Dizzy is a big-band
man. In 1945, he founded his first
own big band. From 1946 to 1950
he had large bands almost
steadily. In 1948 he took one to
Europe. His Paris concert had
long-lasting effects on European
jazz.

It becomes clearer: Dizzy Gillespie in those days was the most
frequently mentioned bebop musician. If he did not bring to this music
the creative impulses that radiated from Charlie Parker, he gave it the

glamour and power without which it could not have conquered the world.

Billy Eckstine says: 'Bird was responsible for the actual playing of [bebop], more than anyone else. But for putting it down, Dizzy was responsible.'

With his Charlie Parker Quintet, Bird made the most important combo recordings of bebop: 'Koko', based on the changes to 'Cherokee', the piece with which he first had attracted attention; 'Now Is the Time', a blues; 'Chasin' the Bird', with the fugato entry of trumpeter Miles Davis – commencing the fashion of fugues and fugati in modern jazz . . . and countless others. Accompanied by Erroll Garner he recorded 'Cool Blues', relating coolness and the blues in the title itself.

'Things to Come' became the most important record of the Gillespie big band, an apocalyptic vision of the things that were to come: a broiling, twitching mass of lava, out of which for a few seconds arise ghostly figurations, to disappear again at once. But above it all the clear and triumphant sound of Dizzy's trumpet. 'Music of chaos', as some people said then, but also music about man's victory over chaos!

Charlie Parker's alto sax became the most expressive voice of modern jazz – each note arising from the blues tradition, often imperfect, but always from the depths of a tortured soul.

Dizzy Gillespie's trumpet became the clearest, most clarionlike and yet most flexible trumpet voice in the history of jazz. Almost every phrase he played was perfect.

Bird became the basic improviser, the chorus-man par excellence, interested more than anything in the flow of the lines he played. Parker made the nineteen-year-old trumpeter Miles Davis a member of his quintet – the man who was to become the dominant improviser of the next phase in

Dizzy Gillespie became more and more interested in the percussive aspects of the new jazz. In the words of Billy Eckstine: 'If you ever listen to Diz humming something, he hums the drum and bass part and everything because it all fits in with what he's doing. Like "Oop-Bop-Sh'Bam". That's modern jazz. Parker encouraged Davis, who had begun *à la* Gillespie and Parker, to find a style of his own.

Years later, when Parker was under contract to Norman Granz, he recorded with Machito's orchestra. But the results were hardly representative Bird. Parker's formula remained the quintet: the smallest instrumentation in which it was possible to create 'form' through the unison statement of theme at beginning and end, while retaining complete improvisatory freedom for the remainder.

In Charlie Parker's words: 'I'd be happy if what I played would simply be called "music".'

On another occasion, Charlie Parker said: 'Life used to be so cruel to musicians, just the way it is today. They say that when Beethoven was on his deathbed he shook his fist at the world because they just didn't understand. Nobody in his own time ever really dug anything he wrote. But that's music.'

In 1946 Charlie Parker had the first major breakdown of his life. It came during the recording of

a drum thing. And "Salt Peanuts" was another. It was a drum lick . . .'

Dizzy was interested in Afro-Cuban rhythms. He played with musicians from the Cuban orchestra of Machito. In 1947 he added the Cuban drummer Chano Pozo to his band and thus brought a wealth of ancient West African rhythms and drum-patterns into modern jazz.

To the question how the future of jazz would develop Gillespie answered: 'Probably it will go back to where it all started from: a man beating a drum.'

According to Leonard Feather, Dizzy Gillespie never took himself, or the music he created, as seriously as did the countless music lovers and musicians who have spent so much time investigating, discussing, and imitating everything.

Leonard Feather: 'The other musicians who took part in the incubating process that evolved

'Lover Man' at the Dial record studios. When Charlie came home after the session, he started a fire in his hotel room and ran – naked and screaming – into the hall.

According to Orrin Keepnews: 'There can be little doubt that he was a tortured man, and there are several who emphasize his loneliness.' Often he would stay up all night, riding aimlessly around on the subway. As a musician, on stage, he never developed the ability to 'sell' himself and his music. He just stood there and played.

into bop today are dead, or struggling intermittently with the drug habit. Gillespie apparently has never suffered any major frustration or neurosis . . .'

The more it became apparent that Dizzy could not keep his big band together permanently, the more consciously he became the comedian of his music. As the 'clown of bebop' he attempted to sell that which otherwise had proven itself unsaleable. He was not only the best trumpeter of bop but also one of its foremost vocalists. Always, he retained controlled superiority.

In the years 1948-50, both Dizzy and Bird made recordings with large string ensembles – Bird in New York, Dizzy in California. This was to become the only major financial success of Parker's career. The fanatics among the fans beat their breasts: Bird and Dizzy had gone 'commercial'. It was revealing how differently the two reacted:

Parker, for whom recording with strings was the fulfilment of a lifelong wish, and for whom the strings represented that aura of the symphony which he had always admired, suffered from the prejudiced judgement of the fans.

Gillespie, for whom the string recordings actually had meant not much more than another record date, made fun of the ignorance of those who talked about 'commercialism'.

Charlie Parker was never satisfied with himself. He never knew how to answer the question of what recordings he thought to be his best. In answer to the ques-

In 1954, at a birthday party for his wife, somebody fell over Dizzy's trumpet and bent the horn so that the bell pointed upwards. 'After his anger had subsided,' Feather

tion about his favourite musicians, a jazz man only came in third place: Duke Ellington. Before him came Brahms and Schoenberg, after him Hindemith and Stravinsky. But more than any musician he loved Omar Khayyám, the Persian poet.

Leonard Feather: 'Charlie drank more and more in a desperate attempt to stay away from narcotics while still avoiding the terrors of sober reality.'

At a time when there was hardly a musician playing anywhere in the world who was not in some degree or fashion under Bird's influence – when this influence had even penetrated into the world of dance and pop-music – Parker was only playing occasionally. According to Orrin Keepnews: 'He had given up the fight towards the end. In 1954 he sent [his former wife] Doris a poem . . . in part it sets forth a credo that might easily have been his own: "Hear the words! Not the doctrine. Hear the speech! Not the meaning . . . Death is an imminent thing . . . My fire is unquenchable".'

On 12 March 1955, he died. He had been watching television, laughing at a joke on the Dorsey Brothers' Show.

reported, 'Dizzy tried to play the horn and found that the sound seemed to reach his ears better . . . The next day he went to a trumpet manufacturer to ask whether he could put the idea into mass production . . .' Dizzy wanted to take out a patent. But it was discovered that a similar instrument had been patented 150 years earlier.

Dizzy Gillespie became the first 'world statesman' of the international jazz tours organized by the American Department of State. With the help of funds from Washington, he managed to put together a big band again. He went on world-wide tours – first to Asia and southeastern Europe, later to Latin America. In Athens he gave the most triumphant concert of his career at the height of the Cyprian crisis of 1956. The Greeks were furious at the Americans. The headlines in the newspapers asked why the Americans were sending a bunch of jazz musicians instead of guns to chase the British out of Cyprus. Dizzy's concert began in a very tense atmosphere. But when the four white and nine black musicians swung into Dizzy's 'Tour de Force', written shortly before the

The Parker myth began almost immediately. Among those who paid him tribute was disc jockey Al 'Jazzbo' Collins: 'I don't believe that in the whole history of jazz there was a musician more recognized and less understood than he.'

'Bird Lives!' This is still true today – and especially today again. In the seventies, all the important altoists were shaped directly by Parker: Ornette Coleman, Phil Woods, Lee Konitz, Charlie Mariano, Sonny Stitt, Gary Bartz, Jackie McLean, Frank Strozier, Cannonball Adderley, Charles McPherson, Anthony Braxton, Oliver Lake . . .; and towards the end of the decade a young musician appeared on the scene who seems like a 'Bird of today', Arthur Blythe.

tour, the audience broke into wild applause. All Athens was filled with enthusiasm over the Gillespie band, and the political climate changed so markedly that a newspaper stated: 'Dizzy Gillespie is a better diplomat than all the diplomats the USA ever had in this part of the world.'

More than anyone else, Dizzy has carried the bop idiom through all subsequent styles and ways of playing: cool and hard bop, free, and rock-influenced – and yet, he remained unmistakably Dizzy Gillespie.

For the young audience of the seventies and eighties, he stands right next to Louis Armstrong. This audience does not realize any more – and justifiably – that John Birks Gillespie once had begun as Satchmo's antipode.

At the beginning of the eighties, the 'new bop' has become a major style. More than ever during the quarter of a century since his death, Charlie Parker's compositions are being played with astonishing frequency by young musicians.

Miles Davis

'Don't we have to admit,' asked André Hodeir as early as 1956, 'that the only complete aesthetic achievements since the great period of Parker and Gillespie belong to Miles Davis?' And the British critic Michael James had stated: 'It is no exaggeration to say that never

before in jazz had the phenomenon of loneliness been examined in so
intransigent a manner [as by Miles Davis].'

Our first quotation establishes the historical situation of Davis's
music, the second its aesthetic situation. Both are contained – at least
up to the beginning of the seventies – in the sound with which he
blows. His tone – one of great purity, full of softness, almost without
vibrato or attack – represents an image of the world; in each sound of
Miles this image is contained . . .

The sound of Miles Davis is the sound of sadness and resignation.
Sadness and resignation, paired with an unconditional, less musical
than personal protest, exist independently of whatever else Miles has
to say. No doubt, he says many amusing, pleasant, and friendly
things, but says it all in this tone of sadness and resignation.

Arranger Gil Evans said: 'Miles couldn't play like Louis [Armstrong]
because the sound would interfere with his thoughts. Miles had to
start with almost no sound and then develop one as he went along, a
sound suitable for the ideas he wanted to express. He couldn't afford
to trust those thoughts to an old means of expression. If you
remember, his sound now is much more highly developed than it was
at first.'

Gil Evans is the man who translated the Miles Davis sound into
orchestral terms. Evans arranged for the Claude Thornhill band
during the forties, when Lee Konitz was in the band. He says: 'At
first, the sound of the band was almost a reduction to an inactivity of
music, a stillness . . . everything was moving at a minimum speed . . .
and was lowered to create a sound. The sound hung like a cloud.'

When improviser Miles Davis and arranger Gil Evans met, it was
one of the great moments in the history of jazz. The result was the
Miles Davis Capitol Band, formed for a two-week engagement in
September 1948 at the Royal Roost, and actually in existence only
for two weeks. 'The instrumentation,' Evans recalled, 'was caused by
the fact that this was the smallest number of instruments that could
get the sound and still express all the harmonies the Thornhill band
used. Miles wanted to play his idiom with that kind of sound.' This
band consisted of Miles on trumpet, a trombone (J. J. Johnson or Kai
Winding), two saxophones (Lee Konitz, alto; Gerry Mulligan,
baritone), and, as sound factors, two instruments rarely used in jazz:
French horn and tuba. In addition, there was a rhythm section of Al
Haig or John Lewis on piano, Joe Shulman or Nelson Boyd on bass,
and Max Roach or Kenny Clark on drums.

Mulligan and Lewis also arranged for this group but its sound was created by Evans in collaboration with Davis, and Evans also arranged its two most significant pieces, 'Boplicity' and 'Moon Dreams'. With these pieces, the texture of sound which became a model for the entire evolution of cool jazz was created. It was, of course, more than just the Thornhill sound with fewer instruments. It was a jazz sound, and if at all comparable to a cloud, the clouds were frequently pierced by rays of improvised sunshine, which struck the listener through the gentle veil of fog.

The most 'modern' piece recorded by this group was 'Israel' by John Carisi, a trumpeter and student of the modern symphonic composer, German-born Stefan Wolpe, with whom many first-rate jazzmen have studied. 'Israel' is a minor blues, and characteristically this piece, which with its harsh, brittle sounds opened new tonal horizons, remains indebted to the core of the jazz tradition: the blues.

This Davis Band, recorded by Capitol in 1949 and 1950, was of a size between combo and big band. Seven years later – 1957 – Miles Davis went a step further. He recorded with a large orchestra, and naturally he asked Gil Evans – of whom little had been heard in the interim – to do the arrangements. 'Gil,' says Gerry Mulligan, 'is the one arranger I've ever played with who can really notate a thing the way the soloist would blow it.' And Miles himself said: 'I haven't heard anything that knocks me out as consistently as he does since Charlie Parker.'

Gil put together a unique big band. There was no saxophone section, but in its place – alongside the conventional trumpets and trombones – there was a strange unreal-sounding combination of French horns, tuba, alto saxophone, clarinet, bass clarinet, and flute. In some of the pieces – like 'Miles Ahead', a theme by Miles Davis – Gil realizes a 'continuation' of the Capitol band's sound; here it becomes apparent which big band sound the old Capitol band aimed at: not the sound of Claude Thornhill in the late forties, but rather the sound of this Gil Evans–Miles Davis big band of 1957. It has consciously been stripped of every trace of heated attack. It is calm, lyrical, static – each climax planned way in advance. Broad lines are always preferred, in terms of melody as well as dynamics. But it moves above the old, swinging, pulsating rhythm, laid down by Paul Chambers, bass, and Art Taylor, drums.

Further climaxes in the Evans–Davis collaboration were reached with the album of Gershwin's music from 'Porgy and Bess' (1958) and

– above all – with the great 'Sketches of Spain' (1959), incorporating Spanish, flamenco-conscious compositions. Here, too, Miles made a decisive contribution to a jazz tendency which since has steadily gained in importance: the opening up of jazz to world music.

There can be no doubt: Miles is an improviser. But he improvises out of a great feeling for arrangement and composition. Probably eighteen-year-old Miles, when he asked Dizzy Gillespie and Charlie Parker how to play right, took Dizzy's advice literally: 'Learn to play the piano, man, and then you can figure out crazy solos of your own.' Marshall Stearns, who tells of this, concludes: 'It was the turning point in the playing of Miles Davis.' This fits in with Evans's story of the Royal Roost engagement: 'There was a sign outside: "Arrangements by Gerry Mulligan, Gil Evans, and John Lewis". Miles had it put in front; no one before had ever done that, given credit in that way to arrangers.'

Until the mid-fifties, Miles had made his most beautiful recordings in quartets, accompanied only by a rhythm section – often with John Lewis or Horace Silver on the piano. Up to that time, he had never had lasting success with audiences. Then, at the 1955 Newport Festival, the turning point came.

All of a sudden, the name of Miles Davis – until then known only to informed fans and critics – could be heard everywhere. Since then success has never left. For the first time in jazz history, the best-paid and most successful musician of an era was not white, but black – Miles Davis. It is self-evident why Miles became the image-setter for a whole generation of black musicians, not only musically, but in terms of personality as well. Proud black parents – even in Africa! – began to name their sons 'Miles', or even 'Miles Davis'.

The quintets Miles Davis has led since then are of crucial importance. The first – with John Coltrane (tenor), Paul Chambers (bass), Red Garland (piano), and Philly Joe Jones (drums) – was especially highly lauded. It set standards for all quintets that were to follow – in fact, for modern jazz quintets between 1956 and 1970 in general. Another greatly influential Davis band was the Kind of Blue group (1959) with pianist Bill Evans. Here the new freedom just recently discovered by musicians like Mingus, Coltrane, Evans, and Miles himself for the first time became a group-integrating force, leading to a lyricism and sensitivity unknown in this kind of music until then. In the chapter about the most important combos, there is an astounding list of all the musicians who gained fame after emerging from a Davis quintet.

An important factor in Miles's great popularity also is his way of playing the muted trumpet – almost as if he were 'breathing' into the microphone. The solo he recorded in this manner on Thelonious Monk's 'Round Midnight' was particularly successful; the muted solo on 'All of You' has been praised, especially by musicians, as one of the most beautiful jazz solos of the fifties. Even more than his open-horn playing, Miles's muted work makes it apparent that there is no definitive attack. No longer does the sound begin in one definite, clearly stated moment, as it does in traditional jazz and particularly with most other trumpets. His sound begins in a moment which cannot be grasped; it seems to come out of nowhere, and it ends equally undefined. Without the listener quite knowing when, it fades into nothingness. Miles's muted trumpet playing close to the microphone showed early traces of two important aspects of his later work: first, his then developing feeling (in the mid-fifties!) that electronics are 'the continuation of music by other means'; and second, the unconditional striving for success he shares with Louis Armstrong, his true antipode. Miles's ambitions have often caused him to listen with special care to and absorb the music of successful players – in the mid-fifties (as Gunther Schuller has shown) to someone like pianist Ahmad Jamal, in the late sixties to Jimi Hendrix and Sly Stone, and later to some of the funk musicians.

But let's return to the fifties: Miles Davis is the most significant creative musician of a movement in jazz best defined as having applied the findings of bop to Lester Young. The basic difference between Young's music and that of Davis and his followers is that Miles plays with the knowledge that between himself and Lester there was bop. André Hodeir's remark, 'Miles Davis is the only trumpeter who could give Parker's music that intimate quality in which lies a considerable part of its charm,' may be interpreted in this sense. The 'intimate quality' is Lester Young.

This intimate quality is also found in the simplicity of Miles's playing. No other musician in jazz has developed simplicity with such refinement and sophistication. The basic contradiction between complexity and simplicity ceases to exist in Miles's playing. In his desire to play simply, Miles (since the second half of the fifties) tends to free his improvisations from the underlying structure of chord changes. He bases his solo work on 'scales'. About his big-band version of Gershwin's 'Porgy and Bess', Miles says: 'When Gil wrote the arrangement of "I love You, Porgy", he only wrote a scale for me to play. No chords. This gives you a lot more freedom and space to hear things.' One of Miles's most influential compositions, 'So What', is based in its first sixteen measures on a single scale; relieved in the bridge by another scale, it returns to the first scale for the final eight bars.

Miles, and with him John Coltrane, who then was in Davis's Quintet, made this method of improvisation based on 'scales' standard practice for the whole jazz world, thus creating the last step required for the total freedom of free jazz. This is also referred to as 'modal' improvisation. (See the chapter dealing with harmonics.)

The simple phrases, often consisting of only a few notes, which Miles makes up on such 'scales', have not only an aesthetic but also a practical basis: From an instrumental point of view the possibilities of Miles Davis, the trumpeter, are limited, especially when he is compared to his chief competitor among modern trumpeters, Dizzy Gillespie, a masterful musician who seems able to execute anything conceivable on his horn. If Miles wanted to maintain himself alongside Dizzy, top him in popularity, he had to make a virtue of his instrumental limitations. Hence the cult of simplicity. Significantly, recording directors agree that Miles always selects for issue those 'takes' from a record date which are instrumentally most perfect, though he may have played with more ideas and inspiration on others. Miles does not seem to want his record audience to know that there are frequent 'clams' in his playing.

This 'sophistication of simplicity' may be related to the fact that Miles – no matter how many avenues for new possibilities in jazz he may have opened – very often chose tradition when faced with a choice between it and avant-garde. He once complained that pianist Thelonious Monk was playing 'wrong chords', though no doubt Monk's chords were not 'wrong', but merely more abstract and modern than was suitable to Miles's conception at the time. Miles complained bitterly to the recording director who had hired Monk for a record date. The results, however – whether Miles likes it or not – were some of the most important and artistically successful recorded works of the fifties (Miles, Monk, and Milt Jackson on Prestige).

A further example of Miles Davis's traditionalism is the sharp words with which for years he assessed one of the most important members of the jazz avant-garde, the late Eric Dolphy – some of them insults which Davis had to retract in later years.

When an ultra-modern fanatic once called Art Blakey 'old-fashioned', Miles said: 'If Art Blakey is old-fashioned, then I'm white.' About the avant-garde of the sixties, he said: 'What's so avant-garde? Lennie Tristano and Lee Konitz were creating ideas fifteen years ago that were stranger than any of these new things. But when they did it, it made sense.'

Once, when tenor saxophonist Stan Getz was making some snide remarks about Coleman Hawkins being basically 'old-fashioned', Davis rebuked him by pointing out that, if it weren't for Hawk, Getz probably would not be able to play as he did.

Often Miles makes harsh judgements – not only about outsiders (which would be understandable), but also about his colleagues. In a 'Blindfold Test' with critic Leonard Feather, Davis voiced such gross insults in connection with many well-known jazz musicians that *down beat* magazine hesitated to spell out all his four-letter words. Reputable musicians like Clark Terry, Ellington, Dolphy, Jaki Byard, Cecil Taylor, and others were insulted by Davis at that time.

On the other hand, it must be seen that – with the exception of Charles Mingus, George Russell, and Dolphy – no other musician led the 'tonal' jazz of the fifties closer and closer to the 'free tonal' jazz of the sixties with such increasing consistency as Miles Davis. Justifiably, Dan Morgenstern calls Miles one of the 'spiritual fathers' of the new jazz. In the mid-sixties, Davis had a quintet whose members – at that time! – played 'free' or almost 'free' on their own records (mostly on the Blue Note label): Tony Williams (drums), Herbie Hancock (piano), Ron Carter (bass), and Wayne Shorter (tenor) – musicians discussed in the instrument chapters. Only Miles himself avoided the final step across the border at that time. But the relevant fact remains that the 'free tonal' musicians also admired him greatly and looked up to him as an example.

Davis's goal in this area of tension between traditionalism and avant-garde is not licence, but rather, controlled freedom. 'Look, you don't need to think to play weird. That ain't no freedom. You need controlled freedom.'

With this 'controlled freedom', Miles Davis was diametrically opposed to many extreme avant-garde musicians of the sixties. But in the context of the new jazz of the seventies, 'controlled freedom' was the actual cue word – no longer just for Miles's music, but for a whole generation of young musicians continuing where Davis's 'electric jazz' only seemingly leaves off.

In 1972, Japanese critic Shoichi Yui went so far as to speak of Davis as the 'absolute apex of the development up to this point.' He held that Davis is superior even to Louis Armstrong and Charlie Parker, each of whom dominated the jazz scene for only a few years, while Davis 'has been the dominating personality from the end of the forties until today – longer than anybody else.' Armstrong's influence, for instance, essentially originates in his playing during the period between his first Fletcher Henderson engagement in 1924, and his first visit to Europe in 1932. The period during which Charlie Parker made his most important recordings is even shorter. (From the Dizzy Gillespie session with 'Groovin' High' and Parker's first own session in 1945 – when, among others, 'Now's the Time' was created – to Norman Granz's session of 1951 with Miles Davis, when 'KC Blues' was recorded: six years!)

It is hard to say which is more admirable: the power with which a musician like Parker made a host of creative, new recordings within such a short timespan in a concentrated, explosive eruption – or the permanence with which Miles Davis, for a quarter of a century, has continued to set new signposts relevant to the majority of jazz musicians.

In order to be able to gain a perspective on this period of a quarter-century, one should remember that Davis has basically gone through four different stylistic phases – including all the overlaps and interconnections which, of course, have existed between these phases:

1. Bebop: from playing with Charlie Parker in 1945 to 1948
2. Cool jazz: from the launching of the Miles Davis Capitol Orchestra in 1948 to the big-band recordings with Gil Evans in 1957/58
3. Hard bop: from the success of the first Davis Quintet with John Coltrane at the 1955 Newport Festival, via the many subsequent Davis Quintets – such as the one with Bill Evans – to 1968 (during this period, an increasingly clear tendency towards model improvisation)
4. Electric: from 'In a Silent Way' in 1969 and 'Bitches Brew' in 1970 until . . .

The term 'electric jazz', coined by an American disc jockey, aptly characterizes the music Davis has been making since 'Bitches Brew' – incorporating electronic sounds. Records like 'Jack Johnson' and 'Live Evil' also belong to this movement – which such musicians as saxophonist

Wayne Shorter and British guitarist John McLaughlin, and, above all, with the collective sound of different pianists playing electric instruments. Among the latter are such players as Chick Corea, Larry Young, Herbie Hancock, Keith Jarrett, the Brazilian Hermeto Pascoal, and – mainly – the transplanted Viennese Joe Zawinul, who has played a special, perhaps even triggering role in this phase of Davis's work.

Even more important, however, were the impulses given by rock musicians Jimi Hendrix and Sly Stone. Filled with self-assurance, Miles declared that he could form a better rock group than even Jimi Hendrix.

What is interesting is the fact that Miles Davis's music – which after 'In a Silent Way' corresponded to its title – became more and more percussive, particularly after he hired the percussion player Mtume, a man inspired by African music. Davis paid tribute to the opening of jazz to world music by using Indian instruments like sitar and tabla drums.

Miles now played trumpet with a wah-wah pedal and through an amplifier. In most cases, the pure, clear, 'lonely', always somewhat sad sound of the earlier Miles is hardly recognizable. But Miles was reaching a youthful mass audience – something no black jazz musician since Louis Armstrong had accomplished. He has given the decisive impulse to a development clarified in the chapter about the jazz of the seventies, which will again be discussed in the combo chapter.

The electrifying success of the 'electronic Miles' led to a point when the world of rock and popular music wanted to seize upon Miles Davis. In the summer of 1970, when he was suppposed to play with rock musicians like Eric Clapton and Jack Bruce at the Randall's Island Festival in New York, Miles had music people all over the world holding their breath for several weeks, but then he said no; he wouldn't play except with his own group: 'I don't want to be a white man. Rock is a white man's word.'

Miles Davis had the same kind of 'leadership' position in the jazz scene of the early seventies as Louis Armstrong or Charlie Parker had during earlier jazz periods. But he does not play his role with Satchmo's natural ease. Miles – exactly like Armstrong – wants to 'make it' with a large audience. But he reflects the pride, self-assurance, and determination to protest that is characteristic of today's black generation; he plays 'black music', but he must also acknowledge the fact that his audience – the buyers of his records and the listeners at his concerts – is mainly white. In a revealing interview with Michael Watts of the London publication *Melody Maker*, Miles said: 'I don't care who buys the records as long as they get to the black people so I will be remembered when I die. I'm not playing for any white people, man. I wanna hear a black guy say, "Yeah, I dig Miles Davis".'

The cover of Miles's album 'On the Corner', for instance, consciously aims – according to the trumpeter's express wishes – at the black market: a comic-strip-style display of a group of dancing, 'hip' street blacks, with slogans like 'Vote Miles', and 'Free me' on their shirts and hats.

Again and again, he has said to dozens of critics and reporters: 'I just do what I feel like doing.' If a man says something like that too often, he obviously has a reason for saying it – he does *not* simply do what he feels like. Miles asked the above-mentioned *Melody Maker* reporter Michael Watts how long he had waited before deciding to ring his doorbell. And then, Miles was noticeably eager for Watts to take a grand tour of his 'rococo house' and enjoyed that his visitor was astonished and impressed by the luxury with which Davis surrounds himself.

Miles Davis mirrors himself in his surroundings and his audience – and he needs this mirror. This is his dilemma: The whites mirror him, but he wants to be heard by the blacks. He may curse at the whites, but he can depend on their applause more than on that of the blacks.

The fact that Miles frequently played with his back to the audience certainly also has to do with that. Miles says: 'What should I do? Smile at 'em?' And then comes the sentence which reappears so often: 'I just do what I feel like doing.'

Any man with so many complexes, so split within himself, must truly have charisma to be successful. Davis's charisma often takes astounding forms.

Twice, Miles has been involved in violent public encounters. Once, gangsters shot at him when he was sitting with a girl in his parked car in Brooklyn. Miles set a reward of $10,000 for the capture of the two assailants. Nobody collected the reward, but a few weeks later the two gangsters were mysteriously shot.

Several years earlier, Miles was standing in front of the Birdland club on Broadway, when a white policeman asked him to move on, then hit him over the head with a club. 'The cop was killed, too. In a subway,' Miles has claimed.

Miles Davis is a devoted sports car fan. In 1972, he broke both legs in an accident. After that – and especially after having to undergo surgery of the hip some time later – he did not appear in public for almost five years, living a life of seclusion, which gave rise to a constant flurry of alarming rumours in the jazz world about the state of his health. Insiders, however, supposed that Miles's seclusion had to do not only with his health, but also with psychological reasons. Miles wants to be 'the greatest' – not only because he is used to it, but also because he needs it. It is the mainspring of his musical and personal development. He would have to cross a high psychological threshold when he returned to the arena, because nobody – including himself – could be sure that he would be 'the greatest' once again.

Miles's accomplishment as a catalyst in jazz since the beginning of the seventies is even more impressive, as it actually took only two records of his – 'In a Silent Way' (1969) and 'Bitches Brew' (1970) – to give the impetus to this development. Critics as well as musicians have pointed out that what came after these two records did not really come up to their high standards. A lot of it was pieced together by Columbia Records from older sessions, even including outtakes, because there were no recent recordings to satisfy the market for more and more 'new Miles'. On several occasions, there was talk of a comeback. During the late seventies, he recorded with guitarist Larry Coryell, but he did only rhythm tracks. The horn lines and improvisations were never added.

In early 1980, Davis made another visit to the recording studios, this time with his twenty-two-year-old nephew, drummer Vincent Wilburn, Jr, from Chicago. One of the musicians involved described the results as 'vocals, electronics, to appeal to young people. It's commercial enough that people who never heard Miles before will get it . . . some tunes are, like, pop . . .'

For months after that, nothing was heard of Miles, and an irritated *down beat* reader wrote: 'Let's all just *forget* about Miles Davis, huh? I'm so sick and tired of readers bitching and moaning about his lack of new recordings and his apparent disdain for his audiences . . . Miles is not a god . . .'

However, Miles was treated like a god when, after six years of mystification, he finally returned in the summer of 1981 with appearances at the Boston and New York jazz festivals. And he played great music, driving his group of mostly young and new musicians to a wild climax of glowing, incandescent beauty. He blew more and better trumpet than in the years preceding his retirement. Finally, it was there again – the warm, dark Davis glow – simultaneously triumphant and resigned.

Yet there was nothing new in Miles's 1981 music. It was a recapitulation of the Miles Davis of the first half of the seventies (if much better played), for a few moments even reverting to the 'Kind of Blue' period of the late fifties.

Typically, the drummer was Al Foster, whom Miles had used before his sabbatical. So even the rhythms were early- and mid-seventies funk-jazz rhythms. Miles just didn't seem to know how much had changed in the meantime – traceable, for instance, to a drummer like Ronald Shannon Jackson (see drum chapter). And anything new in jazz is new first of all in terms of rhythm.

As usual in such cases, the sharks of the media overdid the whole thing. A well-known Madison Avenue man – meaning a man in the know – pointed out that there were more photographers and journalists at Miles's comeback party than at Elizabeth Taylor's Broadway debut. Miles, they claimed, would show the world the musical direction for the eighties, which, considering the music he performed, is nonsense, or true only if nothing new will happen in the remaining years of the decade. But so much has happened already!

People tend to expect the superhuman from Miles. As I have shown, he has changed the course of jazz three times. It isn't fair to demand that he change it a fourth time. He has done enough.

It was obvious that Miles still hadn't overcome his psychological problems. He started his first New York concert forty minutes late, hardly looked at his audience, and played only a fifty-five-minute set, at a concert for which the best seats cost $25, leaving his – yes, his! – fans booing when everyone had expected the performance to end with a standing ovation.

'Miles still needs a lot of nurturing,' said a lady close to him. 'That's why he always wants that façade.' But Max Roach, weeks before the concert, said: 'Miles is a champion. Champs always come back.'

What is clear is that the move from quiet, melodious, impressionistic music to more aggressive, vital, gripping sounds has happened three times in Miles Davis's career: en route from the Capitol Orchestra of the late forties to hard bop in the second half of the fifties; then during the phase developing from 'Kind of Blue' (with Bill Evans in 1959) to the late pre-electric, 'acoustic' quintet recordings (with musicians like Sam Rivers, Wayne Shorter, and Herbie Hancock) and finally on the 'Silent Way' (1969) to 'funky Miles' during the mid-seventies. In fact, in a rudimentary sense, one can recognize this kind of development as early as the forties, when Miles played bebop with Charlie Parker and other important bop musicians – even though it may be that back then he simply was unsure of himself.

In any case, to return to the beginning of this chapter, the conclusion can be drawn that the 'sound of loneliness, sadness and resignation', which Michael James and André Hodeir found in Miles, is Davis's 'actual' sound. In this mood, he made not only most of his revolutionary but also his most beautiful records. And when he then became sure of himself – in the newly developed idiom – he found his way to more dynamic, aggressive recordings that broke through the atmospheric and musical boundaries of the particular idiom. It fits into this picture that Vincent Wilburn, Jr, says that Miles played 'mostly ballads' when – after years of silence – he began to play again in the spring and summer of 1980.

'You want me to tell you where I was born – that old story?' Miles once responded when he was relatively young – in the fifties. 'It was in good old Alton, Illinois, in 1926. I had to call my mother a week before my last birthday and ask her how old I would be.

'There was a very good instructor in town. He was having some dental work done by my father . . . "Play without any vibrato," he used to tell us. "You're going to get old anyway and start shaking." . . . That's how I tried to play – fast and light, and no vibrato.

'By the time I was sixteen . . . Sonny Stitt came to town with a band and heard me play. He told me: "You look like a man named Charlie Parker and you play like him, too. Come with us."

'The fellows in his band had their hair slicked down, they wore tuxedos and they offered me sixty whole dollars a week to play with them. I went home and asked my mother if I could go with them. She said no, I had to finish my last year of high school. I didn't talk to her for two weeks. And I didn't go with the band, either.

'I knew about Charlie Parker in St Louis – I even played with him there, while I was still in high school. We always used to play like Diz and Charlie Parker.

'When we heard that they were coming to town, my friend and I were the first people in the hall, me with a trumpet under my arm. Diz walked up to me and said: "Kid, you have a union card?" I said: "Sure." So I sat in with the band that night. I couldn't read a thing from listening to Diz and Bird.

'Then the third trumpet man got sick. I knew the book because I loved the music so much I knew the third part by heart. So I played with the band for a couple of weeks. I just *had* to go to New York then.

'A friend of mine was studying at Juilliard, so I decided to go there, too. I spent my first week in New York and my first month's allowance looking for Charlie Parker.

'I roomed with Charlie Parker for a year. I used to follow him around, down to 52nd Street where he used to play. Then he'd get me to play. "Don't be afraid," he'd tell me, "Go ahead and play."

'You know, if you can hear a note, you can play it. The note I hit that sounds high, that's the only one I can play right then – the only note I can think of to play that would fit. You don't learn to play the blues. You just play . . .

'Would I rather compose or play? I can't answer that. There's a certain feeling you get from playing, but never from writing, and when you're playing it's like composing, anyway . . .'

John Coltrane and Ornette Coleman

The jazz of the sixties – and certainly most of the jazz of the seventies as well – is dominated by two towering personalities: John Coltrane, who died quite unexpectedly in July of 1967, and Ornette Coleman. One must appreciate the difference between these two in order to realize the extent of their influence and appreciate the scope of the expressive possibilities of the new jazz. Neither man is a revolutionary, and if the effect of their work nevertheless was such, this was not their wish. Both are from the South – Coleman was born in Texas in 1930; Coltrane in North Carolina in 1926. Both are solidly rooted in the blues tradition – Coleman more in the country tradition of the folk blues; Coltrane more in the urban rhythm & blues tradition.

Coltrane had a relatively solid musical education within the limits possible for a member of the black lower middle class – his father was a tailor. Coleman's parents were too poor to be able to afford music lessons for him; Ornette acquired his musical tools on his own. No one told him that a saxophone is notated differently than it is tuned. So, at the age of fourteen to fifteen – a crucial phase in his development – he played everything written 'wrong' in the academic sense. Critic Martin Williams takes this to be a decisive reason for the harmonic uniqueness Coleman displayed from the start.

Whenever young Ornette played, he made a kind of music whose harmonies, sound, and instrumental technique could be placed only with difficulty within the conventional framework of jazz, blues, and rhythm & blues – that is, within the musics to which he related most in terms of style, inclination, expression, and origins. He remembers: 'Most musicians didn't take to me; they said I didn't know the changes and was out of tune.' He says about one of his first leaders, singer–guitarist Pee Wee Crayton, to whose rhythm & blues band he belonged: 'He didn't understand what I was trying to do, and it got so he was paying me not to play.' Nightclub owner and bassist Howard Rumsey recalls: 'Everybody – the musicians, I mean – would panic when you'd mention Ornette. People would laugh when his name was brought up.' This is placed in correct perspective if we remember that Lester Young in the Fletcher Henderson band and young Charlie Parker in Kansas City triggered similar reactions.

In contrast, Coltrane – or, as he was called, 'Trane' – was accepted from the start. His first professional job was in 1947 with the Joe Webb rhythm & blues band from Indianapolis, with singer Big Maybelle. After that, he played mainly in better-known groups, mostly for lengthy periods: Eddie 'Cleanhead' Vinson (1947–48), Dizzy Gillespie (1949–51), Earl Bostic (1952–53), Johnny Hodges (1953–54) . . . until, in 1955, Miles Davis hired him for his quintet and he gained immediate fame with his solo on 'Round about Midnight'. It must be clearly understood: He was accepted and successful within the jazz that was accepted and successful at the time.

Ornette Coleman's emergence, however, came as a shock. He had to take work as an elevator operator in Los Angeles because the musicians would not accept him. Since his elevator was seldom in demand, he would stop it on the top floor and study his harmony books. Then, in 1958–59, producer Lester Koenig recorded the first two Coleman albums for his Contemporary label: 'Something Else: The Music of Ornette Coleman' and 'Tomorrow Is the Question'. A few months later, Coleman attended the Lenox School of Jazz. Many famous musicians were teaching there: Milt Jackson, Max Roach, Bill Russo, Gunther Schuller, John Lewis . . . Yet, after a few days of the summer courses, the unknown 'student' Ornette Coleman had attracted more attention than all the famous teachers.

Right away, John Lewis decided that 'Ornette Coleman is doing the only really new thing in jazz since the innovations of Dizzy Gillespie and Charlie Parker in the forties and since Thelonious Monk.' The leader of the Modern Jazz Quartet described the way Coleman played on his plastic alto with his friend Don Cherry, who used a miniature trumpet, as follows: 'They're almost like twins . . . I can't imagine how they manage to start together. Never before have I heard that kind of ensemble playing.'

Although Coleman was not at all trying to bring about a musical revolution – he always only wanted to make his own music, and otherwise be left alone – there was suddenly the feeling in the jazz world of 1959 that this was a turning point, that a new style was beginning with Ornette Coleman – 'He is the new Bird!'

The harmonic freedom characteristic of all the music played and composed by Coleman has been particularly well described by George Russell: 'Ornette seems to depend mostly on the over-all tonality of the song as a point of departure for melody. By this I don't mean the key the music might be in . . . I mean that the melody and the chords of his compositions have an over-all sound which Ornette seems to use as a point of departure. This approach liberates the improviser to sing his own song, really, without having to meet the deadline of any particular chord . . .' Ornette himself feels that the rules of a music must be based not in harmonic principles applied from the outside, but rather within the instrument and the tune themselves. He called this his 'harmolodic system': each harmony is, as this title suggests, established only by the melodic line. The system has influenced many other jazz musicians, such as guitarist Blood Ulmer, and also the teaching at the Creative Music Studio of German-born vibraharpist Karl Berger, in Woodstock, NY.

The harmonic freedom Coleman had achieved from the start in a manner self-evident to him, John Coltrane had to struggle for in a slow, laborious development spanning an entire decade: from the first cautious attempts at 'modality' with Miles Davis in 1956 to 'Ascension' in 1965.

It is a fascinating, exciting 'adventure in jazz' to follow this development by way of records. In the beginning stands the encounter with Miles Davis and modality. That means: No more improvisation on constantly changing chords, but rather on a 'scale' which, unchangingly, underlies the whole melodic activity. It was a first step into freedom. In spite of the tense, aware attention with which the jazz world was observing this development in all its phases, it was never made clear precisely whether Davis or Coltrane had taken the first step. This is fitting, because the step was not taken consciously. It 'happened' – as something does that is 'in the air'.

The second phase – beginning in 1957 – was the collaboration with Thelonious Monk (though Trane returned to Miles after that: only in 1960 did he permanently separate from him). Coltrane himself is best qualified to discuss Monk: 'Sometimes he would be playing a different set of altered changes from those that I'd be playing and neither one of us would be playing the changes to the tune. We would reach a certain spot and if we got there together we'd be lucky. And then Monk would come back in to save everybody. A lot of people used to ask us how we remembered all that stuff but we weren't remembering so much. Just the basic changes and everybody tried anything they wanted to . . .'

It was around this time that Coltrane developed what Ira Gitler named 'sheets of sounds' – creating the impression of metallic, glassy, crashing, colliding 'sheets' of sound. This was best described by LeRoi Jones (Imamu Amiri Baraka): 'That is, the notes that Trane was playing in the solo became more than just one note following another. The notes came so fast, and with so many overtones and undertones, that they had the effect of a piano player striking chords rapidly but somehow articulating separately each note in the chord, and its vibrating sub-tones . . .'

Many of the recordings Coltrane made in the second half of the fifties for Blue Note or Prestige are exemplary for this way of playing – on Prestige, for example, with the Red Garland Trio; on Blue Note, for instance, 'Blue Train'. The critic John S. Wilson has written that 'he often plays his tenor sax as if he were determined to blow it apart.' In *Jazz Review*, Zita Carno coined that often-quoted sentence: 'The only thing you can, and should expect from John Coltrane is the unexpected . . .' It is one of the few statements about Coltrane which are equally true about all his stages.

The critics at that time overlooked a fact musicians probably felt instinctively – that the 'sheets of sounds' had an immediate rhythmic effect which was at least as important as the harmonic effect: If the notes were no longer definable as eighths, sixteenths, or thirty-seconds, becoming more like quintuplets, septuplets, and nontuplets, then the precision of the relationship to the underlying meter was gone, too. The 'sheets of sounds', therefore, were a step towards substituting for the simple clarity of the conventional beat the flowing, vibrating quality of the pulse – a conception which Elvin Jones, starting in 1960, arrived at in the Coltrane Quartet, and young Tony Williams, beginning in 1963, in the Miles Davis Quintet.

When Coltrane signed exclusively with Atlantic Records in 1960, the 'sheets of sounds' soon moved into the background – although, until his death, Trane on many occasions proved that he had not lost the technical ability necessary to play them. Instead of 'shreds of sounds' and 'sheets of sounds', there was a strong concentration on melody: long, widely curved lines that condensed and dissolved according to an immanent, nonapparent principle of tension and relaxation. One had the feeling that Coltrane first had to supply the harmonic and rhythmic prerequisites so that he could deal more exclusively with the musical dimension that interested him most – melody. It was Coltrane the melody man who for the first time had a real hit with a large audience – with 'My Favourite Things', in its original version a somewhat simple-minded waltz from a Richard Rodgers musical. Coltrane played the piece on the soprano sax with the nasal sound of a zoukra (a kind of Arab oboe); and from the constant, always just slightly altered repetition of the notes of the theme, he built an accelerating monotony previously unknown in jazz, but akin to aspects of Indian and Arabic musics.

Around this time, he claimed that Eastern and Asiatic music interested him, and proved it a year later (1961) with 'Olé Coltrane' (which is also inspired by Spanish–Moorish music) on the Atlantic label. After he had moved to the Impulse label, on the momentum of his success with 'My Favourite Things', he made further records of the same orientation: In 'Africa Brass' (1961) he reflected his impressions of Arab music, and in 'India' (1961), with the late Eric

Dolphy on bass clarinet, of classical Indian music. Just how much he admired Indian music is shown by the fact that a few years later he named his second son Ravi – after Ravi Shankar, the great Indian sitar player.

It is certainly not presumptuous to believe that Coltrane – considering that conventional tonality, stemming from European music, had meanwhile been stretched almost to the breaking point – was searching for a kind of substitute (even in the sense of emotional security) in the 'modes' of Indian and Arab musics.

From 1960 on, Coltrane led a quartet including – with occasional substitutions or additions – Elvin Jones (drums) and McCoy Tyner (piano). The bass spot changed several times – a sign of Coltrane's continually developing conception of the basic harmonic (and rhythmic!) tasks of the bassist: From Steve Davis, he went first to Art Davis, then to Reggie Workman, and finally to Jimmy Garrison – the only musician whom Coltrane retained in his quartet until the end, even after the great change of 1965. Incidentally, Coltrane was fond of using two bassists.

This John Coltrane Quartet – with, above all, Jimmy Garrison – was a perfect group. It followed the intentions of its leader with marvellous empathy – up to the crucial change in 1965. At that point, Coltrane needed a totally 'free' drummer – Rashied Ali – and an equally 'free' pianist – he chose his wife, Alice Coltrane.

Before that, in 1964, a record was created that for many is the apex of Coltrane's work: 'A Love Supreme' – a singular, great prayer of hymnic intensity. Coltrane wrote the lyrics himself: 'Let us sing all songs to God to whom all praise is due . . . I will do all I can to be worthy of Thee O Lord . . . I thank You God . . . Words, sounds, speech, men, memory, thoughts, fear and emotions – time – all related . . . they all go back to God . . .' At the end of this prayer appear the three words which most aptly characterize the music the quartet plays to these lyrics: 'Elation, Elegance, Exaltation.'

An outsider may not have expected such religious testimony from the then most-discussed modern jazz musician. But Coltrane – not unlike Duke Ellington – has frequently dealt with religious matters during his varied career. He said that in 1957 he experienced, through the grace of God, 'a spiritual awakening.' And in 1962, he said: 'I believe in all religions,' to which LeRoi Jones comments that music for Trane was 'a way into God.'

Coltrane saw religion as a hymn of praise to the cosmos which is God, and to God who is the cosmos. The psalmlike monotony which builds whole movements of the four-part 'Love Supreme' on a single chord, and in this manner seems to lead from nowhere to everywhere, is for him an expression of infinity as sound. In many records made after that, Coltrane again took up religious topics, for instance, in 'Meditations'. 'Father, Son, and Holy Ghost' and 'Love' – religious love – are two of the movements on this album.

In the meantime, the culmination of a process that had been going on for years – at first unnoticed by the jazz public – and the real jazz surprise of the winter of 1964–65 had taken place: John Coltrane, personally and musically, had joined the New York avant-garde. In March 1965, he played at the New York Village Gate in a not just musically, but also socially and racially, revealing Free Jazz concert of 'New Black Music', produced as a benefit performance for LeRoi Jones's short-lived Black Arts Repertory Theatre-School.

On several records, Coltrane employed the star quality of his name to help young, little-known, uncompromising free-jazz musicians reach a wider audience. And recordings made by tenor saxophonist Archie Shepp at the Newport Jazz Festival of that year were coupled with a Coltrane performance on the Impulse label. This meant the decisive breakthrough for Shepp.

A few days before the Newport Festival, on 28 June 1965, 'Ascension' was produced. This was Coltrane's first record to be tonally 'free'. Coltrane gathered under his wings almost all the important musicians of the New York avant-garde: three tenormen, 'Trane' himself, Pharoah Sanders and Archie Shepp; two trumpeters, Freddie Hubbard and Dewey Johnson; two altoists, John Tchicai and Marion Brown; two bassists, Art Davis and Jimmy Garrison; and in addition, McCoy Tyner on piano and Elvin Jones on drums. Marion Brown, attempting to describe the mad intensity of 'Ascension' which – at the time – seemed to strain the limits of the appreciable and physically tolerable, said: 'You could use this record to heat up the apartment on those cold winter days.' It is a hymnic-ecstatic music of the intensity of a forty-minute orgasm.

With 'Ascension', Coltrane reached a harmonic freedom Coleman had achieved many years before. However, how much more overpowering, gripping, aggressive is the freedom of 'Ascension'! It is what the title implies: an ascension into heaven, from man to God, taking in both – the divine and mankind, the whole cosmos.

Compared to that, Ornette's freedom seems lyrical, quiet, melodious. It is illuminating that the structure of 'Ascension' – consciously or unconsciously – follows a structural scheme Coleman had used five years earlier on his record 'Free Jazz' (Atlantic). (This was where the term later applied to so much of the jazz of the sixties appeared for the first time: on a 1961 album by Ornette Coleman!) It was a collective improvisation by a double quartet, in which the Coleman Quartet (Don Cherry, trumpet; Scott La Faro, bass; Billy Higgins, drums) faced another quartet (Eric Dolphy, bass clarinet; Freddie Hubbard, trumpet; Charlie Haden, bass; Ed Blackwell, drums). From the dense complexity of collective parts rubbing against each other, a solo emerged that led to another set of collective playing, from which was born – in precisely that sense: free solos born in painful labour – the next solo.

During the years when Coltrane underwent his dynamic development, breathlessly attended by the jazz world, things became relatively quiet for Ornette Coleman. For two years, he lived in nearly total seclusion in New York.

It has been said that he played so little then because he was unable to find work. But the opposite is true: he was showered with tempting offers, but did not want to play in public. He was developing his music; he composed, and learned to play two new instruments: trumpet and violin. He also worked on compositions for string quartet (which he gave Béla Bartók-like sounds) and for other chamber-music ensembles – among them the score for Conrad Rooks's film, 'Chappaqua'. The director found himself wondering if he should use music 'in itself so beautiful'. Rooks commissioned a new score – from Ravi Shankar – and Ornette's 'Chappaqua' – scored for Coleman's trio, Pharoah Sanders (tenor) and a chamber ensemble of eleven musicians – was released on record in Europe only.

In early 1965, Coleman re-entered public life at the Village Vanguard. Only now was the album Coleman had recorded before his voluntary retirement (in 1962 at a concert at New York's Town Hall) released (on ESP). Further Coleman records were made in Europe. It was the year when 'A Love Supreme', though not recorded then, was released; the year that also brought us 'Ascension' – perhaps the richest jazz year since Charlie Parker and Dizzy Gillespie made their great recordings during the forties.

It was also in the year of 1965 that Coleman went on a European tour. It was a surprise to the jazz world that he, who had turned down all offers for years, now signed a contract – accepting this writer's invitation to appear at the Berlin Jazz Days. He arrived with a trio consisting of himself, bassist David Izenzon, and drummer Charles Moffett. At the Berlin Sportpalast he scored such a terrific success that the man who had been expected to make the hit of the evening, Gerry Mulligan, had a fit of anger. In the Stockholm restaurant Gyllene Cirkeln, Ornette recorded two albums that soon appeared on Blue Note, and are comparable in lyrical beauty to Coltrane's 'A Love Supreme'. Swedish critic Ludwig Rasmusson wrote in the liner notes: 'The content of his music is mostly pure beauty, a glittering, captivating, dizzying, sensual beauty. A couple of years ago nobody thought so, and everyone considered his music grotesque, filled with anguish and chaos. Now it is almost incomprehensible that one could have held such an opinion, as incomprehensible as the fact that one could object to Willem de Kooning's portraits of women or Samuel Beckett's absurd plays. Thus Ornette Coleman has been able to change our entire concept of what is beautiful merely through the power of his personal vision. It is most beautiful when Coleman's bass player, David Izenzon, plays bowed bass with him. Then, it is almost hauntingly beautiful . . .'

A comparison of Coleman's 'At the Golden Circle' with Coltrane's 'A Love Supreme' shows most clearly the basic difference between the two musicians: The quiet, naturally balanced, static character of Coleman is opposed by Coltrane's dynamic nature. Both play – in the simple, naïve sense of the word – beautiful music. The music of both is immensely intense. But in Coltrane's music, the dynamic nature of the intensity ranges above the static quality of beauty. In Ornette Coleman's music, the reverse is true.

That is also why it is not surprising that almost all of Coltrane's recordings are conceived from the improvisatory point of view – including his compositions! – while in Coleman's work, composition ranks above improvisation. Coleman is first and foremost a composer. There is an illuminating story – critic John Tynan tells it – that Coleman, in Los Angeles in 1958, was at a point where he simply no longer knew how to make ends meet. Filled with despair, he went to record producer Lester Koenig and asked him to buy some of his compositions. Ornette did not ask for a recording date; he only wanted to sell his compositions. He believed that to be a more promising avenue; his first thought was that the compositions would be a way out. And Ornette's first recording on the Contemporary label was made only because Koenig asked him to play the compositions on the alto saxophone.

Later, when there were heated discussions in the jazz world about the pros and cons of Ornette Coleman's music for years, it became apparent that even the critics who rejected Ornette as an improviser recognized the beauty and competence of his compositions. Coleman the composer was accepted faster than Coleman the improviser. One of the main reasons why Coleman managed to withdraw from the jazz scene for two years was that his creative genius can be satisfied for long periods by composing alone. More often than most other new musicians, he speaks of 'tunes' or 'songs'. He says: 'If I play an F in a tune called 'Peace' I don't think it should be the same as an F that is supposed to express sadness.' The atmosphere of the composition, in other words, the way the composer felt it, determines the atmosphere of the improvisation – a way of thinking that had become rare in jazz after Lester Young.

The fact that Coleman taught himself to play trumpet and violin is also connected with the priority of the compositional element over the improvisational. His music is supposed to be a whole. He would prefer to play everything necessary to make his music into sound himself. In an interview, he once said that he wished he was able to record all the parts himself on multitrack.

In this light one should judge the way Ornette plays his self-taught instruments. Certainly he is a perfect instrumentalist only on the alto sax. But the crux of the matter is missed if one speaks of the 'amateurish' nature of his violin and trumpet playing. The criteria for amateurishness refer back to the 'professionalism' of academic music. Ornette, however, plays the violin left-handed and tunes it as if it were played right-handed; he does not bow it, but rather beats or fiddles it with 'unorthodox' arm movements. He is not interested in the note he might generate, but rather in the sound he can gain from sounding as many strings as possible at once. What is left of the conventional violin when Coleman plays it is only its external shape. He plays it like an independent, newly discovered instrument. And he produces exactly those effects required for his compositions. There – and nowhere else – is where the criterion lies – and that criterion is met brilliantly by Ornette's violin playing. Ornette: 'I can't talk about technique because it is ever-changing. That's why for me the only method for playing any instrument is the range in which it is built. Learned technique is a law method. Natural technique is nature's method. And this is what makes music so beautiful to me. It has both, thank God.'

Ornette Coleman is the master of an immense compactness. This became even clearer when he – finally! – found a horn partner with whom he really enjoyed playing: tenorman Dewey Redman. Through him, Coleman found his way back to quartet music. And two musicians who had already been connected with Ornette in his early days, bassist Charlie Haden (with whom he also made great duo recordings) and drummer Ed Blackwell, joined the new quartet. The latter comes from New Orleans, where Ornette so often played in his youth, and does with the rhythm & blues patterns of the South basically the same thing Ornette did with the Texas blues: he abstracts them.

During the mid-seventies, it became particularly clear that the rhythm & blues background is still important for Ornette Coleman. He appeared in concert and on record with two guitar players, one or two bass guitarists, and drummer Shannon Jackson (and, later, when Jackson went his own way, even with two drummers). *Melody Maker* dubbed him 'Rocking Ornette', wondering whether it now was Coleman's turn to pay tribute to our rock age. Actually, however, he was relating less to contemporary rock than to the music of the black ghettos he had absorbed in his youth. His records 'Dancing in Your Head' and 'Body Meta' became the igniting force for what, in the early eighties, has been termed 'no wave', 'free funk', and 'punk jazz'. Ornette Coleman is the true father of this music – not only because its two main musicians, guitarist James Blood Ulmer and drummer Shannon Jackson, were strongly influenced by him, but also because a continuous stream of Coleman elements flows through this music.

Ornette has little knowledge of the conscious structuring of a composition or an improvisation. But almost everything he plays or composes seems to be cut from the same cloth. For that reason, Coleman's recorded pieces usually are significantly shorter than Coltrane's. Listening to Coltrane meant witnessing a laborious birth. Hearing Ornette means viewing the newborn creature.

Archie Shepp comments on this phenomenon: 'One of the many

things [Trane] accomplished was the breakthrough into the concept that a jazz musician need not – could not – be limited to a solo lasting a few minutes. Coltrane demonstrated that a man could play much longer, and that in fact it was an imperative of his conception to improvise at great length. I don't mean that he proved that a 30- or 40-minute solo necessarily is better than a three-minute one. He did prove, however, that it was possible to create 30 or 40 minutes of music, and in the process, he also showed the rest of us we had to have the stamina – in terms of imagination and physical preparedness – to sustain these long flights . . .'

This indeed touches on one of the more superficial among critical opinions: that the great old musicians – King Oliver, Lester Young, Teddy Wilson – were able to express all they wanted in one or two choruses of sixteen or thirty-two bars, and that it simply indicates lack of conciseness that such contemporary musicians as Coltrane (and many others since him) play such lengthy solos. In fact, the older musicians recorded short solos because records at that time usually only afforded some three minutes of music. But when they were able to play the way they really wanted – in jam sessions or clubs – they preferred, even back then, to play relatively long solos. Great music – from European symphonies to the ragas and talas of India – requires time. Only the commercial top-forty hit is satisfied with two or three minutes.

But back to Ornette Coleman. His aspiration to make his music all by himself as well as his two-year seclusion – which since then has been repeatedly followed by other periods of withdrawal from the public eye – certainly say something about his problems in dealing with the world around him. John Coltrane was a builder of groups. Ornette Coleman is alone. He is filled with a deep mistrust of society. To him, agents and managers automatically are people who want to cheat him. Almost all his managers were originally his friends, but as soon as Ornette would ask them to manage him, the friendship would quickly end. His mistrust – often unfounded – would create such unpleasant situations that soon there would be a reason for his suspiciousness.

In an interview with Dan Morgenstern he said: 'As a black man, I have a tendency to want to know how certain principles and rights are arrived at. When this concern dominates my business relationships, I'm cast into schizophrenic or paranoid thinking . . . I do not wish to be exploited for not having the knowledge or know-how required for survival in today's America. It's gotten so that in your relationships to every system that has some sort of power, you have to pay to become part of that power, just in order to do what you want to do. This doesn't build a better world, but it does build more security for the power. Power makes purpose secondary . . .'

It fits in with his problematic relationship to the world around him that Ornette Coleman is much more concerned with communicating with his audiences at concert or club appearances than, say, John Coltrane was. Occasionally, he appears in brightly coloured outfits that seem more suited to a circus performer than to an avant-garde jazz musician. Then one can sense his roots in a world where jazz musicians were trained to be entertainers.

On the other hand, John Coltrane, who certainly had an even less outgoing personality than Ornette, dealt with the world around him with quiet self-assurance.

I believe Coleman's origin in Texas and the world of country blues cannot be overemphasized. For good reason he made his first record – as a sideman, of course – in the early fifties with blues singer Clarence Samuels (who had been with the Jay McShann Band – the orchestra in which Charlie Parker got his start). Elsewhere (in the free-jazz chapter), we have shown that Ornette's free harmonic conception is a direct result of the harmonic freedom Southern country and blues musicians have always had.

Tenorist Archie Shepp – one of the great musicians of the new jazz – says: 'It was Coleman, who, in my opinion, revitalized and refurbished the blues idiom without destroying its simplistic milieu. Far from taking it beyond its original intentions, Coleman restored [the blues] to their free, classical [*African*] unharmonized beginnings. I have always felt that this early work of Ornette's was much closer to the "old thing" – hoedowns – foot-tappin' – than the new. Certainly Blind Lemon Jefferson and Huddie Leadbetter must have played 13, 17, 25-bar blues. Regardless; no pundit would have been foolish enough to label them avant-garde . . .'

And A. B. Spellman, the critic, says: 'Ornette's music is nothing but the blues.' Ornette is a total blues musician. And if conventional jazz includes only two – or rather, since the advent of bebop's flatted fifth, three – blue notes, it can be said that Coleman has turned the whole scale into blue notes. Almost all his notes are bent up or down, off-pitch, tied, flatted, or augmented – in short: vocalized in the blues sense. Remember his statement that an F in a tune called 'Peace' should not sound the same as an F in a context that is supposed to express sadness? Precisely that is a blues musician's concept. And if, after years of conventional jazz, this concept is found astonishing – because all F's, whether concerned with peace, sadness, or whatever, simply must have the identical pitch – this merely illustrates the influence of the European tradition – an influence that Ornette eliminated, at least in this realm.

The ease with which Ornette deals with free tonality has been contrasted with Coltrane's immensely tense, complex relationship to it. This became clear when, right after 'Ascension', the album 'Coltrane – Live at the Village Vanguard Again' was released. At this point, Coltrane could no longer play just with the musicians who'd been with him for so many years. He founded, as we have mentioned, a new group, a quintet, with Pharoah Sanders as a second tenor sax voice, Trane's wife Alice Coltrane on piano, drummer Rashied Ali and, as the only holdover from the old quartet, bassist Jimmy Garrison. When Coltrane plays on this record well-known themes from his earlier recordings – 'Naima' or 'My Favourite Things' – one feels that he loved these themes and would have preferred to continue playing them as they appeared to him as themes, if only he would have been able to express within them everything he so much wanted to express! If John Coltrane had seen a possibility of reaching, by conventional means, the degree of ecstatic heat he was aiming for, he would have continued to play, 'tonally', to the end.

Coltrane hesitated for a long time. For good reason Martin Williams once called him 'the man in the middle'. Trane needed ten years to take the step he finally took in 1965, and which a whole generation of musicians in this era took in one day. Anybody who hears the sermonlike, sublimely swinging lines of 'Naima' understands: this musician mourned for tonality. He knew how much he had lost with it. And he would have loved to return to it, had he not, during these ten years, again and again run into the limitations of conventional tonality before having been able to express all that seemed necessary to him.

It was only for the sake of increased intensity that Coltrane hired a second tenorist – and in terms of physical power and the ability to bring forth the wildest and most unbelievable sounds on his instrument, the man he chose was certainly the most amazing tenor player in the field: Pharoah Sanders. In interaction with him Coltrane became even more intense, as the great gospel preacher Bishop Kelsey rose to the occasion in his Washingtion, DC, Temple of God in Christ in interaction with a younger preacher – Reverend Little – in the course of their ecstatic double sermons.

Coltrane totally exhausted himself in this process. That was why he had to cancel a European tour in the fall of 1966. That is why he began to need frequent recuperation breaks. Repeatedly, during such shorter or longer breaks, friends would anticipate that this particular one would last a year or so. But just weeks later, Trane would be on the scene again, carrying on with the tearing, ecstatic power of his jazz and love hymns.

The liver ailment doctors determined was the cause of his death may merely have added the final blow to the complete exhaustion resulting from a life led ceaselessly at the edge of humanly possible intensity.

Again and again, he seemed to be totally drained of all energy after his concert appearances. He was like a relay runner: At a certain point, he would hand the torch to Pharoah Sanders, who then had to press forward – even *more* powerfully, intensely and ecstatically, yet without the hymnic power of love that radiated from Coltrane.

Tragically, there was one musician among the persons close to Coltrane who had – and still has – this power of love, but she was not able to express it musically, at least not on the high level associated with Trane. In 1967, when Trane died, she had not yet emerged clearly in the jazz world, but since then, she has become the purest and clearest successor and heir to the spiritual message of John Coltrane. This is his wife, pianist, harpist, organist and composer Alice Coltrane – or, as she was known when vibraharpist Terry Gibbs introduced her in the early sixties, Alice McLeod; or, as she now calls herself in accordance with her religious conviction: Turiya Aparna.

Alice made a pilgrimage to India and studied Hinduism and Buddhism; she took a Hindu name, and she believes that John Coltrane – had he lived longer – would also have gone this way: 'I would like to play music according to the ideals set forth by John and continue to let a cosmic principle of the aspect of spirituality be the underlying reality behind the music as he had . . . I know how badly John wanted to do this work.'

Alice Coltrane – like her husband John years before – knows what she is talking about. She does not merely flirt with ideas that are in the air. For her – as in John's prayer 'Love Supreme' – the great universal Godhead, the 'Universal Consciousness', is a fact that determines life and music; she knows that all those divine names which people use are only transcriptions of the one, identical Great Divine Power.

For her record, 'Universal Consciousness' Alice enlisted – and thus a circle closes – the cooperation of Ornette Coleman. Ornette shaped – or at least essentially determined – a violin sound for Alice without equal among the numerous string experiments in modern jazz, purposely avoiding the standard aesthetics of 'beauty' and homogeneity. The four violinists are from the most diverse schools: two from concert music – Julius Brand and Joan Kalisch; one a free-jazz man – Leroy Jenkins; and the fourth a soul musician – John Blair. These four, in pieces like 'Oh Allah' and 'Hare Krishna', play a dense texture of sounds that combines the complexity of avant-garde concert music with traditional jazz intensity, the spiritual power of Alice Coltrane with the tradition of bebop and blues.

Ornette Coleman loves violins. He admires – as did Charlie Parker twenty years earlier – the great tradition of European concert music. Again and again, he has presented compositions for symphony orchestra, chamber ensembles, and string quartets – most impressively in 'Skies of America', recorded in 1972 by the London Symphony Orchestra conducted by David Measham. However, Ornette Coleman remains a jazz musician – even when composing for symphony orchestra. The symphony orchestra, to him, is an enlarged 'horn' on which he improvises.

Ornette has become a classicist in his improvisations, too. At festivals the world over in 1971, the audiences, with no idea of the new Ornette Coleman, expected the musician who in the early sixties had revolutionized jazz with an immense, overpowering energy and were astonished to hear a man who was simply making 'beautiful music' – clear, singing, wonderfully balanced alto lines.

Jazz needs classicists of this kind. To demand permanent revolution means to demand the impossible – anyone who does, only reveals his immaturity.

Coltrane's music, on the other hand, has become even more effective in the years since his death – triggering developments everywhere, from rock to jazz, in the most diverse of transitional stages.

The hymnlike element prevalent on the entire contemporary jazz and rock scene comes from Coltrane – above all from 'Love Supreme'. When the Miles Davis influence subsided during the mid-seventies, it turned out that Coltrane was now the most intensively influential musician on the jazz scene. In face, a 'John Coltrane classicism' developed which is comparable to the Miles Davis and the Count Basie-Lester Young classicisms of earlier years.

To his friends, Coltrane was a marked man, at least after 'Love Supreme'. He already knew back then that his sounds were shaping the jazz of his times, and he suffered from this responsibility. He saw himself too strongly as a ceaseless seeker to be able to enjoy the fact that the whole jazz world now praised each of his statements as 'the last word'. After 1962 or 1963, I know of no photograph that shows him smiling.

In answer to the question whether there would ever be an end to the development that had already led him through a half-dozen different ways of playing since the mid-fifties and the Miles Davis Quintet, Coltrane told Nat Hentoff: 'You just keep going all the way, as deep as you can. You keep trying to get right down to the crux.'

If Ornette Coleman is the phoenix whose music from the start was revealed to us – if not in its mature form, then at least in its basic conception – as if it had sprung from the head of Zeus, then Coltrane was a Sisyphus, who again and again – from the very bottom up to the mountaintop – had to roll the hard, cumbersome rock of knowledge. And perhaps, whenever Coltrane got to the top, Coleman would already be standing there in his resplendent circus suit, playing his beautiful melodies. But the music John Coltrane would blow then, from the top of the mountain – standing next to Ornette – was imbued with the power of the pilgrim who had reached yet another station on the long, thorny road to knowledge (or might we better say – because it was Coltrane's conviction – to God), and knew there were many more stations to come – though in the months of exhaustion preceding his death he no longer knew how to go on.

John McLaughlin

Preliminary Remarks: No single musician could represent the jazz of the seventies. Jazz has become too wide. McCoy Tyner, Keith Jarrett, Chick Corea, Joe Zawinul and Wayne Shorter, Herbie Hancock, Dexter Gordon, and others are all of equal stature. And above all, Miles Davis (especially during the first half of the decade) and John Coltrane (since the late seventies) are still dominating figures. Beyond them, the jazz scene is split – into acoustic jazz on the one hand, and electric jazz on the other – and actually into many more subgroupings.

And yet, there is *one* musician of that decade – and beyond it also into the early eighties – who belongs to all these groupings. He has played blues and bebop and free and fusion, and above all, he feels bound to electric as well as to acoustic music: John McLaughlin.

The following interview took place in John McLaughlin's Paris home. McLaughlin is among those contemporary musicians who are so articulate that the interviewer merely has to give the cues, so my questions are only included if they are necessary to an understanding of the context. Further information about McLaughlin can be found in the chapters on the seventies, the guitar, and the combos of jazz.

JOHN MCLAUGHLIN: I was born in 1942 in a little village in Yorkshire. My father was an engineer, my mother used to be an amateur violinist. There was always a very good atmosphere towards music in the house, which I am eternally grateful for. Classical music. The Three B's: Beethoven, Bach, Brahms. I think a lot of children are in the wrong environment; they may have a lot of talent, but their parents do not encourage them, they're not interested in music. When I was about nine, my mother sent me to have piano lessons. Later we moved up to Northumberland – close to the Scottish border. Every summer the Scottish bagpipe bands used to come. Sometimes they had six or seven bagpipes, with three or four drummers – they had great drummers. Swinging in their own way. They had a big effect on me.

When I was about ten, there was the beginning of the blues revolution in England. The blues started underground among the students. One of my brothers had a guitar. He taught me three chords, and from that day on, everything was decided. I completely

fell in love with the guitar. I started listening to musicians like Muddy
Waters, Big Bill Broonzy, Leadbelly. [While John said this, I saw that
he still had records by these musicians in his library; they were just
above the record player, so he apparently still plays them. – J.E.B.]
So I had all this music just thrown at me. It was fantastic. Incredible.

When I was fifteen, I was able to take my guitar and a little
amplifier and go to a pub on a Sunday night where they had a jazz
club, and I would say: 'Please let me play a tune with you.' And they
said: 'OK, come in.' And they would play some very fast tunes and
they would burn me out completely, but it was a very good
experience. I went home and I realized I still had much to learn.

Around that time I started to listen a lot to Django Reinhardt and
Tal Farlow. They were my heroes on guitar. They still are. Maybe
that's why I like violinists so much – because I loved Django and
Stephane Grappelli.

When I was sixteen, I went on the road with a traditional jazz
band called 'Professors of Ragtime'. This got me to London – which,
of course, was the centre of jazz in England. In those days there were
two clubs: the Marquee and the Flamingo. They were great.
Everybody met everybody there, and the attitude was that everybody
could play with everybody. So this is what I did. I remember jam
sessions with everybody and anybody.

I remember the Rolling Stones coming in for an audition. I didn't
care much for them. They were out of tune, and I didn't think they
were swinging, but at least they were playing Muddy Waters's blues
tunes.

I started to play with the Graham Bond Organization and with
Alexis Korner. Alexis had everybody in his band at some point. But
Miles Davis's 'Into the Cool' with the Gil Evans big band really did it
for me. Miles crystallized a new school of music, and I immediately
felt: That is my school. But I kept on playing rhythm & blues and it
was great, because they were playing real jazz solos. It was blues, but
at the same time it was much more than blues.

I played with Eric Clapton and Dick Heckstall-Smith and Ginger
Baker and everybody, but I now must talk about Graham Bond. He
meant a lot to me. I had grown up in an ordinary school where the
teacher taught religion in a very dry way. He did not understand
what religion – and Christianity – really means. He was not a living
Christian. I never went to church, but Graham Bond – God rest his

soul – really was a seeker. He was interested in the invisible things in life. He introduced me to a book about ancient Eygptian culture, and I got very interested in this because, for the first time in my life, I realized that a human being is much more than meets the eye. Later, I discovered a book by Ramana Maharshi, and the first thing I saw was a photo of Ramana Maharshi, and this was the first picture of someone I could consider to be enlightened – an enlightened human being, and it meant very much to me. I began to realize that India as a culture and as a nation has treasures waiting to be discovered.

At this time I was friends with a guitar player by the name of Jim Sullivan, a well-known pop musician. So we were hanging out together, and we both became members of the London Theosophical Society. One day he played a record of Ravi Shankar. I couldn't understand it, but there was something which grabbed me. In the notes on the jacket I read the same things I was reading in that book by Ramana Maharshi, so I realized there is a connection between the music and the wisdom. And I knew I had to listen more in order to understand this connection.

I must confess I was taking some drugs at this time – acid and things like this – and it was quite significant for me. There are a lot of subconscious things coming out. Of course, today I am against drugs; my view is that of Aldous Huxley. I think that it is wrong that we have no drug education in our society – in spite of the fact that this society is completely drug orientated. If a kid has a headache you give him a dose of aspirin. An upper wakes you up and a downer gets you back to sleep. This is a terrible education.

At this time I was just scuffling along. Living from hand to mouth. Impossible to make any money. So I had to do sessions: pop sessions with people like Tom Jones, Engelbert Humperdinck and Petula Clark . . . Musically it was terrible, and after some time this session thing was driving me completely crazy. I had to do it in order to survive, and yet more things were happening musically that I wanted to do. Finally, one day I woke up and I said to myself: I cannot do this any more. And I got into my car and just drove, and I didn't stop until I got to Northern England and I stayed with my mother. It was a question of sanity for me.

I didn't want to go back to London. So I decided to go to the Continent and just play the kind of music I wanted to play. The first offer I got was from Gunther Hampel in Germany, so I went there playing free music for about half a year or so.

I am very glad I had the experience with Gunther. I know, idealistically, it is right to play free music but there is always a big 'but'. Because for the most part it is indulgent; this is my real opinion about free music. In order to really play it, first of all, harmonically and melodically you have to know everything, and then you have to be a real big person, a developed human being. Only a developed human being will not indulge himself. But as an ordinary human being – and that's what we mostly are – you indulge yourself. It's not making music, it's self-indulgence, it's not real.

When I was playing with Gunther, I lived in Antwerp, so I could go back to England every now and then. We had a little band with bass player Dave Holland and drummer Tony Oxley, and it was fantastic. I did a record called 'Extrapolation' with Tony Oxley and John Surman on baritone and soprano saxophone. Of course we all were proud when Dave was leaving for New York to play with Miles. Imagine, an Englishman to play with Miles – it was unheard of at that time. A real coup!

A few months later, in November of 1968, I got a call from Dave. He was in Baltimore, and guess who he was with? I said, 'Miles.' 'No,' he said, 'Tony – Tony Williams – and he wants to talk to you.' Tony said he would like to form a band, and he would like to have me. Jack DeJohnette had played him a tape he had done with me a few months before while he was in London with Bill Evans. So I said: 'When you are ready, just call me.'

In early 1969 he called again. So I left the first week of February for New York. Two days later I was in the studio with Miles. That was incredible. You must understand, New York was the ultimate for any European jazz player. And to be able to go there and to play in New York – it was just unbelievable for me!

Tony Williams and Dave Holland were playing with Miles. So immediately I met everybody. Miles and Wayne Shorter and Chick Corea and Jack DeJohnette and Gil Evans! Imagine! Like a dream coming true!

I'll never forget one night in that week. Miles was talking with Louis Armstrong and Dizzy. I wish I had had a camera. The three of them together! Just to see those three guys together was so beautiful for me.

On my second day in New York, Tony had to go to Miles's house to pick up some money. So I went along. Miles had a record date the day after. Miles knew that Tony would leave him in order to have a group with Larry Young on organ and me. But Miles didn't want him to leave. He loves Tony. Miles said to me, 'Why don't you bring your guitar tomorrow?' Tony wasn't terribly happy about that, because suddenly there was a little competition between Miles and Tony. For me, of course, it was the ultimate. It was the last thing I could expect. But now comes the next day. Larry Young was there. And Joe Zawinul and Herbie Hancock. That I was fortunate enough to be invited, to be there at the right moment, was really nothing I could have created. It was just like a blessing.

We had a tune by Joe Zawinul – with lots of chords. Miles said: 'Well, John, why don't you play it on the guitar?' I said: 'Do you want all these chords? That's going to take me quite a while to work it out.' And now I had my first experience with Miles's way of directing. He wanted me to play the tune with just one chord! And then suddenly everybody was waiting for me to start the tune and I didn't know what to do. I had no idea. Miles said: 'Well, you know the chord.' So I gave him the chord. That's all. Two chords, in fact. I started to play, and I realized the light is on; and I played the first solo, Wayne Shorter played the tune, Miles and Wayne played it together. I was confused, but I was playing on instinct. And then we played it back, and I was shocked how beautiful it was. And I realized: Joe Zawinul had brought the tune in, and Miles, in one minute, had brought the real essence, the beauty out of it. I was astonished to see how he could hear all that and just bring it out. That was one of the great things in Miles, how he brought the extraordinary out of his surroundings.

Afterwards, Miles asked me to join his group. Again, it was unbelievable for me. Imagine – I had to turn down Miles! Because it was more important for me to go with Tony Williams. I had compositions. And I realized, with Tony I would have more of a chance to play them than with Miles.

Eventually, Lifetime, our band with Tony Williams and Larry Young, was working. There was very little money involved, but musically, it was fantastic, and we couldn't believe that Columbia was turning us down. We played an audition for a guy called Al Kooper who was with Blood, Sweat & Tears. And he said no. I lost all my respect for him immediately because we were burning.

BERENDT: So this was your first experience with business in America? What do you think about the jazz business?

MCLAUGHLIN: I don't think they understand jazz in America. They are so far from reality. Even after eleven years in the USA, I know they don't understand their own music. They don't know how to market it. In Europe and in Japan it's so much better, because people really love the music. It has always been recognized as an art form over here. In Europe, whoever does business with you deals with you on the psychology that you are an artist. But in America they don't look at it that way. Of course, there are a lot of people who love and enjoy jazz in America. But as far as the business is concerned, it's terrible. There are no festivals as you have them in Europe. So when I first encountered these problems, I was quite surprised, because I thought they would have it much more together. In fact, it was one of the shocks of my life when we made that first record with Tony Williams and when they mixed it and the sound was just terrible, and I realized they had no respect for the music and the musicians. Really, I was shocked.

BERENDT: And of course, later it turned out that everybody was blaming Tony and the musicians for the bad sound. It did a lot of harm to Lifetime . . . However, John, I always felt you have been relatively lucky in your career – businesswise. When I look at what happened to Tony Williams, to Ornette, to Cecil Taylor, to so many others who had bad managers and agents during most parts of their careers, I really think you have been lucky.

MCLAUGHLIN: And yet I have been betrayed, people have taken money from me, and often enough I have been in very difficult positions. I'll never forget my first experience with Douglas Records. I met the man and I thought he's a real nice guy. But the first record I made for him – 'Devotion', with Buddy Miles on drums and Larry Young on organ – was a terrible experience. After I recorded it, I went on tour with Tony Williams, and when I came back, he had finished the album, mixed it, cut this out and that, and there were parts in it which I didn't recognize any more as part of our music. I was in total shock.

BERENDT: How much did they pay you?

MCLAUGHLIN: I got paid about $2,000.

BERENDT: That's all? For a famous record which was sold all over the world and which is still selling?

MCLAUGHLIN: No, not for one record. I got $2,000 for the two records I did for them – for 'Devotion' and 'My Goal's Beyond' . . .

BERENDT: . . . the one with the solo side. This is the record which really established solo guitar playing in jazz – the forerunner of hundreds of solo guitar records which followed – and, in my opinion, it still is the most beautiful of all of them . . . Well, from Douglas you went to Columbia, which is considered the best of all the companies – jazzwise.

MCLAUGHLIN: Well, here I am ten years later, and I have to leave Columbia. They have to pay me for leaving. Because they think that only electric music is worth marketing. Which I think is disgraceful to the American people. And it's patronizing.

BERENDT: Even from a business point of view, it's wrong. That's why the American record business is in such a bad state, because for more than ten years, they have concentrated only on electric music. That's all they have pushed. And in pushing it they have forgotten everything else. Now, the record-buying public is tired of that same electric sound all over again, but the record companies don't know what else to offer and how to market and advertise it.

MCLAUGHLIN: They are looking at it from a hamburger point of view.

BERENDT: Please, tell me about Sri Chinmoy, the guru you had at that time.

MCLAUGHLIN: Well, just before I went to America, I started to do yoga exercises every day in the morning. I arrived in America, and being in Manhattan, I thought I had to get myself more together. So I did more exercises. I was doing one hour and a half in the morning and one hour and a half in the evening. Just yoga. So after a year of doing this I felt great physically, but I thought I was missing the interior thing. So I went to meditate with different teachers, most of them Indians. And then suddenly one day, Larry Coryell's manager introduced me to Sri Chinmoy. Immediately I felt good about him. He said some important things to me. About music and spirituality. My question was: What is the relationship between music and the spiritual consciousness? And he answered: It's not so much what you do, but what's important is the consciousness with which you do it. For instance, a street sweeper can sweep his street perfectly and at the same time have great satisfaction from doing it. He can even get enlightened. The important thing, always, is the state of your consciousness because it determines (1) how you do it; and (2) the quality of what you do; and (3) the quality of what you are. So if you are a musician and you work towards enlightenment, your music will automatically be part of it. Of course, this was a great answer, so I subsequently went to see him several times, and after a few weeks I became a disciple.

BERENDT: But a couple of years later, the jazz media made a big thing out of you leaving Chinmoy.

MCLAUGHLIN: I never left him.

BERENDT: I expected that answer.

MCLAUGHLIN: I will never leave him, because I love him. He is a great man, he is an enlightened man. And that's the greatest thing any human being can be, because it takes an incredible amount of work . . . The only thing that I disagree with are the formalized things . . . This to do and this not to do. I cannot do this because I have to go on as a musician. I have to go on tour.

You know there is this beautiful word by Vivekananda: 'God comes on Earth to found a religion and the Devil comes right behind him and organizes it.' In a sense I am for all religions, but I am against all organized religion. I know this is a difficult problem, because people somehow need organization . . .

Anyway, let's go back to 1971. Miles suggested I should have my own band. I had met Billy Cobham on one of Miles's dates and I looked around for a violin player. I had spoken to Jean-Luc Ponty while I was in Paris. He said no. He wouldn't want to come to America. (Two years later he did!) A few weeks later, I found Jerry Goodman. And Miroslav Vitous, the bass player, called me and said: 'Joe Zawinul and Wayne Shorter are founding a group together, called "Weather Report". We want you to come with us.' And I said: 'Well, that's really nice, but I got something to do myself.' And Miroslav said: 'If you need a piano player, call Jan Hammer. He is also from Czechoslovakia, and he is playing with Sarah Vaughan.' So this was the Mahavishnu Orchestra: Jan Hammer, Billy Cobham, Jerry Goodman, and, of course, I had Rick Laird on bass, because I knew him from way back in England and we used to play a lot together. Right from the beginning, we had a beautiful rapport. One evening I was telling Sri Chinmoy that I got a band together and I wanted to give it a name, and he said: 'Well, call it the Mahavishnu Orchestra.' I said: 'Mahavishnu Orchestra? This is going to take everybody out!' 'Just try it anyway,' he said. So we tried it, and it was great for a year. We really identified with it – with the sound and the energy. And the music was amazing. Of course, I had expected it would work, but I didn't expect a big success like that. We just worked and played and things went great.

Part of the fun was that I kept living my own life the way I wanted to. People were very interested in it. They asked me lots of questions about Sri Chinmoy and all the spiritual things – meditation and India and religion. But of course none of the other musicians went into that. Gradually, they resented it. I felt we would have worked it out, but the real problem was with Jan Hammer and Jerry Goodman. They were really heavily against it. Finally, it became a big psychosis. So we went to Japan and it didn't get better. It got worse. So when we came to Osaka, I said: 'Look, why doesn't anyone say one word to me? If you have something on your mind, just say you hate me, just tell me. It's okay. Tell me and things will get better.' But neither of them would say a word, and Rick Laird told them: 'Why don't you tell him? You are always talking to me when he is not around.' So I felt they were determined to go out, and I realized this is the end of the band. It also had to do with success. You know, success is hard to take.

BERENDT: To me, the Mahavishnu Orchestra – the first one – was the greatest of all the jazz-rock bands. Both its records were just terrific – 'Birds of Fire' and 'Inner Mounting Flame'. Some time later, you had a second Mahavishnu Orchestra, but I always felt you no longer reached that type of height and intensity and inspiration and density.

McLAUGHLIN: We reached it more rarely. It did happen, I think, about two nights in a year. For me, this record 'Visions of the Emerald Beyond' (with the second Mahavishnu Orchestra and a string quartet) was one of the greatest I ever made. And then I did 'Apocalypse' with Michael Tilson Thomas conducting the London Symphony Orchestra.

BERENDT: But meanwhile Shakti had happened. I still remember the sensation – after all that electric high energy: you playing with those Indian guys – all acoustic music, you being the only Westerner in the group.

McLAUGHLIN: In fact, we had played together before the first Mahavishnu Orchestra had finished. I had some friends and they had a music shop and I told them, I am looking for somebody who can teach me about Indian music. So I took some vocal lessons – Indian singing – and the mrindangam player there (South Indian percussion) was L. Shankar's uncle. So I met L. Shankar, the violin player. I'll never forget when Jean-Luc Ponty arrived from California to join the second Mahavishnu Orchestra. Shankar and I had been hanging out that day, so they met – the two violinists, Shankar from India and Jean-Luc from France. And then L. Shankar started to play and I saw that look of amazement on Jean-Luc's face – I've never seen anything like this in my life.

I was so lucky to have some lessons from Ravi Shankar and other masters of Indian music. I love India, its music and its spirituality, its religions. The spirituality *is* the music. You can't separate the two – like you can in the West.

I had met Zakir Hussain, the tabla player, at Ali Akbar Khan's school for Indian music near San Francisco. Khan-sahib, the great master sarod player, was just sitting there in his chair listening to both of us playing, and after we finished I said, I never played with anybody like that.

I did three records with Shakti. But Columbia just didn't go along with it. There was no enthusiasm there. And you have to have enthusiasm, otherwise you can't sell it. Of course, it didn't sell bad, but it didn't sell those enormous quantities – like rock. So, gradually, I realized I was wasting my time with Columbia.

BERENDT: So you went back to electric music because Columbia told you to?

McLAUGHLIN: You can't say this. You know, jazz music and Western harmonies are part of me. I cannot suppress it. Not that I have suppressed it in Shakti, but I was preoccupied with Indian music, which has its own kind of discipline. Shakti really stayed together for quite some time. So I wanted to go back to Western music. It's a part of me I cannot deny. So I really had a desire to play chords and to play with a drummer and a bass player, and that's why I made this record 'Johnny McLaughlin – Electric Guitarist'. In a way it was like going back to my beginnings – and, of course, it also was a reunion with almost all the Mahavishnu players. It was like forgetting all those old problems and just playing music.

BERENDT: For many people there is almost a schism between electric and acoustic music.

McLAUGHLIN: Both are part of me. There is a style of music and a style of playing I can only do on an electric guitar, and there is another style I like to do on acoustic guitar.

BERENDT: Couldn't it be that when you have played electric for some time, you want to go back to acoustic again? And vice-versa? It was like this a couple of times in your career.

McLAUGHLIN: Yeah, maybe that's true. It looks like it. Anyway, at the moment I like to play acoustic guitar. There are such endless possibilities to play acoustic. There is so much to do. It's almost like a cult of simplicity. For me it's just this guitar and nothing else. And it always pushes me to work harder and harder, and that's the only thing I am interested in.

BERENDT: You do a lot of practising?

McLAUGHLIN: I like to work every day – maybe a couple of hours in the morning and three hours in the afternoon. Sometimes I do two hours at night.

BERENDT: When I presented the Mahavishnu Orchestra at the Olympic Games Jazz Festival in Munich in 1972 I considered you, more or less, a European musician, but you talked to me about New York. 'It only could have happened there,' you said. And: 'New York makes you strong. It really is *the* jazz city.' But now, ten years later, you live in Paris. And you have a French wife. And your wife is a classical musician. And you have an apartment at the Pont Neuf in Paris. Are you coming back to your European roots?

McLAUGHLIN: In a sense, yes. I think New York has changed. America has changed. America may, at some point, enjoy a renaissance of music, but I don't know when this will happen. Right now, the situation for music is better in Europe than it is in America. You know, I was in America from 1970 to 1975, but even in 1974 I was beginning to feel it would be nice to live in Europe again – but of course to work in America. Meanwhile I have realized I can work in Europe, and I can do here what I want.

By the way, I met my wife while I was on a Shakti tour in Paris in 1975. It wasn't that I wanted to find a European wife. In fact, I was not interested in finding any kind of wife. I was happy just to go on and play my music with Shakti. But you have no control over that. So we got married in 1976. She plays viola – also viola da gamba. She is interested in the younger contemporary composers. Sometimes, at home, we play together. She plays viola and I play guitar. It feels beautiful. We like to play duets. We have worked on some music by Vivaldi.

BERENDT: How do you feel about fusion?

MCLAUGHLIN: I think a lot of fusion music is not true fusion. If a musician is being pushed to play a certain kind of music or if he feels he has to do something with a different beat in order to become popular, then this is basically against the spirit of music and against the spirit of jazz – that's all. The fusion has to happen inside you, otherwise it's not going to happen at all. It becomes only pseudo-fusion. There is so much pseudo-music around.

You can't say: Let's put it with a disco beat. Or let's do it with a rock beat. It won't have any weight. It won't carry any conviction. That's why I don't listen too much to that kind of music anymore. I'm not deeply touched by it. And I have to be deeply touched, otherwise it's not worth it. I want something to really grab my insides. That's the music I take along when I go on tour.

BERENDT: What do you take along?

MCLAUGHLIN: I take Coltrane, Miles; I take some gypsy music. I have a cassette of a great Indian nagaswaram player. And a beautiful Indian tabla player. And I take some Chopin on the road. And some Schumann.

THE ELEMENTS OF JAZZ

The Elements of Jazz

Sound and Phrasing

What particularly distinguishes jazz from traditional European music is sound. Crudely put, the difference is this: In a symphony orchestra, the members of, say, the string section, will wish to play their passages as homogeneously as possible. This means that each member of the section must have the same ideal of sound and know how to achieve it. This ideal corresponds to transmitted cultural standards or aesthetics: an instrument must have a 'beautiful' sound.

For the jazz musician, on the other hand, it is of no particular importance to conform to a commonly accepted conception of sound. A jazz musician has his own sound. The criteria for this sound are based not so much on aesthetics as on emotionality and expressivity. To be sure, the latter are also found in European music. But in jazz, expression ranks above aesthetics, while in European music, aesthetics ranks above expression.

Thus, one may find in jazz a tendency contradictory to the standards of aesthetics – and opposed to standardized aesthetics – but this tendency does not imply that jazz of necessity must be 'unaesthetic.' It does imply, however, that an artistic music is conceivable which conforms to the highest standards of jazz and yet is contrary to aesthetic conventions.

The self of the musician is clearly reflected – in the most immediate and direct fashion – in the nonstandardized sound of the great jazz improvisers. In jazz, there is no *bel canto*, no 'schmaltzy' violins, but hard, direct sounds – the human voice, plaintive and complaining, crying and screaming, sighing and moaning. The instruments are expressive and eruptive, not filtered through any regulations or rules of sound. That is why the music made by a jazz player is 'true' in a much more concrete sense than that made by the average player of

European music. The majority of the 100 or 200 musicians in a large symphony orchestra probably do not feel the 'titanic struggles' which occur in Beethoven's music, nor do they fully sense the secrets of form which are the basis of symphonic music. But a jazz musician – even in a big band – senses and feels, knows and understands what he plays. The lack of understanding among the 'civil service' musicians in the symphony orchestras, of which so many conductors have complained – especially where modern music is concerned – is unthinkable in jazz.

Because a jazz musician's playing is 'true' in a direct, naïve, and 'primitive' way, it may possess beauty even when it contradicts aesthetic standards. One could say that the beauty of jazz is ethical rather than aesthetic.

To be able to respond to jazz means first and foremost to be able to feel this kind of beauty.

The first word the layman thinks of when jazz is mentioned – 'hot' – is not just a matter of rhythmic intensity. It is first of all a matter of sound. One speaks of 'hot intonation'.

The personal, inimitable sound of a great jazz musician is the reason for something that always astonishes the outsider: that the jazz connoisseur is able to recognize, after relatively few notes of music, who is playing. This certainty does not exist in classical music, where it is only with difficulty, and seldom with complete assurance, that one can guess who is conducting or playing certain parts in a symphonic orchestra.

Sound in jazz is – to give a few examples at random – the slow, expressive vibrato of Sidney Bechet's soprano sax; the voluminous, erotic tenor sax sound of Coleman Hawkins; the earthy cornet of King Oliver; the 'jungle' sound of Bubber Miley; the elegant clarity of Benny Goodman's clarinet; the sorrow and lostness of Miles Davis or the victoriousness of Louis Armstrong; the lyrical sonority of Lester Young; the gripping, concentrated power of Roy Eldridge or the clear glow of Dizzy Gillespie.

In the older forms of jazz the shaping of sound is more marked than in the more recent ones. In the newer forms, an element that often was absent in earlier times is added: jazz phrasing. Trombonist Kid Ory, for example, played phrases that existed in circus and marching music at the turn of the century and are not necessarily jazz phrases. Nevertheless, what he plays is clearly jazz – because of his sound.

Stan Getz, on the other hand – especially the Getz of the fifties – has a sound which, when isolated from its surrounding elements, is not so far removed from 'classical' saxophone sound. But he phrases with a concentrated jazz feeling no symphony player could emulate. There are modern jazz recordings – as, for instance, some by Jimmy Giuffre or by violinist Zbigniew Seifert – which are very close to the chamber music of modern 'classical' composers. Yet the phrasing is so definitely jazz that the music is felt to be jazz even when a regular beat is not present.

Thus one notes a shift in emphasis from sound to phrasing in the history of jazz (and back, to a certain degree, from phrasing to sound with some free-jazz players) – in a sense that will be clarified later in our attempt to define jazz.

Sound and phrasing can represent everything of importance in jazz to the extent that a jazz musician, were he to play a piece of European concert music, could transform it into 'jazz' – even when playing his part note for note.

The sound of jazz and the jazz phrasing connected with it are the 'blackest' elements in jazz. They lead back to the shouts of Southern plantation Negroes, and from there, back to the coast and the jungles of Africa. Along with swing, they are the sole predominantly Negroid elements in jazz.

One might compare the sound which the blacks, in the formative years of jazz, coaxed from their European instruments to the situation in which the Africans deported as slaves to the New World were forced to speak European languages. It has been pointed out that the 'singing' way of speaking peculiar to the Southern United States can be traced back to Negro influence, and it is ironic that even those Southerners who have no other word than 'nigger' for a black person also speak in this manner. Originally, the word was nothing but the black way of saying 'Negro'. In the same sense, jazz sound and jazz phrasing are, or in any case originally were, nothing but the black way of playing European melodies on European instruments. And this way – like black Southern speech – has penetrated the white world so completely that it has conquered audiences in this white world, and is often employed by white musicians as legitimately as by blacks.

From the vantage point of sound it becomes clear that the question of a musician's skin colour remains superficial unless due regard is had for the underlying complexities. From the inner conviction that most of the creative jazz musicians were black, Roy Eldridge once claimed that he could always distinguish a white musician from a black one. Critic Leonard Feather gave him a blindfold test: Eldridge had to listen to a number of unfamiliar records, and judge from them. It turned out that he frequently erred about race. In spite of this, Feather did not – as he believed – disprove Eldridge's point to show that black and white jazz musicians sound alike. He only pointed up the many sides of the problem.

On the one hand: Fletcher Henderson, black, wrote the arrangements without which Benny Goodman, white, might not have become 'King of Swing'. On the other hand: Benny Goodman played these arrangements 'better' with his white orchestra than Henderson did with his black orchestra – according to any standard, and even according to the standard of black musicians.

Furthermore – in reverse: Neal Hefti, white, has written some of the most brilliant arrangements for Count Basie's black band. But Basie's band played them 'better' than Hefti's own band, which consisted mainly of white musicians.

Finally: As early as the fifties – i.e., before the time of today's avant-garde – Charles Mingus, black, was an exponent of an experimental, deliberately abstract tendency one would almost certainly ascribe to a white rather than to a black musician – if all the generalizations we carry to the race problem made any sense. On the other hand, even before the hard-bop movement, white musicians such as Gerry Mulligan or Al Cohn again and again pointed to the importance of beat, swing, and blues – of originality, vitality, and simplicity; in other words, they did what the simplistic average judgement would sooner have expected of black musicians.

Always, there is this duality when the question of race arises in jazz – and not only in jazz. It is impossible, especially for a European writer, to do more than acknowledge both points of view.

Improvisation

'A hundred and fifty years ago our ancestors went to hear Beethoven and Hummel and Thalberg and Clementi improvise richly and splendidly; and before that to the great organists – to Bach, Buxtehude, Böhm, Pachelbel; not forgetting Samuel Wesley, though he came later. Today we have to go for the same sort of musical performance to Lionel Hampton, Erroll Garner, Milt Jackson, Duke Ellington, and Louis Armstrong. I will leave you to digest the implications to be drawn from that curious circumstance.' Thus Burnett James in an article about improvisation in jazz.

Indeed, during the whole history of jazz, from New Orleans to today, jazz improvisation has been accomplished according to the same techniques as employed in old European music – with the aid of harmonic structures (which, however, in free jazz became so 'open' that they are barely structured any longer).

On the other hand, from the beginning of the last century, improvisation atrophied in European music to such a degree that today even leading soloists sometimes are unable to make up the cadenzas left open to improvisation in the great classical concertos. Concert performances today are judged according to 'authenticity', i.e., whether a piece of music is played or sung as the composer 'meant it to be', but if, for example, we were to perform a Vivaldi concerto or a Handel sonata as the composers wrote them, we would simply be 'interpreting' a bare, skeletal framework of notes. The entire improvisatory force and freedom of Vivaldi's and Handel's music – and, in general, of all of baroque and prebaroque soloistically conceived music – have been lost to the ideal of 'authenticity'. Arnold Dolmetsch has said that the omission of ornamentation – the improvised embellishment of the notated music – is as 'barbaric' as would be the removal of the flamboyant Gothic architectural ornamentation from a cathedral with the excuse that one preferred a simpler style. The jazz musician improvises on a given harmonic structure. That is exactly what Johann Sebastian Bach and his sons did when playing a chaconne or an air: they improvised on the harmonics on which the melody was based, or embellished the given melody. The whole technique of ornamentation – the embellishment of melody – which flowered during the Baroque period, still survives in jazz . . . for instance, when Coleman Hawkins played his famous 'Body and Soul'. And the ground bass, organ point, and *cantus firmus* of the old music came into being to give structure to improvisation and to make it easier – in the same sense that jazz musicians today use blues chords and the blues form to give shape to their improvisations. Winthrop Sargeant speaks about harmony in this sense as a 'controlling structural principle in jazz.'

Of course, it is not as if the early jazz musicians had consciously taken over the improvisational techniques of the old music. They knew nothing of Bach and all these matters, and the parallels which exist here are meaningful precisely because they developed unconsciously: the result not of the same but of a related basic musical feeling. On the contrary, the parallels between jazz and old music become suspect when they are practised deliberately, and when, because similarities in improvisational methods do exist, the two forms are thrown into one pot. Nor does the relationship in conception which stands behind all this stem from the old European music. It is a conception basic to *all* musical cultures in which it is 'more important to make music yourself than to listen to the music of others', in which the naïveté of the relationship to music does not allow for any questions of interpretation or conception to arise, in which the music is judged not according to what it means but to what it is. There are such musical cultures and styles in Africa as well as in Europe, in America as well as in Asia – one might even say that almost all musical cultures anywhere in the world have this common basic conception, with the exception of the music which had its flowering in nineteenth-century Europe, and which still rules the musical sensibilities of the white world.

Jazz, then, has improvisation. But the problem of improvisation is not exhausted with this conclusion. It begins with it. The statement 'there is improvisation in jazz' is a truism so widespread that many fans and laymen proceed to draw from it the conclusion that if there is no improvisation in a piece, it is not jazz. Humphrey Lyttelton, the most brilliant representative of traditional jazz in Europe, says: 'In the full sense of "composing extemporarily, that is, without preparation", improvisation has proved to be not essential to, and practically nonexistent in, good jazz.'

Most jazz improvisation is based on a theme. Usually, it is – excluding the free jazz of the sixties and the more complex song forms that came into use in the seventies – a standard song in 32-bar form – the 'AABA' form of our popular tunes – in which the 8-bar main theme (A) is first presented, then repeated, then followed by a new 8-bar idea – the so-called bridge (B) – and in conclusion, the first eight bars are sounded once more. Or it may be the 12-bar blues form, about which more will be said in the section about blues. The jazz musician places new melodic lines over the given harmonies of the song or the blues. He can do this by embellishing or making slight alterations in the songs or blues – André Hodeir calls this manner of improvising 'paraphrasing'. He can also accomplish this by creating entirely new melodic lines over the given harmonies – a manner of improvising which Hodeir calls the 'chorus-phrase'.

The decorative, embellishing 'paraphrase' was the main improvisatory device of the older jazz forms. Clarinetist Buster Bailey relates: 'At that time [1918] I wouldn't have known what they meant by improvisation. But embellishment was a phrase I understood. And that was what they were doing in New Orleans'. The 'chorus-phrase', on the other hand, which creates entirely new melodic lines, is the main improvisatory manner of modern jazz. Its possibilities are vast. Example 1 shows, in the top row, the beginning of the song, 'How High the Moon', the favoured theme of the bop era, with its related harmonies, and below it three different improvisations on it by three leading jazz musicians. One can see at a glance that three completely different melodic lines have come into being. There is no connection between these three lines as far as melody is concerned, but the connection is given through the harmonic structure of 'How High the Moon': the same harmonies constitute the basis for three very different improvisations.

Example 1

This example was transcribed from a record which does not even give a clue to the original theme in its title. This RCA record is entitled 'Indiana Winter'. The three choruses – that is what improvisations on the harmonies of a theme in the number of bars corresponding to that theme are called – cited in the example were played by trombonist J. J. Johnson, trumpeter Charlie Shavers, and tenorman Coleman Hawkins.

The habits of jazz ensure that the most important jazz themes repeatedly become the foundations for the improvisations of jazz musicians. They are played day after day and night after night in hundreds of clubs and concert halls. After 100 or 200 choruses, a musician may arrive at certain phrases which then will crop up more and more frequently in his playing of the tune. After a while something like a 'standard chorus' on the respective theme will have developed.

Many choruses have become so famous that the listener would be disappointed if the musician who made them up were suddenly to play something different. King Oliver's 'Dippermouth Blues', Alphonse Picou's 'High Society', Charlie Parker's 'Parker's Mood', Ben Webster's 'Cotton Tail', Stan Getz's 'Early Autumn', Bix Beiderbecke's 'Singing the Blues', Louis Armstrong's 'West End Blues', Lester Young's 'Song of the Islands,' Chu Berry's or Coleman Hawkins's 'Body and Soul', Miles Davis's 'All of You', Coltrane's 'My Favourite Things' – these (written down as they came to mind) are high points one would be loath to see transplanted to other peaks . . . especially as one cannot be sure they would be peaks. On the contrary, such a result would be unlikely. It would be foolish to claim that choruses which are among the greatest in jazz cease to be jazz when repeated. Thus, what is created by improvising, and, having proved to be of value, is repeated, also belongs to improvisation.

This concept of the once-improvised is important. It makes clear that what was once created by improvising is linked to the man who created it. It cannot be separated from him, notated, and given to a second or third musician to play. If this happens, it loses its character, and nothing remains but the naked formula of notes.

At this point, the distinction between improvisation and composition becomes more differentiated. European music – insofar as it is composed – is capable of limitless reproduction by anyone who possesses the instrumental, technical, and conceptual capacities to grasp it. Jazz can be reproduced solely by the musician who produced it. The imitator may be technically better and intellectually superior – but he still cannot reproduce the music. A jazz improvisation is the personal expression of the improviser and of his musical, spiritual, and emotional situation.

In other words, the concept 'improvisation' is actually inaccurate. A jazz musician who has created a chorus is at one and the same time improviser, composer, and interpreter. In jazz – even in arranged jazz, as will be shown later – these three aspects *must* be in evidence lest the music become questionable. In European music they *can* be separated without affecting the quality of the music. On the contrary: the quality may improve. Beethoven was considered a poor interpreter of his own music; others were able to play it better. Miles Davis in his formative years was, as far as technique is concerned, not an outstanding musician. Yet it is unthinkable that a technically better equipped trumpeter should have copied Miles's phrases and, playing them note for note, have played a 'better Miles Davis' than Miles himself. To express it as a paradox: Miles might have been only a fair trumpet player, but he was the greatest interpreter of his own music one could wish for. Indeed, the spiritual power of his improvisations had impact and influence even on trumpeters who were technically superior.

An improvised jazz chorus stands in danger of losing its authenticity and of becoming dishonest and untrue when it is copied by someone who did not create it. Given the multiplicity of human experience, it is inconceivable that the 'other' could play from the identical situation from which the 'one' improvised his chorus. The relationship between the music heard and the man who created it is more important to jazz improvising than complete lack of preparation. When copying and imitation occur without proper preparation, jazz is in greater danger than when, after hour-long, systematic preparation, phrases are created which belong to the player as expressions of his artistic personality. This is the meaning of the passage from Humphrey Lyttelton quoted above. A musician as different from Lyttelton as Shorty Rogers means the identical thing when he says: 'In my opinion all good jazz musicians are composers. I have utilized them as composers by having parts in which I merely wrote instructions and left the rest to the men to compose spontaneously, mutual instinct being the connecting link between us.' (In other words, between arranger and improviser.) In the formulation 'composing spontaneously' the identity of improviser, composer, and interpreter is expressed in a different way.

This identity of improviser, composer, and interpreter is what is meant when we speak of improvisation in jazz. Not a wild, head-on extemporization. The identity of improviser, composer, and interpreter has to be fulfilled also by the arranger who – aside from relating what is to be improvised to what has been once-improvised – finds the real justification for his position in the fact that he can sometimes respond more satisfactorily to the demand for the identity of improviser, composer, and interpreter than the spontaneously improvising soloist can. Jack Montrose, one of the leading arrangers on the West Coast, said: 'The jazz writer forms a unique contrast to his colleagues in other fields of musical composition in that his ability to *write* jazz music is a direct extension of his having acquired the ability to play it first. He must have shared the experience of creating jazz music, the *jazz experience*. It is my contention that jazz music bearing the stamp of true authenticity has never been written except by composers who have first attained this prerequisite.' Elsewhere, Montrose contended that as long as the music is the work of a jazz musician, jazz will be the result. We shall discuss this more extensively in the next chapter. But at this juncture we propose six points which may serve as a summary of the problem of improvisation in jazz.

1. The once-improvised is equal to improvisation.

2. The once-improvised can be reproduced by the one who produced it, but by no one else.

3. Both improvisation and the once-improvised are personal expressions of the situation of the musician who produced them.

4. The concurrence of improviser, composer, and interpreter belongs to jazz improvisation.

5. Insofar as the arranger corresponds to point 4, his function differs from that of the improvising-composing interpreter merely in terms of craftsmanship and technique: the arranger writes, even when writing for others, on the basis of his experience as an improvising-composing interpreter.

6. Improvisation – in the sense of points 1 through 5 – is indispensable to jazz; improvisation in the sense of complete unpreparedness and unlimited spontaneity *may* occur, but is *not* a necessity.

The Arrangement

Many jazz lovers and almost all laymen believe there is a contradiction between improvisation and arrangement. Because, in their view, improvisation is decisive, the presence of an arrangement must automatically indicate a state of decadence since 'the more arrangement, the less improvisation.'

The jazz musician – not just today, but from the start of jazz, or at least from the great days of New Orleans jazz in Chicago – is of another opinion. He sees the arrangement not as an inhibition of the freedom to improvise but as an aid. For him, it is a matter of experience that the possibilities for free and unlimited improvised solo playing are particularly enlarged when the soloist knows what the musicians playing with him are doing. With an arrangement, he knows. Many of the greatest improvisers – first and foremost Louis Armstrong – have demanded arrangements. Only to a superficial observer does it appear contradictory that Fletcher Henderson on the one hand was the first jazz arranger with a precise conception, while on the other hand his orchestra offered greater freedom of improvisation than almost any other big band of its day.

In the relationship between arrangement and improvisation there is an inherent tension, which can be fertilized to an unimagined extent. Jelly Roll Morton told his musicians: 'You'd please me if you'd just play those little black dots – just those little black dots that I put down there. If you play them, you'll please me. You don't have to make a lot of noise and ad-lib. All I want you to play is what's written. That's all I ask.' And despite this, clarinetist Omer Simeon – long a member of Morton's bands – and guitarist Johnny St Cyr said: 'Reason his records are so full of tricks and changes is the liberty he gave his men . . . He was always open for suggestions.' This is the tension which has to be dealt with in art – and one cannot do much theorizing about it. In the early days of the Ellington orchestra, all the band members felt they were playing what they wanted; and yet each note was 'Ellingtonian'.

Arrangements came into being as early as the formative years of jazz. Even the early jazz musicians – King Oliver, Jelly Roll Morton, Clarence Williams, Louis Armstrong – arrived through improvisation at set, repeatable turns of ensemble playing, and once their effectiveness had been tested, these turns remained. This shows how rapidly improvisation is transformed into arrangement. What was once-improvised yesterday has perhaps already become a permanent arrangement by tomorrow.

George Ball relates how the New Orleans Rhythm Kings – the most successful Dixieland band between 1921 and 1925 – did this kind of thing: '. . . by predetermining definite parts for each man to play; by introduction of patterns, simple though they were, and a more even rhythmic background. Arrangements were, of course, impossible as we know them today, if only from the fact that the most important members of the melody section, Mares, Rappolo and Brunis, could not read music. [Elmer] Schoebel nevertheless spent numberless rehearsals drilling these men in their parts, which we might call arranged, although not a note of music was set down for them, and which the performers had perforce to learn by sheer memory.'

Many other great groups of New Orleans and early Dixieland jazz – not to mention later ones – valued arrangements: the Hot Seven, the Memphis Five, the Original Dixieland Jazz Band, the California Ramblers – groups which have come to represent the incarnation of free, unfettered improvisation to traditional jazz fans.

Perhaps the misunderstanding arises from the fact that the term 'arrangement' has not been precisely defined. There is a tendency to speak of arrangements only when something has been written down beforehand. But it is easy to see that it is actually only a question of procedure whether a certain passage actually has been written down in advance or has merely been discussed. Arrangement begins the moment something is agreed upon in advance. It is immaterial whether this is done in writing or orally. Between the agreements among the New Orleans Rhythm Kings and the complex scores of the modern big-band arrangers, who may have studied with Milhaud, Stefan Wolpe, Ernst Toch, or other great modern composers and who are conversant with the traditional European art of instrumentation, there is only a difference of degree.

Since the thirties, the expression 'head arrangement' has gained currency among big bands. In the bands of Fletcher Henderson and Count Basie, or in the first Woody Herman 'Herd' of the forties it was common practice to establish only the first twenty-four or thirty-two bars of a piece – the remainder was left to the improvisatory capacities of the musicians. This term also makes clear how inevitable and organic is the development from improvisation through the once-improvised to the arrangement.

Since there is no contradiction between arrangement and improvisation, the latter has not faded into the background by reason of the progressive development of the former in jazz history. Improvisation and arrangement have *both* developed equally. Charlie Parker, Miles Davis, and John Coltrane – and later, even more so, Albert Ayler and other free-jazz musicians – command a freedom of improvisation which King Oliver, Louis Armstrong, or Bix Beiderbecke never possessed at the zenith of traditional jazz. This can be determined quite rigorously: often several masters of one title are recorded until recording director and musicians are satisfied. On several available versions of a given piece by Armstrong or Beiderbecke, for example, the solos vary, but they are, by and large, quite comparable; structure and line were changed only rarely. 'Takes' by Charlie Parker, however, differ so markedly that one might say that a new piece was created each time. Of the four masters of Parker's 'Cool Blues', recorded in immediate succession on the same day (only the final one was approved by Parker), three were put on the market under different titles: 'Cool Blues', 'Blowtop Blues', and 'Hot Blues' – and to a certain degree they are all different 'pieces'.

Thus it is not contradictory for musicians who are members of groups dependent on arrangements to speak of improvisation as the 'key word'. John Lewis, the maestro of the Modern Jazz Quartet, where arrangements and composition are of decisive importance, has said: 'Collective improvisation is what makes jazz singular.' And clarinetist Tony Scott, who has undertaken many interesting experiments as arranger and jazz composer, said during a round-table discussion at Newport in 1956 that jazz was more likely to progress through improvisation than through writing.

Clearly, the arrangement can only fulfil its task when the arranger lives up to the demands expressed by Jack Montrose at the end of the last chapter: he must be a jazz musician and a jazz improviser. In the entire history of jazz there is no exception to this basic rule. It is significant that it is not possible to speak of the arrangement in jazz without mentioning improvisation.

Insofar as the arranger has to be an improvising jazz musician, it is only a small step from arranger to jazz composer. Without doubt, the actual contradiction is not between improvisation and arrangement, but between improvisation and arrangement on the one hand and composition on the other. Because improvisation is of such importance in jazz, the music has arrangements but no compositions which are completely 'composed through'; and since European music – at least since romanticism – is composed and compositionally grounded music, it has practically no improvisation aside from 'aleatorics' in modern concert music (but that is a different matter, which, with its theory-laden clumsiness, casts further light on the strained attitude of the concert musicians towards improvisation!).

Thus, the 'jazz composer' is a paradox. 'Jazz' means improvisation, and 'composer' – at least in Europe – means the exclusion of improvisation. But the paradox can be fruitful: the jazz composer can structure his music in the sense of the great European tradition and nonetheless leave room for jazz improvisation. Most of all, he can write what he structures in the sense of the European tradition in a jazz manner. There can be no doubt that jazz is subordinate to European music as far as formal structure is concerned, and that it might gain if mastery of form and structure becomes possible in jazz – provided nothing is lost in respect to the elements in which the singularity of jazz is contained: vitality, authenticity, immediacy of expression . . . in short, all that is jazzlike. From this point of view, Stravinsky's dictum that composition is 'selective improvisation' acquires a much greater degree of importance for the jazz composer than it can have for the composer in the European tradition.

Since the fifties, musicians such as Jimmy Giuffre, John Lewis, Horace Silver, Bill Russo, Ralph Burns, Oliver Nelson, Charles Mingus, Carla Bley, and Chick Corea have given new meaning to the term 'jazz composer', with credit to both elements of the term. But only Duke Ellington, who has been jazz 'composer' since the mid-twenties, stands on the level of the truly great jazz improvisers – the level of Charlie Parker, Louis Armstrong, Lester Young, Coleman Hawkins, John Coltrane, Miles Davis . . .

Beyond all these considerations, of course, stands the kind of composer who could be found in jazz from the very start: the musician who simply writes 12-bar blues or 32-bar song themes, supplying himself and his players with materials for improvisation. This line leads straight from early musicians – Jelly Roll Morton, for example – through, say, Fats Waller in the twenties and thirties and

Thelonious Monk from the forties on to the well-known improvisers of modern jazz who write much of their own material: Sonny Rollins, Miles Davis, John Coltrane, Herbie Hancock, Archie Shepp, Muhal Richard Abrams – in fact, practically everyone who plays improvised jazz. This sort of composing is directly related to the improvisatory process – without detouring through the arrangement. Of course, there are many gradual stages – from simple sets of changes and themes merely setting up a blowing line to the complex jazz composition, formally structured and scored for many voices. All of these steps build on each other so organically that the erection of boundaries appears more or less arbitrary.

The relationship between arrangement and improvisation reflects the frequently posed question about the relationship between the collective and the individual in jazz. Jazz has been called 'the music of the collective' as well as 'the music of boundless individualism'. But the symphony orchestra, in which a hundred musicians subordinate themselves, almost in self-sacrifice, to a single will, is collective to a much greater degree. And a disdain for rules, regulations, and laws would seem to be a prerequisite for 'boundless individualism'. Jazz – except for a few instances of extreme free jazz – shows no signs of such disdain.

What happens in free jazz only *seems* to follow different laws. Certainly, it has none – or only very few – of such exact written-down scores as those written by Oliver Nelson or Gerry Mulligan or Gary McFarland for the big bands. The concept of arranging actually returns to the position it had at the beginning of jazz history – to the orally predetermined arrangements of the King Oliver Band or of the New Orleans Rhythm Kings. And that same fruitful and inspiring tension between the freedom of the improvisatory principle and the order of the arrangement that existed in the other jazz styles is retained. Of course, there is, aside from that, also the kind of improvisation that entails no predetermination, in which there is no trace of arrangement whatsoever; but the impression grows stronger that such total lack of restraint was only a passing stage within the process of liberation during the sixties. After that, the musicians gained a much more relaxed attitude towards composition by learning to harness, structure, and disentangle the experiences of free jazz.

At any rate, since the arrangement had been growing in scope and importance for so many years, it was logical that improvisation – and finally, following the freeing of improvisation, composition as well – should do the same. With his usual cogency, Dave Brubeck summed it up: 'Jazz is about the only form of art existing today in which there is freedom of the individual without the loss of group contact.' This coexistence of collectivism and freedom expresses what we characterized as 'the sociological situation of jazz' at the start of this book.

The Blues

Two jazz critics, a recording director, and a musician were discussing 'if the blues is essential to the jazz idiom.' Pianist Billy Taylor – the participating musician – said: '. . . I don't know of one giant – early, late, mid-thirties, or cool – who didn't have a tremendous respect and feeling for the blues, whether he played the blues or not. The spirit of it was in his playing or he wasn't really a giant as far as jazz was concerned . . .' Nesuhi Ertegun, vice president of Atlantic Records, added: 'Let me ask you one question. Do you think a man like Lester Young would play a tune like "Body and Soul" in the same way if he had never played the blues?' Billy Taylor's answer was 'No.' And Leonard Feather summarized: 'I think what it all boils down to is that the blues is the essence of jazz, and merely having a feeling for blues means having a feeling for jazz. In other words, the chords or the notes of the chords which are essential for blues are the notes that are essential for jazz – the flat third, flat seventh, etc.' To which Billy Taylor countered: 'Well, I hesitate to oversimplify in that particular case because I tend to go back to the spirit. It's not the fact that a man on certain occasions would flat a certain note, bend a note or do something which is strictly a blues-type device. It's just that whatever this nebulous feeling is – the vitality they seem to get in the blues – whatever it is makes the difference between Coleman Hawkins's "Body and Soul" and a society tenor player's "Body and Soul" . . .'

It becomes clear from this discussion that the blues can be defined in several ways: emotionally, racially, sociologically, musically, and formally. Nearest at hand and most useful at this point is the emotional definition. Leadbelly, a singer from the olden days when the blues was wholly a folk art, set down the emotional definition in incomparable fashion: 'Now this is the blues. No white man ever had the blues, 'cause nothin' to worry about. Now, you lay down at night and you roll from one side of the bed to the other all night long – you can't sleep . . . what's the matter? The blues has got you. You get up and sit on the side of your bed in the mornin' – may have your sister and brother, your mother and father around but you don't want no talk out of 'em . . . what's the matter? The blues has got you. Well you go and put your feet under the table and look down on your plate – got everything you want to eat – but you shake you head and get up and say "Lord! I can't eat and I can't sleep! What's the matter with me?" Why, the blues has got you, wanna talk to you . . .'

Bessie Smith sings: 'Nobody knows you when you're down and out.' And John Lee Hooker: 'I've got the blues so bad, it's hard to keep from cryin'.' In 'Trouble in Mind Blues' it goes: 'If you see me laughin', just to keep from cryin' . . .'

This emotional definition also holds true for the blues when it is happy and full of humour – as it often is. The blues artists in whose work there are as many happy as sad blues – such as Big Bill Broonzy or later B. B. King or Otis Rush – have included themselves in this emotional definition of the blues.

Next to the emotional stands the musical and formal definition. T-Bone Walker, the blues singer, has said: 'You know, there's only one blues, though. That's the regular twelve-bar pattern and then you interpret over that. Just write new words or improvise different and you've got a new blues.'

The blues strophe consists of twelve bars, based on the most fundamental of all chords: tonic, dominant, and subdominant.

Example 2

This twelve-bar chord structure is, exceptions aside, consistent – from the earliest blues (insofar as they already conform to the manifest blues pattern) down to the most complex blues improvisations of the modern musicians, who expand the harmonics in the most subtle way but of course without disturbing their basic function.

The blues melodies and blues improvisations which rest on this twelve-bar chord structure derive their peculiar fascination from the 'blue' notes. The music of the blacks brought from Africa to the New

World was largely pentatonic, i.e., their scale consisted not of seven notes like ours, but of five. When these blacks, confronted with European music in America, began to make music of their own, they adapted their pentatonic sensibilities to our tonal system with astonishing rapidity. Only the two steps which were absent from their system remained problematic: the third and seventh steps. In order to make them accessible to their own musical feeling, they had to flatten them. Although this can result in what traditional European functional harmonics would call 'diminution', it is, in principle, a different process. In this process, the 'diminished third' and the 'minor seventh' – to use conventional music terms which actually are out of place here – became blue notes. This happened without recourse to the minor or major keys which in European music govern the 'diminution' of certain steps. In this fashion there came into being a kind of 'contemporaneity' of the feelings which we associate with the major and minor modes. And so the blues became emotionally ambiguous, without this clearly defined contrast between the extremes of joy and sadness to which we are accustomed.

Later when the bebop musicians introduced the flatted fifth, this note, too, became a 'blue' note – at first in the minor blues, then in all kinds of blues music – equal to the blue notes of the third and seventh steps.

In the blues it frequently happens that a conventionally tonic or dominant chord falls under a blue note, so that the major third may be played in the bass, and the minor third in the treble. This creates frictional sounds, which certainly can be interpreted as arising from a friction between two different harmonic systems: the chord structure, which corresponds to the European tradition, and the melodic line, with its blue notes originating in African music.

Example 3

Example 3 shows a very typical melodic line. Every other note is a blue note. The traditional blue notes at the third and seventh steps are marked by a single arrow; the double arrows indicate blue notes originating in the flatted fifth. The C-chord is the basis for the whole cadence – unharmed by the constant friction. Each blue note thus stands before a 'normal' note, into which the blue note resolves – so that the cadence actually is nothing but a sequence of tension and relaxation, repeated six times. The tendency in jazz to create tension only to dissolve it immediately and then to create new tension which is again dissolved here becomes particularly clear. These tensions do not have the broad span they possess in European music.

Since the blues notes are generally resolved by a note which lies one half tone lower, there is a strong tendency in the blues towards descending melodic lines – as Example 3 shows. It is a melodic line which occurs, in this or similar form, in thousands of jazz improvisations – within and outside of blues. It also shows how all jazz is saturated with blues elements – whether an actual blues tune is involved or not.

The twelve blues bars consist of three four-bar phrases, developed in such a way that a statement is made in the first four, repeated (over different harmonies) in the following four, and a 'conclusion' drawn from it in the final four.

Sara Martin sings:

> Blues, Blues, Blues why did you bring trouble to me?
> Yes, Blues, Blues, Blues why did you bring trouble to me?
> O Death, please sting me and take me out of my misery.

This threefold form, with its double question and contrasted answer, creates a finite and compact mode of expression which is comparable to the important 'minor forms' of art – from a literary standpoint as well. The causal interconnection of form and content fulfils the highest criteria of form. It is astonishing that the highest ideal of Western art – the unity of form and content – is approximated in the 'proletarian' and 'Negroid' world of the blues, and so tightly and clearly that the relationship between them becomes 'causal'.

The finite blues form was of course not given from the start – neither musically nor textually. When looking at old folk blues, one must conclude that the threefold four-bar AAB-structure was present in the beginning merely as an 'idea', which was approximated and deviated from. This 'idea' of the blues form became increasingly crystallized over the years, and today it is so pure that nonconformity to it is generally felt to be an error. But in the great, 'classical' period of the blues it was no error not to conform.

Harmonically as well, there were many 'errors' in the old, 'primitive' blues. The singers floated with sovereign ease above certain basic chords, doing much as they pleased. Big Bill Broonzy often pointed out that to be emotionally right was much more important than to be formally and harmonically correct.

The blues singer generally fills the three four-bar phrases only up to the beginning of the third, seventh, and eleventh bar. The remainder of each phrase is at the disposal of an improvisation called a 'break', a short, cadenzalike burst, which sets off the preceding from the following phrase. These one-and-a-half bars of the classic blues-break are the germ cell of jazz improvisation as a whole, with its fascinating interplay of forces between the unbounded freedom of the soloist and the obligation towards the collective of players.

The blues lyrics correspond in level to their form. According to Jean Cocteau, the poetry of the blues is the only substantial contribution to genuine folk poetry in our century. Everything of importance in the life of the blues singer is contained in these lyrics: love and – often disguised – racial discrimination; prison and the law; floods and railroad trains and the fortune told by the gypsy; the evening sun and the hospital (just to mention a few of the favourite subjects of blues singers) . . . Life itself flows into the lyrics of the blues with a surprising straightforwardness and directness to which nothing in Western poetry – and this goes for folk poetry as well – is comparable.

The majority of blues deal with love. Love is viewed, simply and clearly, as that towards which love aims . . . yet it is able to remain love – even when it reflects the kind of war between the sexes sociologists have found to be very frequent in the black ghettos and neighbourhoods, resulting from centuries of disrupted black family structures, during and also after slavery. At a time when everyday love poetry has barely risen above the level of 'Roses are red/violets are blue,' the blues reflects that lofty, unsentimental stature and strength of the emotions and the passions which we know from great literature. Not a single blues is on the housemaid level of 'Too Young' . . . and yet the blues belongs to the world of those who have supplied an entire continent with domestics, butlers and nursemaids!

There are funny blues and fast blues. But mainly blues are the music of a first rural, then urban proletariat whose life is filled with suffering. The social origins of the blues are at least as important as the racial ones. I do not know of a single genuine, authentic blues which does not make it obvious at once that the singer is of the proletariat. It would not make sense for members of the 'aristocracy' to sing the blues. 'They don't have the blues.'

. It is not without reason that references to 'having' or 'not having' the blues are made time and again in blues lyrics. You have to have the blues to be able to sing them. 'The blues are a part of me,' says singer Alberta Hunter.

From its mood and atmosphere the blues achieves continuity – something it seems to be lacking to a notable degree at first glance. It almost seems as if lack of coherence – in other words, diametrical opposition to all that stood for art in the Western sense until the end of the last century – is a mark of the blues (which, of course, also has to do with the oral tradition of the blues). Lines and verses put together from the most varied blues and songs are linked up, unconcerned with what we call logic and context. Sometimes the singer himself seems to be the actor, and then a third person is acting. A moment ago the subject was a 'he', and now it is a 'she' . . . we were in the past, now we are in the future . . . suddenly, we switch from singular to plural.

Even those blues songs clearly created by a single person show that their author was not worried about continuity of content. In the 'Old New Orleans Blues', although unquestionably committed to old New Orleans by title and theme, the next-to-last verse takes us to Memphis, while in the final verse the topic is the lantern swinging in the wind outside the window behind which the singer is sleeping. The 'Two Nineteen Blues' first deals with the railroad and then suddenly with a streetwalker . . . and so on: Dozens of blues furnish examples of this 'blues-discontinuity', while it seems quite difficult to find a blues in which each word follows logically from the foregoing. It would be wrong to conclude that this stems from an inability to create continuity. No, continuity is not the point. The lines and verses have an impressionistic quality. They relate to each other as do the spots of colour in a painting: if you stand close, you cannot tell why there is red next to blue, or green next to orange, but as soon as you take a few steps back, it all blends into a whole. The 'whole' of the blues is the mood, the blues atmosphere. It creates its own continuity. Into the blues mood flows whatever comes up – events, memories, thoughts, fancies – and out comes, always, the blues.

Everything that exists in the world of the singer goes through the blues; all is contemporaneous. Nothing can be outside. Blues singer Big Bill Broonzy tells about how when he was a boy, he and his uncle caught a big turtle: '. . . We drug him home and my uncle told me to make him stick his neck out of his shell. I took a stick and put it in front of him. The turtle caught hold of the stick and couldn't turn it loose. So my uncle said: "Hold his head right there and I'll cut it off." My uncle took the axe and cut the turtle's head off and we went in the house and stayed there a while. When we came back, no turtle. So we looked for him and the turtle was nearly back to the lake where we caught him. We picked him up, brought him back to the house and my uncle said: "There's a turtle who is dead and don't know it." And that's the way a lot of people is today: they got the blues and don't know it.'

At the beginning of the blues stand the work songs and field hollers: the simple, archaic songs sung by the blacks at work in the fields or on the levees. They were sung because it was easier to work to the rhythm of a song than without it. The rhythm had an effect on the singers, and made even those perk up who otherwise would have worked sluggishly or not at all. 'Lawd, cap'n, I's not a-singin' – I's just a-hollerin' to help me with my work.' That's why the white man wanted to see the Negro sing. 'A singing Negro is a good Negro,' is the way French critic François Postif described the attitude of a plantation owner or prison warden.

Folk song and folk ballad, frequently in the 'white' sense, joined with work song and field holler. There were the old rounds with the regular, happy repetition of a refrain of a few lines, sung by the chorus of listeners.

Blind Lemon Jefferson, Big Bill Broonzy, Leadbelly, Robert Johnson, Elmore James, Blind Boy Fuller, Rev Gary Davis, Bukka White, Blind Willie McTell, Big Joe Williams, Sonny Terry, Brother John Sellers, John Lee Hooker, and Lightnin' Hopkins are famous representatives of blues folklore. Most accompanied themselves on guitar, and they often – as, for example, Lonnie Johnson and

Lightnin' Hopkins – are wonderful guitarists. Other blues singers – e.g., Sonny Terry or the late Little Walter and Sonny Boy Williamson – knew how to coax amazing sounds from a harmonica. Others recorded with well-known jazz musicians backing their folk-rooted blues vocals.

In most cases, the accompanying instrument meant more to the blues singer than mere background: It was a partner in conversation. It would inspire and excite; it could make comments in affirmation or protest; it anticipated or completed an idea.

Under no circumstances should the reader assume that we are speaking of things related to a distant past. Almost all well-known commentators on blues have consciously or unconsciously nurtured this feeling, as if they were the last of their profession with just time enough left to document a vanishing folklore art form. A feature of the white man's relationship to folklore of all kinds is that he links it to nostalgia, sentimentality, memories of the 'good old days'. As far as the blues is concerned, this response is wrong.

There are more blues movements and blues styles today than ever before, and they all live side by side. Not one of the old blues forms – folk blues, country blues, prison blues, archaic blues, Cajun blues – has become extinct. In fact, new ones were added: city blues, urban blues, jazz blues, rhythm & blues, soul blues, funky blues . . . In addition there are different styles. The most easily recognizable are Mississippi blues (rough, archaic), Texas blues (mobile, flexible, jazz-related), and East Coast blues, from Florida or Tennessee, for example (often permeated with white country and hillbilly folklore). The folk blues of Texas and of the Midwest (the so-called 'territories') shaped the California big city blues; the folk blues of Mississippi – with Memphis as the core – shaped the Chicago big city blues. But in this case, too, the mixtures are no less interesting than the pure forms, which are illusory in the blues world, anyway – blues is by nature a mixture. The success of the Memphis blues in the sixties – of Albert King, to name one, but also of soul singers like Otis Redding – lies precisely in its combination and urbanization of elements from Mississippi and Texas.

Almost all important blues singers are at home in several forms and styles – not only in the sense that they developed from one form to the other, as from country blues to city blues and on to contemporary urban blues (e.g., Muddy Waters, Howlin' Wolf, B. B. King, Otis Rush) – but also in the sense that they may practise several forms simultaneously (for instance, John Lee Hooker, Johnny Shines, or Louisiana Red, who keep switching between folk, country, and city blues; or Jimmy Witherspoon, T-Bone Walker, Ray Charles, who have all frequently played with jazz musicians; or Gatemouth Brown, who mixes practically everything: blues, jazz, country, Cajun, etc.).

Since the mid-fifties, the blues has penetrated popular music to a degree unimaginable up to then. First, black rhythm & blues – the rocking music of the black South and of the Northern ghettos – led into rock 'n' roll. Bill Haley and Elvis Presley were the first white rock 'n' roll stars, but immediately following came black artists – Chuck Berry, Fats Domino, Ray Charles – who enjoyed an immense success on the white 'pop' scene that would have been considered impossible even shortly before. By 1963, the best of rhythm & blues had become so closely linked to the mainstream of American popular music that *Billboard* magazine temporarily suspended separate listings of 'Rhythm and Blues' and 'Pop'. Separate listing was resumed later, but the magazine kept changing its policy – it had become uncertain, and still is. Outstanding black talent is also now part of the white scene. Younger readers will hardly be able to appreciate how unusual that once would have been. The term 'rhythm & blues' was only introduced in the late forties. Up to then, the term was 'race records'. This label makes it clear that for fifty years, black music had been played in a ghetto that was noticed by the white world only indirectly at best: by letting its own musicians degenerate, play down, drain, what in its authentic black form remained unknown to most of the white audience.

It was through musicians like Bill Haley, Elvis Presley, Chuck Berry, Fats Domino, Little Richard, and others, that the blues literally demolished the popular music of Tin Pan Alley, and its babbling about schmaltzy, kitschy, dishonest feelings. If much of today's popular music is more realistic, clear, honest, and at the same time more poetic, musical, and often emotionally richer than popular music before the mid-fifties (leaving disco music aside), then this must be ascribed to the penetration of white popular music by the blues. Blues – and black music in general – has always *been* what white popular music has only recently become: realistic and full of social involvement, a commentary on the everyday life and problems of those who sang it.

What happened during the fifties was only the preparation for the 'decade of rock', the term frequently applied to the sixties. For the United States, it was Bob Dylan; then, initially in Great Britain and later simply for the whole world, it was the Beatles – and also the Rolling Stones (who took their name from a Muddy Waters blues) – who created a new musical consciousness, so that artists who just shortly before had been the personification of high musical standards – think of Frank Sinatra! – within a few years became 'old fogeys' when confronted with this new consciousness. The musical standards of the world of popular music demolished in the process were the symbols of the moral, social, and political standards of the bourgeois world which had created the old pop music. These standards were the real target of the new movement.

Bob Dylan, the Beatles, the Rolling Stones – they all are unthinkable without the blues. The Beatles came from rhythm & blues, particularly Chuck Berry. Dylan comes from Woody Guthrie and the American folklore at whose centre stands folk blues. For half a year he lived with blues singer Big Joe Williams. It has been said that Dylan was 'the first true poet of popular music.' But in so saying, hundreds of black folk-blues singers, who since the turn of the century – and perhaps even earlier – have been the 'true poets of popular music,' are forgotten.

Both Dylan and the Beatles grew far beyond their respective bases of origin. When Dylan accompanied himself electronically for the first time (at the 1965 Newport Folk Festival), there was a storm of protest from his fans. But three years later, in 1968, he recorded his album 'John Wesley Harding' with acoustic guitar and folk-blues harmonica; and, thus, he programmatically clarified for all his followers – and they did understand – how he viewed his musical and spiritual heritage.

There was a similar development with the Beatles. For years, they had continuously refined their rock 'n' roll heritage, sensitizing their music more and more, and had moved further and further away from the blues. In 'Michelle', 'In My Life', 'Eleanor Rigby', and other songs, they had incorporated baroque elements; in 'Yesterday' they had remembered the old Elizabethan English Madrigal culture; and, in George Harrison's songs, they had made reference to classical Indian music. 'Sgt Pepper's Lonely Hearts Club Band' was a rock symphony. But then, in 1968, their double album, 'The Beatles', was released. And in this album – in reference to Chuck Berry, to early rock 'n' roll and rhythm & blues – they made it clear, as programmatically as Dylan in 'John Wesley Harding', that they knew where they came from, and that they wanted their fans to know it, too. For those who did not hear, John Lennon said it once more: 'If there was another name for rock 'n' roll, it would be Chuck Berry.' (Berry is one of the big stars of blues and rhythm & blues.)

It has been said that the Beatles and Bob Dylan changed the musical and social consciousness of a whole generation. In this context, it is important to realize that this change of consciousness is based on the blues and would have been impossible without it. British guitarist Eric Clapton made this very clear when he said, 'Rock is like a battery. Every so often you have to go back to the blues and recharge.'

To be sure, from the standpoint of jazz and authentic blues, much of the blues derivations played in the rock era of the sixties and the rock 'n' roll of the fifties was inferior to the pure, uncommercialized product. But this holds true only for a minority of jazz and blues connoisseurs. For the majority, the reverse is valid: Through the blues, popular music attained a qualitative level previously unthinkable. This development continues. The stream of black music flowing into white rock and pop music is becoming wider and wider – in fact, it is already so wide that there is no, or almost no, difference anymore between black and white popular music. 'Funkiness' became the fashionable be-all and end-all of commercial rock music during the seventies; funk, though, comes from the black ghetto and the blues. The important stars of funk were black jazz musicians, above all Herbie Hancock and George Benson.

The fact that truly black feeling entered the white world with the blues becomes apparent not only through the music, but also through the kind of dancing that goes with it.

In the world of blues – and in general in the black world, already in Africa – there has always been 'open' and 'individual' dancing. The actual partner of each individual dancer was and is the music: the dancer answers the music with his movements. In the white world, on the other hand, dancing had atrophied increasingly – as a pretext for social and physical contact for which the music merely furnished the barely noticed background. Dancing, like everything else in the rationalized white world, had to 'serve a function'. Dancing in the black world is done only for its own sake. The body becomes a musical instrument – as it has also for the young white rock audience from the mid-fifties on.

American blues specialist Charles Keil (to whom I am indebted in this connection) assumes that, seeing today's young people dance in the US or in Europe, '... a West African villager ... would be delighted to see that Western men and women have at last cast aside the disgusting and lascivious practices of embracing, hugging, shuffling, and grappling in public and have adopted the vigorous, therapeutic pelvic exercise that has always been the pride and joy of his community.'

At first, pure blues consciousness among white audiences and musicians was stronger in Britain than in the US. Most of the successful British pop and rock musicians of the sixties for years had studied, imitated and copied black blues singers and blues instrumentalists, and on that basis found their own styles.

Since the late fifties, there had been a true 'blues movement' in Great Britain – led by a guitarist and vocalist who was born in Vienna, educated in France, and settled in England, Alexis Korner, and later also by John Mayall. One could indulge in all kinds of speculation as to why this contemporary 'blues consciousness' originated in Britain rather than the US, though the British Isles are much farther away from the creative blues centres of the American South or Chicago's South Side than are New York or Los Angeles. The question can be asked: Were there too many prejudices against black blues in the US, and did the American music world jump on the blues wagon only when it was realized how much money British groups like the Rolling Stones – or later Led Zeppelin or John Mayall – were making on the blues?

Another point cannot be made without bitterness: It is white musicians who are making fortunes in today's British and American scenes with black blues, while the black creators of this music – with a growing number of exceptions – are still the relatively obscure voices of a suffering proletariat.

At the beginning of this chapter, we quoted Leadbelly: 'No white man ever had the blues.' For decades, the blues were thought to be the 'last retreat' of black music that no white man would ever be able to penetrate. In all areas of a music originally created by blacks, whites again and again had been more successful, had made more money than the black creators: Benny Goodman and Artie Shaw in Swing, Stan Getz and Dave Brubeck in cool jazz, and all the others. Only in blues did the whites not succeed in producing really convincing sounds.

Since the sixties, parts of this 'last bastion' have also been conquered. There are some white musicians who – at least as instrumentalists – can play authentic black blues. As we said, Britishers Alexis Korner and John Mayall paved the way for this, but both are still far away from the authenticity reached by the musicians following them: guitarists Eric Clapton or Rory Gallagher in Britain, and then also Americans – guitarist Mike Bloomfield and Johnny Winter; or harmonica players Paul Butterfield, Charlie Musselwhite, and Paul Osher, all of whom learned in Chicago's black South Side (especially from Muddy Waters); the late guitarist Duane Allman and pianist–guitarist Dr John; the musicians of the blues-rock group Canned Heat; and others.

Still, there is a difference. White blues – especially where it is artistically serious – is more precious, more 'accurate', cleaner, less expressive, and also more vulgar, less subtle, and less flexible than black blues.

Charles Keil tells of a survey about the nature of blues and soul made by a black Chicago radio station among its audience. In the answers, again and again the word 'mellow' recurred. They're 'mellow', the blues and soul. And 'mellow' is exactly what white blues are not; and when they become mellow, they cease to be blues.

No doubt, the 'authenticity' of most white blues musicians is still relative. As soon as all these white musicians, 'authentic' as they may sound as instrumentalists, open their mouths to sing, the illusion fades away. Then, even the layman can hear who is white and who is black, and there is no bridge over that gap. Not even Janis Joplin (the singer from Texas who died in 1970 and of all white singers the one who came closest to the black sound) was able to bridge that gap. That should be remembered later, particularly when reading the chapters about the white male and female singers. Not without reason, white blues player John Mayall, a man who should know and whom it concerns directly, has said: 'When we talk about blues, we mean black blues. That's the real blues for us.'

However, the sociological and social side of this matter should not be overlooked. The blues is black music for one thing, because the living conditions of blacks in parts of the South and in the Northern ghettos are so different from those of whites, not only in degree, but more important, in essence. The late American critic Ralph Gleason speculated that to the extent that this changes, white blues musicians will gain 'equality' with black blues musicians. At the beginning of the eighties, it seems obvious that it will be a long time before this point is reached.

Spiritual and Gospel Song

The singer who comes closest to Bessie Smith in vocal power and expressiveness is not a blues singer but a gospel singer: Mahalia Jackson, who died in 1972. The gospel song is the modern form of the spiritual, the religious song of the blacks – more vital, more swinging, more jazzlike than the old spiritual, which frequently shows a closeness to European church music, and above all a proximity to the white spirituals of the last century (which are often overlooked by the 'race-romancers').

The blues is the secular form of spiritual and gospel song. Or the other way around: gospel song and spiritual are the religious forms of the blues. Thus it is not only in a relative, but in a literal sense that blues singer Alberta Hunter says: 'To me, the blues are – well, almost religious . . . The blues are like spirituals, almost sacred. When we sing the blues, we're singin' from our hearts, we're singin' out our feelings.' And blues singer T-Bone Walker has said: 'Of course, the blues comes a lot from the church, too. The first time I ever heard a boogie-woogie piano was the first time I went to church. That was the Holy Ghost Church in Dallas, Texas. That boogie-woogie was a kind of blues, I guess. Then the preacher used to preach in a bluesy tone sometimes . . .'

The visitor to a church in Harlem or on Chicago's South Side will not find a great contrast to the ecstatic atmosphere that might be found at a jazz concert – say, by Lionel Hampton. He will find the identical rhythms, the same beat, and the same swing in the music. Frequently, he will find jazz-associated instruments – saxophones, electric guitars, drums; he will hear boogie-woogie bass lines and blues structures and see enraptured people beating time with their hands and feet and sometimes even dancing.

Winthrop Sargeant describes a church service in the South: 'Minutes passed, long minutes of strange intensity. The mutterings, the ejaculations, grew louder, more dramatic, till suddenly I felt the creative thrill dart through the people like an electric vibration; that same half-audible hum arose – emotion was gathering atmospherically as clouds gather – and then, up from the depth of some "sinner's" remorse and imploring came a pitiful little plea, a real Negro "moan" sobbed in musical cadence. From somewhere in that bowed gathering another voice improvised a response; the plea sounded again, louder this time and more impassioned; then other voices joined in the answer, shaping it into a musical phrase; and so on, before our ears, as one might say, from this molten metal of music a new song was smithied out, composed then and there by no one in particular and by everyone in general.'

Modern gospel songs are mostly composed pieces, marketed as sheet music. But these pieces are used freely in church services – certainly not quite as freely as jazz musicians treat a theme, but still as a basis for individual activity and interpretation. Leading black writers like Langston Hughes, who died in 1967, are sometimes authors of gospel lyrics. And the sheet music is often printed in larger editions than commercial tunes.

The most important gospel singer was – and will remain – Mahalia Jackson, born in New Orleans. In 1945 she became famous almost overnight with her recording of 'Move On Up a Little Higher,' a best seller in the category of the big hits: more than a million records sold!

Through Mahalia Jackson, the white world for the first time became familiar with the art of gospel singing on a broader scale. Actually, the whites heard only Mahalia Jackson. Gospel music still is the real underground art form of black America: a flourishing art full of power and vitality – and yet, the average white American has no idea of the wonderfully enraptured life which unfolds in the black churches each Sunday.

Under the impression of the breadth of today's jazz scene, jazz fans will have a hard time accepting the fact that there are far more gospel groups than jazz bands. To give an idea of this wealth of the gospel scene, let me mention here only the most important gospel artists and groups – only those, that is, who are equal to the best jazz players and bands.

Among the female singers: Inez Andrews, Marion Williams, Delois

Barrett Campbell, Bessie Griffin, Shirley Caesar, Dorothy Love, Edna Gallmon Cooke, Marie Knight, Willie Mae Ford Smith, and Clara Ward.

Of the male singers: Robert Anderson, Alex Bradford, James Cleveland, Reverend Cleophus Robinson, R. H. Harris, Jessy Dixon, Isaac Douglas, Claude Jeter, and Brother Joe May.

The outstanding female gospel groups include the Davis Sisters, the Stars of Faith, the Angelic Gospel Singers, the Barrett Sisters, the Robert Patterson Singers, the Caravans, Liz Dargan and The Gospelettes, and the Roberta Martin Singers.

The male gospel groups we should mention are the Five Blind Boys of Mississippi, the Brooklyn All Stars, the Gospel Clefs, the Gospelaires, the Fairfield Four, the Gospel Keynotes, the Highway QC's, the Mighty Clouds of Joy, the Pilgrim Travelers, the Pilgrim Jubilee Singers, the Soul Stirrers, the Swan Silvertones, the Swanee Quintet, the Supreme Angels, and the Violinaires.

And finally, some of the best gospel choirs: the Gospel Singers Ensemble, Rosie Wallace and the First Church of Love, the Staple Singers, the Faith and Deliverance Choir, the Thompson Community Singers, Mattie Moss Clark and the Southwest Michigan State Choir, J. C. White and the Institutional Church of God in Christ Choir, Harrison Johnson and His Los Angeles Community Choir, Walter Hawkins and the Love Center Choir, the Edwin Hawkins Singers, the Garden State Choir, the Brockington Ensemble, and the BC + M Mass Choir.

Of special importance is the aged Bishop Kelsey in Washington, DC. On some of his records – such as 'Little Boy' – one hears how in the course of his sermon, Rev Kelsey gradually becomes the lead singer and how the sermon turns into the gospel singing of the entire congregation.

Many preachers and male gospel singers are masters of falsetto singing, which moves the male tenor or baritone voices far beyond their usual range into that of the female soprano – and even higher than that. This manner of singing was practised in Africa for centuries as a sign of highly potent, bursting manhood. It moved from spiritual and gospel song to the blues and, far beyond that, into modern jazz – as in Leon Thomas – and into contemporary rock and soul music – and it certainly can also be perceived in the high 'falsetto' playing of the post-Coltrane tenor saxophonists.

There are gospel songs with hillbilly and cowboy, mambo, waltz, and boogie-woogie rhythms. But most of all, gospel songs have a strong, full jazz beat. In gospel songs – as in blues – there is everything that can be found in daily life: elections, skyscrapers, railroads, telephones. It may appear naïve to white people – with our characteristic notion of intellectual superiority – when someone expresses in song the wish to talk with the Lord on the telephone, or travel to heaven in a pullman car. Yet, in the great period of our own religious art, it was no different: the Flemish painters transferred the story of the crucifixion to the landscape of the Lowlands, and in the Christmas songs of Silesia, the people sing about the birth of Christ as if it had taken place in the ice and snow of their own mountains.

Spiritual and gospel songs are not, as is often thought, something belonging to history – something that existed at the beginning of jazz somewhere in the Southern countryside. Quite the opposite: in the course of jazz development, they have grown more effective, more dynamic and alive. From the fifties on, gospel and soul have broken into other areas of black music on a wide front; initially into jazz. Milt Jackson – the leading vibraharpist of modern jazz – once answered the question where his particular style and soulful playing came from: 'What is soul in jazz? It's what comes from inside . . . in my case, I think it's what I heard and felt in the music of my church. That was the most important influence of my career. Everybody wants to know where I got my 'funky' style. Well, it came from the church.'

In the liner notes to an early album by Ray Charles, Gary Kramer wrote: 'The importance of the relationship between the religious music of the Negro and jazz is all too rarely emphasized . . .'

Musicians such as Milt Jackson, Horace Silver and Charles generated a 'soul wave' in the second half of the fifties that got its crucial impulse from gospel music and has been breaking into popular music since the sixties. Some of the most successful rock and soul singers of the sixties and seventies would be unthinkable without their gospel background: Otis Redding, James Brown, Aretha Franklin, Little Richard, Wilson Pickett, Isaac Hayes . . .

Soul is secularized gospel music. And many of the best soul singers, even at the high points of their careers, still love to sing in gospel churches for a black audience; Aretha Franklin, for instance.

Some jazz specialists claim that gospel music was more important in the development of the contemporary sounds of rock, pop, and jazz than was the blues. As Charles Keil points out, 'there are still at least 40 store-front churches for every joint where blues or jazz is played in Chicago, the blues capital of the world.'

Jazz and gospel singing are related in yet another respect: Many of the best female jazz singers got their start in church. Sarah Vaughan, for instance, who carried Charlie Parker's conception into jazz singing; or the late Dinah Washington, the successful 'Queen' of rhythm & blues, who not only sang but also played piano in church; or Aretha Franklin.

The late Sister Rosetta Tharpe sang in the thirties with the Swing bands of Cab Calloway and Lucky Millinder and had a successful night-club act, but before she became known in the jazz world she had sung in church – and afterwards she again returned to gospel singing. One of the best-known composers of gospel songs – Thomas A. Dorsey – got his start in Chicago in the twenties and early thirties as a blues lyricist, singer, and pianist.

Danny Barker, the guitarist, says about Bessie Smith: 'If you had any church background, like people who came from the South as I did, you would recognize a similarity between what she was doing and what those preachers and evangelists from there did, and how they moved people . . .'

Harmony

In terms of harmony and melody, jazz does not offer much of a revolutionary nature, at least not until the beginning of free jazz in the sixties. Paradoxically, there is in this very fact a difference between jazz and concert music. In the realm of established musical culture, what is new and revolutionary is always so first and foremost in terms of melody and harmony. Jazz, on the other hand, though among the most revolutionary developments in the arts in our century, is relatively traditional in respect to harmony and melody. Its newness is based on rhythm and sound.

Almost the only novel and singular thing in jazz in the harmonic domain are the blue notes. Aside from these, the harmonic language of conventional jazz – that is, of the jazz prior to and apart from free playing – is identical with that of popular dance and entertainment music. The harmonies of ragtime, Dixieland, and New Orleans jazz are – beyond blue notes – identical with the harmonies of polkas, marches, and waltzes. They are based on the tonic, the dominant, and the subdominant. Bix Beiderbecke brought certain Debussy-like chords and whole-tone effects into jazz. The great Swing musicians added the sixth to the major triad, and 'enriched' sevenths with ninths – or even elevenths. Since bebop, passing chords are placed between the basic harmonies of a piece; or the basic harmonies are replaced by 'alternations'. Jazz musicians are – or at least were during the bebop and cool-jazz periods – proud of the developments in this realm of their music, and among them there was much talk of harmonic problems; but these problems – viewed from the position of European music – are more or less 'old hat'. Only very few chords with augmented or diminished fifths and ninths, characteristic mainly of modern jazz, do not exist in this form in conventional music, especially when such intervals occur in combination. For example, harmonies occur that may have a flatted fifth in the bass and an augmented fifth in the treble, and above this one may occasionally find a diminished or augmented ninth. Example 4 shows two such chord combinations, with their respective resolutions.

Example 4

Example 5 shows the first four bars of the song 'I Can't Give You Anything but Love,' popular since the twenties. (A) indicates the simple, almost primitive harmonies on which the jazz improvisations of that day were based, while (B) shows how the harmonies were altered in later years – during the transition from Swing to bop. No doubt the simple harmonies of 5 (A) might just as well stem from a European folk dance. The more modern harmonies of 5 (B) could also be employed in modern popular music.

Example 5

The development of jazz harmonies from ragtime and New Orleans jazz to bebop and cool jazz are not peculiar to jazz. They run parallel to and are 'synchronized' with harmonic developments in popular music from the polka to the slickly orchestrated sounds of Hollywood movie music. André Hodeir surmises that jazz was influenced by pop music in this respect – a thought which lies near to hand since jazz musicians, who listen open-mindedly to everything which appears to them valid or worthy of imitation in any kind of music, heard that here was something which could be learned and applied to what seemed to them not very highly advanced in their own music. The harmonic language of jazz, according to Hodeir, is 'largely borrowed'. *Because* this is so, it is quite in accord with the main line of jazz tradition. It is peculiar to the genesis of jazz that it 'borrowed' and united the best of two divergent musical cultures: European and African. Even among the first blacks who composed rags, played New Orleans jazz, and sang blues and spirituals, there were some who recognized or at least felt somehow that there was nothing in their own musical past which came even close to the ripe and rich harmonic expression in European music. On the other hand, there was nothing in European music that could come even close to the expressive power of 'black' sonorities and to the vitality of Africa's rhythmic tradition. Thus both musical cultures contributed their 'speciality'.

In bebop and cool jazz, harmonies can be varied just as melodies were the basis for variations in traditional jazz. Thus Example 5 shows eight harmonies in the modern (B) version as compared to four in the old (A). The latter only has chords which are closely related to C-major. The modern version, however, creates a singable bass line which stands in contrapuntal relationship to the melodic line. The entire harmonic picture is loosened up and enriched. The chord sequence itself shows a steady succession of tension and relaxation – in terms of the tensions so important to jazz. Most of the added chords in the modern version 5 (B) are terminal chords, having a tendency to resolve in the subsequent chord. The older version 5 (A) shows only one resolution – in the fourth bar; the modern version shows three such processes. This, too, indicates how jazz history demonstrates an ever stronger and more intense concentration of jazzlike, tension-creating and tension-dissolving elements.

In the modern version a whole new chord structure comes into being. But this chord structure is not so new that it fails to indicate in each chord its relationship to the original harmonies. The new chords, so to speak, stand in place of the handed-down chords. The tonal relationship of the whole remains as ordered and neat as one could desire.

Many laymen and friends of traditional jazz not conversant with the harmonic vocabulary of bop at first reacted to its sounds as 'atonal'. 'Atonality', as the word itself makes clear, means that the music has no relationship to a tonal centre and has no tonal centre of gravity. But this is not the case in the prevalent forms of modern jazz before free music – and even there only in a relatively few instances. If many listeners cannot hear the harmonic centres of gravity, it is not because these centres are lacking, but because the listener's ear is unaccustomed to these harmonies. Indeed, harmony in music is a matter of custom. Any harmonic system, even in its most far-reaching variants, can be assimilated by the ear after a period of listening – even when the initial impression has been that of absurdity.

Altogether, the development of harmony in jazz and modern concert music shows many parallels – with jazz tending to lag considerably behind. The flatted fifth – the bebopper's favourite interval in the forties – in many respects corresponds to the tritone, which plays an important role in modern concert music: in Hindemith, Bartók, Stravinsky, Honegger, Milhaud, etc. Hindemith devoted much space to the tritone in *The Craft of Musical Composition* – one of the main theoretical works on modern concert music. In this work he states: 'With increases in distance the familial relationship is loosened until at the utmost note – the augmented fourth or the diminished fifth – the tritone, it barely remains noticeable.' Elsewhere Hindemith says that the tritone is indifferent to the harmonic base. Thus Hindemith feels that the flatted fifth does not destroy tonality but stands in a neutral – 'indifferent' – relationship to it. This is felt by jazz musicians as well. This 'indifference' is the real reason for the popularity of the tritone in modern jazz. The tritone which, according to Hindemith, 'neither belongs in the region of the harmonious, nor can be regarded as discordant,' has renewed an old jazz tradition: the preference for the shimmering and the ambiguous, which can also be found in the blue notes of the blues. It was no accident that the flatted fifth – as its novelty started to fade – began to take on the function of a blue note. Example 3 (in the chapter on the blues) shows the degree to which blue notes and flatted fifths have become equivalent.

The flatted fifths and blue notes of jazz and the tritone of modern symphonic music thus do not point towards a dissolution of tonality, but towards its loosening and broadening. The presence of the flatted fifth and blue notes in jazz can be explained from the same point of view from which Hindemith explains the tritone in the new symphonic music: 'Harmonic and melodic power are arrayed in opposition.' Where the harmonic power is weakest – in the flatted fifth – the melodic power is strongest. And power of melodic line is what counts.

The bop musicians who were the first to use flatted fifths – Charlie Parker, Dizzy Gillespie, Charlie Christian, Thelonious Monk – certainly did not have the faintest notion of the tritone or of Hindemith's *Craft of Musical Composition*. In their own way they arrived at solutions which Hindemith (whose name stands here for an entire direction in modern concert music) had derived from European musical tradition. This phenomenon, by the way, appears not only in the harmonies but also in the sound character of the music. The sounds of the Miles Davis Capitol Orchestra – in pieces like 'Moves', 'Budo', or 'Israel' – are remarkably similar to those in Stravinsky compositions such as 'Dumbarton Oaks Concerto', 'Symphony in C', or other works from his classicist period.

The first few traces of the dissolution of conventional tonality began to show a couple of years after the initial phase of bebop in some jazz forms of the fifties – as in the work of Lennie Tristano,

Charles Mingus, Teddy Charles, or George Russell. Russell, who wrote the famous 'Cubana Be-Cubana Bop' for Dizzy Gillespie's big band in the late forties, created a system of tonality which he calls the 'Lydian Concept of Tonal Organization'. In many respects it resembles the scales of the old Hellenistic music. Lennie Tristano, with musicians of his school, created a freely improvised piece called 'Intuition', in which Wolfgang Fortner – a well-known contemporary German symphonic composer – found tendencies towards the twelve-tone system.

Musicians like Tristano, Russell, Jimmy Giuffre, and Mingus paved the way for that sudden and explosive harmonic freedom which made jazz burst at the seams around the turn of the fifties. Free jazz, whose first outstanding representatives were Cecil Taylor and Ornette Coleman, finally rejected the laws of conventional functional harmonics. Sounds and lines rub against each other wild and hard, lending an ecstatic character to the music – to a degree that goes far beyond what might have been felt as 'ecstatic' in earlier jazz forms.

On the other hand, even in many of the freest jazz recordings, the music remains related to what musicians call 'tonal centres'. The word 'tonal', however, is not used in the sense of functional harmonics, but is simply supposed to indicate certain crucial points – centres of gravity – from which the musicians take off, and to which they find their way back – or at least try – if they have not lost sight of them in the collective heat of improvisation. (In this context, see also the chapter dealing with free jazz.)

In the chapters about Miles Davis and John Coltrane, we used the term 'modal'. In the manner of improvisation created by Davis and John Coltrane, the harmony is no longer determined by the constantly changing chords of a harmonic structure; every chord that corresponds to the 'mode', to the scale, is allowed. This is a way of playing that has been in existence for centuries in many of the great exotic musical cultures – the Arab and the Indian cultures, for example. On the one hand, it allows harmonic freedom; on the other, it prevents arbitrariness. Modal playing also means a further Africanization of the music; away from the 'dictatorship' of European harmonies towards the free harmonization which exists in many African musical cultures (not only in the Arabianized and Moslemized ones). Modalization thus creates a feeling of belonging in a dual sense: musically and racially – and in mood, too. That is the basis of its success.

The jazz of the seventies combined the freedom of free jazz with the harmonic possibilities of previous jazz styles. The new aspects it achieved in terms of harmonies were rooted mainly in the virtuousity and sovereignty with which harmonies from the most varied sources were dealt with. In pianist Keith Jarrett's playing, for example, one may find side by side, held together by modality, blues chords, Debussylike whole-tone harmonies, traces of medieval ecclesiastical keys, romantic elements, exotic – for example, Arab – elements; and in addition, the whole range of harmonic possibilities of conventional jazz. Often, all these elements occur in such immediate transitions that even specialists no longer are able to localize the sources, but they appear in an order that seems necessary and logical, although no known system could explain the necessities and logic of such an order. That is exactly where freedom is founded: no longer on freedom of tonality but rather in the mastery with which all the elements of tonality and atonality, European, exotic and jazzlike, classical and modern, are utilized. Thus, freedom also includes the freedom to be free – and the opposite: to forego being free, if that is what the musician wants.

This is also how the missionary and sectarian character of the freedom of the free jazz of the sixties was overcome – a conception of freedom which condemned all nonfree playing as not only musically but also politically, socially, and morally regressive.

Melody

If one proceeds from the assumption made by modern musical theory that there is no basic difference between melody and harmony – melody is 'horizontal harmony', harmony is 'vertical melody' – almost everything that can be said about jazz melody has already been said in the preceding chapter. In the early forms of jazz there was hardly anything that could be called a 'jazz' melody – with the exception of melodies containing blue notes. (Example 3 in the blues chapter.) The melodies were fundamentally similar to those of circus and march music, to the piano and drawing-room music of the late nineteenth century. To the degree in which jazz phrasing gained significance, melodies began to evolve in terms of this phrasing – so thoroughly that this manner of phrasing finally changed and shaped the melodic flow itself, and something that might be called jazz melody came into being.

Jazz melody is primarily marked by its flowing character. Insofar as the melodic development is expressed in improvisation, there are no repeats, such as are often used structurally in European music. Repeats are excluded, to begin with, because the soloist mainly improvises from his subconscious, and so is unable to repeat what he has just played without first having recourse to close study of a possible recording. Repeats are part of the relationship of music to time. When a melody is repeated, it is lifted out of the flow of time. It is as if one were to bring back a span of time which has already passed in order to relive it once more. The absence of repetition in the flow of chorus improvisations makes it clear that jazz is more closely related to the realm in which music occurs – time – than is European music. The phenomenon of swing and other peculiarities of jazz also point to this. To give it pointed expression: if music – as almost all philosophies of music hold – is *the* art expressed in time, then jazz corresponds more fundamentally to the basic nature of the musical than European music.

Jazz derives one of its unique traits from the fact that it is instrumentally conceived. André Hodeir, who has expressed the most succinct ideas about the problems of melody and harmony in jazz yet published, said: 'Composers in the European tradition conceive a phrase by itself and then make it fit the requirements of a given instrument. The jazz improviser creates only in terms of the instrument he plays. In extreme instances of assimilation, the instrument becomes in some way a part of him . . .'

Since the instrument and, through it, the musician himself are 'projected into' the melody, things like attack, vibrato, accentuation, rhythmic placement, etc., are so closely connected with a jazz melody that it may become meaningless without them. A European melody always exists 'in the abstract' as well, but the jazz melody exists only in its concrete relationship to the instrument on which it is played and to the musician who plays it. It becomes nonsense (in the literal sense of the term) when it is removed from its creator and his instrument. This is the reason why most attempts to notate jazz improvisations have remained unsatisfactory. The fine points of phrasing, attack, accentuation, expression, and conception cannot be expressed in notation, and since everything depends on these subtleties, notation becomes meaningless. When jazz melodies separated from these subtleties appear on note paper, they often seem primitive and banal.

In the course of jazz development, the improvisers have developed a facility for projecting subtleties into jazz which cannot be expressed in words. In order to accentuate the flowing character of jazz melody, the oppressively dotted quarter- and eighth-notes so typical of the jazz of the twenties have been dispensed with. Ever since the forties, this kind of punctuation has been regarded as 'corny'; it can still be found in popular music, especially when nostalgia for the 'good old days' is in order (but all of a sudden there were several free-jazz musicians, most notably Albert Ayler, who had fun with such 'old-fashioned' march, polka, and circus elements!). Miles Davis, Lee Konitz, and Lennie Tristano have fashioned a manner of improvisation in which eighth-note stands next to eighth-note, almost without punctuation. Here are lines which look in transcription as 'European' and 'symphonic' as one could imagine. But when such lines are played by Davis or Konitz or almost any significant jazz musician today, they become the very essence of concentrated 'jazzness'. The jazz character no longer lies in the crude, external punctuation and syncopation of notes – it lies in subtlety of conception. That is what Fats Waller and so many other jazz musicians mean when they say: 'Jazz isn't *what* you do, it's *how* you do it.'

Because all these refinements – almost ephemeral but extremely important differentiations in attack, phrasing, vibrato, accentuation, etc. – were further developed, it has become increasingly possible to incorporate the beat, i.e., the rhythm section, into the melody line. More and more one can hear unaccompanied jazz solos of similarly concentrated jazz essence as a solo improvisation with a rhythm section. We noted in the chapter on the jazz of the seventies that Coleman Hawkins was the first to record a whole piece without rhythm accompaniment: 'Picasso', in 1947. This record was the real forerunner of those long, free-swinging unaccompanied improvisations and cadenzas played by Sonny Rollins – or, for instance, in Germany by Albert Mangelsdorff – that became something of a trend during the seventies, often filled with hidden romanticism.

One could say that from the mid-fifties on, it became the jazz improviser's prime concern to play long, flowing lines without crudely external jazz effects, and nonetheless to convey real jazz intensity. This is also the source of the 'flowing', 'pulsating' rhythmic conception developed by such musicians as drummer Elvin Jones in John Coltrane's group, or Tony Williams with Miles Davis.

It is only a step from here to the melodies of many free-jazz musicians, who in the realm of melody more than anywhere else retained all elements of post-Lester Young and Charlie Parker jazz phrasing, in addition to an ecstatic intensity which has its roots way back in Africa. With other free-jazz musicians, the pendulum swung in the opposite direction again: away from the emphasis on phrasing to the accent on sound – in the sense of Bubber Miley's 'jungle sounds', for example, of which we spoke in the chapter on sound.

The ability to simply let certain notes 'go by the board' becomes particularly important in the organic course of a jazz melody line. Anyone who has notated jazz improvisation knows of this phenomenon: The note is here, one hears it quite clearly, and it has to be included in the notation. Yet one does not hear it because it was played, but because it was *not* played: it was merely felt and hinted at. Faced with this, many a European musician has capitulated. In the spring of 1958, Marshall Brown went to Europe to recruit a big band of leading European jazz musicians for the Newport Jazz Festival. He consistently admired their high musical standards, yet seldom was truly satisfied. 'For example,' he said, 'it was difficult to find a musician who could throw away a note. Until we listened to these European musicians I had never realized that such subtleties are typical American.'

The theme to be improvised on has become less and less important in the course of jazz development. The embellishment and ornamentation of the theme, so important to the old jazz, recede further into the background. They still exist in the interpretation of 'ballads' – slow pieces, mostly from the realm of popular music, with melodies or chord structures that appeal to jazzmen. Otherwise, improvisation became so free that the melody of a theme is hardly of significance. Often it cannot be recognized even at the start. Since the fifties, the jazz musician who plays fast pieces improvises not so much on a theme as on the harmonies of this theme. And thus – as Hodeir has said – the jazz variation is a 'variation on no theme at all.'

Example 6

Example 6 clarifies the process of untying the jazz improvisation from the theme. The example is transcribed from a record by the Max Roach Quintet, 'Prince Albert'. The actual theme is Jerome Kern's 'All the Things You Are'. The first bars of this melody are in row (a). Above the harmonies of this theme (b), trumpeter Kenny Dorham and tenor saxophone James Moody have placed a riff figure (c) – a new theme closer to their jazz conception. This riff figure is introduced in unison by the two hornmen. Thus the original theme of 'All the Things You Are' is never even heard on the record. The musicians improvise on the new theme which was gleaned from the harmonies (in jazz terminology, chord changes) of 'All the Things You Are', and on which in turn alternated harmonies can be based. One of these improvisations and its related harmonies can be found in rows (d) and (e) (with a flatted fifth in the fourth bar).

Clearly, this chain can be extended. A new riff can be based on the (e) changes, and this riff can become the basis for a different improvisation which in turn possesses alternations. The relationship to the theme is retained in all cases, and the jazz man – if he is knowledgeable – at once feels that somewhere 'All the Things You Are' was the starting point.

This is radical usage of a tenet basic to all forms of music in which improvisation is alive – such as baroque music – and in which the melody (or its harmonies!) is used as material. It is not a cause unto itself, as it is in music of the romantic period. When the melody is a

cause unto itself, it becomes sacrosanct. Since our musical consciousness is romanticized, we are accustomed to regarding melodies as
sacrosanct, and thus many people have no feeling for the 'materiality'
of melody.

Johann Sebastian Bach still had this feeling. It was not the melody
that played a role – as in romantic music – but what one made of it.
Executio took precedence over *inventio*: execution came before
invention, whereas the musical conception of romanticism created a
mystique of invention and placed it above all else. Because Bach
regarded music as working material, he was able to take melodies
from other masters of his time – such as Vivaldi – and use them for his
own purposes without acknowledging his source. According to
contemporary conception this is plagiarism. But to Bach it seemed all
right; and exactly in this sense it seems all right to jazz musicians.
Melody is the material, and so one can do with it as one wishes – with
the *proviso* that what is made of this material should make musical
sense.

The art of inventing new melodic lines from given harmonies has
become increasingly differentiated in the course of jazz development.
Often on older jazz recordings the improvisation actually only
consists of taking the harmonies apart: notes which in the basic
chords were superimposed on one another are strung out in the
melodies. The melodic movement has the flavour of cadenced triads
and seventh-chords. The melodies of modern jazz are more closely
meshed. It no longer depends on interpreting the chord, but on
placing against it a contrasting, independent melodic line. This
creates tension between the vertical and the horizontal – and the old
jazz tendency to find possibilities for tension is thus nourished.

The jazz melody – aside from free playing – obtains its structure
from the 12-bar form of the blues or the 32-bar AABA form of the
popular song – and in the newer stages of jazz, also from several
irregular forms. There is a tendency among jazz musicians to cross
over formal sections. Here, too, the indebtedness of music to time
becomes clear. This crossing over the formal sections would be
misread if one were to conclude that it results in a dissolution of form.
The form – predetermined by the chord structure – remains intact.
(It was dissolved only in certain stages of free jazz). Not following the
formal bar structure is perceived as something special and out of the
ordinary. One might almost say the formal structure is accentuated

by the fact that it is not accentuated. Here, too, a new possibility for creating tension has been discovered: tension between the given, retained form and the free line that swings above it.

Related to the tendency to play across structural sections and displace them unexpectedly is the preference for long melodic lines in modern jazz – lines much longer than in the older forms.

Kenny Clarke and Mary Lou Williams claim that the pioneers of bop consciously crossed bar lines so that musicians who were trying to 'steal' their ideas would not be able to get themselves organized. Thelonious Monk said: 'We're going to create something that they can't steal because they can't play it.' Drummer Dave Tough told of the first time he walked into the place on 52nd Street where Dizzy Gillespie was playing: 'As we walked in, these cats snatched up their horns and blew crazy stuff. One would stop all of a sudden and another would start for no reason at all. We never could tell when a solo was supposed to begin or end. Then they all quit at once and walked off the stand. It scared us.' But, as Marshall Stearns points out, about a year later the selfsame Dave Tough was playing with Woody Herman's band some of the things that had scared him.

Independent of the structuring of 8-bar sections, blues choruses, or 32-bar song strophes is the natural structuring of tension and relaxation. The free-jazz musicians often went as far as to set this 'natural form' in the place of predetermined structures. A collectively improvising free-jazz group creates its own form by 'breathing', by moments of orgiastic intensity followed by moments of quiet and relaxation, which in turn are built up into new 'climaxes'. This achievement of free jazz has also proven of lasting importance for the jazz of the seventies and eighties: Even younger musicians who have returned to conventional, functional tonality love to create their own 'breathed' forms independent of 12-bar, 16-bar, or 32-bar structures. More and more, one can also hear combinations of predetermined and 'breathed' structures.

It is illuminating that the way for this was paved by the Kansas City jazz of the thirties, the so-called 'riff style': The riff creates tension, and the subsequent improvised melodic line creates relaxation. The strong, rhythmic, heavily accentuated phrases called 'riffs', often only two or four bars in length and capable of being repeated until the 32-bar song entity has been filled, are excellently suited to the creation of tension.

Guitarist Charlie Christian – one of the musicians who played a part in the creation of modern jazz – built up his solos in such a way that new riff elements were constantly opposed to new melodic lines. His solos are sequences of riffs and free-swinging melodic lines, the riffs creating tension, the melodic lines relaxation. Charlie Christian's manner of improvising was adopted by many musicians and has had great influence – consciously and unconsciously.

This relaxation – the moment of relief – goes further and deeper than is familiar from European music. Naturally, the aspect of tension and relaxation belongs to every organic musical art. In jazz, however, it is projected into the old call-and-response principle of African music. In the improvisations of Charlie Christian, the riffs are the 'calls', the subsequent free-swinging lines the 'responses'. In other words, the lead singer no longer holds a conversation with the answering chorus of listeners – as in African music or in the spiritual – but the improvising soloist holds a conversation with himself . . . and the loneliness – the 'alienation' – of the creative jazz musician could never be made clearer than through this fact. Everything that goes into the give-and-take between call and response within the communion of a spiritual-singing congregation or a West African cult is now concentrated in the improvisation of a single soloist.

Of course, this thought must not be pursued too far. The principle of call and response is not projected merely in the single individual. The 'call' of the riff is frequently played by the other musicians during the improvisation – which means during the 'response' of the soloist – and it is possible in this way to create an intensity that carries everything with it. This intensity is rooted in concentration. Call and response no longer follow each other, but are sounded simultaneously.

In the preceding, we have repeatedly used the word 'relaxation'. To be 'relaxed' has become a term in the language of musicians as well as of jazz critics – and, as Norman Mailer has shown, an ideal in the life-style of jazz musicians and, in general, of people who want to be 'in'. From that vantage point, it has had a deep influence on the entire American life-style. I've never seen statements on European concert music where 'relaxation' was used as a critical term.

Rhythm, Swing

Every jazz ensemble – be it large or small – consists of a melody section and a rhythm section. To the former belong instruments such as trumpet, trombone, clarinet, and the members of the saxophone family; to the latter, drums, bass, guitar, and piano – only insofar as they do not step out in solo roles of their own, of course.

There is tension between the melody and rhythm sections. On the other hand, the rhythm section carries the melodic group. It is like a riverbed in which the stream of the melodic lines flows. Tension exists not only between the two sections but within each group as well – in fact, this can go so far as to mix up the actual functions of the two sections: It is not uncommon in modern jazz that 'melody instruments' take over rhythm functions while 'rhythm instruments' play the melody part.

Thus a many-layered rhythm is created which thoroughly corresponds to the many layers of melody found in, say, the music of Johann Sebastian Bach. To claim, as many people still do, that the rhythm of jazz is nothing but primitive pounding merely reveals that a person who holds such views is without feeling for the fact that rhythmic possibilities are as inexhaustible as melodic and harmonic ones. The lack of such feeling is of course in line with Western musical development. Hans H. Stuckenschmidt, one of Europe's leading music critics, and thus not a man of jazz but of concert music, once spoke of 'the rhythmic atrophy in the musical arts of the white race.' It is oddly ironic that the oft-heard complaint of primitiveness, directed against jazz and other similar phenomena, here turns back on the world whence it came: against the European–Western world in which there is this strange gap between admirable development of melodic, harmonic, and formal elements and – as Stuckenschmidt said – the atrophy of things rhythmic.

Not that there isn't any rhythm in European music. There are great rhythmic creations – for example in Mozart and Brahms, even more so in avant-garde concert music – but even these pale when compared to the grandiose rhythms of Indian or Balinese music, with traditions of rhythmic mastery as long and honourable as those of Western music in respect to form. One does not have to think only of jazz when it comes to recognizing the inferiority of rhythmic elements in European music.

It is simply an inferiority of rhythmic sense. What every street urchin in the Near East can do – beat out with arms and legs on boxes and pots rhythmic structures in which eight or nine different rhythms are complexly entwined – is within the European tradition not even possible for the percussionist of a symphony orchestra. In symphony orchestras, eight or nine different percussionists are frequently needed to achieve such complexity.

In jazz, the multiplicity of rhythms is anchored in the 'beat': a regularly accented basic rhythm, the beating heart of jazz. As drummer Jo Jones has put it: 'even breathing'. This fundamental rhythm is the organizing principle. Through it, the musical happenings are ordered. It is maintained by the drummer, or in modern jazz often only by the steady 4/4 of the bassist. This regulatory function corresponds to a European need. Certainly swing is connected with an African feeling for rhythm. But in spite of this – as Marshall Stearns has pointed out – there is no swing in Africa. Swing arose when African rhythmic feeling was applied to the regular meter of European music – in a long and complex process of fusion.

In the styles of jazz can be found certain basic rhythms, represented in simplified fashion by Example 7. This example represents the drum parts: the notes in the lower row are played on the bass drum, those on the bottom on the snare drum (in the fusion

Example 7

example: centre row), and the crossed notes on the cymbal. The carrier of the basic beat in New Orleans, Dixieland, Chicago, and Swing style is the bass drum; in bebop and cool jazz it is the cymbal. The rhythmic accents are indicated by >.

In New Orleans style and ragtime (7a), the rhythmic emphasis is on the so-called 'strong' beats: on 1 and 3, just as in march music. From here on, jazz rises to an ever-increasing rhythmic complexity and intensity. Dixieland and Chicago style (7b), as well as New Orleans jazz as played in Chicago during the twenties, shifts the accents to 2 and 4, so that while 1 and 3 remain the 'strong' beats, the accent now is on 2 and 4. Thus the peculiar 'floating' rhythmic atmosphere from which swing takes its name was created.

Both New Orleans and Dixieland rhythms are two-beat rhythms insofar as the bass drum, carrier of the basic beat, is assigned two beats per measure. Of course there were exceptions. Louis Armstrong – always the swing man! – requested drummer Baby Dodds to play an even four beats. Subsequently, Swing style was founded on four beats to the measure (7c), but tends to emphasize 2 and 4. Up to this point, jazz rhythm had a staccato beat – with its concomitant punctuation: the cymbal beat in the Swing example. Bebop brings a further concentration, replacing staccato largely with legato (which is often phrased like a triplet). The rhythm becomes – as French drummer Gerard Pochonet has said – a '*son continu*', a continuous sound. The cymbal sounds steadily – thus the '*son continu*'. On his other instruments – primarily on the bass drum – the drummer executes all kinds of rhythmic accents which serve to emphasize the basic rhythm: it is not so much 'beat out' as it is 'encircled'. Compared to this bop rhythm, the rhythm of cool jazz seems like a step backward, combining rhythmic features of Swing and bop.

At the bottom of example 7(e), there is a rhythm sample of fusion music (one of many possible ones!). Here the two-beat rhythm returns – in disguise. The snare drum (centre row) hints at it. The bass drum accents the basic rhythm by encircling it.

For free jazz, there is no basic formula that can be notated. The beat is replaced by what many jazz musicians call 'pulse': a pulsating, percussive activity so fast and nervous that single beats, standing by themselves, can no longer be perceived. The physiological shift of the beat from a correspondence to the heartbeat to the faster, more nervous, jerky throbbing of the pulse has been repeatedly pointed out by musicians and listeners (although the pulse, of course, is also based on the heartbeat; but what counts here are the different levels of awareness). Frequently, the melodic parts are played at quite moderate-medium tempo – to a basic beat which, though no longer marked by any one instrument, is clearly perceived as medium-fast – while the drummer contrasts to that a frenzied, multi-layered sounding of all his instruments. This certainly offers a new way of creating tension, and with stimulating results: several tempi – all different from each other – co-exist next to and on top of each other! The free-jazz drummers use many rhythmic formulae that have been developed through jazz history, and also a host of new rhythms taken from African, Arabian, Indian, and other exotic musics – occasionally also from European concert music. Many musicians for whom the freedom of free jazz not only represents a liberation from conventional harmonies, but also has racial, social, and political implications, emphasize African elements – from pride in the traditions of their own race.

It is often proposed that within free jazz, swing – that basic constituent element without which jazz is unthinkable – has ceased to exist. But what has ceased to exist is merely a certain metric symmetry. Our musical instincts used to perceive swing as rooted just in the friction between the symmetry of conventional, fundamental rhythm and the asymmetry of the various counter- and cross-rhythms that move above this fundamental rhythm and 'contradict' it. Actually, what happened was that, in an even more concentrated and radical manner than when bebop rhythm was created, swing has been moved more 'inward'. Some contemporary musicians have learned to produce swing through phrasing (and thus to include it in the flow of the melody line) to such an extent that they find the kind of swing that depends on the mere symmetry of a steady, basic beat – or on just a steady bass beat – much too obvious, and even 'primitive' and outmoded. (But since the seventies, there is also the sheer lustful joy of accenting – and overaccenting! – conventional swing – and Swing – rhythms again.)

When bebop came into being, the majority of critics and fans also responded: This music doesn't swing any more! But just a few years later, when they had grown accustomed to the new rhythms, these same critics and fans said: It swings more than ever. And even Dixieland bands used bebop drummers in their rhythm sections.

Jazz of the seventies and eighties is in a similar position vis-à-vis the jazz of the sixties as, twenty years earlier, cool jazz was vis-à-vis bebop: The use of elements of earlier jazz forms is - in light of the newly gained freedom - once again held in high esteem. In addition, there are the rock elements, of which we spoke in the chapter about the seventies.

In these computerized times, we have come to call jazz–rock or fusion rhythms 'binary', differentiating them in this way from the 'ternary' ones of conventional jazz forms. Jazz–rock is based on steady eighths - a fact which explains the close relationship of rock, jazz–rock, and fusion rhythms to Latin music. Drummers like Billy Cobham and Pierre Courbois pointed this out at an early stage of the development. Conventional jazz rhythms, in contrast, are based on a triplet structure, that is, on a 'ternary' rhythm feeling.

And yet what happens rhythmically in many contemporary jazz groups is still shaped after bebop models as they crystallized in the earlier years of modern jazz. They can be found everywhere in today's jazz - even in those contemporary jazz forms which are all but totally out of contrast with bop in terms of sound, melody, and harmony.

The tension-filled complexity of these bop structures was clarified many years ago by Miles Davis, when he said: 'Like, we'd be playing the blues, and Bird [Charlie Parker] would start on the eleventh bar, and as the rhythm section stayed where they were and Bird played where he was, it sounded as if the rhythm section was on 1 and 3 instead of 2 and 4. Every time that would happen, Max [Roach, the drummer] used to scream at Duke [Jordan, the pianist] not to follow Bird but to stay where he was. Then, eventually, it came around as Bird had planned and we were together again.' Davis called this - according to Marshall Stearns - 'turning the rhythm section around,' and adds that it so bewildered him at first that he 'used to quit every night.'

Stearns has shown, on the basis of African recordings, that no style of jazz before free jazz was rhythmically closer to Africa than bebop. The simple, marchlike meters of New Orleans and of Dixieland were replaced by rhythmic structures in which ancient African practices seem suddenly to have come to life again.

All this took place without any direct contact between the urbanized modern jazz musician and West African rhythms. It is as if the musicians have subconsciously relived once more an evolution which their ancestors had gone through centuries ago – or conversely: as if they have shaken off habits rooted ultimately not in their own, but in European tradition – becoming increasingly 'free', rediscovering, consciously *and* unconsciously, their true rhythmic heritage. This is also supported by the fact that in free jazz – as with drummers Sunny Murray or Rashied Ali – there was a further 'Africanization' of jazz rhythms.

As early as the fifties, Art Blakey travelled to West Africa to become acquainted with old African rhythms. Even earlier, in the late forties, Dizzy Gillespie had hired the conga drummer Chano Pozo, who was still a member of an African sect in his native Cuba, where West African traditions remained alive to a much greater degree than in North America.

Meanwhile, what used to be the exception has almost become the rule on a host of jazz recordings: Frequently, percussionists who are exponents of Africanizing rhythms – Latin Americans, above all Cubans and Brazilians, and Africans – are included in the rhythm sections of jazz groups. No longer do we have to face a flaw that used to be so prevalent in earlier combinations of jazz and African rhythms – a rhythmic gap.

But all these remarks are insufficient. It may be possible to write down and notate the most complex rhythms by Max Roach or Art Blakey – or today, Tony Williams, Billy Cobham, and Jack DeJohnette – only to discover that what has been written down and copied is merely a miserable skeleton of what the music really sounded like. You see, it swung – and swing cannot be notated. It cannot even be grasped in words. 'It's a real simple thing,' says Jo Jones, 'but there are some things you can't describe, some things that never have been described . . . The best way you can say what swinging is, is you either play with a feeling or you don't. It's just like the difference between receiving a genuine handshake or a fishy one.'

Jo Jones thinks that the difference between jazz and European music lies in swing. In European music – 'that approach to music is scientific' – the musician plays the notes that are placed before him. If one is sufficiently musical and has studied music, one can play the required parts. But in order to play jazz it is not sufficient to be musical and to have studied music long enough. Here lies the problem of all the jazz courses at conservatories and music schools, where jazz musicianship supposedly is taught. Surely much can be learned there. Almost all important representatives of modern jazz have studied music, and it is part and parcel of a good musician that he should know and understand his craft. But the decisive part cannot be taught: swing. One can hardly say what it is.

Thus the opinion gains ground that 'symphonic jazz', if it is at all possible, will have to come from within jazz rather than from European music. It is only possible when the elements of both musical realms are joined together and preserved. But symphonic musicians who wish to write jazz have until now been unable to capture what jazz is – precisely because these things cannot be taught and because these musicians, coming not from jazz but from the European tradition, do not possess them.

But – back to swing. In the course of jazz development swing became ever more far-reaching and concentrated. 'The phenomenon of swing,' says André Hodeir, 'should not be regarded as the immediate and inevitable result of a confrontation between the African rhythmic genius and the 2/2 beat. What we know about primitive jazz excludes the hypothesis that swing sprang into being like a spark at the collision of two stones. Pre-Armstrong recordings reveal, on the contrary, that swing was merely latent at first and took shape progressively over a long period . . .'

The aspect of tension and relaxation belongs to swing. Jo Jones says: 'Another thing about rhythm is that when an artist is performing on his instrument he breathes in his normal fashion, and he has a listening audience that breathes along with him.'

Steadiness of natural conditions of breathing create the uniqueness of swing. There are never two possibilities. 'The only way I can describe swing,' says ragtime pianist Wally Rose, 'is it's the kind of rhythmic movement where you can place a note where and when it is due. The only thing that keeps you together is when the whole band meets on this beat, meets on the split second you all think the beat is due. The slightest deviation from that causes tension and frustration . . .'

Swing gives jazz its peculiar form of precision, which cannot be compared with any kind of precision in European music. Conductors and composers of symphonic music have been among the first to admit this. The difference between the precision found in Count Basie's band and the precision of the best European orchestras – jazz as well as symphonic – is due to the fact that Basie's precision stems from swing, whereas the other kind of precision is the result of academic drill. Basie's musicians feel that the note is due, and since they all feel this at the identical moment, and from the basis of swing, everything is precise in a direct, unfettered way. The kind of precision gleaned from academic tradition, on the other hand, is neither direct nor unfettered.

To swing belong, furthermore, the multiple layers of rhythm and the tension between them – the displacements of rhythmic accents and all that we have said about them. This displacement is called 'syncopation' in European music. But the use of this term in jazz reveals an essential misunderstanding of the nature of jazz. Syncopation can only arise when the syncopated displacement of a note is something irregular. In jazz it is something regular – and to such a degree that the absence of syncopations may have 'syncopating' (if this word had any meaning in jazz) effects.

It must be clear by now: swing is not the task of a drummer who has to 'swing' the soloists. A jazz musician who does not swing – all by himself and without any rhythm section – is no jazz musician. Thus the considered opinion of many modern musicians that it is almost as possible to swing without a drummer as with one: 'The drive that creates the pulsation has to be within yourself. I don't understand why it should be necessary to have someone else drive you,' says Jimmy Giuffre. Nat Hentoff states in this context: 'The ability to swing must first be contained within each musician. If he is dependent on a rhythm section . . . he is in the position of the rejected suitor who can't understand that one must be capable of giving love if one wishes to receive it.'

It becomes increasingly clear that such paraphrases, by the musicians themselves or by sympathetic critics, are more satisfactory elucidations of the phenomenon of swing than 'exact' explanations made by musicologists who have no feeling for swing. It is particularly unedifying to see swing explained as off-beat accentuation, which is so often the case. Off-beats – in other words, the accentuation away from the beat into the 'weak' beats commonly unaccented in European music – does not of necessity produce swing. Much of contemporary popular music – even when it does not swing – is full of off-beats.

Some of the most concise thoughts concerning swing have been expressed by the Swiss musicologist Jan Slawe. In his *Versuch einer Definition der Jazzmusik*, in the context of rhythm and meter, he states: 'The main concept of jazz theory is "formation of conflict"; originally, these formations of conflict were rhythmic in nature, existing in the antagonism between simultaneously executed, different segments of music-filled time.' And later he adds: 'The fundamental nature of swing is expressed in the rhythmic basis of the music as a whole . . . in particular, swing postulates a regularity of time in order to simultaneously be able to negate it. The particular nature of swing is the creation of rhythmic conflicts between the fundamental rhythm and the rhythm of the melody; this is the musical-technical cornerstone of jazz.'

But these definitions, too, remain unsatisfactory. Meanwhile, so much has been written about swing that one might tend to accept once and for all the dictum that swing cannot be verbally expressed. Maybe this is because swing involves a feeling for time for which there is no precedent in European music. Ethnology has shown us that the African's sense of time – and, generally, that of 'primitive' peoples – is more holistic and elementary than the differentiated time sense of Western man. Swing developed when the two concepts of time met. In all the polyrhythms of African music, often much more complex than those in jazz, there is still no swing – as is the case in European music. One might assume that its nature is rooted in the overlapping of two different conceptions of time.

Musicology knows well that music may occur in two different conceptions of time. Stravinsky calls these 'psychological' and 'ontological' time. Rudolf Kassner speaks of 'lived' and 'measured' time. These two kinds of time cannot be equalized in those aspects of our being which count most: one second of pain becomes an eternity, and one hour can be but a fleeting moment in a state of happiness. This is of significance to music. Music is art in time . . . as sculpture is art in space, and painting the art of the plane. But if music is art in time we may ask which time: psychological or ontological, relative or absolute, lived or measured?

This question can be answered only in respect to one particular musical style. It has been said that the relationship between lived and measured time is of considerable formative consequence to music. Thus romantic, and particularly late romantic, music is almost exclusively an art of lived, psychological time. Private and subjective experience of time is primary here. On the other hand, the music of a Bach is almost exclusively in measured, objective, ontological time, related in each note to the movement of the cosmos, to which it is of no concern whether a minute seems to us like an eternity, or eternity like a minute.

The question is: which is the time of swing? And here it becomes clear why Western man must 'leap over the shadow of his time sense' if he wants to find out about swing. For there can be no doubt: swing is related to both levels of time at once – to measured, objective time and to lived, psychological time. By the same token, it is also related to both an African and a European sense of time. Swing is rooted in the awareness of a simultaneously desperate and joyous inability to find a common denominator for lived and measured time. More precisely: a common denominator for lived and measured time has been found, but the listener is aware of a duality – in other words, he is aware of swing.

THE INSTRUMENTS OF JAZZ

The Instruments of Jazz

The Trumpet

The trumpet has been called 'the royal instrument of jazz' – because its sound is so piercing and brilliant that in almost all ensemble passages in which a trumpet takes part the lead almost automatically is assigned to it. This happens in the New Orleans collective as well as in the ensembles of the big bands, which are almost always dominated by the trumpet section.

With the trumpet belong, on the one hand – particularly in the older forms of jazz – the cornet, and, on the other – in the newer styles – the fluegelhorn. In the early days of jazz, 'trumpet' almost always meant cornet. Later on, there were few cornetists – probably because the trumpet offers greater range and technical possibilities. Nevertheless, cornetist Rex Stewart ranks as one of the greatest technical virtuosos of the 'trumpet' up to the beginnings of bop. Other technically able 'trumpeters' – mainly in the realm of Dixieland – stayed with the cornet, among them *Wild Bill Davison* and *Muggsy Spanier*. In modern jazz the cornet is used by, among others, *Nat Adderley* and occasionally also by *Clark Terry*; in free jazz, by *Butch Morris*. In some modern forms of jazz, however, the fluegelhorn became popular due to its round, flowing sound. There are fluegelhorn players in jazz who manage to lend their instrument a saxophonelike suppleness, and yet are able to preserve the brilliance of the brass sound. Among the best fluegelhorn players are *Art Farmer, Thad Jones, Jimmy Owens*, the Dutch player *Ack van Rooyen*, and – here, too – *Clark Terry.*

The first generation of jazz cornetists is that of *Buddy Bolden* – the legendary progenitor of New Orleans jazz, who regrettably played before the time of recorded jazz music – and his contemporaries, active around the turn of the century and immediately thereafter.

They played jazz, or similar music – we might call it ragtime and march music with hot intonation. To this generation belong *Freddie Keppard, Emmanuel Perez, Bunk Johnson, Papa Celestin, Natty Dominique,* and primarily *King Oliver.* His recordings provide rich material for study. They have that rough, earth-bound, hard sound, still lacking the triumphant tone which Louis Armstrong gave to the jazz trumpet.

Tommy Ladnier links this sound to a strong and expressive blues feeling, accentuated primarily in the lower registers of the instrument. Initially, Ladnier stems wholly from Oliver. In the twenties, he travelled as far as Moscow, billed as 'Tommy, the talking cornet.' Later he participated – with Mezz Mezzrow and Sidney Bechet – in the famous New Orleans recordings organized in 1938 in New York by the French jazz critic Hugues Panassié. His solo on one of these ('Really the Blues') enjoys great reputation among friends of traditional jazz. Ladnier – born in 1900 – belongs to *Louis Armstrong*'s generation, but one feels inclined to place him earlier in terms of musical conception. We have spoken of Armstrong in a special chapter: He did not switch from cornet to trumpet until 1928. Armstrong is the measure for all jazz trumpeting up to this day.

Among the musicians who played most *á la* Armstrong were *Hot Lips Page*, Teddy Buckner, and Jonah Jones. Page, who died in 1954, was active in the Kansas City circle of musicians from the late twenties to the mid-thirties. An exceptional blues player, he sometimes played so much like Armstrong that he could be mistaken for him. As a singer, too, he was astonishingly close to Armstrong. *Jonah Jones*, who was among the most reliable big-band trumpeters of the Swing era – in Cab Calloway's band, for instance – with his solid and humorous quartet recordings won himself a following in the fifties and sixties among those who found modern trumpet too complicated and Dixieland trumpet too cliché-ridden.

Now, back to the first generation of white trumpet (and cornet) players, beginning with *Nick La Rocca*, founder of the Original Dixieland Jazz Band. His cornet in a way retained the sound of the circus trumpeters of the turn of the century, in paradoxical contrast to his preposterous claims that he and his white orchestra had been the first jazz band.

In the realm of the old Dixieland, but considerably more musical and differentiated, was the trumpeting of *Sharkey Bonano*. He and

Muggsy Spanier are among the white trumpeters who frequently are counted by traditional jazz fans among black New Orleans rather than white Dixieland. *Muggsy Spanier*, who died in 1967, made the first Chicago-style recordings in 1924 with his Bucktown Five. In 1939 he had a short-lived band – Muggsy Spanier's Ragtime Band – which made a deep and lasting impression with its musicianly and original Dixieland music. In 1940 he made records with Sidney Bechet – accompanied by guitar and bass only – which are a kind of 'chamber music' of traditional jazz.

Along the line originating from La Rocca, but more polished and musical, are *Red Nichols* and *Phil Napoleon*, two musicians representative of 'New York style'. This term is common usage for the music of the white jazzmen in New York during the twenties and early thirties, who did not have the privilege of steady, stimulating contact with the New Orleans greats, as did their colleagues in Chicago. On the other hand, they were often ahead of them in terms of academic training, technique, and craftsmanship. Comparison between Nichols and Bix Beiderbecke illuminates this point: Nichols's blowing was perhaps even more clean and flawless than Bix's, but he could not approach Bix where sensitivity and imagination were concerned. Both Napoleon's Original Memphis Five and Nichols's Five Pennies found great favour with their kind of 'purified' jazz, especially with 'commercial' audiences.

Bix Beiderbecke brought elegance and cool sensitivity to the sound of the jazz trumpet. He had more followers than any other white trumpeter of his time. *Bunny Berigan*, *Jimmy McPartland*, and *Bobby Hackett* are among these. The Bixian conception can be pursued well into cool jazz. Many solos by Miles Davis, and even more by Chet Baker, sound as if Beiderbecke's Chicago style had been 'transformed' into modern jazz – although, of course, there is no direct link between Bix and Miles.

The most successful musician of the Beiderbecke succession was Bunny Berigan, who died much too young in 1942. A pronounced big-band trumpeter, he worked with Benny Goodman and Tommy Dorsey in the mid-thirties and then formed his own band, with which he scored a hit that was bigger than Coleman Hawkins's 'Body and Soul', even though it did not have the long-lasting effect of the latter: 'I Can't Get Started'.

Stylistically, the most significant of Beiderbecke's followers was

Bobby Hackett, who died in 1976. Hackett was a genuine master of the art of playing 'standards', the great songs of popular music in America. His 'traditional' jazz playing was spiced with many harmonic and rhythmic experiences from much more 'modern' periods of jazz.

Indebted to Beiderbecke, but more closely related to Armstrong, are *Max Kaminsky* and Wild Bill Davison. Max emerged from the Chicago circle. *Wild Bill Davison* for years was the most exciting trumpeter of the Eddie Condon groups that became the focal point for traditional jazz in New York during the mid-forties and the fifties. Without Davison's vitality and originality, Condon's music often might have been not much more than 'warmed-over' memories of old Chicago.

Beiderbecke had some influence on black musicians as well – for instance, on *Joe Smith*, a member of Fletcher Henderson's band. The contrast between the melancholy elegance of Smith's trumpet and the hard sounds of the Henderson band remains intriguing to this day. Henderson called Smith 'the most soulful trumpet I ever had.'

Rex Stewart, although not a Beiderbecke successor, copied some of Bix's solos during the years when Beiderbecke was the talk of all jazz musicians; mainly – with the Henderson band of 1931 – Bix's celebrated 'Singing the Blues', one of the most famous trumpet solos in jazz history.

With Stewart we arrive at a group of trumpeters who might be described as 'Ellington trumpets'. These are first and foremost the 'jungle-style' trumpeters.

The first in this group was *Bubber Miley*, who died in 1932 and who gave the Ellington band of the twenties the characteristic colouration which until this day is associated with Ellington. Bubber was first influenced by King Oliver: If one recalls Oliver's most famous solo – 'Dippermouth Blues' – it illuminates how direct the link is to Miley's famed solo on Ellington's first version of 'Black and Tan Fantasy', which Bubber co-composed.

Ellington remained interested in the retention of the 'Miley colour'. Stewart, *Cootie Williams*, *Ray Nance*, *Clark Terry*, and others had to see to this during various epochs in Ellington's career. Cootie Williams plays growl trumpet with particular expressiveness and strength. He is the soloist on one of Ellington's most significant recordings, 'Concerto for Cootie' (1940). Stewart, who died in 1967, has often been admired for the lightness and assurance with which he could play at even the most rapid tempi – and very expressively, at that.

An element of Stewart's style was the half-valve technique: the valves of the trumpet are pressed down only halfway. *Clark Terry* transplanted this style of playing into modern jazz. He has created a unique, completely personal style and is perhaps the only modern trumpeter outside free jazz who did not become enmeshed in the back-and-forth between Dizzy Gillespie and Miles Davis. And, above all, Terry is master of intelligent musical humour.

All trumpeters mentioned up to now actually belong to the immediate Armstrong school. In contrast to this school stands what might be called – for simplification – the Gillespie school. It, too, is a product of what had come before. The Gillespie tradition actually begins long before Dizzy, with *Henry 'Red' Allen*. Allen, who died in 1967, took King Oliver's place in the Oliver band when it was taken over by Luis Russell in 1929. In his playing, the shift in emphasis from sonority to phrasing was indicated for the first time – if only in spurts. Allen – when compared to his contemporaries – plays more legato than staccato, in a more flowing manner, connecting rather than separating his phrases.

The tendency towards this kind of playing becomes more marked with a group of trumpeters who came after Allen: *Roy Eldridge*, Buck Clayton, Harry Edison and Charlie Shavers. Eldridge became the most important exponent of his instrument between Armstrong and Gillespie. Fluidity now became an ideal for jazz trumpeters. The saxophone is the most 'fluid' of jazz instruments, and here was revealed for the first time the impact of the saxophone on the sonority of modern jazz. Eldridge once said: 'I play nice saxophone on the trumpet.' He later abandoned this saxophone emphasis in his playing, but it remained an active influence.

Roy Eldridge excels in creative impulsiveness, *Charlie Shavers* in technical brilliance. Shavers, who died in 1971, was an all-round trumpeter to a degree matched perhaps only by Harry James at that time. The latter, known through his connection with Benny Goodman, led a dance band that was popular from the late thirties all the way to the fifties.

Buck Clayton and *Harry Edison*, finally, play the most gentle and tender trumpets of all the Swing musicians. Edison earned his nickname, 'Sweets', because he loved to eat anything sweet. But his nickname applies also to the supple tenderness of his playing. Harmonically speaking, he is the most 'modern' trumpet before Gillespie, while Clayton still tends more towards traditional harmonies. Both were among the star soloists of the classic Count Basie band of the late thirties. In the fifties, Edison became a busy Hollywood studio musician who participated in recording sessions with stars like Frank Sinatra, and later in New York in jazz and rock productions. No other trumpeter so completely expresses the sensitivity of modern jazz in the idiom of Swing style.

Edison influenced a trumpeter who later played much the same role in the Basie band he himself had played from 1937 to 1950: *Joe Newman*. And Clayton is frequently mentioned when *Ruby Braff's* antecedents are under discussion. Braff is a unique stylistic phenomenon: a trumpeter of the jazz generation of the fifties who took his cues not from Dizzy or Miles, but from the trumpeters of the earlier jazz tradition – a perfectionist of the Swing trumpet, full of grace and charm in Swing and Dixieland. In the seventies he co-led a quartet with guitarist George Barnes, whose Swing was characterized by a floating weightlessness. This Swing tradition is still alive – as in *Warren Vaché*, who, although prominent only since the end of the seventies, remains very much indebted to it in everything he plays.

Jazz trumpeters began early to make use of the stimulating effects of the highest registers of the instrument – playing far above conventional trumpet range. As with everything else in the history of the jazz trumpet, this, too, begins with Louis Armstrong. But Charlie Shavers was the musician who most influenced the high-note specialists: 'Cat' Anderson and Al Kilian with Duke Ellington, and eventually *Maynard Ferguson*, who became known as a member of Stan Kenton's orchestra. Kenton scored with the record sales of Ferguson's skyscraper-climbing escapades, but the critics were almost unanimously antagonized by the tastelessness of this way of playing. Later, Ferguson showed that he is a musician with real jazz feeling and tremendous swing – mainly with his wildly swinging big bands, which he led in the late fifties in the US, later in Great Britain (more about that in the chapter on the big bands).

From the point of sheer technique and craftsmanship, Ferguson is the absolute peak among jazz trumpeters. With astonishing ease and assurance, he plays things other trumpeters would consider impossible.

Most of all he does not just scream and screech when playing at skyscraper heights; even up there he hits each note accurately and phrases musically. Not until the end of the seventies did he meet with a real competitor in this field: *Arturo Sandoval*, who lives in Cuba and plays in the Irakere big band.

Dizzy Gillespie based his style of playing on the instrumental achievements of Eldridge and on the stylistic contributions of the other bop pioneers: antipodal to Armstrong and yet only comparable to him in power and brilliance. Gillespie, too, has been discussed in a special chapter.

Just as all trumpeters of traditional jazz come from Armstrong, so do all modern trumpeters stem from Gillespie. The four most important in the forties were Howard McGhee, Fats Navarro, Kenny Dorham, and young Miles Davis. The early death of *Fats Navarro* was as lamented by the musicians of his generation as Bunny Berigan's and Bix Beiderbecke's passing had been mourned by the musicians of the Swing and Chicago periods. Fats' clear, assured playing was a forerunner of the style practised by the generation of hard bop since the late sixties, combining the melodic arcs of Miles Davis with the fire of Dizzy Gillespie. In his autobiography, *Beneath the Underdog*, Charles Mingus makes Fats Navarro into an emblematic figure of modern jazz.

Miles Davis began as a Dizzy imitator, just as Dizzy had begun by imitating Eldridge. But he soon found his own, completely new style. Miles is the founder and chief representative of the second phase of modern jazz trumpeting: lyrical arcs of melody, in which the sophistication of simplicity is admirably cultivated, even less vibrato than Dizzy – and all this with a tone less glowing than loaded with coolly smouldering protest. After Davis, the development of jazz trumpeting is contained in the interplay between Dizzy and Miles, frequently spiced with a shot of Fats Navarro (into whose place Clifford Brown later stepped). *Kenny Dorham* (who died in 1972) proved himself to be a musician in this mould who by no means received the recognition due his talent.

Chet Baker, Johnny Coles, and Art Farmer are all stylistically close to Miles Davis, but only Chet was directly influenced by Miles. Baker played his way to sensational success with his solo on 'My Funny Valentine', recorded in 1952 with the Gerry Mulligan Quartet. For a short time he dominated all jazz polls. His phrasing is so supple that he occasionally was chided as 'feminine'. In the course of the sixties, however, Baker developed into a trumpeter with a gripping attack, who impresses with the logic and form of his improvisations. Since the Gerry Mulligan–Chet Baker cooperation was reconstructed for a Carnegie Hall concert in 1976, Baker has been enjoying something of a comeback. On muted trumpet, *Art Farmer*, who lived mostly in Europe for many years, combines liquid mobility with soulful expressiveness and strong jazz feeling. Art – and along with him *Johnny Coles* – are the only modern trumpeters who can equal the lyrical intensity of Davis without imitating him – in their own unmistakable ways. And it is indeed illuminating that just these two trumpeters, who are above any attempt at copying Miles, come closer to him in expressiveness than all the many musicians directly influenced by him. Art Farmer also emerged in 1952 from the same Lionel Hampton band which brought to light the most highly praised trumpeter next to Miles Davis: *Clifford Brown*, who died in 1956 in a tragic automobile accident. 'Brownie', as he was called, further developed the playing style of Fats Navarro. In many respects, he – and, of course, Navarro – are the 'fathers of the hard-bop trumpet.' The black musicians untouched by cool jazz had continued to play bop in the first half of the fifties. Only hardly anybody took notice. It was Brownie's success that initiated the breakthrough of hard bop. After his untimely death, a Clifford Brown myth developed, comparable to the Beiderbecke legend. And Brown's influence became noticeable again, even more strongly, at the end of the seventies with the rise of neo-bop.

The musical experience of cool jazz in the first half of the fifties and the vitality of the bop of the forties merged in hard bop. *Donald Byrd, Thad Jones, Joe Gordon, Lee Morgan, Bill Hardman, Nat Adderley, Benny Bailey, Carmell Jones, Idrees Sulieman, Dizzy Reece, Ira Sullivan*, Yugoslavian *Dusko Gojkovic, Ted Curson, Woody Shaw, Blue Mitchell, Booker Little*, and *Freddie Hubbard* and all trumpeters in this mould. Of the younger generation, *Hannibal Marvin Peterson, Bobby Shew, Wynton Marsalis, Tom Harrell, Charles Sullivan, Jimmy Owens, Eddie Henderson*, the Japanese *Terumasa Hino, Jack Walrath* (who became known through his work with Charles Mingus), *Cecil Bridgewater*, and *Jon Faddis* (who brilliantly reminds one of Dizzy Gillespie) belong to this type of player. Some of them moved away again from the orientation towards hard bop in the course of the years, or developed it in other directions. Many of them share the overriding influence of John Coltrane – the younger they are, the more strongly.

Donald Byrd combined a certain academic solidity with so much professional flexibility that he became one of the most frequently recorded trumpet players of hard bop. In the seventies, he was successful in 'funk jazz', even though many critics objected to it. Byrd is one of the great teachers of jazz. *Thad Jones*, an exceptional arranger, was co-leader of the Thad Jones–Mel Lewis Big Band from the late sixties. He stems from the Basie Orchestra, and he blew some of his first remarkable solos in the then 'experimental'-sounding Jazz Workshops of Charles Mingus. Since the early eighties, he has lived in Copenhagen, Denmark, sounding even more mature than when he was a busy studio musician in New York. *Lee Morgan*, who died in 1972, and *Joe Gordon* worked with Dizzy Gillespie's big band in the mid-fifties. Morgan, who as an eighteen-year-old was featured extensively by Dizzy, became (as a member of Art Blakey's Jazz Messengers) a frequently recorded hard-bop musician. *Carmell Jones*, who comes from Kansas City, plays tender, sensitive trumpet lines with a charm and amiability that scarcely any other trumpeter of this often so angry and protest-laden generation has matched. Carmell was in the Horace Silver Quintet for some time, but his conception did not blend very well with its funk and soul-oriented music. Since 1965, he has made his home in Berlin.

Among other creative jazz trumpeters living in Europe is *Benny Bailey*, who has won many friends with his great, full sound – a true trumpet stylist and, in addition, one of the best lead trumpeters one could wish for in a big band. If Bailey were living in New York, he would probably be as busy as Clark Terry, because his particular combination of inimitable improviser and perfect studio and section musician is rare.

Terumasa Hino gave up a successful career in his native Japan in order to live in New York. In Japanese, *hino* means 'burning from a fire within', and that's the way he plays. No other trumpeter born outside the United States can compare with his power and his 'blast'. In the course of the seventies he became interested in jazz–rock. *Hannibal Marvin Peterson*, who was first presented by Gil Evans, has mastered the entire range of jazz from Bessie Smith to Coltrane with so much energy and fire that the *New York Times* dubbed him 'Muhammad Ali of the trumpet.'

The development of the trumpet, as far as it took place within 'tonal' jazz, brought little that was new until the early eighties – aside from a further, often astounding perfection of the fire of bop. After the much too early death of the very promising *Booker Little* in 1961 (who had made some of his most beautiful recordings with Eric Dolphy), *Freddie Hubbard* and *Woody Shaw* became by far the best-known representatives of this way of playing. Hubbard is the most brilliant trumpeter of a generation of musicians who stand with one foot in hard bop and the other in fusion music. He played as inspiredly in Max Roach's ensembles as (for example) in a studio band Friedrich Gulda put together, as well as on numerous records under his own name which vividly reflect the development of jazz from hard bop through free playing of the sixties to the electric sound of the seventies. Many critics have deplored the stereotyped character of Hubbard's jazz–rock and fusion productions. For years, he kept wavering between making convincing jazz music and more commercially oriented records. Woody Shaw, on the other hand, has been going his own way without making compromises. At the turn of the seventies, he is probably the most inspired trumpeter of hard bop.

When you realize how many young musicians have turned to the new bebop, it becomes clear how strongly their generation is fascinated by it. Among the most interesting trumpeters in this mould are young *Tom Harrell* and *Wynton Marsalis* (who was presented first by Art Blakey, later by Herbie Hancock); and some bebop trumpeters of the middle and older generation have also unexpectedly found new attention, among them *Red Rodney* and *Ira Sullivan*. Sullivan (who also plays tenor saxophone) has a particularly vital feeling for the music of Charlie Parker. Rodney was already on the scene with some of the great big bands of the forties – Jimmy Dorsey, Gene Krupa, Woody Herman.

Now, let's move on to free playing; to do so we have to go back in time. *Don Cherry*, the groundbreaking, free brass-player, blows a cornetlike 'pocket trumpet' – more or less a child's trumpet. When he became known in the late fifties as a member of the Ornette Coleman Quartet, he seemed to most critics merely a good friend of Ornette's who also happened to play the trumpet. Since then, he has become a 'poet of free jazz' of great, intimate, glowing expressiveness, commended even by so strict a critic as Miles Davis. Since the mid-sixties, Cherry has been living in Europe, where he has made notable achievements – in a twofold sense. On the one hand, he created particularly unusual realizations of new large-orchestral jazz that excel over all other attempts in this direction with their melodiousness and charm. On the other hand, he became an exponent of 'jazz meets the world' – of the incorporation into jazz of elements of the great exotic musical cultures. Cherry assimilates Balinese, Indian, Tibetan, Arabic, and Chinese elements – often not only on his trumpet, but also on various flutes and other instruments.

The immensity of Cherry's importance is illustrated by the fact that all other free-jazz trumpeters stood in his shadow for years – *Lester Bowie*, *Clifford Thornton* (who has made a name for himself on the valve trombone, too), *Dewey Johnson*, *Bobby Bradford*, *Leo Smith*, *Butch Morris*, and *Raphe Malik* among the black musicians; *Don Ellis* and *Mike Mantler* among the whites; and *Toshinori Kondo* among the Japanese.

Ellis, who died in 1978 and who became known in the late fifties as a member of George Russell's sextet, scored a sensational success at the 1966 Monterey Festival, where he introduced his new big band. He played a custom-made 'quarter-tone trumpet' which allows for the finest tonal nuances (before him, the Czech trumpeter *Jaromir Hnilička* had already employed such an instrument, stimulated by the quartet-tone music of Czechoslovakian composer Alois Hába). *Mantler*, who hails from Vienna, made his name mainly as leader of the New York Jazz Composers Orchestra and as collaborator of composer (and pianist) Carla Bley. *Lester Bowie*, who grew out of the avant-garde circles in Chicago (the so-called AACM – Association for the Advancement of Creative Musicians), often sounds like a 'Cootie Williams of the avant-garde' with his expressive solos, sometimes on the muted instrument. He once said: 'The history of our music does not just go back to 1890 or to New Orleans. It goes back thousands of years! We try to express this with our music.'

The rediscovery of tradition moves straight across all playing styles. It can be felt in neo-bebop as much as in free playing. *Bobby Bradford* and *Leo Smith*, for instance, both from the old blues state of Mississippi, sound reminiscent of their home state even in their freest excursions. Bradford, who mostly plays cornet, became known in California as the partner of clarinetist John Carter. Leo Smith (he, too, a composer in search of new sounds) co-led a group with German bassist Peter Kowald in the early eighties.

It is interesting how many connections exist between American trumpeters of this direction and many of their European colleagues. The most important are *Kenny Wheeler*, *Harry Beckett*, *Ian Carr*, and *Marc Charig* in Britain; *Enrico Rava* in Italy; *Tomasz Stańko* in Poland; *Manfred Schoof* in West Germany; hard-bop-oriented *Franco Ambrosetti* in Switzerland. Of these musicians, Wheeler has the biggest name and the largest musical range: from free jazz to the aestheticized playing of the sort that many jazz fans connect with the output of ECM Records. Enrico Rava is a master of coloratura playing – certainly in the Italian tradition – with a love for Brazilian music. Tomasz Stańko is a truly unique figure. He is one of the very few trumpeters in the world who give solo concerts – without a rhythm section – with an impressive wealth of expressions and sounds. Ian Carr became known for the intelligent, harmonically exciting ensemble sound of his group Nucleus.

Among the trumpeters who have incorporated rock elements, *Randy Brecker*, *Eddie Henderson*, *Lew Soloff* (in the early seventies, with Blood, Sweat & Tears), *Chuck Mangione*, and Danish player *Palle Mikkelborg* require special mention. *Doc Severinsen*, known among the mass audience as a television personality, has tried on some of his big-band records to open the concept of the classic big jazz orchestra towards contemporary rock. Mangione, with his catching, effectful music, is successful particularly on the American college and university circuit. Randy Brecker – also an outstanding fluegelhorn player – became known through his work in Art Blakey's Jazz Messengers and in the Horace Silver Quintet. He probably is the trumpeter best versed in a technically complex kind of electric jazz; and he is one of the busiest New York studio musicians, so he really knows about 'jazz-rock': 'Playing trumpet is often difficult in rock because you have to compete with all that electricity ... Certain elements of jazz have come to rock, but rock people still can't improvise on the level of a jazz artist. As a jazz musician, you feel like yourself. As a rock musician, you feel like a star.'

The Trombone

The trombone began as a rhythm and harmony instrument. In the early jazz bands it was hardly more than a 'blown bass'. It supplied an additional harmonic background for the melody instruments –

trumpet and clarinet – above which they could move, and it stressed the rhythmic accents. In big bands, the trumpets and trombones form the 'brass section' which stands opposite the 'reed section', the saxophone group. Both, brass and reeds together, form the 'horn section', whose counterpart and partner is the 'rhythm section'.

In view of the substitute-bass role the trombone had to play in the marching bands of early New Orleans, it can be said that the style of the first jazz trombonist worth mentioning was already a sign of progress. This style is called 'tailgate'. The name stems from the fact that the trombonist took up more space than other musicians on the 'band wagons' – the carts on which the bands rode through the streets of New Orleans on festive occasions – and had to sit as far back as possible, on the tailgate. There he had room to work his slide. The tailgate position made possible effective, glissandolike fills placed between the melodic phrases of the other horns. *Kid Ory*, who died in 1973, was the most important representative of this style.

A trombonist of very personal conception within the New Orleans tradition is *Charlie Green*. Bessie Smith liked his accompaniments – as in 'Empty Bed Blues' – which gives an indication of his style: blues trombone. He was a kind of Tommy Ladnier of his instrument.

George Brunies is an important early white trombonist. He was in the New Orleans Rhythm Kings, and his contribution can best be evaluated when one compares the trombone parts in the NORK recordings with those of the Original Dixieland Jazz Band. While the ODJB trombone functions almost exclusively as a bass, in the NORK it plays a subordinate but definitely important part in the Dixieland counterpoint ensemble.

The first jazz musician to play musically conceived, expressive, and melodically rich solos on the trombone was *Jimmy Harrison*, who died in 1931. Critics have called him the most important trombonist in the realm of the older styles. He was one of the leading soloists in Fletcher Henderson's band. And he was the first to at least come close to, if not yet attain, the biting sound of the trumpet on the trombone.

Miff Mole is in many respects a white 'counterpart' of Jimmy Harrison. Perhaps he lacked the former's mighty inspiration, but he was a flawless technician, and the white musicians of the day were made aware by his playing rather than Harrison's of the fact that the trombone was about to achieve 'equal rights'. Miff's trombone was an important voice in the Original Memphis Five led by Phil

Napoleon, and along with the latter and Red Nichols, he made up the 'triumvirate' of memorable New York-style brass musicians.

The Chicago-style trombonists were also influenced by Mole – for instance, *Tommy Dorsey* and Jack Teagarden. Dorsey evolved in the thirties into the 'Sentimental Gentleman', leader of a successful big band and eventually hardly a jazz musician anymore. Yet he always remained a player of great technical ability and soulful feeling. *Jack Teagarden* came from a Texas family which gave three other talented musicians to jazz. He was one of the few traditional jazz players who were especially respected by the cool jazz musicians of the fifties for his controlled, expressive sound and his supple lines. Bill Russo – a former Stan Kenton arranger and an excellent trombonist himself – praised him as 'a jazzman with the facility, range and flexibility of any trombonist of any idiom or any time; his influence was essentially responsible for a mature approach to trombone jazz.' Teagarden – or Big 'T', as he was called – was Louis Armstrong's favourite trombonist. Together, they played and sang on some of the most spirited and enjoyable duo-recordings in jazz. Both as singer and instrumentalist, Teagarden was a blues man – with a very modern, reflective attitude towards the blues.

There is a Duke Ellington group among the trombones as well, although they are not as closely related, stylistically, as the Ellington trumpets. These are *Joseph 'Tricky Sam' Nanton*, Juan Tizol, and Lawrence Brown. 'Tricky Sam' is *the* great man of growl trombone. *Juan Tizol* (co-author with Ellington of the famous 'Caravan', considered to be the first real Latin jazz tune, though there were already Latin elements in Jelly Roll Morton's 'New Orleans Blues' and in W. C. Handy's 'St Louis Blues' around the time of World War I) does not play the slide trombone – as do most important jazz trombonists – but the valve trombone. He plays it softly and sweetly, and occasionally becomes a trifle saccharine. His sound has been compared to that of a cello. *Lawrence Brown*, stylishly melodic and sometimes not very intense, is a musician of strong personal warmth with a preference for tuneful (sometimes almost sentimental) melodies.

Benny Morton, J. C. Higginbotham, Vic Dickenson, Dickie Wells, and Trummy Young are the great trombonists of Swing style. Their playing shares a vibrant vehemence. Morton, Wells, and Dickenson were all heard with Count Basie's band. Morton had previously worked with Fletcher Henderson; his playing has an intense, blueslike quality – something on the order of a Swing fusion of Jimmy Harrison and Charlie Green. *Dickie Wells* has been described as a musician of 'romantic imagination' by André Hodeir. He is a romanticist not in the sense of overblown pathos but in terms of a forceful, imaginative sensitivity. Much of this romanticism is contained in the incomparable vibrato of his trombone sound.

J. C. Higginbotham, who died in 1973, was the most vehement, powerful trombone of the Swing period – his tone sometimes reminiscent of the earthy, tight sound known in the twenties as 'gutbucket' trombone. Sometimes he played with an abrupt explosiveness, as if the trombone had been struck rather than blown. *Vic Dickenson* has a lusty, pleasing sense of humour which sometimes seeps into even his slow solos. With his appealing and singable ideas, he is among those Swing musicians who – across all boundaries of style – enjoyed a remarkably active career well into the seventies. Dan Morgenstern once wrote about Dickenson: 'When he picks up his trombone he tells you a story that's personal through and through. His horn seems to be an extension of his body. The complete ease with which he masters it makes the instrument, which actually is a bit cumbersome, appear like the embodiment of elegance . . .'

Trummy Young is to the trombone what Roy Eldridge is to the trumpet. From 1937 to 1943 he was one of the principal soloists in the Jimmie Lunceford band. His 'Margie' was a particular success from that period. Louis Armstrong brought Trummy Young into his All Stars in 1952 as the replacement for Jack Teagarden. With this group Trummy popularized – and sometimes banalized – his style.

Directly linked to Trummy Young – and in terms of tone related to the vehement verve of Swing trombonists like Benny Morton or J. C. Higginbotham – is the trombonist who created modern trombone style and remains its personification: *J. J. Johnson*. Before discussing him, we must mention a white trombonist, *Bill Harris*, master of a brilliant virtuoso technique. Harris was a member of Woody Herman's band from 1944 to 1946, again from 1948 to 1950, and later played with Herman again from time to time. His solo on 'Bijou', recorded with Herman in the mid-forties, was the most admired trombone solo of the time. His personality was marked by the contrast between the piercing, springy style of his fast work and the polished, studied vibrato of his slow solos. The contrast is so pronounced one might think two musicians were involved, if one did not know that Harris, with his slightly professorial looks, was responsible for both. Next to J. J. Johnson, Harris, who died in 1973, was for years the strongest influence on trombonists.

J. J. Johnson became to trombonists what Dizzy Gillespie is to trumpet players; what he plays is not just bop trombone but also 'trumpet-trombone'. He plays his instrument with that brilliant glow long associated with the trumpet; no other trombone player before him accomplished this feat. Contrast to this the muted playing of J. J.: earthy, tight; reminiscent of Charlie Green's blues trombone but with all the mobility of modern jazz. Johnson went through the same development as Gillespie: from the nervousness of bop to great sobriety and quiet sovereignty. J. J., also an outstanding arranger, went to Hollywood in the late sixties to start a new career as film and television composer and arranger. When bebop returned in the late seventies, he started again to play solo trombone – even *more* mature and mellow than during the period of his great success. This maturity shows in his statements, too: 'A change in art shouldn't take place for novelty's sake, as in fashion. New styles in music or painting or poetry should result from a new style of thinking in the world. The next style in music will come from the heads and hearts of real artists and not from opportunists.'

Kai Winding is the white counterpart of J. J. Johnson. Independent of J. J., he found a style often so reminiscent of J. J. that time and again they were mistaken for each other. It must be counted among the marvels of jazz that two musicians as different as Winding and Johnson should have arrived at similar styles. Kai, born in Denmark, was a member of Benny Goodman's band and later came to the fore through his playing with Stan Kenton; thus he was first and foremost a big-band musician. J. J. Johnson, from Indiana, black, combo-man of the bebop groups, came to the fore through his playing on 52nd Street.

In 1954–55 the two joined forces in the two-trombone combo, Jay and Kai, which turned out to be pretty much the opposite of what had been expected: that a group in which the only two horns were the same – and, moreover, played in similar style – would be colourless and monotonous. Actually, the charm of this two-trombone combo was specifically rooted in the many colours created by the two trombonists, with the aid of a whole arsenal of mutes employed in the most artful combinations.

Ten years later – among the musicians of hard bop – *Curtis Fuller*, Jimmy Knepper, Julian Priester, Garnett Brown, and Slide Hampton (also notable as an arranger) are especially worthy of mention. Fuller is particularly typical of the Detroit generation of hard bop. *Jimmy Knepper*, associated for many years with Charles Mingus, blows a 'piercing', vital trombone style in which Swing and bop elements are equally alive. Knepper and *Garnett Brown* are all-round trombonists who master everything from conventional big-band work to avant-garde experimentation. *Julian Priester* became known primarily through his work with the pianoless Max Roach Quintet of the sixties. In the seventies, he played with Herbie Hancock, as did Garnett Brown, who had begun with George Russell in the early sixties and was a brilliant soloist in the Thad Jones–Mel Lewis Band. *Slide Hampton*, with his octet of 1959, 'modernized' the classic Miles Davis Capitol band of 1949, giving it a touch of soul. For years Slide lived in Europe, playing in the most diverse groups, from quartet to big band. He was connected with the great tenorman, Dextor Gordon, in a very fruitful cooperation that initially took place in Europe in the sixties. Ten years later, in the United States, Slide Hampton was also the man behind the most impressive mass trombone effort in jazz so far: his 'World of Trombone', recorded in 1979, with no fewer than nine excellent trombonists, among them Janice Robinson and Curtis Fuller.

J. J. Johnson and Bill Harris had an almost inestimable influence on all trombonists who came after. *Frank Rosolino* stems primarily from Johnson. His typically Italian feeling for effects, his temperament, and his sense of humour often stood out in Stan Kenton's 1953–54 band. In his countless appearances and recordings, he remained a bebop man until his tragic death in 1978. *Carl Fontana* plays without Frank's striving for effects, but with great flexibility and feeling for harmonic subtleties. He, too, is a big-band musician and emerged from the bands of Kenton and Woody Herman. Further trombonists of this line are *Frank Rehak* and *Eddie Bert* – the latter a particularly temperamental Bill Harris-influenced improviser.

Redak, Bert, Al Grey, Bill Watrous, and, most of all, *Urbie Green* are flexible trombonists, able to cope with any style or demand – the 'Vic Dickensons' of modern jazz. Urbie, who became known through his work in the Benny Goodman band of the fifties (during which stint he often 'stood in' for Benny) has said: My playing has been compared to almost every trombonist who ever lived. The reason probably is that I had to play in so many different styles – Dixieland, lead á la Tommy Dorsey, and later, modern jazz . . .' To this flexibility, *Al Grey* adds the aspect of humour which has always had an especially live tradition among the trombonists – from 'tailgate style' through Vic Dickenson and Trummy Young up to Albert Mangelsdorff and Ray Anderson, whom we will discuss later. Grey is a big-band veteran: from Benny Carter and Jimmie Lunceford to Lionel Hampton and Dizzy Gillespie up to Count Basie.

Particularly individual was *Willie Dennis*, who died in 1965. He emerged from the Tristano school and was the actual trombone exponent of the Tristano conception. Since he formed most of his notes with his lip, he did not have to move his slide very much, and in this way he achieved a fluidity on the slide trombone which few others have approximated even on the valve trombone. In addition, his tone gained much in singing grace.

Among the most significant trombonists of the sixties are *Jimmy Cleveland*, the above-mentioned Curtis Fuller, and Bob Brookmeyer. Cleveland is a 'super J. J.', whose brilliant tromboning often seems almost explosive, especially since this explosiveness is combined with the fluency of a saxophone in the most natural way.

Valve trombonist *Bob Brookmeyer*, on the other hand, is a man of modern Lester Young classicism, who 'cooled off' the tradition of his home town, Kansas City, in quite a remarkable way. With Jimmy Giuffre, he recorded an album entitled 'Traditionalism Revisited' which demonstrates the classicist position: the jazz tradition viewed from the standpoint of modern jazz. Here famous old jazz themes – such as Louis Armstrong's 'Santa Claus Blues' and 'Some Sweet Day', King Oliver's 'Sweet Like This', Tommy Ladnier's 'Jada', and Bix Beiderbecke's 'Louisiana' – are transported into the world of modern jazz. Like J. J. Johnson – and many other bop and cool musicians – Brookmeyer enjoyed a comeback with the emergence of neo-bop in the late seventies.

Among the trombonists of the younger generation who carry on, refine, and play the J. J. Johnson tradition in a contemporary way are *Janice Robinson*, *Bruce Fowler*, *Tom Malone* (who plays thirteen instruments besides the trombone), and *Jiggs Whigham*, who lives in Europe, heading the Jazz Department of the Cologne Music Academy. *Wayne Henderson*, *Glen Ferris*, and Brazilian *Raoul de Souza* have taken this playing style into jazz–rock, funk, and fusion, in many records that are highly electronicized.

In free jazz, *Grachan Moncur III*, *Roswell Rudd*, and *Joseph Bowie*, among others, gained prominence – all musicians who widen and inflect the sound spectrum of their instrument, including noise elements in their music. *Roswell Rudd* deserves special attention in this field as he has a certain Dixieland and blues approach to his tonally free excursions. Through the vocal qualities Rudd incorporates in his playing, he discovered the folk music of the world: 'Suffice it to say that vocal techniques I had associated at one time only with the jazz singers of my own country were revealed to be common to the oldest known musical traditions the world over. What I had always considered the epitome of musical expression in America, the blues, could be felt everywhere in the so-called "folk world".' Roswell Rudd, who is also an excellent college teacher, says this in a *down beat* article with the fitting title 'The Universality of the Blues'. Rudd is connected with soprano saxophonist Steve Lacy in a particularly fruitful partnership. Characteristically, both got into free playing directly from Dixieland, skipping the stages in between.

Actually, the trombone scene – more so than any other instrument, with the exception of the clarinet – had atrophied during the sixties. Some of jazz's best trombone players, among them J. J. Johnson, Kai Winding, and Bill Harris, were practically absent from the scene. In the jazz polls, no instrument had fewer entries than the trombone. In this situation, European trombone players, somehow, took over: *Paul Rutherford* in Great Britain, *Eje Thelin* in Sweden, and, most important, *Albert Mangelsdorff* in West Germany. They developed new styles of playing, creating a lively, flourishing trombone scene again.

Mangelsdorff emancipated the long lines of alto player Lee Konitz – under whose influence he began in the fifties – in a gradual and seemingly necessary process, becoming ever freer harmonically, until they were – in the exact sense of the word – 'freed'. Since the beginning of the seventies, Mangelsdorff has been developing a technique which permits him – as the first trombonist in jazz – to play 'chords' on his instrument. By blowing one tone and simultaneously singing another, lower tone, Mangelsdorff gives the vocal tone the sound quality of the trombone. In addition to these two tones, Mangelsdorff creates – simultaneously! – three-, four-, and five-tone chords by playing with the overtone scales generated through the friction between the blown and the sung tones. This conscious use of overtones is a specific discovery of the free jazz of the sixties – it occurred especially among the saxophonists, where overtones (as for tenorists Pharoah Sanders, Dewey Redman, and Albert Ayler) frequently became more important than the *de facto* blown tones.

Mangelsdorff made many of his best records with important American drummers like Elvin Jones, Alphonse Mouzon, and Shannon Jackson. In his long solo appearances – without rhythm section – he manages to keep audiences attentive to his music through the wealth of his ideas and sounds. Since the sixties, his name constantly appears in the leading spots of the American jazz polls – even though he does not live in the United States. (Generally, Europeans achieve this kind of recognition in America only if they decide to live there.) In 1980, Mangelsdorff was voted the world's best trombonist in the annual *down beat* 'critics' poll'.

Many musicians feel that the European trombone scene is richer than the American one. In Sweden, Eje Thelin reached a mature soloistic and chord-filled trombone style similar to, but independent of, Mangelsdorff. Among the younger trombone players, particular mention is due the West German *Günther Christmann*, the Dutch *Willem van Manen*, and the East German *Connie Bauer* – and Japanese, bop- and fusion-oriented *Shigeharu Mukai*.

In the seventies, the trombone scene was revitalized in America in the realm of contemporary mainstream mainly through *Bill Watrous*; in free jazz especially through *George Lewis*, who was first introduced by Anthony Braxton. Watrous blows with fantastic power and brilliance and with astounding technical virtuosity. Lewis, who belongs to the AACM, has studied philosophy, especially the German philosophers Heidegger and Husserl. The level of abstract thinking required for that can also be felt in his music. Lewis is also interested in electronic sounds: 'With the synthesizer, you have a whole new source of available sounds, rhythms, timbres, and colours. It's just a matter of organizing them rhythmically. I want to be able to do everything with it on the same level as on my trombone . . .'

Another powerful trombonist to become known during the seventies is *Ray Anderson*. He, too, was first presented by Anthony Braxton, but lacks his abstractness. Anderson, a strong player of gripping melodic lines, reminds us that one element has been more important in the history of the jazz trombone than in that of any other instrument – and it certainly has been part of the nature of the trombone from the start: humour.

The Clarinet

In all stages of jazz development, the clarinet has been a symbol of interrelation. The function of the clarinet in the old New Orleans counterpoint, filling in the space between the contrasting trumpet and trombone, and entwining them like ivy, is characteristic for its position. Not coincidentally did the clarinet have its greatest period during the Swing era, when jazz and popular music were largely identical.

Alphonse Picou (1879–1961) is the first clarinetist from New Orleans whose style has become known. His famous chorus on 'High Society' is one of the most copied solos in jazz history. Down to this day, almost every clarinetist who plays 'High Society' is quoting Picou – just as every trombonist who plays 'Tin Roof Blues' is quoting from George Brunis's solo with the New Orleans Rhythm Kings, or playing it entire.

The second important clarinetist from old New Orleans is *George Lewis* – though his influence was felt much later, in the New Orleans revival of the forties and fifties. Lewis (1900–68) participated in New Orleans jazz life from the time he was sixteen. In the thirties, he worked on the docks until the New Orleans revival movement in the forties carried him to world-wide fame. In the music recorded by George Lewis then and in the fifties – initially with trumpeter Bunk Johnson, later with his own bands staffed with the best New Orleans-style musicians – the listening public, which was inundated with amateurish or commercialized New Orleans and Dixieland records, was reminded of the really authentic New Orleans jazz. Lewis's tenderly fragile clarinet playing, as in his classic 'Burgundy Street Blues', on his many long, world-wide concert tours, found admirers in many countries, including Japan.

It points up the multiple layers of jazz development that the great triumvirate of the jazz clarinet, *Johnny Dodds-Jimmie Noone-Sidney Bechet*, preceded Picou and Lewis in recording, while in a certain sense building musically and stylistically on their way of playing. Picou, Lewis, and, of course, Bechet, actually were merely the final representatives of a style cultivated in old New Orleans by many other Creole clarinetists. As late as 1964 – on the island of Martinique, the centre of the large French Creole area that originally reached from Louisiana in the north to French-Guyana in the south –

I heard an eighty-year-old man play at a fair who sounded virtually like Sidney Bechet, and yet he had never heard the name of that great clarinetist. On the other hand, Bechet, when he came to Paris and was introduced to music from Martinique, played many pieces of Martiniquan folk music as if they were – as they really actually could be – old Creole dances from New Orleans.

But back to the triumvirate: Dodd-Noone-Bechet. Noone is best known for the gentleness and subtlety of his tone. Compared to him, the improvisations of Johnny Dodds seem almost wild and brutal. Dodds – a master of the lower register of his instrument – was Louis Armstrong's preferred clarinetist during the time of the Hot Five and Hot Seven recordings. Bechet, finally, of whom we shall speak again in the soprano chapter, is the embodiment of the jazz *espressivo*. The strong, moving vibrato of his clarinet produced a sound recognizable even to the jazz layman. In France, where Bechet lived during his final years (he died in 1959), he was as popular as any *chanteur*. And even when much in his playing seemed to have become mannered, it was one of the especially moving human experiences in jazz to see this white-haired, dignified man from old New Orleans play amid the young Dixieland existentialists in Saint-Germain-des-Prés.

In Paris, too, *Albert Nicholas*, the last great New Orleans clarinetist, made his home (he later moved to Switzerland, where he died in 1973) – playing in a clearly 'clarinetistic', technically masterful style which in the fifties became somewhat Bechetlike, yet always retained that wealth of ideas and mobility which Bechet often seemed to have lost in the final years of his life. Nicholas – also a Creole – emerged from the orchestras of King Oliver and Luis Russell, while the Bechet of the twenties is primarily represented by records made with the Clarence Williams Blue Five. In the thirties Bechet recorded with his own New Orleans Feetwarmers. Among his most important clarinet recordings are those he made with pianist Art Hodes in the forties.

Nicholas – along with Omer Simeon and Barney Bigard – belongs to what might be called the third generation of the jazz clarinet. *Omer Simeon* was Jelly Roll Morton's favourite clarinetist, while *Barney Bigard* became known mainly through the flowing, supple solos he recorded as a member of Duke Ellington's band from 1928 to 1942, and with Louis Armstrong's All Stars from 1946 to 1955, as one of the few jazz musicians who spent considerable time with both of these giants. Bigard, who died in 1980, was a sorcerer of melody – playing with strong feeling and with dynamics almost equal to those of Benny Goodman.

Bigard, though indebted to the New Orleans tradition, in his great period already belonged among the Swing clarinetists. Before going on to these, we must recapitulate the history of the white jazz clarinet. It begins with *Leon Roppolo* of the New Orleans Rhythm Kings, that famous white group of the early twenties. Roppolo is one of the Beiderbecke types so frequent in jazz who seem to burn themselves out in their music and their lives. The most important of his successors in the realm of Chicago style are *Frank Teschemacher*, Jimmy Dorsey, and Pee Wee Russell. All three played with Bix Beiderbecke. Teschemacher, who died in 1932, loved to connect and smear his notes – perhaps subconsciously feeling that this would make him sound more like a black musician. He was a great influence on the young Benny Goodman. *Jimmy Dorsey* rose to fame with his big band, which he led from the thirties on, and through his collaborations with his trombonist brother Tommy, which were frequently interrupted by fights. Jimmy had a certain influence as a clarinetist, and perhaps even more as an alto saxophonist, due to his technical assurance and craftsmanship. Charlie Parker, for example, always had praise for Jimmy Dorsey – showing that touching tendency to overrate technical ability so frequent among musicians. *Pee Wee Russell*, who died in 1969, preferred the lower registers of the clarinet. He played with a vibrato and way of phrasing which puts him in a similar relationship to Lester Young and Jimmy Giuffre as Bix Beiderbecke seems to be to Chet Baker. Willis Connover dubbed him 'the poet of the clarinet.'

Finally, *Mezz Mezzrow*, a musician who gained renown through his friendship with the French jazz critic Hugues Panassié, must be mentioned among the Chicago clarinetists. From the standpoint of technique, he was mediocre, and as an improviser often had to limit himself to stringing triads together. Still, he played with a feeling for the blues surprising in a white musician of his generation.

'The race,' Mezzrow wrote, 'made me feel inferior, started me thinking that maybe I wasn't worth beans as a musician or any kind of artist, in spite of all my big ideas.' Mezzrow's most important contribution is not so much his clarinet playing as his autobiography, *Really the Blues*, in which the flavour of Chicago in the twenties, and even more, of Harlem in the thirties and forties, has been so well captured that even Henry Miller expressed his enthusiasm. Though white, Mezzrow again and again described himself as a Negro, and on the several occasions when he was put in jail, he insisted on being placed in the black section. For a while he made his living selling marijuana in Harlem, and he described the effect of the drug with an exceptionally powerful language and on a high literary level. The philosophy of his book is one of unbounded vitality: 'That was what New Orleans was really saying – it was a celebration of life, of breathing, of muscle-flexing, of eye-blinking, of licking-the-chops, in spite of everything the world might do to you. It was a defiance of the undertaker. It was a refusal to go under, a stubborn hanging on, a shout of praise to the circulatory system, hosannas for the sweat-glands, hymns to the guts that ache when they are hollow. Glory be, brother! Hallelujah, the sun's shining!'

It may be part of the instrument's nature that traditional jazz elements have stayed alive for the clarinetists way into the seventies and eighties, much more so than for most players of other instruments. This is true, for instance for *Bob Wilber*, initially inspired by Bechet, and for *Kenny Davern*. Both combine the warmth of traditional playing and a contemporary kind of elegance. Wilber once said: 'I felt then [in the fifties] and even more so now that there's a *oneness* about jazz. Style shouldn't be a barrier between musicians.'

But back to the thirties: The clarinetist of whom the layman thinks first when jazz clarinet is mentioned is *Benny Goodman*. He, too, stems from the circle of Chicago style. He is the 'King of Swing' whose scintillating and polished clarinet playing is the reason why the clarinet and the Swing era are largely synonymous. 'B. G.' – as he is known – is one of the great stylists of jazz, a musician of superlative charm, spirit, and gaiety. His clarinet playing is associated in equal degrees with his big-band recordings and those he made with various small combos: from the Benny Goodman Trio, with Teddy Wilson at the piano and Gene Krupa on drums, through the quartet in which Lionel Hampton first found public recognition, to the Benny Goodman Sextet in which guitarist Charlie Christian helped pave the way for modern jazz. In terms of expression, Goodman accomplished on the clarinet almost everything other instruments could not achieve until the advent of modern jazz. But he did this – and here is the heart of the matter – without the harmonic finesse and rhythmic complexity of modern jazz. This may be one reason for the disadvantageous position occupied by the clarinet in modern jazz. On the other hand, 'B. G.' is a master of subtleties. His dynamics range smoothly – as those of no other clarinetist – from softest pianissimo to jubilant fortissimo. Particularly astonishing is the skill with which Goodman manages to play even the softest notes and still – even when playing with a big band – capture the attention of the listeners in the very last row of a large concert hall.

Other well-known clarinetists of the Swing era were *Artie Shaw* and *Woody Herman*, both of whom had big bands to celebrate their clarinets in Goodmanesque fashion. *Jimmy Hamilton*, *Buster Bailey*, and, indirectly, Edmond Hall were also influenced by Goodman, as were all clarinetists who played alongside and after him – except Lester Young and the modern clarinetists who stem from him. Hamilton has played solos with Duke Ellington which are softer and more restrained than even Goodman. If the theories of the jazz-racists were correct, one would have to conclude – comparing Hamilton and Goodman on purely aural evidence – that the former was white and Goodman black, though the opposite is true. During the fifties, Hamilton evolved into an important clarinet voice in modern jazz, and it is regrettable that his name was so rarely mentioned in the same breath with Buddy DeFranco, Tony Scott, and Jimmy Giuffre. Perhaps this is because Hamilton, as a member of the Ellington band, was overshadowed by so many better-known Ellington soloists: Harry Carney, Johnny Hodges, etc. Two other good clarinetists of the Duke Ellington Orchestra were *Russell Procope* and *Harold Ashby*, whose main instruments, however, are alto and tenor saxophone, respectively.

Edmond Hall, who died in 1967, was the most important black Swing clarinetist and – alongside Benny Goodman – the towering Swing stylist on this instrument. He had a sharp, biting tone which often stands in contrast to Goodman's suppleness. During the forties and fifties, Hall played with Eddie Condon's New York Dixieland bunch. *Peanuts Hucko*, a clarinetist who plays 'dixielandish Benny Goodman,' also belonged to this group.

It is indicative of the organic rightness of jazz evolution that the approaches to the playing of different instruments have evolved on a parallel course. Nearly every instrument has its Roy Eldridge or Charlie Parker. The 'Eldridge' of the clarinet is Edmond Hall; the 'Parker' of this instrument became *Buddy DeFranco*, the first clarinetist who could outdistance Benny Goodman in terms of technique. He is an improviser of vital force – which led impresario Norman Granz to team him with Lionel Hampton and other great Swing musicians on numerous recordings. The brilliance of his playing is of such clarity it has sometimes been regarded as 'cold'. It is one of the paradoxes of jazz that the playing of so 'hot' and basic an improviser as DeFranco should have impressed so many listeners as 'cold'. It symbolizes the difficult, almost hopeless situation of the clarinet in modern jazz that so brilliant a musician as DeFranco finally resigned himself to taking over the direction of the Glenn Miller Orchestra '. . . for reasons of economic survival . . . playing tiresome music and adding nothing to his own development,' as Leonard Feather put it. In 1973, he left the band to try jazz once again, with relatively little public success.

It does not contradict Buddy DeFranco's position as the 'Charlie Parker of the clarinet' to point out that a European musician was the first, strictly speaking, to play bebop on the clarinet. This was the Swede *Stan Hasselgard*. Benny Goodman made him a member of his sextet in the spring of 1948, the only clarinetist he ever tolerated alongside himself. A few months later – in November of the same year – Hasselgard was fatally injured in an automobile accident. Hasselgard was the second European jazz musician of stylistically creative consequence. The French gypsy guitarist Django Reinhardt, who had a considerable influence on almost all jazz guitarists between the late thirties and the late forties, was the first.

After DeFranco's 'coldness', the 'warmth' of *Jimmy Giuffre* seemed even stronger. Initially, Giuffre played almost exclusively in the low register of his instrument – the so-called Chalumeau register. He has on occasion pointed out that he did this because he was technically unable to do anything else. In fact, making the transition from low to high register fluently is the greatest problem involved in playing this instrument.

Giuffre's technical handicap became a stylistic identification. The dark warmth of his playing at last seemed to embody what had been missed for so long: a modern clarinet conception somehow corresponding to the 'Four Brothers' sound of the tenor saxophonists. But Giuffre played his clarinet much as *Lester Young* had played his twenty years before – on the few recordings Pres had then made on this instrument: in 1938 with the Kansas City Six, and around the same time with Count Basie's band. Many experts do not doubt that Lester, had he played it more often, would have become as important on the clarinet as he was on the tenor. Lester himself said he played clarinet so rarely mainly because he could not find an instrument that suited him.

The paradox of the situation is that cool jazz actually has only two clarinetists whose playing corresponds to the cool conception in a narrower definition: Lester Young and Jimmy Giuffre; whereas among the tenor saxophonists the Lester Young sound was multiplied to such a degree that Lester Young, the tenor man, seemed to be living in a world of mirrors. Indirectly, however, a few tenor men have extended the cool Lester Young-conception when occasionally playing clarinet: *Zoot Sims*, *Buddy Collette*, and others. But this was usually perceived only as a surprising side effect, not as a genuine style – as, for example, Sims's way of playing tenor. Much later – in the early seventies – a musician who had come to attention through Miles Davis's 'Bitches Brew', *Benny Maupin*, reminded us on clarinet and bass clarinet that the quiet balance of the Lester Young heritage can be particularly attractive even among the electronicized contemporary jazz sounds.

But back to Giuffre. During the second half of the fifties, he moved away from his preference for the low register of his instrument – probably because the success of his dark-toned playing forced him to play clarinet so much that he overcame his technical handicap. By the sixties and seventies, finally, Giuffre stood out as a sensitive musician of a cool free jazz, with a restrained, chambermusiclike conception.

A further level of abstraction of clarinet playing – almost bordering on a flutelike sound – was reached by *John La Porta* and *Sam Most*. As early as the fifties, both were considered avant-garde, before the free jazz of the sixties had shown to what limits the avant-garde concept could go in jazz. La Porta, also an exceptional arranger, won high acclaim through his work in American jazz education.

Two other important musicians who took up the struggle with the difficult position of the clarinet in jazz are the German *Rolf Kühn* and the American *Tony Scott*. From 1956 to 1969, Kühn lived in the United States, and John Hammond called him 'a new Benny Goodman' then. Leonard Feather found that 'Kühn had the misfortune to enter the jazz scene at a time when his chosen instrument had suffered an apparently irreversible decline in popularity. Had it not been for these circumstances, he might well be a major name in jazz today.' In the sixties and seventies, Kühn incorporated a lot of modern impulses, at first from Eric Dolphy and later elements of fusion music.

Tony Scott is a true 'jam session' musician, one of the few still extant, with an immense drive to play – and, above all, with the 'loudest sound of all clarinetists' (Perry Robinson). He is a genuine clarinetist who feels the music through his horn, undisturbed by the unfavourable stylistic situation of the instrument. 'I don't like funerals,' said Scott when it seemed in the late fifties that the jazz clarinet was finally laid to rest. 'That's why I went to Asia.'

In Asia, Scott inspired and trained dozens of musicians. What all those 'Americans in Europe' – the American musicians who today live in every large and in many smaller towns of Europe – accomplished together, Scott achieved almost alone in the much more extended Asian territory. From Taiwan to Indonesia, from Okinawa to Thailand, he passed the message of genuine jazz on to a whole generation of young jazz musicians. Since the beginning of the seventies, Scott has been living in Rome.

Of course, the dilemma of the clarinet – that it simply didn't seem to fit into the 'saxophonized' sound of modern jazz – was not solved by Scott's flight to Asia. A solution was initiated by the great avant-gardist *Eric Dolphy*, who died in Berlin in 1964 – however, not so much on clarinet as on bass clarinet.

Never before has the bass clarinet been a true jazz instrument. Dolphy turned it into one – with searing, wild emotional expression and also with a physically immense power that gave his listeners the feeling that he was not playing the traditional bass clarinet, which had always appeared somewhat old-fashioned, but rather a totally new instrument that had never been heard before. (Harry Carney, baritone saxophonist with Duke Ellington, and a few others had occasionally used the bass clarinet in more conventional contexts.)

Dolphy's way of playing bass clarinet quickly found followers, more so in Europe than in America. Dutchman *Willem Breuker*, Briton *John Surman*, German *Gunter Hampel*, Luxembourgian *Michel Pilz*, Frenchman *Michel Portal*, and Italian *Gianluigi Trovesi* have been playing bass clarinet – some of them clarinet as well – with Dolphy's conception, yet with their own individual styles. Hampel, who spends about half of the year in Germany, the other half in New York, is a master of complex interwoven filigree – on the bass clarinet as well as on several other instruments (flute, vibraphone, piano) with his own group. Breuker alienates the popular music of the nineteenth century – polkas, operettas, waltzes, marches, tangos, and Dutch folk music. He has been called a 'Kurt Weill of jazz'. Trovesi studied prebaroque medieval folk and dance music, combining this knowledge with his love for jazz.

American musicians to mention in this context are *Doug Ewart*, *L. D. Levy*, *Walter Zuber Armstrong*, and *David Murray*. Levy became known through his convincing duo records (on bass clarinet, alto sax, and flute) with bassist Richard Davis. Ewart was the partner of, among others, George Lewis and other AACM musicians. Murray, a member of the World Saxophone Quartet, has written some outstanding music for theatre and plays off and on Broadway.

Beyond that, the mainstream of jazz in the seventies became as important among clarinetists as among players of other instruments. Musicians belonging to this field are *Bobby Jones* (who died in 1980), *Eddie Daniels*, and *Roland Kirk* (about whom more in the chapter on tenor sax). Jones, who came to the fore through his work with Charles Mingus, occasionally seemed like an 'Edmond Hall of the seventies,' with Hall's swinging expressiveness, but with greater, more contemporary mobility. Daniels tends towards a healthy, contemporary bebop, which he plays with virtuoso perfection.

In the fusion field, *Tom Scott* and *Alvin Batiste* have realized clarinet sounds of interest from a jazz point of view. Particularly unique is Batiste's work with the electric clarinet, full of recollections of the great old New Orleans clarinet players.

Let's finally return to free playing, citing *Anthony Braxton*, *John Carter*, *Michael Lytle*, and *Perry Robinson*. Multi-instrumentalist and composer Braxton creates iridescent, abstract lines on the different instruments of the clarinet family, which many listeners perceive as complicated and which yet have brought him world-wide success. Even though John Carter was a Texas companion of Ornette Coleman, he did not become known until the seventies, when the clarinet showed the first signs of being revitalized, first in Europe, then in America. He is a jazz chamber musician of free tonality whose playing has solid roots in the great tradition of the jazz clarinet. A man of the most recent generation, in contrast, is Michael Lytle, who is part of the Creative Music Studio in Woodstock, New York. The most radical clarinet player of his generation, he produces sounds with his instrument which even to the specialist sound anything but clarinetlike; and yet he unearths a hidden lyricism from the collages and clusters of his music.

Last but not least we should mention the musician who today comes first to mind when contemporary clarinet playing is discussed across all styles: *Perry Robinson* has played with the Jazz Composers Orchestra; with Roswell Rudd, Charlie Haden, and Sunny Murray; with Gunter Hampel and Dave and Darius Brubeck – and all these names illustrate his universality. Universality is different from versatility. Unlike Eddie Daniels, Robinson is not a well-schooled, professional studio musician conversant with everything (which is not meant to be derogatory). He has joined the different styles and playing techniques of free and cool jazz, bop, Swing, and rock into the new style that is the style of the seventies and eighties: 'We want to be able to play any kind of music, yet we want to be ourselves . . . The clarinet, it's incredible, because you have these different sounds. The only frustrating thing about it that has to be overcome somehow is that it's too small; it won't carry the weight when you're trying to get through. That's why, when I went into the energy playing on clarinet, I made a study of it, and I learned a lot of things about sound, about overblowing. Like the need to express ourselves is sometimes such an urge, but there's other ways, the psychic ways, of breath control, thinking big, and thinking way out there.' (Perry Robinson in an interview with Bob Palmer.)

The Saxophones

The ideal jazz instrument is an instrument that can be as expressive as the trumpet and as mobile as the clarinet. The instruments of the saxophone family combine these two qualities, which are in extreme opposition where most other instruments are concerned. That is why the saxophone is important to jazz. But it became important only at the start of the thirties. One can hardly speak of a New Orleans saxophone tradition – at least not to the same degree as with other instruments. The few saxophonists active in New Orleans were looked upon with the expressions reserved today for sousaphone or theremin players, regarded as odd characters rather than musicians. Generally, the saxophone belonged to sweet bands and popular dance music rather than jazz. During the days of Chicago style, things changed. It is noteworthy that the New Orleans Rhythm Kings were without a saxophone when they came to Chicago from New Orleans in 1921; yet when they obtained the engagement at Friar's Inn that was their springboard to fame, they were urged to include a saxophone. The saxophonist stumbled and staggered about amid the collective ensemble of the NORK, and never really found his place – and as soon as the band quit the job at Friar's Inn, he was let go.

Since no jazz tradition existed for the saxophone, the clarinet tradition had to do for jazz-minded saxophonists. The importance which the saxophone – primarily the tenor – has achieved in modern jazz immediately becomes clear when one realizes that at the outset of its jazz career, the saxophone was played more or less like a peculiar sort of clarinet, whereas since the fifties jazz clarinetists often have had a tenor-sax approach to their instrument.

The saxophones range downward from soprano (and sopranino) through alto, tenor, and baritone to bass (and contrabass). The most important in jazz are the first four.

Adrian Rollini played Dixieland and Chicago-style music on the bass sax with its hollow, somewhat burping sound – with great agility and basically with the same intention that motivated Boyd Raeburn to use the instrument as the lowest voice in the sax section of his modern big band: to give depth and bottom to the sound spectrum. Joseph Jarman and Roscoe Mitchell use the bass sax in free jazz, creating similar 'honking', exotic sounds as those produced at the beginning of the saxophone development in New Orleans on the other saxophones. Thus, there still is hope for the bass saxophone – and even for the huge contrabass instrument, which Anthony Braxton uses every so often.

The Soprano Saxophone

The soprano saxophone continues where the clarinet leaves off – because of its loudness, for one. It has the most disproportionate history of all instruments in jazz – even more disproportionate than the violin. In the beginning, there was only Sidney Bechet. Today, there are hundreds of sopranoists. A tenor man is no longer acceptable in countless big bands and studio orchestras if he does not double on the soprano. In fact, things have been somewhat reversed since the seventies: often the soprano became the main instrument and the tenor the second one.

For decades, we were told that soprano sax was used so rarely because of the difficulty in playing it 'clean'. Its overtone scales necessarily sound out of tune. Today, however, we know that this is the very advantage of the instrument: The 'dirtiness' of sound, which has been of great importance in all phases of jazz history, is an integral part of the soprano. One could almost say that the soprano tends to flatten each note, to turn it into a 'blue note', to turn the whole scale 'blue'. This is a tendency immanent from the start in folk blues and the archaic jazz forms. The three classical blue notes of jazz are compromises with the European harmonic system. Actually, the music of the African and Afro-American tends towards slanting each individual tone, towards not accepting a note as it is, towards reinterpreting each note as a personal statement. The soprano does all this in an exemplary manner: It 'Africanizes'. The thesis that this is its actual strength can even be verified in a test: There are sopranoists who have managed to produce 'clean' sounds in spite of all the technical difficulties of the instrument – *Lucky Thompson*, for example, who in the sixties transferred the perfect beauty of his tenor sound to the soprano. But he has remained relatively unsuccessful, in spite of the high degree of sophistication of his playing. He is admired, but fails to truly excite and move.

Sidney Bechet is the Louis Armstrong of the soprano saxophone – he has Armstrong's majestic expressiveness. During the span of his rich life, which led from the New Orleans of pre-World War I days to the Paris of the fifties, he changed – gradually at first, but then more and more decidedly – from clarinet to soprano sax. It has been said he did so because with advancing age the soprano became easier for him, since it requires less air for full-volume play. His main reason, however, was that the soprano makes possible a wider range of expression, and the maximum of *espressivo* was Bechet's main goal. For good reason he has been called the forefather of the great ballad tradition of jazz. For the outsider, this tradition begins with Coleman Hawkins's 'Body and Soul' in 1939. But actually, it began much earlier – with Sidney Bechet (and, of course, like all things in jazz, with Louis Armstrong!).

Bechet had only a few soprano students: *Johnny Hodges, Don Redman, Charlie Barnet, Woody Herman, Bob Wilber* – and in a certain sense, even in the Coltrane era, *Budd Johnson* and *Jerome Richardson*. They all applied their Bechet experiences to the stylistic periods to which they belonged. Hodges, the most famous soloist of the Duke Ellington Orchestra, was devoted to expressiveness in a way similar to Bechet. But the soprano solos he played with Ellington in the twenties and thirties seem pale compared to the power of his alto sound. Hodges gave up the soprano altogether after 1940. Perhaps he also felt that playing the soprano would always keep him somewhat in the shadow of the great Bechet, to whom he was indebted in many ways. Towards the end of his life, when the soprano sound became fashionable, Ellington wanted Hodges to give it another try, but there was not time. Hodges died in 1970.

When the black music tradition was rediscovered in the seventies, especially through the activities of the AACM musicians, interest in Sidney Bechet was renewed. Tenor man *David Murray*, for instance, recorded his 'Bechet's Bounce,' a convincing combination of the old Bechet styles and contemporary free sounds.

The close proximity between Hodges and Bechet in this aspect is made clear by Woody Herman: If he derives from Hodges as an alto player, he stems from Bechet as a soprano man.

We said that Bechet had only a few soprano students. But *John Coltrane*, too, is among Bechet's students on this instrument. I know from personal experience: Around the turn of the fifties into the sixties, Coltrane repeatedly had me send him soprano records by Bechet, especially from his French period, so he could study them. With his solo on 'My Favourite Things' in 1961, Coltrane created a sweeping breakthrough for the soprano saxophone (see also the chapter on Coltrane).

The development of the soprano saxophone again displays the continuity of growth so very characteristic of jazz: from New Orleans – from Sidney Bechet in this case – to the modern and complex creations of Coltrane and Wayne Shorter and to their 'students' and contemporaries.

Coltrane retained the expressiveness and 'dirtiness' of Bechet. But for Bechet's majestic clarity, which is reminiscent of Louis Armstrong, he substituted an Asiatic meditativeness. Coltrane's soprano sound calls to mind the shenai of northern Indian music, the nagaswaram of the music of southern India, and the zoukra of Arabian music. His soprano sound virtually demands modality – and it becomes particularly clear at this point what modality actually is: the equivalent in jazz to the 'modes' of Arabic music and the Indian ragas.

Without Coltrane's soprano work it is hard to conceive of the whole Asiatic movement in jazz – not only in the area of the soprano, but transcending to all other instruments. This is particularly true of those instruments which, since the sixties, have increasingly been incorporated into jazz or were imbued with a new approach: violin, flute, bagpipes, oboe, English horn, etc. In fact, we must say that these instruments were incorporated into jazz or experienced changes in approach precisely because Coltrane's way of playing the soprano became the great example.

Still, Coltrane was not the first to play a modern type of jazz on the soprano sax. The first musician to do so was *Steve Lacy*. We have already mentioned his peculiar development in the chapter on the trombone, in connection with Roswell Rudd. He moved from Dixieland directly to free jazz – bypassing the usual way stations of bebop and cool jazz. Quite to the contrary, he did not discover bop until after he had been playing free jazz. In 1952, he played Dixieland with musicians like Max Kaminsky, Jimmy McPartland, and Rex Stewart: in 1956, he played with Cecil Taylor; and in 1960, with Thelonious Monk. He is one of the few horn players – and probably the only white among them – who fully understood and assimilated Monk.

The stations of Lacy's development – Kaminsky, Cecil Taylor, Monk – indicate his originality. He is the first well-known sopranoist in jazz who made the soprano his main instrument right from the start. Accordingly, he did not derive his way of playing from the clarinet, tenor, or alto sax. Lacy, who lived in Paris from 1963 to 1980, stands outside the three main currents in soprano playing – Sidney Bechet, John Coltrane, and Wayne Shorter. To the best of my knowledge, he was the first to produce sounds by blowing 'in reverse': not by blowing into the instrument, but by sucking air 'backwards' through the horn. Many others have since adopted this way of playing.

Leonard Feather surmises that Coltrane first became interested in the soprano saxophone through Steve Lacy. This is suggested by the fact that before Lacy joined the Thelonious Monk Quartet, Coltrane had played with Monk. The club in which Monk then could be heard regularly was the Five Spot in New York, the meeting place of the in-group of jazz. No doubt Coltrane must have heard Lacy there.

'My Favourite Things', as we have said, became a hit. Soon, big bands and studio orchestras jumped on the soprano bandwagon. The range of the saxophone section was extended. Some arrangers became specialists in incorporating soprano sounds into this range: Oliver Nelson, Quincy Jones, Gil Evans, Gary McFarland, Thad Jones, and, later, Toshiko Akiyoshi.

The soprano not only took up the legacy of the clarinet - in a certain sense it was also heir to the tenor saxophone. Since free jazz, many tenor men love to 'overblow' their instruments in a way reminiscent of the falsetto sound of blues and gospel vocalists - driving into the range of the alto and soprano sax. In this way the tenor becomes 'two or even three instruments in one': tenor, alto, and even soprano. This tendency to play 'high' has always been part of jazz. A hot way of playing is frequently achieved by playing 'high' - in a way which prompted the German ethnomusicologist Alphons Dauer to suspect that the term 'hot' actually was derived from the French *haut* - high. It is obvious that the overblown tenor saxophone is a very ecstatic, intensive instrumental sound on the one hand, but that it is musically rather limited on the other. No doubt, the soprano continues where the overblown tenor leaves off. In this way a tenorist who overblows his instrument and also plays the soprano commands the entire range, from the lowest tenor tones to the flutelike heights of the overblown soprano saxophone. Thus it is no surprise that there is a host of soprano players who were initially specialists of falsetto tenor, among them *Pharoah Sanders, Archie Shepp, Roscoe Mitchell, Joseph Jarman, Sam Rivers,* and Englishman *John Surman* (whose main instrument at first was the baritone, and who first used the soprano only as a 'falsetto baritone' - until he made an increasingly decisive switch from baritone to soprano). Further discussion of the musicians whose main instruments are tenor, alto, or baritone, will be found in the chapters dealing with those instruments.

Other important soprano saxophonists after Coltrane are altoists *Oliver Nelson, Charlie Mariano,* Britisher *Barbara Thompson, Jerry Dodgion,* and *Cannonball Adderley,* who died in 1975 (all of whom often realize typical alto phrases on the soprano sax); and tenor players *Dave Liebman, Steve Grossman, Roland Kirk* (who included among his instruments the sopranolike manzello), *Jerome Richardson*, *Budd Johnson*, *Carlos Garnett*, *Azar Lawrence*, *Zoot Sims*, *René McLean*, *Joe Farrell*, *Sam Rivers*, and – most important – *Wayne Shorter* (who influenced many of those named above).

Shorter, who came out of one of Art Blakey's Messenger groups, became known as *the* saxophonist of the Miles Davis Quintet from 1964 to 1970. 'In a Silent Way' of 1969 was the first record on which he played soprano. Apparently, he and the producers thought this to be such a minor point that not even the personnel identifications on the record indicate his soprano contribution. But the jazz world immediately noticed and listened. 'Bitches Brew', produced a year later, is unthinkable without Shorter's soprano sound. Shorter aestheticized Coltrane's legacy. Miles + Trane = Shorter, that is: Shorter combines Coltrane's meditativeness with Miles's lyricism. His soprano sound has, in a way, the expressiveness described in the beginning of the chapter on Miles Davis: loneliness, forlornness, 'the sound floats like a cloud'. As a soprano player – but not as a tenorist! – Shorter ranks among the truly great improvisers in jazz: The tone alone implies the music and the complete musical personality of the improviser.

Shorter loves Brazilian music. One of his masterpieces is the transformation of 'Dindi' – one of the earliest bossa compositions, dedicated by Antonio Carlos Jobim to the late Sylvia Telles, the first singer of bossa nova – into an exciting, hymnal free-jazz excursion, which yet retains in every note some of the Brazilian tenderness. Shorter has been part of the most successful of all fusion groups from its beginnings in 1971: Weather Report. Amid all the electronics of this group, his characteristic sound is often hard to pick up, but Shorter definitely is a main force behind the soprano's rise to the spot of most favoured horn in jazz–rock and fusion music. Some of the musicians who have blown the soprano in records with fusion, rock, and funk music are *Ernie Watts*, *Tom Scott*, *Steve Marcus*, *Ian Underwood*, *Ronnie Laws*, *Grover Washington*, and, in Europe especially, *Barbara Thompson*, whom we have mentioned.

Some of these players, and even more so those belonging to free jazz, make it especially clear that the soprano comes closer to an 'African' sound and intonation than the other saxophones. Important free players to gain attention as sopranoists can be found mainly in and around the AACM: *Anthony Braxton*, *Joseph Jarman*, *Roscoe*

Mitchell, as well as *Oliver Lake* and *Julius Hemphill*. Occasionally, Jarman produces that typical growl sound which Sidney Bechet so movingly employed in the lower registers to create his blues and ballad renditions. Hemphill dedicated one of his works to the West African Dogon tribe, which lives in total seclusion in Upper Volta, making references not only to the music but also to the mythology of this tribe.

But the 'pure' Bechet legacy also remains alive, touched more by Swing than by Coltrane and Shorter. It is represented in an exemplary manner by *Bob Wilber* and *Kenny Davern*, on individual records as well as in their joint 'Soprano Summits' since 1975.

'Pure' soprano playing, in the vein of the contemporary aestheticism, is cultivated especially by Norwegian *Jan Garbarek* and by *Paul Winter*, but also in unaccompanied duos and chamber-musiclike formations by some of the musicians named above, as for instance Dave Liebman. Particular attention has been aroused by the clear and yet melancholy sound of Jan Garbarek, who is one of those European players who have also influenced American musicians - more so in fact than their European colleagues.

The Alto Saxophone

The history of the alto saxophone actually begins in the Swing period. To the clarinet triumvirate 'Jimmie Noone–Johnny Dodds–Sidney Bechet' of the twenties corresponds a trio of altos that set the pace for everything played on this instrument during the thirties: Johnny Hodges–Benny Carter–Willie Smith.

The Duke Ellington musician *Johnny Hodges*, who died in 1970, was a melodist of the rank of Armstrong or Hawkins. His warm, expressive vibrato and his way of melting notes in erotic glissandos made the Hodges sound one of the best-known instrumental signatures in jazz. Dark, tropical warmth seems to lie in this sound, which may occasionally approach sentimentality on slow pieces. At faster tempi, Hodges remained the great, gripping improviser he had been since joining Duke Ellington's band in 1928.

Among the many Hodges disciples, *Woody Herman* for many years was one of the best known. Herman still blows Hodges-inspired solos which stand in pronounced and sometimes amusing contrast to the more modern conceptions of the young musicians in his band.

Benny Carter is Hodges's opposite. Where the latter loves melancholy and earthiness, Benny Carter has a buoyant clarity and airiness. During the forties Carter settled in Hollywood, where he started a second career as arranger and composer for film and television studios. Carter is one of the most versatile musicians in jazz, of equal importance as alto saxist, arranger, and orchestra leader, and also a notable trumpeter, trombonist, and clarinetist. We shall have more to say about Carter in the chapter on big bands.

Willie Smith, lastly, who died in 1967, was a particularly powerful, strong and expressive improviser – and, in addition, an excellent lead saxophonist in big bands. In the thirties, Smith was a soloist in Jimmie Lunceford's band; his solo in Lunceford's 'Blues in the Night' was highly acclaimed.

The maturity of the Hodges–Carter–Smith constellation seems all the more astonishing when one considers how few notable alto players preceded them. There was *Don Redman*, who as an arranger had a great impact on the development of the big-band sound of the twenties and early thirties, and who played occasional alto solos with his bands; and then there was *Frank Trumbauer* among the Chicago-style musicians, who recorded with Bix Beiderbecke. Trumbauer did not play the E-flat alto, but its relative, the C-melody saxophone.

After the Hodges–Carter–Smith constellation the whole development of the alto saxophone is concentrated in one towering personality: *Charlie Parker*. In the chapter dedicated to him and Dizzy Gillespie, I have attempted to clarify his singular position. Parker's importance was so great initially that there was hardly another bop altoist worth mentioning. The sole exception was *Sonny Stitt*, who vacillated between alto and tenor, and who – strangely enough – developed independently of Parker a Bird-like alto style of great clarity and bluesy expressiveness.

There was one realm which stayed relatively free from bebop way into the fifties: 'Jump' – a style of playing (and dancing!) popular in Harlem and other big city ghettos. Three of its outstanding players were alto saxophonists: *Earl Bostic*, *Pete Brown*, and *Johnny Hodges*. The latter was – mainly in those few years of his career when he was not a member of the Ellington band – a player of dynamic Jump rhythms, as in records with organist Wild Bill Davis. In the late forties, long before the great rock 'n' roll era, Bostic scored hits of rock 'n' roll proportions with his 'Flamingo' and other records. And Pete Brown found a way of playing in which the contrast between old-fashioned staccato and the modern conception is unintentionally – and sometimes intentionally – humorous.

While all the other instruments during the great days of bop produced important musicians in addition to the leading representative on the respective horn, the alto saxophone had to wait for the start of the cool era for a considerable figure to emerge: This was *Lee Konitz*, who came out of the Lennie Tristano school. The abstract, glittering alto lines played by Konitz around the turn of the forties on his own and Lennie Tristano's recordings later became more singable, calmer, and more concrete. Of this change, Lee says that then 'I played more than I could hear'; he'd feel better when 'I really can hear what I'm playing'. In the meantime, Konitz has absorbed and incorporated into his music many of the jazz elements since then – and some of Coltrane and of free jazz – and yet he has always remained true to himself. He is one of the really great improvisers in jazz. In the seventies he gained special attention with a unique nonet.

After Charlie Parker and Lee Konitz, the development of the alto saxophone takes place in the interplay between them. *Art Pepper* found his way towards a mature, Parker-influenced style of deep emotionality. Pepper, who has spent more time in jails and reformatories than outside them, is an especially distressing example of the disastrous effect that heroin has had on the lives of some jazz musicians. He tells about it in his autobiography, *Straight Life*, which appeared in 1979 and initiated his comeback. The book is a moving document of the depressing conditions under which so many jazz musicians have to live.

Paul Desmond, who died in 1977, was a particularly successful figure of the Konitz line as altoist in the Dave Brubeck Quartet – and surely the most significant jazz talent in this well-known group: a lyricist of the alto sax.

The most significant altoists of West Coast jazz were Bud Shank, Herb Geller, and Paul Horn. *Shank* was one of the first jazz musicians to play with one of the great masters of classical Indian music. As early as 1961 he was recording with sitar master Ravi Shankar. *Herb Geller*, who moved to Germany, has much of the clarity of Benny

Carter, but of course it is a Carter style that is touched by what came afterwards, especially by Bird.

The power of Parker's personality gains full clarity when it is realized that the 'Bird-influence' – after the ideas originating with Konitz had been digested – did not recede during the late fifties, but rather increased steadily: *Lou Donaldson* with his strong blues emotions; *Leo Wright*, who used to play with the Dizzy Gillespie Quintet and now resides in Germany; *Cannonball Adderley*, who until his death in 1975 was highly successful with the soul and funk-inspired music of his quintet; *Jackie McLean*, who joins Parker's blues feeling with a 'freer', less restrained expressiveness; *Sonny Criss*, who combined the archetypical world of the old blues tradition with that of Charlie Parker; *Charles McPherson*, who stems from the Detroit hard-bop circle; *Gigi Gryce* and *Oliver Nelson*, who are also outstanding arrangers (Nelson died in 1975); and, finally, *Frank Strozier* and *James Spaulding*, who both mark the transition to free jazz – all of them have, in the final analysis, their roots in Charlie Parker. This is true of *Phil Woods*, too: No other altoist transformed the Charlie Parker heritage so consistently into contemporary jazz. Swiss critic Peter Rüedi called him (in 1972) 'the most complete alto player in today's jazz.' It is significant to note that this completeness is shaped by the awareness of all the way stations Woods passed through in twenty-five years: Lennie Tristano's institution, Jimmy Raney's cool jazz, George Wallington's bop, Dizzy Gillespie's and Quincy Jones's big bands . . .

While Bird's way of playing still dominated the scene, *Ornette Coleman* appeared at the Lenox Jazz School, which was under John Lewis's direction, in the summer of 1959. In the chapter devoted to him, the musical revolution this towering musician instigated is discussed in detail. The fact that he – as is true of all genuine innovators – did exactly what was 'in the air', is significantly illustrated by other musicians taking similar roads at about the same time, or just after him, without being directly influenced by him. Among the alto saxophonists in this group, we should particularly mention *Eric Dolphy*, who died in 1964, but whose influence still affects the scene of the eighties. Dolphy (who based his playing somewhat more on functional harmonics than Coleman) came out of Chico Hamilton's and Charles Mingus's groups and made recordings of lasting value with the late trumpeter Booker Little and with his own groups. With his emotionally charged intonation and the wild, free flight of his ideas, he created effects on a par with those of Ornette Coleman.

The breakthrough created by Ornette Coleman and Eric Dolphy had an especially liberating effect on the alto players. Among the first to be affected were *John Tchicai*, *Jimmy Lyons*, and *Marion Brown* (who combines the virtuosity and the clarity of a man like Benny Carter with the possibilities of free jazz) – followed by *Byard Lancaster*, *Mark Whitecage*, *Carlos Ward*, and *Ken McIntyre*, as well as, more or less connected with the AACM scene, *Anthony Braxton*, *Joseph Jarman*, *Roscoe Mitchell*, *Oliver Lake*, *Julius Hemphill*, *Henry Threadgill*, *John Purcell*, and *Dwight Andrews*. Brown's development is typical: from a 'wild' free player when he entered the scene in the mid-sixties to a musician who now commands the entire stylistic range of his instrument. Dan Morgenstern wrote of Oliver Lake that he sounded 'like Dolphy into Hodges'. Hemphill, on the other hand, could be called a 'multimedia man' among the alto players; he collaborates a lot with actors and dancers, with film and video and theatre. Jarman and Mitchell are founding fathers of the Art Ensemble of Chicago (which will be mentioned in the Combo chapter). The former has combined his improvisations with modern black poetry; the latter developed into an outstanding solo performer on unaccompanied alto saxophone.

Having similarly wide stylistic range in their playing are the following non-Americans: Japanese players *Akira Sakata* and *Kenjo Mori*, Englishmen *Trevor Watts* and *Mike Osborne*, and South African *Dudu Pukwana* with his exciting combination of Bantu music and Bird.

More than anyone else, *Anthony Braxton* has introduced thousands of people all over the world, who would never have heard such sounds without him, to the music of the jazz avant-garde. As we have mentioned in our chapter about the seventies, he was the first free player to attain commercial success.

Braxton's main instrument is the alto saxophone, but he also plays clarinet, sopranino, bass clarinet, contrabass clarinet, flute, alto flute . . . Says Braxton: 'I consider myself a composer first and an instrumentalist second.'

Anthony Braxton the jazz improviser comes from Charlie Parker and Paul Desmond; Braxton the composer has been shaped by Schoenberg, Anton Webern, John Cage – and Johann Sebastian

Bach: 'Listening to Desmond led me to Konitz. And listening to Bird led me to Ornette. And listening to Bach led me to Schoenberg. My thing has always been that I like a particular style of music as long as it keeps me interested . . .'

In fusion music, special attention has been attracted by *David Sanborn*, *Ian Underwood*, *Fred Lipsius*, as well as *Elton Dean* in Great Britain and *Sadao Watanabe* in Japan. The latter is a senior player of his instrument who has gone through its entire development, beginning with Charlie Parker, and has come to master it all.

Beyond all that, there also is a powerful mainstream movement of the alto sax, fed not only by Swing music, but also by bop and Coltrane. Some of its representatives are *John Handy*, *Sonny Simmons*, *Eric Kloss*, *Richie Cole*, *Gary Foster*, *Bobby Watson*, *Jerry Dodgion*, *Joe Ford*, *Arnie Lawrence*, *Sonny Fortune*, *Arthur Blythe*, and *Charlie Mariano*. Ford and Fortune came to the fore through their collaboration with pianist McCoy Tyner. Musicians like Kloss and Cole are timeless improvisers in line with the great saxophone tradition of jazz – as is Polish player *Zbigniew Namyslowski*. All these musicians are proof that 'Bird lives' – in the seventies as well as in the eighties. *Arthur Blythe*, who plays a particularly powerful alto, reveals a unique kind of Bird influence, but he also has been touched by Johnny Hodges and Ornette Coleman. He is an amazing musician with a moving expressiveness, from whom we will certainly hear a lot more in the future. Blythe is an especially convincing example of the phenomemon that today it is more often the 'traditionalists' than the avant-gardists who, in their own way, 'revolutionize' the scene.

The widest range of styles among all the alto players is commanded by Boston-born *Charlie Mariano* (which might surprise American readers, because, as Charlie puts it, 'My American career was finished when I went to Japan with Toshiko in 1962'). Mariano got his start in 1941, still under Johnny Hodges's influence. He played with Charlie Parker, initially forming his style in Bird's mould. In the mid-fifties, he played in the Stan Kenton band, in the early sixties with Charles Mingus. He moved to Japan with his then wife, Toshiko Akiyoshi; there, and in Malaysia and India, he studied and incorporated Indian music. Under the Coltrane influence and that of Indian wind instruments, he got into the soprano saxophone and studied the nagaswaram, a sort of Southern Indian oboe. Finally, in the early seventies, he moved to Europe, opening up to jazz–rock and fusion in its more demanding, musicianly varieties – a growth that has not stopped in forty years and most certainly will continue.

The Tenor Saxophone

'The best statements Negroes have made of what their soul is, have been on the tenor saxophone.' – Ornette Coleman

The evolution of the tenor saxophone is the reverse of that of the clarinet. While the latter begins with a wealth of brilliant names and then seems to ebb off into a decrescendo – albeit a wavy one – the history of the tenor sax is one imposing crescendo. At the beginning stands a single man. Today there are so many tenor saxists that it sometimes becomes difficult even for the expert to survey the subtleties which distinguish them. We have said before: the sound of modern jazz was 'tenorized' – which it actually was after Lester Young – until in the course of the late sixties it was 'guitaricized' and later 'electronicized'.

The single figure at the beginning is *Coleman Hawkins.* Until the end of the thirties, all jazz tenor playing took its cues from him: from his dramatic melodic structures, his voluminous sonority, and his rhapsodic improvisations. A Hawkins pupil then was quite simply anyone who played tenor. The most important are *Chu Berry, Arnett Cobb, Hershel Evans, Ike Quebec, Ben Webster, Al Sears, Illinois Jacquet, Buddy Tate, Don Byas, Lucky Thompson, Frank Wess, Eddie 'Lockjaw' Davis, Georgie Auld, Flip Phillips, Charlie Ventura,* and *Benny Golson.* Chu Berry came closest to the master. During the second half of the thirties – while Hawkins was in Europe – he was a much-sought-after musician, the man who first came to mind when a tenor was needed. One of his most famous solos was on 'Ghost of a Chance'. *Arnett Cobb* was a member of the Lionel Hampton band in the early forties. His playing can best be characterized by the way he was advertised after quitting Hampton: 'The Wildest Tenorman in the World.' *Hershel Evans* was Lester Young's opposite in the Count Basie Band. Though Lester was the greater musician, Evans played the most renowned tenor solo in the old Basie band: 'Blue and Sentimental.'

'Why don't you play alto, man?' Evans used to tease Lester. 'You got an alto sound.' And Lester would tap his forehead: 'There are

things going on up there, man. Some of you guys are all belly.' Basie
found the contrast between the styles of Lester and Hershel so
effective that he saw to a similar contrast in most of his bands from
then on. In his fifties band, for instance, these roles were taken by the
'two Franks': *Frank Foster* representing the 'modern' trend, *Frank
Wess* the Hawkins school. Later *Eddie 'Lockjaw' Davis* took Wess's
place. Davis is a typical 'Harlem' tenor, with hard, striking presence.
Later in his career, into the eighties, Foster gained fame as an
arranger and leader of a first-rate big band.

Before Hershel Evans, there was a tenor man in Count Basie's first
Kansas City band whose place he took: *Buddy Tate*. When Evans died
in 1939, Buddy returned to Basie. Later he dropped into comparative
obscurity, until the Mainstream wave of the fifties and sixties brought
him renewed attention. For many years, he led his own band in
Harlem, enriching the style of the classic Harlem big bands (as
played in the old Savoy Ballroom) with modern rhythm & blues
tendencies. Tate and Arnett Cobb, the two 'Texas Tenor Men', are
among the few musicians of their generation who even today – in the
early eighties – are still active.

Lucky Thompson is a master of sweeping, tuneful melodic lines. He
often worked with Charlie Parker, Dizzy Gillespie, Oscar Pettiford,
and other modern jazz musicians, and his improvisations unite, in a
very personal fashion, the best of both jazz tenor styles, Hawkins and
Young. *Don Byas,* who died in 1972, became known primarily for his
'sensuous' vibrato and ballad interpretations. He played with Basie,
was one of the first Swing musicians to work with the then young
bebop people, and made his home in Holland from the late forties on.

Ben Webster – who died in Europe in 1973 – was two things: a
musician with a throaty, harsh vibrato on fast pieces, and a master of
erotic, intensely felt slow ballads. Of all the musicians of the Hawkins
school, his has been the strongest influence – on many musicians of
modern jazz as well. In the early forties, Webster was a member of
the Ellington orchestra, with which he recorded one of his most
famous solos – 'Cottontail'. *Al Sears* took Webster's chair with
Ellington in 1943. His stylistic bent is indicated by a rhythm & blues
piece, 'Castle Rock', he wrote for Johnny Hodges, which became a
hit. Later *Paul Gonsalves* (who died in 1974) became Ellington's
featured tenor in the Webster tradition. Gonsalves's marathon tenor
displays were legendary: fast, torrid runs in flowing motion, almost

free from repeated notes and honks, yet more exciting – and musically more logical – than many solos played by tenor men whose honking ecstasy was outside the realm of music. Ellington took care to always have a musician who could take the spot of the great and, in the final analysis, unreachable Ben Webster.

A stylistic phenomenon is *Benny Golson*: a tenorist and arranger who emerged from the Dizzy Gillespie band of the mid-fifties and played with all the young modern musicians at the time. Nonetheless, he is cast in the mould of the rich, mature ballad style of Byas–Webster–Hawkins. 'Out of the Past' is the title of one of Golson's most beautiful pieces – and out of the past, full of sadness and long-lost magic, are his tenor improvisations and melodious compositions. In the past decade, relatively little – apart from a few appearances – has been heard from this 'romanticist of jazz'.

Illinois Jacquet, finally, is perhaps the 'hottest', most exciting musician of the Hawkins school. Long before the modern free-jazz tenorists, he was able to extend the range of his instrument into the extreme heights of the flageolet. Jacquet came from Lionel Hampton's band, where he played his famous solo on 'Flyin' Home'. He is also renowned for his triumphs with the early tours of Norman Granz's Jazz at the Philharmonic. Jacquet says: 'Granz owes the worldwide success of JATP to me!'

Georgie Auld, Flip Phillips, and *Charlie Ventura* are the leading white tenor men of the Hawkins school – the first two via Ben Webster. A substantial craftsman, Auld played more *à la* Pres with a medium-sized group at the height of the bop era; later, he made Jimmie Lunceford-inspired big-band recordings with more of a Hawkins orientation. For years, *Flip Phillips* was used as an effective crowd-pleaser with the Jazz at the Philharmonic troupe. But in Woody Herman's band in the mid-forties, and later also on records and in concerts, Phillips has played excellently structured ballads with a polished and 'reduced' Hawkins sound. *Charlie Ventura*, lastly, became known through the medium-sized groups he led on and off from 1947 into the fifties. During the bop era he performed under the banner of 'Bop for the People' and contributed much to the popularization of bop.

Bud Freeman, the tenor voice of Chicago style, who touched Lester Young in his earlier period, preceded Coleman Hawkins. Bud, still active in the early eighties, became the most compelling Dixieland tenor – a state of affairs which did not prevent him from studying with Lennie

Tristano in the fifties. *Gene Sedric* might be called a black counterpart of
Freeman, known from his playing on many Fats Waller records of the
thirties.

With these musicians we have for the present exhausted the
Hawkins chapter of tenor history. *Lester Young* became the great man
of the tenor in the forties, and particularly in the fifties, but then,
tension between Hawk and Pres has remained alive – to the degree
that a renewed predominance of the Hawkins tradition could be
detected among the tenorists of the Sonny Rollins school after the late
fifties.

What fascinates tenor players about Hawkins is, first of all, the big,
strong, voluminous tone. What fascinates them about Lester Young
are his lyrical, sweeping lines. Simplified, the tension that underlies
the history of the tenor sax is the tension between Hawkins's sonority
and Lester's linearity. This tension is already present in some of the
tenor players who have been mentioned as representatives of the
Hawkins line – Thompson, Byas, Gonsalves, Phillips, and Ventura.
To these must be added a group of tenor men who, stylistically
speaking, are firmly in the Lester camp, but show a noticeable
tendency towards the Hawkins sonority. *Gene Ammons*, who died in
1974, is the most important. The son of boogie-woogie pianist Albert
Ammons, he was in the Billy Eckstine and Woody Herman bands of
the forties and moved into the limelight through the 'battles' (those
popular contests between two practitioners of the same horn) he
fought with Sonny Stitt (on tenor!). He has the biggest, mightiest tone
outside the Hawkins school: 'Big as a house, a fifteen-storey apartment
dwelling, and very vocal, too,' says Ira Gitler, who goes on to
compare his playing with the blues singing of Dinah Washington.

Otherwise, the tenorists of the Lester Young school may be
grouped – in much simplified terms – in two sections: the musicians
who have linked Lester's ideas to the ideas of bop, and the school of
modern Lester Young classicism, in which the bop influence receded
in proportion to the youth of the musicians. The most important
tenorists of the 'Lester Young plus bop' direction are *Wardell Gray*,
James Moody, *Budd Johnson*, and *Frank Foster*, as well as the forerunners
of Sonny Rollins we shall mention later.

James Moody, altoist and flutist as well as tenor man, was one of the
more remarkable musical personalities of the bop era, often filled
with a rollicking humour that was replaced by maturity and

mellowness during the seventies. Dizzy Gillespie hired him for his quintet in 1960 and again in 1980. *Budd Johnson* emerged from the most influential big bands of the bop era – Earl Hines, Boyd Raeburn, Billy Eckstine, Woody Herman, Dizzy Gillespie – and was probably the only musician to play in all these great bands. Under this influence, he repeatedly reoriented his approach to playing to contemporary trends. Born in 1910, he belongs to the handful of musicians of his generation still to deal with the musical movements of the seventies and eighties.

Wardell Gray, who died in 1955 under mysterious circumstances (his body was found in the desert near Las Vegas), was a musician of supreme importance. He had Lester's linearity, the phrasing of bop, and his own distinctive hardness of attack and sparkling mobility, all joined in convincing stylistic unity. It is fitting that such genuine Swing musicians as Benny Goodman and Count Basie were attracted by Gray, but became aware of stylistic conflict when he began to play in their combos or bands. 'The Chase', that characteristically titled tenor battle recorded in 1947 by Gray and Dexter Gordon (who is of similar importance and will be discussed later), still ranks among the most exciting musical contests in the history of jazz.

It should be noted that, initially, there were only a few tenor players who could be considered bebop musicians (in a strict sense). Wardell Gray, James Moody, Sonny Rollins (in his early career!), Dexter Gordon, and Allen Eager were the only ones at the time. Lester Young's stature was still too great to allow a different development. Even a man like Sonny Stitt, who was – on alto – pure bop, clearly showed the Lester Young influence when he changed to tenor saxophone. In fact, up to the middle of the fifties, Lester's – not Charlie Parker's – importance for the tenor scene continued to grow!

Wardell Gray occupies a central position between the two tenor movements of the fifties: the 'Brothers', and the Charlie Parker school led by Sonny Rollins. In the former, Lester Young celebrated his real triumphs. The abundance of names belonging to this Lester Young classicism will be categorized according to the manner in which the Basie–Young tendency has made itself increasingly felt: At the beginning of our list the bop influence is noticeable – Allen Eager, Stan Getz, Herbie Steward, Zoot Sims, Al Cohn, Bob Cooper, Buddy Collette, Dave Pell, Don Menza, Jack Montrose, Richie Kamuca, Jimmy Giuffre, and Bill Perkins. A remarkably large segment of these musicians either have worked with Woody Herman or are more or less connected with the California jazz scene. That is where the 'Four Brothers sound' developed in 1947. 'We had a band,' *Stan Getz* tells, 'in the Spanish section of Los Angeles. A trumpeter named Tony de Carlo was the leader, and we had just his trumpet, four tenors and rhythm. We had a few arrangements by Gene Roland and Jimmy Giuffre.' Roland and Giuffre, in other words, created the 'Four Brothers sound'. The four tenors in this band were *Getz, Herbie Steward, Zoot Sims,* and *Jimmy Giuffre.*

At the time, Woody Herman was about to form a new band. He happened to hear the four tenors and was so taken with the sound that he hired three of them: Sims, Steward, and Getz. In place of the fourth tenor he put Serge Chaloff's baritone, to add warmth to the tenor combination. The new sound was made famous by a piece written for Herman in 1947 by Jimmy Giuffre. It was called 'Four Brothers' - whence the name of the sound. Along with the Miles Davis Capitol sound it became the most influential ensemble sound in jazz up to Miles Davis's 'Bitches Brew' - and even after that it remained effective. Its warmth and suppleness symbolized the sound-ideal of cool jazz.

In the years to follow, a succession of tenorists passed through the Four Brothers sax sections of various Herman bands. The first was Al Cohn, who took Steward's place as early as 1948. Then came Gene Ammons, Giuffre, and many others, down to Bill Perkins and Richie Kamuca (who died in 1977). Getz, who from the start of the 'Brothers' counted as the *primus inter pares,* made some combo recordings (for Prestige) in 1949 with Sims, Cohn, Allen Eager, and Brew Moore in which the Four Brothers sound was celebrated by five tenorists.

The following passage by Ira Gitler - a critic with particular affinity for the modern tenor scene - will give an impression of the fine distinctions among these tenor players: 'An excellent example of inner differences in a similar area can be found in examining the work of Zoot Sims and Al Cohn and comparing it to the playing of Bill Perkins and Richie Kamuca. In the broad sense, all would be considered modernists in the Basie-Young tradition, but Sims and Cohn, who were originally inspired by Lester Young, grew up musically in the forties when Charlie Parker was at his peak and his influence at its most powerful. Although they do not play like Parker, they have been affected somewhat stylistically and very much harmonically.

'Kamuca and Perkins (active from the fifties) who for inspiration go back to the Pres of the Basie period and also to the Brothers (Sims, Cohn, Getz) are only touched by Bird through osmosis from the Brothers, and since it is twice removed, the traces are intangible.'

The Parker traces are strongest in *Allen Eager*, as shown by the splendid, stimulating solos he played with the Buddy Rich big band around 1945. *Getz* is the towering figure in this school, an improviser in the sense of truly great jazz improvising and altogether one of the outstanding white jazz musicians. He is a virtuoso who can play anything possible on the tenor sax. It is this technical element that distinguishes him from most of his Brothers-colleagues and their sophistication of simplicity (which, in a sympathetic way, hides the fact that these players, too, are masters of technique!). Stan became known mainly through his ballad interpretations. Nonetheless, during the fifties, he had a Parker-inspired affinity for very fast tempos. Some of the most exciting recordings of his career were made in 1953 at the Storyville Club in Boston with guitarist Jimmy Raney, and at a 1954 concert at the Shrine auditorium in Los Angeles with trombonist Bob Brookmeyer. It is characteristic of a musician like Getz that he seems to unfold more freely in contact with a nightclub or concert audience than in the cold studio atmosphere.

In 1961, when bossa nova with its poetic, charming songs from Brazil entered the United States, Getz was introduced to this music by guitarist Charlie Byrd, just returned from Brazil. Initially with Byrd, later without him, he scored a number of great hits with Brazilian music.

It has been said so many times that Getz was 'inspired' by the bossa nova and that he 'owes everything' to it, that it is necessary to point out that earlier there had been a reverse influence: from cool jazz (where Getz has his roots) to the Brazilian samba. Only from the interaction between cool jazz and samba did the bossa nova emerge. Thus, a circle was closed when Getz 'borrowed back' (as he himself expressed it) Brazilian elements. This may be one of the main reasons for the fascination of his 'Brazilianized', melodic cool-jazz transformations, although some creative Brazilian musicians called these recordings 'falsifications' or 'bastardizations'. It is interesting to remember that the characteristic switch from the choralelike *cantilena* to intensely rhythmic passages, so typical of Brazilian music, also existed in a different form in Getz's cool improvisations from the early fifties on – long before the emergence of bossa nova.

Since the mid-sixties, after the bossa nova wave died down, Getz has been combining his classicist Lester Young legacy with some harder, more expressive ingredients, originating mainly in Sonny Rollins. The expressive range of this great jazz musician seems continuously to become even more universal and towering.

Zoot Sims is considered the most swinging of the Brothers. He is an untrammelled, vital improviser with a certain knack for emphasizing the upper ranges of his instrument, lending to his tenor an occasional alto sound; characteristically, he has played the alto, too; later, under the influence of Coltrane, he also played soprano with very personal inflections. *Al Cohn* mirrored the *conscious* turn towards Basie–Young classicism – not only in his playing but also as arranger and leader on many recordings. The little twists and turns he gives to his smooth Lester Young tone make his playing especially expressive. For several years Cohn and Sims co-led a two-tenor quintet which – within the confines of their similarity – gained attractiveness from their subtle dissimilarity.

Most of the remaining musicians on our list of Lester Young classicists are representatives of West Coast jazz. *Bill Perkins* plays perfect, beautifully felt Lester phrases one is tempted to call 'noble'. *Jimmy Giuffre*'s tenor playing has something of the quality of his clarinet – a great affinity for cool, 'distilled' blue notes. His is a Young classicism based on a keen knowledge of modern 'classical' chamber music and a deep love of folk melodies. *Buddy Collette* is one of the few black musicians in West Coast jazz – but his black roots are shown more by his alto playing, veering towards Parker, than by his relatively polished tenor sound. And *Don Menza,* who also is an excellent big-band arranger (for Buddy Rich, for instance), is among those who carried the 'Four Brothers sound' into the vicinity of Sonny Rollins.

There is a European who belongs in this illustrious list of otherwise American players: Austrian *Hans Koller.* He began in the early fifties in Lee Konitz's line, was impressed by Sims and Cohn, and later – through Coltrane – developed his own expressive conception.

Several musicians will not fit into either of the categories into which we have attempted to divide the Lester Young tenors. Among them are *Paul Quinichette*, Brew Moore, and Warne Marsh. Quinichette, who came out of Count Basie's band, was mentioned as a fascinating 'mirror-image' of Pres in the chapter on Hawkins and Young. *Brew Moore*, who died in 1973, also belongs in Lester's immediate vicinity – without the detour via modern classicism. *Warne Marsh* is a product of the Tristano school. Marsh has been said to play 'tenorized' Lee Konitz, but he does have his own fluid style, which has become so up-to-date again in the seventies and early eighties that Marsh has been able to attract much attention with his duet records with musicians many years his junior, such as Pete Christlieb and Lew Tabackin.

So far, it might seem as if the contest between the ideas of Hawkins and Young in the evolution of the tenor sax had ended with complete victory for Young. This picture became blurred in the course of *Sonny Rollins*'s overwhelming influence during the second half of the fifties. Rollins the improviser became so important one tended to mention him right after Miles Davis. Nonetheless, neither Sonny himself nor his way of playing were 'new' in the strictest meaning of the word. From 1946, he played with many important bop musicians: Art Blakey, Tadd Dameron, Bud Powell, Miles Davis, Fats Navarro, Thelonious Monk, and others. His style involves combining Charlie Parker lines with the voluminous sound of Coleman Hawkins – which Sonny developed into his very own, angular, edged, immensely individual sound – plus that slight Lester Young influence which hardly any tenor player since Pres can completely escape.

This combination, which appeared so novel in the second half of the fifties, was *comme il faut* during the bop years. Not only Sonny Rollins played that way then, *Sonny Stitt*, and, most of all, *Dexter Gordon* are musicians of this lineage, related in many respects to the previously mentioned 'Lester-plus-bop' line (James Moody, for instance). Gordon was *the* bop tenor man, with all the quicksilver nervousness belonging to bop. In 1944, in a recording of Billy Eckstine's big band ('Blowing the Blues Away'), Gordon and Gene Ammons founded the musical practice of 'battles' and 'chases' of which we have spoken already in this chapter. (More about Gordon is given later in this chapter.)

That Sonny Rollins nevertheless achieved primary importance so suddenly was due less to his innovations than to the temperament and vitality he brings to his improvisations – in short, to his stature. Thus, he can afford to treat the harmonic structures on which he improvises with an astonishing lack of constraint and great freedom, and often indicate melody lines only with widely spaced staccato notes, satirizing and ironicizing them in this manner. It is a freedom similar to that of Thelonious Monk's piano improvisations. Both Monk and Rollins are New Yorkers, and there's that typically quick and dry New York sense of humour in their music. 'Sonny Rollins fears nothing,' said the French tenorist Barney Wilen at a time when he was one of the many young musicians of the Rollins school.

This school remains alive in the eighties, too. Rollins, who visited India in the meantime and studied yoga and Asiatic religions, now makes most of his records in the fusion vein – which displeases the jazz purists. But that is his way of gaining a hearing also by a young audience, and he still displays his most important asset: his sound – and his (occasionally somewhat sarcastic) humour. His family has roots in the Caribbean. Again and again, he has composed and included in his music calypsos, and Latin themes and rhythms in general.

Before turning to John Coltrane and the musicians of his school, we have first to mention a number of tenor players who are more or less independent of both the Rollins and the Coltrane schools – even though some of them may, in the course of their careers, have received impulses particularly from John Coltrane. They are *Hank Mobley, J. R. Monterose, Johnny Griffin, Yusef Lateef, Billy Mitchell, Charlie Rouse, Stanley Turrentine, Booker Ervin, Teddy Edwards, Roland Kirk, Clifford Jordan, Bobby Jones, Jack Montrose*, and others.

Hank Mobley has a velvety tone which hangs like a veil over his long, seemingly self-perpetuating lines. *Stanley Turrentine* applies a 'rocking soul' approach to the 'jumping' lines of Ben Webster and Coleman Hawkins. The late *Booker Ervin* – who first became known through his association with Mingus – was one of the most solid improvisers of the early and mid-sixties with a marvellous wealth of blues-inspired and vehement swing. *Johnny Griffin*, with his melodic, humorous improvisations, has enthused many an audience.

Yusef Lateef stems from the Detroit circle of modern bop musicians. As early as the fifties, he became the first jazz musician to try to incorporate elements from Arabic and oriental musics into jazz – making inspiring, exciting recordings, on which he (aside from tenor) blows such instruments as diverse flutes of often exotic origin, and oboe and bassoon (used only rarely in jazz). *Harold Land*, who first became known through his work in the Max Roach–Clifford Brown Quintet that helped initiate the transition from West Coast jazz to hard bop in the mid-fifties, still is one of the most dynamic and freshest improvisers of California jazz. Most of these musicians have been active for a relatively long span – from the early fifties until today – proving that they are playing a kind of music that is, in the best sense of the word, 'timeless', independent of passing fashions.

And then, there is *Roland Rahsaan Kirk*: a blind musician who came to Chicago from Columbus, Ohio, in 1960, with three saxophones hanging around his neck, sometimes playing them all simultaneously – and, on top of that, a flute and about a dozen other instruments – blowing on a siren between choruses.

Kirk, whose death in 1975 was mourned by the entire jazz world, was one of the most vital, most communicative of the modern jazz musicians. He was like the old folk musicians who packed up their bundle and wandered through the world. And, no doubt, he was a symbol of many things that have occurred in jazz during these years: sophistication rising from roots, naïveté from a genuine childlike attitude, sensitivity from vitality. Said Kirk, 'People talk about freedom, but the blues is still one of the freest things you can play.'

For Kirk, jazz was 'black classical music'. In his compositions and improvisations, he deliberately elevated this tradition into a programme, not in the sense of historicizing backward looks, but quite to the contrary by incorporating it into the sounds of the seventies. A few times he played with pop and rock groups: 'I just want to play. I'd like to think I could work opposite Sinatra, B. B. King, the Beatles, or a polka band, and that people would dig it.' Roland Kirk has referred to so many of the great black musicians – Duke Ellington, Charles Mingus, Sidney Bechet, Fats Waller, Don Byas, John Coltrane, Clifford Brown, Lester Young, Bud Powell, Billie Holiday, etc. – that it may be said with special emphasis: Kirk played 'on' the black tradition as if it were an instrument. He said: 'God loves black sound.'

A distinction of many of these musicians – certainly of Sonny Rollins and Roland Kirk – is their relationship to rhythm. They play beyond the rhythm with the same free sweep that characterizes their approach to harmony; but since on the one hand they move far away from the basic beat while on the other never losing contact with it, they develop an intense, exciting rhythmic tension in which the real stimulation of their playing resides. In this respect, too, Rollins continues Charlie Parker's heritage. 'Charlie Parker's Successors Play Tenor' said the headline in a French jazz magazine as the Rollins influence reached its peak in the late fifties.

At this peak the Rollins influence changed over into the perhaps even more engulfing *John Coltrane* influence. Coltrane (see the chapter devoted to him and Ornette Coleman) became the teacher and master of most of the tenorists of the sixties, seventies, and (until now) the eighties as well – and not only of the tenorists.

The Coltrane 'students' can be classified into two groups (similar to the grouping of the players of other instruments): those within the boundaries of tonality and those outside (with all the intermediate shades that must be called expressly to mind in such a generalized classification). Among the former the Coltrane model is stronger and more immediately perceptible, whereas the latter see Coltrane's impulses as 'liberation' only in general terms, bringing their own individuality into play that much more clearly.

Members of the first group are musicians as diverse as *Joe Henderson, George Coleman, Charles Lloyd, Carlos Garnett, Joe Farrell, Sam Rivers, Billy Harper*, and among the younger generation, *Pat LaBarbera, Ricky Ford, Michael Stuart*, and others. Henderson led the great bop tradition exemplarily into the jazz of the post Coltrane era. Farrell couples the power of a more conservative tenor style with contemporary sensitivity, which certainly was one reason why Chick Corea repeatedly used him for recordings. Charles Lloyd led a group in the late sixties that was one of the forerunners of the jazz-rock bands. Harper, who has been incorporating elements of gospel music, carries on John Coltrane's message in a hymnlike manner, both musically and spiritually. Like George Coleman, Sam Rivers played with Miles Davis during the sixties and with Cecil Taylor later on. Something like a father figure to the New York avant-garde in the seventies, he bridges over to the next group of tenor players. The attention of the jazz world was directed to Ford by his work with Charles Mingus, to Stuart by his playing with Elvin Jones, and to Pat LaBarbera by his association with Buddy Rich's big band and with Elvin Jones. All three tend towards that 'John Coltrane classicism' of the seventies and eighties which has become the true contemporary mainstream of jazz (to be discussed a bit later).

Archie Shepp, Pharoah Sanders, Albert Ayler, John Gilmore, Fred

Anderson, Dewey Redman, Frank Wright, Joe McPhee, Charles Tyler, Charles Austin, as well as – among the younger generation – *David Murray, Chico Freeman,* and *David S. Ware* stem from the camp of the 'free tonal' – to some ears even 'atonal' – avant-garde jazz. Shepp, an especially devoted 'angry' free-jazz man in the beginning, has meanwhile come to infuse the traditions of Coleman Hawkins, Ben Webster, and Duke Ellington with the experiences of free playing. 'My sax is a sex symbol,' Shepp once said.

Albert Ayler, who often appeared with his trumpet-playing brother, Don Ayler, had a different motto: 'We play peace.' Ayler's involvement was less political than religious, even philosophical. In the freedom of his tenor breaks, Ayler (who developed his style more or less independently of Coltrane) referred back to tradition in an especially peculiar, folk-musiclike manner, incorporating march and circus music of the turn of the century, folk dances, waltzes and polkas, or the 'dirges' – the music of the old New Orleans funeral processions. Ayler, who died in 1971 at the age of thirty-four (his body was found in New York's East River after he had been missing for twenty days), was 'in many ways closer to [the old sound] of Bubber Miley and Tricky Sam Nanton than to Parker, Miles, or Rollins. He brought back to jazz the wild, primitive feeling which deserted it in the late thirties . . . His technique knew no boundaries, his range from the lowest honks to the most shrill high harmonies being unparalleled.' (Richard Williams)

Pharoah Sanders is the tenor man bursting with musicianly and physical power whom John Coltrane engaged in 1966 as the second horn player of his group, in order to grow through his challenge. Like others among the newer tenorists, he extends the range of the tenor sax, by means of overblowing, into the highest registers of the soprano. For a couple of years, Sanders stereotyped and banalized his way of playing, but since the late seventies it has become obvious again that Trane knew why he chose him.

Around the turn of the decade from the sixties to the seventies, *Dewey Redman* finally became the congenial musical partner whom Ornette Coleman – and later also Don Cherry – had been seeking for so long. Old and New Dreams is the name of the group Redman co-leads with Cherry – and that is exactly what they are presenting: new dreams of an old and basically timeless black tradition. *Charles Austin* has gained attention in a very original collaboration with synthesizer player Joe Gallivan, abstracting his Coltrane roots. And *Chico Freeman* has been called by critic Patrick Irwin 'perhaps the most inside-outside player'. 'Inside' implies: Freeman knows his tradition. 'Outside' means: He ventures into free sounds. The 'Inside' aspect comes from his father, Von Freeman (whom I will discuss in a little while); the 'outside' comes from his links to the AACM, the avant-garde grouping of musicians in his hometown, Chicago.

The free way of playing struck especially fertile soil among Europe's tenorists. Some of them play in a style totally their own, not comparable to any American musician. Dutchman *Willem Breuker*, whom we have mentioned as a bass clarinet player, utilizes the European musical tradition - not coincidentally, also the tradition of Dutch and Low German folk music - in a way that corresponds to Roland Kirk's utilization of the black tradition. German tenorist *Peter Brötzmann* blows his 'tenor clusters' with an intensity usually found only among black musicians. Brötzmann nevertheless realizes this drive in a totally European - in fact, actually German - manner. British critic Richard Williams and other international observers felt Brötzmann's way of playing to be 'teutonic'. Clusters - 'all notes at the same time' - are popular in the entire realm of free playing, but nobody plays clusters as radically as Brötzmann. Norwegian *Jan Garbarek* has, in a very European sort of way, 'spiritualized', romanticized and aestheticized free jazz, which was his original musical root, and developed a playing style of melodious and catchy clarity. Briton *Evan Parker* is perhaps the most individual of European tenor players. Evan really created a new style: abstract and avant-garde, fluently melodizing in falsetto, and without recognizable influence from Coltrane or Coleman.

Other important European tenorists are Briton *Allen Skidmore*, Polish players *Tomasz Szukalski* and *Leszek Zadlo*, the Swede *Bernt Rosengren*, the Finn *Juhani Aaltonen*, Frenchman *François Jeanneau*, and the Germans *Heinz Sauer* and *Gerd Dudek*.

Let's now move on to the musicians influenced by rock and fusion music. Of these we should name *Wayne Shorter*, *Benny Maupin*, Argentinian *Gato Barbieri*, *John Klemmer*, *Tom Scott*, *Wilton Felder*, *Mike Brecker*, and – the youngest tenorist in this group – *Bob Malach*. *Wayne Shorter*, the most prominent of these, has already been introduced in the soprano saxophone chapter. His roots are in bebop, but for a couple of years one could no longer hear them, until Shorter started to show them again in the late seventies. *Mike Brecker* is an outstanding neo-bob musician, even though he has made more fusion records than 'acoustic' jazz albums. There are statements by him (and other musicians) indicating that their fusion, soul, and funk records are actually made primarily for commercial reasons and that they would really prefer to play true acoustic jazz. *Bob Malach* transfers the great tenor tradition in a particularly convincing manner to fusion and jazz-rock music. He occasionally sounds like a 'tenorized' Charlie Mariano, although his junior by almost two generations.

Proceeding to neo-bop, we must first discuss retrospectively a senior figure in jazz whose name has come up several times in this chapter: *Dexter Gordon*. Dexter belongs to the generation of the great bop musicians. John Coltrane named him as one of the few musicians to whom he was indebted. Gordon's playing has often been called 'dry' and 'sardonic'; the wealth – and the originality! – of his ideas seem inexhaustible. Like so many other American jazz men disappointed by the US scene, he moved to Europe in the early sixties, making his home at first in Paris, and later in Copenhagen. For years he was one of the central figures on the European jazz scene. In 1976 he returned to New York for a short engagement, and by doing so became a catalyst of the renaissance of bebop. Gordon, already strongly influential on the tenor scene, now became important to a large segment of today's jazz scene in general – on all instruments.

Now so many tenorists play bebop again that we can only name the most important here: *Dave Schnitter, Carter Jefferson, Larry Schneider, Eric Schneider, Bob Berg*. It is one of the special ironies of this development that, with the comeback of bop, *Von Freeman* (born in 1922 and thus only a year older than Gordon) finally gained the recognition due him thirty years ago. During all those intervening years, Von Freeman lived in Chicago, more or less separated from the main jazz scene, and only jazz insiders who had heard him spoke of him as a 'giant on a par with the really great tenor players of Dexter Gordon's, Wardell Gray's and Gene Ammons's generation.' Chico Freeman, as we have mentioned already, is Von Freeman's son; and indeed the international jazz fraternity took notice of the father only after recognizing the son.

We can carry the irony even further: Dexter Gordon and Von Freeman do not appear as senior citizens on today's scene, but rather as timeless musicians. And so these two can be named in connection with a generation of musicians most of whom are half their age.

Indeed, there is no other instrument which demonstrates the timelessness of the great black tradition so well as the tenor saxophone. On today's scene, it is represented by musicians like *Bennie Wallace, George Adams, Dave Liebman, Pete Christlieb, Ray Pizzi, Frank Tiberi, Sal Nistico, Hadley Caliman, Odean Pope, Garry Windo, Lew Tabackin* and many others mentioned before (especially among the first group of Coltrane players and among the neo-bop musicians) who, though their roots are different, grew into this group. Tabackin, by the way, shows an interesting Sonny Rollins influence, whereas in the music made by most of the others John Coltrane remains alive in an endless, inexhaustible number of different possibilities. Never before in jazz – and, of course, never since – has there been a jazz musician who could count so many other excellent – and in some cases even great – musicians among his 'pupils' and 'students' and 'successors' as Coltrane could, if this giant were still alive.

On the other hand, even good old Swing jazz is back again. After all that has been said in this chapter, it should not be surprising that the front man of the young Swing generation should be a tenor player (whom we already have mentioned in the chapter on jazz of the eighties): *Scott Hamilton.*

The Baritone Saxophone

For decades, *Harry Carney* represented the baritone saxophone, more monopolistically than any other jazz musician ever represented any other instrument. In 1926 Duke Ellington received permission from the Carney family to keep sixteen-year-old Harry in the band, and from that point until the Duke died in 1974 Carney remained with Ellington; five months later, Carney, who was almost synonymous with the history and the sound of the Ellington orchestra, died too. Carney was to the baritone what Coleman Hawkins was to the tenor – of equal power, volume, and expressivity. He played his instrument with all the dark force and roughness it embodies. 'No baritone player should be scared of the noise his horn can make. Carney isn't scared,' said Pepper Adams, a baritonist of the generation which in the late fifties took up the Carney tradition again. Until the mid-forties, Carney ruled royally over the baritone scene. Aside from him there was only *Ernie Caceres*, who managed to play Dixieland on the cumbersome horn, and *Jack Washington*, who provided a similarly professional and powerful foundation for Basie's sax section as did Carney for the Ellington band – without, of course, Carney's brilliance and stature.

Then came bop. And paradoxical as it might seem to play the nervous, mobile phrases of bop on the big horn – suddenly there was a whole row of baritonists. *Serge Chaloff*, who came from a Russian Jewish family, was first. He applied to the baritone all the new things played by Charlie Parker – as Buddy De Franco did on the clarinet and J. J. Johnson on the trombone. Chaloff is among the musicians who played big-band bop with Woody Herman's important 1947 band. Ten years later – when the original 'Brothers' section was reconstructed for a recording date – he had to be taken to the studio in a wheelchair. A few months later, he was dead of cancer.

The restless expressiveness of Charloff's baritone was smoothed out into cool sobriety by *Gerry Mulligan*. Mulligan began quite *à la* Charloff in the combos of Kai Winding and Chubby Jackson toward the end of the forties. He worked in the big bands of Claude Thornhill and Elliot Lawrence, and was one of the important participants in the Miles Davis Capitol sessions – also as an arranger. From 1951 on, he became the increasingly influential baritone voice of Basie-Young classicism. Mulligan is of great importance as baritone saxophonist, arranger, band leader, but most of all as a catalytic personality. Few modern musicians are so firmly rooted in the 'mainstream' of the Swing era. His 'meetings' on record (Verve) with such Swing musicians as Harry Edison, Ben Webster, and Johnny Hodges are impressive proofs of this. The famous pianoless quartet which first made the name Mulligan popularly know in the early fiftes and will be discussed in our combo chapter was organized on the West Coast. Though he himself didn't want to be called a West Coast man, he had lasting influence there. Since the end of the sixties, Mulligan has repeatedly taken the place of altoist Paul Desmond in the Dave Brubeck Quartet for different lengths of time.

The true baritone sound of West Coast jazz came from *Bob Gordon*, who – fatally injured in an automobile accident in 1955 – was an improviser of sweeping vitality – he, too, was a musician of Basie-Young classicim. The records he made with tenorist-arranger Jack Montrose are among the most memorable combo recordings in West Coast jazz.

Influenced more by Charlie Parker and the other great bebop musicians than by his own baritone colleagues, on the East Coast – and later in Europe – *Sahib Shihab* developed into a baritonist who has received much too little recognition. Shihab plays his instrument with power and conviction, and often also with ironic humour, totally free of any mannerisms, and beyond the three modern 'baritone styles' signified by the names Chaloff, Mulligan, and Pepper Adams.

Another excellent bebop baritone saxophonist is *Cecil Payne*, who has played a lot with Dizzy Gillespie. *Charlie Fowlkes* earned himself a solid reputation as a 'Jack Washington of the fifties and sixties' among the players with whom he made music firmly grounded in the healthy Basie tradition.

However, the man who got the whole new wave of interest in the baritone saxophone rolling is *Pepper Adams*. Before him, it seemed as if the possibilities of the baritone had been exhausted with Mulligan and the musicians of his generation, and that the only thing yet to come could be an increase in perfection. This opinion was blown down by Pepper Adams's 'sawing' sound. Pepper emerged in 1957 from the Stan Kenton band. There he was nicknamed 'The Knife'. Drummer Mel Lewis says: 'We called him "The Knife" because when he'd get up to blow, his playing had almost a slashing effect on the rest of us. He'd slash, chop, and before he was through, cut everybody down to size.' Adams is one of the musicians who ebulliently negate the belief that one can distinguish between 'black' and 'white' in jazz. Prior to the appearance of his first photographs in the jazz magazines, almost the entire European critical fraternity thought him to be black. They were supported in this opinion by the fact that he comes from Detroit, the 'Motor City', which is the birthplace, physically and musically, of many black musicians of this style. Says Pepper: 'Hawkins made a tremendous impression on me.' Since Pepper Adams came on to the scene, he has been the most powerful baritone voice in bebop and hard bop – and he still is in the neo-bop of the eighties.

Meanwhile, however, there is a whole generation of excellent baritone players in the different fields of contemporary bebop – among them *Ronnie Cuber, Charles Davis, Bruce Johnstone, Bob Militelo, Jack Nimitz*, and – especially brilliant – *Nick Brignola*. Most of them have worked in big bands, above all in Woody Herman's orchestra – which has been something like a breeding ground for good baritone players in modern jazz, from Chaloff in the forties to Brignola in the seventies. The latter musician has become even more impressive since neo-bop came into existence in the early eighties.

Among the musicians inclined towards free playing, only two baritonists became internationally known during the sixties: *Pat Patrick* as a member of the Sun Ra Arkestra and, in Europe, Briton *John Surman*, whom Japanese critics of those days called 'the most important baritone saxophone player of the new jazz.' In the early seventies, Surman made the soprano – until then his supplementary horn – his main instrument.

Surman explained that, much more than the other saxophones, the baritone by nature gravitates towards certain standard phrases and standard effects; particularly in free playing, it tends quite noticeably towards cliché formation. This may be the reason why, initially, there was relatively little happening in free baritone playing. This situation changed during the seventies, mainly because of two musicians: *Henry Threadgill* and *Hamiet Bluiett*.

Both are connected to well-known groups of the new jazz – Threadgill to Air, Bluiett to the World Saxophone Quartet. Threadgill, especially, blows the baritone with impressive ease, as if it were a flute – and indeed he is also prominent as a convincing stylist on the flute. Bluiett, who loves to accent the powerful low registers of his horn, plays with a vital awareness of the African roots of black music. Threadgill and Bluiett are not simply 'free players'. They – like many other musicians in their mould on other instruments – play 'everything': free and blues, bop and Swing, Dixieland and soul – commanding all these styles as if they were '*one* music' (which in fact they are). The aspect of freedom primarily rests in the sovereignty with which this process is carried out.

The Flute

As recently as the fifties, the flute ranked among 'Miscellaneous Instruments'. But in proportion to the decline of the clarinet came the flute's ascendancy. At least since the late fifties, this instrument has taken the position of playful, airy, triumphant heights on jazz recordings which had been the domain of the clarinet during the Swing era . . . to which, since the mid sixties, was added another 'clarinet successor': the soprano sax under John Coltrane's influence.

Still, the flute has only a relatively short tradition in jazz. The earliest flute solo I know of is on a 1933 recording by Spike Hughes and His All American Orchestra, 'Sweet Sue'. Here, flutist *Wayman*

Carver plays with a suppleness that seems astonishingly modern. Chick Webb, too, occasionally used a flute in his orchestra of the early Swing era. But back then, the instrument still was a curiosity. Strange how suddenly this state of affairs changed when, in the early fifties, the appearance of a half-dozen jazz flutists – literally overnight – established the instrument in jazz.

The first musician to record modern flute solos – with a direct, vital bop feeling – was tenor player *Jerome Richardson*. Immediately after him, *Frank Wess* and Bud Shank stepped into the limelight. Wess (mentioned in the tenor saxophone chapter) was in Count Basie's orchestra. And in this band, whose name stands for Swing *par excellence*, he played the flute – still thought to be alien to Swing by many jazz fans – with the natural ease of his saxophone.

Wess symbolizes the breakthrough that led to the acceptance of the flute. Of course, it could only become important in the post-Lester Young era of the fifties, after the priority of jazz phrasing over jazz sonority had reached the general consciousness. Lester Young is the 'main culprit' in this shift of accent from sonority to phrasing, and thus jazz flutists are initially shaped in his mould. Wess illustrates this point almost ironically: as a tenorist, he clearly is of the Hawkins tradition, while as a flutist, he is just as clearly of the Young line. Wess recorded some of his most interesting flute solos on a date with Milt Jackson (vibraphone), Hank Jones (piano), Eddie Jones (bass), and Kenny Clarke (drums): 'Opus de Jazz.'

Bud Shank was the most important West Coast flutist. He emerged from Stan Kenton's band, where, in 1950, he had already recorded an interesting flute solo showing Latin influences, 'In Veradero'. Later, his duets with Bob Cooper, into which Max Roach drummed swing, stirred much discussion. A strong Arabic and oriental tendency is detectable in *Yusef Lateef* – on flute as on his numerous other instruments. Aside from the usual concert flute, he has used a whole store of other, exotic flutes: Chinese bamboo flute, a flute of Slovak folk origin, cork flute, the Arab 'nai' flute, Taiwan flute, and a 'ma ma' flute he himself constructed.

Other good jazz flutists are *Sahib Shihab*, *James Moody*, *Leo Wright*, *Herbie Mann*, *Sam Most*, *Buddy Collette*, *Paul Horn*, *Rahsaan Roland Kirk*, *Charles Lloy*, *Joe Farrell*, *James Spaulding*, *Eric Dixon*, and *Sam Rivers*. It should be noted here that many of these musicians are saxophonists first and foremost and play the flute as a second instrument. This is true, for instance, of tenor and alto player *James Moody*, whom we have mentioned in the tenor chapter, and who came out of the first bop circle of the forties. Although the flute is only one instrument among others for him, he has been considered one of the best jazz flutists for thirty years – a bebop man par excellence also on this instrument.

For a long time, the most successful jazz flutist was *Herbie Mann*. He incorporated many different exotic elements into his jazz recordings: Latin, Brazilian, African, Arabian, Jewish, Turkish – and in the seventies, of course, rock, and finally even disco.

Herbie Mann won the Readers' Poll of *down beat* magazine – *the* authoritative popularity poll of the jazz world – from 1957 to 1970 – for thirteen years! To everyone's surprise, *Hubert Laws* took over this spot as best-liked jazz flutist with a real 'classical' sound. He has successfully attempted to create a number of jazz adaptations of classical music – compositions of Bach, Mozart, Debussy, Stravinsky, and others – but he also made many jazz-rock and fusion records.

Paul Horn, who became known in the second half of the fifties for his work with the Chico Hamilton Quintet, in the early seventies made unaccompanied flute recordings in the Taj Mahal, on which the flute sounds echo back from the one hundred-foot dome of the marvellous edifice 'like a choir of angels', multiplied a hundredfold, as in an acoustic hall of mirrors: meditational mantras transformed into flute music. The success of this Horn record, 'Inside', was so great that it was later followed by a second one, this one recorded in the burial chambers of Egyptian pyramids (among them the famous Cheops pyramid).

New flutists keep coming. The reservoirs seem inexhaustible. More and more saxophonists choose the flute as a supplementary horn – only to discover one day that it has become their main instrument – as has occasionally happened to James Moody.

A special place is occupied by the outstanding avant-garde player *Eric Dolphy* (who died in 1964). His influence as an alto and bass clarinet player was felt immediately, from the early sixties on, while on flute the importance of his message was not realized by other musicians until the mid-seventies. The genius of his ideas already included all of what 'jazz flute' means on today's scene. His flute 'message' – quite in contrast to what he expressed on his other instruments – was one of lightness and airiness. For people who knew Dolphy the man, there is reason to feel that his flute playing expressed more of his humanity – his soft-spoken gentleness and amiability – than the bursting expressivity of his alto style and the pain-filled eruptions of his bass clarinet improvisations.

Strangely enough, the first to understand and elaborate on Dolphy's flute style were European musicians. They distinguish themselves through an awareness of classical traditions – musicians like the Bulgarian *Simeon Shterev*, Czechoslavakian *Jiří Stivin*, German *Emil Mangelsdorff*, Briton *Bob Downes*, and Dutchman *Chris Hinze*. Downes, who has also stepped out as a composer of contemporary ballets, belongs to the realm of 'classics' as much as to jazz. Hinze plays mainly jazz-rock. Mangelsdorff has an especially full, rich sound. Stivin, also an excellent composer and altoist, is a virtuoso with Bohemian musicians' roots. Shterev commands the whole rich musical heritage of his Balkan homeland.

Many of the flutists named above cultivate the 'overblowing' technique, where, through simultaneous blowing and singing or humming, two voices become audible – and often, through overtones, even three or four voices – creating jazz intensity of an astonishing degree. Anybody who knows the flute from classical music – from baroque music, for instance – may not immediately think of the flute as an instrument that lends itself to jazzlike intensity in the same terms as, say, the tenor saxophone. Only by way of the technique of overblowing has it gained this intensity, and only in that way could it have achieved its success on today's scene.

The first jazz musicians to overblow the flute, as early as the mid-fifties, were *Sam Most* and *Sahib Shihab* (whom we discussed in the chapter on baritone saxophone). Ever since the sixties, this technique has been employed by a growing number of flutists, most intensely, most 'hot' by Rahsaan Roland Kirk (whom we have already talked about in the tenor sax chapter). He sometimes seemed to explode in a dozen different directions with the many different sounds he created simultaneously while blowing the flute (and, at the same time, blown through the nose, his so-called nose flute).

A master of overblowing is *Jeremy Steig*. He was the first flutist to structurally incorporate air and functional and finger noises into his music – while Kirk still used them mainly to increase ecstatic vitality. Steig recorded some highly interesting chamber-musiclike duos with bassist Eddie Gomez.

Flutists in the actual rock–jazz field are, among others, *Chris Wood*, *Tom Scott*, *Gerry Niewood*, and the two jazzwomen *Bobbi Humphrey* and Briton *Barbara Thompson*. It may be presumed that the flute horizon of jazz and jazz-rock will experience a further widening in the coming years.

The flute does not exist: no instrument is more universal. The history of the flute begins symbolically with Pan, the Greek god of the shepherds and of 'the whole', the god who gives a soul to 'everything'. Every musical culture on earth has developed its own particular types of flutes. To the degree to which jazz musicians incorporate the musical cultures of the world do they discover flutes. I once did a record date with *Don Cherry* to which he brought 35 different flutes – among them a Chinese shuan flute made from ceramic, a Latin American Maya bird flute, a Bengali flute, a bamboo flute, a metal flute (in B-flat), a plastic flute in C, American Indian flutes, Japanese flutes, etc.

The flute has always been an instrument with a special affinity for world music – as early as the fifties through Yusef Lateef and Bud Shank, later particularly impressively through Paul Horn, and in the seventies, for instance, through Brazilian *Hermeto Pascoal*, who overblows the flute with truly 'passionate' intensity.

Some of the musicians who play 'free' flute (in that universal sense of 'free' which evolved in the seventies) – all of them influenced by Eric Dolphy – are *Douglas Ewart, Henry Threadgill, Oliver Lake, Prince Lasha, Ronald Snyders*, and – with a particularly well-rounded, big tone schooled in classical music – *James Newtown*. He continues Dolphy's legacy in an especially original and convincing manner.

Contemporary mainstream is played on the flute by, among others, *George Adams, Steve Slagle, Robin Kenyatta, Joe Ford, Dwight Andrews, Jerry Dodgion*, and the co-leader of the Akiyoshi–Tabackin Big Band, *Lew Tabackin*. Once in a while, Tabackin produces sounds in his virtuoso, amazing flute excursions played in a quartet or in his big band reminiscent of Japanese shakuhachi flutes. (Tabackin: 'No wonder. With my wife being Japanese, you absorb these sounds automatically.')

But one of the greatest shakuhachi players in Japan (perhaps the greatest of them all), *Hozan Yamamoto*, has also played this immensely expressive bamboo flute – probably the most expressive instrument of the world-wide flute family – in a jazz context with his own kind of mastery. He has done so with, for instance, singer Helen Merrill and percussion player Masahiko Togashi.

Tabackin is also part of those sections consisting of four or five flutes which have produced some of the most interesting and novel sounds of the Akiyoshi–Tabackin Big Band. In an earlier edition of this book we had surmised that one day combinations of this sort involving several flutes would exist in jazz music. Now they do exist, and they seem so rich and differentiated that – now that the ice is broken – it is to be hoped that other jazz composers and arrangers, too, will try their hand at them.

The Vibraphone

'Percussion' instruments – that is, instruments which are struck or hit – tend to be used primarily as rhythm instruments. If such instruments additionally offer all kinds of melodic possibilities, it can be assumed that they would make ideal jazz instruments. In this sense, the vibraphone is an ideal jazz instrument. The fact that so vitally rhythmic a musician as Lionel Hampton incorporated it in jazz – or at least helped to do so – points in this direction. If it nevertheless has been slow to assert itself, it may be due to its inability to allow for the production of a hornlike jazz sound. The sound of the vibraphone can only be influenced indirectly, by way of its electrically adjustable vibrato – or by foregoing any electrical adjustment – or through the force – or sensitivity – with which it is struck.

Lionel Hampton and *Milt Jackson* are the outstanding vibraphonists of the jazz tradition. Hampton is a volcano of energy who, like hardly anyone else, can carry thousands of people to a trancelike state of ecstasy by the sheer power – and, of course, showmanship – of his playing and performing. He loves to have a big band with trumpet, trombone, and sax sections behind him. His big bands often pound away without consideration for intonation, blend, or precision, but Lionel Hampton, the vibraphonist, derives from the rhythmic riff-orgies of his big bands even more inspiration and fire and power than he possesses on his own.

Hampton and – a couple of years before him – *Red Norvo* introduced the vibraphone to jazz at the beginning of the Swing era. Hampton had come from the drums, Norvo from the xylophone. Norvo developed in a remarkably open way from Chicago style through Swing, bebop, and cool to contemporary jazz – with a special sensitivity for small chamber-musiclike jazz groups.

As Hampton's vibraphone career had started with Louis Armstrong, so *Milt Jackson*'s began in 1945 with Dizzy Gillespie, in his ground-breaking bebop big band. From 1951 until 1974 (when the group disbanded) Jackson was a member of the Modern Jazz Quartet, which originated as the Milt Jackson Quartet and to begin with was hardly more than the combination of Milt Jackson's vibes and a rhythm section. The Milt Jackson Quartet became the Modern Jazz Quartet under the influence of John Lewis, and it has sometimes been said that the shape and form given by Lewis to this ensemble restricted Jackson's flow of ideas and improvisatory freedom. The fact is, however, that Jackson has played the most beautiful solos of his career as a member of the Modern Jazz Quartet. As so often happens in jazz, the tension between the rigidity of the arrangements and the freedom of improvisation did not hinder the artist, but inspired him.

Milt Jackson's improvisations deserve the adjective 'flowing' – more than any other kind of jazz. A provocative element of Jackson's playing is the seemingly unconscious way in which he makes the most complicated harmonies seem natural and organic. That is also one of the reasons why he is one of the great ballad players in jazz. Already in the mid-fifties, Jackson was one of the first soul musicians.

However far vibraphonists may have developed away from Milt's style, whoever plays vibraphone in modern jazz speaks of him with respect and admiration. It is improbable that his legacy will soon be forgotten. Indeed, since the late seventies one musician has made a name for himself by continuing the tradition of Milt Jackson – and that of bebop – in an especially convincing manner: vibraphonist *Charlie Shoemake*.

Of course, Jackson is not the only vibraphonist of his generation; others are *Terry Gibbs, Teddy Charles, Cal Tjader, Vic Feldman*, and the somewhat younger *Eddie Costa, Tommy Vig, Lem Winchester, Larry Bunker*, and *Mike Mainieri*. Gibbs became known through his brilliant solo work with the Woody Herman band of the late forties. Even in later years, he remained interested in big bands – and in the contrast between his vibraphone and the big-band sound. *Cal Tjader's* blend of jazz phrasing with mambo, conga, bolero, cha-cha-cha, and other Latin rhythms is a valid and intelligent development and sophistication of Cuban jazz, as initiated by Dizzy Gillespie, Chano Pozo, and Machito in the great days of bop. Teddy Charles belongs among those musicians who, in the fifties, were already expanding tonality and preparing the way for free playing.

Lem Winchester, who died in 1961, was the first to display a feeling for the glittering, 'oscillating' sound quality of his instrument – at first only in initial intimations. In the ensuing years, this manner of

playing became more and more pronounced through musicians like
Gary Burton, *Walt Dickerson*, *Tom van der Geld*, and *Bobby Hutcherson*.
These are the players who after fifteen years of unchallenged Milt
Jackson reign have revolutionized the style of their instrument as
dramatically as has happened only to the bass during this timespan.
These musicians accomplished what Ornette Coleman had wanted to
see replace the 'old rules of playing': 'a continuous exploring of all
possibilities of the instrument.' They found that the flittering,
'oscillating' quality of sound which we mentioned in connection with
Lem Winchester fits their instrument better than simply 'a continuation of standard bop by means of the vibraphone.'

Gary Burton plays with a fascinating combination of tender, floating
lyricism and great virtuosity. He is the vibraphonist who has
developed further than anyone else the ability to play with three or
four mallets simultaneously, creating chordal effects similar to those
of pianist Bill Evans, who influenced him. Another influence was the
country and hillbilly music of his home state, Indiana. Burton joins
all these elements into a new, independent whole so securely that he
has become successful far beyond jazz. It was Burton, too, who
initiated the contemporary trend towards playing without a rhythm
section, and who led this trend to its first big triumphs.

Walt Dickerson has transferred ideas of John Coltrane to the
vibraphone. He is another vibraharpist who loves exploring new
sounds – and he, too (like all these other players of the vibraphone), is
an impressive improviser without accompaniment. But the real 'star'
among the more recent vibraphonists (since the late sixties) is *Bobby
Hutcherson*. He is a sovereign improviser, combining bebop and
Coltrane, the Milt Jackson tradition and the new vibraphone sound.

Tom van der Geld is the most sensitive, 'most tender' player among
the new vibraphonists. Once in a while his improvisations sound as if
the bars of his instrument were set vibrating not by being struck with
mallets, but by a mild, warm wind. *David Friedman* has a brilliant,
gripping sound, occasionally like a 'Lionel Hampton of the eighties',
with a pronounced fondness for surprising technical effects. Off and
on, he includes a second vibraphonist (and marimba player), *David
Samuels*, in his group, 'multiplying' the vibraphone sound in this way.
What Friedman and Samuels play together sometimes sounds like an
entire 'metallophone ensemble', reminiscent to a certain extent of
Balinese music.

A few vibraphone players have become interested in the sounds of jazz-rock and fusion music, among them *Roy Ayers, Dave Pike, Mike Mainieri, Ruth Underwood,* and *Jay Hoggard.*

Radically new ways of playing have been discovered by two German musicians who have made their home in the United States: *Gunter Hampel* and *Karl Berger.* Hampel (who has also distinguished himself as flutist, clarinetist, bass clarinetist, and pianist) is the more sensitive of the two, Berger (who heads the Creative Music Studio in Woodstock, NY) is the more dynamic – with bop roots that he has been developing in the direction of a wide and deep interest in 'world music'. With his different groups, Hampel has created mesmerizing webs of sound, combining the vibraphone with flutes and saxophones played in the high registers.

A synthesis of all these tendencies has been created by three American players, who on the one hand play 'free' and on the other command the entire tradition of their instrument: *Bobby Naughton, Earl Griffith* and, above all, *Jay Hoggard.* Jay is a ravishing improviser – '*the* new man on the vibes', as many New York musicians felt at the beginning of the eighties. He also is interested in finding sounds and possibilities for his instrument in fusion music.

These are the two main tendencies of vibraphone playing in the eighties: the percussiveness in the Hampton tradition of Jay Hoggard (and also of David Friedman) and the 'oscillating' sensitivity initiated by players like Winchester, Dickerson, and Hampel and carried on by Tom van der Geld and Bobby Naughton.

The Piano

On the one hand: Since the history of jazz begins with ragtime, and ragtime was a pianistic music, jazz begins with the piano. On the other hand: The first bands on the streets of New Orleans had no pianos – perhaps because pianos could not be carried around, but perhaps also because the piano could not produce the jazz sound that seemed essential to the early hot players.

The history of jazz piano is acted out between these two poles. The piano offers more possibilities than most other instruments used in jazz. It is not limited to playing one note at a time, as are the horns. It can not only produce rhythm but can also harmonize this rhythm. It can not only state the harmonies, as can the bass, but also connect them with other musical possibilities. But a horn line is more intense than a piano line. In summary, we find:

On the other hand: The more the pianistic possibilities of the piano are exploited, the more the piano seems overshadowed by the hornlike, intense phrasing of jazz blowers.

On the other hand: The more the pianist adopts the phrasing of the horns, the more he relinquishes the true potential of his instrument – up to a point which can represent 'pianistic suicide' for anyone familiar with pianistic virtuosity in European music.

Art Tatum and Bud Powell (who was too great to be capable of such 'pianistic suicide', though it did exist within the piano school he represents) signify the extremes of this last dichotomy. These extremes have been sharpened since the eighties of the past century, when *Scott Joplin* began to play ragtime in the Midwest. Joplin was a 'pianistic' pianist. He played his instrument clearly within the conventions of the romantic piano tradition. (See the chapter on ragtime.)

Since New Orleans bands had no use for 'pianistic' piano players, and since a hornlike piano style had not yet been 'discovered', there was hardly one pianist in the jazz bands of old New Orleans. But there were pianists in the saloons and the bars, in the 'houses' and cabarets – pianists in abundance. Every house had its 'professor', and the professor was a pianist. He played ragtime piano. And even when he played blues and stomps and honky-tonk piano, ragtime was always in the background.

The great 'professor' of New Orleans piano was *Jelly Roll Morton*, who died in 1941. Morton played ragtime piano with awareness of the marching bands on the New Orleans streets. Filled with pride at his certainly considerable accomplishments, he became almost paranoid: 'I have been robbed of three million dollars all told. Everyone today [1939] is playing my stuff and I don't even get credit. Kansas City style, Chicago style, New Orleans style – hell, they're all Jelly Roll style . . .'

The 'professors', the 'honky-tonk' and 'barrelhouse' pianists existed in New Orleans not only before and during the period of the actual New Orleans style, but also after – into our times. However, only a few of them gained fame beyond the limits of the Delta City – for instance, *Champion Jack Dupree*, *Huey 'Piano' Smith* and *Professor Longhair* (who died in 1980). Fats Domino (mentioned in the blues chapter and later again in the singers chapter), who stood at the centre of the rock 'n' roll movement of the fifties, emerged directly from this tradition. Indeed, in the section dealing with jazz vocalists, we shall discuss the fact that New Orleans created styles twice in the history of black music – not only during the era of New Orleans jazz, but also fifty years later in rhythm & blues and in rock. The New Orleans piano 'professor' bridges these two fields. Jelly Roll Morton made New Orleans jazz with his band; Fats Domino or Professor Longhair made rhythm & blues and rock 'n' roll – and although separated by half a century, they all belong to the same 'professor' and 'honky-tonk' tradition.

Ragtime as played in the Midwest by Scott Joplin was clearly different from ragtime in New Orleans as played by Jelly Roll Morton – but both were music in which one could feel the elements of rag – the elements of 'ragged time'. Soon, there was ragtime in New York, and again it was different from the piano sounds in the Midwest and in New Orleans. From New York ragtime developed the great era of the Harlem jazz piano. But even if Scott Joplin played in Sedalia, Missouri, from the 1890s, and Jelly Roll Morton named 1902 as the year he 'invented' jazz, and the first ragtime pianists played in New York and Harlem around 1910, this still does not prove that the line of evolution led directly from Sedalia over New Orleans to Harlem. Styles – as we have mentioned – develop when the time is ripe, independently of causal schemes of evolution.

James P. Johnson, who died in 1955, was the first important Harlem pianist. He was a schooled musician; from the beginning there were many academically trained musicians among the pianists, in contradistinction to the players of other instruments. James P. Johnson had studied with a pupil of Rimsky-Korsakoff, and late in his career – during the thirties – he composed a series of symphonic and quasi-symphonic works.

With Johnson is revealed for the first time an aspect of jazz piano at least as important as all the brilliant solo achievements: the art of accompaniment . . . the art of adapting oneself to a soloist, to stimulating him and giving him a foundation on which to build. Johnson did this in unsurpassed fashion for Bessie Smith – on 'Preachin' the Blues' 'Backwater Blues', for instance.

Harlem of the twenties was a breeding ground for jazz piano. *Duke Ellington* related: 'Everybody was trying to sound like the "Carolina Shout" Jimmy [James P. Johnson] had made on a piano roll. I got it down by slowing up the roll . . . We went out every evening regardless of whether we had money or not . . . I got a big thrill when I found *Willie "The Lion" Smith* [one night] . . . We made the rounds every night looking for the piano players . . .'

Willie 'The Lion' Smith is another great pianist of the Harlem tradition of the twenties – a master of charming melodies, which he set off with the mighty rhythm of his left hand.

The Harlem pianists – Johnson, Smith, Ellington, Luckey Roberts, and young Fats Waller – played for 'rent parties' and in 'cutting contests', all part of the whirling jazz life of Harlem. At the rent parties, jazz was a means of getting up the rent for one's apartment in a friendly atmosphere, and the cutting contests were play-offs among the leading pianists, ending only when one man had definitively 'cut' all the others. The most characteristic of their various styles was called stride piano. 'Stride' means a constant, swinging alternation of a bass note (played on one and three) and a chord (played on two and four).

The most important pianist to come out of this Harlem tradition was *Fats Waller*, who died at thirty-nine in 1943. Louis Armstrong said: 'Right now, every time someone mentions Fats Waller's name, why, you can see the grins on all the faces . . .' Fats was two men: one of the greatest pianists in jazz history and one of the funniest and most entertaining comedians of popular music – both of which he managed to combine with inimitable relaxation.

'Livin' the Life I Love' was the theme of his life and his music. He did not always bring it off . . . for all his comic sense, he still suffered when the public seemed to appreciate his showmanship more than his music. Gene Sedric, Fats's tenor man, relates: 'Fats was sometimes very unhappy about his music. You see, he was appreciated for his showmanship ability and for that amount of piano that he played on records, but very few of Waller's record fans knew how much more he could play than what he usually did on records. He didn't try to prove anything by his singing. It was a matter of fun with him . . . Yet, he wanted to do great things on organ and piano – which he could do . . .' Elsewhere, Sedric says: 'As for the record sessions, it seems like they would always give him a whole lot of junk tunes to play because it seemed as if only he could get something out of them . . .'

As composer, Waller wrote some of the most beautiful jazz themes, equally agreeable to all styles. 'Honeysuckle Rose' and 'Ain't Misbehavin'' are the most important. 'Waller,' says Coleman Hawkins, 'could write tunes as fast as he could play the piano.'

As a pianist, Fats had the strongest left hand in traditional jazz – a left hand which could replace not only a rhythm section but a whole band. He was altogether an 'orchestral' pianist. His piano sounded rich and full like an orchestra. Quite relevantly, the most orchestral of all jazz pianists, Art Tatum, invoked Waller: 'Fats, man – that's where I come from . . . Quite a place to come from, too!'

The other great pianist to come from Fats Waller is *Count Basie*. Basie tells of his first meeting with Fats: '. . . I had dropped into the old Lincoln Theatre in Harlem and heard a young fellow beating it out on the organ. From that time on, I was a daily customer, hanging on to his every note, sitting behind him all the time, fascinated by the ease with which his hands pounded the keys and his feet manipulated the pedals . . .'

Today, one can sometimes still hear in the piano solos Basie plays with his band that he comes from Fats Waller. He plays a kind of 'economized' Fats: an ingeniously abstracted structure of Waller music in which only the cornerstones remain – but they stand for everything else. Basie became one of the most economical pianists in jazz history, and the way he manages to create tension between often widely spaced single notes is incomparable. Many pianists have been influenced by this: *Johnny Guarnieri* in the Swing era, and during the fifties *John Lewis*, the maestro of the Modern Jazz Quartet, in whom one senses behind Basie's unconscious economy of means a sage knowledge of all that economy and abstraction imply in music and art. When musicians like Basie or John Lewis leave open spaces in their improvisations it is more than just empty space, it is a medium of tension and relaxation every bit as important as any note they play.

In many of the Basie tributes of the fifties, West Coasters *Marty Paich* and *Pete Jolly* and Easterner *Nat Pierce* (with, among others, Woody Herman's big band) have played a modernized – sometimes a cool – Basie style. *Sir Charles Thompson*, too – the composer of 'Robbin's Nest', a popular bop and Harlem-jump theme of the forties and fifties – shows a Basie influence.

However, another stream of jazz piano development flowed into Count Basie: the stream of great boogie-woogie pianists. Basie not only plays 'economized' Fats Waller, but 'economized' boogie as well.

In the early days, the ragtime and Harlem pianists always looked down a bit condescendingly on the 'poor boogie-woogie piano players.' Chicago became the centre of boogie-woogie – where Harlem rent parties and cutting contests jumped to the sound of stride piano, their counterparts on Chicago's South Side rocked to the beat of blues and boogie piano. Boogie-woogie, too, has its roots in the Midwest and Southwest, down to Texas. From Texas comes one of the few remarkable pianists who still play genuine, uncommercialized boogie and blues piano: *Sam Price*. Memphis, St Louis, and Kansas City were important boogie-woogie towns. *Memphis Slim*, who comes from Memphis, and now lives in Paris, is among the more recent masters of boogie. He made a name for himself primarily as a blues shouter. There are many blues singers in the black sections of Northern and Southern cities who accompany themselves with convincing boogie-woogie piano, or even are outstanding boogie soloists – as, for example, *Roosevelt Sykes*, *Little Brother Montgomery*, and above all, *Otis Spann* (who died in 1970).

The boogie-ostinato – the sharply accented, continuously repeated bass figures – may have developed in the South from the banjo or guitar figures with which the blues singers accompanied themselves. Anyhow, blues and boogie belong together since their origin. The first boogies were played as blues accompaniments, and to this day almost all boogies are in the twelve-bar blues pattern. Often, the difference between blues and boogie is anything but distinct; and as might be pointed out here, the notion that all boogie-woogie is fast and bouncy is an erroneous generalization. It is just as false as the idea that all blues are slow.

If the search for the origins of boogie-woogie takes us beyond the early banjo and guitar blues accompaniments, we arrive at a time when the differentiation between Latin American (rumba, samba, tango, etc.) and North American (ultimately jazz-influenced) music was not yet so distinct. *Jimmy Yancey*, the 'father of boogie-woogie', and other boogie pianists have based some of their pieces on the bass figures of Latin American dances – Yancey's 'Lean Bacon Boogie', for example, is based on a tango figure. In the last analysis, boogie is a sort of 'arch-rhythm' of black music, which is why one encounters it again and again in modern times – as 'in disguise' in rhythm & blues of the fifties and in soul music of the sixties or in Muhal Richard Abrams's piano improvisations of the seventies; of course often in an alienated, abstract manner. That authentic boogie-woogie can still be alive and effective became apparent when a number of British rock and blues musicians formed Rocket 88 in 1978 on the occasion of the fiftieth anniversary of boogie-woogie (in 1928 Pinetop Smith had recorded his 'Pinetop's Boogie-Woogie', which gave the whole style its name). Rocket 88 included, among others, Rolling Stones drummer Charlie Watts, British boogie team George Green and Bob Hall (on two pianos), as well as Alexis Korner, the father of British blues – in all, ten musicians who play boogie with the same cooking intensity that heated up the old boogie joints in Chicago in the twenties.

At the time, Jimmy Yancey, *Pinetop Smith, Cow-Cow Davenport*, and *Cripple Clarence Lofton* were the first important boogie-woogie pianists. Yancey was originally a tap-dancer, which might have inspired his eight-to-the-bar playing.

Most brilliant of the boogie-woogie pianists was *Meade Lux Lewis*, who lost his life in an automobile accident in 1964. His 'Honky Tonk Train Blues', first recorded in 1929, achieved legendary fame. In the mid-thirties, when the Negro audience for whom boogie-woogie had been played in the twenties on Chicago's South Side and elsewhere had long since gone beyond this style, the white world began to warm up to it. At that time, jazz critic John Hammond searched for Lewis and found him as a car-washer in a suburban Chicago garage. At New York's Café Society Hammond brought him together with two other pioneers of boogie-woogie piano: *Albert Ammons* and *Pete Johnson*. The records made by these three masters of boogie at three pianos are among the most exciting examples of boogie-woogie.

As James P. Johnson and the other Harlem pianists belong to the ragtime branch, although they soon ceased to play the old, original rags and finally can only be designated as rag-influenced, so Chicago had pianists who clearly belong to the boogie-woogie branch and yet were only boogie-woogie influenced. The first of these is *Jimmy Blythe*, who was employed frequently in the Chicago recording studios of the twenties. Blythe was tasteful, experienced, versatile – even though he may seem rough, monotonous, and untutored to listeners of today. In the meantime, our notions of what is tasteful, experienced, and versatile in jazz have simply become more demanding. Blythe, long before Basie, knew how to achieve boogie effects without really playing boogie-woogie – as in his 'Sunshine Special', where he 'hides' the ostinato lines, usually played by the bass, in the melody line.

As a stomp pianist, Blythe was not much different from the great Harlem pianists. The stomp is the connecting link between boogie-woogie and the Harlem branch, and eventually also links up with the third line of pianistic development – hornlike playing. Before speaking of this, we must mention the white pianists of Chicago style and its wider radius. They more or less stand between the rag and boogie branches – *Joe Sullivan*, for instance, leaning more towards Waller, *Art Hodes* more towards the blues piano of the South Side pianists. The former has wonderful humour, the latter persuasive blues feeling.

The third branch of pianistic development – hornlike piano playing – was the latest to evolve. *Earl Hines* has been called the first musician of this direction; in any case he is its most important pathbreaker. His playing has been called 'trumpet style piano' – the mighty octave movements of his right hand sounded like a translation of Louis Armstrong's trumpet lines to the piano. But Hines is a musician in his own right: filled with energy and humour and revealing musical and human development even in his old age. He is one of those fascinating personalities of jazz who have become legends in their own time.

No piano can sound 'like a horn', but Hines is the founder of a school whose pianists realized lines – little by little at first, but more and more generally later – which may not have attained a hornlike expression, but surely the contours of hornlike phrases. This school leads via Mary Lou Williams, Teddy Wilson, Nat 'King' Cole, and – of special importance – Bud Powell, up to countless pianists of contemporary jazz.

Of special interest is *Mary Lou Williams*, since she lived through this entire school and developed parallel to it. Mary Lou (who died in 1981) is surely the most important female figure in the whole history of instrumental jazz. She began to play around 1927, in the blues and boogie-woogie style of the day. In Kansas City she became arranger and pianist for the Andy Kirk band. She wrote some significant arrangements – for Kirk, Benny Goodman ('Roll 'Em'), and Duke Ellington ('Trumpet No End') – which cannot be left out of any history of the arrangement in jazz. As a pianist she evolved through Swing and bop into a mature representative of modern jazz piano – which caused some to say that this 'First Lady of Jazz' had no style of her own. She herself said with justified assurance: 'I consider that a compliment, although I think that everyone with ears can identify me without any difficulty. But it's true that I'm always experimenting, always changing, always finding new things. Why, back in Kansas City I found chords they're just beginning to use now. What happens to so many good pianists is that they become so stylized that they can't break out of the prison of their styles and absorb ideas and new techniques.' She demonstrated this openness towards new developments as recently as 1977, when she played a noted duo concert with the best-known player of free-jazz piano, Cecil Taylor.

In the Swing style of the thirties the Earl Hines direction is embodied first of all in *Teddy Wilson*. He connects it with the format of the great black Swing horn players and with the elegance and affability which Benny Goodman brought to the jazz of that day. It is this connection which has led to a point, forty years later, when one seems to be hearing Teddy Wilson in every other cocktail pianist. Wilson, as a member of the Goodman combos and as a leader of his own ensembles, participated in some of the best and most representative combo recordings of the Swing era. During the thirties, he influenced almost every pianist – among others *Mel Powell, Billy Kyle, Jess Stacy,* and *Joe Bushkin.* Bushkin, of course, was also influenced by the 'grand old man' of all jazz pianists: *Art Tatum. Marian McPartland* has transferred the elegance of Wilson – with whom she recorded a duo album – to the contemporary scene, incorporating many of the musical insights since then. She is one of those players who in the course of their lives keep growing in format and stature.

Everything created in the course of the history of jazz piano up to the time of his renown – the mid-thirties – comes together in Art Tatum, with the addition of a pianistic virtuosity which has been compared to that of the great concert pianists, such as Rubinstein or Cherkassky, and which before him was unheard-of in jazz. The cadenzas and runs, the arpeggios and embellishments of the virtuoso piano music of the late nineteenth century are as alive in his playing as is a strong feeling for the blues – which he demonstrates in, say, his recordings with blues singer Joe Turner. Nurtured on the piano techniques of the nineteenth century, Tatum shows a certain preference for the salon pieces of that time – such as Dvořák's 'Humoresque,' Massenet's 'Elégie,' and others of this genre – a choice which might not be wholly compatible with the ultimate in taste. But it is characteristic of the high esteem in which Tatum is held by almost all jazz musicians that a storm of protest arose when French jazz critic André Hodeir brought up this question of taste. Even musicians who otherwise could not be moved to write took pen in hand to send in glowing defences of Tatum.

Tatum, who died in 1957, was a soloist – period. Aside from a few combo recordings with all-star personnel, or the previously mentioned sessions with blues singer Joe Turner, he was accustomed to playing solo or with his own trio. Tatum continues to be influential – as on French pianist *Martial Solal* or *Adam Makowicz* from Poland, and indirectly also on dozens of piano players who today play virtuoso solo piano. In this sense it might be said that Art Tatum's universal piano approach is experiencing its real triumphs in the seventies and eighties – almost twenty-five years after this great musician's death.

After Tatum, the counterplay between the pianistic and the hornlike conceptions of jazz piano becomes particularly marked. *Bud Powell*, who died in 1966 under tragic circumstances, was the primary exponent of the hornlike approach and, in general, the most influential pianist of modern jazz. At eighteen, he had already played with Charlie Christian and Charlie Parker at Minton's. He has been called 'the Bird of jazz piano' – and was similarly tormented and threatened as a human being. After his creative period – from the mid-forties to the early fifties – he spent more than half his time in asylums. During this relatively long time he often was only a shadow of the greatness he displayed in those few years when he actually created the modern piano style.

The problem of Powell is an intensification of the problem of the jazz musician in general: the problem of the artist who is creative within a socially and racially discriminatory world whose aggressiveness and lack of sensibility cannot possibly be borne by those artists who are neither willing nor able to play the game.

Powell created those sharply etched lines which seem to stand free in space like glowing metal that has hardened. Yet Bud is also a romanticist, whose 'Glass Enclosure' (an original composition) or whose ballad interpretations – for instance, 'Polkadots and Moonbeams' – have the gentle charm of Robert Schumann's 'Scenes from Childhood'. This tension between the hardness of his hornlike lines and his romantic sensibility is always present, and perhaps it was this tension between two ultimately incompatible extremes which also contributed to the tragedy of this wonderful musician. Lennie Tristano said of Powell that he got 'the piano past being the piano . . . There's hardly anything anybody could say about Bud Powell which could emphasize how great he was.'

From Tatum comes the technique; from Powell, the style. Tatum set a pianistic standard which for a long time seemed unattainable. Bud Powell founded a school. Thus, there are more pianists in modern jazz who are 'Powell students' than there are 'Tatum students'. Descended from Tatum are first of all *Billy Taylor*, *Martial Solal*, *Hank Jones*, *Jimmy Rowles*, *Phineas Newborn*, and *Oscar Peterson* (who, of course, are also influenced to a certain degree by Bud Powell and other pianists). Taylor, as pianist and as observer of the jazz scene, possesses a wily and penetrating intelligence. Jones combines bebop and Tatum, leading this combination to ever greater maturity

– since the seventies also in impressive solo appearances. Solal possesses French brilliance and Gallic humour and esprit. Sometimes the wealth of his ideas and intimations explodes like fireworks.

When in the course of the seventies Polish pianist *Adam Makowicz* came to the fore, it became apparent how strong the Tatum tradition still is. Makowicz plays a very concertlike, 'Chopinesque' kind of Tatum style. Guided by John Hammond, the greatest talent scout of jazz, he moved to New York in 1978, where he stated: 'What I am learning here is mainly rhythm.'

The most successful pianist of the Tatum school, however, is *Oscar Peterson*; time and again he has pointed out how strongly indebted he feels to Tatum. Peterson is a swinger of immense energy and gripping attack. In the seventies, when he started to give solo concerts (without the small groups with whom he had appeared until then), it could be heard that the Harlem pianists had also left their mark on him: Fats Waller and James P. Johnson with their mighty bass lines, who in turn are the ancestors of Tatum. In the meantime, Peterson has formed a school of his own. One of the pianists in this school is *Monty Alexander*, who combines an attack *á la* Peterson with the charm of his native Jamaica.

From Bud Powell come *Al Haig, George Wallington, Lou Levy, Lennie Tristano, Hampton Hawes, Pete Jolly, Claude Williamson, Joe Albany, Dave McKenna,* Japanese émigré *Toshiko Akiyoshi, Eddie Costa, Wynton Kelly, Russ Freeman, Harold Mabern, Cedar Walton, Mose Allison, Red Garland, Horace Silver, Barry Harris, Duke Jordan, Kenny Drew, Walter Bishop, Elmo Hope, Tommy Flanagan, Bobby Timmons, Junior Mance, Ramsey Lewis, Ray Bryant, Horace Parlan, Roger Kellaway, Roland Hanna, Les McCann,* Austrian *Fritz Pauer,* and a legion of other pianists, among them also those we will mention as representatives of contemporary neo-bop (into which many of those listed here have grown).

Al Haig, Duke Jordan, and George Wallington played in combos on 52nd Street during the formative years of modern jazz. *Lennie Tristano* (who died in 1978) is the head of the previously mentioned Tristano school, which had such great importance at the time of the crystallization of cool jazz. He played long, sweeping, sensitive melodic lines (often almost in the sense of Bach's linearity) over complex harmonic structures. As Lynn Anderson put it: 'He was the first piano player to spontaneously improvise extended chord stretches . . . He was the first to improvise counterpoint . . . Another of his innovations was his conception of bypassed resolution, so that

harmony does not always move in the way you think it should . . .'
Tristano anticipated the harmonic freedom of free jazz by as much as
ten years.

Tristano's influence reaches across many styles. Among those
pianists who have paid allegiance to him are *Don Friedman*, *Clare
Fischer*, and, above all, *Bill Evans*; among the younger ones are *Alan
Broadbent*, *Connie Crothers*, and *Ken Werner*, all of whom show how alive
the Tristano influence still is. Werner is a young pianist who has
become known in the early eighties, commanding the wide range of
contemporary jazz piano playing with Tristano-like linearity.

Russ Freeman, *Claude Williamson*, and *Pete Jolly* are the main pianists
of West Coast jazz. *Hampton Hawes*, who also lived on the West Coast
(he died in 1977), does not fit in the West Coast bag. He had a strong
blues and Charlie Parker feeling, which was very much rooted in his
black heritage. *Mose Allison* (see also the chapter on male vocalists)
represents an intriguingly direct connection between old blues and
folk songs and modern Bud Powell piano. *Red Garland* is a hard-bop
pianist who sparkles with ideas. He became known through his work
with the Miles Davis Quintet in the mid-fifties. After he left Davis, his
place was taken first by Bill Evans (of whom more later) and then
Wynton Kelly. Kelly, and even more so *Junior Mance*, *Les McCann*, and
Bobby Timmons, belong to the funk- and gospel-inspired hard-bop
pianists. Timmons's compositions 'Moanin',' 'This Here,' and 'Dat
Dere,' written in the late fifties when he was in Art Blakey's
Messengers and Cannonball Adderley's quintet, became highly
successful. In the early seventies, Les McCann combined his soul
piano conception, which he had presented with great success in the
fifties, with contemporary electric sounds. *Ray Bryant*, a master of
expressive, weighty blues improvisations, initiated a dance fad around
1960 with his pieces 'Little Susie' and 'Madison', which – like so
many of its predecessors – began in Harlem and went around the
world. *Ramsey Lewis* for many years led a trio which combined gospel
and hard bop in a pleasant, often somewhat commercialized manner,
then switched to fusion. *Tommy Flanagan*, a musician of the Detroit
hard-bop generation, has found a delicacy in the 'hardness' of hard
bop that few others have. His duo album 'Our Delight', recorded
with Hank Jones in 1978, is for this writer one of the most beautiful
duo piano records in all of jazz. *Barry Harris* has always been
designated a 'genius' by the musicians to come out of Detroit. He was

the strongest and most individual personality behind the Detroit jazz scene and a highly respected teacher of many musicians. *Horace Silver* has extended the Powell heritage particularly convincingly – to a funk and soul-inspired playing style, coupled with an audacious sense of form and affable vitality, which has become a success formula for himself and his quintet.

Thelonious Monk, who died in 1982, also belongs among the hornlike pianists. He was one of the important musicians from the in-group of the bop creators, but his influence was realized only from the second half of the fifties on. Monk, a pioneer of modern jazz from Minton's, played '*al fresco*-like', widely spaced, often barely indicated lines. In terms of the dissolution of the phrase as a unit and harmony as a functional system, he went further than almost anyone before free jazz. His great harmonic freedom was rooted in knowledge and in a strong and original creativity. Much of what leads to Ornette Coleman, John Coltrane, Eric Dolphy, and all the other avant-gardists of jazz was heard for the first time in his music – anchored in a strong blues feeling and saturated with a mocking, burlesquing sense of humour. Monk's own themes, with their rhythmic displacements and irregular structures, are among the most original themes in modern jazz.

Randy Weston, *Herbie Nichols* (who died in 1963), and *Mal Waldron* are pianists who seem to operate along similar lines, whether consciously influenced by Monk or not. Weston, who besides Monk names Ellington as an influence, lived in North Africa for years, where he also worked with Arab music. *Nichols* played in traditional and blues bands before he had an opportunity to present his bizarre and novel compositions (which, regrettably, have attracted little attention). He was one of the true originals of jazz piano. *Mal Waldron* had great success in Japan during the seventies, though he lived in Munich. His way of playing was referred to as 'telegraph style': his phrases sounded something like 'long-long-short-long', like a mysterious Morse code. Waldron was the last accompanist for the great Billie Holiday. He developed an increasingly individual style in which 'space' is very important.

An especially successful pianist was *Bill Evans*, who died in 1980. Evans was one of the few white musicians accepted within the narrower circles of hard bop – and yet his style was completely different from that of other hard-bop pianists, much more sensitive and fragile; in today's terms, he was the first 'modal' pianist. He might be designated a 'Chopin of the modern jazz piano', with the eminent skill – without comparison in jazz – to make the piano 'sound' in a way that places him (in terms of sound) in the vicinity of a pianist like Rubinstein. It is no wonder that such a unique and interesting combination of heterogeneous elements has been successful in commercial terms as well (in the Bill Evans Trio). Evans's work with other musicians – with Miles Davis or bass player Scott LaFaro, for instance – says German pianist Michael Naura, shows him to be 'a musician who seems to register his environment in an almost spiritualistic manner. Only someone capable of total devotion can play a piano like that.'

It is illuminating that Evans has been a point of departure for a whole line of pianists, among them *Don Friedman* on the East Coast, with his sensitive and clear piano improvisations, and *Clare Fischer* on the West Coast, who also has made a name for himself as an arranger (and who also is interested in Latin music).

Jaki Byard holds a special position. He emerged from the Mingus group and on the one hand plays very modern, nearly free improvisations with abrasive sounds; but on the other hand, he is rooted in the stride piano of the twenties. He is a musician with that total grasp of the black tradition which Mingus and Roland Kirk set up as an ideal.

There are a few musicians who do not fit into the system we have tried to use in classifying the pianists. They should be discussed now, before going on. As a member of Lionel Hampton's band, *Milt Buckner* (who died in 1977) created a 'locked hands style' – with intertwined, parallel octave movements – that has a strong, stimulating effect. He sometimes sounded as if he were transferring a whole trumpet section in all its sweeping brilliance to the piano.

British-born *George Shearing* incorporated Buckner's style into the sound of his quintet. Combined with the bop lines of Bud Powell, he developed this style into a success formula, but he also has a 'Chopinesque' sensitivity.

Characteristically, the most sensational success has been enjoyed by the two pianists who are least definable in terms of schools: *Dave Brubeck* and Erroll Garner. Brubeck has incorporated a wealth of European musical elements, from Bach to Darius Milhaud (with whom he studied), in his playing – elements which in his music seem to be enveloped within a certain romanticism. The question whether Brubeck 'swings' has been debated for years. Critics and musicians have attacked him for 'pounding' the piano. But Brubeck is a marvellously imaginative and individual improviser. He and his alto saxophonist Paul Desmond mutually inspired one another almost in the intuitive way of sleepwalkers. Brubeck often finds his way to great, moving climaxes. The way in which he builds to these climaxes over wide stretches and seemingly 'shores up' to them is unique and original. However, when Leonard Feather initiated an inquiry as to who was the most overrated musician, Brubeck took the lead with ease. Thirty-seven per cent of all those polled offered his name. Particularly in Brubeck's case, a behaviour pattern among the 'jazz fraternity' is evident, as can also be seen in other musicians in jazz history – even in Louis Armstrong's case: In the first half of the fifties, Brubeck was one of the most highly praised musicians on the jazz scene. Again and again, he was chosen as best pianist and combo leader – or, in more general terms, as 'Musician of the Year.' At that time, he was considered *the* embodiment of avant-garde piano playing. Then he became successful – far beyond the limits of what can be considered 'normal' in jazz. And increasingly, the jazz fraternity began to move away from him – though he hardly plays any different today from back then. On the contrary: his playing has become more swinging, harder, more mature. Has the jazz world, one is forced to ask, become so caught up in its cliquish self-isolation that it interprets any success that goes beyond the usual limits as proof of treason?

Since Fats Waller, there has been no pianist whose name was so synonymous with happiness and humour as that of *Errol Garner* (who died in 1977). Garner is also comparable to Fats – and to Tatum – in his orchestral approach to the piano. He sovereignly commands the entire keyboard. 'Concert by the Sea' is the title of one of his most successful records; and the title is appropriate not only because this concert was recorded on the Pacific Coast, but also because Garner's piano cascades bring to mind the roar of the sea. Garner was a player of fascinating relaxation. When he played, the listener sometimes felt that the beat had been delayed too long, but when it came, you knew it fell just where it belonged. Also masterful were Garner's introductions, which – often with cadenzas, often also with humorous intimations – seemed to delay the start of the theme and the beat further and further. Garner's world-wide audiences applauded enthusiastically when pianist and audience finally arrived 'back home' again, in the well-known melody and the even better-known 'Garner beat'.

Garner was so singular and original that only two pianists are really related to him: *Ellis Larkins* and *Ahmad Jamal*. Larkins played some of the most beautiful piano accompaniments in jazz history, on a record of Ella Fitzgerald singing Gershwin. The younger Jamal occupies a curious position, evaluated in sharply contrasting fashion by musicians and critics. While most of the latter hardly consider him more than a gifted cocktail pianist, many musicians – primarily Miles Davis – have called him a towering 'genius'. Jamal's timing and combination of embellishment and economy are masterly. Gunther Schuller believes that Miles's high regard for Jamal is mainly due to the fact that the Davis of the fifties adopted certain ways of embellishing and, to a certain degree, his sophisticated simplicity from Jamal, and that Miles's great success began with this adoption.

The next step in the development was taken by *Cecil Taylor*, in a manner that had not been thought possible by even the most farsighted critics. In his clusters, racing across the entire keyboard of the piano, swings the world of Bartók's 'Microcosm'. Martin Williams claims that Taylor transforms modern concert music into the idiom and technique of jazz as surely as Jelly Roll Morton transformed John Philip Sousa's marches.

Taylor himself, on the other hand, has pointed out that he feels more at home in his own black tradition – above all, in Duke Ellington – than in European music. If you listen to him carefully, you can detect in his playing dozens of elements from the history of black piano music: blues cadenzas and bop phrases and boogie basses, but all of them only intimated, estranged, abstract, and – as soon as they are sounded – transformed into the next element in the gushing stream of idea after idea. His intensity consists not just of racing across the keyboard; it is fed by, as he put it, 'the magical lifting of one's spirits to a state of trance . . . It has to do with religious forces' – in the sense of the African tradition.

There are musicians who have placed Taylor's influence above that of Ornette Coleman – and in any case we must remember that Taylor was already introduced at the 1957 Newport Festival, after he had learned his trade in the groups of Swing musicians like Hot Lips

Page, Johnny Hodges, and Lawrence Brown, and thus chronologically stands before Coleman. The actual, overwhelming aspect of
Taylor's improvisations lies in the physical power with which he
plays. German pianist Alexander von Schlippenbach, strongly
influenced by Taylor, has pointed out that any other pianist would be
capable of generating such burning and bursting intensity for only a
few minutes, and that it is incredible that Taylor is able to keep up
such playing for an entire evening in long concerts or club
appearances. It is one of the most refreshing – and revealing –
characteristics of the jazz scene at the turn of the seventies that a
musician playing a kind of music as difficult and uncompromising as
Taylor's is now, at last, enjoying a 'commercial' success, too.

Cecil Taylor may be the outstanding pianist of free jazz, but there
are – independently of him or coming from him – a host of other
piano avenues in this field. They have been travelled by *Paul Bley*,
Carla Bley, *Ran Blake*, *John Fischer*, *Sun Ra* (famous mainly as the leader
of his free big band), *Narada Burton Greene*, *Dave Burrell*, *Bobby Few*,
Muhal Richard Abrams, *Don Pullen*, *Anthony Davis*, and *Amina Claudine
Myers*; as well as by Britons *Howard Riley* and *Keith Tippett*; Dutchmen
Fred van Hove, *Leo Cuypers*, and *Misha Mengelberg*; the German
Alexander von Schlippenbach (leader of the Globe Unity Orchestra, the
most consistent free big band in Europe); the Austrian *Dieter
Glawischnig*; the Japanese *Yosuke Yamashita*; the Swiss *Irene Schweizer*;
the Italian *Giorgio Gaslini*; and *Friedrich Gulda*. We can mention only a
few of these pianists in detail.

Paul Bley plays free jazz with humour and affability. A critic once
called him a 'James P. Johnson of free playing'. *Ran Blake* and Carla
Bley are especially sensitive players. Ran, who has been influenced by
Thelonious Monk, is a master of estranging standard tunes by the
great writers of American popular music. He tears, shreds, and
abstracts these tunes, transplanting them to a new musical world
diametrically opposed to their original world (which certainly
involves a socio-critical process). *Carla Bley* (more about her in the big
band chapter) became known mainly as a player of her own tender,
delicate compositions, perhaps the most original jazz compositions this
side of Thelonious Monk. Carla's 'chronotransduction', which she
created with writer Paul Haines, 'Escalator over the Hill', is a kind of
jazz opera: With its six record sides, it is the largest complete work that
has so far emerged from within jazz – by far transcending the limits of

jazz, to be sure, in the direction of a 'total music' incorporating elements of rock, Indian and European classical musics, etc. The linguistic creation 'chronotransduction' illuminates the point: time and space are being transcended in a musical and poetic sense.

Also interesting in this connection is the music of the Japanese pianist *Yosuke Yamashita*. American critics have chided him for imitating Cecil Taylor, but Yamashita draws his seemingly ritualistic power and intensity, which are reminiscent of Taylor, not from the American but from the Japanese tradition, which for centuries has had a special, very Japanese culture of intensity.

Muhal Richard Abrams is the 'chief' (a term he would surely object to) of the AACM, which we have mentioned several times. He is a pianist who incorporates the entire black tradition, from ragtime and boogie on into free playing. *Amina C. Myers*, who is a close associate of the AACM, plays free music out of the ancient black 'classic blues' and spiritual tradition. Two further 'free' pianists with a strong consciousness of the black tradition are *Don Pullen* and Anthony Davis – Pullen especially dynamically in fascinating recordings with tenor player George Adams (both Pullen and Adams are, characteristically, products of Charles Mingus's groups).

Anthony Davis is a cool, aware, and articulate player who was also influenced by romantic and classical music, above all chamber music, which he heard in his parents' home. He said: 'Although Ornette Coleman's melodic and linear innovations are important because they freed music from the regularly occurring bebop changes and bar lengths, we're now getting into a new period of music where the harmonic dimensions are coming back. I hear almost everything I play as being tonal, with certain stressed areas rather than more traditional resolutions. At times, I'll even use several contrasting tonal areas at the same time.' This statement characterizes not only the position of Anthony Davis, but also that of many other young musicians at the beginning of the eighties (as, for example, Jay Hoggard – mentioned at the conclusion of the vibraphones chapter – who has often played with Anthony Davis).

Just as the American pianists mentioned here incorporate their tradition into their playing, so their European colleagues build on their tradition, while at the same time feeling inspired by the great contemporary American piano players, especially Cecil Taylor. *Friedrich Gulda*, who is considered one of the great Mozart, Beethoven, and Debussy pianists of our time, is a particular master of the European tradition – although, *only* of this tradition. He has transposed fugue and sonata structures into modern jazz in the most convincing way so far realized, but since Gulda's name usually is dropped when people talk about important 'classical' players being 'equally successful' in playing jazz, it has to be pointed out that his jazz feeling is quite limited.

In any case, jazz piano playing is becoming more and more individualized – not only on the free side of Cecil Taylor but also among nonfree players. Among the latter there are also a number of pianists who defy categorization. *Andrew Hill*, originally from Haiti, has infused African elements from his Caribbean homeland into modern piano compositions and improvisations. 'Really listen to the avant-garde, and you can hear African rhythms. You hear the roots of jazz,' he said. The fact that the African, Negroid, black nature of jazz not only is not being suppressed as the music's development continues, but on the contrary gains increasingly concentrated and valid prominence as the black music of America progressively throws off the shackles of European musical laws, becomes impressively clear in musicians like Hill – and also in Muhal Richard Abrams, Don Pullen, and others.

Even more direct in his relationship to Africa is *Dollar Brand*, a musician from Capetown, South Africa. Pianistically, his playing may be not much more than self-sufficient, but the spiritual strength of the emotions he gets across is amazing. Dollar's father belonged to the Basuto tribe, his mother to the Bushman tribe. Brand fuses this heritage with a deep knowledge of Ellington and Monk, but also with the songs and chorales of the Dutch and Low German Boers who colonized his South African homeland.

Herbie Hancock has progressively turned to 'commercial funk' music, hardly jazz anymore – and yet the jazz world keeps considering him one of its own, not only because his Blue Note records 'Empyrean Isles' and 'Maiden Voyage' from the sixties are among the few convincing 'tone poems' jazz has brought forth, aside from Duke Ellington. They are 'tone paintings of the sea' comparable to Debussy's 'La Mer' in concert music. Hancock is one of the important musicians who became known through their work in the Miles Davis Quintet in the sixties. His own sextet of 1973 presented one of the most interesting and musically most demanding solutions to the entire problem posed by electronics in jazz. The fact that Hancock remained a jazzman even after he changed over to 'commercial funk' became apparent with the group VSOP that he led for a few concert tours during the second half of the seventies (with Freddie Hubbard, Wayne Shorter, Tony Williams, and Ron Carter – all on acoustic instruments). And it became even more apparent when he appeared with Chick Corea on two grand pianos – a great, world-wide concert event which also appealed to those who normally would not have attended such a concert, but were lured by the names Hancock and Corea, well-known from their 'commercial' and 'electric' recordings. It also has to be realized that Hancock, in his youth, heard a lot of rhythm & blues. That is among his roots. So when he plays popular funk, it's not so much a matter of becoming 'commercial' as of going back to his own heritage.

Chick Corea is another musician from the Miles Davis circle. Interestingly enough, before getting into fusion music he played free jazz. Corea is an affable musician with a fondness for childlike fairy-tale moods. He knows Bartók, loves Latin American and Spanish music, and is an outstanding composer. Critics have compared his charming tunes with famous piano pieces of the nineteenth century – with Schumann and Mendelssohn – but failed to notice the immanent, highly sensitized jazz tension with which Chick Corea 'fills' his romanticism. Far from being an unusual phenomenon today, this 'filling' of romanticism with modern tension became very contemporary. It can also be found in the work of other important pianists of the seventies and eighties, for example in *Keith Jarrett, Richie Beirach, Stu Goldberg, Art Lande, Danny Zeitlin, Lyle Mays, Warren Bernhard, Walter Norris, Bob Degen, Ken Werner,* Norwegian *Bobo Stenson,* Frenchman *Jean-Pierre Mas,* Briton *John Taylor,* and – years before this trend began – *Steve Kuhn.* The first player who 'filled' romanticism with modern tension was Bill Evans. Beirach's music often has the lovely simplicity of folk songs; his record company has presented him mainly with such aestheticized music. But he is also a dynamically powerful player of more far-reaching piano possibilities. That, too, is often a part of romanticism: an attitude of moderation and often even self-sufficiency.

Romanticism without the air of moderation is the main characteristic of the most successful pianist of this direction (and, next to McCoy Tyner, the most successful jazz pianist of the seventies): *Keith Jarrett.*

He is a 'pianistic totalizer' whose fingers – and, above all, head and heart – command almost everything ever played on a piano. His 'Solo Concerts' are musical voyages not only through several centuries of piano history, but also through many 'landscapes' of an ever more complex human psyche. But there are also aspects of 'pretentiousness' and 'arrogance' in Jarrett's playing – two terms used by critics when Jarrett played at Carnegie Hall for the Newport–New York Festival in 1976. In Jarrett's personality – and in his music – there are some of those mannerisms of certain late-Romantic artists, reminiscent of the Wagner Festivals in Bayreuth, which seem to breed an atmosphere of admiration and devotion by admiring themselves.

With Herbie Hancock and Chick Corea we have already mentioned two of the most important fusion pianists. Others are *George Duke, Joe Zawinul, Patrice Rushen, Ben Sidran, Milcho Leviev, Stu Goldberg, Bob James, Jan Hammer*, as well as Dutchman *Jasper van t'Hof* and the two Germans *Joachim Kühn* and *Wolfgang Dauner*. Most of these pianists have also employed electric pianos and synthesizers and will be introduced in the following chapter. But on the other hand almost all of them insist on playing on their records, electronic as they may be, at least one piece on the acoustic concert grand – a token of their continued allegiance to the piano tradition (which many of them, were it not for commercial consideration, would much rather nurture and develop exclusively). Among those named above, Stu Goldberg has found particularly interesting avenues, with a hard, angular romanticism sometimes faintly reminiscent of Thelonious Monk. Joachim Kühn has been voted 'Best European Jazz Pianist' seven times by now. And Milcho Leviev loves to incorporate the polyrhythms of his Balkan homeland into his playing.

Behind all these styles and streams, in fact feeding them all, flows the mainstream (in the sense of that main development line of jazz history which leads from bebop via Coltrane to contemporary music): Here, *McCoy Tyner* is the towering figure, since the early seventies the Number One Pianist in most jazz polls of the world. He is the essence of jazz in the most powerful, swinging sense of that word. 'McCoy Tyner plays piano like a roaring lion,' said critic Bill Cole.

Tyner became known in the early sixties as the pianist of the classic John Coltrane Quartet. In the meantime (we have talked about it), the whole scene – jazz, jazz–rock, fusion, pop – has become unthinkable without Coltrane. And, today McCoy Tyner represents the Coltrane tradition more validly than any other musician. In fact, Tyner *is* that tradition: quietly serving, filled with seriousness and religiosity.

The first Tyner album voted 'Record of the Year' – more would follow – was 'Sahara' in 1972. In connection with it, McCoy quoted the Arabian historian Ibn Khaldoun: 'This desert is so long it can take a lifetime to go from one end to the other, and a childhood to cross at its narrowest point.' This quote is characteristic, because for McCoy Tyner, all of music is 'a journey of the soul into new, uncharted territory.' He says: 'I try to listen to music from many different countries: Africa, India, from the Arabic world, European classical music . . . All kinds of music are interconnected.'

It is an enigma to other pianists how McCoy Tyner manages to get so much power out of the piano. Cecil Taylor's piano is similarly powerful, but he plays free music, where it is easier to reach that kind of energy level. Other pianists may pound the piano keys as hard as they can, they would sound only half as powerful as McCoy. He explains: 'You've got to become one with your instrument. Like, you start learning an instrument – and at first the piano is nothing but an instrument. But after a while it becomes an extension of yourself, and you and your instrument become one.'

It must be this 'union' with his instrument that has enabled McCoy Tyner to find his own characteristic sound on the piano – very much in line with the great jazz horn players. Naturally, this is much more difficult on the piano than on a horn. McCoy is one of the few piano players who have done this successfully, which, he says, is one of the reasons why he does not use electric instruments: 'Electric music is bad for your soul.'

Many pianists are influenced – directly or indirectly – by Tyner; examples are *Hal Galper*, *John Hicks*, *Hilton Ruiz*, *JoAnne Brackeen*, and from Belgium, *Michel Herr*, the European pianist who has incorporated McCoy Tyner's style most convincingly.

Among these, JoAnne Brackeen has become especially successful. 'Mythical Magic' is the title of one of her records – which is exactly what one feels when listening to her music: a ritual of mythical-magical power. Brackeen played with Art Blakey and Stan Getz and later with Joe Henderson prior to appearing in solo performances and with her own groups. She studied with Lennie Tristano – one of the many students in whom this great jazz teacher brought out their own identity. (Said Lennie: 'Teaching is an art – as much as playing.')

JoAnne Brackeen has created a new image of the woman in jazz: the woman as a jazz musician – simply a jazz musician, without asking whether this musician is a man or a woman – and yet still a woman who will not let herself be exploited by men and by a male-dominated society, or even by the male-chauvinist music business; the woman and jazz musician who does not feel the need to escape from the implications of her situation into glamour or into flirting with the supposedly inescapable female inferiority in the man's world of jazz, or – as was somewhat the case with Mary Lou Williams – into religious faith: all this has never existed so purely, so totally, and so convincingly as with JoAnne Brackeen. She is the first representative of a new type of female jazz musician, who does not merely talk about emancipation but *is* emancipated.

Of course, the spirit (and a spirit it really is!) of Coltrane and Tyner can be also felt among those piano players who are affiliated with contemporary neo-bop. *Onajee Allen Gumbs, Kenny Barron, Kenny Kirkland, George Cables, Mickey Tucker, Mike Wofford, Andy Laverne, John Coates, Jim McNeeley,* and *Mark Soskin* are some of these – each with his personal approach and, of course, not only influenced by McCoy, but by other musicians, too; Mickey Tucker, for instance, by Monk, or Kenny Kirkland by the solid, 'down home' style of Harlem piano playing. This is the largest stylistic grouping of contemporary pianists, particularly since they are directly related to those players whom we have mentioned as members of Bud Powell's school. In a certain sense, *Stanley Cowell* is one of them, too, but we could have also included him among the 'free' pianists, as he bridges both fields. He, too, is a musician who is aware of the totality of the black tradition.

A large number of European players also belong in this context – in fact, so many that I can mention only three pronounced individualists here: Britons *Stan Tracey* and – as a real virtuoso – *Gordon Beck,* as well as the Spaniard (or as he would call himself: Catalonian) *Tete Montoliu.* Montoliu once said: 'Basically we Catalonians are all blacks.' And that's the way he plays – perhaps the 'blackest' of the European pianists, and yet rooted in the tradition of his native Catalonia, whose folksongs he has given moving interpretations. *Tracey* has occasionally been called a 'British Thelonious Monk,' but he is more than those words can express. His humour is typically British, full of understatement and intimations and often of sarcasm, too.

It is in keeping with the ever widening and universal consciousness of the piano tradition that the last great, authentic ragtime pianist, *Eubie Blake*, should have enjoyed an astounding comeback during the seventies. 'I wrote this piece in 1899,' is how Eubie – born in 1883! – introduces (in 1981!) his performances of 'Charleston Rag'. Louis Armstrong was yet to be born.

Organ, Keyboards, Synthesizer

The organ: Originally, it was the dream of exalted church music, resounding in hallowed cathedrals, the 'royal instrument' of the European tradition (Ligeti: 'the largest prosthesis in the world').

The realization of this dream was the starting point of the organ in jazz. It began with *Fats Waller*.

John S. Wilson wrote: 'Like the inevitable clown who wants to play Hamlet [Fats] had a consuming desire to bring to the public his love of classical music and of the organ . . .' And Waller himself, in reference to a Chicago music critic who had written that 'the organ is the favourite instrument of Fats' heart, and the piano only of his stomach,' said: 'Well, I really love the organ . . . I have one at home and a great many of my compositions originated there . . .'

To be sure, the organ was also the instrument of escape for Fats Waller: It symbolized a world – a distant, unattainable world – in which the artist is accepted solely on the basis of his musical abilities, without racial or social prejudice, and also without regard for his talents as a showman and entertainer. If one hears the organ records made by Fats Waller – such as his famous version of the spiritual, 'Sometimes I Feel Like a Motherless Child' – one encounters an element of sentimentality that makes it clear that Waller had only a fuzzy notion of the world into which he wanted to escape.

The instrument truly loved by Fats Waller was the great church organ of the European tradition, the pipe organ. Once, in Paris, he had an opportunity to play the organ in the cathedral of Notre Dame. It was, as he put it, 'one of the greatest moments in my life.'

Fats Waller passed his love for the organ on to his best known pupil – *Count Basie*, whose organ playing is (almost) as light and spare as his piano style. Basie, however, played the electric organ because it had become obvious in the meantime that the pipe organ can be used in jazz only with great difficulty. The pipes sound too slowly because the distance between the console and pipes is too long and mechanically involved. That's why it is very hard to swing on a pipe organ. 'On a normal pipe organ,' *Clare Fischer* said, 'the lag is about half a beat behind, which plays hell with your mind when you're trying to play rhythmic music. It makes it impossible to play jazz.'

It was Fischer who (in 1975) made probably the most swinging (and musically most interesting) pipe organ recordings, on a small 'chamber organ', where the distances the air column has to travel are relatively short. *Keith Jarrett* has also made recordings on a church organ – with less satisfying results. Among the Europeans, Belgian *Fred van Hove* has developed his own style of playing (free) jazz on a pipe organ – with gigantic sound columns and imposing clusters.

Meanwhile, and in a general sense, the term 'organ' in jazz refers to the electric organ, in any of the many different types available on the market. At first the electric organ was a favourite instrument in the bars and the cocktail lounges of America's black ghettos. The first musicians to gain prominence there derived their organ styles directly from Fats Waller and Count Basie: *Wild Bill Davis* and *Milt Buckner*. Under their influence, the organ-guitar and organ-tenor combination (with drums respectively) became popular in black neighbourhoods all over the country. Meanwhile, there are many other organ players who have developed their own personal styles in this 'rhythm & blues context' of the organ – among them *Jack McDuff*, *Johnny Hammond*, *Don Patterson*, *Lou Bennett*, *Richard 'Groove' Holmes*, *Lonnie Smith*, *Jimmy McGriff*, *Charles Earland*, and many others. *Shirley Scott* has brought some of the relaxation and amiability of Erroll Garner to this way of playing. Since *Ray Charles* (who also plays organ) became successful, not only the blues, but also the soul and gospel element of the black churches has become significant for practically dozens of organ players.

A host of rock organists have taken over the traditions of rhythm & blues and of gospel music; among others, *Stevie Winwood* (in his early phase), *Al Kooper*, and the black, particularly soul-oriented musicians *Billy Preston* and *Booker T. Jones*.

Musicians like Richard 'Groove' Holmes, Jimmy McGriff, Charles Earland, Booker T., Billy Preston, and many others, bring to mind that the technique of playing the Hammond organ was already well developed in the gospel churches when it was only in its infancy in jazz. It is, generally speaking, significant to note that for both black and white audiences, the organ has – superficially – a similar tradition; but that this tradition implies a totally different musical background for each. For both, the organ comes from church. But 'church' for black listeners is associated with the cooking sounds of the gospel churches, while white listeners might have Johann Sebastian Bach in mind.

We have gone somewhat ahead in time to clarify the position of the blues and soul tradition in jazz organ playing. Before the road was free to travel by all the organists coming after Wild Bill Davis and Milt Buckner, *Jimmy Smith* had first to appear on the scene. Smith did for the organ what Charlie Christian had achieved for the guitar; he emancipated it. Only through him did the organ gain equal footing with the other instruments in jazz. Probably his most important record, made in 1956, is an improvisation of Dizzy Gillespie's 'The Champ'. Nobody had accomplished this before: achieving effects on the organ reminiscent of a big band – in this case of the most exciting Dizzy Gillespie big band of the late forties – by employing a high, overpowering dynamic range built on wide, steadily rising arcs of sound.

Smith can also be compared to Christian because he was the first to consciously play the organ like an electronic instrument – similar to Christian's transition from acoustic to electric guitar. Certainly, Wild Bill Davis, Milt Buckner, and others played Hammond organ before Jimmy Smith. But they played it more like a piano with an electric organ sound. It was left to Smith to realize that the electric organ is an independent, new instrument that has only the keyboard in common with the piano or the conventional organ. Indeed, the realization that electronics do not simply electronicize and amplify an instrument, but rather make of it something new, took a long time to be generally accepted. Electronics – I emphasize again – meant a revolution – for organs, guitars, violins, bass, and other instruments.

Later, during the sixties and seventies, Smith made many commercial pop-jazz recordings of doubtful value. But that does not detract from his historic achievement: He made the organ a vehicle for jazz improvisations of the highest artistic quality.

Smith came on the scene in 1956. Nine years later came the next step in the development of the organ: through *Khalid Yasin* (at that time still known as *Larry Young*). Yasin, who died in 1979, played the organ in the spirit of John Coltrane. It is illuminating that he became well known at the moment when Smith, through continuous repetition of blues and soul clichés, more and more seemed to have become a roaring 'Frankenstein of Hammond Castle'. Understandably, organists and audiences initially became enraptured with the instrument's immense range of dynamics, its fortissimo possibilities. Yasin discovered the potential of the organ played pianissimo.

Yasin belongs to the generation of musicians that carried the Coltrane legacy into advanced rock. It is regrettable that he never got to enjoy great commercial success. But his influence is omnipresent in the organists of modern jazz and rock. It is especially notable in the two British players *Brian Auger* (who – like Yasin – also made recordings with Tony Williams) and *Mike Ratledge* (of the group Soft Machine).

In Europe, Frenchman *Eddie Louiss* (whose family comes from Martinique) has developed the Coltrane influence into an individual, hymnal, singing, triumphant style – with some Caribbean–Creole overtones. Interesting organ sounds have also been created during the seventies by musicians like *Carla Bley, Amina C. Myers, Clare Fischer,* Cuban *Chucho Valdez* (of the group Irakere), and, especially originally, by *Arturo O'Farrill*. But in general it must be said that organ playing in jazz has been stagnating since Khalid Yasin. This is so mainly because since the turn of the sixties, a new group of musicians has developed who do play the organ, but whom I hesitate to call organists in the sense of the term as used so far in this chapter. For them, the organ is one instrument among several others: acoustic and electric piano, synthesizer, clavinet, and such accessories as wahwah pedal, fuzz, vibrator, Echoplex and Echolette, phase shifter, ring modulator, etc. These musicians are referred to as 'keyboard artists'. And indeed, the only thing all the instruments they play actually have in common is the keyboards.

Joe Zawinul, a prototype of these new keyboard players, sits at the centre of half a dozen different instruments, like an astronaut in the cockpit of his spaceship, surrounded by a mass of electronics that can hardly be increased. Almost ironically, the good old sound of the acoustic piano is also there, produced by a Yamaha *Electric*(!) Grand Piano.

These are keyboard artists who have become internationally known (some have been mentioned in the piano chapter): *Joe Zawinul, Herbie Hancock, George Duke, Jan Hammer, Chick Corea, Stu Goldberg, Kenny Kirkland,*

Patrice Rushen, Bob James, Richard Tee, Jeff Lorber, Barry Miles, Mike Mandel, Lyle Mays, Dave Grusin, Milcho Leviev, Dave Sancious, Ian Underwood, Joe Sample, Mark Soskin; as well as, from the Netherlands, *Jasper van t'Hof*; from Denmark, *Kenneth Knudsen*; from Great Britain, *Geoff Castle, Gordon Beck*, and *John Taylor*, and, from Germany, *Wolfgang Dauner* and *Joachim Kühn* – and many, many more. Basically, this field of keyboard playing has become so vast that it is impossible to categorize. The wave of keyboard artists that has been inundating the scene since the early seventies has produced surprisingly few individualists. Musicians with a sound unmistakably their own can be counted on two hands.

And yet, the electronic keyboard instruments are indispensable for today's jazz – as we have shown with what we said about electronics in the section about jazz styles. Modern man lives in an electronic world, which implies electronic sounds, which in turn imply electronic keyboards. It also is a phenomenon of volume; electronic instruments can be heard better because they are easier to amplify and to control. In a way, the sound of the electric piano is to that of its acoustic sister instrument what the vibraphone is to the marimba; it is clearer, more sparkling, more precise – i.e., more percussive. That is certainly one of the main reasons why the electric piano made its breakthrough so swiftly.

Carla Bley has pointed out that the lack of individualism has to do not only with the instruments, but also with the record industry: 'There is such a trend towards superclean sound in the industry that all these things will become depersonalized. If you happen to have a personal sound, it would interrupt the cleanness and disturb everybody . . . The producer would stop and have it done over again. They are trying to get rid of personalities, to make everyone sound like a million other people. Maybe that's so people can be replaced by other people and nobody will have the industry over a barrel.'

This situation is even more paradoxical when you consider that the synthesizer is part of the keyboard family – the instrument that offers millions and billions of different sounds, making it the perfect tool for unmistakably personal expression. And yet on the synthesizer there are even fewer players who seem to be able to find their own personal style. The wealth of variety the synthesizer offers is also its most crucial problem: it is too easily used for pure effects, cheap sound-imitations and incongruous playing around with the sound. It is the dialectic of the great instruments in the history of music that they offer their players resistance. Personalities grow with the resistances they meet and deal with. And exactly because the electronic instruments make many things so easy – because they initially level out resistance – individuality is difficult to achieve on them.

It fits into this picture that the overwhelming number of keyboard artists play fusion music, in other words a kind of music which is primarily produced from a commercial point of view. This music is not only supposed to be successful as fast as possible, most of it is also supposed to be off the market again soon in order to make room for new 'products'. And it also fits this picture that, interestingly enough, those musicians who found a personal expression on keyboards had already developed this personality on the acoustic piano – musicians like *Kenny Barron, Barry Miles*, and *Bill Evans.* The latter succeeded in realizing the entire rich and brilliant sensitivity of his acoustic piano on the electric instrument as well.

Because of the complexity of the production process, personal styles that this or that keyboard player may have developed often are only seemingly personal. In the last edition of this book, in 1973, I wrote that Herbie Hancock 'made particular strides, truly using electronics as a new means of expression subject to its own laws . . . creating that kind of *Klangfarbenmelodie* established in modern concert music by Arnold Schoenberg.' Insiders learned that Hancock had his synthesizer programmed by Patrick Gleeson, a pioneer of synthesizer music. So the music was as much Gleeson's as Hancock's (Gleeson also created the much lauded synthesizer music for Francis Ford Coppola's film *Apocalypse Now!*)

The synthesizer, developed by R. A. Moog in the late fifties, gained sudden popularity in 1968 through the world-wide success of Walter Carlos's record 'Switched-On Bach', which presented electronic versions of some of Johann Sebastian Bach's compositions. Here, the electronics 'simulated' the original instrumental voices – there were hardly any signs yet of a truly autonomous use of the new sounds and new instrumental possibilities. In his next work, however – the soundtrack to Stanley Kubrick's *Clockwork Orange* – Carlos took a crucial step forward.

The first artists, besides Carlos, to experiment with the synthesizer in an effort to create really new and original sounds were not jazzmen, but musicians of different types of music – for example, John Cage and Terry Riley.

In jazz, the new possibilities of the synthesizer which make up its actual attraction were used most creatively by players like *Paul Bley*, *Sun Ra*, *Richard Teitelbaum*, *George Lewis*, *Joe Gallivan*, *Pete Levin*, and by the German *Wolfgang Dauner*. These musicians have refuted the argument levelled so often against the synthesizer, and against electronics in general, that they sound mechanical and 'inhuman'. This was done most convincingly by Sun Ra through the boiling intensity of his synthesizer improvisations, and also by a player like Terry Riley through his spirituality, and by Richard Teitelbaum through his very personal intellectual level.

The really fascinating aspect of the synthesizer is that the player can make music 'with' and 'on' the overtone scales much more easily than ever before. In music so far, overtone scales have always involved an element of vagueness, secrecy, and incalculability. The overtones produced by a synthesizer, on the other hand, have a purity that radiates something artificial and aseptic. A symphony orchestra or a big band employing conventional acoustic instruments has a 'floating' sound, caused by the fact that instruments like the trumpet or the trombone, the violin or the cello, produce similar overtones, similar but not exactly alike (and that means different). In the physics of sound, this leads to 'impurity', but it is precisely this impurity that produces that brilliant wealth of sound colours of those musical aggregates – their 'floating' character, in other words. The synthesizer transforms the 'secret' world of overtones into a new world of purity and calculability.

There are constant additions on the synthesizer and accessory market. Specialists have pointed out that even after twenty years the development is only in its beginning stages. There is a new kind of jargon that goes along with electronics. Insiders use it as a sort of ritual language: pink noise, white noise, phasing, sawtooth sound, sequencer, shatter quadrophone, sinus tone, trigger, trigger impulse, low-pass, high-pass, tape-pass, and so on. In the mid-seventies the first monophonic generation of synthesizers was followed by polyphonic synthesizers and, since the early eighties, by digital ones. The latter instrument multiplies by millions the already existing millions of sound possibilities. As we said, the problem lies precisely in this wealth of possibilities. 'The instrument is a lot further ahead than most of the players,' said British rock synthesizer-player Rick Wakeman; 'the technology is racing ahead of the musicians.' Consider that even instruments which have developed a tradition over centuries – the trumpet, the trombone, the violin, or the cello – still offer new possibilities of playing to be discovered and to be perfected. In that light, it must appear normal that synthesizer players, on the one hand, feel challenged by the technological possibilities at their disposal, but, on the other hand, seem to be racing after these possibilities like exhausted long-distance runners.

Finally, let me return once more to the organ. Outside the realm of jazz, although with clear repercussions on it, an organ style has developed which goes beyond Larry Young: the music of *Terry Riley*. Riley's music cannot be categorized – neither as jazz nor as rock nor as avant-garde concert music – but it has influenced musicians from all these fields (Don Cherry, for example, or the British group Soft Machine or composer Steve Reich, to mention three names from three fields). Riley is far from playing the organ with the kind of technical brilliance and loudness taken for granted among contemporary organists. He plays at a low volume, carefully, moderately, as a sort of aid to meditation. His music is supposed to be felt more than heard. It is music as much for the aura of a person as for his ears. Riley's music is modal, but it is not so much Coltrane's modality – even though 'jazz ears' may perceive it as such – as it is the modality of Asia, above all of Indian ragas. And yet it is Western music, played on modern Western electronic instruments. Riley's music has been called 'minimal music', since it hardly seems to change. The listener has the impression that the same tonal movements are constantly being repeated, but in the course of these repetitions imperceptible changes take place, so that at the end of a Riley piece something new, something different is reached, while the listener is still under the impression of hearing the same tonal movements, phrases, and sounds with which the piece began a long time ago. Riley's phrases are 'mantras' that develop and grow in meditation – hardly noticed by the meditating subject – and begin to be effective in a spiritual world, according to their own laws. Riley has dematerialized the organ – certainly a significant accomplishment with an instrument that just a short while before (as with Jimmy Smith and Jack McDuff or with rock players like Keith Emerson or Rick Wakeman) had seemed to be one of the most material, robust, and solid of all instruments. But he also brought the organ back to where it had been before it became electronic: to the spiritual realm – not, however, to a regressive spirituality, but rather to one that progresses into new spaces not only of sounds, but of consciousness.

The Guitar

The history of the modern jazz guitar begins with Charlie Christian, who joined Benny Goodman in 1939, and began to play in the Minton circles shortly thereafter. He died in 1942. During his two years on the main jazz scene, he revolutionized guitar playing. To be sure, there were guitarists before him; along with the banjo, the guitar has a longer history than any other jazz instrument. But it almost seems as if there are two different guitars: as played before Charlie Christian, and as played after.

Before Christian, the guitar was essentially an instrument of rhythm and harmonic accompaniment. The singers of folk blues, work songs, and blues ballads accompanied themselves on guitar or banjo. In the whole field of jazz prehistory – the field of the archaic, West African-influenced folk music of the Southern slaves, the guitar (or banjo) was the most important and sometimes sole instrument. This was the beginning of the tradition which singers like *Leadbelly* and *Big Bill Broonzy* carried into our time, playing rich and long melodic lines which jazz guitarists per se discovered considerably later.

The surveyable history of the jazz guitar begins with *Johnny St Cyr* and *Lonnie Johnson*. Both are from New Orleans. St Cyr was an ensemble player – with the bands of King Oliver, Louis Armstrong, and Jelly Roll Morton in the twenties – while Johnson, almost from the start, concentrated on solo work. The contrast between the rhythmic chord style and the soloistic single-note style which dominates the evolution of the guitar, is emphasized from the very beginning in St Cyr and Johnson. *Bud Scott*, *Danny Barker*, and later, in the Swing era, *Everett Barksdale* descended straight from St Cyr. Barker recorded with Charlie Parker, and the collaboration between the New Orleans guitarist and the great bop musician was not at all as paradoxical as one might assume. Everett Barksdale is known primarily for his work with the Art Tatum Trio.

The supreme representative of the rhythmic chord style of playing is *Freddie Green*, most faithful of all Count Basie band members: from 1937 to present times. Indeed, what is meant by the concept 'Basie' is in no small degree to Freddie Green's credit: the tremendous unity of the Basie rhythm sections. Nowhere else in jazz did rhythm become 'sound' to the degree it did with Basie, and this sound, basically, is the sound of Freddie Green's guitar. He hardly ever plays solos or is featured, yet he is one of the most dependable guitarists in jazz history. Green is the only guitarist who surmounted the breach created by Charlie Christian as if there had been no breach at all. Green, by the way, has a very prosperous successor on today's rock, jazz–rock, funk, and soul scene: *Cornell Dupree*, who plays the kind of dependable rhythm guitar which Green has played for six decades in the Basie band. His playing, of course, is enriched by the many developments in the music since then.

The guitarists of the New Orleans tradition who combined the chord style of St Cyr and the single-string style initiated by Lonnie Johnson in the most personal way are *Teddy Bunn* and Al Casey. Bunn made some of his most beautiful recordings with Tommy Ladnier in 1938 – among them 'If You See Me Comin'', on which he also proved himself an expressive vocalist. *Al Casey* is more in the Swing tradition. He became known through his many recordings with Fats Waller and played the – in his time – most inventive single-note solos outside the Charlie Christian realm.

Lonnie Johnson was the main influence on *Eddie Lang*, the most important Chicago-style guitarist, and also made duet recordings with him. Lang came from an Italian background, and reflects the tendency towards the *cantilena* and the *melos* of the Italian musical tradition noticeable in so many jazz musicians of Italian origin. The other important Chicago-style guitarist is *Eddie Condon*, more influenced by St Cyr, purely a rhythm player and, until his death in 1973, the tireless guiding spirit of the Chicago-style scene in New York.

If one had heard everything played by these guitarists well into the second half of the thirties, and then had gone to Europe to hear *Django Reinhardt*, he would have understood the appeal that Django had. Django came from a gypsy family which had trekked through half of Europe. He was born in Belgium, but the Reinhardts, as the name implies, are a large German gypsy family, and even today there are Reinhardt gypsy groups in Germany playing *à la Django*.

Django's playing vibrates with the string-feeling of his people – whether they play violin, like the Hungarian gypsies, or flamenco guitar, like the Spanish gypsies of Monte Sacre. All of this – combined with his great respect for Eddie Lang – came alive in Django Reinhardt's famed Quintet du Hot Club de France, consisting solely of stringed instruments: three guitars, violin, and bass. The melancholy strain of the ancient gypsy tradition lent a magic to Reinhardt's music; down through his last years (he died in 1953), he found his greatness in slow pieces. Often the very titles of his compositions capture the enchanted atmosphere of Django's music: 'Douce Ambiance', 'Mélodie au crépuscule', 'Nuages', 'Songs d'automne', 'Daphne', 'Féerie', 'Parfum', 'Finesse' . . . In 1946, none other than Duke Ellington took Django Reinhardt on an American tour.

Django was the first European whose influence could be felt on the American scene, in countless guitarists. In fact, even a nonguitarist like pianist John Lewis named Django as a man who had influenced him through the climate of his music: Lewis named 'Django', one of the Modern Jazz Quartet's most successful pieces, in memory of Reinhardt. And even in the seventies, many guitarists showed allegiance to Reinhardt; in the United States, for instance, Earl Klugh, mandolin player David Grisman (see 'Miscellaneous Instruments'), Larry Coryell and, in Europe, French guitarist Christian Escoudé and Boulou Ferré (both also from gypsy families), as well as Belgian guitar virtuoso Philip Catherine. It was above all Philip's sound that made Charles Mingus call him 'Young Django'.

The phenomenon of Django has often been cause for amazement. How was it possible for such a musician to emerge from the European world? In all probability, the only possible explanation – if one is not satisfied with the statement that Django simply was there – is sociological: European gypsies were in a social situation comparable to American blacks. Again and again, ethnic minority groups have been the sources of great jazz musicians – in the United States (besides the blacks), Jews and Italians; and in the Europe of the thirties and forties, particularly Jews. Jazz in its authentic form is a cry for freedom, whatever the racial environment and whatever the style.

Django's position as an outsider is somewhat related to that of *Laurindo Almeida*, a Brazilian musician of the rank of the great concert guitarists, such as Segovia or Gomez. Almeida employed the Spanish guitar tradition within jazz – initially, in the late forties, as a member of Stan Kenton's band. The solos he played on some of Kenton's recordings emanate more warmth than almost anything else in the cold and glittering music of that phase of Kenton's development. Since the seventies, he has been one of the 'LA4', with altoist Bud Shank, bassist Ray Brown and drummer Jeff Hamilton. They have been quite successful with their mixture of classical and Latin American music plus jazz.

Another guitarist who loves to mix different kinds of music is *Charlie Byrd*, who lives in Washington. He really is in command of everything that can be expressed on the guitar – from Bach to Brazilian Bossa Nova.

The connection of the Iberian baroque guitar tradition with the modern age (and also with a West African rhythmic feeling coming from the Yoruba tradition) was made even more convincing by the great guitarists of Brazil. The three best known are *Baden Powell, Bola Sete*, and *Egberto Gismonti*. Powell is the most original and rhythmically most dynamic of them. Sete, who has been living in the United States since 1960 and who played with Dizzy Gillespie, names Reinhardt and Segovia as his important influences. In the seventies, Gismonti appeared with Norwegian saxophonist Jan Garbarek and American bassist Charlie Haden. They played a kind of music that transcends style and geographical borders – 'world music' in the best sense. As a writer, Gismonti has developed his own kind of chamber music, which intelligently combines classical and Latin American (especially Brazilian) music.

But back to Django Reinhardt (who also featured, in a totally different cultural environment, but in a similar process of acculturation, many Ibero–Spanish elements). The melodic lines he initially played on unamplified guitar seemed almost to cry out for the technical and expressive possibilities of the electrically amplified guitar. *Charlie Christian* gave the electric guitar such renown that almost all guitarists switched from acoustic to amplified instruments at the turn of the thirties. Yet Christian was not the first to play amplified jazz guitar. First came *Eddie Durham*, the arranger, trombonist, and guitarist in the bands of Jimmie Lunceford and occasionally Count Basie. In Basie's 1937 recording of 'Time Out', the contrast between Freddie Green's rhythm guitar, acoustic, and Durham's solo guitar, electric, is charming. More recent guitarists as well – for example, Tal Farlow in the fifties and John McLaughlin in the seventies – have frequently made use of the possibilities for contrast between electric and acoustic guitar. As far as Durham is concerned, however, he did not yet know how to exploit fully the potential of the electric guitar. He continued to play it as if it were the old acoustic instrument, only electrically amplified – as in the seventies many pianists initially approached the electric piano as if it were a grand, but with an electric sound. An outstanding musician with especially keen foresight was needed to recognize the new possibilities of the electric guitar. Charlie Christian was that man.

Christian is comparable to both Lester Young and Charlie Parker. Like Young, he belongs to the Swing era and to the pathbreakers; like Parker, he belongs to the creators of modern jazz.

Christian is the outstanding soloist on some recordings made privately at Minton's around 1941: 'Charlie's Choice' and 'Stomping at the Savoy'. These records were later issued publicly and must be regarded as the first of all bebop records.

Christian charted new territory in terms of technique, harmony, and melody. Technically, he played his instrument with a virtuosity that seemed incredible to his contemporaries. The electric guitar in his hands became a 'horn' comparable to the tenor sax of Lester Young. His playing has been described as 'reed style' – he played with the expressiveness of a saxophone.

Harmonically, Christian was the first to base his improvisations not on the harmonies of the theme, but on the passing chords which he placed between the basic harmonies.

Melodically, Christian smoothed out the tinny staccato which almost all guitarists prior to him had employed into interconnected lines which radiated some of the atmosphere of Lester Young's phrases. Not surprisingly, Christian had played tenor sax before becoming a guitarist.

Whoever comes after Charlie Christian has his roots in him. To begin with, there is the first generation of 'post-Christian' guitarists: *Tiny Grimes, Oscar Moore, Irving Ashby, Les Paul, Bill de Arango, Barney Kessel*, and *Chuck Wayne*. The most important is Barney Kessel, who – as a member of the Oscar Peterson Trio and with his own groups – made many Swing-oriented recordings in the United States and in Europe. Strange how that which had seemed revolutionary in Christian appeared in Kessel, since the end of the fifties, conservative and not very daring. In the early fifties, Les Paul had an immense commercial success with recordings in which he overdubbed different sounds and tracks of electronically manipulated guitar voices. At the time, these techniques were put down in jazz circles as 'extramusical trickery'. Only from today's vantage point is it clear that – long before Jimi Hendrix and all the others about whom we will talk later – Les Paul was the pathbreaker of modern electronic manipulation of sound. That is why – twenty years after his big success – many young guitarists still refer back to him.

If Kessel could be designated the most rhythmically vital guitarist of the jazz of the fifties, Jimmy Raney is harmonically the most interesting and Johnny Smith the one with the most subtle sound. But before Raney and Smith comes *Billy Bauer*. He emerged from the Lennie Tristano school, and in the early fifties played the same abstract, long lines on the guitar that Wayne Marsh played on tenor or Lee Konitz on alto. With Konitz, Bauer made duet recordings – just guitar and alto sax – among them, the slow, deeply felt 'Rebecca' – one of the first duets in modern jazz which, even at that time, pointed towards the rich duo culture that evolved during the seventies. *Jimmy Raney* is also indebted to the Tristano school, but his melodies are more concrete and singable. Where Bauer played 'dissonant' chords and pointed leaps in which the thresholds are barely exploited, Raney featured richly nuanced harmonies, whose interrelatedness seems rounded, logical, often almost inevitable. *Johnny Smith* unfolded these harmonies to the last note. A whole universe of satiated, late-romantic sounds evolved – the world of *L'Après-midi d'un faune* brought into jazz; a fatigued, decadent faun who relaxes in the warm sun of late summer . . . or in 'Moonlight in Vermont'. The mood of this ballad has never been more subtly captured than by Johnny Smith.

All this comes together in *Tal Farlow*. Farlow initially stems from Raney, but with his big hands he had possibilities quite different from those of Raney, who only played single-finger style. After Tristano, and before Sonny Rollins, hardly any jazz musician swung such long, ceaseless, seemingly self-renewing lines above the bar lines of choruses, sequences, and bridges as Farlow. But these are not the abstract lines of Tristano; they are the concrete lines of modern jazz classicism. It is regrettable that Farlow has withdrawn so much from the scene. Only George Wein, the jazz impresario, managed to lure

him into occasional, albeit highly successful, appearances at his
Newport–New York festivals during the seventies. In the early
eighties, he was reunited very successfully with Red Norvo, on
records and in person.

Beyond the constellation Bauer–Raney–Farlow, yet inspired by it,
stand the other guitarists of modern jazz: *Jim Hall*, *Herb Ellis*, *Les
Spann*, *Gabor Szabo*, *Grant Green*, the early *George Benson*, *Kenny Burrell*,
Larry Coryell and finally the most significant: *Wes Montgomery*. Jim
Hall – with his beautifully melodious, tuneful improvisations –
gained renown, initially, through his work in the Chico Hamilton
Quintet and in Jimmy Giuffre's trio; Herb Ellis, through his long
cooperation with Oscar Peterson. Ellis often combines the stylistic
elements of Christian with a shot of blues and country music (in
which he has roots).

Jim Hall, when less and less was heard from the other great cool-
jazz guitarists (Farlow, Raney, and Bauer), became a master of
delicate, sensitive guitar improvisations that have long left behind the
confines of cool jazz and, since the seventies, can be considered the
truly ageless jazz guitar style. In this sense, Hall has become *the*
timeless jazz guitarist par excellence.

Detroit-born *Kenny Burrell* could be designated *the* outstanding
hard-bop guitarist, but – on electric as well as Spanish guitar – he has
grown in the most diverse directions. He has played with Dizzy
Gillespie, Benny Goodman, Gil Evans, Astrud Gilberto, Stan Getz,
and Jimmy Smith – which proves his versatility and openness.

Ralph Gleason, the San Francisco critic, said that *Wes Montgomery*,
who died in 1968, was 'the best thing to happen to the guitar since
Charlie Christian.' Wes was one of three musical Montgomery
Brothers from Indianapolis (the others are pianist–vibraphonist
Buddy and bassist Monk), who first became known in San Francisco.
He combined a fascinating, at the same time almost inconceivable
octave technique with hard and clear self-restraint, in statements in
which the blues and the Charlie Christian tradition figured
prominently – even when he moved into pop-jazz, as he did
frequently during the last years of his life.

Wes Montgomery's development exemplifies the way in which so
many jazz musicians become subject to the marketing process of the
industry. His producer, Creed Taylor, produced him strictly from a
market point of view – with string orchestras and commercial tunes.

He did not even allow him to play the kind of music really near and dear to him on every third or fourth album – which would have been the least you could have expected, as critic Gary Giddins once remarked. In 1962, Wes said in a *Newsweek* interview: 'I know the melody and you know the melody – so why should I turn around to play the melody?' But only a few years later, he did nothing but play melody. Towards the end of his life, Wes said: 'I'm always depressed by the result of my playing . . .'

Wes Montgomery's legacy was carried on by many musicians, but especially so by two players who are diametrically opposed to each other: *Pat Martino* and *George Benson*, the latter in a commercial direction, the former in the opposite. Martino is one of the great outsiders on the contemporary guitar scene; he is one of the few players who have not only copied Wes Montgomery's octave technique, but made their own style out of it. George Benson, at first solidly within the great black guitar tradition, in the course of the seventies became the guitar superstar with recordings selling in the millions. Along with Herbie Hancock he is the bestselling musician of modern jazz. Singer Betty Carter commented in a *Rolling Stone* interview: 'It's like George Benson . . . the way he can play, why does he have to sound like Stevie Wonder to make money?' And Benson himself said: 'I'm not there to educate an audience, I'm there to play for them.' It is Benson's singing, of course, that made him so popular on records.

But we have advanced too far. In the meantime, a 'guitar explosion', as the British *Melody Maker* called it, had taken place – a widening of the guitar scene by a factor of hundreds, if not thousands, within the span of a few years. Up to that point, the tenor sax had been the major instrument, now suddenly it was the guitar. Even psychologists have dealt with this phenomenon. Both instruments, they claim, are 'sex symbols' – the tenor being a male symbol, the guitar, with its shape reminiscent of the human female figure, the female.

Three musicians were the actual igniters of the sixties' guitar explosion, each in a different field of music: Wes Montgomery in jazz, B. B. King in blues, and Jimi Hendrix in rock.

B. B. King (more about him also in the chapter on the seventies) is the father of all guitar playing in rock and popular music of the sixties and seventies. He 'rides' on the guitar sound: He lets it approach, jumps in the saddle and bears down on it, spurs it on and gives it free rein, bridles it again, dismounts – and jumps on the next horse: the next sound. It was King who fully realized the development that began with Charlie Christian: the guitar sound grew increasingly longer, was further and further abstracted from the instrument. Of course, this development began in fact before Christian; at the moment when first the banjo, then the guitar were used in Afro-American music. It leads straight from the metallic chirpings of the banjo in archaic jazz (so brief in duration one often could barely hear them), through Eddie Lang and Lonnie Johnson, who (still without electric potential) waged a constant battle against the brevity of their sounds, and via the saxophone style of Charlie Christian and the great cool guitarists of the fifties, to B. B. King – and from him, as we shall see, on to Jimi Hendrix. This development has a single goal: the continuous, determined elongation and the related individualization and malleability of the sound (which, however, as it became easier and easier to realize technically and electronically, finally began to lose its attraction). The aim of this development – the fact that one can do almost whatever one wants with the sound of the guitar, more so than with any other instrument – may have been the main reason for the immense progress and popularity of guitar playing in the sixties and seventies.

In the sixties and early seventies, B. B. King represented the apex of a development that points back to the history and prehistory of the blues. A particularly significant role in the transformation of the rural blues guitar into the 'riding' guitar phrases of B. B. King was played by *T-Bone Walker*, who died in 1975. As we mentioned in the blues chapter, the South Side of Chicago has been a centre of the blues tradition – with guitarists like *Muddy Waters, Jimmy 'Fast Fingers' Dawkins, Buddy Guy*, and recently especially *Otis Rush*. There is a white guitarist who stems from the Chicago school of guitar playing, influenced greatly by Muddy Waters, and who stands solidly in this tradition: *Mike Bloomfield*. About Otis Rush it is said that he carries on where B. B. King left off, playing the King style even harder and more charged with electric and emotional tension. Among the guitarists bridging the gap to rock are *Albert King, Albert Collins*, and *Johnny 'Guitar' Watson*. Says Collins: 'I wanted to play jazz. I wanted to sound like Kenny Burrell . . . I've been known as a blues player, but I wanna be more than a "rock–blues" guitarist.' Watson has incorporated his guitar style, which still is very much oriented towards the blues tradition, into the funk and fusion music of the seventies.

The third great musician who – with Wes Montgomery and B. B. King – ignited the guitar explosion is *Jimi Hendrix*. Hendrix – born in 1947 as a 'black Indian' in Seattle, Washington, died in 1970 in London as a world star – is surrounded by a halo of myths. Among instrumentalists, he was the real genius of the rock age of the sixties. The exact cause of his death is still not entirely clear. An overdose of heroin, said the sensationalist press; suffocation in his own vomit was the coroner's verdict. 'I don't know whether it was an accident, suicide or murder,' is what his friend, musician Noel Redding, said. And it is still unclear where all the money, certainly millions, that Jimi had earned with his music went to.

Hendrix was the musical symbol of the counterculture of the sixties, comparable only to Bob Dylan. At the legendary Woodstock Festival, he shredded the American National Anthem – but what he really meant was America itself: He ripped the anthem with machine guns, tore it to shreds with bomb explosions and the sound of children moaning.

Hendrix has been dead for only a decade, but already there are half a hundred books about him. There are complicated analyses of his playing technique: his use of wah-wah pedals and vibrato arms; how he used rings and bottle necks and occasionally even his teeth; how he played not only on his guitar, but also 'on' his amplifier, with switches and controls; how he retuned his instrument, fast as lightning, in the middle of a song, employing totally unusual tunings; the way he seemed to drum his guitar rather than pick it; the way he played with his own feedback, waiting for it and then answering it, returning it to the amplifier, as if asking questions which he then would try to reply to, which would lead to further questions. Often it seemed as if the feedback was his real partner, more so than the rhythm sections that never really satisfied him.

Jimi's actual accomplishment was to open the music to electronics. Electronics became his instrument, while the guitar served only as a control device. He was the first to explore the wide, unfathomable land of electronic sounds, the first to play 'live electronics' – more than all of those who use this catch phrase today – and he was the first to transform electronics into music with the instinct of a genius, as if plucking the strings of an instrument made of waves, rays, and currents. Whatever can be called electronics in today's music – in jazz, rock–jazz, fusion, rock, and pop – comes from Jimi Hendrix. And that applies to guitarists as much as to electric piano and synthesizer players, and even to horn players who use electronics, as long as they employ them as more than a gimmick or a gag.

Jimi Hendrix spoke of his guitar as his lover. He got high just from playing it. But he also beat it, destroyed it, burned it – on stage. It was love and hate at the same time, a kind of sadism that was also masochism, as if someone were losing his mind, a lover who could neither give nor receive true love.

So these are the pillars of today's guitar playing: Wes Montgomery, B. B. King and Jimi Hendrix. Many guitarists have built their structures on these pillars, but none as brilliantly as *John McLaughlin*. His range extends from folk blues and Django Reinhardt through the great guitarists of the fifties – in particular Tal Farlow – to the Indian sitar (see also the chapters about jazz of the seventies, about McLaughlin himself, and about the combos of jazz).

McLaughlin has played the most diverse kinds of music – free jazz in Europe (with Gunter Hampel, for example), fusion with Miles Davis, highly electronicized music with his Mahavishnu Orchestra, Indian music with his group Shakti, solo guitar and duets with French guitarist Christian Escoudé. But whatever he plays cannot be thought of separate from his spirituality. 'God,' he says, 'is the Master musician. I am His instrument.'

One of the electronic devices employed by John McLaughlin is the guitar synthesizer, which he helped to a solid place on the guitar scene within a short time. Its fascination is especially convincing when the natural, warm guitar sound is superimposed on the synthesizer sound. The synthesizer can be programmed to couple each of the six guitar strings with a different sound – for example, the high strings with the sound of the flute or the trumpet, the middle ones with that of the trombone or tenor sax, the bottom ones with the sound of the baritone sax or the bass.

The guitar scene continues to explode. In order to get an even halfway correct picture, we can form the following groupings (remembering that they all blend into one another): rock, rock–jazz and fusion, folk jazz, free, cool, traditional, and bop–mainstream–neo-bop.

Most directly rooted in Hendrix (and in the blues) are the rock players whom we can only mention summarily in this context: *Eric Clapton*, *Duane Allman*, *Carlos Santana* (who is influenced by Latin music and who has made recordings with McLaughlin), *Jeff Beck*, *Nils Lofgren*, and, perhaps the most individualistic rock guitarist of them all, *Frank Zappa* – to name only a very few.

In diametrical opposition stand those players who have transposed the tradition of the cool guitarists from the fifties to today's jazz. The most important of them, the one who was already active during those years, is *Jim Hall*, whom we discussed earlier. 'The quiet American' is what *Melody Maker* called him when he appeared in London. And Hall himself has said: 'Even though I never got to work with Lester Young, that's the sound I try to get from my guitar.'

Other guitarists who deserve mention in this context are Hungarian-born *Attila Zoller*, Canadian *Ed Bickert*, and Americans *Howard Roberts*, *Michael Santiago*, *Doug Raney* (the son of Jimmy Raney, whose tradition Doug carries on), and *Jack Wilkins*. Zoller was initially indebted to the Lennie Tristano school. As the first among the guitarists, he transferred the long, singable melody lines he had learned back then into the freer realm of the new jazz – as in his collaborations with pianist Don Friedman. Zoller is a master of sensitive, romantic restraint, and it is hard to understand why a man of such talent is still known only to insiders. Bickert made recordings with Paul Desmond, the 'poet of the alto saxophone', and Bickert's style is just as 'poetic'. Wilkins, perhaps the most talented of the younger guitarists of this direction, has become known through his work in trombonist Bob Brookmeyer's group.

Let's move on to the largest grouping, the jazz–rock and fusion guitarists. This grouping incorporates extreme positions: rock and blues on the one hand, cool and bebop on the other. In this instance, too, our list can claim anything but completeness: *Joe Beck* (chronologically the first), *Larry Coryell*, *Steve Khan*, *Eric Gale*, *Earl Klugh*, *Al DiMeola*, *Pat Metheny*, *Lee Ritenour*, *Vic Juris*, *Baird Hersey* (cf. the big-band chapter), *Larry Carlton*, *Janne Shaffer*, as well as Dutchman *Jan Akkerman*, Briton *Allan Holdsworth*, Finn *Jukka Tolonen*, Norwegian *Terje Rypdal*, and the Germans *Volker Kriegel* and *Toto Blanke*.

Larry Coryell was already playing fusion music in the mid-sixties, when nobody even knew the term, in the Gary Burton Quartet and in the group Free Spirits. His major influences were Jimi Hendrix and John McLaughlin: 'Jimi is the greatest musician who ever lived, as far as I'm concerned . . .' But then he adds: 'I hate him, because he took everything away from me that was mine . . .' and about John McLaughlin: 'McLaughlin heard me in England and I still hear some of my own style coming back at me. Then, when he came to the United States, I started listening to him. It's a two-way street.' Coryell hails from Texas, which is his third major influence: 'If you listen to me carefully, it must come through that I'm from Texas.'

With keyboard player Richard Tee, drummer Steve Gadd, and the already mentioned Cornell Dupree on rhythm guitar, *Eric Gale* formed the successful group Stuff. *Steve Khan* gained prominence through his recordings with the Brecker Brothers and with the fusion recordings of arranger Bob James, but he also paid tribute to Thelonious Monk in a congenial solo suite. At the outset of his career, *Al DiMeola* recorded a wonderful duet album, transcending all musical cultures, with the great Spanish flamenco guitarist Paco de Lucia; but he never subsequently fulfilled the promise of this duet. *Pat Metheny* scored a world-wide success with his smooth, catchy jazz–rock sounds. 'Miracle sounds, trips through the spheres, magic rituals, music as appeal shrouded in secrecies, pop-jazz as hypnosis,' is what critic Klaus Robert Bachmann found in his music. And he himself feels: 'I love Wes Montgomery and Jim Hall . . . but obviously what I do is quite far from what Wes was doing. It's much more, I hate to say it, "white". Wes was bluesier . . .' *Lee Ritenour* probably is the busiest guitarist on the Los Angeles fusion scene. *Jan Akkerman* has created a fascinating combination of Johann Sebastian Bach with rock, a combination that sounds anything but paradoxical on his guitar. *Terje Rypdal*, finally, is a guitarist who creates tone paintings that remind one of the fjords and dark mountain lakes of his Norwegian homeland.

Related in many ways to the players of rock–jazz and fusion are the folk–jazz guitarists. Considering how deeply rooted the guitar is in the folk music traditions of many different cultures, it is no wonder that this direction has evolved. Among the guitarists of this style, there are players as diverse as *Alex de Grassi*, *William Ackerman*, *Leo Kottke*, *Ry Cooder*, *John Fahey*, and *Robbie Basho*. The latter is also indebted to the meditative music of India; one of his tunes he termed a 'neo-gothic construction for six-string guitar, combining East and West.'

Proceeding to the free guitarists, the first musician to play free-jazz guitar in the sixties was *Sonny Sharrock*, who played with Pharoah Sanders, Don Cherry, and others. He was followed by *Michael Gregory Jackson* (certainly the most important and creative of them all), *James Emery*, *Spencer Barefield*, *James Blood Ulmer*, and Briton *Derek Bailey*. Probably the most radical of these free players is Bailey; working on his instrument in all imaginable ways, he is one of the most original players on the European free-jazz scene. James Blood Ulmer, who came out of an Ornette Coleman group and studied and uses Coleman's 'harmolodic system', has become the pathbreaker of 'no wave' music (see the chapter 'The Eighties'). He bridges from free to funk, concretizing the former and musicalizing the latter. Ulmer's motto: 'Jazz is the teacher, funk is the preacher.'

Diametrically opposed to the free players, to use another pair of contrasts, are the guitarists who remained connected with the Swing tradition. Among them are *George Barnes* (who died in 1977) and *Bucky Pizzarelli*, who formed a wonderful guitar duet, *Cal Collins*, and the best known of them, *Joe Pass*. In the early seventies, Barnes co-led a quartet with Ruby Braff, in whose stylistic mould both he and Pizzarelli belong. Pass made recordings with many of the important jazz people of Norman Granz's Pablo label, among them Ella Fitzgerald and Oscar Peterson. He is a master of ballad playing as well as of swinging jam sessions. Like tenor man Scott Hamilton and trumpeter Warren Vaché, Collins is part of the new Swing movement that has been crystallizing since the turn of the seventies.

Finally, we have to mention some of the players of the contemporary mainstream which leads from bebop via Coltrane to neo-bop; *John Scofield*, *John Abercrombie*, *Roland Prince*, *Ted Dunbar*, *Rodney Jones*, *Ed Cherry*, *Joe Diorio*, *Monette Sudler*, *Ron Eschete*. The most prominent is Abercrombie, an improviser full of ideas. He has played with two great drummers – two very different ones: Billy Cobham and Jack DeJohnette – and indeed, his playing is marked by an astounding rhythmic variety and assurance.

At the very end, however, we must discuss a musician who fits into none of the groupings we have suggested: *Ralph Towner*, leader of the group Oregon, which disbanded in 1981. Towner began as a pianist and still plays piano. His guitar style is moulded by this piano element. Towner studied in Vienna, and he admits to not being quite sure which side he is more indebted to: European music – in

particular music from Vienna, that is, Viennese classicism, romanticism, and avant-garde (Schoenberg, Webern, etc.) – or jazz. 'I
wasn't on the jazz scene until I got a classically oriented technique on
the guitar . . . I do find acoustic instruments more sympathetic than
electric instruments . . . I treat the guitar quite often like a piano trio.
If I'm playing alone, it's almost like a one-man band approach . . .'

The guitar has come a long way – from the African banjo to the
instrument of John McLaughlin and Ralph Towner, from folk blues
to the guitar synthesizer. Like the flute, the guitar is an archetypical
instrument. The Greek god Pan, the Indian god Shiva, and Aztec
gods have blown on flutes; angels and Apsaras – the female heavenly
beings of Hindu mythology – have played guitars. Psychologists have
pointed to the phallic image of the flute and the similarity of the
guitar to the female body. Like a lover, the guitarist must woo the
body of his mistress, stroke and caress it, so that she not only receives
love, but also returns it. The guitarist and his instrument symbolize
the couple *per se*, symbolize love.

The Bass

In 1911, Bill Johnson organized the Original Creole Jazz Band, the
first real jazz band to go on tour from New Orleans. He played
bowed bass. In the course of a job in Shreveport, Louisiana, he broke
his bow. For half the night, he had to pluck the strings of his bass.
Ostensibly, the effect was so novel and interesting that the jazz bass
has been played pizzicato ever since.

This tale, told by jazz veterans from New Orleans, is probably an
invention, but has the advantage of reflecting much of the spirit of
those years. Thus, it is 'true' on a higher level. On the everyday level,
it is true that the string bass had much competition from the tuba in
old New Orleans. The tuba tradition was so strong that, even thirty
years later, many of the great Swing bassists – such as John Kirby and
Red Callender – still played tuba.

The bass provides the harmonic foundation for the jazz ensemble.
It is the backbone of a jazz group. At the same time, the bass has a
rhythmic task. Since bop, the four even beats to the measure played
by the bass are often the only factor keeping the basic rhythm firm.

Since the plucked string bass can fulfil this rhythmic function with more precision than the blown tuba, bass replaced the tuba at an early date. Thirty-five years later, the electric bass has established itself next to the 'acoustic' contrabass. The evolution thus moves from tuba via stand-up bass to electric bass guitar: In the course of this evolution, the rhythmic impulse has become more precise, shorter, sharper. In the course of the same development, on the other hand, the sound has become less personal and direct. Many of the great bassists have pointed out that the acoustic bass is such a sensitive, highly developed instrument that it will never be replaced by modern electronics. It might well be that the stand-up bass has an ideal median position between the two extremes of the tuba on the one hand and the electric bass guitar on the other, because it fulfils the needs of sound and rhythm optimally.

All bassists of traditional jazz refer back to *Pops Foster*. Foster worked with Freddie Keppard, King Oliver, Kid Ory, Louis Armstrong, Sidney Bechet, and all the other New Orleans greats, and can easily be identified by his 'slapping' technique. This way of letting the strings snap back against the finger-board of the bass – rejected by the bassists of the fifties as a sign of extreme technical inability, but used again by the free-jazz bassists to increase sound and intensity – gave Foster's playing much of its rhythmic impact. During the thirties, Foster was chosen several times as the 'all-time bassist' of jazz. In 1942 – the year when Jimmy Blanton, the man who had 'emancipated' the bass, died – he went to work for the New York subway system, but resumed his playing career when the traditionalist revival began. He died in 1969.

John Kirby and *Walter Page* are the great bassists of the Swing era. Kirby, who emerged from the Fletcher Henderson band in the early thirties, was leader of a small group in the late thirties which cannot be omitted from the history of the jazz combo. Walter Page (who died in 1957) was a member of the classic Basie rhythm section. Jo Jones says that it was Page who really taught him to play in Kansas City: 'An even 4/4.'

Further Swing-era bassists who should be mentioned are *Slam Stewart* and *Bob Haggart*. Haggart was the backbone of the Swing-attuned Dixieland – or the Dixieland-attuned Swing – of the Bob Crosby band, and is continuing this tradition as co-leader of the 'World's Greatest Jazz Band'. Stewart is best known for the way he sings in octaves with his *arco* playing: the humming effect of a bee, which can be very amusing if not heard too often. Later, *Major Holley* also played in a similar manner, but Holley sings in unison with his bowing.

Generally speaking, the history of the bass can be approached from the same point of view as that of the guitar. As modern guitar history begins with Charlie Christian, so the story of modern bass starts with *Jimmy Blanton*. Both Christian and Blanton stepped on to the main jazz stage in 1939. Both died of lung disease in 1942. In two short years, both revolutionized the playing of their respective instruments, made 'horns' of them. This function was established as clearly in the duo recordings made by Blanton in 1939–40 with Duke Ellington at the piano as it was by Charlie Christian with Benny Goodman during the same period. The Ellington band of the early forties is considered the best band of Ellington's career primarily because Jimmy Blanton was on bass. He gave the Ellington Band an especially high degree of rhythmic–harmonic compactness. Blanton was twenty-three when he died. He made the bass a solo instrument.

From Blanton stretches the impressive line of modern jazz bassists: *Oscar Pettiford* is the second. Soon after the death of Blanton he became Ellington's bassist. And as Duke had recorded duets with Blanton's bass, he now made quartet recordings with Pettiford on cello. *Harry Babasin* was the first jazz cellist, but Pettiford was the man who gave the cello its place in jazz. The road from the deeper sounds of the bass to the higher range of the cello seemed a natural consequence of the evolution of the bass from harmonic to melodic instrument. Since then, there have been other bassists, too, who have chosen the cello as secondary instrument, as did the late *Doug Watkins*, and later *Ron Carter* and *Peter Warren* until finally, in today's jazz, the cello has become an autonomous solo instrument. Musicians like *Abdul Wadud*, *Diedre Murray*, *David Darling*, *Tristan Honsinger*, *Kent Carter*, and Frenchman *Jean-Charles Capon* play it. (For more details, see the chapter 'Miscellaneous Instruments'.)

Pettiford, *Ray Brown*, and *Charles Mingus* are the great post-Blanton bassists. Pettiford, who died in Copenhagen in 1960, played on 52nd Street in the mid-forties with Dizzy Gillespie, and at that time really disseminated the new 'Blanton message'. In the fifties, he was the busiest bass player on the New York scene. Several times during his career Pettiford organized big bands for recording purposes. His mobility on the bass was consistently amazing. He knew how to create tones on the bass that sounded as if he were 'talking' on a horn. There may be more perfect bassists, but nobody could 'tell a story' as O. P. could. In the two years before his death, when he lived in Europe – first in Baden-Baden, then in Copenhagen – he had a strong and lasting influence on many European musicians. (And if the author is permitted a personal word of gratitude here, I should like to say that I have not learned more from any great jazzman than from those night-long talks and record-listening sessions with O. P., who always considered it a special challenge to spread the 'message' – as he called it – of jazz.)

Ray Brown is considered the most dependable and swinging of the first generation of bebop bass players. He was featured in a bass concerto, 'One Bass Hit', recorded by Dizzy Gillespie and his big band in the late forties. Later, he recorded an album with a big band of California musicians led by arranger–pianist Marty Paich, which is nothing less than a complete, grandiose 'concerto' for bass and big band. This record also contains a solo for bass alone: it has the aura of 'Picasso', Coleman Hawkins's equally unaccompanied tenor-sax solo. Brown is the preferred bassist for Norman Granz's record productions. Compared to the technical stunts of today's bassists, he may not be one of the modern virtuosos; but his unerring way of infusing swing and relaxation into a band still is unbeatable in the early eighties.

Charles Mingus, who died in 1979, is of overriding significance, not only as a bass player, but also as a band leader. Mingus, who called jazz 'black classical music', had an especially keen awareness of the black musical tradition, and he really lived this tradition: In the early forties, he briefly played traditional jazz with Kid Ory. Then he joined Lionel Hampton, whose best band – that of 1947 – gained much from Mingus's arrangements and personality. Through his work with the Red Norvo Trio in 1950–51, he won renown as a soloist. Subsequently, he increasingly turned his attention to breaking new paths for jazz, never fearing powerful and exciting harmonic clashes. There was probably more collective improvisation in the Mingus groups of the fifties and early sixties than in any other significant jazz combo of that time. As a bassist, Mingus led and held together the many different lines and tendencies that took shape within his groups with the certitude of a sleepwalker. More than any other musician, he paved the way for the free, collective improvisations of the new jazz. The duets of Mingus on bass and the great avant-gardist Eric Dolphy on bass clarinet offer some of the stongest emotional experiences in all of jazz.

During the mid-sixties, Mingus lived in comparative seclusion. But from 1970 until his final illness, he enjoyed a world-wide comeback. It did not start in the United States, but on a great European tour, prompted by years of repeated invitations to appear at the Berlin Jazz Days. The new Mingus of the seventies looked back on the whole history of jazz.

The triumvirate Pettiford–Brown–Mingus seems even more brilliant when seen in the light of a host of other outstanding jazz bassists of that generation, among them *Chubby Jackson, Eddie Safranski, Milt Hinton, George Duvivier, Percy Heath, Tommy Potter, Curtis Counce, Leroy Vinnegar, Red Mitchell, Paul Chambers, Wilbur Ware, Israel Crosby . . .*

Safranski and *Chubby Jackson* (who plays a specially built five-string bass) became known primarily through their work in the bands of Stan Kenton and Woody Herman. *Duvivier* and *Hinton* are 'musicians' musicians', highly regarded by musicians for their assurance and dependability. *Percy Heath* has become a much-admired musician through his superior, firm playing in the Modern Jazz Quartet. *Leroy Vinnegar* turned the California-based rhythm sections built around Shelly Manne upside down, insofar as Shelly found many melodic potentials in the drums, while Leroy's bass delivered the rhythmic foundation that made the swing felt. He, and before him *Curtis Counce*, who died in 1963, and later *Monty Budwig, Carson Smith*, and *Joe Mondragon* were among the most frequently recorded bassists on the West Coast. *Red Mitchell* is a wonderful soloist who phrases with saxophone-like intensity and mobility. In the seventies he had a fabulous comeback, particularly with Japanese audiences. The late *Paul Chambers* had the expressiveness and vitality of the Detroit hard-bop generation. He was also a master of bowed bass, and played *arco* with intonation and phrasing reminiscent of Sonny Rollins's tenor sax. *Wilbur Ware*, who died in 1979, was a unique soloist and the chosen bassist of Thelonious Monk – probably the most empathetic Monk ever had.

With Chambers and Ware, we have arrived within the circle of hard-bop bassists: *Jimmy Woode* (who emerged from the Duke Ellington band, and since has become one of the most indispensable 'mericans in Europe'), *Wilbur Little, Jymie Merritt, Sam Jones*, the late *Doug Watkins*, *Reginald Workman*, and others belong to this group. Some of them have been pathbreakers for the development that was carried out by *Charlie Haden* and *Scott LaFaro*: the second phase of the emancipation of the bass – after the first one associated with Jimmy Blanton and Oscar Pettiford.

Since the turn of the fifties, *Haden* has frequently worked with Ornette Coleman, and he was – in the beginning perhaps even more so than Don Cherry – an essential partner of Coleman. His Liberation Music Orchestra, for which Carla Bley wrote arrangements, expands not only musical but also political consciousness: music conceived as the guiding torch of freedom – using themes and recordings from East Germany, Cuba, and the Spanish Civil War. Notable also is Haden's cooperation with Keith Jarrett and – in the group Old and New Dreams – with Don Cherry. In a number of duo recordings, Haden proved himself to be one of the most empathetic and stimulating duo partners of today.

Scott LaFaro, tragically killed in a 1961 auto crash at twenty-five, was a musician on the order of Eric Dolphy, creating new possibilities not from disdain for the harmonic tradition, but from superior mastery of it. Hearing LaFaro improvise with the Bill Evans Trio makes clear what the bass has become through its second emancipation: a kind of super-dimensional, low-register guitar, whose sound has so many diverse possibilities as would have been thought impossible for the bass only a short time before, but which still fulfils the traditional functions of the bass. Says bassist Dave Holland: 'The bass has become something like the fourth melody voice in the quartet. Wasn't Scott LaFaro the major reason for that?' John Coltrane's bassist *Jimmy Garrison*, who died in 1976, developed Scott LaFaro's 'guitar sound' into a 'flamenco guitar sound' – for example, in the long solo which he plays at the beginning of the 1966 recording of Trane's hit, 'My Favourite Things'. Perhaps even more amazing technically was the bass work of *David Izenzon* (who died in 1979) in the Ornette Coleman Trio during the mid-sixties. He presented his 'guitarlike' bass sounds with the drive of a percussionist.

These, then, are the 'headwaters' from which the mainstream of the bass flows through the sixties and seventies into the eighties – with musicians like *Richard Davis*, *Ron Carter*, *Chuck Israels*, *Gary Peacock*, *Steve Swallow*, *Barre Phillips*, *Eddie Gomez*, *Cecil McBee*, *Buster Williams*, *Stafford James*, *Mark Johnson*, *Clint Houston*, *Dave Williams*, *Calvin Hill*,

Cameron Brown, Michael Moore, Mike Richmond, David Friesen, Glen Moore, Harvie Swartz, Frank Tusa, Gene Perla, Wayne Dockery, French *Henry Texier,* Hungarian *Aladar Pege,* German *Günter Lenz,* Swede *Palle Danielsson,* Dane *Niels-Hanning Ørsted Pedersen,* Briton *Dave Holland,* and Czechs *George Mraz* and *Miroslav Vitous.*

Because of this wealth of players, we can give special mention to only a few. *Richard Davis* is perhaps the most versatile of all bassists. He is one of those universalists who have mastered with equal perfection everything from symphonic music to all kinds of jazz, all the way from bop to free playing. *Ron Carter* and *Dave Holland* became known through their work with Miles Davis. Holland, who has also played with Chick Corea, Anthony Braxton, and Sam Rivers, made a statement characterizing the situation of many contemporary musicians: 'What produced tension ten years ago now no longer produces tension, because it has become commonplace to one's ear. In order to create that same kind of tension now, you have to use something which is even further removed from the original idea of consonance . . .' Carter is an improviser with such a wealth of ideas that, as critic Pete Welding put it, it 'occasionally seems as if he is playing duos with himself.' Coming from the acoustic bass, he has mastered a wide range of instruments: first the cello, more recently a 'piccolo bass' – an instrument of baroque music – in cellolike tuning. Carter plays the piccolo bass, which is to the contrabass approximately what the violin is to the viola, with the brilliance and lightness of a *pizzicato* concert violin and, at the same time, with the drive of a jazz player like Oscar Pettiford. It is fascinating how, in the quartet he led from 1977 to 1980, his piccolo bass and the conventional acoustic bass – initially played by Buster Williams, later by others – complemented each other, creating the impression that the group employed a single eight-string bass – probably the richest bass sound on today's scene. Ron Carter in a *downbeat* interview: 'The term "liberation of the bass" has such negative overtones to it – it means that someone has been in bondage up to this point . . . I've never felt inhibited in what I was trying to play. I didn't necessarily feel that I was a bass in a rhythm section that played behind or accompanied a soloist, that my function was just a function . . . Since the music the electronic bass is predominantly used in is so different from the acoustic bass, it's like comparing apples and oranges. I don't see the electric bass as having any major input in regard to the development of the upright bass at any time . . .'

Chuck Israels also made a name for himself as leader of an excellent big band. *Gary Peacock*, *Steve Swallow*, and *Barre Phillips* (who lives in Europe) are particularly sensitive and immensely flexible bassists. *Eddie Gomez* was one of the busiest acoustic bass players on the New York scene of the seventies and remains so in the early eighties. He has also shown himself to be a ravishing duet partner: of pianist JoAnne Brackeen and of flutist Jeremy Steig, for instance.

Cecil McBee and *Buster Williams* cultivate and update the Coltrane tradition on the bass in a way similar to McCoy Tyner on the piano. *David Friesen* and *Glen Moore* have come to the fore with a number of chamber-musiclike recordings – the former, for example, in a duo with John Stowell, the latter in the group Oregon. *Aladar Pege*, bass teacher at the Hungarian National Conservatory in Budapest, has been praised in Europe since the first half of the sixties as an 'unbelievable bass miracle in terms of playing technique'. In 1980, he had a sensational success at the Jazz Yatra in Bombay, the great Indian festival. Since then, he has also been recognized and praised on the American scene, and Pege repeatedly took the place of the late, great Charles Mingus in the posthumous group Mingus Dynasty. *Miroslav Vitous* was a founding member of Weather Report in 1971. He has a special sensitivity to advanced fusion music. *George Mraz* and *Mike Richmond* seem like 'Ray Browns of the contemporary scene' through their dependable swinging rhythms.

The most-recorded bassist in Europe is the Dane *Niels-Henning Ørsted Pedersen*. During the last two decades, whenever an American soloist on tour in Europe needed a bassist, Niels-Henning was almost always the musician to get the call. In this way, he came to play with Bud Powell, Quincy Jones, Roland Kirk, Sonny Rollins, Lee Konitz, John Lewis, Dexter Gordon, Ben Webster, Oscar Peterson, and dozens of other famous musicians.

Ørsted Pedersen summarized the situation of the bass on today's scene in the following way: 'The bass has become more and more independent as an instrument. In the older jazz there was a very strong connection between instrument and solo, and it's my opinion that a solo should not be determined by the instrument. What I like today is that you've left the point behind where you have technical difficulties; there's no reason to be impressed by anything, just go for the music . . .'

Beyond the mainstream, we find – as with the other instruments – players of free music on the one hand, and fusion and jazz–rock players (who mostly use the electric bass) on the other. (Here, too, one must realize that, particularly today, many musicians have become so versatile that they can belong to the most diverse stylistic camps. We will list them in the grouping where they are most often found.) Important free bassists are *Buell Neidlinger*, *Peter Warren*, *Jack Gregg*, *Sirone*, *Henry Grimes*, *Alan Silva*, *Malachi Favors*, *Fred Hopkins*, *Mark Helias*, *John Lindberg*, *Rick Rozie*, *Francisco Centeno*, Briton *Brian Smith*, Japanese *Yoshizawa Motoharu* and *Katsuo Kuninaka*, Austrian *Adelhard Roidinger*, Norwegian *Arild Anderson*, Italian *Marcello Mellis*, Dutchmen *Arjen Gorter* and *Maarten van Regteren-Altena*, Germans *Peter Kowald* and *Buschi Niebergall*, and finally, South African *Johnny Dyani*. Musicians like Neidlinger, Sirone, and Silva belong to the first generation of free players. Neidlinger and Sirone worked with Cecil Taylor, Silva with Sun Ra's orchestra. Malachi Favors plays bass in the Art Ensemble of Chicago, Fred Hopkins in the group Air. John Lindberg has played with Anthony Braxton and is now a member of the New York String Trio. Arild Andersen could be called an especially 'romantic' player. Yoshizawa Motoharu's immensely intense bass is deeply rooted in the Japanese tradition – as is Johnny Dyani's in the tradition of his native South Africa. And Rick Rozie, finally, has managed in the early eighties to open up again new dimensions of free-bass playing.

It took years for electric bass players to solve the problems they had with their sound – the dull, somehow always empty tone of the instrument. Their dilemma was this: on the one hand, the electric bass had more flexibility, its sound – and its volume! – fit better into electric groups; on the other hand it lacked expressivity, it didn't sound 'human', but technical. The first player to initiate a change in the early seventies was a rock bassist: *Larry Graham* of Sly and the Family Stone. He did something that bass teachers of the academy would strictly forbid: He played – incredibly percussively – with his thumb. In the black rock and rhythm & blues productions of Motown Records, this thumb style became something like a trademark: the bass played with such intensity that its strings occasionally hit the wood of the instrument, just like the old New Orleans slap bass. *Stanley Clarke* combined this thumb style with Scott LaFaro's technique (and was immensely successful with his fusion music). LaFaro's technique had already been used on the electric bass by *Steve Swallow*, but it was up to *Jaco Pastorius* from Florida – he became famous overnight in 1976 when he first played with Weather Report – to solve the problem. He combined the thumb approach and LaFaro's flexibility with an octave technique that had been associated with guitarist Wes Montgomery, but considered out of reach for bassists, and to this he added his very personal flageolet style of playing. In this way, Pastorius has become the bass sensation of the past decade, because through him the electric bass finally has become fully 'emancipated'. Now, all of a sudden, the electric bass had that attribute which Oscar Pettiford had made the main criterion for all bass playing: 'Humanity, expressivity, emotionality, the ability to tell a story.' Says Pastorius: 'I play the bass as if I were playing a human voice. I play like I speak. I like singers . . .'

Among other electric bass players, we first have to mention two musicians who predate the development just discussed: *Jack Bruce* and *Chuck Rainey* – and then the German *Eberhard Weber, Miroslav Vitous, John Lee, Mark Egan, Alphonso Johnson, Don Pate, Abe Laboriel, Ralphe Armstrong, Michael Henderson, Bob Cranshaw, Jamaaladeen Tacuma,* as well as the Dane *Bo Stief* and Briton *Hugh Hopper.* Bruce was a member of the legendary group Cream, which in the sixties realized blues-inspired rock improvisations in a jam-session style. Though a true member of the British rock scene, Bruce has made several recordings with such jazz musicians as Charlie Mariano and Carla Bley. *Weber* has pointed to his sense of allegiance to the European tradition; he has included elements of this tradition – above all, from the period of romanticism – in his playing and in that of his group Colours. With drummer Gerry Brown, *Lee* formed one of the most dependable fusion rhythm sections on the New York scene. *Johnson,* formerly with Weather Report, is an especially elegant, flexible player who is very active on the West Coast fusion scene. *Hopper* is associated with the music of the British group Soft Machine. And *Stief* must be considered the most sought-after electric bassist on today's European scene.

Jazz has made the bass, the 'clumsy elephant' of the symphony orchestra, into a highly sensitive instrumental voice commanding the whole range of expressive possibilities – to a point where bassists like Rick Rozie, Jaco Pastorius, or David Friesen can successfully play solo concerts which are filled with musical tension and beauty. When you consider that Pastorius can handle Charlie Parker's 'Donna Lee' – a tune which has driven many a horn player to exasperation – as if it were the easiest thing in the world, then you start to realize what kind of development the jazz bass has gone through since the days of Jimmy Blanton.

At the conclusion of this bass chapter, let's once again quote the veteran bassist *Ray Brown*: 'Take a guy like myself, who's been playing the bass since he was fourteen. I've seen this instrument go from a slapped, two-beat instrument into complete freedom with people like Stanley Clarke . . . I have been cast in situations where the guy says, "You're free." I said, "Wait a minute. I don't know if I want to be free." I've talked to kids who don't know anything but freedom. They don't know what it's like to play time and enjoy it . . . And yet, I like what's happening to the bass. Some of the young people I have heard play the bass like a guitar and it's fantastic. But I also still enjoy going someplace and seeing somebody playing time with a good sound – that will never be replaced! It's like a heartbeat.' The young Swing generation (we have repeatedly mentioned it) will see to it that this 'heartbeat' will not be forgotten. These musicians play Swing very much in the tradition, and yet are also very much part of the eighties. Their central player (aside from their senior Ray Brown) is *Brian Torff*, who is an astounding match for Brown.

The Drums

To the person raised in the tradition of European concert music, jazz drums initially appear to be noise-making devices. But – paradoxical as it may seem – this is because the drums serve this very purpose in European music. The tympani parts in Tchaikovsky or Richard Strauss, in Beethoven or Wagner, are 'noise-makers' insofar as they are intended to create additional intensity and *fortissimo* effects. The music 'happens' independently of them; the musical continuity would not break down if they were left out. But the beat of the jazz drum is no mere effect. It creates the space within which the music 'happens': the musical continuity would become disrupted if it could not be constantly 'measured' against the beat of a swinging drummer. Jazz rhythm, as we have already shown, is an ordering principle.

It was no accident that there were no drum solos in the early forms of jazz – indeed, there were no drummers then with developed individuality. Concerning early jazz history, we know of Buddy Bolden and Freddie Keppard and the Tio family, we know of trumpeters, trombonists, even violinists – but we hardly know anything of drummers. Since the beat was the ordering principle – and only that! – the drummer had no task but to mark the beats as steadily as possible, a task which was performed the worse the less neutrally (i.e., the more individually) he drummed. Only later was it discovered that an additional element of the tension so important to jazz could be gained from the individuality of a drummer – without loss to the ordering function. Quite the contrary: unvaried, metronomic regulation developed into organically nuanced artistic order.

At the beginning stand *Baby Dodds* and *Zutty Singleton*, the great drummers of New Orleans. Zutty was the softer, Baby the harder. Zutty created an almost supple rhythm; Baby was vehement and natural – at least in the terms of that day. Dodds was the drummer in King Oliver's Creole Jazz Band, later with Louis Armstrong's Hot Seven. He can be heard on many records with his brother, clarinetist Johnny Dodds. Baby was the first to play breaks: brief drum eruptions, which often fill in the gaps between the conclusion of a phrase and the end of a formal unit, or set off solos from each other. The break is the egg from which drummers – primarily Gene Krupa – hatched the drum solo.

Oddly enough, white drummers initially expressed more strongly the tendency towards accentuating the weak beats (2 and 4) so characteristic of jazz. The first two are the drummers of the two famous early white bands: *Tony Spargo* (Sbarbaro) of the Original Dixieland Band and *Ben Pollack* of the New Orleans Rhythm Kings. Pollack later founded one of the first larger jazz-oriented dance bands in California (1925) in which many musicians who began in Chicago style – among them Benny Goodman, Jack Teagarden, and Glenn Miller – first became known. In the late twenties, *Ray Bauduc* held the drum chair in the Pollack band. Ray is one of the best white drummers in the New Orleans–Dixieland tradition.

Within the Chicago-style circle 'white' drumming developed in a different direction: towards virtuoso play with rhythm, in which the play occasionally became more important than the rhythm. The three most important Chicago drummers were *Gene Krupa*, *George Wettling*, and *Dave Tough*. George Wettling was the only one who remained true to the musical tradition of Chicago style until the end of his life – he died in 1968. Wettling was also a gifted abstract painter. He remarked that jazz drumming and abstract painting seemed different to him only from the point of view of craftsmanship: in both fields, he felt rhythm to be decisive. To someone who expressed amazement that Wettling should be both abstract painter and jazz drummer, he conveyed his own surprise that he should be the only one active in both spheres, since in his opinion they belonged together. George Wettling was one of those fascinating personalities who demonstrate the unity of modern art simply through their work.

Gene Krupa, who died in 1973, became the star drum virtuoso of the Swing era. 'Sing Sing Sing', his feature with the Benny Goodman band, in which he played a long solo (in part with Benny's high-register clarinet soaring above him), drove the Swing fans to frenzy. Technically, Krupa was topped only by the drummers of modern jazz. He was the first who dared to use the bass drum on recordings in the twenties. It had been the practice to dispense with recording this part of the drummer's equipment, due to the danger that its reverberations would cause the cutting-needle to jump on the still rather primitive recording equipment.

The most important drummer of the Chicago circle is *Dave Tough*, who died in 1948. He, too, was a man who knew something about the unity of modern art – if not as a painter, then as a would-be writer. Throughout his life, he flirted with contemporary literature as Bix Beiderbecke had flirted with symphonic music. Tough was one of the most subtle and inspired of drummers of his time. To him, the drums were a rhythmic palette on which he held in readiness the right colour for each soloist. He gained his greatest fame around 1944 as the drummer in Woody Herman's 'First Herd'. He helped pave the way for modern jazz drumming, as did *Jo Jones* with Count Basie's band, and it is interesting to note how a white and a black drummer arrived at similar results more or less independently of each other.

More about Jo Jones later, but let us point out that here is a fact vividly illuminating the element of inevitability in jazz evolution. Aside from Baby Dodds, the white Chicago drummers hardly drew much from other black drummers. Even though there were constant relations with black musicians, one could say that for twenty years 'white' and 'black' drumming in the main developed independently of each other. Nevertheless, the two evolutionary branches arrived at similar results. Dave Tough prepared the way for the new style in Tommy Dorsey's band, which he joined in 1936. At the time, Jo Jones was doing basically the same thing with Count Basie.

Jo Jones developed under the influence of the great black New Orleans and Swing drummers. Along the line leading from Baby Dodds to Jo Jones, there are four important drummers. The most important is *Chick Webb*, whose elemental power conjures up a giant rather than the crippled, dwarfish man he actually was. Chick Webb and, among white drummers, Gene Krupa were first in the line of the 'drummer leaders', big band leaders whose instrument was drums. This line was later continued brilliantly by Mel Lewis, Buddy Rich, and Louie Bellson. Webb was a drummer with a magnetizing aura. There are recordings of his band in which his drums are barely audible, and yet each note conveys the excitement which emanated from this amazing man.

Big Sid Catlett, *Cozy Cole*, and *Lionel Hampton* follow Webb. Big Sid and Cozy, who died in 1981, are Swing drummers par excellence. Cozy made his first recordings in 1930 with Jelly Roll Morton. In 1939 he became the drummer with Cab Calloway's band, in which he was frequently featured in solos. In the late forties, he was the drummer in Louis Armstrong's best All-Star group, and in 1954 he founded a drum school with Gene Krupa in New York.

Cole and Catlett were for a long time considered the most versatile drummers in jazz, equally in demand for combo or big-band work, for New Orleans, Dixieland, and Swing recordings (and Catlett even in a few records important in the history of bop) – in other words, in all the different fields in which other drummers specialized. Catlett, who died in 1951, was with Benny Carter and McKinney's Cotton Pickers in the early thirties, then worked with Fletcher Henderson. At the turn of the thirties, he was Louis Armstrong's preferred drummer. 'Swing is my idea of how a melody should go,' he said – not a scientific definition, but a statement which the musicians of the time, and jazz fans of all times, have understood better than all the fancy theories.

The difference between traditional and modern drumming becomes clear when one compares Cozy Cole and *Jo Jones*. Both are great musicians, but Cole is completely absorbed in the beat, staccato-fashion, and relatively unconcerned with musical shading of what the horns are playing. Jones also creates an imperturbable, driving beat, but in more legato fashion, carrying and serving the musical happenings. The Count Basie rhythm section in its classic period (with Jones's drums, Freddie Green's guitar, Walter Page's bass, and Basie's piano) was known as the 'All American Rhythm Section'.

Jo Jones is the first firmly committed representative of the even four-bar unit. He says: 'The easiest way you can recognize whether a man is swinging or not is when the man gives his every note its full beat. Like a full note four beats, and a half note two beats, and a quarter note one beat. And there are four beats to a measure that really are as even as our breathing. A man doesn't swing when there's anticipation.' *Kenny Clarke* followed this dictum through: The even four beats became the *son continu* – the ceaseless sounding of the rhythm. The basic beat was displaced from the heavy, pounding bass drum to the steadily resounding ride cymbal.

Clarke, the drummer of the Minton circle which included Charlie Christian, Thelonious Monk, Charlie Parker, and Dizzy Gillespie, is the creator of modern drum technique. It seems to me that he is often overlooked in this capacity by jazz friends in the United States, perhaps because he has been living in Paris since 1956 and has become the respected father figure of all the many 'Americans' in Europe. *Max Roach*, of course, has developed this manner of playing to its most complete maturity. He is the prototype of the modern percussionist: no longer the more or less subordinate 'drummer' who must beat out his even 4/4, but an accomplished musician who has studied, generally is able to play an additional instrument, and often knows how to arrange. It is almost the opposite of what used to be: once, drummers almost always were the least schooled musicians in the band; today they are often the most intelligent, as interesting in personality and education as in their playing. Roach once said: 'To do with rhythm what Bach did with melody.' This was not just meant as an impressive slogan; jazz rhythm has literally achieved the multilinear complexity of baroque play with melodic lines.

Roach was the first to drum complete melodic lines. There are private recordings, made at the historic bop sessions at the old Royal Roost in New York in the late forties, on which Roach, in dialogue with Lee Konitz, consistently completes phrases Konitz has started. You can sing along with Roach's drumming just as well as with Konitz's alto playing. And vice versa: What Lee plays on alto is rhythmically as complex as what Max plays on the drums. The drums are no longer exclusively a rhythm instrument, and the alto sax is no longer just a melody instrument. Both have enlarged their range in a complex joining of what earlier could more readily be distinguished as 'melody', 'harmony', and 'rhythm' than today. Thus, Roach could manage without a piano in his quintet of the late fifties. His sidemen said: 'He does the piano player's comping on the drums.'

Roach has effectively destroyed the belief that jazz can swing only in 4/4 time. He plays entire drum solos in thorough, accurately accented waltz rhythm and swings more than many a musician who limits himself to 4/4. And he superimposes rhythms tightly and structurally – almost as in polyrhythmic counterpoint – such as 5/4 over 3/4. Roach does all this with a lucidity and restraint which gives meaning to his expression: 'I look for lyricism.' No one has proved more clearly than Roach that lyricism – poetic lyricism – can be conveyed through a drum solo. His 'Freedom Now Suite' is one of the most moving jazz works dedicated to the black liberation struggle in America.

Max Roach formed entire drum groups, achieving within jazz what, for example, the 'Percussions de Strasbourg' did for modern concert music. He displayed his melodic–rhythmic communicative power in spectacular duo concerts and recordings around the turn of the seventies, with players like Cecil Taylor, Anthony Braxton, Archie Shepp, and Dollar Brand. The Max Roach group was one of the germ-cells of the neo-bop scene, as the Max Roach–Clifford Brown Quintet had been in the fifties for hard bop. Almost forty years after he first became known, Max Roach was voted the leading jazz drummer in the 1980 *down beat* Critics' Poll!

Meanwhile, it has become obvious: The drums became a melody instrument . . . or more precisely, became a melody instrument *as well*. Certainly the drums did not suddenly give up their rhythmic function. Through the increasingly complex, more musical conception of rhythmic function, the melodic function arose almost by itself. Logically and inevitably, the drums went the way of all the instruments in and around the rhythm section. First came the trombone, which had only furnished the harmonic background in New Orleans; Kid Ory, with his tailgate effects, began and Jimmy Harrison, with his solo work with Fletcher Henderson, completed the emancipation of the trombone. Then came the piano, which insofar as it was used at all in New Orleans bands, was purely a rhythm-and-harmony instrument. Earl Hines emancipated it: not relinquishing the rhythmic-harmonic function, but opening the way towards a hornlike one. Guitar and bass went a similar way. The evolution of the guitar from Eddie Lang to Charlie Christian is one of increasing emancipation. On the bass, Jimmy Blanton brought about this emancipation with one stroke. And finally, Kenny Clarke and

Max Roach made the drums an 'emancipated instrument'.

The interest expressed by Roach and the bop musicians in drumming and in Cuban rhythms (which also are in principle West African) thus appears logical. *Art Blakey* was the first jazz drummer to go to Africa, in the early fifties, and study African rhythms and incorporate them into his playing (see also the chapter on percussion). He has made duet recordings with the Cuban bongo drummer Sabu which are a constant interplay between jazz and West African rhythms – 'Nothing But the Soul' (1954) is the characteristic title of one of these recordings. (It was the first time that the word 'soul' was used in a jazz title; a couple of years later it designated a playing style in jazz – and later in rock and in pop music). In the late fifties (that is, before Roach) Blakey put together whole percussion orchestras: four jazz drummers – Jo Jones among them – and five Latin drummers, using all kinds of rhythm instruments and playing together under the slogan 'Orgy in Rhythm'. And, of course, once the drums were emancipated – that is, once they have acquired melodic possibilities from the complexity of the rhythms – orchestras of percussionists had to become possible, just as there are orchestras made up of bass players or saxophonists.

What is characteristic about these efforts is the fact that the African influence has continually gained in importance for jazz drummers. Many theoreticians and ethnomusicologists believe that the African heritage was strongest in the original jazz forms and has been lessened ever since. In reality, however, jazz instrumentalists – and mainly drummers, in parallel with their growing political and sociological awareness and identification – have infused more African elements into jazz since the days of free jazz than the instrumental, urban jazz music from New Orleans via Chicago to Harlem ever had to show.

Blakey is the wildest and most vital of all the jazz drummers to emerge from bop. His rolls and explosions are famous. Compared to this, Max Roach seems more subdued and intellectual. Philadelphia-born '*Philly*' *Joe Jones* attempted to merge the two approaches. He plays with the explosive vehemence of Blakey, but he also has elements of Max Roach's musical cosmopolitanism. Even more 'sophisticated' – in the refined sense this word has acquired in the terminology of jazz musicians – is the playing of *Joe Morello*. He had the maturity, if not the vitality, of Max Roach, with a nearly somnambulistic feeling for the improvisations of his colleagues. Morello joined the Dave Brubeck Quartet in 1957. Through him, Brubeck gained a rhythmical awareness which he had lacked before. Ten years later, *Alan Dawson* replaced Morello for a while. Dawson also taught percussion at Berklee College in Boston, the most famous of jazz schools. He combines intellect and spirit with a swing and drive that hark back to the great drummers of the jazz tradition. Particularly integrated into melodic play is the drum work of *Connie Kay* with the Modern Jazz Quartet (see also the section dealing with jazz combos).

The drummers of hard bop - *Art Taylor*, *Louis Hayes*, *Dannie Richmond*, *Pete LaRocca*, *Roy Haynes*, *Albert Heath*, and (although he has gone far beyond hard bop) *Elvin Jones*, to mention only the most important - link back to Blakey and Roach. Dannie Richmond was the only musician to remain affiliated with Charles Mingus for a considerable time. In the combo section, we will point out how important he was for the togetherness of Mingus's music (and is today for the continuation of his legacy). *Roy Haynes* gave the successful, bossa-nova-influenced Stan Getz Quartet of the sixties its true jazz feeling. Roy possesses that certain hipness so important not only for the music but also for the jazz musician's life style. He made recordings in the seventies which are heard as jazz-rock rhythms by fusion fans, but which can be perceived as ironic questioning of jazz-rock, too. *Elvin* - the third member of the *Jones* family from Detroit, which gave us two other remarkable talents in pianist Hank and trumpeter-composer Thad - plays a kind of 'super-bop' which musicians felt to be a new way of 'turning the rhythm around' - after all that has already been done in this area by Charlie Parker and Kenny Clarke. In a period when one could hardly imagine that further concentration and compression of the rhythmic happenings in jazz were possible, Elvin Jones and his cohorts proved that the evolution continues. There has been further development, too, in the field of 'encircling' the basic rhythm. The less drummers play 'on' the beat and the more they play 'around' it, the more elemental is the perception of the basic rhythm - almost paradoxically. 'It's less - and yet more,' said John McLaughlin about Elvin Jones.

Before we can attempt to show where this development has led, we must refer back to a number of drummers who stand outside the realm of these tendencies, and represent a basically timeless modern Swing approach, in which new developments are less of a stylistic nature, but tend more towards even greater professionalism and perfection. *The* main representative of these drummers is *Buddy Rich*, a *ne plus ultra* of virtuoso technique. His astonishing drum solos and no less astonishing personality were highlights of the big bands of Artie Shaw, Tommy Dorsey, and Harry James, as well as of his own brilliant big bands. At a drum workshop at the 1965 Newport Festival, he 'stole the show' from all the other drummers – and among them were Art Blakey, Jo Jones, Elvin Jones, Roy Haynes and Louie Bellson. However, Rich often gives one the impression that he is a great vaudeville artist – a circus artist who performs the most breath-taking *salti mortali* without a net – rather than a genuine jazz musician in the sense of Roach, Blakey, or Elvin Jones. It certainly is of psychological interest that Buddy Rich was born into a family of vaudevillians.

Louie Bellson, also an excellent arranger, put *two* bass drums in the place of one, and played them with an agility comparable to the footwork of an organist. During his years with Duke Ellington – 1951 to 1953 – the band gained a new, typical 'Bellson' sound. Ellington's *Sam Woodyard* retained the two bass drum setup, and fifteen years later double bass drums became standard equipment for many rock drummers.

The name *Denzil Best* stands for a way of playing known as 'fill-out' technique. Kenny Clarke, Max Roach, and Art Blakey 'fill in' the musical proceedings, placing their accents wherever they deem appropriate. This is the 'fill-in' technique. But Best 'fills out' the musical space evenly, placing no (or hardly any) accents, but stirring his brushes continuously on the snare drum, and thus creating his own special *son continu* swing. This, too, is an end result of the legato evolution initiated by Jo Jones and Dave Tough. After the great success of the George Shearing Quintet around 1950, where Best was a member, his way of drumming has been copied in hundreds of modern cocktail-lounge groups.

From Dave Tough descend a number of excellent big-band drummers, such as *Don Lamond*, Dave's successor with Woody Herman, or *Tiny Kahn*, who died much too young and also was a gifted arranger whose themes are still being played. Other drummers of this lineage are *Gus Johnson*, *J. C. Heard*, the late *Osie Johnson* and *Shadow Wilson*, as well as *Oliver Jackson*, *Grady Tate*, *Mel Lewis*, *Sonny Payne*, and *Rufus Jones*.

Wilson, Gus Johnson, and Payne were Jo Jones's successors in the

Basie band, a lineage continued into our present time by *Butch Miles*. Heard participated in many of Norman Granz's Jazz at the Philharmonic tours and is in some respects a 'modernized' Cozy Cole or Sid Catlett. Grady Tate is much in demand for modern Swing recordings. Mel Lewis (see also the big band chapter) has turned the great big-band drum tradition of men like Chick Webb, Dave Tough, or Don Lamond into a contemporary art.

On the West Coast, *Shelly Manne* took a step which was as logical as Art Blakey's, though it led in the opposite direction. Manne is the absolute melodist among jazz drummers. His way of playing is spare and subtle, spirited and animated, but frequently quite removed from what swing means in terms of the line leading from Webb to Blakey. On the other hand, Manne has shown that he can swing – as in the famous quartet recording of 'The Man I Love' (with Coleman Hawkins and Oscar Pettiford) from the mid-forties, or in the many combo recordings he made on the West Coast – from the fifties right up to the eighties, when he began to include fusion elements, too. He became well known through many dozens of records which made the term 'West Coast jazz' a trademark.

The other way of drumming worked out on the West Coast is connected with the name *Chico Hamilton*. With his quintet, Chico recorded two drum solos in the mid-fifties, 'Drums West' and 'Mister Jo Jones'. His ideas really become clear when one combines these titles. Chico plays a 'West Coast Jo Jones'. In 1953, he was a founding member of the Gerry Mulligan Quartet, and he represents the strongly 'cooled' drumming style of modern Basie–Young classicism – often, however, doing somewhat self-consciously what comes naturally to the others. Since the seventies Hamilton has moved into fusion.

One of the works displaying the characteristic tendencies of all these jazz drummers between Buddy Rich and Shelly Manne and which became symptomatic for the work of many studio drummers in New York is 'Drum Suite', written in 1956 by Manny Albam and Ernie Wilkins, two of the leading arrangers of modern jazz, for big band and four solo drummers. The four drummers are Osie Johnson, Gus Johnson, Teddy Sommers, and Don Lamond. Gus generally lays down the fundamental beat. The others play around him. No drum solo is more than eight bars in length. Each beat is integrated into the musical proceedings. In one of the six movements of the suite the four drummers play in *concertante* with four horns – Joe Newman (trumpet), Hal McKusick (alto), Al Cohn (tenor), and Jimmy Cleveland (trombone). In another, the cymbals are used coloristically with unusual instrumental combinations of oboe, French horn, and woodwinds. Throughout, there are spirited exchanges among the four drummers, or among individual drummers and single horns or sections. Nowhere are the drums used differently from any of the horns.

The 'in group' of New York jazz – that small elite from whence almost everything important in jazz originates – has gone even further. Its development leads from *Elvin Jones* – here we tie up with the paragraph in this chapter where we first mentioned this outstanding drummer – via Tony Williams to Sunny Murray, and from there to Billy Cobham.

Elvin took the *son continu* that began with Kenny Clarke to the extreme limits of what is possible within the framework of a symmetrical meter. He went to the extreme limits, but not beyond. When Coltrane wanted him to go further, Jones resigned from the Coltrane group in an act of great inner consequence. He was replaced by *Rashied Ali*, in whose playing the meter initially was totally dissolved (but who has since returned to recognizable meters). Jones, however, has remained one of the great, independent jazz drummers even in the eighties – a musician who refers to Coltrane on the drums as convincingly as does McCoy Tyner on the piano.

Meanwhile, in 1963, Miles Davis had hired *Tony Williams* (only seventeen at the time) for his quintet. Williams arrived – from a different point of origin – at a similar reduction of the jazz beat to a nervelike vibration and swing. In the chapter about jazz rhythm, we spoke of the fact that there is a certain physiological parallel to this reduction: from heartbeat to 'pulse'. Thus, a new physiological level, heretofore virtually blocked to musical approaches, was made accessible. The physiological level of great classical music was breathing, that of 'classic' jazz reflects the heartbeat, that of the new jazz the pulse.

Before all this, however, three drummers who had worked with Ornette Coleman since 1959 had already shown that the 'liberation' of the rhythm does not mean a liberation from the function of the drummer. These three were *Billy Higgins*, *Ed Blackwell*, and *Charles Moffett* (who has been described as a 'Sid Catlett of free jazz'). Blackwell is from New Orleans, and has said that he sees no contradiction between what the drummers of his home town have always been doing and the new conception. In general terms, it is important to realize that Higgins and Blackwell – to a certain extent also Moffett – played mainly metrically with Ornette. It only sounded 'revolutionary', while it was 'traditional' at the same time. Higgins and Blackwell have remained significant jazz drummers, the former in countless record sessions on the West Coast, the latter in his work with, for instance, Don Cherry and Dewey Redman.

The most extreme representative of the possibilities of free-jazz rhythm, however, was and still is *Sunny Murray*. In a radical fashion, the marking of the meter is here replaced by the creation of tension over long passages. When Murray was with Albert Ayler in the mid-sixties, especially when Ayler was playing folk-music themes, there were clearly perceptible metric pulses in the horn melodies, but Murray just didn't seem to consider them. He played above – and often enough even against – the meter with pulsating beats that seemed to be collecting energy, and suddenly broke out into wild rolls utilizing the entire spectrum of his instrument. 'Murray,' wrote Valerie Wilmer, 'seems obsessed with the idea of strength and intensity in music.'

There can be no doubt that Murray's music swings with an immense density and power. It swings without beat and measure, meter and symmetry – all that which only recently was thought indispensable to swinging – simply by virtue of the power and flexibility of its tension-arcs. One is tempted to wonder whether this fact might not call for revision of all previous swing theories, because this way of playing creates tension, too; in fact, it increases tension, in an ecstatic sense, far beyond anything previously known. And swing in earlier jazz can be subsumed under this, too; swing as an element of tension-building.

Murray says: 'I work for natural sounds rather than trying to sound like drums. Sometimes I try to sound like car motors or the continuous cracking of glass . . .'

Obviously, Murray is not the only drummer of this kind. Other drummers of the 'first generation' of free jazz are *Milford Graves*, *Beaver Harris*, *Barry Altschul* (in the beginning of his career), as well as the previously mentioned *Charles Moffett* and *Rashied Ali* – and (worthy of special attention) *Andrew Cyrille*, who gave important rhythmic impulses to Cecil Taylor from 1964 to the mid-seventies. He played with Illinois Jacquet as well as with West African drum groups from Ghana and is conversant with the different kinds of

European percussion music. At the risk of oversimplification, he could be called 'the intellectual' among free-jazz drummers.

Cyrille captured the attitude of many of these drummers to swing: '"Swing" is the natural psychic response of the human body to sound that makes a person want to move his or her body without too much conscious effort . . . In a more abstract sense, "swing" is a completely integrated and balanced sound, forming a greater, spiritual-like, almost tangible magic sensibility of being – the conscious knowledge that something metaphysical is happening.'

This 'first generation' of free drummers was the point of departure for a second and third generation, of whom we will speak later.

When the seventies began, the great synthesis took shape – more perhaps among drummers (and guitarists) than among any other instrumentalists: the freedom of free jazz was preserved, but it was recognized that freedom can turn into chaos. On the contrary, one is genuinely free if one is able – if he so desires – to play not only free, but also bop, cool, hard bop, Swing, and even Dixieland: in other words, what had been considered taboo among a certain group of musicians for ten years as 'square' and 'un-hip'.

Rock rhythm is not very flexible. In some respects, it returned to Cozy Cole and Sid Catlett of the thirties: it reverted the accent away from the cymbals and back to where it had been – to the bass drum and the tomtoms. Thus, it cannot react as easily and effortlessly to the soloists' playing as a rhythm 'played on top'. But it is direct and clear. One can always tell where 'beat one' is – which occasionally was no longer possible in the playing of jazz drummers in the sixties.

The task of the new type of drummer to gain significance since the beginning of the seventies was, in other words, to merge the emotionalism and communicative power of rock with the flexibility and complexity of jazz. The drummers who first accomplished this – and, in a certain sense, are still accomplishing it most perfectly today – are *Tony Williams*, *Alphonse Mouzon* and *Billy Cobham*. We have already mentioned Williams. It is significant to realize that his playing tended initially in two directions, towards free jazz and towards jazz–rock. Tony Williams's span today becomes clear in his choice of sidemen for his 1978 recording, 'The Joy of Flying': jazz–rock musicians as well as jazz players (even Cecil Taylor!), Europeans as well as Americans coming from the most diverse styles.

Billy Cobham accomplished his pathbreaking contribution in John McLaughlin's first Mahavishnu Orchestra. He led his own groups after that, but he hasn't reached the level of his Mahavishnu playing. Mouzon's development shows a similar problem. He was, on the one hand, a founding member of Weather Report and, on the other, one of McCoy Tyner's sidemen in the early seventies, playing 'acoustic' jazz in the Coltrane tradition – both of these styles on the highest level. During the late seventies Mouzon repeatedly said that he considered himself not a jazz but a rock musician; the rock world, however, obviously has problems accepting him as one of its own, because his playing is too complex and too demanding for a rock context.

The panorama of contemporary jazz–rock and fusion drummers built on the foundation laid down by Williams, Cobham, and Mouzon, is so wide that, again, only a few can be named: *Steve Gadd, Peter Erskine, Harvey Mason, Lenny White, Gerry Brown, Steve Jordan, Ndugu Leon Chancler, Eric Gravatt, John Guerin, Dan Gottlieb, David Moss,* and *Terry Bozzio.* Among the Europeans of this grouping (even though they play with a kind of 'European understatement' that differentiates them from their more aggressive American colleagues) are Dutchman *Pierre Courbois*, the French-Italian *Aldo Romano*, and *Fredy Studer*, from Switzerland.

Steve Gadd, known for his work in the group Stuff and in countless studio productions, is the best versed of these drummers. Developing Tony Williams's style, he created the 'dry' studio sound that became characteristic of many of these drummers. A special position is held by *Bernard Purdie*, who gains his remarkable musical and communicative powers from gospel, soul, and blues. When he joined Weather Report in the second half of the seventies, *Peter Erskine* (who also has had his big band experiences) helped solve the rhythm problems with which this group had been beset for years. *Harvey Mason* has become a star through his work with George Benson. *Lenny White*, who comes from Jamaica, was part of Miles Davis's 'Bitches Brew' in 1969 and has played with Larry Coryell and Chick Corea. *John Guerin* and *Dan Gottlieb* stand out as particularly sensitive players, as evidenced by the names of the musicians they have played with: Guerin with singer Joni Mitchell; Gottlieb with Gary Burton, Eberhard Weber, and Pat Metheny. *Pierre Courbois* was a significant influence on the entire European scene in the early seventies with his group Association PC, but he has since grown away from this style of music. This is true also

of several other players we named, of Lenny White, for example, who
first played fusion with Chick Corea's 'Return to Forever', but then
also bebop and even experimental bop with Heiner Stadler.

*Jon Hiseman, Robert Wyatt, John Marshall, Bill Bruford, Simone
Phillips*, and *Phil Collins* are part of the British scene. Hiseman drums
in the successful United Jazz & Rock Ensemble. As early as the late
sixties, Robert Wyatt, in the British group Soft Machine, was
creating a network of sensitive rhythms which were ahead of what
most other drummers on the early jazz–rock scene were able to play
then, even in America. Bruford, Aldo Romano, and Fredy Studer
were among the most interesting European fusion drummers at the
turn of the seventies. Briton *Ken Hyder* has been incorporating
elements of Scottish and Celtic folk music into his playing in a most
original fashion.

The 'daddy' of European jazz–rock drummers is *Ginger Baker*. After
he became world famous in the sixties in the blues–rock group
Cream, he spent several years in Nigeria studying African percussion
music. Later, he tried a comeback, but did not succeed, because (like
his colleague on bass, Jack Bruce) Baker has power and musical fire,
but has not been able to keep up with the playing standards
meanwhile achieved.

The panorama of the free drummers is similarly complex. Among its
second- and third-generation players are *Phillip Wilson, Don Moye,
Steve McCall, Pheeroan Ak Laff* (Paul Maddox), *Thurman Barker, Bobby
Battle, Warren Smith, Stanley Crouch, Ronald Shannon Jackson*, et al . . .

Wilson, Moye, and McCall are close to the AACM, even though
Wilson changed to a different kind of music in the late sixties: He
played in the Paul Butterfield Blues Band, but returned to free music
in the second half of the seventies when his AACM colleagues finally
had found recognition not only in Europe, but also in the United
States. Today he is one of the most open and interesting of free
drummers. McCall lends a light, airy quality to the rhythm of the
group Air. Ak Laff has played with Anthony Davis, James Newton,
and Oliver Lake. Baker, Battle, and Smith all became known
through their work with Sam Rivers. And Stanley Crouch has
become prominent as critic and producer.

Turning to the European scene, we must first mention the
'daddies' of free drumming there: the Swiss *Pierre Favre* and

Dutchman *Han Bennink*, the former perceptive and sensitive, the latter vital and gripping. More than any other drummer today, Favre is able to produce percussion 'sketches' so vividly that one can almost 'see' them as pictures: a Sunday morning in Switzerland or a young girl on her way to school. While Bennink's sound is especially convincing and developed on the skins, Favre is particularly impressive on cymbals, gongs, and other metal percussion instruments. Even before their American colleagues, both Favre and Bennink utilized the rich arsenal of percussion instruments employed today by so many drummers: instruments from Africa, Brazil, Bali, Tibet, India, and China. Favre and Bennink can certainly be considered founders of something like a European percussion lineage. From that lineage stem the Swiss *Peter Giger* and *Reto Weber*, the Finn *Edward Vesala* (who has also studied Balinese music), Briton *Tony Oxley* (who has constructed his own set of instruments, including electronic sound sources), as well as Germans *Paul Lovens* (who became known through his involvement with the Globe Unity Orchestra), *Detlef Schönenberg* (who plays in one of the most interesting European duos, with *trombonist Günter Christmann), and* – from East Germany – *Günter 'Baby' Sömmer.*

Finally, we must mention the Japanese free drummers *Masahiko Togashi, Shota Koyama,* and *Takeo Moriyama.* Togashi plays 'spiritual' percussion music in which can be found elements from the Japanese musical and spiritual tradition, including Zen. There is hardly another percussionist today in whose music 'space' – the emptiness between the beats – has such significance and is filled with so much content. Moriyama and Koyama are very wild and intense players – with a kind of intensity which is fed not only from blacks but also from traditional Japanese sources.

An important step beyond all these drummers – Americans, Europeans, and Japanese – is being taken around the turn of the seventies by *Ronald Shannon Jackson.* One of the musicians at the 1980 Moers Festival in Germany said: 'In a sense, Ronald is doing what Elvin Jones did in the early seventies. As Elvin emancipated the bop rhythms then, so Ronald Jackson is emancipating the rock and funk rhythms today.' Jackson is the main drummer of what guitar player James Blood Ulmer calls 'no wave' – not only because of his new, impressive polyrhythms, but also because he has managed to transmit these polyrhythms to his compositions and to the music of his group

Decoding Society. As with most such styles, the novel aspect of 'free funk' is the rhythm. Jackson has succeeded in realizing this rhythm in his melodies, too – almost as Dizzy Gillespie did with 'Cubop' rhythms in the forties. Jackson, who has worked with Albert Ayler, Ornette Coleman, and Cecil Taylor (Ornette influenced him especially), plays 'free funk' in a way comparable to *Barry Altschul*'s 'free bop' – which leads us to the next grouping of drummers. Altschul, a master of the rim shot, has an inimitable knack for creating intensity and impulsiveness especially through his restraint. His playing spans free music to swinging neo-bop, but his speciality is precisely the combination of both fields.

The 'hostile' camps of fusion and free music are reconciled in the field of drumming, too, by the players of contemporary mainstream (also the reason why an especially large number of them have been in the limelight of both styles): *Billy Hart Stu Martin, Victor Lewis, Eddie Gladden, Ben Riley, Clifford Javis, Al Foster, Peter Donald, Adam Nussbaum, Peter Apfelbaum, Don Alias, Eddie Moore, Alvin Queen, Woody Theus, Ronald Steen, Freddie Waits, Horacee Arnold, Wilbur Campbell, Ed Soph, Mickey Rocker, Leroy Williams, Bruce Ditmas, Frank Butler, Jake Hanna, Jeff Hamilton, Paul Motian, Joe LaBarbera, Elliot Zigmund, Michael Di Pasqua,* Norwegian *Jon Christensen,* South African *Makaya Ntshoko* (who lives in Europe), as well as the Pole *Janusz Stefanski* . . .

Billy Hart is an immensely empathetic drummer, one of the most intensive as well as swinging on the scene today, who plays a kind of 'sensitized Elvin Jones'. Also having their base in Elvin Jones are *Eddie Moore, Janusz Stefanski, Woody Theus,* and *Al Foster.* Foster accomplished the feat of welding together two musicians as different as Sonny Rollins and McCoy Tyner when he accompanied them on a tour for Milestone Records. He was also the chosen drummer at Miles Davis's much heralded 1981 comeback – which, however, showed that Miles had not understood in which direction rhythm and drumming had developed during his quasi retirement.

Stu Martin (who died in 1980) came out of Quincy Jones's band of the early sixties. He commanded a particularly wide musical spectrum, including even Eastern European and Jewish music. *Freddie Waits, Horacee Arnold,* and *Wilbur Campbell* are members of the Max Roach percussion group mentioned earlier. *Mickey Rocker* was Dizzy Gillespie's favourite drummer in the seventies. *Victor Lewis, Eddie*

Gladden, and *Ben Riley* are *the* drummers on the modern neo-bop scene, all having played with both its central figures: Dexter Gordon and Woody Shaw. *Jake Hanna* and *Jeff Hamilton* are true Swing men, referring back to the music of the great classic Swing tradition. *Makaya Ntshoko* is creating a very personal combination of bebop with percussion elements of his native South Africa.

Three of these drummers have played with Bill Evans, and all are characterized by the sensitivity of Evans's music: *Paul Motian*, *Elliot Zigmund*, and *Joe LaBarbera*. Motian is another drummer in whose music space – the space between notes – plays a distinct role; he, too, received impulses from Asian percussion techniques.

Jack DeJohnette holds a special position: he is probably the most universal of all these drummers, and an incredibly complex musician. His group New Directions is certainly opening new directions for the music of the early eighties. DeJohnette's style of playing was described particularly well by critic Lois Gilbert: 'To a synthesis of the virtues of Tony Williams and Elvin Jones, DeJohnette has brought his own acute sense of time – with Philly Joe Jones, he is virtually the only drummer who comfortably plays both sides of the beat – anticipating it or lagging behind as the situation demands – and he has an unprecedented sense of detail.' It is interesting to note that DeJohnette began as a pianist and still sometimes plays piano on his group's recordings. If there is any justification in calling a drummer's style 'pianistic', then it is most certainly true of his. DeJohnette is also an outstanding writer, but in contrast to most other drummers, his words do not immediately reveal themselves as 'drummer's compositions'. Indeed, a certain type of very obvious 'drummer's writing' has been quite prevalent in almost all tunes composed by drummers so far – from Sid Catlett and Cozy Cole to Billy Cobham and Alphonse Mouzon.

It is strange how the development of the drum has taken place in pairs, from the beginning until today. We discussed how Jo Jones came up with results in the thirties in Count Basie's band that were quite similar to those reached independently by Dave Tough with Tommy Dorsey. Among the bop drummers, there is on the one hand 'wild' Art Blakey and on the other intellectual Max Roach. During the sixties, Elvin Jones stood in opposition to Tony Williams. Or among the free drummers: 'racing' Sunny Murray here and complex Andrew Cyrille there. Or in Europe: dynamic Han Bennink and sensitive Pierre Favre. Similarly poised in opposition among the drummers on the contemporary scene are Billy Cobham (or, if you wish, Alphonse Mouzon) and Jack DeJohnette. In fact, this polarity can be found right from the beginning of drum development – even in New Orleans: 'wild' Baby Dodds on the one hand, and Tony Spargo, who incorporated European elements into the music of the Original Dixieland Jazz Band, on the other. ('European elements' back then, however, meant marching band and circus music.)

The Percussion Instruments (Cuban, Salsa, Brazilian, African, Indian, Balinese)

The percussion instruments used to be side instruments for the drummers. However, in the course of the sixties, the store of percussion instruments became so immense that a new type of musician, the percussion player, evolved. The percussionist must be distinguished from the drummer, even though there are countless drummers who are *also* percussionists – and vice-versa.

Initially, most of the percussion instruments came from Latin America: claves, chocallo (also referred to as shaker), guiro (also named gourd or, in Brazil, reco reco), cabaza, maracas, quijada, cencerro (or more simply, cow-bells), guica, bongos, conga, timbales, pandeira, and so on. Then other instruments were added: from India, Tibet, China, Japan, Bali, and Africa (where most of the Latin American percussions originated anyway). Airto, the renowned Brazilian percussionist, spent years before his move to the United States travelling through Brazil – through the Amazon jungle, the dry Northeast, and the Matto Grosso prairie – where he collected and studied about 120 different instruments.

The father of all percussionists relevant to the modern jazz scene is *Chano Pozo* from Cuba (his complete name was Luciano Pozo y Gonzales). He infused Cuban rhythms into Dizzy Gillespie's big band of 1947–48 and thereby became the great catalyst for so-called 'Cubop'. The creator of this music, however, is Dizzy Gillespie, the only jazz improviser of his generation who could improvise as comfortably on Latin rhythms as on jazz rhythms (often favouring the former because he considered them less 'monotonous').

Some of the tunes the Gillespie band recorded with Chano Pozo –

'Cubana Be-Cubana Bop', for instance, or 'Manteca', 'Woody'n You', 'Afro Cubano Suite', or 'Algo Bueno' – are bacchanals of rhythmic differentiation. Chano Pozo died in a stabbing in 1948 in East Harlem's Rio Café. There have been rumours that he was slain because he had made public – and thus desecrated – the secret rhythms of the Nigerian Abaquwa cult, to which he had belonged in Cuba. The rhythmic power of this mysterious Cuban conga player is illuminated by the fact that Gillespie, though he often employed several Latin American percussionists at one time, never again was able to achieve the effects he had reached with Chano Pozo alone.

The percussion players can best be grouped according to where they, their instruments, or their styles come from. In this way, we have percussionists with Cuban (and, later, Puerto Rican), Brazilian, African, and Asian roots. Those are the groupings to which most percussionists belong. There are others from Mexico (active mainly on the West Coast of the United States), Trinidad, Jamaica, Haiti, and other countries.

The Cuban wave reached its first high point between the late forties and the mid-fifties. Not only did Dizzy Gillespie play Cuban rhythms again and again, but so did the favourite white big band, Stan Kenton's: In 1947, for example, with their successful version of 'The Peanut Vendor', in 'Chorale for Brass, Piano and Bongo', or in the 'Fugue for Rhythm Section' with bongo player *Jack Costanzo*; later Kenton used *Carlos Vidal* on conga, *Machito* on maracas, and others in pieces like 'Machito', 'Mambo in F', 'Cuban Carnival', and 'Cuban Episode'. In 1956, Kenton devoted to Latin (and above all Cuban) music a grand suite: 'Cuban Fire', written by Johnny Richards and featuring six Latin percussionists.

The Latin bands enjoying the greatest recognition in the jazz world of the fifties were, in New York, the orchestra of *Machito* (alias Frank Grillo) with the inspired and jazz-experienced arranger and trumpeter Mario Bauza (who had done arrangements also for Chick Webb's and Cab Calloway's bands), and that of timbales player and arranger *Tito Puente*; and on the West Coast, the band of *Perez Prado*, with Kenton-like brass effects and a new kind of rhythm, the mambo – the first Latin dance to originate in the States (influenced by Mexican rhythms): 'rumba with jitterbug' is how *down beat* defined the mambo, which was quite a hit in the mid-fifties.

It was Machito who frequently played and recorded with jazz men

– first with Charlie Parker (starting in 1948), and later with Brew Moore, Zoot Sims, Stan Getz, Howard McGhee, Herbie Mann, and others. Machito's alliance with Parker was instigated by jazz impresario Norman Granz, mainly because 'Cubop' was a widespread fashion back then. Parker was not nearly as accomplished on Cuban rhythms as Gillespie. Above all, it was Machito who nurtured the realization in the jazz world that it is wrong simply to add a Latin percussion player to a conventional jazz rhythm section – as was usually the case then (and often later). Instead, complete Cuban rhythm sections must be formed where the Latin percussionists are conversant with jazz, and the jazz drummers with Latin American music. Such a group usually would employ several Latin percussion players – and the bassist has to command the bass lines of Latin music with as much ease as those lines he normally would play.

Among the significant Cuban percussionists of those years were conga players *Carlos Vidal*, *Candido*, and *Sabu Martinez*, and bongo player *Willi Rodriguez*. They made recordings with many jazzmen: Vidal with Stan Kenton, for instance; Candido with Gillespie; Sabu (who died in 1979) with Gillespie and Art Blakey.

On the West Coast, the vibraphonist and bongo player *Cal Tjader* has worked since 1954 on an intelligent and spirited combination of jazz with Latin music, often revealing Mexican elements. Tjader came from the George Shearing Quintet of 1949. Jazz critics have written a lot about the peculiar sound of this group, but the Shearing Quintet was also important in terms of rhythm, as a jumping-off point for a number of Latin percussionists who later became known through their own recordings: timbales player *Willie Bobo*, conga player *Mongo Santamaria*, and conga and bongo player *Armando Peraza*.

During the late fifties, Cuban music lost considerably in attractiveness. A second wave came in the seventies in the shape of salsa, which since then has been sustained not only by Cuban musicians, but also by players from Puerto Rico (and by some from the Dominican Republic). Its centres are where most of these ethnic groups are concentrated in the United States, New York and Miami. Salsa means 'sauce' and has been defined as 'Cuban plus jazz', with elements of blues and rock. Fania Records has been quite successful in bringing together salsa and jazz musicians for studio dates and also for large concerts, as in New York's Yankee Stadium and in Madison

Square Gardens. Among the best-known 'Fania All Stars' are *Mongo Santamaria*, *Ray Barretto*, *Larry Harlow*, *Willie Colon*, and the musical director of Fania Records, *Johnny Pacheco*. He patterned the All Stars primarily on the Cuban *conjuntos* (medium-size ensembles composed of percussionists and horn players). Pianist Larry Harlow is also the writer of the first salsa opera, *Hommy*. Pianist and bandleader *Eddie Palmieri* (who was inspired first by Bud Powell, later by McCoy Tyner) created a salsa concerto style with pieces in larger forms, earning him the title of a 'Duke Ellington of salsa'. In the late seventies, the developments on the salsa scene were repeatedly documented at the Newport–New York Festival.

Conga player *Mongo Santamaria* has been the most influential Cuba-style percussionist for more than twenty years, with a host of recordings in the fields of Cuban as well as jazz and rock music (plus all imaginable mixtures). Santamaria also scored the first real salsa hit in the mid-sixties with his version of Herbie Hancock's composition 'Watermelon Man'. Since that time his music has been studied by Latin percussionists (and also by many jazz drummers) as diligently as Chano Pozo's work was studied in the forties and fifties. Also of great significance is timbalero *Willie Bobo*, who has made records with, among others, Miles Davis, Stan Getz, and Cannonball Adderley.

Meanwhile, there is a whole generation of Latin musicians born not in Cuba or Puerto Rico or elsewhere in Latin America, but in New York, mostly in the Barrio district of East Harlem. Ray Barretto, Johnny Pacheco, and Eddie Palmieri are among this group of players. As can be easily understood, these musicians have an additional interest in North American music, particularly jazz. But the dictum that you have to be a Latino to play outstanding Latin music still holds – with a few exceptions. The first such exception was Cal Tjader, whose heritage is Swedish (certain non-Latin elements can be perceived in the 'coolness' of his music). Drummer *Don Alias* is another exception. Alias is Anglo, but grew up with Cubans; he is not only an excellent jazz drummer – as in the group Stone Alliance – but also a brilliant conga player. The successful fusion drummer *Billy Cobham*, who has also played with the Fania All Stars, has a highly developed feeling for Latin music. Cobham hails from Panama and thus – like many other Panamanian musicians – has two cultural roots, Anglo and Latin.

The rule that only a Latino can play convincing Latin music is true not only for percussionists, but also – even though less strictly – for horn players. Trumpeter Fats Navarro, who died in 1950, and tenorist Sonny Rollins were among the first important jazz improvisers on Latin rhythms. Navarro came from a Florida Latino family; Rollins (though born in New York), from a family from the Virgin Islands. Navarro played especially well over Cuban rhythms; Rollins – as composer and also as improviser – infused the amiable charm of Caribbean music, particularly of calypso music from Trinidad, into jazz long before today's tendencies in that direction. On the other hand, since the sixties, it has become more and more obvious that a growing number of non-Latin horn players are interested in Latin music (more Brazilian than Cuban!) – particularly since two non-Latins, Charlie Byrd and Stan Getz, enjoyed success along this line.

Nowadays, there is a vast number of mixtures of Latin American and North American music: 'Latin rock', 'Latin soul', 'rock salsa', in dozens of different combinations. After the mambo, the boogaloo was the second Latin dance to be created in the United States – the latter, however, with English lyrics, not Spanish like the mambo. The boogaloo is a mixture of mambo with rock 'n' roll and – depending on who is playing – with undercurrents of jazz and blues. An especially successful, highly differentiated combination of rhythms from the spheres of rock and Latin music (above all salsa) was created on the West Coast during the early seventies by *Carlos Santana*, who originally came from Mexico. The rock group Earth, Wind & Fire is so successful mainly because it includes conga and timbales players, producing a ravishing mixture of soul (or gospel) elements with salsa rhythms. Percussionist *Ralph McDonald* (born in Harlem in a family of Trinidad calypso musicians) has become successful with his 'Latin fusion', including also aspects of the African tradition.

Latin rhythms are almost ubiquitous on the jazz and rock scenes – certainly also because, as we have shown, rock and fusion rhythms are basically latent Latin rhythms. John Storm Roberts (to whose book *The Latin Tinge* I am indebted in this context) quotes salsa bandleader Ray Barretto: 'The whole basis of American rhythm . . . changed from the old dotted-note jazz shuffle rhythm to a straightahead straight-eighth approach, which is Latin.' Or, to put it more precisely, it is ambivalent – referring to rhythms from North America as much as to those from Latin America.

'Salsa' has become a sort of catch phrase that should be used with caution. No longer does it refer only to Cuban rhythms, but also to the 'bomba' from Puerto Rico, the 'meringue' from Santo Domingo, and to other dances and rhythms from the Caribbean and Mexican sphere. In a 1977 *downbeat* interview, Mongo Santamaria pointed out that some of these rhythms still are '*nañigo*', that is, 'coming from secret religious cults'.

Let's move on to Brazil. The interest of the jazz musicians in Brazilian music was instigated by guitarist *Charlie Byrd*, who went there in 1961. A year later, in 1962, he recorded the album 'Jazz Samba' with *Stan Getz*, including the famous song 'Desafinado' written by Joao Gilberto and Antonio Carlos Jobim. The Grammy Award for this tune was not given to Charlie Byrd, but to Stan Getz, because Byrd's guitar solo was cut from the version shortened for single release! As a result of this, Charlie Byrd's decisive contribution was neglected – and from that point on, Getz stood at the centre of the bossa nova wave. The Brazilian musicians defined the bossa as 'samba plus cool jazz'. A first hint of the potential of Brazilian music was given on the West Coast as early as 1953 by the album 'Brazilliance', recorded by a quartet featuring Brazilian-born guitarist *Laurindo Almeida* and alto saxophonist and flutist *Bud Shank* (the two are still collaborating in this field).

But the percussive side of Brazilian music was realized on the American scene only in 1967, when Brazilian percussion player *Airto Moreira* and his wife, singer *Flora Purim*, moved to New York. Airto was involved in two tunes on Miles Davis's pathbreaking album 'Bitches Brew'. Along with the many other impulses this record gave rise to, it caused the in-group of jazz musicians to become aware of Brazilian rhythms. Many leading jazz groups of the seventies used Brazilian percussionists, among them Chick Corea, McCoy Tyner, Dizzy Gillespie, Weather Report, and others. The percussionists in these groups were – and still are – Airto, *Dom Um Romao, Paulhino da Costa, Guilherme Franco*, and one of the most sensitive and flexible players, *Nana Vasconcelos*. Mainly because of his fusion recordings and the albums he made with Flora Purim, Airto has become the best known of these percussionists. Nana is a real master of the berimbao, an instrument that looks like 'bow and arrow': a single metal string stretched over a staff is played with a coin, using a coconut pressed against the player's body as resonator and modulator. On this simple instrument, which comes from Bahia, the 'New Orleans of Brazilian music', Nana has discovered a fascinating wealth of expressive possibilities. On one of his records, he makes 'body music', employing no instruments, but using his entire body as a percussion instrument, producing the most diverse sounds with his hands, fingers, and feet on his chest, stomach, and trunk, as well as on his arms, legs, and shoulders.

Another interesting percussion instrument from Brazilian music is the guica, an open drum with a pipe inside which is rubbed – mostly with a moist cloth – producing a strange 'giggling' sound. More than any other country in Latin America, Brazil has an immense wealth of these different instruments, and a vast number of them – typical of Brazilian music – directly connect the rhythmic and the melodic elements.

The Brazilian rhythms are softer, more supple, more elastic, and less aggressive than the Cuban ones. That's why the Brazilian percussion players have been able to create a perfect integration of jazz and Latin rhythms, so perfect that often the constituent elements – jazz here, Brazilian there – can no longer be singled out. Another reason why this could be achieved is the fact that there are stronger ties between the basic rhythm of Brazilian music, the samba, and that of North American jazz than between jazz and Cuban rhythms. The fascination of combinations of jazz with Cuban music lies in the tension between the two, which creates power, aggressiveness, explosiveness. Combinations of jazz and Brazilian music fascinate through their softness and suppleness and an almost unnoticeable blend of their rhythms which creates elegance and charm.

A new union of jazz and Brazilian rhythms was achieved in a truly masterful way by *Guilherme Franco* in the Coltrane-inspired music of McCoy Tyner's group. In a sense, this represents the final point – so far – of a development that began in 1949 when Nat King Cole added bongo player *Jack Costanzo* to his successful trio. But Nat soon let Costanzo go again, because he remained alien to the group's music. A satisfactory integration of jazz and Latin rhythms simply seemed unattainable at the time.

In the course of the growing new awareness of their African roots, many American jazz musicians have adopted African percussion instruments, rhythms, techniques, and musicians. The forerunner of this development was *Art Blakey*, who on his record 'Orgy in Rhythm' was already forming entire drum orchestras as early as the fifties. Wayne Shorter once said: 'Dizzy Gillespie's thing was Afro–Cuban.

Then Art Blakey took off the Cuban and said "Afro" and the whole jazz world understood.' A Blakey record released in 1962 is entitled 'The African Beat'; it employs, among others, the following musicians with their African instruments: *Solomon Ilori* (African talking drum), *Chief Bey* (conga, telegraph drum, double gong), *Montego Joe* (bambara drum, double gong, corboro drum, log drum), *Garvin Masseaux* (chekere, African maracas, conga), *James Folami* (conga), and *Robert Crowder* (batá drum, conga). Later, *Max Roach* and others formed similar percussion groups.

The first African percussionist to gain recognition in the jazz world, as early as in the beginning of the sixties, was Nigerian *Olatunji*, who also worked with John Coltrane. For his recording dates, he employed musicians like Clark Terry, Yusef Lateef, and George Duvivier. For years, his composition entitled 'Uhuru' – the Swahili word for 'freedom' – with lyrics by the Nigerian poet Adebayo Faleti, was the 'in-song' of the New York musicians and music fans – even in United Nations circles – interested in African problems and the liberation struggle of African peoples.

In the seventies, percussionists like *Kahil El Zahbar*, *Don Moye* (from the AACM circle), and *Mtume* (made known by Miles Davis), as well as the aforementioned *Ralph McDonald*, referred directly to African rhythms. El Zahbar, leader of his African Heritage Ensemble, plays the 'mbira': the old African 'thumb piano', which, in a slightly different version, is also called 'kalimba' and, in other parts of Africa, 'nsimbi' or 'zanza'. This instrument is also played by *Paul Berliner*, who has researched African music and its connection to jazz.

Repeatedly, Carl Berger's Creative Music Studio in Woodstock, New York, has employed African percussionists from Ghana, Lagos, etc. to play and teach 'world music'. Two highly respected Haitian drummers are *Ti-Roro* (who died in 1980, and was connected with Haitian voodoo cults), and his somewhat younger colleague, *Ti-Marcel*. Ti-Roro once said that a person cannot understand Haitian – and that means African – drumming without realizing that drums and drummer are 'two different beings'. The 'loa' – the sacred spirits – do not speak to the drummer, but to the drums. A drum must be 'baptized' – and for the ceremony, it is dressed like a baby. The drums are fed and put to bed at night. They have their own will, which can be quite contrary to that of the drummer – to such an extent that they refuse to 'talk' to their player on certain days or under certain circumstances. Ti-Roro: 'If you don't consider your drums as "beings", you can play technical tricks on them at best, but not meaningful music.'

The next group of percussionists we have to consider are those with Asian roots. The most satisfying integration of Indian rhythms with jazz was achieved by Indian tabla player *Zakir Hussain*. The son and student of famous tabla drummer Alla Rahka, Hussain grew up with jazz from the beginning: 'I heard Charlie Parker when I was twelve. My father made records with Buddy Rich and Elvin Jones, and he also worked with Yusef Lateef. Thus Indian music and jazz came together for me by themselves.' Hussain made ground-breaking recordings with John Handy and Ali Akbar Khan as well as in John McLaughlin's group Shakti. In a way, he integrated Indian tabla rhythms and sounds as perfectly into jazz as did Guilherme Franco (and others) in terms of Brazilian rhythms.

Other Indian percussionists who have worked with jazz musicians are *Trilok Gurtu* and *Badal Roy*, the latter, for instance, with Miles Davis. Gurtu, also known as a teacher at the Creative Music Studio, has made recordings with Don Cherry and Charlie Mariano and is an outstanding tabla player and an excellent jazz drummer – a combination that would have been unthinkable just a few years ago. *Collin Walcott*, lastly, is the first American-born musician to gain recognition as a tabla (and sitar) player, as with the group Oregon and with *Don Cherry*. Cherry himself has played Balinese and Tibetan percussion instruments, among others.

In view of the cosmopolitan, world-music spirit of today's jazz, it goes without saying that percussion techniques from other musical realms and cultures have also been incorporated into jazz. *Andy Narell*, for instance, and guitarist *Roland Prince* brought steel drums from Trinidad into the jazz context. *Okay Temiz* has carried the rhythms of his native Turkey into jazz. Karl Berger is of the opinion that 'Turkish music is world music *par excellence*, because in it Asian, European, and African sources come together.'

The impact and the 'totality' of percussive rhythms from many countries of the earth becomes clear when you realize that Weather Report, the most successful fusion group of the seventies, employed one or more percussionists in addition to the drummer during most of that decade. The first percussion player in the group was also the first with Miles Davis and Chick Corea: *Airto*. After him come *Dom Um Romao, Alejandro Neciosup Acuna, Manolo Badrena, Alyrio Lima*, and *Muruga* (the latter not only on Latin American, but also on Moroccan and Israeli drums) – musicians, in other words, who belong to or have mastered the most diverse musical cultures.

Another characteristic of this 'totality' of percussive rhythms is that a new type of percussionist has evolved. He is no longer indebted to one of the different musical cultures, but feeds on many of them. Musicians like *Kenneth Nash, Sue Evans, Armen Halburian, Bill Summers, David Moss*, and others belong in this category.

A modern percussion player uses dozens of different instruments. Each has its own tradition and demands its own playing technique. It is no longer anything out of the ordinary that a percussionist commands Cuban and Brazilian instruments as well as Indian and Tibetan ones, and Turkish and Moroccan. In order to play them congenially – or at least professionally – he has to be familiar with the way they were originally played in their native cultures. That's how universal jazz has become today.

It would be a misunderstanding to consider all that has been discussed in this chapter a radically new development. It is new in a gradual sense at best. The tendency for the jazz musician to include and incorporate anything he is confronted with has been immanent from the beginning of jazz. Many of the things discovered by jazz in the past few years and decades simply were not known by the early jazz musicians – for example Indian music. But Latin American music was known from the start. The main reason why New Orleans was the most important city in the development of jazz was not only because it is the southernmost city in the North American cultural sphere, but because it is the northernmost city of the Latin American – Latin and Creole – cultural sphere. Both converged there almost as intensely as in Miami or New York's Barrio today. The 'Latin tinge' Jelly Roll Morton spoke of in respect to his 'New Orleans Blues' was from the start more than just a tinge. It was an integral part of jazz, because the black rhythms of both North and South America were based on African rhythms – and mainly from the same African cultures, above all, from the Yorubas. It is important in this context that African rhythms and instruments were less tainted, kept purer and more alive, in the Latin sphere (above all, in Cuba, Haiti, and Brazil) than in North America, where they underwent stronger changes and mutations – mainly because the white masters suppressed the black heritage of their slaves. At the risk of oversimplification, it can be said that Latin music is 'Africanized European dances and melodies', whereas North American music can be considered 'Europeanized African rhythms'.

John Storm Roberts has shown that 'the Latin ingredients in early New Orleans jazz are more important than has been realized.' He writes that Papa Laine, leader of the first known white jazz band, had a trumpeter at the turn of the century named 'Chink' Martin, whose parents were Spanish and Mexican. In interviews, Martin said that Royal Street between Dumaine and Esplanade – a central point in New Orleans' old French Quarter – had been inhabited mainly by Spanish and Mexican people. Jelly Roll Morton never saw a duality of only black and white elements, but from the beginning a trinity: 'We had Spanish, we had coloured, we had white . . .'

'Spanish' in old New Orleans is what we would call 'Latin' today. Jelly Roll Morton went so far as to claim that the 'Spanish tinge' was the essential ingredient that differentiated jazz from ragtime. New Orleans author Al Rose believes that ragtime came into being when black bands tried to play Mexican music. And the old journal, *New Orleans*, surmised that the word 'jazz' was a bastardization of the Mexican expression 'Musica de jarabe'. We don't have to take all these speculations at face value, but they point to the significance of Latin elements in old New Orleans – a significance neglected by most jazz historians to date.

The Latin elements are not only significant to the music of old New Orleans, but also to the New Orleans of today. Contemporary New Orleans rock, by people like Fats Domino, Professor Longhair, Allen Toussaint, Dr John, and others is (as we pointed out in the piano chapter) different from Northern rock music because it is Latinized and Creolized: a 'combination of offbeat Spanish beats and Calypso downbeats', as Professor Longhair put it. This, then, is a constant element in the musical tradition of the city. It points not only towards Mexico and Cuba, but directly towards the Spanish history of New Orleans – all part of the same cultural sphere, encompassing Cuba and Mexico as well as the entire Creole realm right down to Trinidad and French Guiana.

It has also become clear that in this field (as in all the others) jazz developed according to the law under which it came into being. Everything was *in nuce* – was already potentially present – in the early forms of jazz.

The Violin

What had happened to the flute during the fifties has come true for the violin since the end of the sixties: All of a sudden, it was at the centre of attention – there was talk of a 'violin wave'. This seems particularly paradoxical in view of the inferior role the violin had previously played in the history of jazz. Though the violin is by no means new to jazz – it is as old as the cornets of New Orleans – its softness of sound long kept it from playing an equal role in the swinging consortium of trombones, trumpets, and saxophones.

Early New Orleans and ragtime bands frequently included a violinist, but only because it was a nineteenth-century custom to have a violin in that sort of a band. The violinist in the old New Orleans orchestras was the counterpart of the 'stand-up fiddler' of Viennese *Kaffeehaus* music. As late as the fifties, this *Kaffeehaus* tradition still cast its shadow over the jazz violinists. As soon as they were no longer 'modern', they wound up where their instrument – as far as jazz was concerned – came from: in commercial music.

The first important violinist in jazz was *Joe Venuti*. Rediscovered in the decade preceding his death in 1978, the 'old man' generated an amazing vitality, outplaying many of the younger violinists – a phenomenon breaking through all generational boundaries, comparable to Earl Hines among the pianists. *Eddie South*, born in Louisiana in the same year as Venuti (1904; died in 1962), never achieved Venuti's fame. South, who had ties to the European scene as early as the twenties, spent time in Paris during the thirties and played there with Django Reinhardt and Europe's most important jazz violinist, *Stephane Grappelli*. An amazing recording made by these three is the 'Interprétation swing et improvisation swing sur le premier mouvement du concerto en ré mineur pour deux violons par Jean Sebastian Bach.' Here, South and Grappelli play the main segment of the first movement of the Bach D-minor concerto for two violins, with Reinhardt taking the orchestra part on guitar. This recording is one of the earliest, and perhaps the most moving, testimonies to the admiration so many jazz musicians have for Bach's work. During World War II, the German occupation authorities in Paris melted down all available copies of this record as a particularly monstrous example of 'degenerate art' (*Entartete Kunst*). Fortunately, a number of copies in private hands survived, and the recording was later reissued.

Stephane Grappelli is the 'grandseigneur' of the jazz violin with a very French sort of amiability and charm. From 1934 on, he was, with Django Reinhardt, a key member of the famous 'Quintet du Hot Club de France', the first important combo in European jazz. During the German occupation, he lived in England. During the late forties and after, he played with many well-known European and American musicians in Paris. Then he faded from the scene for a while, but when the 'violin wave' started in the late sixties, he made a true comeback. Among his most beautiful recordings are those the seventy-year-old Grand Old Man made with musicians half his age – for example, with Larry Coryell, Philip Catherine, and Gary Burton.

In the meantime, in the United States – beginning with his 1936 record of 'I'se a Muggin' – *Stuff Smith* had become the great jazz violinist. He was the first to use electronic amplification. With the sovereignty of a master, he ignored all the rules of the conservatory. A well-bred concert violinist might cringe at Stuff's violent violin treatment, but he achieved more jazzlike, hornlike effects than any other player prior to today's 'violin wave'. Smith, who died in Munich in 1967, was a humorist of the calibre of Fats Waller. During the second half of the thirties, he led a sextet on 52nd Street in New York with trumpeter Jonah Jones which combined jazz and humour in a wonderful way. In the fifties, Norman Granz teamed Smith's violin with the trumpet of Dizzy Gillespie.

For years, *Ray Nance*, who died in 1976, was a trumpeter in Duke Ellington's orchestra and also played occasional violin solos. But on violin he played mostly moody, sentimental melodies, while his trumpet solos belong with the great examples of the genre in jazz. On the other hand it is an illustration of the growing importance of the jazz violin that the instrument became increasingly essential to Nance in the years before his death. Now, in smaller groups, he played happy, swinging violin solos that showed his roots in terms of style and phrasing to be where he originated as a trumpeter as well: in Louis Armstrong.

Interestingly enough, it was a European who initiated the great success of the violin in the new jazz; *Jean-Luc Ponty*, born in 1942, the son of a violin professor, really and definitely electrified the violin. His position is thus the same as Charlie Christian's among guitarists or Jimmy Smith's among organists.

Ponty, who studied classical violin (he was a first-prize winner at the Conservatoire Nationale Supérieur de Paris), began with true jazz recordings, as in the 'Violin Summit' with Stuff Smith, Stephane Grappelli, and the Dane Svend Asmussen. He moved to the United States in 1973, where he played first with Frank Zappa, then in John McLaughlin's second Mahavishnu Orchestra. In the late seventies, Ponty developed the impulses he had received there into his own kind of fusion music: 'Lighter, warmer, more romantic and more accessible' (Tim Schneckloth) than McLaughlin, which made him successful with a wide audience extending beyond the actual realm of fusion. But he also developed a tendency – as *down beat* put it – to become 'quite predictable' and 'corral both his playing and arrangements into the most narrow of bags'. Ponty uses a vast number of accessories to produce the electronic sounds on his violin and his music has become a case of constant brinkmanship between extramusical effects and high quality.

As the musician who actually initiated the contemporary interest in the violin – with his jazz recordings around the turn of the sixties – Ponty became indirectly responsible for the comeback of the music of veteran masters Venuti and Grappelli.

Around the same time as Ponty, *Don 'Sugar Cane' Harris* became known, only to disappear from the scene again – regrettably – after a couple of years. As Ponty stems from the classical violin tradition, Harris comes from the blues. For years he toured the United States with Johnny Otis's Blues Show, where he acquired his funky blues style.

But the list of extraordinary contemporary violinists only begins with Ponty and Harris. Immediately after – and in part also parallel to them – come *Mike White, Jerry Goodman, Steve Kindler*, Polish players *Zbigniew Seifert* and *Michal Urbaniak, John Blake*, Frenchman *Didier Lockwood*, Indians *L. Shankar* and *L. Subramaniam*, as well as – in free jazz – *Leroy Jenkins, Alan Silva, Billy Bang*, and *Ramsey Ameen*.

White made Coltrane-inspired recordings with Pharoah Sanders. *Goodman* is an especially eclectic player, uniting rock–jazz, country, and hillbilly music, the Nashville sound, Mingus, gypsy and classical musical. *Urbaniak* plays a very personal kind of fusion music which often reveals traces of the folk music of his native Poland.

Of particular significance is *Zbigniew Seifert*, whom critic Patrick Hinely compared directly to John Coltrane: 'What links Seifert and Coltrane, besides total dedication to their instruments, is a quality one might call "controlled drift" or "responsible freedom". In both men's music, there is no way you can tell what is going to happen next, but you can trust them to take it all the way to the edge.'

And from Seifert himself: 'What I play on the violin, I imagine being produced by the saxophone. I admire Coltrane and try to play as he would if his instrument were the violin. That's probably the reason that I avoid playing my instrument in the usual way, with all the well-known effects . . .' And McCoy Tyner said at the 1976 Berlin Jazz Days: 'I've never heard a violinist like him before!'

Seifert is among the outstanding Polish jazz musicians who have made their country one of the most interesting jazz nations in the world. His music lives in the tension between his classical roots and his love for Coltrane. There is, in other words, a Zbigniew of chamber music and one who is 'Trane-like'. Seifert made recordings with Eddie Gomez, Jack DeJohnette, John Scofield, Joachim Kühn, Cecil McBee, Billy Hart, Charlie Mariano, and others. Towards the end of 1978, only a few weeks before his tragic death early in 1979, the members of the group Oregon, who had just become acquainted with his style, invited him to the studio. The resulting record, 'Violin', was dedicated to his memory.

The jazz world had just lost Zbigniew Seifert when another European jazz violinist arrived on the scene and was immediately hailed as 'the new Zbiggy': *Didier Lockwood*, who comes from France, the classical land of great jazz violinists. The first of them was Michel Warlop, as early as in the late twenties. When Django Reinhardt and Stephane Grappelli made their first big-band jazz recordings in the early thirties, it was with an orchestra led by Warlop. When Warlop concluded in 1937 that Grappelli was a greater violinist than himself, he gave him one of his violins as a present. By doing so, he initiated a tradition. And since then the most promising French jazz violinist has been presented with the Warlop violin. Grappelli passed it on to Ponty. In early 1979, Ponty and Grappelli decided that Didier Lockwood had become worthy of possessing Warlop's instrument. It was handed on to Lockwood at a Paris concert.

Says Lockwood: 'No other violinist has moved and influenced me more than Zbigniew Seifert.' In Lockwood's music, too, the Coltrane tradition remains alive, but he is more interested in fusion music than Seifert was. He possesses an elegance and charm matched by only a very few musicians on today's fusion scene.

It is remarkable that Coltrane has had such a strong influence on violinists. However, his legacy led to quite different results with players like Ponty, Mike White, Seifert, and Lockwood. It resulted in yet another style in Philadelphia-born *John Blake*, who was presented by McCoy Tyner in 1979 as a member of his group. Blake is an improviser with the burning power of the saxophonists who could be heard in Tyner's groups during the seventies; he has a noticeable interest in black soul and funk music.

It is fitting that with the opening up of jazz towards Indian music, two significant Indian violinists have become successful on the jazz and fusion scene: *L. Shankar* and *L. Subramaniam*, the former known through his work in John McLaughlin's Shakti, the latter through recordings with Larry Coryell, Stu Goldberg, Herbie Hancock, Maynard Ferguson, John Handy, and Ali Akbar Khan. Both Shankar and Subramaniam hail from the same families of southern Indian musicians; that means they belong to the Carnatic musical culture of India (the other being the Hindustani, in the northern part of the country). Subramaniam currently possesses the title 'Violin Chakravarti' ('Emperor of the Violinists'), a title given to only one violinist in each generation.

The outstanding and far too little known violin voice of free jazz is *Leroy Jenkins*. His clusterlike, 'pounded' violin sounds have a kind of manic drive. Jenkins uses the violin as percussion instrument or noise producer – without scrupling about the traditional rules of violin and harmony. *Ramsey Ameen* became known in the late seventies through his work with Cecil Taylor, *Billy Bang* with the New York String Trio. He has recorded a highly interesting solo violin album which shows that, even on an instrument with a tradition as great and old as that of the violin, new ways of playing can still be found.

No other instrument in jazz has as many European players as the violin. Among the violinists mentioned in this chapter, there are seven Europeans (plus eleven Americans and two Indians). In addition, the American players Eddie South, Stuff Smith, and Alan Silva all lived in Europe for extended periods; and 'Sugar Cane' Harris, L. Subramaniam, and Billy Bang made some of their most important recordings in Europe. The ironic dot on the 'i' is the fact that the very first of the well-known jazz violinists, Joe Venuti, was European by birth. Venuti used to claim that he had been born of Italian parents on the Atlantic Ocean, en route to America. But when Joe was in his seventies, he admitted that he was born in northern Italy, near Lago di Como, where Venutis still lives to this day.

Miscellaneous Instruments

For fifty years – until about 1950 – only a relatively small 'family' of instruments was employed in jazz. They were basically the same instruments that had been used in early New Orleans jazz: two instruments from the brass group (trumpet and trombone), saxophone and clarinet from the reed group, and, of course, the rhythm-section instruments – drums, bass, guitar, and piano.

Nevertheless, there have been shifts in emphasis within jazz instrumentation – to such a degree that the entire history of jazz can be viewed in terms of shifting emphases placed on particular instruments. In this scheme, the piano would stand at the beginning; it ruled the ragtime period. Then the trumpet blew its way to the forefront: first in New Orleans, where the 'Kings of Jazz' always were trumpeters (or cornetists), then in the great Chicago period, when trumpeters like King Oliver, Louis Armstrong, and Bix Beiderbecke came to the fore. The Swing era was the time of the clarinet. And with the appearance of Lester Young and Charlie Parker, the saxophone became the main instrument – initially tenor, then for a while alto, and after that tenor again. In the early seventies, finally, electronics became the determining sound factor – first in the shape of the electric guitar, but soon to such a degree that the electronic sound has frequently become more important than the original sound of the instruments electronically amplified or manipulated. Electronics similarize the sound of instruments. This is true even for instruments as diverse as organ and guitar. There are rock groups which have disbanded because the musicians thought that the electric organ and electric guitar sounded so much alike they felt they could do without one of them. Differentiation within similarity, on the other hand, is one of the most attractive chapters in the annals of jazz. It is a fascinating challenge to differentiate the various players of the Coltrane heritage. And it is just as fascinating to differentiate the various electronic sounds of the seventies and eighties.

There have been three major changes in jazz instrumentation – first, through the Lester Young-initiated switch of jazz-consciousness from sonority to phrasing; then, as we indicated, through electronics; and, finally, through the opening of jazz to world music.

After Lester Young had cleared the path for the recognition that the jazz essence was no longer tied, for better or worse, to sonority, jazz could be played on practically any instrument offering possibilities for sufficiently flexible, clear jazz phrasing. Thus, instruments were 'discovered' for jazz which previously had hardly ever (or never) been in jazz use. The flute, the French horn, and the violin are examples of this phenomenon.

While some of these instruments could be summarily discussed under the heading 'Miscellaneous Instruments' in prior editions of this book, they have since become so important that they require chapters of their own: flute, violin, organ and keyboards, percussion instruments.

Another motive behind this ongoing process of discovering new instruments for jazz is the musicians' interest in sound. In the section 'The Elements of Jazz' it was shown that sound is an indispensable jazz element, and in the course of jazz history, the interest in sound has grown continuously. There are musicians and groups today for whom involvement in and joy of sound seem to have become of paramount importance.

Discovering new sounds has been a crucial motivating factor for jazz musicians. In the late sixties it seemed as if electronics were especially suited to take over this function. But then it became clear that precisely the 'oversupply' of sound possibilities in electronics – we discussed this in the chapter on organ and keyboards – caused problems regarding individuality and personal style. As we have seen, the chief aim of the interest in sound is to arrive at a *personal* expression. That is why, paradoxically, the sound-consciousness associated with electronics led to a revival of acoustic jazz from the late seventies on.

But let us return to the topic of 'miscellaneous instruments'. Many of them are used as secondary instruments, and we have mentioned them where a certain musician's primary instrument was discussed:

the cello in connection with bassist *Oscar Pettiford*; the bass clarinet introduced by *Eric Dolphy* in the clarinet chapter; oboe and bassoon in connection with *Yusef Lateef* in the tenor and flute chapters. There we also discussed *Roland Kirk*, who in addition to all his other instruments played two archaic saxophones, used mainly in turn-of-the-century Spanish military bands: the stritch and the manzello.

How the limits of jazz instrumentation have expanded becomes clear when one hears the harp improvisations of *Alice Coltrane*. In the fifties, *Corky Hale* from the West Coast and *Dorothy Ashby* from New York had already attempted to play in a jazz vein on this instrument. (A curiosity: The first traceable jazz harp was played by *Caspar Reardon* in 1934, on Jack Teagarden's recording of 'Junk Man' [with Benny Goodman], and after that by *Adele Girard* in Joe Marsala's 'Jazz Me Blues' [with Eddie Condon and Joe Bushkin!].) But only the modality of the new jazz seems to have cleared the way for this difficult instrument, which has to be constantly retuned. Alice Coltrane was the first to develop a jazz-harp sound into something more than just a curiosity.

Two instruments have come full circle: harmonica and tuba. In old New Orleans, the tuba – as mentioned – was a kind of forerunner of the string bass. Today, musicians like *Howard Johnson, Don Butterfield, Bob Stewart, Joe Dailey,* and *Earl McIntyre* are playing tuba solos of almost trumpetlike agility. Blues singer Taj Mahal used an entire tuba section as accompaniment on one of his records. Howard Johnson briefly led a tuba band in the seventies. Since one tends to forget the man who initiated this whole development, it should be pointed out that as early as the fifties, in Los Angeles, bassist *Red Callender*, Charles Mingus's teacher, incorporated the tuba into the then-dominant West-Coast sounds.

The harmonica is the 'harp' of the folk–blues singer. The two *Sonny Boy Williamsons*, as well as *Sonny Terry, Junior Wells, Shakey Jake, Little Walter, Big Walter Horton, James Cotton, Carey Bell, Whispering Smith,* and many others have played marvellously expressive 'talking' harmonica solos – usually in the blues groups that existed (and continue to exist) in the South or on Chicago's South Side. Nevertheless, this instrument was always afflicted with the stigma of a certain folklorelike primitiveness. Belgian *Toots Thielemans* liberated the harmonica from this affliction. He plays it with a mobility and wealth of ideas reminiscent of the great saxophonists of the cool-jazz era.

Since the emergence of electronic amplification, the harmonica has been given equal rights in the family of instruments. It has also made inroads in contemporary blues–rock music where it is played by white musicians like *Paul Butterfield* or *John Mayall* in the style of the great black blues 'harp' men. *Magic Dick* has contributed exciting harmonica solos in a pure rock context. *Stevie Wonder* has combined Thielemans's refinement with the 'harp' sound of the old blues. *Mauricio Einhorn* has incorporated the Thielemans sound into his native Brazilian music, adding the specific Brazilian rhythm feeling.

Next are such instruments as French horn, oboe, English horn, and bassoon. Their 'fathers' (in terms of jazz) were, as early as the fifties, *Julius Watkins* and *Yusef Lateef*. Watkins played the French horn on recordings with important musicians like Kenny Clarke, Oscar Pettiford, and Quincy Jones, reaching a remarkable jazzlike intensity difficult to find on this difficult instrument. Lateef – who is as outstanding on tenor sax, flute, oboe, and bassoon as he is on diverse exotic instruments such as the argol (an Egyptian kind of oboe) – was the precursor, even before Coltrane, of the opening up of jazz to world music. In the fifties, tenorist *Bob Cooper* played oboe and English horn on West Coast jazz recordings, including some with Max Roach on drums. Perhaps the most interesting bassoon solos in today's jazz are by *Frank Tiberi*. *Paul McCandless* has come to the fore in the group Oregon on oboe and English horn; he is a musician with roots in the romantic tradition of these instruments. *Vincent Chancey* has played intelligent French horn solos in Carla Bley's ensemble, which also reflect romanticism.

A clever mixture of horn and electronics is the lyricon, a saxophonelike wind instrument which controls a synthesizer. It has been played by *Tom Scott, Michal Urbaniak, Sonny Rollins, Wayne Shorter* and other musicians, clearly 'humanizing' electronic sounds.

Let's move on to some miscellaneous string instruments. The mandolin is so engulfed by the serenade-sound of Italian mandolin groups that it might seem paradoxical that it has made its way into jazz. But it has happened – characteristically at first by way of musicians close to country and western music (who, at the same time,

are real 'Swingers'): *Tiny Moore* and *Jethro Burns*. The latter made his
first mandolin recordings as early as the forties, with Bob Wills' Texas
Playboys. In a modern context, guitarist *John Abercrombie* (especially
convincing in his quartet recordings with McCoy Tyner) and above
all *David Grisman* have employed the mandolin. Grisman, who has
enjoyed steadily growing success since the turn of the seventies,
creates string sounds that seem like a contemporary counterpart of
Django Reinhardt's Quintet du Hot Club de France.

The 'fathers' of cello playing in jazz have already been mentioned
in the chapter about the bass. But it was up to *Abdul Wadud* (who has
recorded with quite a few AACM musicians) and *David Darling* to
realize the full potential of this instrument in today's jazz – Darling
with romanticizing and aestheticizing sounds and a lot of overdubbing,
Wadud with convincing jazz feeling and an astonishing talent for
improvisation (and yet complete awareness of the classical and
romantic cello tradition). Another outstanding cellist in the mainstream of today's jazz is *Jean-Charles Capon* from France. Free jazz on
cello is played by *David Eyges*, *Irène Aebi* (mainly in Steve Lacy's
group) and *Tristan Honsinger*, the latter with a radical disdain for
compromise reminiscent, to a certain degree, of Derek Bailey's guitar
style. Eyges, who says he is influenced by country blues, Ornette
Coleman, and the great jazz violinists, has recorded exciting cello-sax
duos with Byard Lancaster.

Another way of discovering new possibilities in sound is by the
invention of new instruments. *Emmet Chapman* invented the 'stick', an
electric ten-string instrument capable of producing such a rich sound
that it seems as if several string instruments had been overdubbed.
Chapman has recorded with Michal Urbaniak, the Transfusion Big
Band of drummer Les DeMerle, and others.

The horizon of instruments was extended even further by the
exotic instruments that became available in the course of the opening
up of jazz to the other great musical cultures of the world. *Don Cherry*,
for example, has used instruments from Lappland, Africa, Tibet,
India, China, and elsewhere. *Han Bennink* occasionally uses the
dhung, a giant Tibetan Alpine horn. *Collin Walcot*, *Bill Plummer*, and
others have played the Indian sitar for jazz records. Saxophonist
Charlie Mariano studied the nagaswaram, an oboelike instrument from
Southern India, for years, first in the city of Kuala Lumpur, then in a

small Indian village. He has created a unique union of Carnatic (South Indian) spirituality and the Coltrane tradition.

One of the most interesting among these musicians is *Stephan Micus*, a 'world musician' in the full sense of the word. Micus commands a zither from Bavaria, bamboo flutes from Japan, a rabab from Afghanistan and instruments from Bali, India, and Tibet – plus a Scottish bagpipe. For years, he travelled in Asia, studying these instruments. He plays them with a profound internationalization of their tradition and spirituality, uniting their sounds in a musical river which makes the stream of inner consciousness audible. At the end of the chapter on jazz in the seventies, we discussed a new type of musician who plays world music. Many players who represent this type have been mentioned. But hardly anyone represents it in so ideal, so visionary a way as Micus. The inner space of sounds in search of which so many musicians dared to venture into electronics: Micus not only imagines it, he realizes it – not with electronics, but on instruments thousands of years old.

THE VOCALISTS OF JAZZ

The Vocalists of Jazz

The Male Singers

Before jazz, there were blues and shouts, work songs and spirituals – the whole treasury of vocal folk music sung by both black and white in the South. There was what Marshall Stearns has called 'archaic jazz'. From this music jazz developed. In other words, jazz developed from vocal sources. Much about the sounds peculiar to jazz can be explained by the fact that horn-blowers imitate the sounds of the human voice on their instruments. This becomes obvious in the growling sounds of trumpets and trombones in the orchestra of Duke Ellington, for example, or in Eric Dolphy's bass clarinet.

On the other hand, jazz today is so exclusively an instrumental music that its standards and criteria derive from the realm of the instrumental, even the standards of jazz singing. The jazz vocalist handles his voice 'like an instrument' – like a trumpet or trombone or – today especially – a saxophone. Thus the criteria important to European vocal music, such as purity or range of voice, are inapplicable to jazz. Some of the most important jazz singers have voices which – according to 'classical' criteria – are almost ugly. Many have a vocal range so limited that it would hardly encompass a Schubert song.

The dilemma of jazz singing can be expressed as a paradox: all jazz derives from vocal music, but all jazz singing is derived from instrumental music. Significantly, some of the best jazz singers – at least among the males – are also players – above all, Louis Armstrong.

In the literature of jazz, critics of the most diverse persuasions mean to be laudatory when they say of an instrumentalist – such as alto saxophonist Johnny Hodges – that his sound 'resembles that of the human voice'. On the other hand, nothing more flattering can be said of a singer than that he or she knows how to 'treat the voice as an instrument'.

The symbol of the jazz-vocal dilemma is that almost all the jazz polls in the fifties gave first place to a man who is not a jazz singer – *Frank Sinatra*. The reason for this was not the oft-claimed intrusion of commercial values on the jazz field. Many uncompromising jazz instrumentalists voted for Sinatra. And undoubtedly, no 'modern' singer *within* jazz at that time sang with the sensitivity and musicality of Sinatra. In the field of 'commercial' music, Sinatra set the standards for almost all who came after him. Thus, 'Frankie's' place in the jazz polls is not based on erroneous judgements, but is a direct result of the jazz-vocal dilemma.

Only one domain is beyond this dilemma of jazz singing: the blues. But precisely this makes the vicious circle clear. For decades, almost all jazz singers who found favour with the general public were outside the stream of real blues, whereas the first-rate singers of authentic blues and gospel – at least until the big success of blues in rock music from the sixties on – were hardly known. This breakthrough began – as early as the late fifties – with *Ray Charles*, a real blues singer in the tradition of folk blues and gospel, who was accepted by the whole world of modern jazz, and found a wide audience beyond both blues and jazz. It has been rightly said that no one did more to assure the return of the blues to the common consciousness of America than Ray Charles in the fifties. But Charles was only the final link – at that time – in an unending chain of blues singers whose earliest representatives disappear somewhere in the darkness of the South of the past century. And simultaneously, he was the first link in the still growing chain of black singers who sing authentic blues, and yet have great success even with white audiences.

The first well-known representatives of this blues folklore are probably *Blind Lemon Jefferson*, a blind street musician from Texas, and *Huddie Leadbetter* – called *Leadbelly* – who served time in Angola State Penitentiary in Louisiana, first for murder and a few years later for manslaughter. From them, the line runs via *Robert Johnson*, who came from Mississippi and was poisoned in Texas, to *Big Bill Broonzy* and *Son House* and the many blues singers who made Chicago the blues capital of the USA (though all are natives of the South): *Muddy Waters, Little Brother Montgomery, St Louis Jimmy, Sunnyland Slim, Sonny Boy Williamson, Little Walter, Memphis Slim, Howlin' Wolf* and many others. *John Lee Hooker*, who lives in Detroit, also belongs here. Almost all the blues singers are also excellent guitarists. And when they play piano, they accompany themselves with exciting boogie-woogie bass lines. (Other important folk-blues singers are mentioned in the blues chapter.)

In an unending stream, over the decades, more and more new blues singers became known as they migrated from the South to the cities of the North and West. There are two main streams in this great blues migration, and two main states: Mississippi and Texas. Mississippi-born blues people generally migrate to Chicago, those from Texas go to California. The two streams differ musically, too: The Mississippi stream is rougher, 'dirtier'; the Texas stream softer, more flexible and supple. It was the Texas stream that merged with the Midwestern big bands during the Swing era, leading to Swing blues and jazz blues. But here, too, there are of course all imaginable kinds of crossings and mixtures.

The blues stream from Mississippi and Texas (and all the other Southern states) has been flowing uninterruptedly for more than fifty years. But the South remains full of great blues talent. Many blues people resist all the temptations of North and West - such as the wonderful *'Lightnin''* *Hopkins* from Texas. To this day he sings his songs in the bars and hangouts of Houston, his lyrics mirroring the life of his city.

The blues was as alive in the seventies as it was during the twenties and thirties. Since the sixties, a new generation of blues singers has appeared, filled with the consciousness of race and social protest that can be found in many contemporary jazz musicians as well. Members of this new blues generation include singer–harmonica player *Junior Wells*, singer–guitarists *Buddy Guy, Albert King, Albert Collins*, and - above all and still growing in significance - *Otis Rush*, as well as *Taj Mahal*, who has found success with contemporary rock audiences. They no longer hope - as did Trixie Smith and many other 1920s blue vocalists, filled with the despair and irony which co-exist in the blues - that some day 'the sun will shine in their back door'. (The irony is in the avoidance of the front door!) Rather, filled with sense of self, they demand - like singer-pianist *Otis Spann* in 1967 - 'I Want a Brand-New House'.

When I visited Angola State Penitentiary in the summer of 1960, I heard several young blues singers every bit as good as the well-known

Chicago names – among them *Robert Pete Williams*, who was later released and made a name for himself in blues circles prior to his death in 1980. The day before my visit, there had been a thunderstorm. One of the prisoners told us he had nearly been struck by lightning. He was still under the spell of the fear which had possessed him. I suggested that he might someday write a blues about his experience – and right away, he strummed a few chords on his guitar and improvised his 'Lightning Blues'. The surprise was the lyrics, which reflected his experience in intensely realistic expression. These blues lyrics are the real 'jazz and poetry'. Here the difference between 'jazz' and 'poetry' is one of terminology, not substance.

One of the most successful singer–guitarists of authentic big-city blues for more than twenty years now is Mississippi-born *B. B. King*, a cousin of Bukka White, one of the great old folk-blues men. In the 1966 edition of Leonard Feather's *Encyclopedia of Jazz*, it is stated that King 'would like to see Negroes become unashamed of blues, their music.' Indeed, King himself has been an essential factor in the fulfilment of this wish, though (especially in the middle class) there still are many blacks who look down on blues as rustic, primitive, and archaic, and want to dissociate themselves from it. The black American will have found the road to full awareness of his own identity – and thus to true equality – only when he takes as much pride in the blues as a German does in Beethoven or an Italian in Verdi . . .

From the start, the borderline between folk blues as a realm distinct from jazz and the domain of jazz itself has been fluid. A number of singers who are authentic blues singers have been counted as belonging to the jazz world at least as much as to the world of blues. The first of these – and founder of this vocal swing tradition – was *Jimmy Rushing*, who died in 1972. Rushing, from Oklahoma – a state that always was within the sphere of Texas blues influence – became *the* blues singer par excellence of Swing style. He was the first not to sing 'on the beat' – as the folk–blues people did – but in front or behind the beat, to 'sing around' the rhythmic centres and counter them with his own accents, thus creating greater tension. During the thirties and forties, Rushing was Count Basie's singer, and his singing was the exact vocal expression of Basie's instrumental theme of those years: 'Swingin' the Blues'. Other singers of this brand are *Jimmy Witherspoon*, who lives in California, and *Big Miller* from Kansas City.

In the Basie band of the fifties, *Joe Williams* took the place of Rushing. He is a fine musician, who on the one hand endows his ballads with a blueslike intensity and on the other sings the blues with the sophistication of a modern jazzman.

Big Joe Turner, who lives in New Orleans, is the blues shouter of boogie-woogie. In the thirties he worked with the great boogie pianists; a generation later, he had a second round of success – as did many other bluesmen – with the emergence of rock 'n' roll, creating one of its biggest early hits, 'Shake, Rattle and Roll'. *'Champion' Jack Dupree*, *Fats Domino*, and *Professor Longhair* (who died in 1980) – all three born in New Orleans – *Roosevelt Sykes* from Louisiana, *Memphis Slim* (resident in Paris), and the late *Otis Spann* are all convincing, expressive singer–pianists of blues and boogie-woogie.

One – or even two – steps further is *Leon Thomas*, combining the blues tradition with the music of the post-Coltrane era in free, cascading falsetto improvisations, for which he also found inspiration in exotic folklore – such as the music of Central African pygmy tribes. Thomas shows the acute political awareness of the new blues generation in a particularly exemplary manner: 'How much does it cost to fly a man up to the moon? I think of the hungry children that I see every afternoon . . .' It is regrettable that in recent years this excellent singer has only been heard in a rock context – where he often is not even credited with a mention of his name.

The line that leads from Blind Lemon Jefferson through the South Side of Chicago to the modern blues of Otis Rush and B. B. King is the backbone of all jazz singing. This line could be designated the 'blues line' of jazz singing to differentiate it from the 'song line'. But it is important to see the continuous, intensive interrelationship between these two. This is illustrated by the first and most significant singer of the 'song line', *Louis Armstrong*. Armstrong's music remains related to the blues even when it is not blues – and in the orthodox sense of the word, it rarely is. Armstrong's singing is exemplary of the instrumental conception basic to all jazz singing, a conception revealed particularly clearly by vocalists who are also instrumentalists: from the old blues singers, who usually also played the guitar, via trombonist Jack Teagarden, to today's singer–instrumentalists.

Some years ago, on the occasion of an Armstrong visit, the *London Times* noted: 'Of course, this voice is ugly when measured against what Europe calls beautiful singing. But the expression which

Armstrong puts into his voice, all the soul, heart, and depth which swing along in every sound, make it more beautiful than most of the technically perfect and pure, but cold and soulless singing in the white world of today.'

Hot Lips Page, who died in 1954 – at times almost an Armstrong double – came close to Satchmo not only as trumpeter, but also as singer. Trombonist *Jack Teagarden* (who died in 1964), sang some of the most humorous and spirited vocal duets in jazz with Armstrong. Teagarden was a master of 'sophisticated' blues singing, and was so as early as in the thirties, long before the ironic sophistication of the blues became 'modern' in the late fifties. Later, in a more modern field, one finds in *Woody Herman* a similar sophistication, tasteful and musicianly, but not as expressive as Teagarden or the great black vocalists.

Most male singers who have maintained a position in the realm of jazz *per se* have been instrumentalists. The others who began somewhere within jazz or close to it have gone over to commercial music: *Bing Crosby, Frankie Laine, Perry Como, Matt Dennis*, and the musically outstanding *Mel Tormé*, who – wavering between jazz and commercial music – tries to combine both; he belongs among the best and most swinging interpreters of the songs by America's great popular composers. Appropriately, *Nat 'King' Cole* was a first-rate jazz vocalist as long as he was mainly a pianist. Later, as he became a successful singer in the commercial field, his piano playing – and his jazz interest – were pushed further and further back. Nevertheless, his jazz roots and a certain jazz *espressivo* remained noticeable in his singing up to his death in 1965. His influence has extended over a whole generation of singers between Ray Charles and Stevie Wonder. This is one reason why American commercial music is the world's best: so many of the popular stars have a jazz background and 'paid dues' in jazz before attaining commercial success. (Outside the vocal realm, Glenn Miller, Harry James, and Tommy and Jimmy Dorsey are examples of this.)

The jazz instrumentalist, as we said, is especially qualified also to be a good jazz singer. Examples of this can be cited not only from the times of Hot Lips Page and Jack Teagarden, but also from today: drummer *Grady Tate*, trombonist *Richard Boone*, tenor saxophonist *George Adams*, guitarist *George Benson*, and trumpeters *Chet Baker* and *Clark Terry* are notable singers in their stylistic area – Terry with lots of joy and humour, Boone with a combination of traditional blues and contemporary satire, Baker with an almost 'feminine' kind of fragility, Benson (he, too!) with a lot of the King Cole tradition, Adams with the masculine attack known from his tenor playing.

In the forties *Billy Eckstine* was to male singers what Sarah Vaughan was to the females. Eckstine had the greatest vocal gift since Louis Armstrong and Jimmy Rushing. He belonged to the bop circle around Gillespie and Parker, and was so full of enthusiasm for their music that he took up an instrument – the valve trombone. 'Jelly, Jelly' was the big (and still popular) hit by 'Mr B', relating bebop to the blues tradition.

With Billy Eckstine we have reached bop, and we should mention *Babs Gonzales* (who died in 1979), whose fun-filled group Three Bips and a Bop was successful in the late forties, and who later – as the writer of 'Oop-Bop-A-Da', for instance – was one of bebop's entertaining voices; *Earl Coleman*, whose sonorous baritone was once accompanied by Charlie Parker; and *Kenneth 'Pancho' Hagood* and *Joe Carroll*, who both worked with Dizzy Gillespie. Carroll reminded people of Dizzy in mobility of voice and sense of humour. Of course, one must not forget Dizzy Gillespie himself when speaking of bop vocalists. Dizzy's high-pitched, slightly oriental-sounding voice corresponds as closely to Dizzy the trumpeter as Satchmo's voice corresponded to *his* trumpet. *Jackie Paris* carried the bop vocal conception into cool jazz. *Oscar Brown, Jr*, a personality of great radiance, is a singer, nightclub artist, and lyricist. *Johnny Harman* is a 'musicians' singer', whose supple, flowing phrasing – as in his ballad recordings with John Coltrane – has been much admired by connoisseurs. *Bill Henderson* and *Mark Murphy* sing with a healthy, Basie-inspired Mainstream conception; the latter has put a whole era of jazz into song with ravishing sophistication. *Mose Allison* transforms, in a totally personal style, black and white blues and folk songs into his own compositions with a modern soul character. In fact, when soul singing became an 'in-thing' in the sixties and seventies, some white singers who didn't know the black tradition at all referred to white Mose Allison – who, to be sure, comes from an overwhelmingly black town in Mississippi, and has absorbed black folk music since childhood.

No doubt the yield of great male jazz singers – aside from the blues singers and Louis Armstrong – is not impressive. This fits our conception of the jazz vocal dilemma. Jazz singing, beyond blues, is the more effective the closer it approximates instrumental use of the voice. The female voice has the greater potential in this respect. It certainly is characteristic that quite a few male singers have had voices that seemed deformed by nature or at least sounded unusual – beginning with Louis Armstrong. Often deformation increases expression.

Also from the realm of bebop stems a development which led to a highly successful vocal group, the *Lambert–Hendricks–Ross Ensemble*. *Eddie Jefferson* – as early as at the start of the forties – was the first to equip recorded jazz solos with his own lyrics. He was followed by *King Pleasure* (whose adaption of a James Moody recording, 'Moody's Mood for Love', became a big hit in 1953) and British-born *Annie Ross* (whose song 'Twisted', based on a tenor improvisation by Wardell Gray, was a hit in 1952). *Jon Hendricks* carried this approach to its peak. He was the actual 'poet of the jazz solo', a 'James Joyce of Jive', as *Time* magazine called him. *Dave Lambert* (who died in 1966) had arranged and recorded a group vocal in 1945 with Gene Krupa's big band, 'What's This?', which was the first recorded bebop vocal. So in a sense, Dave Lambert, Jon Hendricks, and Annie Ross belonged together musically even prior to forming Lambert, Hendricks and Ross in 1958. The trio began with vocalizations of Count Basie records, and went on from there to develop an entertaining, spirited vocal ensemble style that has remained unique, vocalizing the entire spectrum of modern jazz. When these three sang solos by Charlie Parker, Lester Young, Sonny Rollins, Miles Davis, Oscar Pettiford, John Coltrane, and others to Jon Hendricks's lyrics, one had the feeling that this was what all those great musicians had wanted to say. When Annie Ross returned to England in 1962, Ceylon-born Yolande Bavan took her place until the trio finally broke up in 1964. Hendricks, however, and Eddie Jefferson (who died in 1979), carried on this style into recent times – Hendricks also in a musical based on the much-lauded 'Evolution of the Blues' he had created for the Monterey Jazz Festival; Jefferson in an inspired collaboration with the young alto player Richie Cole.

But the 'song line', as we called it, of male jazz singing also continues to develop. It has been carried into our times by singers like the aforementioned *Mark Murphy*, as well as by *Bob Dorough*, *Joe Lee Wilson*, *Gil Scott-Heron*, *Lou Rawls*, *Ben Sidran*, and *Tony Middleton*.

Murphy and Dorough sing songs by the great composers of American popular music with the special intensity of contemporary jazz. Rawls has developed soul music in his own way, and Wilson is the male singer of the New York avant-garde – he worked with Archie Shepp and Rashied Ali, among others. Scott-Heron is a poet of the ghetto with an acute political and social consciousness. Sidran, who also has come to the fore as a pianist, has created a peculiar kind of 'speech-song' in the fusion field. With his husky voice, Middleton (who recorded with master accompanist Ellis Larkins on piano) sometimes sounds like a modernized and vocalized Ben Webster.

We have mentioned the strong influence of Brazilian music on modern jazz, so we ought to name some of the singers from that country: first the two great 'father figures' of modern Brazilian music, *Antonio Carlos Jobim* and *João Gilberto*; later, among the younger vocalists, *Edu Lôbo*, *Gilberto Gil*, *Caetano Veloso*, and above all *Milton Nascimento*. They all possess that melodic enchantment and poetry which makes Brazilian music so unmistakable; the younger ones also with a more contemporary manner and socially critical approach.

Finally, there is the most successful and most frequently named of all contemporary male vocalists, *Al Jarreau*. Singing, gargling, clucking, moaning, screaming, whispering – he commands an incomparable arsenal of vocal possibilities. Born in Milwaukee, Jarreau comes from an old Creole- and French-speaking Louisianian family: 'Sure, there's a lot of New Orleans in my music; a lot of Louisiana, and that also means a lot of Africa . . .' Jarreau says he took his cues from Billie Holiday and Nat King Cole and especially from the Lambert–Hendricks–Ross trio. That connection is even visible: when Al sings his saxophonelike phrases he moves his fingers and his hands as if he were playing some imaginary instrument – just the way Jon Hendricks used to do years ago. Jarreau's throat produces an entire orchestra of sounds: drums and saxophones, trumpets and flutes, congas and basses – all from the mouth of one man, from the lowest bass to the highest falsetto, as if he had a dozen or more different male and female voices at his disposal.

We have said a great deal about the tradition of black music in this book. Among the instrumentalists, the avant-garde musicians – like those from the AACM circle – are often the ones who maintain this tradition. The situation is quite different with the vocalists. Especially among the female singers, avant-garde musicians have almost nothing to do with the tradition. Here, the black tradition is largely cultivated in a field outside of jazz – the area of pop-music. This was already underway with the successful soul singers of the sixties (unthinkable without Ray Charles): *Otis Redding* leading on by way of *James Brown* (whose cry, 'Say it loud: I'm Black and I'm Proud!' did more for the new self-confidence of the black masses than all the words of people like Eldridge Cleaver, Rap Brown, or Stokeley Carmichael) and *Marvin Gaye* ('Save the World–Save the Babies– Save the Children!') to *Stevie Wonder*. What these vocalists sing is, very much in the sense intended by Charles Mingus and Roland Kirk, 'black music' – in fact, in particular with Stevie Wonder, 'black classical music'. Wonder has been compared as a composer with Duke Ellington. His albums, some of them consisting of several records – 'Songs in the Key of Life', 'Hotter Than July', and 'Journey Through the Secret Life of Plants' – are suitelike compositions conceived as large works with an inner coherence; they summarize and recapitulate today's stock of black music in a way similar to Ellington. Wonder is a musician of fascinating universality and flexibility. He is a composer and arranger as well as a singer, plays almost every imaginable instrument on his records – and commands all the modern studio techniques: overdubbing, all kinds of synthesizers and sound manipulators, etc., as if the studio with all its electronic gadgetry were an additional instrument on which to play music (which, in fact, it is).

The Female Singers

The history of female blues singing starts later than male blues singing. No female singers from 'archaic' times are known to us. Folk–blues singers like Blind Lemon Jefferson, Leadbelly, or Robert Johnson did not have female counterparts; nor do their contemporary successors. The simple, rural world of folk blues is dominated by man – woman is an object.

This changed as soon as the blues moved into the big cities of the North. At that time – in the early twenties – the great era of classic blues, whose 'mother' was *Ma Rainey* and whose 'empress' was *Bessie Smith*, began. In the chapter on Bessie, we discussed the classic blues period in detail. Singers like *Bertha 'Chippie' Hill*, *Victoria Spivey*, *Sippie*

Wallace, and *Alberta Hunter* carried on the message of classical blues, while *Big Mama Thornton* incorporated it into rhythm & blues. But it is important to note that in the late twenties the musical climate was already changing, shifting the accent away from the blues and towards the song.

The first female singers important in this field (who are worth listening to even today) are *Ethel Waters*, *Ivie Anderson*, and *Mildred Bailey*. Ethel Waters was the first to demonstrate – as early as the twenties – the many possibilities for jazz singing in good commercial tunes. Ivie Anderson became Duke Ellington's vocalist in 1932 and remained for almost twelve years; Duke called her the best singer he ever had. Mildred Bailey – of part Indian origin – was a successful singer of the Swing era with great sensitivity and mastery of phrasing. She was married to Red Norvo; and with him, Teddy Wilson, and Mary Lou Williams she made her finest recordings. Her 'Rockin' Chair' became a hit of considerable proportions; it was a blues, but an 'alienated', ironic blues.

The songs of the female singers in this 'song line' were – and are – the ballads and pop tunes of 'commercial music', the melodies of the great American popular composers – Cole Porter, Jerome Kern, Irving Berlin, George Gershwin – sometimes even tunes from the 'hit parade', all sung with the inflection and phrasing typical of jazz.

In this area, improvisation has retreated to a final, irreducible position. The songs must remain recognizable, and of course the singers are dependent upon the lyrics. But in a very special sense there can be improvisation here, too. It lies in the art of paraphrasing, juxtaposing, transposing – in the alteration of harmonies, and in a certain way of phrasing. There is a whole arsenal of possibilities, of which *Billie Holiday*, the most important figure in this branch, had supreme command. Billie was the embodiment of a truth first expressed by Fats Waller (and after him by so many others): in jazz it does not matter so much what you do, but *how* you do it. To pick one example among many: In 1935, Billie Holiday recorded (with Teddy Wilson) a banal little song, 'What a Little Moonlight Can Do' – and what resulted was a completely valid work of art.

Billie Holiday sang blues only incidentally. But through her phrasing and conception, much that she sang seemed to become blues.

Billie Holiday made more than 350 records – among them 70 with

Teddy Wilson. She made her most beautiful recordings in the thirties with Wilson and Lester Young. And in the intertwining of the lines sung by Billie Holiday and the lines played by Lester Young, the question which is lead and which is accompaniment – which line is vocal and which instrumental – becomes secondary.

Billie Holiday is the great songstress of understatement. Her voice has none of the volume and majesty of Bessie Smith. It is a small, supple, sensitive voice – yet Billie sang a song which, more than anything sung by Bessie Smith or the other female blues singers, became a musical protest against racial discrimination. This song was 'Strange Fruit' (1939). The 'strange fruit' hanging from the tree was the body of a lynched Negro. Billie sang this song as if she were stating a fact: That's the way it is. Any blues by Bessie Smith, even a simple, everyday love song, was sung with more emphasis and pathos than this: the most emphatic and most impassioned musical testimony against racism to become known before Abbey Lincoln's interpretation of Max Roach's 'Freedom Now Suite' of 1960.

Charm and urbane elegance, suppleness and sophistication are the chief elements in the understatement of Billie Holiday. These elements can be found everywhere – for example, in 'Mandy Is Two' (1942), the song about little Mandy, who is only two years old but already a big girl. And this is expressed so straightforwardly and warmly! How simple and unpretentious it is! Nothing rings false, as is the rule with commercial ditties attempting childlike naïveté. It is almost inconceivable that something seemingly destined by every known law to become *kitsch* could be transformed into art.

Billie's singing had the elasticity of Lester Young's tenor playing – and she had this elasticity prior to her first encounter with Lester. Billie was the first artist in all of jazz – not just the first woman or the first jazz singer – in whose music the influence of the saxophone as the style and sound-setting instrument became clear. And this took place, only seemingly in paradoxical fashion, before the beginning of the saxophone era, which actually only began with the success of Lester Young in the early forties. The 'cool' tenor saxophone sound is apparent already in Billie Holiday's first recording – 'Your Mother's Son-in-law', made in 1933 with Benny Goodman. It can be said that because of Billie Holiday, modern jazz had its beginning in the realm of singing earlier than in the field of any instrument.

It had its beginning with Holiday also because she was the first to realize – certainly subconsciously – that not only was her voice the instrument, but also the microphone. Holiday was the first vocalist to understand that a singer using a microphone has to sing in a totally different way from one not using a mike. She humanized her voice by 'microphonizing' it, thus making subtleties significant which had been unknown in all singing up to that point – in fact, had been unnecessary, because they could not have been made audible.

The life story of Billie Holiday has been told often, and even more often has been effectively falsified: from servant girl in Baltimore through rape and prostitution to successful song star – and through narcotics all the way downhill again. In 1938 she worked with Artie Shaw's band, a white group. For months she had to use service entrances, while her white colleagues went in through the front. She had to stay in dingy hotels, and sometimes couldn't even share meals with her associates. And she had to suffer all this not only as a black, but also as the sole woman in the band. Billie felt she had to go through all this to set an example. If it could work for *one* black artist, others could make it too. She took it . . . until she collapsed.

Before that, she had appeared with another great band, that of Count Basie – and had suffered the reverse kind of humiliation, possibly even more stinging than what she had to endure in Shaw's band: though Billie was as much a Negro as any of Basie's musicians, her skin colour might have seemed too light to some customers and it was unthinkable at that time to present a white girl singer with a black band. At a theatre appearance in Detroit, Billie had to put on dark make-up.

In the last years of her life – she died at the age of forty-four in 1959 – Billie Holiday's voice was often a mere shadow of her great days. She sang without the suppleness and glow of the earlier recordings; her voice sounded worn, rough, and old. Still, even then her singing had magnetic powers. It is extraordinary to discover just how much a great artist has left when voice and technique and flexibility have failed and nothing remains except the spiritual power of creativity and expression. To hear this on recordings made by Billie Holiday in the fifties is an almost eerie experience: a vocalist devoid of all the material and technical attributes of her profession who still remains a great artist.

Billie Holiday stands at the centre of great jazz singing. Her important recordings with Teddy Wilson, Lester Young, and other greats of the Swing era are convincing testimony to the fact that the dilemma of jazz affects only lesser practitioners. Indeed, it is from the almost paradoxical overcoming of this dilemma that great art can be wrought. That is why we have concerned ourselves with Billie Holiday at such length.

After Holiday comes a host of female singers whose common denominator was – and still is – their application of Billie's accomplishments to the particular stylistic field to which they belong.

Before that, however, *Ella Fitzgerald* must be discussed. She also stems from the Swing era. But Ella, born in 1918 and thus only three years younger than Billie Holiday, is not only a great Swing vocalist, but also one of the great voices in all of contemporary jazz. No other female singer – and hardly any other great jazz musician – commands a wider range of music. In the thirties, her big hit 'A-Tisket, A-Tasket' – done with the Chick Webb band – was a naïvely playful song dressed up in the Swing sounds of the day. In the forties, her scat vocals on such themes as 'How High the Moon' or 'Lady Be Good' led to the core of bop. In the fifties, Ella developed a mature ballad conception. Her interpretations of the 'songbooks' of the great American songwriters – Gershwin, Kern, Porter, Berlin – are among the lasting documents of American music. From the sixties to the eighties she has retained supreme mastery of all the different styles through which she has lived and sung.

Even today, no matter how much she may have changed during all these years, Ella still has some of the simplicity and straightforward-ness of the sixteen-year-old girl who was discovered in January, 1934, in an amateur contest at Harlem's Apollo Theatre – as were so many other great jazz talents (for example, her greatest competitor, Sarah Vaughan). The 'prize' Ella won back then was a 'short' engagement with Chick Webb's band, but the engagement did not end even with Webb's death five years later. In 1939, Ella took over nominal leadership of the Webb band for a while.

Ella Fitzgerald's long artistic life, spanning so many decades, has led us far ahead – right past an era which must be treated at this point.

The most important women singers of the forties and fifties were initially connected with the three successful centres of that period's instrumental jazz: the circle surrounding Woody Herman, the one around Stan Kenton, and the one around Charlie Parker and Dizzy Gillespie.

Mary Ann McCall was the vocalist of Woody Herman's Herd of the late forties. She had a musicianly conception corresponding to that of Woody's soloists at the time, for instance Serge Chaloff or Bill Harris.

June Christy was the voice of Stan Kenton's band, and the warm, human climate of her singing won her many friends time and again, even when one could not go along with her all the way as far as intonation was concerned. June Christy replaced *Anita O'Day* with Kenton in 1947. Anita is still, after thirty years, considered to be the 'greatest white female jazz vocalist' – with a musical assurance of virtuoso calibre and great improvisational capacity.

Even more important female vocalists came from the circle surrounding Charlie Parker and Dizzy Gillespie: *Sarah Vaughan, Carmen McRae,* and – somewhat later, because she initially was with Lionel Hampton's band – *Betty Carter.* Like so many jazz singers, Sarah received her first impulses in a gospel church. She said: 'You have to have a little soul in your singing, the kind of soul that's in the spiritual . . . It's a part of my life.' In 1943, she became the singer of Earl Hines's band; in 1944, of Billie Eckstine's. Both bands were 'talent cradles' for the important bebop musicians of those years – and Sarah knew immediately: 'I thought Bird and Diz were the end. I still do. I think their playing influenced my singing.'

Sarah Vaughan was the first real jazz singer with a vocal range equal to that of an opera singer. Her rich, dark contralto brought a new sound into jazz singing. Her ability to change this sound in the most diverse manner and to literally charge it with emotional content even today surpasses anything done by any other female jazz singer.

Sarah Vaughan's stature is so towering that other singers of her generation remained in her shadow. This is particularly regrettable with *Carmen McRae* (who was once married to Kenny Clarke, the creator of bebop drum style). She is also one of the great individualists of modern jazz singing. Especially impressive is the way Carmen sounds so 'definitive'. Nat Hentoff once compared her with a 'sternly exotic figurehead over the cutwater of a New England whaling ship,' referring both to her personality *and* to the powerful individualism of her singing.

McRae's junior by eight years, *Betty Carter* was recognized only relatively late by the jazz world as belonging among the great bop singers. Only in the course of the seventies did she become an embodiment of bebop singing – in fact, of jazz vocalizing in general. Critic Peter Rüedi described her as 'aware of herself and her social situation, humorous, urbane, bluesy, "dirty", of explosive aggressiveness and then again totally succumbing to her song, and always direct, without frills, to the point of crudity. Her tone has some of the lyrical as well as gripping "dryness" of the early Dexter Gordon . . .'

Other female singers of this generation are *Chris Connor, Jackie Cain, Dakota Staton, Ernestine Anderson, Lorez Alexandria, Abbey Lincoln, Helen Merrill, Carol Sloane, Nina Simone, Nancy Wilson,* and *Sheila Jordan.* Ernestine Anderson's comment, 'If I had my way, I'd sing true like Ella and breathe like Sarah Vaughan,' is in many ways the musical creed of most of them: They want to sound like Ella Fitzgerald in terms of expression, and like Sarah in terms of phrasing, though some of them also want it the other way around, combining Ella's phrasing with Sarah's expression.

Jackie Cain first became known in Charlie Ventura's band. With her husband, pianist–arranger Roy Kral, she forms the most perfect vocal duo in jazz history – spirited, pleasant, humorous. *Helen Merrill* is a much underrated singer. She has often been accompanied by John Lewis, the former leader of the Modern Jazz Quartet, and indeed has some of his sensitivity and sophistication. *Nina Simone*'s is an especially passionate voice in the struggle for black dignity and identity, a struggle she supports as a woman, singer, pianist – as an entire human being. She once referred to the blues as 'racial memory', and this memory is the source for her songs, however modern they may sound. Another voice in the black struggle is that of *Abbey Lincoln*, especially in songs by Max Roach, her former husband, whose 'Freedom Now Suite' she sang with poignant and moving emotion. *Sheila Jordan* is of special significance. She has 'emancipated' song-singing, thus paving the way for all the female vocalists in free jazz whom we will discuss later. Sheila became known through her work with George Russell – above all, in the grandiose-satirical 'You Are My Sunshine', a spoof full of sharp cynicism.

Once more, we have to backtrack: In his uncompromising endeavours to use the human voice as instrumentally as possible, Duke Ellington first employed *Adelaide Hall*, then *Kay Davis*, the former in the twenties, the latter in the forties. Kay Davis's voice was used as a kind of coloratura above the orchestra, often scored in parallels with clarinet, creating a fascinating meshing of sounds. Later, this combination of a jazz voice with the sound of an ensemble or full band was used by others, but few remember that this, too, began with Duke.

One result of the instrumental conception of jazz singing is the development of scat vocals: stringing together 'nonsense' syllables with complete absence of lyrics. *Louis Armstrong* 'invented' scat singing way back in the twenties; the story goes that he hit upon it when he forgot the lyrics while recording. *Anita O'Day*, *June Christy*, *Sarah Vaughan*, *Carmen McRae*, *Dakota Staton*, *Jackie Cain*, *Annie Ross*, *Betty Roché*, *Betty Carter*, and others have created excellent scat vocals, but the mistress of this domain, often also referred to as 'bebop vocal', still is *Ella Fitzgerald*. Both vocalizing and scat singing necessarily led to today's 'free' singing (to be discussed later).

To be sure, there is also a 'blues line' among the female vocalists, which refers back to the blues singers mentioned at the beginning of this chapter. The last of the great classic blues singers, *Alberta Hunter*, made some wonderfully expressive recordings in 1980 – at age eighty-three! – which is even more astounding when you realize that it was Alberta who wrote 'Down Hearted Blues', Bessie Smith's first hit, in 1923! In the twenties, she sang with Louis Armstrong, Sidney Bechet, and Fletcher Henderson.

Among the female singers, too, the blues proves to be the constant element of black music, always changing but always the blues, whose message is passed on from one generation to the next. Among those who have done so are *Helen Humes* (with Count Basie in the late thirties; she, too, singing better than ever in the seventies), *Dinah Washington* (who died in 1963), *Betty Carter* (who began with the blues as Dinah Washington's successor in Lionel Hampton's band), *Ruth Brown*, *LaVerne Baker*, *Etta Jones*, and many others. Dinah Washington was called the 'Queen of the Blues'. She, too, had her start in gospel music, and these gospel roots remained audible in many of her blues recordings. Her sardonic humour – sometimes even cynicism – gave her performances an additional dimension.

Janis Joplin carried the art of classical blues into rock. Almost nothing she sang can be thought of without Bessie Smith – and yet, Janis's singing always sounded harder, cruder, louder, more obtrusive. She was driven by a fierce will to live and love – up to her untimely death in 1970, which prompted the media to all sorts of wild speculations. Joplin's singing made particularly clear how many white performers – often even those who appear 'authentic' in their relationship to black music – have vulgarized and coarsened the message of their black models. Speaking of Bill Haley's relationship to the great black blues artists – Big Joe Turner, for example – in 1954, at the beginning of the rock 'n' roll era, Karl Belz states in his *Story of Rock*: 'He tended to shout his lyrics rather than clearly "vocalizing" them.' This is similarly true of dozens of other white singers and instrumentalists who derive from black music. They only *seem* authentic, but in reality they are not.

Janis Joplin was an immensely impulsive person, a woman who seemed to live in a continuous state of explosion. When she sang, in an unaccompanied solo, about wanting a Mercedes-Benz because all her friends drove Porsches, or a colour TV to be delivered by three – this (certainly also humorous) request sounded like a mystic incantation, a desperate prayer. The listener has the feeling the world might come to an end if the Mercedes and colour TV are not there on time.

There are echoes of Janis Joplin in many female rock singers, for example in *Maggie Bell*, who comes from Glasgow, or in Polish-born *Genya Ravan*, who lives in the United States.

In the course of the sixties, the heritage of the black spiritual and gospel tradition entered even more strongly into the mainstream of female singing. The white world had become conscious of this heritage through the recordings of *Mahalia Jackson*, who died in 1972 – but Mahalia was only one of the many wonderful singers of black religious music. Others are *Dorothy Love Coates*, *Marion Williams*, the late *Clara Ward*, *Bessie Griffin* (see chapter on spirituals).

When the gospel tradition finally made its way into popular music, soul music came into being. Its representatives are singers like *Tina Turner*, *Diana Ross*, and, above all, an artist who has been called the 'Billie Holiday of the seventies,' *Aretha Franklin*. Aretha is the daughter of Rev C. L. Franklin, the preacher of New Bethel Baptist Church in Detroit. From childhood on, she heard the rousing gospel songs in her father's church. When she was able to carry a tune, she joined the church choir; and at twelve or thirteen, she became a soloist. As her first important influence she named Mahalia Jackson; later, she pointed in particular to the significance of jazz musicians in her musical development: Oscar Peterson, Erroll Garner, and Art Tatum. Aretha herself is also a good, soul-inspired pianist.

Aretha's hit records are among the best that seventies pop music has to offer, but one of her recordings is of exceptional interest from a jazz point of view: 'Amazing Grace', recorded in 1972 at the New Temple Missionary Baptist Church in Los Angeles, in front of and with the congregation: it is nothing less than a swinging, ecstatic gospel service. This was not only a homecoming to the musical and spiritual world from which she originates – that alone would have meant much – but a conscious, jubilant rediscovery of her own roots.

Having emerged from the Supremes, *Diana Ross*, too, is more than just a soul specialist. As early as 1969, Lennie Tristano said: ' I think Diana Ross is the greatest jazz singer since Billie Holiday' – a statement that was greeted with incredulity in the jazz world. However, opinions have changed since Diana Ross's excellent singing (and acting) in the role of Billie Holiday in the film 'Lady Sings the Blues'. Regrettably, her performance in this movie is its sole redeeming feature.

It is only a short step from the female vocalists just mentioned to those in fusion and on the borderline between jazz and fusion. There are so many singers of the most diverse directions in this field that they can be named here only summarily: *Phoebe Snow, Dee Dee Bridgewater, Ricky Lee Jones, Bonnie Herman* (the rich, 'sensual' voice of the vocal group Singers Unlimited), *Marlena Shaw, Ann Burton, Jean Carn, Lorraine Feather, Gayle Moran* (known through her recordings with Chick Corea) and *Angela Bofill*. Ron Welburn said about Angela: 'She could become the first singer to bring real artistic dignity to the fusion idiom.'

Betty Carter has pointed out that today it is next to impossible to be a female jazz singer: 'I guess, I'm the last of the Mohicans. It's understandable: jazz singing is not profitable. Young singers tend towards commercial singing – and let's face it, it's one way or the other: if what you're singing becomes commercial, it's no longer jazz.' Many of the singers we just named have discovered this – often quite painfully. One example is Dee Dee Bridgewater. She became known with the Thad Jones–Mel Lewis big band in the early seventies and made some breathtaking records – some of them along avant-garde lines – such as a duet with bassplayer Reginald Workman. In the early seventies, she was in the same position as Angela Bofill today: the most promising young jazz singer. Meanwhile, Bridgewater has all but left the jazz world.

Among folk singers, too, there are some of interest to the jazz scene. Just as the black singers refer back to the gospel, soul, and blues tradition, so the folk singers have their roots in white Anglo-American music. The two representatives of this direction of most interest from a jazz viewpoint are *Judy Collins* and *Joni Mitchell.* Collins did a superb job of incorporating the wistful songs, cries, and signals of whales into her song, 'Farewell to Tarwathie'. Mitchell's album 'Mingus', released in 1979, is the most beautiful, moving memorial to this great jazz musician to date. Critics have called Mitchell's singing much too ethereal and fragile to have anything to do with Mingus's music; and yet this very fact makes it clear how far Mingus's message carries. Mitchell has always been fond of employing jazz musicians on her studio dates, among them bassist Jaco Pastorius and drummer Don Alias. Just how much she is associated with jazz is illustrated by her statement that the most important record in her musical development was the Count Basie album by Lambert, Hendricks and Ross.

What the tradition of Anglo-American folk music is to singers like Collins and Mitchell, the samba tradition (which, in turn, is rooted in West African Yoruba music) is to the Brazilian singers. *Flora Purim* has become the most famous in the northern hemisphere because she moved to the United States in 1968. But back home in Brazil there are even more impressive voices, practically unknown in the States or in Europe – *Ellis Regina* and *Maria Bethânia*; the former having Ella Fitzgerald's flexibility, the latter Billie Holiday's emotional energy.

Purim and her husband, percussionist Airto Moreira, were at the centre of a 'Brazilian movement' on the American scene of the seventies. Flora was first introduced by Stan Getz and Gil Evans, then by Chick Corea (in his first Return to Forever group of the early seventies). One of her most beautiful recordings is 'Open Your Eyes, You Can Fly' (1976), the entire record being a triumphant song of liberty. One senses that the song mirrors personal experience. Flora had just been released from prison where she had been put on a drug charge that was never proven.

Flora Purim: 'I learned how to make sounds travel from my diaphragm to my throat to my nose, through my head . . . When I went to the USA, my friends warned me: "Don't sing jazz or

American music. There will be too much competition." I took that to heart. I simply sing human music.'

Flora Purim leads us to our final grouping of female vocalists: those who sing free music. The first to do so, as early as the sixties, were American *Jeanne Lee* and Norwegian *Karin Krog*. Then came the British singers *Norma Winstone*, *Julie Tippetts*, and *Maggie Nichols*; Polish *Urszula Dudziak*; American *Jay Clayton*; French *Tania*; Israeli-born *Rimona Francis*; Greek-American *Diamanda Gallas*; and American *Lauren Newton*. These singers have extended the 'voice as an instrument' into realms which would have seemed inaccessible only a few years ago. Singing to them is not only vocalizing songs, but everything else: screaming, laughing, and crying; the moaning of sexual experience and childlike babbling. The entire body, from the abdomen to the sinuses and the skull, becomes an instrument, a vibrating source of sounds, a 'body of sound'. The entire range of human – and specifically female – sounds is employed; nothing human or organic seems to be alien to it. These singers are unrestrained in the way they scream, moan, and belt out whatever fits the particular song, the mood, or the atmosphere – and yet this lack of restraint is only an apparent one, because all these sounds have to be formed, mastered, and musically integrated in order to become meaningful.

'The voice as an instrument' – this expression can be used sensibly only in relative terms: What seemed a *ne-plus-ultra* of instrumental vocalizing in the twenties with Adelaide Hall in Duke Ellington's band was surpassed by Ella Fitzgerald in the forties, by Indian singer Yma Sumac in the fifties, by Jeanne Lee and Karin Krog in the sixties, by Urszula Dudziak in the seventies, and by Lauren Newton and Diamanda Gallas in the eighties. In their time, each of these voices was hailed as the unbeatable final stage of the development – and that's the way it will continue to be.

Jeanne Lee has become known primarily through the artful musical textures she weaves in the group of her husband, multi-instrumentalist Gunter Hampel. Her singing flows from a musical as much as from a literary feeling. Jeanne has vocalized modern poetry. There is no other singer with her acute and detailed sense for words, listening and following the sound of each word, each single syllable. *Karin Krog* made one of her most beautiful albums in a duo with tenorist Archie Shepp – and as paradoxical as it may sound, the young woman from cool Scandinavia and Shepp with his highly developed consciousness of black music play together in perfect empathy. For the sake of a few tunes, band leader Don Ellis had Karin Krog flown in from Oslo to Hollywood. Said Ellis: 'There is no singer in the States who could have done what she does.' *Norma Winstone* combines the experiences of the new jazz with classical song forms, above all the ballad. She has done so particularly impressively in the group Azimuth, with pianist John Taylor (Norma's husband) and trumpeter Kenny Wheeler.

Julie Tippetts's career went against the current: She didn't move from jazz to pop music, but from pop to free jazz. In the second half of the sixties, singing as Julie Driscoll, in recordings with organist Brian Auger – including her hit 'This Wheel's on Fire' – she was one of the most frequently heard and most sensitive and musically flexible of female rock singers. In the seventies, it often seemed as if she – now under the name Julie Tippetts – was hiding from her old identity in a music of a most demanding and complex kind of abstractness. Polish-born *Urszula Dudziak* electronicizes her voice – and she 'percussionizes' it. She channels her voice through a number of different synthesizers and uses a custom-built electronic percussion instrument. An American critic wrote: 'Imagine that the "Girl from Ipanema" comes from Warsaw instead of Rio and is now living in New York – then you'll have an idea of how she sounds.' *Jay Clayton*, who is also interested in minimal and modern 'classical' music, has worked with Steve Reich, Muhal Richard Abrams, and John Cage. *Tania* (who lives in Paris) has performed with Swiss drummer Pierre Favre and Japanese dancers, but, most of all, she likes to give solo concerts. She has, writes *Le Monde de la Musique*, 'a voice beyond the simple fact of singing.' *Rimona Francis* incorporates into her singing the Israeli musical tradition and the irregular meters of Bulgaria (where her family stems from), but also remembers Bartòk and Arab vocalizing. *Lauren Newton* from Oregon commands what must be the largest range of styles of all these singers. She has studied baroque music as well as modern concert music – Schoenberg and Ligeti, for instance – and she includes all these experiences in an immensely light and witty kind of improvisation that sparkles with fresh ideas. Says Lauren: 'I can dare to do things in jazz that you just wouldn't think of doing in modern concert music. Jazz gives you more freedom, but jazz is also more demanding.' *Diamanda Gallas* (from San Diego) starts where other singers usually leave off. Immediately – without requiring any time to arrive – she reaches a level of almost insane, shocklike intensity, assaulting her listeners' ears with her screams and vocalized eruptions. She is like a raving bacchante from Greek mythology transposed into modern times (and indeed she does have a Greek family background!). And if one Diamanda isn't enough for you, she's singing to multiple tapings of her own voice.

As we have said, Betty Carter feels that jazz singing – in the strict sense – is a dying art. And indeed, it is difficult to find on today's scene a young singer who simply sings swinging jazz music – in the vein of Mark Murphy or Bob Dorough among the male vocalists. But for years people also said that big bands were dead – and then big bands made a glorious comeback. It may just be that female jazz singing will do the same someday. What the scene needs is a young, contemporary kind of Betty Carter and – just as important – a record company which will let her sing jazz – pure jazz – without all the (explicit or unspoken) demands for 'commercial potential'. *Then* it will have commercial potential.

THE BIG BANDS OF JAZZ

The Big Bands of Jazz

It is difficult to determine where big bands begin. What a moment ago was New Orleans music in the next moment has become big-band jazz, and we stand at the doorstep of the Swing era. In 'The Chant' by Jelly Roll Morton's Red Hot Peppers (recorded in 1926), there are traces of big-band sounds, though the idiom is purest New Orleans jazz. And when King Oliver yielded his band to Luis Russell in 1929, the orchestra, though it had scarcely changed, turned from a New Orleans group into a Swing band. How fluid these transitions were can be clearly seen in the case of *Fletcher Henderson*. The real big-band history of jazz begins with him. From the early twenties to 1938, he led large orchestras and exerted an influence comparable only to Duke Ellington. (We are omitting Ellington from this section because his spirit runs through nearly all stages of big-band jazz; an entire chapter about Duke may be found in the first part of the book.)

At the outset, Fletcher Henderson played a kind of music which differed little from the New Orleans music of the time. Between 1925 and 1928, he fittingly made records under the name of The Dixie Stompers. Slowly and almost imperceptibly, sections were formed, joining related instruments in groupings. From that point on, the sections were to be the characteristic of the classical jazz big bands. Among the first 'sections' were the clarinet trios. They can be found in Henderson, and in Jelly Roll Morton as well – and, of course, in Duke Ellington. The development from the nine or ten men Henderson had at the start – a personnel which today would be called a combo, but then was the ultimate in 'bigness' – to the typical ensemble work of the compact trumpet, trombone, and saxophone sections of the height of his career, is smooth and barely perceptible.

Fletcher Henderson and the Beginning

Fletcher Henderson had a real instinct for trends. He was not a man like Ellington, who spearheaded evolution. He followed – but not without giving format and content to what the trend happened to be. It is fitting that he did not retain his musicians for long periods of time, as Ellington did, but changed personnel frequently.

In Henderson's various big bands the musicians found a freedom which seems contrary to the general opinion of big-band work. This freedom extended to external matters: In 1932, John Hammond supervised a recording session with the Henderson band. It was called for 10 A.M. By 11.30, five men had arrived. At 12.40, the last man showed up: John Kirby with his bass. The freshness and spontaneity of Henderson's music is the sunny side of such goings-on, which, however, are not unfamiliar in jazz recording work up to today.

Henderson, who died in 1952, was a great arranger; there are experts who rate him as the most important arranger of traditional jazz, next to Duke Ellington. At any rate, he and Duke were the first who knew how to write for big bands with a sure feeling for jazz improvisation.

The versatility of the Henderson band was great. Around 1930, a programme might have consisted of Jelly Roll Morton's old 'King Porter Stomp', 'Singin' the blues', with Rex Stewart soloing à la Beiderbecke; a number featuring the big sound of Coleman Hawkins's tenor sax or the fluent trombone of Jimmy Harrison; then perhaps a showpiece from the repertoire of the old Original Dixieland Jazz Band such as 'Clarinet Marmalade': and finally 'Sugar Foot Stomp', patterned on King Oliver's famous 'Dipper-mouth Blues', with Stewart playing Oliver's original trumpet solo. And in between, some real stomp numbers tailored to the taste of the Harlem audience (a taste which since then has changed, if at all, only in terms of an even stronger beat and – related to this – a preference for the traditional rhythm and blues elements), pieces like 'Variety Stomp', or 'St Louis Shuffle' – and now and then also one of the commercial tunes of the day, such as 'My Sweet Tooth Says "I Wanna" But My Wisdom Tooth Says "No".'

Henderson always had an amazing knack for using the right soloists. Musicians who played in his band have been mentioned in almost every chapter on instruments in this book. Among the most important are alto saxophonists Don Redman and Benny Carter; tenorists Coleman Hawkins, Ben Webster, and Chu Berry; clarinetist Buster Bailey; trumpeters Tommy Ladnier – the one with the blues sound – Rex Stewart, Red Allen, Roy Eldridge, and Joe Smith; trombonists Jimmy Harrison, Charlie Green, Benny Morton, Claude Jones, and Dickie Wells; drummers Kaiser Marshall and Sid Catlett; and Fletcher's brother Horace Henderson, who played piano (as did Fletcher) and often lent his name to the band. Many of these musicians later became band leaders, most prominently, Redman and Carter.

Don Redman is one of the names that might well be offered in answer to the oft-asked question about the most underrated musician in jazz history. 'I changed my way of arranging after hearing Armstrong,' he has said. From 1928 on he made recordings with McKinney's Cotton Pickers; from 1931 to 1940 (and intermittently after that until his death in 1964) he led his own band. Many of the musicians who played with Henderson have also been with Redman's bands. Redman refined the music of Henderson. But then, this is a common denominator for the whole evolution of orchestral jazz: a steady, uninterrupted refinement of the 'classical' ideas of Fletcher Henderson.

In 1931, Redman put together the first big-band line-up in a modern sense. It consisted of three trumpets, three trombones, a four-piece saxophone section and a rhythm section of piano, guitar, bass, and drums. The four saxophones soon grew to five – for the first time in Benny Carter's band in 1933. This constitutes the standard big-band instrumentation – with the qualification that the brass section, occasionally in the late thirties and generally from the forties on, might consist of four or even five trumpets and four trombones. That would add up to a total of 17 or 18 musicians, and it is characteristic of the nature of jazz that such an instrumentation is conceived of as a 'big' band. From the standpoint of European music, this is still a chamber ensemble. 'Big' would mean the 100-man apparatus of the symphony* orchestra. Thus the reproach of overdone trappings certainly does not fit jazz. The impressive multiplication of the same voices, employed in the great symphonic forms – a multiplication often purely for the sake of volume or effect – is contrary to the nature of jazz. Jazz tends towards linear instrumentation of each voice: each instrument has a distinctive, perceivable musical purpose, it is used as a 'voice'.

Benny Carter briefly led McKinney's Cotton Pickers – the manager was named McKinney – after Redman had left. Carter became the prototype of the band leader as he would appear with increasing frequency from then on: leaders who were first and foremost arrangers, and led bands primarily because they wanted to hear their ideas translated into the kind of sounds they had in mind. Carter's career as a band leader, accordingly, was unhappy and full of interruptions, and yet he became the true specialist of the saxophone section – and a master of melodic delineation. No one knows how to make a saxophone section 'sing' like Carter . . . like a multivoiced 'saxophone-organ'. The saxophone sounds discovered by Carter in 1933 – on such recordings as 'Symphony in Riffs' or 'Lonesome Nights' – signified an entirely new tone colour, which was to gain ever-increasing importance in jazz. It is in no small measure due to the wealth of possibilities discovered by Carter in the five-piece saxophone section that some modern band leaders have made do with a trombone or a trumpet less rather than do without one of their saxophonists.

The Goodman Era

From Fletcher Henderson came first of all the most successful big-band man of the thirties – *Benny Goodman*, 'the King of Swing'. Then came all the Henderson- and Goodman-influenced big white orchestras of those years, such as the bands of *Tommy* and *Jimmy Dorsey*, and the Artie Shaw band mentioned below. They combined the Henderson influence with that of white bands of the twenties more or less close to Chicago style: Ben Pollack, The Wolverines, Jean Goldkette.

The Goodman band played a polished Henderson music, cleansed of 'impurities' of intonation and precision. It became the symbol of the Swing era. The crest of the B G wave (which began in California in 1935 when Goodman and his musicians had almost given up hope of ever breaking through) was the famous 1938 Carnegie Hall concert – the decisive entrance of jazz into the hallowed halls of 'serious' music. Goodman (and John Hammond) had hired members of the Duke Ellington and Count Basie bands for this concert. They performed alongside the well-known soloists of the big Goodman band: trumpeters Harry James and Ziggy Elman, drummer Gene Krupa, pianist Jess Stacy – and the soloists of Goodman's small groups: pianist Teddy Wilson and vibraphonist Lionel Hampton. In point of fact, Goodman – and later Artie Shaw – were the first who dared to feature black musicians in white bands; if at first only in the 'diplomatic' form of added solo attractions, so the racists would not have to face the fact that white and black musicians were sitting side by side in the same band.

In its early years, Fletcher Henderson was the most important arranger for the Benny Goodman orchestra, and the band actually retained its Henderson stamp, no matter how many other arrangers Goodman employed. Only Eddie Sauter gave the Goodman band of the early forties a 'new sound' – in such pieces as 'Superman', with Cootie Williams as trumpet soloist, 'Clarinet à la King,' a showcase for Benny's clarinet, and 'Moonlight on the Ganges'. Sauter no longer used the sections in contrasting opposition throughout, as had Henderson, but sometimes merged them and sometimes created new 'sections' by combining instruments from different sections only to dissolve them again – all according to the flow of the music. Here Sauter began what he would carry to greater perfection – in collaboration with arranger Bill Finegan – in the *Sauter–Finegan Band* of the fifties. In this band, much of the artistry of concert music – not least the frequent use of percussion instruments beyond the jazz beat – was combined with a thoroughly Americanized, jazz-minded sense of humour. (It should be understood, however, that this process of 'dissolving' sections was just beginning with Eddie Sauter. It was to be continued – in a much more radical way – by orchestra leaders like Gil Evans and Sun Ra.)

Clarinetist *Artie Shaw* – after a not very successful 1936 attempt to use a string quartet within a big band – played the most refined and subtle big-band jazz of the late thirties and forties – with the exception of Duke Ellington, of course. Shaw liked a certain impressionistic sensitivity – and yet, often enough, retained the powerhouse vigour of the big Swing bands. Again and again, he used black musicians in his band: Billie Holiday, and trumpeters Hot Lips Page and Roy Eldridge. The indignities these musicians had to suffer during the successful tours of the Shaw band – when hotels refused to admit them, restaurants where the others ate refused to serve them, and the establishments where the band was performing would let them in only through the back entrance – have been touched on before, when speaking of Billie Holiday.

Three white Swing bands are outside the Henderson–Goodman circle in certain respects: the *Casa Loma Band*, and the orchestras of Bob Crosby and Charlie Barnet. Glen Gray's Casa Loma Band was a hit with the college crowd before Benny Goodman. In the stiffness of its arrangements and its mechanical ensemble playing it was a forerunner of the Stan Kenton band of the late forties – the band for which Pete Rugolo was the arranger and which was connected with the 'progressive jazz' slogan. Gene Gifford was the 'Rugolo' of the Casa Loma Band. He wrote pieces which then seemed as imposing and compact as did the Kenton 'Artistry' recordings fifteen years later: 'White Jazz', 'Black Jazz', 'Casa Loma Stomp'.

Bob Crosby played Dixieland-influenced Swing, pointing back to the Ben Pollack band (which he took over in 1935) and the New Orleans Rhythm Kings, and ahead to the modern brand of commercialized Dixieland music. He had an ideal Dixieland rhythm section consisting of Nappy Lamare (guitar), Bob Haggart (bass), and Ray Bauduc (drums). Since the late sixties, *The World's Greatest Jazz Band* has been bringing the old Bob Crosby tradition back to life.

Charlie Barnet founded his first big band in 1932, and led bands almost continuously until the sixties – bands which were all shaped by Barnet's strong feeling for the music of Duke Ellington. Perhaps it is fair to say that Barnet's relationship to Ellington corresponds to that of Goodman to Henderson. 'Cherokee', recorded in 1939, was the theme song of the Barnet band, also used as a theme by dozens of radio programmes the world over.

The Black Kings of Swing

Fletcher Henderson not only influenced most of the successful white bands of the thirties, but himself led the first successful Harlem band. This concept, the 'Harlem' band, became a stamp of quality for jazz bands, just as the word 'New Orleans' is a stamp of quality for traditional jazz. Even Benny Goodman had the desire to play for the expert and excited – and exciting – audiences of Harlem, which had made the Savoy Ballroom into a famous centre for music and dance in the Swing era. In l937, Goodman played a musical battle with the then most popular band in Harlem, that of Chick Webb – and lost! Four thousand people jammed the Savoy Ballroom, and five thousand more stood outside on Lenox Avenue to witness this friendly battle.

From Henderson the 'Harlem' line leads straight through Cab Calloway, Chick Webb, and Jimmie Lunceford to Count Basie and the various Lionel Hampton bands; and beyond these to the bebop big bands of Harlem in the forties and finally to the jump bands of the fifties *à la* Buddy Johnson; or to the back-up band for *Ray Charles*'s appearances.

Cab Calloway, the comedian of scat singing, took over a band in l929 which had come to New York from the Midwest: The Missourians. From then on through the late forties he led consistently good bands of which the later ones are important primarily for the musicians who played in them: Ben Webster, Chu Berry, Jonah Jones, Dizzy Gillespie, Hilton Jefferson, Milt Hinton, Cozy Cole.

Tiny, hunchbacked *Chick Webb* presided over Harlem's Savoy Ballroom. Duke Ellington says: 'Webb was always battle-mad, and those guys used to take on every band that came up to play there. And most times they did the cutting, regardless of the fact that half the time the other bands were twice the size. But the unforgettable and lovable Chick ate up any kind of fight, and everybody in the band played like mad at all times.' Gene Krupa, who was 'drummed out' by Webb while with Benny Goodman, said: 'I was never cut by a better man.' And pianist–arranger Mary Lou Williams remembers: 'One night, scuffling around Harlem, I fell in the Savoy. After dancing a couple of rounds, I heard a voice that sent chills up my spine . . . I almost ran to the stand to find out who belonged to the voice, and saw a pleasant-looking, brown-skinned girl standing modestly and singing the greatest. I was told her name was Ella Fitzgerald and that Chick Webb had unearthed her from one of the Apollo's amateur hours.'

Of at least equal importance was *Jimmie Lunceford*, orchestra leader par excellence. Through him 'precision' started to gain ever-increasing significance in the playing of large jazz bands. From the late twenties until his death in l947, he led a band whose style was mainly developed by arranger Sy Oliver, who also played trumpet in the band. This style is marked by a two-beat 'disguised' behind the 4/4 Swing meter, and by the effective unison work of the saxophone section, with its tendencies towards glissandi. Both the Lunceford rhythm and the Lunceford sax sound were widely copied by commercial dance bands in the fifties, most of all by Billy May. The Lunceford beat was so potent in its effect that the general designation of 'Swing' did not seem to suffice. The Lunceford beat became 'bounce'. Lunceford's music 'bounced' from beat to beat in a way that emphasized the moment of 'lassitude', as Erroll Garner did, for example, in his piano playing. Oliver's section writing was the first really new treatment of the sax section since the work of Redman and Carter. From this developed the first typical orchestra sound – aside from Ellington's growl sounds and the clarinet trios of Fletcher Henderson's and Ellington's bands. Such sounds and tricks of instrumentation, which struck to a band like a trademark and made it identifiable after just a few bars, now became increasingly popular.

With *Count Basie*, the stream of Kansas City bands merges with that of the successful Harlem bands. To Kansas City belong the *Bennie Moten* band (which Basie himself took over in 1935); the bands of *Jay McShann* and *Harlan Leonard*, in both of which Charlie Parker played; and, prior to these, primarily *Andy Kirk and His Twelve Clouds of Joy.* All were blues- and boogie-oriented, with a well-developed riff technique, using short, reiterated blues phrases as themes or to heighten tension, or employing such riff phrases as contrasting elements. Andy Kirk's pianist and arranger was Mary Lou Williams, and it was mainly due to her influence that the Kirk band developed beyond the simple blues–riff formula of the other Kansas City Bands.

At first (and in some of his recordings even today), Basie retained the Kansas City blues–riff formula, but he made much more than a formula of it. In it, he found the substance which gives his music – which in the course of the years has absorbed many of the elements brought forth by the evolution of big-band jazz – its power. Basie has led big bands since 1935, with but a few short interruptions. In the Basie bands of the thirties and forties the emphasis was on a string of brilliant soloists: Lester Young and Hershel Evans (tenors); Harry Edison and Buck Clayton (trumpets); Benny Morton, Dickie Wells, and Vic Dickenson (trombones); and the previously mentioned 'All American Rhythm Section'. In the modern Basie bands, the emphasis is on an effortless, resilient kind of precision, but of a sort which develops in the most natural way from swing. It has been said that Basie is 'orchestrated swing'. The Basie band of the fifties also had good soloists: trumpeters Joe Newman and Thad Jones; saxophonists Frank Foster, Frank Wess, and Eddie 'Lockjaw' Davis; trombonists Henry Coker, Bennie Powell, and Quentin Jackson; and, last but not least, Basie himself, whose sparing piano swings a band as no other pianist can.

In the seventies, Basie presented recordings with arrangements by Bill Holman and Sam Nestico. Basie's still indestructible 'Swing machine' consisted of trumpeters Sonny Cohn, Frank Szabo, and Bobby Mitchell; trombonists Al Grey, Curtis Fuller, and Bill Hughes; saxophonists Eric Dixon, Bobby Plater, and the late Jimmy Forrest and Charlie Fowlkes. Freddie Green was still lending the band his unmistakable guitar sounds; and with Butch Miles, Basie had again found an outstanding Swing drummer.

Above all, Count made a number of excellent combo recordings: jam sessions with Eddie Lockjaw Davis, Joe Pass, Clark Terry, and Benny Carter; quartet efforts with Zoot Sims; a date with blues singer Joe Turner; and - especially remarkable - a trio album featuring Basie the pianist.

Woody and Stan

Elements of the Swing era have remained more important for the styles of modern big bands than for the improvisations of individual soloists. In 1936 *Woody Herman* became front man for a collective of musicians from the disbanded Isham Jones orchestra. Swing *à la* Benny Goodman was the last word then. Nevertheless, Herman did not play conventional Swing, but blues. He called his band '*The Band That Plays The Blues*.' 'The Woodchopper's Ball' was the band's most successful record. When the war broke out, the band that played the blues began to dissolve, but soon thereafter the brilliant line of 'Herman Herds' began. The '*First Herd*' was perhaps the most vital white jazz band ever. 'Caldonia' was its biggest hit. When Igor Stravinsky heard this piece on the radio in 1945, he asked Herman if he could write a composition for his band. Thus the 'Ebony Concerto' came into being; a piece in three movements in which Stravinsky, in his own way, combines his classicist ideas with the language of jazz. And though most jazz people might not like the piece (because it does not 'swing'!), it should be said that the 'Ebony

Concerto' is by far the best 'jazz-inspired' composition so far written by one of the great classical composers of the twentieth century.

Bassist Chubby Jackson was the backbone of the First Herd. The drummers were first Dave Tough, then Don Lamond. Flip Phillips was on tenor; Bill Harris established himself with one stroke as a significant new trombone voice with his solo on 'Bijou'; John La Porta played alto; Billy Bauer, guitar; Red Norvo, vibraphone; and Pete Candoli, Sonny Berman, and Shorty Rogers were among the trumpets – in short, a star line-up which no other jazz band of the time could match.

Indicative of the spirit of this band is Chubby Jackson's recollection that the musicians frequently would congratulate each other on their solos after a night's work.

In l947 came the Second Herd. It grew into the *Four Brothers Band*, mentioned in our tenor saxophone chapter. This, too, was a bebop band – with Shorty Rogers and Ernie Royal (trumpets); Earl Swope (trombone); Lou Levy (piano); Terry Gibbs (vibraphone); the previously mentioned tenor men, and singer Mary Ann McCall. 'Early Autumn', written by Ralph Burns, was the big hit of the Four Brothers sound. George Wallington's 'Lemon Drop' was characteristic of the Second Herd's bop music.

In the fifties the *Third* and *Fourth Herman Herds* – and so on; the transitions are blurred. Herman himself once said: 'My three Herds? I feel as if there'd been eighty.' Ralph Burns wrote a 'book' (i.e., library of arrangements) for the Third Herd in which the Four Brothers sound became the trade-mark of the band. (This had not been the case in the actual Four Brothers band, where the typical Brothers section of three tenors and one baritone was used alongside the traditional five-voiced sax section with the alto as lead.)

In spite of all the talk about the end of the big bands, Woody Herman has swung so successfully through the sixties and seventies that even his closest followers have stopped counting Herds. Herman adapts the more musical rock themes to his big-band conception – pieces like the Doors' 'Light My Fire' or Chick Corea's Latin hit 'La Fiesta'. And he discovered a fascinating new arranger: New Zealand-born *Alan Broadbent*, a musician who studied at the Berklee School in Boston and with Lennie Tristano, and proves that even today new, exciting sounds can be generated from the tried and true big-band instrumentation. Broadbent also wrote a concerto that the Herman Herd performed with the Dallas Symphony Orchestra.

Stan Kenton, who died in 1979, had also led various bands of differing styles, and so more space must be devoted to him than to any single bands. Perhaps the most typical Kenton piece is 'Concerto to End All Concertos' – typical in title as well. It opens with poorly copied Rachmaninoff-like bass figures by pianist Kenton. The whole late-romantic musical climate lurks behind these figures, along with the notion that sheer size and volume equal expressive power – this seemed to be the peculiar Kentonian world of ideas. From this climate sprang Kenton's first well-known piece, 'Artistry in Rhythm', in 1942. It was followed in subsequent years by a series of other 'Artistries': in Percussion, in Tango, in Harlem Swing, in Bass, in Boogie. Arranger Pete Rugolo is often linked with this effect-laden and elaborate style, but Kenton himself clearly had already established the 'Artistry' style when Rugolo, then still in the army, first offered him an arrangement in 1944. Rugolo, who studied with Darius Milhaud, the important modern French composer, is primarily responsible for the second phase of Kenton's music, 'Progressive Jazz' in the narrower sense, even more powerful and elaborate, laden with massive chords and multilayered clusters of sound. During the late forties – the main period of Rugolo's influence – Kenton was enormously successful. His soloists led in the jazz polls: drummer Shelly Manne; bassist Eddie Safranski; tenorman Vido Musso; trombonist Kai Winding – and most of all, singer June Christy. Hers was the most engaging voice in the band.

Encouraged by success, Kenton built himself a large concert orchestra in 1949, reinforcing his jazz line-up with a string section and extra woodwinds. For this project, Kenton again found a pretentious title: 'Innovations in Modern Music'. But these were 'innovations' which Hindemith, Bartók, Stravinsky, and the other great modern composers had introduced twenty or thirty years earlier. Typical was Pete Rugolo's 'Conflict', with June Christy's voice used as an instrument and stark contrasts between etherealized string sounds and roaring brasses – or, from the second series of 'Innovations', the late Bob Graettinger's 'House of Strings', with sounds reminiscent of Bartók's 'Music for Strings'. Graettinger's impressive suite, 'City of Glass', conjured up the images of the title with coldly abstract, shimmering, ghostly sounds.

Then – in 1952-3 – came the most significant Kenton band from a jazz standpoint. Kenton seemed to have forgotten some of his past and decided to make a swinging music, perhaps not directly

influenced by Count Basie, but nevertheless extremely well suited to a
time in which the Basie spirit had come to life to a degree that hardly
anyone in jazz could escape it. Kenton had many gifted soloists in this
band, and the emphasis was on swinging solo work as never before in
Kenton's career. Zoot Sims and Richie Kamuca played tenors; Lee
Konitz was on alto; Conte Candoli on trumpet; Frank Rosolino on
trombone. Gerry Mulligan wrote such arrangements as 'Swinghouse'
and 'Young Blood', and Bill Holman – obviously inspired by
Mulligan – furnished artfully simple examples of sections employed
in contrapuntal ensemble play. Bill Russo maintained the Kenton
tradition of a highly demanding music based on complex section
interplay.

In the following years, Kenton involved himself more and more
deeply in work at American colleges and universities. He established
'Kenton Clinics', in which he and his musicians acquainted
thousands of young students with the fundamentals of contemporary
jazz, particularly of big-band music. In the process, Kenton did not
shrink from personal sacrifices, often furnishing arrangements and
musicians free of charge or below usual rates. 'Stan is the driving
force in jazz education in America,' said Dr Herb Patnoe of De Anza
College in California.

Towards the end of the sixties and in the early seventies, Kenton
experienced a comeback hardly anyone had expected. He surrounded
himself with young, contemporary musicians with whom he played
more direct, simple, and straightforward music than in his 'Progressive' and 'Artistry' periods, if still with the Kentonian power
and his own incomparable pathos. He recorded some of his best later
work at concerts held at universities, such as Redlands and Brigham
Young.

In the meantime, Kenton had severed relations with Capitol
Records, the label with which he had been affiliated since the start of
his career, and began to market his records by mail on his own
'Creative World of Stan Kenton' label. This prompted an entire
wave of independent record companies to distribute their records in
the same way. Experience has shown that mail-order often can reach
customers faster, more simply, and more effectively than conventional marketing methods which, even after eighty years of jazz, seem
unable to serve demanding jazz record buyers.

The Bop Big Bands

In the meantime, bebop had arrived, and there were various attempts at big-band bebop. The first signs could be discovered in the *Earl Hines* big band of the forties. The great pianist, identified with the trumpet style of piano in Louis Armstrong's second Hot Five, led big bands almost uninterruptedly from 1928 to 1948 – along lines in which Harlem Jump and bop could merge smoothly. *Billy Eckstine*, a Hines alumnus, made the first deliberate attempt to play big-band bop when he formed a band in 1944. He and Sarah Vaughan were the vocalists (see the chapter on singers). Dizzy Gillespie, Fats Navarro, and Miles Davis successively played in the band – the three most important modern trumpet voices; Art Blakey was on drums; and the saxophones at various times included Charlie Parker, Gene Ammons, Dexter Gordon, and Leo Parker.

In 1947, the orchestra had to disband, but by then *Dizzy Gillespie* – who for a time had been musical director of the Eckstine band – had brought about the final transformation of bop into big-band jazz. Gillespie, Tadd Dameron, John Lewis, and Gil Fuller furnished the arrangements. Lewis was at the piano, Kenny Clarke on drums, Milt Jackson on vibraphone, Al McKibbon (later Percy Heath) on bass, James Moody and Cecil Payne among the saxes; and Chano Pozo added the incredibly exciting Cuban rhythms so characteristic of this band – rhythms that remind one of the *Machito* band, which must be cited among the important big bands of the time. It was the witches' cauldron in which the mixture of Cuban rhythms and jazz phrases was most thoroughly brewed. At times, its horns would consist of North American musicians and the rhythm section of Cubans (see also the chapter about the percussion instruments). In fact, one of Dizzy's reasons for hiring Chano Pozo (and, later, other Cuban percussionists) was that he wanted to capture the excitement of Machito's music.

Gillespie was in the process of forming his big band when President Truman warned the Japanese in the summer of 1945 that they must surrender or experience 'ultimate destruction'. When the first atomic bomb was dropped, the Gillespie band was just about ready to play. This fact takes on almost ghostly symbolism when listening to a piece like 'Things to Come'. This is the Gil Fuller 'Apocalypse in Jazz' mentioned in our Parker–Gillespie montage, with its jabbing, hectic, decaying phrases.

It is illuminating that the accents of 'Things to Come' were not taken up again until twenty years later - in the big-band attempts of free jazz.

A string of bands worth mentioning existed in the realm between Kenton and Herman. *Les Brown* provided dance music, but it was so sophisticated and musical that jazz fans, especially jazz musicians, often responded to it. *Claude Thornhill* played his calm, atmospheric piano solos amid a big-band sound that inspired the conception of the Miles Davis Capitol Orchestra in the late forties. *Elliot Lawrence* played swinging arrangements by Gerry Mulligan, Tiny Kahn, and Johnny Mandel - both simple and musically interesting.

Boyd Raeburn led a band in the mid-forties that in many respects paralleled Kenton's. 'Boyd Meets Stravinsky' was a representative title. Soloists such as pianist Dodo Marmaroso, bassist Oscar Pettiford, and drummer Shelly Manne (on one occasion even Dizzy Gillespie), brought much jazz feeling to the complex arrangements by, among others, George Handy and *Johnny Richards*. The latter wrote the arrangements for Dizzy Gillespie's 1950 recordings with strings - the most jazz-oriented string arrangements created up to that time - and in the mid-fifties he put together a band that attempted to extend the ideas of Progressive Jazz. The Richards band featured huge, piled-up blocks of sound and focused on irregular meters.

Basie as Basis

In the mid-fifties, the conviction that there is a contradiction between swing and elaborate production effects which cannot be bridged beyond a certain point seemed to gain ground everywhere. This conviction is quite in line with what we have called 'Basie classicism'. Big bands of this persuasion make music beyond experimentation. *Maynard Ferguson*, who emerged in 1950–53 from the Kenton band, organized his 'Dream Band' in the mid-fifties for an engagement at Birdland in New York. It really was a dream band. Every musician in it was a famous exponent of his instrument, and all these musicians had the same musical ideal: to play swinging, blues-based jazz - vital and musically interesting in equal measure. Jimmy Giuffre, Johnny Mandel, Bill Holman, Ernie Wilkins, Manny Albam, Marty Paich, and others furnished the arrangements. Eventually, Maynard decided to form a permanent band instead of a studio orchestra whose members were unable or unwilling to leave New York. He found a bunch of excellent young musicians who made a brand of big-band jazz as fiery and wild as Woody Herman's First Herd, yet more clearly rooted in the language of modern Basie–Young classicism. 'Fugue', written by trombonist-arranger Slide Hampton for Ferguson, is perhaps the most swinging fugue yet to have emerged from jazz.

Ferguson lived in Great Britain during the sixties (where he also led a successful band), but in the seventies he had a commercial comeback in America. Ferguson said: 'I'm not interested in nostalgia. You have to move along with the times . . . you just have to take and use the current rhythms. In the so-called golden era of the big bands, the great bandleaders of the day all played the better tunes of the day - so why not now?' And so Ferguson plays contemporary pop tunes in jazz–rock arrangements filled with effects that hardly elicit applause from the jazz crowd but reach a large young audience. There is more and more evidence of a tendency towards operalike pathos, almost as if Ferguson had become a 'Puccini of big-band music'.

But back to the fifties, when Basie's influence was stronger than Ellington's. *Shorty Rogers* made a kind of Basie jazz with a West Coast conception, full of original, spirited inventiveness. Arranger Quincy Jones, bassist Oscar Pettiford, trombonist Urbie Green, Boston trumpeter Herb Pomeroy, and others made big-band recordings in which the Basie influence is strongly apparent.

Quincy Jones called his first orchestral album, with such marvellous soloists as Art Farmer (muted trumpet), Lucky Thompson and Zoot Sims (tenors), Phil Woods (alto), Herbie Mann and Jerome Richardson (flutes), Jimmy Cleveland (trombone), Milt Jackson (vibraphone), Hank Jones and Billy Taylor (pianos), and Charles Mingus and Paul Chambers (bass): 'This is How I Feel About Jazz.' He wrote in the liner notes that the music reflected his feelings about 'the less cerebral and more vital or basic elements contained in jazz'.

He continued: 'I would prefer not to have this music categorized at all, for it is probably influenced by every original voice in and outside of jazz, maybe anyone from blues singer Ray Charles to Ravel . . . We aren't trying to prove anything except maybe that "the truth doesn't always hurt." . . . Our prime objectives in this album were soul, groove and honesty . . .'

Jones always had a great liking for Europe. In 1959 he brought to the Old World the first modern American big band to be permanently based in Europe. The band was to supply the music for the show *Free and Easy*, but the show folded. With great difficulty Quincy managed to keep the band together for a time - with work in Paris, Sweden, Belgium, and Germany. Among the members were Phil Woods, Sahib Shihab, Budd Johnson, and Jerome Richardson in the sax section; Quentin Jackson, Melba Liston, Jimmy Cleveland, and Sweden's Ake Persson in the trombone section. The music was moving and healthy, simple and honest; in many ways the most enjoyable big-band jazz of the turn of the fifties next to Ellington and Basie. To be sure, Quincy offered nothing very new. But he perfected the old, and made it shine as hardly anyone managed to do. Too bad that Jones - after his band returned from Europe and continued to work for several months in the US - gave up fighting for its survival in the face of lack of commercial possibilities.

Meanwhile, Jones has become one of Hollywood's most successful film and television arrangers and composers. One can feel the jazz tradition in everything he writes, and occasionally a big-band or fusion record by Quincy is released, joining commercialism and jazz quality with a cleverness and 'hipness' totally Quincy's own.

Of similar interest in this context are the big-band recordings of *Gerry Mulligan* - almost like a 'sophistication' of Basie. Around that same time, *Bill Holman* was the first to attempt something on the order of a big-band realization of hard bop - with intense and concentrated arrangements of such bop themes as Sonny Rollins's 'Airegin'. A little later (in 1960), there was, for the first time, a big band of 'funk' and soul and gospel jazz, if only for recording purposes: tenor man *Johnny Griffin*'s 'Big Soul Band' with arrangements by Norman Simmons.

On the West Coast during the sixties, *Gerald Wilson* came to the fore with a big band that found great admiration among musicians. Wilson, who had written arrangements for Lunceford, Basie, Gillespie, and other important orchestras also did not want to 'prove anything new', but rather summed up with power and brilliance the 'mainstream' of the development of orchestral jazz up to that time.

Gil Evans and George Russell

The one man whose big-band jazz really seemed 'new' in this period was *Gil Evans*. Gil, who emerged from the Claude Thornhill band, wrote for the Miles Davis Capitol Band, and once again teamed up with Davis in 1957 - to produce those warmly glowing, impressionist orchestral sounds discussed in the Miles Davis chapter. The Evans band became the big-band realization of Miles Davis's trumpet sound. Occasionally - regrettably much too seldom - Evans also created similar sounds for other soloists, among them trumpeter Johnny Coles and guitarist Kenny Burrell.

Later, Evans - meanwhile a grey-haired veteran - also opened himself to free music and even to the compositions of rock guitarist Jimi Hendrix. But Gil, who broke up the classic big-band sections in a very sound-conscious way, is not a 'diligent' arranger - as, say, Quincy Jones is. He lets his music ripen within himself, and seldom writes anything finished and final. Even during recording sessions, he often whittles away at changes and reconstructs entire compositions and arrangements. In many cases, his music is born while it is being played - almost in the sense of the early Ellington. That is why there are - regrettably - far too few records by this immensely personal and incomparable musician (who is still in close personal contact with Miles Davis).

The other great loner among arrangers is *George Russell*, already mentioned several times. He also emerged from the jazz revolution of the forties. During the fifties, Russell created his 'Lydian Chromatic Concept of Tonal Organization', the first work deriving a theory of jazz harmony from the immanent laws of jazz, not from the laws of European music. Russell's concept of improvisation, 'Lydian' in terms of mediaeval church scales, yet chromatic in the modern sense, was the great pathbreaker for Miles Davis's and John Coltrane's 'modality'. Russell came to Europe for the first Berlin Jazz Days in

1964, and subsequently lived in Scandinavia. Today he teaches at the distinguished New England Conservatory in Boston. With European as well as American musicians, he has created numerous works which are as individual, as different from the mainstream of what most jazz arrangers write, as the works of Gil Evans.

Free Big Bands

Meanwhile, free jazz had entered the scene, and the question was: What does the new free jazz sound like when played by big bands?

The musician who stood out most clearly in the transition from tonal to free tonal orchestral jazz was bassist *Charles Mingus* with his big-band concerts. These infrequent concerts occasionally bordered on chaos in terms of organization, and yet produced results - above all, exciting collective improvisations - which moved the jazz world for years to follow.

The most highly praised big band of Mingus's career was probably the band with which he recorded his 1971 album, 'Let My Children Hear Music'. Mingus commented: 'Jazz is black classical music . . . Let my children hear music - for God's sake - we've heard enough noise . . . Now I, myself, came to enjoy the players who didn't only just swing, who invented new rhythmic patterns, along with new melodic concepts. And those people are Art Tatum, Bud Powell, Max Roach, Sonny Rollins, Lester Young, Dizzy Gillespie, and Charlie Parker, who is the greatest genius of all to me because he changed the whole era around. But there is no need to compare composers. If you like Beethoven, Bach or Brahms, that's okay. They are all pencil composers. I always wanted to be a spontaneous composer . . .'

In 1965, composer (and pianist) Carla Bley and trumpeter Mike Mantler presented their *Jazz Composers Workshop* first in New York and then at the 1965 Newport Festival.

From this, the *Jazz Composers Orchestra* evolved, with soloists such as Don Cherry, Roswell Rudd, Cecil Taylor, Pharoah Sanders, Larry Coryell, Charlie Haden, Gato Barbieri - in general, the cream of the New York avant-garde - under *Mike Mantler*'s direction. If one realizes how difficult it is to find an audience for such avant-garde productions in the US - definitely much more difficult than in Europe

- he can speak of Mantler's personel contribution with only the greatest respect.

The Jazz Composers Orchestra was also involved in the Jazz Opera, 'Escalator Over The Hill', by Carla Bley and Paul Haines, which was mentioned in the chapter on pianists. In the meantime Carla Bley has become increasingly prominent with medium-sized groups of her own. Her compositions and orchestrations are imaginative collages of swinging jazz elements and national anthems (ridiculed, of course!), of world music and children's songs and massive clusters - all this permeated with sensitive, often socially critical humour (as in a piece she wrote in 1980, after Ronald Reagan had been elected to the American presidency).

The other, perhaps even more important name in free big-band jazz is *Sun Ra*. As early as the mid-fifties, Sun Ra, who had learned his trade thoroughly as relief pianist with the Fletcher Henderson band of the late forties, had formed a big band in Chicago, incorporating percussive and other sounds totally new for the time – sounds which their composer and creator perceives as 'cosmic sounds', as 'music of the outer galaxies' and of the 'Heliocentric Worlds'. On one of his album covers, Sun Ra had himself depicted with Pythagoras, Tycho Brahe, and Galileo.

Sun Ra's music is more than just avant-garde, free big-band jazz. It certainly is that, but behind it stands the whole black tradition: Count Basie's Swing riffs and Duke Ellington's saxophone sounds; Fletcher Henderson's 'voicings'; old blues and black songs; African highlife dances and Egyptian marches; black percussion music from South, Central, and North America, and from Africa; Negro show and voodoo ritual; trance and black liturgy - celebrated by a band leader who strikes one as an African medicine-man skyrocketed into the space age.

Sun Ra's music is even more free from the sections common to conventional big bands than that of Gil Evans or the Jazz Composers Orchestra. The instruments play together in ever changing combinations. Especially notable are the saxophone players of the Sun Ra Cosmic Arkestra, among them John Gilmore, Marshall Allen, Pat Patrick, and Danny Davis. Their saxophone and woodwind sounds are as new and revolutionary as Benny Carter's saxophone sections were in the early thirties. The Arkestra includes, among other rarely used instruments, original constructions by band members, such as the 'Sun Horn', as well as oboe, bassoon, bass clarinet, English horn, violin, viola, cello, and a group of dancers, occasionally even a fire-eater.

Sun Ra's compositions have titles like 'Next Stop Mars', 'Outer Spaceways Incorporated', 'Saturn', 'It's After the End of the World', 'Out in Space', etc. Many uninitiated listeners have smirked at such titles and at the show Sun Ra puts on as naïve. They joke about the dancers and acrobats Sun Ra has jumping all over the stage; or about a film which he has shown with his music: Sun Ra as a Christ figure, a dozen times in twenty minutes. They mock the glittering 'Saturn gowns', 'galaxy caps', and 'cosmic rosaries', which the Sun Ra musicians and dancers wear. Occasionally, the culmination of a Sun Ra show involves a telescope which the master sets up next to his organ, and through which he searches for his 'home planet Saturn' during special 'cosmic climaxes'.

But naïveté does not exist where black art is concerned. It did not exist when the chorus girls of the Cotton Club in Harlem during the twenties took on the hullaballoo of white Broadway musicals, accompanied by Duke Ellington's jungle sounds; it does not exist when the preacher of a black Revivalist church expresses his hope that his parishioners may 'go to Heaven tonight! right now! by subway'; it did not exist when Louis Armstrong sang 'I Hope Gabriel Likes My Music'. It existed only in the heads of white critics; and while they diagnose him as a naïf or even a charlatan, they say nothing about Sun Ra's music - and definitely nothing about the man Sun Ra - but a lot about themselves. Sun Ra's music - to LeRoi Jones - is the most precise expression of ancient black existence today. And Sun Ra himself says: 'I paint pictures of infinity with my music, and that's why a lot of people can't understand it . . .'

Unlike the US, Europe offers a mass of free big-band jazz: by *Alexander von Schlippenbach*, for instance. His 'Globe Unity' evolved from the 1965 New Jazz Meeting Baden-Baden and was only given a chance for a short life span back then. Yet in the eighties it is still playing its arrangements, which often satirize the jazz tradition while at the same time paying tribute to it, and its wild collective improvisations. The gap between free jazz and modern concert music is bridged by the *London Jazz Composers Orchestra* of bassist Barry Guy, who structures his music almost in the sense of classical compositions.

John Coltrane's pathbreaking 'Ascension' and the preceding double-quartet record 'Free Jazz' by Ornette Coleman (both cited in the chapter on Coleman and Coltrane) have been key experiences for many free big bands. Here the form was created: exciting, hectic collective improvisations, from which emerges a solo which - in turn - intensifies to the point that the next collective improvisation (which, again, will 'give birth' to a new solo) comes into existence. This form has been further developed by others - differentiated, sublimated, and structured - with especially personal results indicating future directions by musicians like *Anthony Braxton* (with his Creative Music Orchestra), *Karl Berger* (with his Woodstock Workshop Orchestra), *Leo Smith, Roscoe Mitchell*; and in Europe by *John Tchicai, John Stevens, Willem Breuker, Mike Westbrook, Keith Tippett*, and *Loek Dikker*, who all, of course, added their personal solutions and experiences. Braxton, for instance, offers radical abstractions and alienations; Berger works with world music; Breuker critically and satirically turns Dutch folk and nineteenth-century popular tunes into free music; and Mike Westbrook creates large and moving sound visions, sometimes integrating poems by the great classic and romantic British lyricists.

Rock Big Bands

There were three main currents in the big-band jazz of the early seventies:

1. Continued development of free big-band jazz.
2. Continued development of conventional big bands, utilizing contemporary themes and tendencies.
3. So-called 'rock big bands'.

And of course there were widely varying combinations of these three.

Let us first discuss rock big bands, ensembles like *Blood, Sweat & Tears, Chicago, Dreams*, or *The Flock*. The word 'big' should actually have been put in quotation marks because we are here dealing mostly with groups of seven to eleven members - in other words, relatively small according to the conventions of big-band jazz. Still, it became customary to call them 'big bands', because - with the help of electronics - they show tendencies to play in 'sections'. Keep in mind, too, that the big jazz band, in its early stages, also consisted of no more than eight to eleven musicians. Quite possibly, an evolution could have come full circle here. At least theoretically, there was a possibility for a while that the rock big band was standing at the beginning of a development similar to that of the jazz big band from the twenties on. Meanwhile, however, this chance has been lost.

There is no - or hardly any - development among these so-called rock big bands. Frequently they strike the listener with a strange stiffness and immobility, reminiscent in many respects of Stan Kenton during the forties. Since so many young big-band rock musicians have emerged from the university and college bands shaped by Kenton and his clinics, one might perhaps find a connection here.

The rock big band that has shown more growth than any other is *Blood, Sweat & Tears*, which - for a while - became more and more flexible and jazzlike from one record to the next, from one line-up to the other. 'Chicago' sounded promising at first, but has bogged down in stereotyped repetition of what already was on the first record. It is interesting to note that many rock big bands existed only for very short time spans - among them *Dreams* with trumpeter Randy Brecker and drummer Billy Cobham (who later joined John McLaughlin's Mahavishnu Orchestra), and *The Flock*, which practised collective improvisation in such a refreshing manner - reminiscent of free jazz (and of Mingus!) - and lost its most important musician (violinist Jerry Goodman), also to the Mahavishnu Orchestra.

The initial problem for all these groups is technical: the balance between acoustic horns and the basic electronic instrumentation of the rock groups. While conventionally staffed big bands can often record a whole LP in two to three sessions, rock big bands require weeks - often months - to obtain suitable results. Thus the high degree of human fatigue and exhaustion among the members of these groups. Blood, Sweat & Tears changed its personnel three times in a few years, until in 1974 only one of the original musicians was left.

The musical results often are in grotesque contrast to the effort involved. Unlike most other forms of rock, its big bands have failed to utilize and sophisticate tradition, particularly the jazz tradition. On the whole, their horn parts are hardly more than orchestrated guitar riffs. The use of horns is often so primitive that the impression is that beginners who do not have the slightest idea of the mysteries of orchestral arrangement - neither in jazz nor concert music - are at work here.

In a way, *Santana* belongs to the rock big bands. The group added to the usual rock instrumentation Latin percussion instruments and occasional horns, and thus created a true pandemonium of exciting rhythms. Especially impressive is Santana's album 'Caravanserai', an allegorical musical caravan moving in future dimensions of space and time - the caravan of the human self on its eternal voyage from reincarnation to reincarnation. John Coltrane's meditativeness and Gil Evans's many dimensions have here been artfully contrasted in the percussiveness of Santana's music.

Until recent years, only *Frank Zappa* has found in rock music - in real rock, that is - musical avenues which reach the level and complexity of big-band jazz. Significantly, Zappa did not start with jazz or blues or rock, as did all the others. In interviews he has repeatedly said he was prompted to become a musician by the works of Edgar Varese, the great modern composer who as early as in the twenties treated and solved many problems relevant to modern classical music in the fifties and sixties: problems of noise integration, electronics, percussion, collage techniques, musical density, etc. In the early fifties, Zappa, then unknown and unnoticed, attended the '*Kurse für Zeitgenössische Musik*' (Courses in Contemporary Music) in Darmstadt, Germany, where many of the composers who have so radically changed the contemporary avant-garde music scene lectured or studied: Boulez, Stockhausen, Nono, Zimmermann, Ligeti, Henze, Kagel, Berio . . . That is the world that shaped Zappa - and which he longs for even today - though you are not supposed to notice: thus his eccentricity, his bizarre humour, his pose - at once ironic and sincere. In this day and age, doesn't he seem like a Don Quixote struggling against windmills? And doesn't he love to appear this way?

Many critics feel that with the album 'The Grand Wazoo', released in 1972, Zappa's music reached its culmination. The production is said to show influences by - I will simply list the names - Miles Davis, John McLaughlin, Manitas de Plata, Gil Evans, Kodaly, Prokofiev, Stravinsky, Kurt Weill, etc. Critic Harvey Siders calls one of the pieces from 'The Grand Wazoo' one of the 'most successful weddings of jazz and rock in the book.'

Big Bands Forever: The Seventies and Eighties

Anyone who realizes how few convincing rock big-band records have appeared until now, and on the other hand takes into account the excellent productions featuring the conventional big-band setup released in growing numbers from the early seventies on, certainly cannot speak of the 'end of big bands'. Many outstanding leaders and arrangers have proven that the big band still has noteworthy possibilities. Among these musicians are *Don Ellis*, *Buddy Rich*, *Louie Bellson*, *Thad Jones–Mel Lewis*, *Oliver Nelson*, *Doc Severinsen*, *Toshiko Akiyoshi–Lew Tabackin*, and – in Europe – *Kenny Clark–Francy Boland* and *Chris McGregor* and his *Brotherhood of Breath*. In addition, there is a whole line of arrangers and band leaders who have been active for decades and have kept their music alive as times changed – among them Woody Herman, Count Basie, Maynard Ferguson . . .

The scope of contemporary big-band music has become so broad because on the one hand new possibilities are continually being discovered, while on the other nearly all the possibilities that have been discovered in forty years of big-band history have remained alive.

Don Ellis (who died in 1978) came out of the George Russell sextet of the early sixties, and later studied Indian music with Hari Har Rao. He was especially interested in using new meters and rhythmic sequences. Other musicians, to be sure, had employed asymmetrical meters in jazz before Ellis – Thelonious Monk and Max Roach, then Dave Brubeck and Sonny Rollins, and as early as in the thirties, Fats Waller and Benny Carter – but nobody went as far as Ellis, who said: 'I reasoned that since it was possible to play in a meter such as a 9, divided 2-2-2-3, it would then be possible to play in meters of even longer length, and this led to the development of such meters as 3-3-2-2-2-1-2-2-2 (19). To arrive at this particular division of 19, I tried many different patterns, but this was the one that swung the most. The longest meter I have attempted to date is a piece in 85.'

Some of Ellis's meters look like mathematical equations – for instance, the blues in 11 that Ellis played as three times $\frac{3\frac{2}{3}}{4}$ with natural, swinging ease. Ellis once said, ironically, that if his orchestra had to play a traditional 4/4 beat, one had best explain it to the band as '5/4/1', otherwise it would be no fun.

On one of his records, 'Tears of Joy', Ellis also incorporated a string quartet and a woodwind quintet in the big-band line-up. Through a novel technique of electronic amplification and adjustment – the Barcus-Berry Transducer System – it had become possible to give as much volume and power to the strings and woodwinds as to the bass and sax sections.

Buddy Rich, on the other hand, does not experiment at all. His big band 'celebrates' his spectacular drum artistry effectively. An evening with the Rich Big Band is show business in the conventional sense, but in its utmost perfection. The band's repertoire includes evergreens, classic jazz themes, originals, and good contemporary tunes.

Another drummer, *Louie Bellson*, occasionally also makes big-band recordings, but he does not appear so much as the star in the centre; he takes on a functional role on drums in order to present musicianly convincing arrangements (frequently his own) which combine the great big-band tradition with, sometimes, the contemporary rock atmosphere.

Many of these bands – those of Rich, Bellson, and Maynard Ferguson, for example – recruit their musicians among the graduates of jazz courses at American colleges and universities. In a sense, it can be said that with the fine training of these young musicians, the bands tend to reach an even higher professional level than most of their forerunners. There is nothing in terms of technique they cannot handle. They are unbeatable readers and can play higher and faster than ever. But strangely enough, what often is lacking is the magic goal of the jazz musician: individuality. A basic problem of music education is revealed here: individuality cannot be taught. It has to grow organically, like a plant. In our modern world of media – with radio and television programmes all sounding alike – the plant called 'individuality' has a hard time thriving. The American educational system, a model for the world, and its jazz educators should address themselves more strongly to this problem.

But we have to backtrack once more by a couple of years – to Europe. Here, the *Clarke–Boland Big Band* proved how alive the big-band tradition can be even when no concessions are made to the *Zeitgeist*. In the sixties, under the co-leadership of drum patriarch Kenny Clarke and Belgian arranger Francy Boland, some of the best-known American expatriates – among them trumpeters Benny Bailey, Art Farmer, and Idrees Sulieman; saxophonists Herb Geller and Sahib Shihab – united with European musicians of the calibre of Swedish trombonist Ake Persson (who died in 1975), German trumpeter Manfred Schoof, and British sax men Ronnie Scott and Tony Coe. The band's second drummer was a British musician similar to the famous Clarke not only in playing, but also in name: Kenny Clare. He impressively supplemented Clarke's musicianship and stylistic feeling with his professional dependability, occasionally also disguising a lack of stamina in Clarke, the grand old master.

For years, pianist Boland's arrangements were considered the 'most traditional contemporary big-band arrangements' on the jazz scene. Especially characteristic of this are the albums 'Sax No End' (with tenorists Johnny Griffin and Eddie Lockjaw Davis) and 'Faces' (with musical portrait sketches of the band members). It is too bad that just when the orchestra was becoming successful with a larger audience in the early seventies, it disbanded.

About that time, *Peter Herbolzheimer* formed his *Rhythm Combination & Brass*. All through the seventies and also into the early eighties, this has been Europe's most professional big band – certainly making many concessions to fads of the day, but again and again showing a high degree of musicianship and a swinging power generated by some of the best musicians in Europe and a few American guests.

The musically most convincing of all more recent big bands was, for most of the seventies, the *Thad Jones–Mel Lewis* Orchestra. For many years, it played New York's Village Vanguard every Monday night. Without making compromises with the rock spirit of the times, the two co-leaders, trumpeter and arranger Thad Jones and drummer Mel Lewis, managed to appeal to a large audience and to create an orchestral jazz which, as swinging as it was in the traditional sense, was full of sounds and ideas never heard before. Jazz from all periods – including the jazz of the sixties and the music of John Coltrane and the post-Coltrane era – merged in the arrangements, furnished mainly by Thad Jones and played by an elite troupe of New York's finest musicians.

Regrettably, Jones and Lewis separated in 1979. Jones became the leader of a Copenhagen-based band staffed with Scandinavian and American players, one of the most swinging big bands in Europe today. And Mel Lewis carries on the tradition of the New York band, attempting to broaden its scope.

Meanwhile, however, another orchestra had made its breakthrough, the *Toshiko Akiyoshi–Lew Tabackin Big Band* in Los Angeles. Since 1978, most of the critics have been voting it the number one big band. The orchestra gets its stamp from the compositions and arrangements of Japanese-born pianist Toshiko Akiyoshi. She says: 'When I look back and analyse what I've done, I find that in many cases I seem to have had a tendency to write in what you might call layers of sound. In other words, I will have one thing, then I will hear another that goes along with it. It's just like a photograph with a double exposure, you know?' Particularly original is a five-part flute section which Toshiko formed with members of her orchestra – with her husband Lew Tabackin taking the lead voice. She has also been successful in widening the scope of the sax section by adding different kinds of flutes and clarinets in new and original combinations. In some of her pieces, she has drawn on Japanese tradition, for example, on *gagaku*, the ancient court music of the Japanese emperors.

The stream of the great big-band tradition continues to flow. Many orchestras all over the world are a part of it. Some of the more important ones are *Jaki Byard's Apollo Stompers*, *Frank Foster's Jazzmobile Orchestra*, *Ed Shaugnessy's Energy Force*, the *Dave Matthews Big Band*, and *Nat Pierce* and *Frank Capp's Juggernaut*.

Aside from these established big bands, a number of arrangers make an occasional orchestral jazz recording, and have in this way helped to shape the contemporary big-band scene. Among them are some who have been mentioned before as well – above all, *Oliver Nelson*. Nelson, who died in 1975, is best characterized by a list of his favourite musicians: Charlie Parker, John Coltrane, Gil Evans, George Russell. The title of one of his best-known works, 'The Blues and the Abstract Truth', signifies Nelson's position: the tension-field between the tradition of the blues and the truth of avant-garde abstractions.

In Britain, South African pianist *Chris McGregor* has 'applied' the Ellington tradition to free jazz in his *Brotherhood of Breath*, to which he added, as a further element, Bantu and Zulu rhythms and melodies and motifs of his homeland. South African emigrés play alongside British musicians – certainly not with the usual studio precision, but the friction of intonation and harmony within the Brotherhood of Breath may even have an Africanizing and intensifying effect. There is lots of folk music in the Brotherhood's sounds.

All in all, clearly a comeback of tradition can be found on the big-band scene of the late seventies and early eighties. It is no longer free-jazz orchestras or rock big bands, but the conventional big-band instrumentation (four trumpets, four trombones, a five-piece saxophone section, with minor deviations, alterations, and additions) that today again is the focal point of big-band attention – thirty years after the period when there first was talk of the 'death' of the big bands.

And finally, there are also big bands that put rock elements to creative use – without the stiffness and lack of inspiration we talked about earlier. Two such bands are the *Les DeMerle Transfusion* and *Baird Hersey's The Year of the Ear*. Guitarist Hersey incorporates synthesizer and other electronic sounds into the powerfully swinging style of his band. And Lee Underwood wrote about drummer Les DeMerle's orchestra: 'A band that fuses East Coast intensity with West Coast savoir-faire, and jazz sophistication with rock and roll urgency.'

There are at least two big bands of this type in Europe, too: the *United Jazz & Rock Ensemble*, initiated by pianist Wolfgang Dauner, with musicians like Charlie Mariano, Barbara Thompson, Albert Mangelsdorff, and Jon Hiseman; and the *Vienna Art Orchestra*, founded by Swiss composer Mathias Rüeggi, with its (often typically Viennese) humour and chutzpah. These bands have proven that big-band jazz can be immensely successful – especially with a young audience – if innovation and original paths are followed.

Even further away from the usual big-band sound is an orchestra which became known in 1979 at CBS Records' so-called Havana Jam in Cuba and which since then has found world-wide recognition: *Irakere*, led by pianist–composer Chucho Valdés. Irakere plays 'Cuban jazz' along the lines sketched earlier in connection with the Machito band, but even more exciting, engaging, contemporary than the Cuban bands in the United States. Chucho Valdez' 'Missa Negra' is a ritual of black music that refers at the same time back to Africa and ahead to a new type of Latinized big-band sound. But Irakere actually represents only the tip of an iceberg: Cuba is full of such music. The American–Western European world simply has not yet realized it.

Lastly, one other big-band scene should be mentioned that also is 'underground' – in both senses of that word: all the big bands at America's high schools, colleges, and universities. There are hundreds of big bands of all imaginable (and certainly also some unimaginable) shadings. These orchestras form the vital 'underground', the basis, for tomorrow's professional big bands. Some of them are good enough to bear comparison with some of the best-known big bands of today. If you know this scene – with its volcanic vitality – you have to laugh when someone asks if big bands are dead.

THE JAZZ COMBOS

The Jazz Combos

Jazz is initially a music of small ensembles. Jazz was a combo music long before the word 'combo' existed. This word came into being when it became necessary to distinguish between big bands and small groups. Before that, any jazz band was automatically a combo, and if one did not know from hindsight what would evolve from the bands of Fletcher Henderson and Duke Ellington in the twenties, these ensembles, too, could be regarded as 'combos'.

Since jazz from the start has been an art of small ensembles, a history of combos must be written differently from a history of big bands. Since practically every jazz man has played in combos, such a history would turn into an endless listing of names. The required selective principle rests in the fact that a combo should be more than merely a group of musicians who have come together to play. By way of the Modern Jazz Quartet and John Lewis, 'integration' has become a key term in jazz criticism. Here indeed is the key to our history of the combo in jazz. Integration – in terms of mathematics or music – means that everything belongs to a whole, that all elements are subordinate to one main idea.

In this sense, Dave Brubeck made a relevant statement about the combo situation: 'The important thing about jazz right now is that it's keeping alive the feeling of the group getting together. Jazz, to make it, has got to be a group feeling . . .' This describes what we have referred to as the sociological situation of jazz – as at the beginning of the section dealing with Swing style and in the chapter about the arrangement. Jazz is at once music of the individual and music of the collective. No other art has attained both in such extreme measure. In such simultaneity the sociologist may find philosophical, political, and historical aspects. With jazz, this simultaneity of the individual and the collective, of – if you will –

freedom and necessity, has acquired musical aspects for the first time. Rarely can jazz be seen so clearly as a legitimate artistic expression of our time as in this point. And since this is so, the combo history of jazz is almost something like a concentration of jazz history *per se*.

In the selective sense in which we wish to concentrate combo history, Jelly Roll Morton's *Red Hot Peppers* (1926 to 1930) and Louis Armstrong's second *Hot Five* with Earl Hines (1928) are the first significant jazz combos. Morton was the first to map out pieces from beginning to end and give them the stamp of a formative personality; Armstrong's Hot Five recordings achieved integration through the somnambulistic rapport between Louis and his musicians, above all pianist Earl Hines.

Orrin Keepnews writes in the liner notes to a Morton album: 'This is complex, intricate music. The musicians reputedly did not play from written scores but each number was preceded by perhaps a half-hour of studying the tunes, deciding on the placements of solos, memorizing the basic arrangements. It is the definitive answer to anyone who would claim that jazz is deficient in counter-point or in depth of musical structure. It is a remarkable combination of improvisation and arrangement . . . These are all talented musicians, but nevertheless, the voice that is heard here, the single, unified sound, is Morton's. This is the mark of his greatness . . .'

In the Armstrong Hot Five with Hines (they consisted of six and sometimes even seven musicians) and in the Morton Red Hot Peppers we see for the first time a coming together of elements which previously had only existed separately: the collective improvisation of the old New Orleans bands in which soloistic achievement, and the individuality of the improviser in general, had barely begun to develop; this soloistic achievement itself; and, lastly, the conscious or intuitive creation of form through an outstanding personality.

The Swing Combos

What the thirties brought was, compared to this, initially a step backwards. In 1935 Benny Goodman formed his *Benny Goodman Trio*. It became the germ cell and model not only for all the other

Goodman combos – the Quartet with Lionel Hampton and eventually the Sextets with Charlie Christian and Cootie Williams – but also for all the combos which developed as 'bands within bands' in all the important large orchestras. Thus, Artie Shaw formed his *Gramercy Five* with himself on clarinet and first Billy Butterfield and then Roy Eldridge on trumpet. Tommy Dorsey, Bob Crosby, and Jimmy Dorsey formed Dixieland combos within their big bands: Tommy Dorsey his *Clambake Seven* with Pee Wee Erwin (trumpet), Bud Freeman (tenor sax), Dave Tough (drums), and others; Bob Crosby his *Bob Cats* with Matty Matlock (clarinet), Eddie Miller (tenor), Yank Lawson (trumpet), and the rhythm section mentioned in the big-band chapter. Later, towards the end of the forties, Jimmy Dorsey formed his *Original Dorseyland Jazz Band* with Ray Bauduc on drums. Chu Berry recruited his *Stompy Stevedores* primarily from the ranks of Cab Calloway's band, of which he was a member. Count Basie's band had its *Kansas City Six* and *Seven* and Woody Herman his *Woodchoppers*.

The most important of these 'bands within the bands' originated in the *Duke Ellington* orchestra. Trumpeters Cootie Williams and Rex Stewart, clarinetist Barney Bigard, and altoist Johnny Hodges all made recordings in which the atmosphere of Ellington's music was, amazingly, projected into ever-changing small instrumental combinations. The 'Ellington spirit' served as the integrating factor. It was so strong that even some records made by Lionel Hampton with musicians drawn mainly from this band acquired a noticeable Ellington aura.

The opposite of the integration which permeates the recordings made by the Ellington musicians can be found in the recording groups put together by *Teddy Wilson* from 1935 on. In a sense, these groups should not be mentioned here, in view of our selective combo principles. Here solo follows solo, but precisely on this account it is amazing how often the musical climate creates its own unity – especially when Billie Holiday and Lester Young are among the participants. In a record like 'Easy Living' (1937) there is certainly nothing 'integrated' – and yet, from first note to last, we are in the unifying climate created by the tune, the lyrics, and the way in which Billie Holiday sings and the musicians, obviously, feel with her.

It is remarkable how the turning point in jazz evolution, which came towards the end of the thirties and beginning of the forties, not only involved the harmonic, melodic, and rhythmic innovations of the bop musicians, but also initiated new concepts of integration. In 1938 bassist *John Kirby* formed an ensemble which in every respect made Swing music in the best sense of the term, yet was a combo in a sense which did not become the rule until the fifties. With Kirby – and with the *King Cole Trio* as well – begins the real 'integration' line of combo history which leads through the *Art Tatum Trio* and the *Red Norvo Trio* to the characteristic combos of the fifties and sixties: the Gerry Mulligan Quartet, the Modern Jazz Quartet, the Jimmy Guiffre Trio, the Max Roach–Clifford Brown Quintet, the Miles Davis Quintet, the Horace Silver Quintet, Art Blakey's Jazz Messengers, the various Charles Mingus groups, the Ornette Coleman groups – and further on to Weather Report and John McLaughlin's Mahavishnu Orchestra, and still further (in the late seventies) to Air and the World Saxophone Quartet . . .

Kirby's 'Biggest Little Band in the Land' created airy, complementary frameworks of sound within which trumpeter Charlie Shavers, clarinetist Buster Baily, altoist Russell Procope, and pianist Billy Kyle improvised pretty and pleasing solos. The band had a clearly identifiable sound. It was the first ensemble to find success as a completely integrated combo in the sense that the Gerry Mulligan Quartet or the Modern Jazz Quartet achieved it fifteen years later.

Many of these successful later combos sprang up on the West Coast, and perhaps it is fitting that the combo which, alongside Kirby, initiated this whole development also started there: the *King Cole Trio*. It is the first combo of the modern piano-trio type: not merely a pianist accompanied by a rhythm section, but three instruments constituting a single entity. The Nat 'King' Cole Trio was formed in 1940, with Oscar Moore on guitar and Wesley Prince on bass. Later, Cole had guitarist Irving Ashby and bassist Johnny Miller. But in the course of the forties, the success of Cole the singer gradually began to overshadow the pianist, until Nat gave up his trio and became a singer of popular songs.

Bop and Cool

In the meantime, bop had arrived. The *Charlie Parker Quintet*, with Miles Davis on trumpet, set the standard for both the music itself and for the format of the combos who played this music. For the first time it was again as it had been in the old Dixieland jazz: music and structure belonged together. Then it had been the free counterpoint of trumpet, trombone, and clarinet over a two-beat rhythm; now it was trumpet and saxophone in unison over the new legato rhythm. This unity of music and structure remained obligatory for the combos of hard bop: *Art Blakey's Jazz Messengers*, the *Horace Silver Quintet*, the *Max Roach Quintet* (with trumpeter Clifford Brown and then with other musicians), and – above all – from the mid-fifties to the end of the sixties, the *Miles Davis Quintet* – and then again (that's how durable this structure has proven) in neo-bop around the turn of the seventies, in groups like Dexter Gordon's, Woody Shaw's, and many others.

It is only natural that in the course of this long timespan many musicians have tried to widen and vary song and group structures, while at the same time preserving their basic format. In the mid-fifties, pianist Horace Silver was especially successful in this respect through the individualistic construction of his themes. Thus, he might use two 12-bar blues phrases, follow them up with an 8-bar bridge taken from song form, and then repeat the blues phrase, thus combining blues and song form; or he might combine a 15-bar main theme with a 16-bar interlude – 'even though it's not even, it sounds even,' as Horace has said – and so on in many similarly conceived compositions. And it should be said clearly: If today's music, even in the more demanding forms of rock, has often become free of the schematic nature of the conventional 32-bar song form, this is due in no small measure to Silver, who was the first to pave the way for this development. To be sure, there were unique forms deviating from conventions even in the early days of jazz – as in Jelly Roll Morton's music or in William Christopher Handy's (e.g., 'St Louis Blues') – but awareness of this had meanwhile been buried. Horace Silver unearthed it.

A number of years before the first Silver success in this field – around the turn of the forties – Lennie Tristano had already refined and abstracted the Parker format. He also had two horns, but they were both saxophones – Lee Konitz (alto) and Warne Marsh (tenor) – and to this he added a third hornlike line through Billy Bauer's guitar. In the *Lennie Tristano Sextette* could be found a very mobile linearity, moving over highly differentiated harmonies. After bop had broadened the harmonic material, Lennie Tristano 'widened' the line – in the conscious conviction that jazz musicians had been concerned enough with harmonic problems for years and that the time had come to strengthen this awareness of line and melody. There were recordings such as 'Wow', with a vigour that only hard bop would return to the general jazz consciousness in the late fifties; but above all there was a thoughtful, inspiring coolness with something of the atmosphere of the mediaeval cloisters in which scholastic debates were held at dusk.

Even before Tristano, bop musicians had attempted to broaden the structure of the Parker Quintet – in terms of sound. Primarily, *Tadd Dameron*, *James Moody*, and *Charlie Ventura* were involved in this effort – Dameron in his recordings for Blue Note, for which he used such musicians as trumpeter Fats Navarro and tenorists Wardell Gray and Allen Eager; James Moody with his significant and much-too-neglected recording of 'Cu-Ba' (also on Blue Note); and – most successfully – Charlie Ventura with his Bop for the People combo, in which vocalist Jackie Cain and pianist Roy Kral (later to become her husband) sang humorous, spirited vocal duets. All this culminated in the *Miles Davis Capitol Band*. In it, sound became definitively established as a structuring element. (In the Davis chapter, the ensemble is discussed in detail).

What followed consists of manifold combinations and developments of these three elements: the harmonic, connected with the name of Charlie Parker; the element of sound, for which Miles Davis's Capitol Band created an ideal; and the element of integration, for which the John Kirby Band and the King Cole Trio had already broken ground.

On the West Coast, for example, *Shorty Rogers* with his Giants and *Gerry Mulligan* with his Tentette made recordings which further perfected the sound of the Davis Capitol Band, though sterilizing it a bit in the process. Later, Rogers reduced the Giants to the size of a quintet and created polished West Coast music within the Parker

format – as did drummer *Shelly Manne*. He is one of the few West
Coast musicians flexible enough to keep their own musical concept
alive by continually reorienting themselves in the changing musical
stream – right into the eighties. Today, with young musicians, he
makes records that are partially rock-influenced, but retain the solid
tradition of the jazz of the fifties.

On the East Coast, *J. J. Johnson* and *Kai Winding* found an
impressive solution. They joined their two trombones in a quintet,
and thus on the one hand preserved the two-horn format of bop, and
on the other discovered a structuring sound in the subtleties of
differentiated trombone tones. This structure was so intriguingly
simple that it was frequently copied. Winding himself did it – after
the original combo disbanded – by combining four trombones instead
of two. *Al Cohn* and *Zoot Sims* followed suit, combining two tenors –
and on occasion, two clarinets – instead of trombones. *Phil Woods* and
Gene Quill did something similar when they teamed up on alto
saxophones. Tenormen *Eddie 'Lockjaw' Davis* and *Johnny Griffin*
projected the idea into the world of hard bop around the turn of the
fifties. And in the early seventies, drummer *Elvin Jones* transplanted
this concept of the 'duplicated instrument' into the post-Coltrane era,
using two tenor players.

High Points of Integration

At an earlier date – in the late forties – vibraphonist *Red Norvo* had
formed a trio with guitarist Tal Farlow and bassist Charlie Mingus
which, more so than any other group, established what one could call
'chamber jazz'. In light, relaxed, transparent interplay, the lines of
vibraphone, guitar, and bass flowed into, opposite, and around each
other, and if Norvo – as a representative of the older jazz generation –
didn't play quite as 'modern' as Farlow and Mingus, the twofold
stylistic plateau thus created lent an added charm. The linear
function Norvo had assigned to the bass of Mingus (later Red
Mitchell) was adopted in *Gerry Mulligan*'s successful Quartet from
1953 on. Gerry did away with the piano, let the changes be indicated
by a single bass line which took on additional contrapuntal

significance, and set the lines of his baritone sax and Chet Baker's trumpet above that. Later, after Chet Baker (who became famous almost overnight through his playing in this quartet) had made himself independent, valve trombonist Bob Brookmeyer or trumpeters Jon Eardly and Art Farmer took his place. In a manner which has been described as 'busy', Mulligan played contrapuntal counter-melodies or riffs on his baritone behind the improvisations of the second horn in his quartet. So it became apparent that even the riff – one of the most rudimentary of jazz elements – could be used structurally in terms of modern combo integration. Of course, after some time it became obvious that the more one became used to the surprising sound of this quartet, the more clearly the formulalike nature of its music was revealed. So Gerry Mulligan, who is not only a great musician, but also a far-sighted man, enlarged his quartet to a sextet. And it is this lineup to which he has returned again and again for more than twenty-five years.

The most often cited of all these combos is pianist John Lewis's *Modern Jazz Quartet*, with Milt Jackson, vibraphone; Percy Heath, bass; and first Kenny Clarke, then Connie Kay, drums. Founded in 1951 and disbanded in 1974, it was by far the longest-lived combo in jazz history. Lewis, one of the melodically most gifted of all jazz composers, found much stimulation in the contrapuntal art of Johann Sebastian Bach. At the beginning, he often took over classical forms almost literally – above all in 'Vendome', a precise and knowledge-able version of a baroque invention – with the one difference that in the place of the 'episodes' in the form of the invention are put improvisations by the members of the Modern Jazz Quartet. Later, Lewis discovered contrapuntal possibilities more germane to jazz than to old music. As he said: 'In the little piece entitled "Versailles", which also used a "classical" form – the fugue – as a model, I don't feel that this has anything to do with the model, the best-known examples of which are Bach's. We have started to work on some new concepts of playing which give freer rein to the creativity of the improviser and yet produce an even stronger form . . .' In those terms, Lewis also worked on an incorporation of the percussion part into the linear and contrapuntal play of his quartet. His percussionist, Connie Kay, was equipped with a whole arsenal of auxiliary rhythm instruments: finger cymbals, triangles, small Chinese drum, etc . . .

And if drum instrumentation in general has become increasingly enlarged since the sixties, Connie Kay was among those who gave this direction its first impetus.

Characteristic of Lewis's jazz-minded relationship to baroque music are these thoughts, expressed by him in connection with his suite, 'Fontessa': ' "Fontessa" is a little suite inspired by the Renaissance Commedia dell'Arte. I had particularly in mind their plays, which consisted of a very sketchy plot and in which the details – the lines, etc. – were improvised . . .'

The MJQ – as Lewis's combo is abbreviated – had gone through a clearly perceivable development. During the sixties, the Bach elements became rare, but this was compensated for by a much more swinging jazz intensity. Lewis's 'Django', for example, became less and less melancholy in the successive recordings available, and more and more swinging and intense.

The MJQ had great influence. Even in the hard-bop combos with their Parker Quintet structure, one suddenly could detect echoes of John Lewis's will to form. And even *Oscar Peterson*, whose trio at first was a kind of modernized King Cole or Art Tatum Trio, has paid respect to John Lewis's integration principle.

A similarly long development was undergone by the *Dave Brubeck Quartet*, formed in 1951, after Brubeck had first gained experience with a highly interesting octet (1946) and a trio (1949). Brubeck has probably had more hits than any other jazz musician, and yet – and certainly because of this – he has been harshly criticized, but Brubeck has charisma, which has carried him from one success to another for more than thirty years (see piano chapter).

Brubeck's most important partner was Paul Desmond, a 'poet of the alto saxophone', whose improvisations have been valued much more highly by critics than Brubeck's piano playing. When Desmond withdrew in the late sixties, Gerry Mulligan stepped into his place. Mulligan has always been an immensely swing-oriented, 'busy' improviser, and it is obvious that through his participation the until then somewhat pastoral, cool Brubeck Quartet definitely became a more intense, 'hotter' group. Since the seventies, Brubeck has often appeared with some or all of his three sons, who have added an occasional fusion element to his music.

From Hard Bop to Free

We have already mentioned hard-bop combos in connection with the Charlie Parker Quintet. It is apparent that an evolution towards greater integration took place here as well. Even the most vital hard-bop group, the *Jazz Messengers* – thrust forward by *Art Blakey*'s wild percussion work – tends to have at least one (sometimes even two) musical 'integrator' in the sense of the function of John Lewis within the MJQ, if in hard-bop terms. Horace Silver, then Benny Golson, Bobby Timmons, Wayne Shorter, Cedar Walton, George Cables, etc., had this function with Blakey, whose groups have been of central significance for more than thirty years – right into the eighties. (More about contemporary bop later in this chapter).

Marvellous integration is also a characteristic of the various groups *Max Roach* has led since his work with Clifford Brown and Sonny Rollins in the mid-fifties – ensembles partially with full, rich three-part horn sounds, without piano; later with pianist Ron Mathews and trumpeter Freddie Hubbard; frequently also with Roach's then wife, Abbey Lincoln. Max's main work, 'Freedom Now Suite', is exemplary not only for content but also in structure. Even more dense and concentrated is the music Roach made with his groups in the seventies – with gripping two-horn sounds (by, among others, trumpeter Cecil Bridgewater and saxophonist Bill Harper). Roach also is one of the few musicians – if not the only one (outside the gospel churches) – who has solved the difficult problem of how to integrate a choir into a jazz context.

At the centre of all these combos stands the *Miles Davis Group* (featuring many different musicians), which was a kind of backbone for the entire jazz development from the mid-fifties to the early seventies. It has been said that Miles, in the process, developed into *the* 'star-maker'. Here is a list of musicians who have emerged from his groups: saxophonists John Coltrane, Cannonball Adderley, Hank Mobley, Wayne Shorter, George Coleman, Sam Rivers, Dave Liebman, and Steve Grossman; bass clarinetist Bennie Maupin; pianists Red Garland, Bill Evans, Wynton Kelly, Herbie Hancock, Chick Corea, Joe Zawinul, and Keith Jarrett; guitarist John McLaughlin; bassists Paul Chambers, Ron Carter, and Dave Holland; drummers Philly Joe Jones, Tony Williams, Jack DeJohnette, and Billy Cobham; and percussionist Airto Moreira – truly a list defying comparison! In the chapters about the seventies and Miles Davis himself, the role this great musician has played is depicted from different viewpoints.

From the point of view of our combo-selection principle, it is important also to see that the concept of 'modality', introduced by Miles and John Coltrane, creates a high degree of connection – and thus integration. The integration factor here is the 'scale' – no longer many, continuously varying chord changes, but only a single chord (or very few chords).

John Coltrane transplanted this principle into 'freer' jazz – in a sense shown in the chapter about him (and elsewhere throughout the book). One of the most beautiful recordings of the 'classic' Coltrane Quartet – with McCoy Tyner on piano and Elvin Jones on drums – is the famous 'A Love Supreme', which combines spiritual fervour with formal completeness in a way not heretofore achieved in jazz. This group, with its high standards of improvisation and interplay, with the lasting value of its themes (composed mostly by its leader) and its 'togetherness' is still a model for many jazz groups way into the eighties.

Before Coltrane there were those groups which helped pave the way for free jazz. Next to him in stylistic terms (in the sense of the criteria used in this section) were initially only the *Ornette Coleman Quartet* and *Trio*. It was not until the seventies that the impulses given by Coleman and Coltrane merged – but even then only in certain cases, as with the musicians of the AACM (to be discussed later).

Among the groups which paved the way for the new jazz, three are important: the *Jimmy Giuffre Trios* of the fifties, *Charles Mingus*, and *George Russell*. In the early fifties, Jimmy Giuffre recorded his 'Tangents in Jazz', in which the drummer – as percussionist – is drawn into the melodic and structural development of the music to such an extent that a continuous beat is largely dispensed with. In the trio organized by Giuffre in 1954 there was no drummer at all, and one may surmise that this outcome was near at hand: once the drums are used more or less as melody instruments, there surely must be other instruments capable of serving this purpose better. In this trio, Giuffre used guitarist Jim Hall and bassist Ralph Peña. Giuffre went one step further when he joined with valve trombonist Bob

Brookmeyer in a trio without a rhythm section – two horns plus guitar in an exhilarating web of lines that elaborated on both chamber music and folk music.

Even more important for further developments were the various groups led by *George Russell* from the second half of the fifties on – above all, his sextets with musicians like trombonist Dave Baker, multi-instrumentalist Eric Dolphy, and trumpeter Don Ellis. In the freely swinging modality of Russell's music a hymnic tone is achieved – a tone which reached a larger audience only years later through John Coltrane's 'A Love Supreme' – but also shows an aspect of abstraction which often seems like a premonition of Anthony Braxton's work.

The most important pathbreaker of the new jazz, however, was *Charles Mingus*. As we discussed earlier, his music returned the feeling of collective improvisation to jazz. To be sure, there has always been collective improvising in jazz, but ever since jazz had given up the three-part New Orleans counterpoint, the emphasis had shifted to solo improvisation, the work of single players accompanied by a rhythm section. Through Mingus, improvising became collective again, and to an extent unknown since the days of New Orleans jazz – which was not only indicative of a process in music, but also in society. It is no accident that the revolutionary Mingus recordings we are referring to were made around the turn of the fifties, i.e., immediately preceding the new awakening of social and political awareness in the sixties. Again and again, jazz has anticipated and heralded such social developments. 'Polyphonic music says: We', is what Theodor Adorno, the philosopher, once wrote. In those terms, New Orleans and Dixieland jazz on the one hand, and Charles Mingus and the free, collective jazz of the sixties and seventies on the other, all say 'we'. The music of the great individuals – of, for instance, Charlie Parker, Lee Konitz, and, earlier, Coleman Hawkins and Lester Young – says 'I'.

Among Charles Mingus's most important recordings in this context are 'Better Git It in Your Soul', 'Goodbye, Pork Pie Hat', 'Open Letter to Duke', 'Mingus, Mingus, Mingus' (with Eric Dolphy), and 'Tijuana Moods' (with Clarence Shaw, trumpet) and 'The Black Saint and the Sinner Lady' (with Charlie Mariano). Drummer Dannie Richmond played a crucial part in the success of almost all of Mingus's productions. With the assurance of a sleepwalker he kept up with his leader's many tempo changes (still rather new and unusual in jazz at the time), and thus held the music together.

Ornette and After

Aside from Lennie Tristano's 'Intuition' and 'Digression' (which, in 1949, were lone precursors of much later developments), the *Ornette Coleman Quartet* of 1959-60 was the first group to play 'free', yet from the start meet the integration criteria of this section. Appearing at a New York club, the Five Spot, Coleman and his trumpeter Don Cherry enraptured audiences night after night for months. The many musicians always present in the audience were fascinated by the precision with which Ornette and Don entered in unison after their long, free solo excursions – though it wasn't recognizable to the majority of even the specialists why they came in at this particular spot and not somewhere else. One of the musician–listeners said then: 'You can't hear it, but there is no doubt: Ornette and his men know what they're doing. In a couple of years, everybody else will know it, too' (which of course, has become true). Bassist Charlie Haden had an especially integrating effect in his group, with his totally free bass lines that dispensed with conventional harmonies, yet created connection and structure.

A few years later, Ornette did away with the second horn, forming a trio. It may certainly be surmised that he himself took on the roles of trumpeter and violinist – however much he was criticized in them – in addition to his alto work because he needed further sound colorations but nevertheless wanted to mould the music of his group as directly and immediately as possible. Only towards the end of the sixties did Coleman succeed in finding another congenial horn partner in tenor saxophonist Dewey Redman. Redman, in turn, joined Don Cherry in the group *Old and New Dreams* – again a number of years later – further developing Coleman's music towards the world-music consciousness of the seventies. Here Redman also blows the musette, an Arabian instrument, while Cherry incorporates elements of Indian and Tibetan, and occasionally American Indian, music.

From Coleman and Coltrane spring all the free-jazz groups that emphasize the collective experience of their music to an extent heretofore unknown. Dismayed by the isolation of the individual in modern society, these musicians feel that their improvisations unite them to a degree 'as otherwise, among humans, only love can do' (Don Cherry). Cherry's piece 'Complete Communion', realized in 1965, first in Paris and then in New York, indicates this concept of 'total communication' even in its title.

Other groups that compensated for the isolation of the individual expressing himself without restraint (which is where a music that knows no harmonic or formal ordering factor may easily lead), with much stronger and more intensely personal collective relationships were the *Archie Shepp Quintet* with trombonist Roswell Rudd; the *New York Art Quartet* with altoist John Tchicai (and also with Rudd); the *Albert Ayler Quintet* and many European groups: around Tchicai in Copenhagen; Jan Garbarek in Oslo; Tomasz Stańko in Warsaw; Albert Mangelsdorff, Manfred Schoof, Peter Brötzmann, and Gunter Hampel in Germany; Michel Portal in Paris; John Stevens, John Surman, Allan Skidmore, Paul Rutherford, Tony Oxley, and others in London . . .

Special attention in this connection is merited by the various groups of the AACM, which has been repeatedly mentioned.

The AACM

As early as at the beginning of the sixties, pianist *Richard Abrams* had founded the AACM in Chicago, the Association for the Advancement of Creative Musicians: a grouping of musicians which has had much significance, not only musically, but also in terms of consciousness in the self-identification process of black musicians. The AACM first met with real success in Europe, aside from the much too limited local resonance it found in Chicago. In the late sixties, in a deliberate reaction against the lack of interest in free music on the part of the American public (and against its political and social implications!), some of the most important AACM musicians moved

to Paris – among them saxophonists Joseph Jarman and Roscoe
Mitchell, trumpeter Lester Bowie, bassist Malachi Favors, and multi-
instrumentalist Anthony Braxton. From there, the *Art Ensemble of
Chicago* quickly became known all over Europe. Since Jarman,
Mitchell, Bowie, and Favors did not have a regular drummer (Phillip
Wilson, Don Moye and Steve McCall worked only briefly with the
group), they soon began to play percussion themselves: Bowie on the
bass drum and Mitchell, Jarman, and Favors on the entire range of
various percussion instruments which, around that time, became
customary in the new jazz. In this way, the percussion parts – played
alternately by musicians whose main instruments were trumpet,
saxophone, and bass – were integrated completely in the melodic
activity. This was also a crucial contribution of the Art Ensemble of
Chicago.

As far as I know, there has never been a jazz combo that had so
many different instrumental colours at its disposal as the Art
Ensemble. On their European tours, the four musicians carried whole
busloads of instruments. Particularly versatile are Mitchell (who
plays alto, soprano, tenor, and bass saxophone; clarinet, flute,
piccolo, sirens, whistles, bells, steel drum, congas, gongs, cymbals,
etc., etc.) and Jarman (whose instruments include sopranello; alto,
soprano, and tenor sax; alto clarinet, oboe, flute, piano, harpsichord,
guitar, marimba, accordion, vibraphone, and several dozen percussion
instruments). With this instrumentation, the AACM players made
numerous records in France, Germany, and Great Britain, including
the first big-band realization of AACM music, at the 1969 New Jazz
Meeting Baden-Baden.

The majority of the American jazz audience became aware of the
significance of the AACM almost ten years later. It was a slow
process, beginning with Anthony Braxton's success and resulting in
many AACM musicians being rated in top positions of the 1979 *down
beat* Critics' Poll.

In the meantime, two further groups rooted in the AACM had
been formed: *Air* (Henry Threadgill on saxes and flutes; Fred
Hopkins, bass; Steve McCall, drums) and the *World Saxophone Quartet*
(Hamiet Bluiett, baritone sax and flute; Julius Hemphill, alto and
soprano sax; Oliver Lake, alto and soprano sax and flute; David
Murray, tenor saxophone and bass clarinet).

One of the most successful Air records is 'Air Lore' (1980). It is dedicated to Scott Joplin's early rags and to Jelly Roll Morton's New Orleans compositions, which is a remarkable demonstration of indebtedness to tradition in view of the avant-garde character of this music. The sound of Air corresponds to the group's name: it is airy, light, loose, clear, and transparent. The *World Saxophone Quartet*, too, makes music corresponding to its name: The overwhelming majority of the critical fraternity considers it the best saxophone group in the world today – equally embedded in the jazz tradition (as in early New Orleans or in the Harlem jazz of the twenties) and indebted to French woodwind-ensemble music of the nineteenth and twentieth centuries. Above all, the World Saxophone Quartet plays 'hip', with a low-key kind of humour that continually transmits a stream of coded or uncoded signals.

Of course, there has also been combo music on a high level by other AACM musicians (and also by members of a similar grouping founded in St Louis, BAG, as well as by musicians close to these two groupings): These include players like saxophonist *Oliver Lake*; trumpeter *Leo Smith*; the four members of the World Saxophone Quartet in recordings and appearances under their own names; *Richard Abrams*, the great innovative spirit of the AACM; and the best-known AACM musician *Anthony Braxton*. Braxton came to the fore particularly with his quartets, which included trombonist George Lewis, and later his colleague Ray Anderson, in a gradual process of abstracting music to the limit.

The attitude of most of these musicians towards tradition is illuminated by a motto formulated by the players of the Chicago Art Ensemble: 'Ancient to the future.' This not only means (in the Western rationalistic sense) 'pointing towards the future from the ancient past,' but it also refers (in the sense of ancient concepts of African mythology) to a 'suspension of time.' Said Abrams: 'My thoughts . . . are my . . . future . . . now and forever . . . symbolizing . . . the past . . . present . . . and future – in the eternal now . . .' This is an African thought. Or Asian. Definitely not Western.

It fits in with the initially mentioned process of sensitization that Muhal Richard Abrams should have influenced the musicians of the AACM not just in terms of music. Trombonist George Lewis said that he was even prompted to his extramusical studies – mainly German philosophy – by Muhal. And Joseph Jarman stated that before meeting Abrams he had been 'like all the rest of the "hip" ghetto niggers' on the streets of Chicago's South Side. Quite possibly, his future would have been bleak, as it is for so many young people trapped in the ghettos. But then he met Muhal, and his life acquired a sense of direction. It seems that Abrams, who remained more or less in the background for years, was much more interested in furthering the careers of other AACM musicians than his own. It was only in the second half of the seventies – in fact, after his appearance at the 1978 Montreux Festival – that he has found the recognition as a pianist and composer which other, much younger AACM players had gained earlier.

It is characteristic of the awareness of form, which is of basic importance to most of these musicians, that they have again and again referred to Duke Ellington. Muhal Richard Abrams told critic Gary Giddins: 'If it keeps going the way it's going, I think things will reach a point similar to where Duke was . . . with, of course, some added criteria . . .'

The Seventies

Between the early seventies and the early eighties, the combo situation has been similar to that of the big bands. There are four streams and various cross-connections between them:

1. The combos playing along the lines of today's mainstream jazz, among which the hard-bop and neo-bop groups occupy a special place – of growing significance around the turn of the seventies.

2. The groups playing free music, discussed in connection with the AACM.

3. The jazz–rock and fusion groups, whose development was initiated by Miles Davis's 'Bitches Brew'.

4. Chamber musiclike groups, who further refine the tradition of the Red Norvo Trio or the Jimmy Giuffre Trio. The prototype of these is Ralph Towner's group *Oregon* (disbanded in 1980) with Paul McCandless (oboe and English horn), Glen Moore (bass), and Collin Walcott (sitar, tabla, percussion). In a sense, Oregon constitutes *the*

culmination of integrated, chamber musiclike jazz playing in all of jazz history so far – as the trio which Keith Jarrett led around 1971–72, with bassist Charlie Haden and drummer Paul Motian, constitutes an apex in the history of that type of group which has come to be called 'piano trio'. As we said, the point of the piano trio is that the pianist's sidemen do more than merely furnish accompaniment: their music is integrated as equally as possible into the musical whole.

Mainstream

Among the groups of the mainstream of the seventies, there are, on the one hand, those whose 'first editions' were formed twenty years ago (and thus have been mentioned already) and on the other, newly formed ensembles. Of course, the groups whose leaders had formed ensembles in the fifties have integrated the subsequent musical experiences as much as those groups which were first formed in the seventies. For this reason, we list both kinds of groups together: *Art Blakey's Jazz Messengers*, the *Dizzy Gillespie Quintet*, the *Max Roach Quartet*, the *Cannonball Adderley Quintet*, *McCoy Tyner's group*, the *Phil Woods Quartet*, the *Woody Shaw Quintet*, and *Herbie Hancock's VSOP*. Most of these are groups with ever-changing lineups.

McCoy Tyner is a central figure among them, as a source of strength and inspiration for the entire scene. Especially successful in incorporating elements from soul, funk, and rhythm & blues into his combo music was Cannonball Adderley, who died in 1975. His brother, cornetist Nat Adderley, carries on this tradition with his group *Cannonball Adderley Brotherhood*.

Cannonball Adderley, of course, had his roots in Charlie Parker. Med Flory's *Supersax* from California consists of five saxophonists who play Bird's unforgettable tunes and solos harmonized, instrumented, and orchestrated – an astounding feat in terms of technique when you consider that a single sax player may have considerable problems trying to realize Parker's music. How much more difficult must this be for five saxophones together – and above all with the brilliant precision Supersax achieves! On the other hand, it must be said that this precision does produce a polished smoothness that lends a certain 'streamlined' character to Bird's music. The World Saxophone

Quartet, too, has played some of Parker's compositions. There, Bird's music truly comes to life, much more so than with Supersax, where it often seems merely reconstructed.

In all these groups, the bop character is alive; but this character has gained a new significance since the turn of the seventies which not even farsighted observers had expected. During most of the seventies it appeared as if bebop were slowly fading away. But now, suddenly, the exact opposite seemed to be occurring: bop was coming back with full force. Neo-bop of the seventies and eighties (of which we have repeatedly spoken) produced a host of new groups. Towering above them all are the combos of the great veteran tenorist *Dexter Gordon*, the initiator of this whole movement.

Electric Jazz, Jazz–Rock, Fusion

The integration of jazz and rock – long awaited, often prematurely announced during the sixties, and accomplished by Miles Davis's 'Bitches Brew' – shaped the style of the best-known (and best-selling) jazz groups of the seventies. The groups which broke ground for this development in the United States and in Britain have already been discussed in the chapter on the seventies. The outstanding jazz–rock and fusion groups of the decade were *Weather Report*, Larry Coryell's *Eleventh House*; John McLaughlin's *Mahavishnu Orchestra*; *Lifetime*, led by drummer Tony Williams; the *Gary Burton Quartet*; Chick Corea's *Return to Forever*; *Herbie Hancock*'s groups of the first half of the seventies; the *Pat Metheny Quartet*; the *Jeff Lorber Fusion*; and trumpeter Ian Carr's *Nucleus* and saxophonist Barbara Thompson's *Paraphernalia* in Britain; the *Association PC* of drummer *Pierre Courbois* and keyboard player Jasper van t'Hof's *Pork Pie* in Germany and the Netherlands; *Magma* in France; and, finally, the groups of guitarist *Volker Kriegel* and saxophonist *Klaus Doldinger* in West Germany.

In the early seventies, it was mostly former Miles Davis-players who carried forward the development beyond 'Bitches Brew'. They include soprano and tenor saxist Wayne Shorter; keyboard players Joe Zawinul, Chick Corea, and Herbie Hancock; drummers Tony Williams and Jack DeJohnette; guitarist John McLaughlin . . .

Some of the first steps in this direction – surprising in light of how little was to follow from this great musician as composer and arranger

– were taken by *Wayne Shorter* with his two albums 'Super Nova' and
'Odyssey of Iska'. Shorter is the only hornman (on tenor and soprano)
on both records; with him are guitarists, bassists, a vibraphonist,
percussionists. The 'Odyssey of Iska' is the mythical journey of a
black explorer – a Nigerian Ulysses – who becomes a symbol of the
human soul. Shorter said about the album: 'Perhaps you can relate
the enclosed [music] to the journey of your own soul.'

'Odyssey of Iska' is an impressive 'tone poem' in jazz, calling to
mind the Herbie Hancock tone poems mentioned in the piano
chapter. And, indeed, since Hancock's 'Maiden Voyage', there has
been an increasing tendency towards compositions in larger forms,
complete within themselves, towards suites and tone poems. This is
reflected, for instance, by Zappa's 'Grand Wazoo' (mentioned in the
big-band chapter) or by 'Zawinul', released around the same time as
Shorter's two records: 'Impressions of Joe Zawinul's days as a
shepherd boy in Austria . . . A tone poem reminiscent of his
grandfather's funeral on a cold winter day in an Austrian mountain
village . . . Zawinul's first impressions of New York when he arrived
here as a boy on a ship from France . . .' Three horns (flute, trumpet,
soprano sax) confront two bassists and three percussionists; and this
ensemble joins with two electric pianos – Zawinul's and Herbie
Hancock's. Miles Davis was enthusiastic.

Great things were expected from the start when Joe Zawinul and
Wayne Shorter founded the group *Weather Report* in 1971. In the first
Weather Report, Miroslav Vitous played bass and Alphonse Mouzon
drums, but elemental Mouzon and intellectual Vitous did not fit
together. During most of the seventies, the rhythm players of the
group kept changing, until a consolidation was reached towards the
end of the decade when bassist Jaco Pastorius became the most
important member of the group next to Zawinul, while Shorter no
longer seemed to function as co-leader. Shorter's friends have often
regretted that he was featured so rarely on the various Weather
Report albums in solos commensurate with his significance as an
outstanding saxophonist.

No doubt, after Miles's 'Bitches Brew' and along with John
McLaughlin's Mahavishnu Orchestra, Weather Report is the most
important and the most influential group in fusion. But again and
again, 'WR' has polarized the scene. After publishing a devastating
review of its album 'Mr Gone' in 1979, *down beat* was inundated for

months with letters from fans and adversaries of the group. The review of 'Mr Gone' said, in part: 'Weather Report has done to jazz in the seventies what Paul Whiteman did to it in the twenties . . . Like Whiteman, Weather Report has overorchestrated its sound. Where Whiteman's band made hot jazz saccharine, Weather Report has made experimentation sound processed . . . By not taking chances they have nothing to lose, but conversely they have nothing to gain . . .' This criticism was so vehemently attacked by Weather Report fans that a final evaluation of this record – perhaps not their best – seems next to impossible at this time.

Zawinul emphasizes that his Weather Report music is embedded in the tradition of jazz, above all, in bebop. One of his most successful compositions is 'Birdland', named after the famous jazz club on Broadway, which in turn was named for Charlie Parker. Around the turn of the fifties, Zawinul was in the Birdland almost daily. Twenty years later, in 1980, he said: 'The old Birdland was the most important place in my life'. He believes this to be evident in all stages of Weather Report's music. Most critics are inclined to doubt it, but in 1980 'WR' issued a new record full of bebop roots (possibly inspired by the neo-bop wave): 'Night Passage'.

Herbie Hancock (see also piano chapter) had left Miles Davis before 'Bitches Brew'. In 1972, he created the record 'Crossings' with its rich electronic instrumentation (electric piano, melotron, Moogsynthesizer), into which three horns are interwoven: Benny Maupin (soprano saxophone, alto flute, bass clarinet, piccolo), Eddie Henderson (trumpet), and Julian Priester (trombone). With his electronics and the three horns, Hancock achieved sounds reminiscent of Gil Evans's rich orchestral palette. 'Quasar', the title of one of his pieces, is representative of the music: mystical, primordial cosmic explosions, in which time seems to be standing still.

Drummer *Tony Williams* had also left Miles Davis in 1969 to devote himself more intensely to the integration of jazz and rock than seemed possible to him with Miles at the time. The different ensembles he formed under the heading of Lifetime were advanced jazz-oriented rock groups, whose integration problems Williams failed to solve – less for musical than for psychological reasons. But in Tony Williams's Lifetime, John McLaughlin gathered the tools he needed for his Mahavishnu Orchestra.

Not even Larry Young (alias Khalid Yasin) was able to realize the full potential of his organ artistry in Williams's Lifetime. Groups like Lifetime – and Weather Report and the Mahavishnu Orchestra, too – illuminate particularly well the complexity of the musical and human (and technical!) mechanisms of such groups. It is truly a stroke of luck when such organisms produce great music: a string quartet has it much easier.

The process of attrition to which jazz–rock and fusion groups are subject can also be seen in *Chick Corea*'s music. In the opinion of most critics, of the various groups he has led – at first under the name *Return to Forever* – the first of 1972 (with singer Flora Purim, percussionist Airto Moreira, saxophonist and flutist Joe Farrell, and bassist Stanley Clarke) was by far the best. It was one of the happiest, lightest products of contemporary jazz. But his later groups have also retained the playful, communicative aspect so characteristic of Corea's music.

Possibly the most dense, artistically most satisfying fusion music so far has come from guitarist *John McLaughlin*, with his *Mahavishnu Orchestra* – here, too, with the first (1971–72) of the Mahavishnu groups (with Jan Hammer, keyboards; Billy Cobham, drums; Jerry Goodman, violin; and Rick Laird, bass). Nowhere else has it been demonstrated so convincingly, what astounding, liberating, and delightful – and spiritual – effects fusion music can create.

The tunes by the first Mahavishnu Orchestra had titles like 'The Dance of the Maya', 'A Lotus on Irish Streams', 'Sapphire Bullets of Pure Love', 'Meetings of the Spirit', 'Awakening', 'Sanctuary', and 'Vital Transformation', characterizing the meditative spirit at the core of those pieces. To the strength of this meditative spirit belonged – which only seems to be a paradox – the high volume at which this music was played; it brought forth a kind of stillness precisely by virtue of being so overpowering. The Mahavishnu music created a 'cathedral of sounds' that admitted nothing but these sounds.

One negative result of the density of this music was that within a short time the musicians had worn each other out in personal and musical tensions and conflicts, causing the group to break apart. With his later Mahavishnu groups, McLaughlin never again reached the level of this first orchestra. From 1976 on, he began to appear with a new group *Shakti* (which disbanded in 1978). Shakti was a remarkable turnabout after McLaughlin's electronic 'high energy' phase. The four Shakti musicians – McLaughlin on guitar and three Indians, among them violinist L. Shankar and tabla player Zakir Hussain – played low-volume acoustic music. It was a meeting of jazz not only with the musical culture of India, but also with Indian spirituality and religiousness – at a level of perfection reached only by one other group: the cooperation between sarod master *Ali Akbar Khan* (with Ravi Shankar possibly the most famous of all living practitioners of classical Indian music) and alto saxophonist *John Handy*, who had become known through his work with Charles Mingus. Khansahib (as he is called by his students in his Ali Akbar Khan music school near San Francisco) and Handy began to play together in 1971 and took up their collaboration again in 1980–81, when South Indian violinist Dr L. Subramaniam joined their group *Rainbow*. Rainbow is especially outstanding in the intensity of its wild climaxes, while Shakti's forte was density and interplay.

Critics have perceived Shakti – after John McLaughlin's Mahavishnu music – as an 'abrupt break'. But McLaughlin's devotion to Indian music and spirituality had been obvious during his Mahavishnu phase. And above all, Shakti's music was of similar density, and as interwoven as the Mahavishnu records had been. Says McLaughlin: 'India is part of my home on this planet . . . India is a part of me, not only psychologically but also physically.' This is also indicated by the names of his two bands: Mahavishnu means 'divine compassion, power, and justice'; Shakti, 'creative intelligence, beauty, and power.'

After Shakti disbanded, it was not followed by another truly integrated McLaughlin group. At first, McLaughlin returned to electric music – with his *One Truth Band* in its different lineups. Since then, he has primarily done solo work, including acoustic duos with French guitarist Christian Escoudé and others.

The process of attrition of jazz–rock and fusion music is, in a way, a frightening development. Never before in the history of jazz has anything similar occurred. Actually, only two groups of a worthy artistic level became known during the second half of the seventies: the *Jeff Lorber Fusion* and the *Pat Metheny Group*. With its 'beautified', perfect, and somewhat polished integration, the latter is almost like a 'Modern Jazz Quartet of fusion music'. Most of the other successful groups – *Spyro Gyra* for instance – carried fusion close to disco and other commercial pop trends. They are interested in creating products for the marketplace – and so have themselves become products.

There is hope, however, in a new way of playing introduced primarily by black musicians. In an ironic reference to 'new wave' rock, guitarist James Blood Ulmer – one of its main exponents – called it 'no wave'; others refer to it as 'free funk' or even 'punk jazz'. It was born less out of speculative raves by the music business (which, however, took over immediately) than in an underground coming-together of free jazz, traditional jazz, and new-wave rock. In this field, it has primarily been *Shannon Jackson* with his *Decoding Society* who has succeeded in creating integrated combo music – by melodifying the polyrhythmic patterns of his drumming, and transferring them to the playing of his group. (More about 'no wave' and 'free funk' can be found in the chapter on the eighties.)

A DEFINITION OF JAZZ

A Definition of Jazz

The question, 'What is jazz?' calls for a dictionary and an encyclopedic answer. But a search through dictionaries and encyclopedias yields some odd examples. I was unable to find a single even halfway satisfying definition of jazz in the recognized, distinguished scientific encyclopedias.

In a strangely paradoxical way, this illustrates that the method often suggested to jazz critics as exemplary for arriving at an understanding of the phenomenon of jazz – the method of Western musicology with its entire impressive tradition – fails when it comes to jazz. Jazz can only be understood in terms of a genuine comprehension of its nature, about which jazz musicians generally are better informed than the theoreticians. All attempts at a definition from other points of view – such as European music, or, as has been repeatedly attempted since the sixties, African music – remain unsatisfactory. That is why people involved with jazz took it upon themselves to find a useful definition of jazz. These attempts also have a history, and it is worth noting that each new attempt was based on all that preceded it. Important steps in this process were taken by Marshall Stearns and the California critic Woody Woodward. Bearing in mind their definitions, and the entire preceding body of work, I should like to suggest the following definition of jazz:

Jazz is a form of art music which originated in the United States through the confrontation of blacks with European music. The instrumentation, melody, and harmony of jazz are in the main derived from Western musical tradition. Rhythm, phrasing and production of sound, and the elements of blues harmony are derived from African music and from the musical conception of the Afro-Americans. Jazz differs from European music in three basic elements, which all

serve to increase intensity:

1. A special relationship to time, defined as 'swing'.

2. A spontaneity and vitality of musical production in which improvisation plays a role.

3. A sonority and manner of phrasing which mirror the individuality of the performing jazz musician.

These three basic characteristics, whose essentials have been – and will continue to be – passed on orally from one generation to the next, create a novel climate of tension. In this climate, the emphasis is no longer on great arcs of tension, as in European music, but on a wealth of tension-creating elements, which continuously rise and fall. The various styles and stages of development through which jazz has passed since its origin around the turn of the century are largely characterized by the fact that the three basic elements of jazz temporarily achieve varying degrees of importance, and that the relationship between them is constantly changing.

For one thing, this definition stresses the fact that jazz developed in the confrontation between 'black' and 'white', and thus is neither a completely European nor a completely African concern. In connection with this, the origin of the various musical categories – melody, harmony, rhythm, sound – in such differing musical cultures as the European and the African is indicated. Occasionally, since definitions demand brevity, it has been necessary to simplify. Thus, for instance, jazz instrumentation no doubt derives from Europe; but, for example, the banjo, which took the place of the guitar in early jazz, was a black invention. And the percussion apparatus developed by jazz in the course of its evolution differs significantly from that common to European music – then and now. From the opposite point of view, similar conclusions hold true for sonority. The jazz sound, as we have shown, is largely a black creation, but at the same time there are a multitude of vocal and instrumental sounds in jazz which are familiar to European music.

In all these points, we have related our findings to what has been stated in the section on 'The Elements of Jazz'. There the three significant characteristics – swing, improvisation, jazz sound/phrasing – were arrived at. The six points at the end of the chapter on improvisation may be taken as a further interpretation of Point 2 in the definition.

The final paragraph of our definition contains a thought not present in previous definitions of jazz. A history of jazz could certainly be written from the point of view of the three jazz characteristics – swing, improvisation, and sound/phrasing – and their relation to each other. All these characteristics are important, to be sure, but their relationships change, and these changing relationships are a part of jazz evolution.

That jazz sound and jazz phrasing stand in dialectic opposition has been pointed out already. In old New Orleans jazz, phrasing still largely corresponded to European folk and circus music. On the other hand, typical jazz sonority was particularly highly developed here. Later, this kind of sonority came to be regarded as exaggerated. No major musician in any phrase of jazz has had a purely European No major musician in any phase of jazz has had a purely European music occasionally have come very close. By way of compensation, jazz phrasing has become increasingly important. Thus, modern jazz, since cool jazz, is as far removed from European music in terms of phrasing as old jazz was in terms of sonority.

In their extremes, jazz phrasing and jazz sonority seem mutually exclusive. Where jazz sonority is at its strongest – for example, in the 'jungle' solos of Tricky Sam Nanton, Bubber Miley, or Cootie Williams with Duke Ellington's band – jazz phrasing stops. The 'jungle' sound dictates the phrasing, and this sound exists for its own sake – beyond jazz phrasing. On the other hand, where jazz phrasing appears at its most highly cultivated stage – as in the tenor improvisations of Stan Getz, the flute solos of Hubert Laws, or the alto lines of the Lee Konitz of the fifties – jazz sonority seems largely suspended. The musical proceedings are so unilaterally dictated by the phrasing that it does not appear possible to produce sounds which have an expressive meaning outside the flow of the phrase.

A similar, if not quite so precise, relationship exists between swing and improvisation. Both are factors of spontaneity. Thus it may come about that when spontaneity is expressed in the extreme through the medium of swing, improvisation will recede. Even when a record by Count Basie's band does not contain a single improvised solo, no one questions its jazz character. On the other hand, when improvisation is given too free a rein, swing recedes, as in many unaccompanied solos or in some free-jazz recordings. This suppression of swing by freedom is already illustrated by the very first totally 'free' record in jazz history – Lennie Tristano's 'Intuition'.

Thus the relationships among the elements of jazz change constantly. In the thirties, when sonority in terms of New Orleans jazz had already receded and fluent phrasing in terms of modern jazz had not as yet been fully developed, swing celebrated such unquestioned victories that swing – the element – and Swing – the style – were not even differentiated in terminology. There have always been forms of jazz which seek to project the jazz essence into a single element of jazz. The ragtime pianists had swing, but neither improvisation nor jazz sonority. The early New Orleans bands did have jazz sonority, but they had more march rhythm than swing, and a form of collective improvisation which sooner or later led to ever-repeated head arrangements. In the realm of Swing style there is a kind of big-band music in which improvisation, sonority, and sometimes even phrasing largely take a back seat – and yet it swings marvellously. During the fifties Jimmy Giuffre often projected the whole jazz essence into a single Lester Young-inspired phrase. On the other hand – as is made clear by just these 'exceptional examples' – at the real peaks of jazz, all three jazz elements are present simultaneously, if in varying relationship to one another: from Louis Armstrong and Jimmy Harrison through Coleman Hawkins and Lester Young to Charlie Parker, Miles Davis, and John Coltrane.

It is important to note, too, that swing, improvisation, and sonority (or phrasing) are elements of intensity. As much as they may differ from each other, just so much do they concur in creating intensity.

Swing creates intensity through friction and superimposition of the levels of time.

Improvisation creates intensity through the fact that the road from musician to sound is shorter and more direct than in any other type of musical production.

In sonority and phrasing, intensity is produced by the immediacy and directness with which a particular human personality is projected into sound.

It may thus be assumed that the main task and real meaning of the basic jazz elements rest in the creation of structured intensity. This understanding is also contained in free jazz with its ecstatic heat, as idiosyncratic as the interpretation of the three basic elements in this music may often appear.

In all these differentiations the question of quality – stature – is decisive. One might almost be tempted to adopt it as a fourth 'element of jazz' within our definition (implicitly it is included, in any case, through the word 'art' in the first sentence of the definition). If, for example, Stan Kenton or Keith Jarrett has found a place in jazz – a place that was perhaps disputed at some points of their development, but nevertheless basically is accepted – this is due to the quality and stature of their music, which are indisputable, even though much might be said against these two musicians in terms of jazz essentials. Moreover, this point similarly applies to the European – or to any other – musical culture. Even if it were possible to give a precise definition of what 'classical' music is, a music which contained all the elements of this definition and yet lacked the stature – the quality – of the great classical works would still not be 'classical'.

It is important in this context to discuss some thoughts which were developed – as far as I know, for the first time – by the American writer and scholar Robert M. Pirsig. Pirsig (in his book *Zen and the Art of Motorcycle Maintenance*) has shown that definitions are 'square', because quality is defined 'entirely outside the analytic process'. Thus the aspect of quality, necessarily, is excluded from any attempt at definition. Pirsig: 'When you subtract quality you get squareness.'

Jazz fans may feel that such considerations are too intellectual, and yet they explain why we who belong to the jazz world are left strangely dissatisfied with any definition (including the one I have proposed). Jazz scholars may develop ever more extensive and refined definitions, but the real point eludes them: indeed, it *must* necessarily elude them, for reasons which Pirsig has shown (more extensively than can be summarized here). What remains excluded from the range of the definition musicians know better than all scholars. We have quoted Fats Waller before: 'It's not *what* you play, but *how* you play it.'

Pirsig says: *Any* definition is unsatisfactory, because quality cannot be defined. The term 'square' – and its antonym 'hip' – come from the language of jazz. Jazz is 'hip music'. But the aspect of the 'hip' (as Norman Mailer has shown in his important study 'The White Hipster') eludes language. That is why it applies to jazz, more so than to other fields, that definitions can only fulfil a demand for approximation – no more.

This state of affairs explains why thousands of cocktail, pop, and rock groups all over the world play a kind of music which might fulfil all – or almost all – requirements of our definition (and of all the other jazz definitions to date), and which yet cannot be called jazz. In countless 'commercial' groups, there *also* is improvisation, sometimes even jazz phrasing and jazz sounds; they often even swing – and yet their music is not jazz. On the other hand, as we have shown, with genuine jazz musicians the presence of only *one* element of 'jazzness' is often sufficient to insure the jazz character of their music.

It is necessary to understand this: Jazz has to do with quality. Quality is felt rather than rationally comprehended. This has been realized subconsciously by musicians for as long as jazz has existed. For them music has to be first and foremost 'good' to be perceived as jazz. All other criteria play a secondary role, however important they may be.

There is another fact which must be considered in this context. The constant use of the elements, styles, musicianship, techniques, and ideas of jazz in commercial music forces the jazz musician unceasingly to create something new. In this sense André Hodeir remarked that today's innovation is tomorrow's cliché.

The flair for the cliché, however, is not only connected with the abuses of jazz in commercial music; it lies in the nature of jazz itself. Almost every blues strophe has been turned into a cliché. All the famous blues lines exist as ever-recurring 'entities': 'I've been drinkin' muddy water, sleepin' in a hollow log . . .' 'My baby treats me like a low-down dog . . .,' 'Broke and hungry, ragged and dirty too . . .,' ''cause the world is all wrong . . .,' 'But the meanest blues I ever had . . .,' 'I'm just as lonely, lonely as a man can be . . .,' 'Can't eat, can't sleep . . .,' 'I wanna hold you, baby, hold you in my arms again . . .,' 'I'm gonna buy myself a shotgun . . .,' 'Take me back, baby . . .,' 'I love you, baby, but you sure don't treat me right . . .' – and so forth. The great blues singers used them as they pleased, taking a line from here and another from there, adapting them to each other, and often not even that.

What holds true for the lyrics also applies to the music. When Jimmy Smith or Horace Silver records a blues, both the arrangement and the improvised solos are saturated with structural elements from half a century of blues history. Everything played by the modern bop musicians is saturated with elements from Charlie Parker records which, though not in themselves clichés, certainly lend themselves to cliché-making. Or, to reach back into jazz tradition: in every third or fourth blues by Bessie Smith one hears phrases, or even entire lines, which might just as easily have been heard in other contexts from other blues singers. Every boogie consists of nothing but a constantly changing montage of 'entities' made up of ostinatos and largely standardized melodic phrases. Almost every improvised break on old records by the Hot Five or Hot Seven, by Johnny Dodds or King Oliver, by Jimmie Noone or Kid Ory, is mutually interchangeable. So are the breaks which set off the four-bar blues phrases from each other – whether they be played by singers accompanying themselves on the guitar or by the most famous of jazz musicians. There are half a hundred – perhaps not even that many – 'model breaks' from which all others are derived.

The further one goes back, the more apparent this model character becomes. What Marshall Stearns, Alan Lomax, and Alfons Dauer discovered of African elements in jazz consists almost without exception of such connective models and 'entities'; they were not only taken over from African music as 'entities' but often had this character within African music itself. Their model nature is so compact that they have survived through centuries almost without changing. Consider the tango: the rhythm was brought by the slaves from Africa, and today it exists in African folklore as much as in the great Argentinian tango tradition, in temperamental folk dances, lasciviously slow dance and bar music, in boogie-woogie basses, and in hundreds of intermittent stages. Everywhere there is the identical ostinato figure – the model with its tendency towards the cliché.

All jazz consists of such 'models'. They are fragments – such as the downward-descending lines of old blues or modern 'funk' – which have something of the aura of the words with which fairy tales begin: 'Once upon a time . . .' This, too, is a model element. And as it is in the fairy tales, where elements-turned-symbols become content, so it is in jazz: the evil witch casts a spell on the noble prince, and hard-hearted king turns soft when he catches sight of the lovely shepherdess, and at last prince and shepherdess find each other and the shepherdess turns out to be a bewitched princess – witch and prince, magic and hardheartedness, king and shepherdess . . . all of these are elements of motives which can be joined together in inexhaustible combinations.

While Western concert music in the process of its ever-increasing tendency towards abstraction has lost almost all the old models and entities; while there is hardly a structural and formal element that has not been questioned – theme and variation, the sonata form, the triad – while we now long for the attainment of new and connective models and elements in concert music, and can only attain them by taking up once again the old models and elements which in the meantime have become questionable; and while in doing this we are historicizing – meanwhile, all these things are present in jazz in the most natural, self-evident, and living way.

Model, element, entity, cliché, may coincide – literally and note for note. But as model, as element, and as entity they have meaning; as cliché they are meaningless. But *since* they can coincide there is a constant tendency towards the cliché inherent in the models, elements, and entities. To a great extent, it is on the basis of this tendency that jazz constantly renews itself. The most fascinating thing about jazz is its aliveness. Jazz runs counter to all academicism – that very academicism which has made great European music the exclusive concern of the well-bred bourgeoisie.

The aliveness of jazz is such that standards are constantly overthrown – even where the old models and entities remain relevant. This complicates the position of jazz criticism. It has been reproached for being without standards.

In reality, it is remarkable that jazz criticism has so many standards. Often the evolution of jazz proceeds so rapidly that the kind of standards arrived at in European music – frequently formed one or two generations after the particular music has been alive – are meaningless. Jazz standards without flexibility tend to acquire violent and intolerant aspects.

We insist: The point is not to define standards and to test an art form against them; the point is to have the art and constantly reorient the standards in its image. Since this is inconvenient, one attempts to avoid it – within and outside of jazz. But it is above all jazz, as a music of revolt against all that is too convenient, which can demand of its listeners that they revise standards valid years ago and be prepared to discover new norms.

Nearly one hundred years after it began, jazz is still what it was then: a music of protest – that, too, contributes to its aliveness. It cries out against social and racial and spiritual discrimination, against the clichés of picayune bourgeois morality, against the functional organization of modern mass society, against the depersonalization inherent in this society, and against that categorization of standards which leads to the automatic passing of judgements wherever these standards are not met.

Many American musicians, particularly blacks, understand protest as a matter of race. No doubt it is that. But their music would not have been understood all over the world, and it would not have received almost immediate acceptance by musicians of all races, colours and political systems, if the racial aspect were the crucial factor. Here as elsewhere the racial element of jazz has long transcended itself and become universal. It has become part of the world-wide protest against a domination-oriented society, which is perceived as a threat by millions of cultured people in all fields all over the world in every country and social system – in short, by those who are shaping the judgement to be passed on our epoch by future generations: a threat not only to themselves and their creative productivity but to essential human dignity and worth.

POSTSCRIPT

Postscript

I

It has been my aim, in all the editions of this book, to show the *whole* range of jazz – from ragtime and New Orleans until today. Thus the span covering everything to be presented had to be stretched wider and wider: The first edition of 1953 dealt with forty years; this one covers a century. Frequently, as I was writing, I had to ask myself: How many readers can appreciate the music of Jelly Roll Morton as well as the sounds of Weather Report?

Mainly with this in mind, I have radically shortened some sections. From the chapters on the instruments of jazz, quite a few musicians' names have been eliminated – not only players from the old days, but also rock musicians (if they have no relevance to today's jazz). This self-limitation was also forced upon me by the sheer quantity of material on the one hand, and by the available number of pages on the other.

In many instances, it was painful to mention important musicians only briefly or summarily – as in the many groupings of soprano and tenor saxophone players, pianists, and guitarists. Today's scene in these fields has become so broad that anything more than a listing of names often has been impossible.

Another problem is that of language: In the older styles, almost every musician stands by himself, as more or less independent of his colleagues. Consider this: There were fewer musicians playing *all* instruments used in the Chicago style of the twenties than there are players of a *single* instrument in some of today's styles – as, for instance, tenor saxophonists in the Coltrane tradition. Language cannot possibly differentiate them all. The basic problem of music criticism and literature is that music is more differentiated than language. As Mendelssohn, the great romantic composer, saw in the early nineteenth century, it is difficult to write about music – not because music is vague, but because it is more precise than words.

Many players belong to more than one category. Musicians change and develop. Still, most of them can be introduced under only one heading, in order to keep the flood of names and facts manageable. This bothers me especially in the chapters about tenor saxophone and piano, where countless musicians had to be dealt with. But I see no way out of this dilemma. Criticism and historiography are not possible without generalizations. Egon Friedell, the eminent Austrian cultural historian, once said: 'All classifications made by man are arbitrary, artificial, and false. But an equally simple consideration shows that these classifications are useful and indispensable; and above all, that they are unavoidable because they correspond to an innate tendency in our way of thinking.'

Any musician mentioned in the instrument section of this book is necessarily seen at a particular point of development. In reality, however, a human life is not a point but a line, leading from a starting point by way of many further points to an end point – in other words, a sequence of countless points. What can be described, however, is in most cases nothing more than a single 'point': a single playing style, a specific grouping into which the player is categorized. It has been my aim to place him in the grouping where a majority of critics perceive him – and above all (and ideally) where the musician sees himself.

II

It is important to transmit an impression of the totality and unity of jazz. That is why all the fanaticism and sectarianism which the followers of different jazz styles have approached each other with had to be avoided. I, too, have been made aware that they are still at it. Stanley Dance, the senior critic I have always especially admired, complained that the 1973 edition of this book contained rock musicians like Janis Joplin, Frank Zappa, the Allman Brothers, Cream, Julie Driscoll-Tippetts (today clearly a jazz musician), Jimi Hendrix, Nina Simone, and Soft Machine. Younger critics, on the other hand, particularly praised this feature as a strong point of the book. It is always difficult to find the right middle path.

Someone who writes things like 'Eclecticism with taste', forgets that jazz is by nature an eclectic music – and has been so from the start. Jazz would never have come into existence without eclecticism. The basic point is this: As in almost all other art forms, the difference between 'purity' and 'eclecticism' is the simple fact that purity existed so far back in the past that one tends to forget how eclectic it once was.

Of course we have a different attitude towards rock in today's jazz world than in the early seventies. When rock music still was more creative, there were more rock players of interest to the jazz world than today. (Not just a subjective opinion: The Rolling Stones' Mick Jagger, a man who should know about this kind of thing, feels that rock 'n' roll has become 'only recycled past.')

Rock is unthinkable without jazz (because jazz – and black music in general – is the main source of rock), but jazz is thinkable without rock. There are a hundred times more jazz musicians who have influenced the rock scene than rock players who have had an influence on the jazz scene. To be sure, the latter do exist: Contemporary guitar playing cannot be conceived of without rock star Jimi Hendrix, neither can contemporary bass playing be imagined without rock bassist Larry Graham. To an extent, the same seems true also of certain drum patterns of jazz–rock and fusion music; however, in the final analysis they do not stem from rock but from blues and rhythm & blues, from funk and soul and the music of the black ghettos. On the other hand, there can be no doubt that within the realm of rock – if you can apply that kind of category here – Frank Zappa has formed more convincing and artistically more demanding large ensembles than those of the so-called fusion scene. So Zappa and Hendrix and Graham are the kind of rock musicians who belong in this book – as, on the other hand, do Johnny Dodds and Jimmie Noone, King Oliver and Jelly Roll Morton.

III

I have deleted the chapter on European jazz: European musicians no longer need to be consigned to a 'ghetto'. The most important of them – and *only* those, the creative ones – are part of today's universal scene. That means that they are included in the chapters pertaining to their instruments. Only those Europeans (and Japanese) are mentioned who in the opinion of this author (which of course is relative: it is only *one* opinion among others) meet the high standards of American jazz upon which the concept of this book is based. Even in view of the great advances in European and Japanese jazz since the sixties one should not forget that the pathbreaking and style-setting musicians still come from America. And there are no indications that this will change in the foreseeable future.

For this writer – as for most non-Americans who love jazz and write about it – jazz has become a world music. It is American and it is universal – which only seems to be a contradiction. You must have roots in order to be universal. Mozart and Haydn, Schubert and Strauss, Schoenberg and Webern, are as Viennese as can be – and yet they are universal.

That is how I've tried to see jazz: as American – that's why 90 per cent of the musicians in this book are Americans – and as universal; that's why the few creative musicians from Europe and Japan, from Brazil and Africa I've included are dealt with on equal terms.

In fact, the term 'world music' applies to jazz more than to anything else played today. (Of course, this term, as used in this book, always implies an artistic level). Americans should be more aware – and prouder – of the fact that they have created the true world music of the twentieth century.

IV

The question has been raised: Why does this book about jazz come from Germany? To be quite honest, I don't know. Like many Germans, I have my difficulties with my country. But the question, at least in the United States, is not so much, why this book comes from Germany, but rather: Why does it come from Europe? And that is a question I think I can answer.

As much as jazz comes from America, jazz literature and jazz criticism are unthinkable without Europe. The first serious evaluation of jazz came from the Swiss conductor Ernest Ansermet, in 1919. The first book on jazz was written by a Belgian, Robert Goffin, in 1932. The first jazz magazine was edited by a Frenchman, Hughes

Panassié, starting in the late twenties. And the first jazz discography was also compiled by a Frenchman, Charles Delaunay, from 1936 on. At the time, jazz was already accepted as a serious art form by many of Europe's intellectuals. Great European artists, from Hindemith to Stravinsky and from Picasso to Matisse, had already dealt with jazz and paid tribute to it in their works. In its homeland, however, jazz was then – and for quite some time to come – seen as some sort of circus music. In fact, even in 1976, at the huge conference 'The United States in the World' (organized in Washington, DC, as part of the American bicentennial activities), scientists, artists, writers, and intellectuals from Poland, Hungary, France, Germany, India, Thailand, and Japan supported my thesis that jazz is America's most important contribution to world culture. The participating Americans bluntly denied it!

In 1965, when John Coltrane won his first *down beat* Critics' Poll, the principal jazz poll of leading critics from all over the world, he was ranked in the top spot by 64 per cent of the European critics, but only by 32 per cent of the Americans. In fact, the Europeans had been giving him their votes for years, but had been outvoted by their American colleagues. A few years later, in the late sixties, European critics were the first to point out that the musicians of the Chicago AACM, the Association for the Advancement of Creative Musicians, were taking the crucial steps in the further development of the music. In America, this realization came years later. And only in the late seventies, ten years after that, did a respectable number of AACM musicians win polls in the United States. Albert Ayler, Cecil Taylor, Eric Dolphy, Ornette Coleman, Chick Corea, Lester Bowie, Joseph Jarman, Roscoe Mitchell, Anthony Braxton, were stars in Europe before American media even started mentioning them.

The world's largest jazz magazine is not, as one would expect, an American publication but Japanese: *Swing Journal*, published in Tokyo – followed by *Jazz Forum*, the magazine of the International Jazz Federation, which is published in Warsaw, Poland.

When John McLaughlin went to the United States in 1969, he said: 'There is only one place where it's all happening: New York.' That certainly is true. But seven years later, the same John McLaughlin decided to live in Paris, and now he said: 'The Americans still haven't realized that jazz is an art. The Europeans have understood that. For the Americans, jazz only means business.

In America the record industry does to the musicians what it wants.'

And it also is a fact that three of America's leading jazz critics, Leonard Feather, Dan Morgenstern, and Stanley Dance, were born in Europe.

V

Some critics – Barry Tepperman in Canada, for instance (to whom I am indebted for suggestions and corrections) – have pointed out that the totality of jazz today has become too broad to fit between the covers of a single book. He said that the weaknesses of my book were 'generic problems', founded in 'the nature of work, and not the author'. I have to accept that point of view.

Musicians, on the other hand – and I note this with gratitude – have been favourably inclined towards this book from the beginning. The 'musician teachers' among them have been using it in their classrooms at colleges and universities – from Marion Brown in Atlanta to Richard Davis at the University of Wisconsin, from Anthony Davis at Yale to John Handy in San Francisco.

Creative artists have always seen the main function of the critic not as criticizing but as describing the situation and helping to make it understood. I have always felt this to be my principal goal. Certainly this book is filled with criticism – in literally hundreds of cases, from Mezz Mezzrow to Dave Brubeck and on to Keith Jarrett. But I believe that attempting to arrive at a personal critical judgement on each musician mentioned would mean nothing less than totally overestimating the job of the critic. It would show the critic in the light in which musicians (and other artists) have seen him ever since (jazz) criticism came into existence: as a know-it-all schoolmaster.

The aim of this book has been to present only facts in accordance with the present internationally accepted position of jazz criticism and scholarship. The many 'side theories' were not dealt with. My own theories are clearly identified as such; this applies especially to the swing phenomenon and to the definition of jazz, as well as to some thoughts on improvisation, the shift of sound production towards phrasing, the problem of tension in jazz, the development of the drums, and to certain opinions about jazz–rock and fusion music.

VI

The various editions of this book have been published in sixteen languages, and altogether more than one million copies have been printed. It was only natural that criticism and suggestions should have come from all sides. Much of it has found its way into this book, for which I am thankful. I am especially grateful to my translators, Helmut and Barbara Bredigkeit and – in Japan – Shoichi Yui, as well as to Dan Morgenstern in the United States, without whom this edition would not exist.

Of necessity, a book like this draws on works which preceded it. I am especially indebted to Leonard Feather's *Encyclopedia of Jazz* (Quartet Books, London); to André Hodeir's *Jazz – Its Evolution and Essence* (Da Capo); to the two anthologies by Nat Shapiro and Nat Hentoff, *Hear Me Talkin' to Ya* (Dover) and *The Jazz Makers* (Rinehart & Company, Inc, New York); to Charles Keil's *Urban Blues* (University of Chicago Press); and to John Storm Roberts's *The Latin Tinge* (Oxford University Press). Information not taken from these works for which a source is not specifically mentioned comes from articles in the jazz magazines *down beat* (USA), *Melody Maker* (Great Britain), *Jazz Hot* and *Jazz Magazine* (France), *Jazz Podium* (Germany), and *Jazz Forum* (edited in Poland) – and, above all, from the source which still is (and should be) the most important for a jazz critic: personal contact with musicians.

It is the musicians to whom I owe gratitude first and foremost – for literally thousands of hours of conversations, for years of good relationships with many, for friendship with some, and above all: for their music. It is important to me to close this book with this word of gratitude.

J.E.B.

DISCOGRAPHY
by
Brian Priestley

A Jazz Discography
by Brian Priestley

The reason why this is 'A Jazz Discography' rather than 'The Jazz Discography' is, quite simply, the apparent impossibility of recommending everything one would like to recommend.

There was a brief moment near the end of the 1970s when it seemed that all the important jazz records ever made had been recently reissued. Since then, on the one hand some classics and near-classics at that time hard to obtain have reappeared (e.g. Coltrane's 'A Love Supreme' or John McLaughlin's 'My Goal's Beyond') but many more of the essential reissues which came out in the last decade have now been withdrawn, not only here but in the countries from which they could be imported.

Because this discography is intended to be of immediate practical use in conjunction with the rest of the book, everything known to be definitely unavailable has been omitted. (This, regrettably, does not preclude items listed here also becoming unavailable in the near future.) The only exceptions to this rule are a few of the albums on the Prestige, Blue Note and MPS labels, some of the last-named produced by Joachim Berendt himself, since these series are undergoing selective re-importation at the time of writing (and, except in the case of Prestige, under the original catalogue numbers).

The basic criterion for inclusion in this listing, apart from availability, is of course a favourable mention of the artist in the text. In the case of non-American musicians, only those with a substantial reputation outside their own land have been mentioned, and it is hoped that this judgement is not deemed too selective. In a great number of cases, I am indebted to the work of Werner Wunderlich, jazz presenter on Südwestfunk, who compiled the discography for the German edition of the book.

I am also grateful for the assistance of friends who work in jazz record shops, notably Pete Fincham, Graham Griffiths and Tony Middleton. The benefit to the reader of using specialist dealers, either by personal visit or by mail, can hardly be emphasized too strongly. If any of the numbers, album titles, etc., that I have given change (which is not impossible) or if sudden unavailability makes secondary choices necessary (which is all too likely), the specialist shop will be able to help while the general shop will probably not have a clue.

JOHN ABERCROMBIE (g)
  'M' (1980)   ECM 1191
  'Five Years After' (1981, with Ralph Towner)   ECM 1207
  See also Jack DeJohnette, Collin Walcott.
MUHAL RICHARD ABRAMS (p)
  'Spihumonesty' (1979, with George Lewis, Roscoe Mitchell a.o.)
                                                  Black Saint BSR 0032

GEORGE ADAMS (ts)
  'Don't Lose Control' (1979 with Don Pullen, Dannie Richmond a.o.)
                                                    Soul Note SN 1004

  See also Gil Evans, Hannibal Marvin Peterson.
PEPPER ADAMS (bars)
  'Twelfth & Pingree' (1975)   Enja 2060
  See also Donald Byrd, Thad Jones, Thelonious Monk.
CANNONBALL ADDERLEY (as)
  'Somethin' Else' (1958, with Art Blakey, Miles Davis, Hank Jones)
                                                  Blue Note BST 81595
  'Phenix' (1974, with George Duke, Airto Moreira a.o.)
                                                  Fantasy 5995 (2 LP)

  See also Miles Davis, Milt Jackson.
AIR (group): '80° Below 82' (1982, with Henry Threadgill)
                                                    Antilles AN 1007

TOSHIKO AKIYOSHI (p)
  'Sumi-e' (1979, with big band incl. Lew Tabackin a.o.)
                                                    RCA PL 37537

RASHIED ALI (d, perc)
  See John Coltrane
RED ALLEN (tp)
  See Sidney Bechet, Fletcher Henderson.
LAURINDO ALMEIDA (g)
  'L.A.4 Live in Montreux' (1979, with Ray Brown, Bud Shank)
                                                    Concord CJ 100

  See also Stan Kenton
BARRY ALTSCHUL (d)
  'Another Time Another Place' (1978, with Arthur Blythe, Anthony Davis,
    Dave Holland, Abdul Wadud a.o.)   Muse MR 5176
  See also Chick Corea.
ALBERT AMMONS (p)
  'Boogie Woogie and the Blues' (1944, with Don Byas, Sid Catlett, Vic
    Dickenson a.o.)   London 6.24297
GENE AMMONS (ts)
  'Ammons/Stitt' (1961, with Sonny Stitt)   Reactivation JR 150
  See also Woody Herman.
RAY ANDERSON (tb)
  'Harrisburg Half Life' (1980)   Moers Music 01074
LOUIS ARMSTRONG (tp, vcl)
  'Louis Armstrong Memorial' (1926–56, with Barney Bigard, Baby Dodds,

Johnny Dodds, Edmond Hall, Earl Hines, Albert Nicholas, Kid Ory a.o.)
CBS 66247 (2 LP)

'Satchmo at Symphony Hall' (1947, with Barney Bigard, Sid Catlett, Jack Teagarden a.o.) MCA 510.047

'Ella and Louis Again, vol 1' (1957, with Louis Bellson, Ray Brown, Herb Ellis, Ella Fitzgerald, Oscar Peterson) Verve 2304.501

See also Fletcher Henderson, King Oliver, Bessie Smith.

ART ENSEMBLE OF CHICAGO (group)

'Urban Bushmen' (1980, with Lester Bowie, Joseph Jarman, Roscoe Mitchell a.o.) ECM 1211/12 (2 LP)

ALBERT AYLER (ts)

'Great Moments with Albert Ayler' (1965-7)

MCA 2-4129 (2 LP)

DEREK BAILEY (g)

'Aida' (1980) Incus 40

See also London Jazz Composers Orchestra

CHET BAKER (tp)

'Live in Europe' (1956) Jazz Anthology JA 5240

'Daybreak' (1979, with N.-H. Ørsted Pedersen)

SteepleChase SCS 1142

See also Gerry Mulligan.

GATO BARBIERI (ts)

'Alive in New York' (1975, with Ron Carter a.o.) Jasmine JAS 54

See also Carla Bley, Charlie Haden.

COUNT BASIE (p, org)

'The Best of Count Basie' (1937-9, with Buck Clayton, Harry Edison, Jo Jones, Jimmy Rushing, Dicky Wells, Lester Young a.o.)

MCA 2-4062 (2 LP)

'Sixteen Men Swinging' (1953-4, with Frank Foster, Thad Jones, Joe Newman, Frank Wess a.o.) Verve 2610.040 (2 LP)

See also Benny Goodman, Lester Young.

BILLY BAUER (g)

See Woody Herman, Lee Konitz.

SIDNEY BECHET (ss, cl)

'The Complete Sidney Bechet, vols 1/2' (1932-41, with Red Allen, Sid Catlett, Kenny Clarke, Baby Dodds, Earl Hines, Tommy Ladnier, Mezz Mezzrow, Rex Stewart a.o.) RCA PM 42409 (2 LP)

'Le Grand Album de Sidney Bechet' (1945-7, with Sid Catlett, Pops Foster, Mezz Mezzrow a.o.) Festival ALB 139 (2 LP)

GORDON BECK (p, synth)

'French Connection 2' (1982) JMS 2473. 959

See also Didier Lockwood, Phil Woods.

BIX BEIDERBECKE (co)

'The Bix Beiderbecke Story' (1927-9, with Eddie Lang, Pee Wee Russell, Joe Venuti a.o.) CBS 66367 (2 LP)

LOUIE BELLSON (d)
   'London Scene' (1980, with big band)   Concord CJ 157
   See also Louis Armstrong, Ella Fitzgerald, Art Tatum.
HAN BENNINK (d)
   See Peter Brötzmann.
GEORGE BENSON (g)
   'George Benson' (1971-5, with Ron Carter, Billy Cobham, Jack
      DeJohnette, David Friedman, Herbie Hancock, Airto Moreira a.o.)
                                         CTI 43.002
   See also Jimmy Smith.
KARL BERGER (vib, p)
   'Woodstock Workshop Orchestra' (1979, with Don Cherry, Leroy
      Jenkins, Lee Konitz, Oliver Lake, George Lewis a.o.)
                                     MPS 68.250
   See also Carla Bley, Don Cherry.
BUNNY BERIGAN (tp)
   See Tommy Dorsey.
CHU BERRY (ts)
   'A Giant of the Tenor Sax' (1938-41, with Sid Catlett, Roy Eldridge a.o.)
                                  London 6. 24293
   See also Lionel Hampton.
BARNEY BIGARD (cl, ts)
   See Louis Armstrong, Benny Carter, Duke Ellington, Jelly Roll
      Morton.
ED BLACKWELL (d)
   See Anthony Braxton, Ornette Coleman, Eric Dolphy, Old and New
      Dreams.
ART BLAKEY (d)
   'Kings of Drums' (1938-62, with Kenny Clark, Lionel Hampton, Jo Jones,
      Gene Krupa, Buddy Rich, Max Roach a.o.)   CBS 88136 (2 LP)
   'Au Théâtre des Champs-Elysées' (1959, with Lee Morgan, Wayne
      Shorter a.o.)   RCA PM 37451
   See also Cannonball Adderley, Benny Golson, Milt Jackson, Thelonious
      Monk, Fats Navarro, Charlie Parker, Horace Silver.
JIMMY BLANTON (b)
   See Duke Ellington.
CARLA BLEY (p, org)
   'Escalator over the Hill' (1968-71, with Gato Barbieri, Karl Berger, Don
      Cherry, Charlie Haden, Leroy Jenkins, John McLaughlin, Dewey
      Redman, Perry Robinson, Roswell Rudd a.o.)
                        Virgin 3LP-EOTH (3 LP)
   'Social Studies' (1980, with Steve Swallow a.o.)   Watt 11
   See also Charlie Haden.
HAMIET BLUIETT (bars)
   See Lester Bowie, World Saxophone Quartet.
ARTHUR BLYTHE (as)
   'Blythe Spirit' (1980, with Abdul Wadud a.o.)   CBS 85194
   See also Barry Altschul, Jack DeJohnette, Gil Evans.

FRANCY BOLAND (p)
See Kenny Clarke.
LESTER BOWIE (tp)
'The Great Pretender' (1981, with Hamiet Bluiett a.o.) ECM 1209
See also Art Ensemble of Chicago, Jack DeJohnette.
JOANNE BRACKEEN (p)
'Mythical Magic' (1978) MPS 68. 211
See also Stan Getz.
DOLLAR BRAND (ABDULLAH IBRAHIM) (p)
'Ode to Duke Ellington' (1973) Philips 6385.656
'Africa – Tears and Laughter' (1979) Enja 3039
ANTHONY BRAXTON (saxes, cl)
'Elements of Surprise' (1976, with George Lewis)
  Moers Music 01036
'Six Compositions: Quartet' (1981, with Ed Blackwell, Anthony
  Davis) Antilles AN1005
See also Chick Corea, Jack DeJohnette, Max Roach.
WILLEM BREUKER (saxes, cl)
'The European Scene – Live at the Donaueschingen Music Festival' (1975)
  MPS 68.168
BOB BROOKMEYER (tb)
'Composer/Arranger' (1980, with Mel Lewis big band, Clark Terry)
  Rhapsody RHAP 11
See also Gerry Mulligan.
BIG BILL BROONZY (vcl, g)
'If You're Black Get Back' (1956) Storyville 6.23703
PETER BRÖTZMANN (saxes, cl)
'Ein halber Hund kann nicht pinkeln' (1977, with Han Bennink)
  FMP 0420
See also Globe Unity Orchestra.
CLIFFORD BROWN (tp)
'Pure Genius, vol 1' (1956, with Max Roach, Sonny Rollins a.o.)
  Elektra/Musician MUSK 52.388
See also Sonny Rollins.
RAY BROWN (b)
'Tasty' (1979, with Jimmy Rowles) Concord CJ 122
See also Laurindo Almeida, Louis Armstrong, Dizzy Gillespie, Coleman
  Hawkins, Illinois Jacquet, Barney Kessel, Howard McGhee, Oscar
  Peterson, Stuff Smith, Ben Webster, Lester Young.
DAVE BRUBECK (p)
'Dave Brubeck Quartet at Carnegie Hall' (1963, with Paul Desmond a.o.)
  CBS 66234 (2 LP)
'We're All Together Again For The First Time' (1972, with Paul Desmond,
  Gerry Mulligan a.o.) Atlantic ATL40489
MILT BUCKNER (p, org)
'Milt Buckner Chordpunch' (1966–70, with Jo Jones a.o.)
  MPS 88.017 (2 LP)
See also Lionel Hampton.

KENNY BURRELL (g)
   'Guitar Forms' (1964-5, with Gil Evans a.o.)   Verve 2304.158
   'Ellington is Forever' (1975, with Joe Henderson, Thad Jones, Jimmy
      Smith a.o.)   Fantasy 68.520 (2 LP)
GARY BURTON (vib)
   'Country Roads' (1968, with Roy Haynes, Steve Swallow a.o.)
                         RCA PL45139
   'Easy as Pie' (1980, with Steve Swallow a.o.)   ECM 1184
   See also Chick Corea.
JAKI BYARD (p)
   See Booker Ervin, Rahsaan Roland Kirk, Charles Mingus.
DON BYAS (ts)
   'Two Kings of the Tenor Sax' (1944-5, with Sid Catlett, Ben Webster a.o.)
                        London 6.24058
   See also Albert Ammons, Charlie Christian, Dizzy Gillespie.
CHARLIE BYRD (g)
   'Blues Sonata' (1961)   Riverside 68.910
   See also Woody Herman.
DONALD BYRD (tp)
   'Hip-intertainment, vol 1' (1961, with Pepper Adams, Herbie Hancock a.o.)
                        VGM 0002
   See also Thelonious Monk, Sonny Rollins.

CAB CALLOWAY (vcl)
   'Minnie the Moocher' (1933-4, with big band)   RCA INT 5121
HARRY CARNEY (bars)
   See Duke Ellington, Benny Goodman, Lionel Hampton.
IAN CARR (tp)
   'Awakening' (1980, with Nucleus)   Mood 24000
   See also United Jazz & Rock Ensemble.
BENNY CARTER (as, tp)
   'Jazz Off the Air, vol 3' (1944-7, with Barney Bigard, Miles Davis, Dexter
      Gordon, J. J. Johnson, Max Roach, Rex Stewart a.o.) Spotlite SPJ 147
   'Further Definitions' (1961, with Jimmy Garrison, Coleman Hawkins, Phil
      Woods a.o.)   Jasmine JAS 14
   See also Lionel Hampton, Coleman Hawkins, Fletcher Henderson,
      Art Tatum, Chick Webb.
BETTY CARTER (vcl)
   'Betty Carter' (1970)   Bet-Car MK 1001
JOHN CARTER (cl)
   See Clarinet Summit.
RON CARTER (b)
   'Magic' (1961, with Eric Dolphy, Mal Waldron a.o.)
                        Prestige (2 LP)
   See also Gato Barbieri, George Benson, Miles Davis, Gil Evans, Herbie
      Hancock, Joe Henderson, Lee Morgan, Jimmy Smith, McCoy Tyner.

PHILIP CATHERINE (g)
  'Sleep My Love' (1978–9, with Charlie Mariano, Jasper van't Hof)
  CMP 5 ST
  See also Stephane Grappelli, Peter Herbolzheimer, Rolf Kühn N.-H. Ørsted Pedersen, Jean-Luc Ponty.
SID CATLETT (d)
  See Albert Ammons, Louis Armstrong, Sidney Bechet, Chu Berry, Don Byas, Coleman Hawkins, Billie Holiday.
SERGE CHALOFF (bars)
  'Boston Blow-Up' (1955) Affinity AFF 63
PAUL CHAMBERS (b)
  See John Coltrane, Miles Davis, Benny Golson, J. J. Johnson, Wes Montgomery, Art Pepper, Sonny Rollins.
RAY CHARLES (vcl, p)
  'The Ray Charles Story, vol 1' (1952–6) Atlantic 40264
DON CHERRY (tp, fl, perc)
  'Eternal Rhythm' (1968, with Karl Berger, Albert Mangelsdorff a.o.)
  MPS 68.225
  'Codona 2' (1980, with Nana Vasconcelos, Collin Walcott) ECM 1177
  See also Karl Berger, Carla Bley, Ornette Coleman, Charlie Haden, Steve Lacy, Old and New Dreams.
CHARLIE CHRISTIAN (g)
  'Live at Minton's Playhouse' (1941, with Don Byas, Kenny Clarke, Dizzy Gillespie, Thelonious Monk a.o.) Jazz Anthology JA 5122
  See also Benny Goodman.
CLARINET SUMMIT (group)
  'You Better Fly Away' (1971, with John Carter, Didier Lockwood, Perry Robinson, Eje Thelin, Stan Tracey, Gianlùigi Trovesi a.o.) MPS 68.251
KENNY CLARKE (d)
  'Live at Ronnie Scott's' (1969, with big band incl. Francy Boland, Johnny Griffin a.o.) MPS 88.019 (2 LP)
  See also Sidney Bechet, Art Blakey, Charlie Christian, Miles Davis, Dizzy Gillespie, Lee Konitz, Modern Jazz Quartet, Thelonious Monk, Fats Navarro.
BUCK CLAYTON (tp)
  'Copenhagen Concert' (1959, with Jimmy Rushing, Buddy Tate a.o.)
  SteepleChase SCC 6006/7 (2 LP)
  See also Count Basie, Benny Goodman, Lester Young.
ARNETT COBB (ts)
  'Live at Sandy's' (1978, with Buddy Tate a.o.) Muse MR 5191
BILLY COBHAM (d)
  'Observations &' (1981) Elektra/Musician MUSK 52386
  See also George Benson, John McLaughlin.
AL COHN (ts)
  'Non-Pareil' (1981) Concord CJ 155
  See also Woody Herman, Jimmy Knepper.

NAT KING COLE (p, vcl)
'From the Very Beginning' (1936–41)   MCA MCL 1671
See also Lester Young.
ORNETTE COLEMAN (as, tp, vln)
'Free Jazz' (1960, with Ed Blackwell, Don Cherry, Eric Dolphy, Charlie Haden, Billy Higgins, Freddie Hubbard, Scott La Faro)
Atlantic ATL 50240
'At the Golden Circle, vols 1 and 2' (1965)
Blue Note BST 84224 & 84225
JOHN COLTRANE (ts, ss)
'Giant Steps' (1959, with Paul Chambers, Tommy Flanagan a.o.)
Atlantic ATL 50239
'A Love Supreme' (1964, with Jimmy Garrison, Elvin Jones, McCoy Tyner)   MCA MCL 1648
'Ascension' (1965, with Jimmy Garrison, Freddie Hubbard, Elvin Jones, Pharoah Sanders, Archie Shepp, John Tchicai a.o.)
Jasmine JAS 45
'Live at the Village Vanguard Again' (1966, with Rashied Ali, Alice Coltrane, Jimmy Garrison, Pharoah Sanders)   Jasmine JAS 16
See also Miles Davis.
CHICK COREA (p, synth)
'Circle – Paris Concert' (1971, with Barry Altschul, Anthony Braxton, David Holland)   ECM 1018 (2 LP)
'Return to Forever' (1972, with Airto Moreira, Flora Purim a.o.)
ECM 1022
'Chick Corea and Gary Burton in Concert' (1979)   ECM 1182 (2 LP)
See also Miles Davis, Herbie Hancock, Joe Henderson.
LARRY CORYELL (g)
'Standing Ovation' (1978)   Mood Records 22888
See also Stephane Grappelli, Herbie Mann.
ANDREW CYRILLE (d, perc)
'Special People' (1980)   Soul Note SN 1012
See also Charlie Haden, Leroy Jenkins.

KENNY DAVERN (cl, ss)
See Soprano Summit
ANTHONY DAVIS (p)
'Under the Double Moon' (1980, with Jay Hoggard)   MPS 68.267
See also Barry Altschul, Anthony Braxton, Leroy Jenkins, George Lewis, David Murray, James Newton.
EDDIE LOCKJAW DAVIS (ts)
'Jaws' Blues' (1981)   Enja 3097
See also Fats Navarro.
MILES DAVIS (tp)
'Birth of the Cool' (1949–50, with Kenny Clarke, Gil Evans, J. J. Johnson, Lee Konitz, John Lewis, Gerry Mulligan, Max Roach, Kai Winding a.o.)
Capitol CAPS 1026

'Miles Davis Classics' (1956-64, with Cannonball Adderley, Ron Carter, Paul Chambers, John Coltrane, Bill Evans, Herbie Hancock, Philly Joe Jones, Tony Williams a.o.) CBS 88138 (2 LP)

'Sketches of Spain' (1959-60, with Gil Evans big band) CBS 32023

'Bitches Brew' (1969, with Chick Corea, Jack DeJohnette, Dave Holland, John McLaughlin, Wayne Shorter, Joe Zawinul a.o.) CBS 66236 (2 LP)

See also Cannonball Adderley, Benny Carter, Charlie Parker.

RICHARD DAVIS (b)

See Eric Dolphy, Booker Ervin, Earl Hines, Rahsaan Roland Kirk, Ben Webster.

WILD BILL DAVISON (tp)

'That's A-Plenty' (1943, with Edmond Hall, Pee Wee Russell a.o.)
London 6.24059

BUDDY DeFRANCO (cl)

'The Liveliest' (1980) Hep HEP 2014

JACK DeJOHNETTE (d)

'Special Edition' (1979, with Anthony Braxton, David Murray a.o.)
ECM 1152

'New Directions in Europe' (1979, with John Abercrombie, Lester Bowie, Eddie Gomez) ECM 1157

See also George Benson, Miles Davis, Collin Walcott.

PAUL DESMOND (as)

'Paul Desmond' (1978) Artists House AH 9402

See also Dave Brubeck.

VIC DICKENSON (tb)

See Albert Ammons, Billie Holiday.

WALT DICKERSON (vib)

'Visions' (1978, with Sun Ra) SteepleChase SCS 1126

BABY DODDS (d)

See Louis Armstrong, Sidney Bechet, Johnny Dodds, Jelly Roll Morton, King Oliver.

JOHNNY DODDS (cl)

'The Immortal Johnny Dodds' (1926-8, with Baby Dodds, Kid Ory a.o.) VJM VLP 48

See also Louis Armstrong, Jelly Roll Morton, King Oliver.

ERIC DOLPHY (as, bcl, fl)

'Fire Waltz' (1961, with Ed Blackwell, Richard Davis, Booker Little, Mal Waldron) Prestige 68.330 (2 LP)

'Berlin Concerts' (1961) Enja 3007/9 (2 LP)

See also Ron Carter, Ornette Coleman, Charles Mingus.

KENNY DORHAM (tp)

'Short Story' (1964, with Tete Montoliu, N.-H. Ørsted Pedersen a.o.)
SteepleChase SCC 6010

See also Thelonious Monk, Fats Navarro, Sonny Rollins, Horace Silver.

TOMMY DORSEY (tb)

'The Best of Tommy Dorsey' (1935-40, with big band incl Bunny Berigan, Bud Freeman, Buddy Rich a.o.) RCA INTS 5017

GEORGE DUKE (p, synth)
  'George Duke & Feel' (1974, with Airto Moreira, Flora Purim a.o.)
                                                              MPS 68.023
  See also Cannonball Adderley.

HARRY EDISON (tp)
  'The Swinger' (1958)   Verve 2304.538
  See also Count Basie, Ella Fitzgerald, Billie Holiday, Buddy Rich, Lester
    Young.
ROY ELDRIDGE (tp)
  'At the Arcadia Ballroom New York' (1939)
                                             Jazz Anthology JA 5149
  'Little Jazz and the Jimmy Ryan's All Stars' (1975)   Pablo 2310.869
  See also Chu Berry, Coleman Hawkins, Illinois Jacquet.
DUKE ELLINGTON (p)
  'The Indispensable Ellington, vol 1/2' (1927–9, with Barney Bigard, Harry
    Carney, Johnny Hodges, Bubber Miley, Joe Nanton, Cootie Williams
    a.o.)   RCA PM 43687 (2 LP)
  'Masters of Jazz, vol 6' (1929–73, as above plus Jimmy Blanton, Paul
    Gonsalves, Ray Nance, Oscar Pettiford, Rex Stewart, Ben Webster, a.o.)
                                                  RCA CL 42237 (2 LP)
  'The Indispensable Ellington, vol 5/6' (1940, as above)
                                                  RCA PM 45352 (2 LP)
  'Money Jungle' (1962, with Charles Mingus, Max Roach)
                                                  Blue Note BN 25113
HERB ELLIS (g)
  See Louis Armstrong, Coleman Hawkins, Oscar Peterson, Ben Webster.
BOOKER ERVIN (ts)
  'The Freedom and Space Sessions' (1963–4, with Jaki Byard, Richard
    Davis a.o.)   Prestige 68.360 (2 LP)
  See also Charles Mingus.
BILL EVANS (p)
  'Village Vanguard Sessions' (1961, with Scott LaFaro)
                                             Milestone 68.101 (2 LP)
  'Affinity' (1978, with Toots Thielemans a.o.)   Warner WB 56617
  See also Miles Davis, J. J. Johnson.
GIL EVANS (p)
  'Out of the Cool' (1960, with Ron Carter, Elvin Jones a.o.)
                                                        Jasmine JAS 52
  'The Rest of Gil Evans' (1978, with George Adams, Arthur Blythe,
    Hannibal Marvin Peterson)   Mole Jazz MOLE 3
  See also Kenny Burrell, Miles Davis.

TAL FARLOW (g)
  'The Swinging Guitar of Tal Farlow' (1956)   Verve 2304.211
  See also Red Norvo.

ART FARMER (tp)
'Portrait of Art Farmer' (1958, with Roy Haynes, Hank Jones)
Contemporary S 7554
See also Wardell Gray, Peter Herbolzheimer.
PIERRE FAVRE (d)
'Santana' (1968, with Irene Schweizer)   FMP 0630
MAYNARD FERGUSON (tp)
See Stan Kenton.
CLARE FISCHER (org)
'Clare Declares' (1975)   MPS 68.148
ELLA FITZGERALD (vcl)
'Ella Swings the Band' (1936-9, with Chick Webb band)   MCA 1327
'Whisper Not' (1965, with big band incl Louie Bellson, Harry Edison,
Shelly Manne, Jimmy Rowles a.o.)   Verve 2304.393
'Ella and Oscar' (1975, with Oscar Peterson)   Pablo 2310.759
See also Louis Armstrong, Chick Webb.
TOMMY FLANAGAN (p)
'Super Session' (1980, with Elvin Jones, Red Mitchell)   Enja 3059
See also John Coltrane, Roy Haynes, Sonny Rollins, Bennie Wallace.
FRANK FOSTER (ts)
See Count Basie, Milt Jackson.
POPS FOSTER (b)
See Sidney Bechet, James P. Johnson.
BUD FREEMAN (ts)
'Three's A Crowd' (1938)   London 6.24061
See also Tommy Dorsey, Rex Stewart.
CHICO FREEMAN (ts)
'Spirit Sensitive' (1979, with Cecil McBee a.o.)
India Navigation IN 1045
See also Cecil McBee, Don Pullen, Edward Vesala.
VON FREEMAN (ts)
'Young and Foolish' (1977)   Daybreak D 002
DAVID FRIEDMAN (vib)
'Double Image' (1977)   Enja 2096
See also George Benson.

JAN GARBAREK (ts, ss)
'Belonging' (1974, with Keith Jarrett a.o.)   ECM 1050
See also Charlie Haden.
ERROLL GARNER (p)
'Concert by the Sea' (1955)   CBS 62310
See also Charlie Parker.
JIMMY GARRISON (b)
See Benny Carter, John Coltrane.
STAN GETZ (ts)
'Stan Getz at Storyville' (1951, with Jimmy Raney a.o.)
Vogue VJD 554(2 LP)

'West Coast Jazz' (1955, with Shelly Manne a.o.)   Verve 2304.330
'Getz/Gilberto' (1963)   Verve 2304.071
'Live at Montmartre' (1977, with JoAnne Brackeen, N.-H. Ørsted Pedersen
   a.o.)   SteepleChase SCS 1073/4 (2 LP)
See also Woody Herman.

DIZZY GILLESPIE (tp)
  'Dizzy Gillespie' (1945-6, with Ray Brown, Kenny Clarke, Milt Jackson,
    John Lewis, James Moody, Charlie Parker, Sonny Stitt a.o.)

                                                Saga 6920

  'Dizzy Gillespie, vol 1/2' (1946-9, with Ray Brown, Don Byas, Kenny
    Clarke, Milt Jackson, J. J. Johnson, Yusef Lateef, John Lewis, James
    Moody, Chano Pozo a.o.)   RCA PM 42408 (2 LP)

  'Musician, Composer, Raconteur' (1981, with Milt Jackson, James Moody
    a.o.)   Pablo 2620.116 (2 LP)
  See also Charlie Christian, Red Norvo, Charlie Parker.

EGBERTO GISMONTI (g, p)
  See Charlie Haden, Nana Vasconcelos.

JIMMY GIUFFRE (cl, ts)
  '7 Pieces' (with Jim Hall, Red Mitchell)   Verve 2304.438
  See also Woody Herman.

GLOBE UNITY ORCHESTRA (group)
  'Live in Wuppertal' (1973, with Peter Brötzmann, Alex von Schlippenbach,
    Manfred Schoof, Kenny Wheeler a.o.)   FMP 0160

BENNY GOLSON (ts)
  'Groovin' with Golson' (1959, with Art Blakey, Paul Chambers a.o.)
                                       New Jazz 68.346

EDDIE GOMEZ (b)
  See Jack DeJohnette, Jeremy Steig, Bennie Wallace.

PAUL GONSALVES (ts)
  See Duke Ellington, Earl Hines.

BENNY GOODMAN (cl)
  'Carnegie Hall Jazz Concert' (1938, with Count Basie, Harry Carney,
    Buck Clayton, Bobby Hackett, Lionel Hampton, Johnny Hodges,
    Gene Krupa, Cootie Williams, Teddy Wilson, Lester Young a.o.)
                                       CBS 66202 (2 LP)

  'Live 1939-41' (1939-41, with Count Basie, Charlie Christian, Lionel
    Hampton, Fletcher Henderson, Gene Krupa, Cootie Williams a.o.)
                             Jazz Anthology JA 5181

  See also Lester Young.

DEXTER GORDON (ts)
  'The Chase' (1947, with Wardell Gray, Jimmy Rowles a.o.)
                                    Spotlite SPJ 130
  'American Classic' (1982)   Elektra/Musician MUSK 52392
  See also Benny Carter, Wardell Gray.

STEPHANE GRAPPELLI (vln)
  'Young Django' (1979, with Philip Catherine, Larry Coryell, N.-H. Ørsted
  Pedersen)   MPS 68.230

'Live' (1979, with David Grisman)   Warner WB 56903
See also Quintet of the Hot Club of France, Django Reinhardt.

WARDELL GRAY (ts)
'Central Avenue' (1949-53, with Art Farmer, Dexter Gordon, Clark
     Terry a.o.)   Prestige 68.334 (2 LP)
See also Dexter Gordon.

JOHNNY GRIFFIN (ts)
'Little Giant' (1959)   Riverside 68.918
See also Kenny Clarke, Wes Montgomery.

DAVID GRISMAN (mandolin)
See Stephane Grappelli.

BOBBY HACKETT (tp)
See Benny Goodman.

CHARLIE HADEN (b)
'Liberation Music Orchestra' (1969, with Gato Barbieri, Carla Bley,
     Don Cherry, Andrew Cyrille, Dewey Redman, Perry Robinson, Roswell
     Rudd a.o.)   Jasmine JAS 55
'Folk Songs' (1979, with Jan Garbarek, Egberto Gismonti)   ECM 1170
See also Carla Bley, Ornette Coleman, Keith Jarrett, John McLaughlin, Old
     and New Dreams, Art Pepper.

EDMOND HALL (cl)
See Louis Armstrong, Wild Bill Davison, Coleman Hawkins, Art Tatum,
     Lester Young.

JIM HALL (g)
'Jim Hall/Red Mitchell' (1978, with Red Mitchell)
     Artists House AH 9405
See also Jimmy Giuffre, Baden Powell.

SCOTT HAMILTON (ts)
'Back to Back' (1978, with Buddy Tate a.o.)   Concord CJ 85

GUNTER HAMPEL (vib, fl, bcl)
'That Came Down on Me' (1978, with Jeanne Lee, Perry Robinson a.o.)
     Birth 0027

LIONEL HAMPTON (vib, d, p)
'Historical Recording Sessions, vol 1' (1937-9, with Chu Berry, Harry
     Carney, Benny Carter, Coleman Hawkins, Johnny Hodges, John Kirby,
     Gene Krupa, Mezz Mezzrow, Rex Stewart, Cootie Williams a.o.)
     RCA PM 43293 (3 LP)
'Vol 1' (1947, with Milt Buckner, Barney Kessel, Charlie Shavers a.o.)
     Reactivation JR 102
'Hamp in Harlem' (1979, with big band incl Joe Newman a.o.)
     Timeless SJP 133
See also Art Blakey, Benny Goodman, Gene Krupa.

HERBIE HANCOCK (p)
'Maiden Voyage' (1965, with Ron Carter, Freddie Hubbard, Tony
     Williams)   Blue Note BST 84195
'An Evening with Herbie Hancock and Chick Corea' (1978)
     CBS 88329 (2 LP)

See also George Benson, Donald Byrd, Miles Davis, Wayne Shorter.

JOHN HANDY (as)
  'Karuna Supreme' (1975)   MPS 68.114
  See also Charles Mingus.

BILLY HARPER (ts)
  'Trying to Make Heaven My Home' (1979)   MPS 68.234
  See also Thad Jones.

BILL HARRIS (tb)
  See Woody Herman.

COLEMAN HAWKINS (ts)
  'Dutch Treat' (1936–8)   Xanadu 189
  'The Chocolate Dandies and Leonard Feather's All Stars' (1940–43, with
    Benny Carter, Sid Catlett, Roy Eldridge, Edmond Hall, John Kirby,
    Oscar Pettiford, Art Tatum, Cootie Williams a.o.) London 6.24056
  'The Essential Coleman Hawkins' (1948–59, with Ray Brown, Roy
    Eldridge, Herb Ellis, Percy Heath, Hank Jones, John Lewis,
    Oscar Peterson a.o.)   Verve 2304.537
  See also Benny Carter, Lionel Hampton, Fletcher Henderson, Max
    Roach, Bessie Smith, Rex Stewart.

ROY HAYNES (d)
  'Out of the Afternoon' (1962, with Tommy Flanagan, Rahsaan
    Roland Kirk a.o.)   Jasmine JAS 24
  See also Gary Burton, Art Farmer, J. J. Johnson, Bud Powell, Sonny
    Rollins, Pharoah Sanders, Lester Young.

PERCY HEATH (b)
  See Coleman Hawkins, Milt Jackson, Modern Jazz Quartet, Sonny
    Rollins.

JULIUS HEMPHILL (saxes)
  See World Saxophone Quartet.

FLETCHER HENDERSON (p)
  'First Impressions' (1924–31, with Louis Armstrong, Coleman Hawkins,
    John Kirby, Rex Stewart a.o.)   MCA 1310
  'Swing's the Thing' (1931–4, with Red Allen, Benny Carter, Coleman
    Hawkins, John Kirby, Rex Stewart, Ben Webster a.o.) MCA 1318
  See also Benny Goodman, Bessie Smith.

JOE HENDERSON (ts)
  'Mirror Mirror' (1980, with Ron Carter, Chick Corea, Billy Higgins)
                                    MPS 68.255
  See also Kenny Burrell.

PETER HERBOLZHEIMER (tb)
  'Wide Open' (1973, with big band incl Philip Catherine, Art Farmer, N.-H.
    Ørsted Pedersen a.o.)   MPS 68.040

WOODY HERMAN (cl, as)
  'Early Autumn' (1948–50, with Gene Ammons, Billy Bauer, Al Cohn, Stan
    Getz, Jimmy Giuffre, Bill Harris, Shelly Manne, Oscar Pettiford a.o.)
                                  Capitol M 11034

'Live at Monterey' (1960, with Charlie Byrd, Zoot Sims a.o.)
                                                Atlantic ATL 50236

'The New Thundering Herd' (1976, with Al Cohn, Stan Getz, Jimmy
    Giuffre, Jimmy Rowles, Zoot Sims a.o.)   RCA PL 02203

BILLY HIGGINS (d)
    See Ornette Coleman, Joe Henderson, Steve Lacy, Jackie McLean,
    Thelonious Monk, Lee Morgan, N.-H. Ørsted Pedersen.

EARL HINES (p)
    'Once Upon a Time' (1966, with Richard Davis, Paul Gonsalves,
        Johnny Hodges, Elvin Jones, Ray Nance, Pee Wee Russell a.o.)
                                                    Jasmine JAS 42

    'At Sundown' (1974)   Black & Blue 33.116
    See also Louis Armstrong, Sidney Bechet, Jimmie Noone.

TERUMASA HINO (tp)
    See Mal Waldron.

JOHNNY HODGES (as)
    See Duke Ellington, Benny Goodman, Lionel Hampton, Earl Hines, Lester
    Young.

JAY HOGGARD (vib)
    'Solo Vibraphone' (1978)   India Navigation IN1040
    See also Anthony Davis.

BILLIE HOLIDAY (vcl)
    'Fine and Mellow' (1939-44, with Sid Catlett, Vic Dickenson, a.o.)
                                                    London 6.24055

    'Songs for Distingué Lovers' (1957, with Harry Edison, Barney Kessel,
        Red Mitchell, Jimmy Rowles, Ben Webster a.o.)   Verve 2304.243
    See also Artie Shaw, Lester Young.

DAVE HOLLAND (b)
    See Barry Altschul, Chick Corea, Miles Davis, Sam Rivers, Collin Walcott.

JOHN LEE HOOKER (vcl, g)
    'Sittin' Here Thinkin'' (c 1955-9)   Muse MR 5205

FREDDIE HUBBARD (tp)
    'Born to be Blue' (1981)   Pablo 2312.134
    See also Ornette Coleman, John Coltrane, Herbie Hancock, Bobby
    Hutcherson.

BOBBY HUTCHERSON (vib)
    'Spiral' (1965-8, with Freddie Hubbard, Sam Rivers a.o.)
                                                Blue Note LBR 1029

    See also Woody Shaw, McCoy Tyner.

MAHALIA JACKSON (vcl)
    'Mahalia Jackson, vol 1' (c 1948-52)   Reactivation JR 115

MILT JACKSON (vib)
    'Plenty, Plenty Soul' (1957, with Cannonball Adderley, Art Blakey, Frank
        Foster, Percy Heath, Quincy Jones, Joe Newman, Oscar Pettiford,
        Horace Silver, Lucky Thompson a.o.)   Atlantic 8811

See also Dizzy Gillespie, Howard McGhee, Modern Jazz Quartet, Thelonious Monk.

RONALD SHANNON JACKSON (d)
'Nasty' (1981)   Moers Music 01086
See also Albert Mangelsdorff, Cecil Taylor, James Blood Ulmer.

ILLINOIS JACQUET (ts)
'Swing's the Thing' (1957, with Ray Brown, Roy Eldridge, Jo Jones
a.o.)   Verve 2304.434

JOSEPH JARMAN (saxes)
See Art Ensemble of Chicago.

KEITH JARRETT (p)
'Bop-Be' (1974, with Charlie Haden, Dewey Redman a.o.)
                                                           Jasmine JAS 29
'The Köln Concert' (1975)   ECM 1064/5 (2 LP)
See also Jan Garbarek.

EDDIE JEFFERSON (vcl)
'The Live-liest' (1976)   Muse MR 5127

LEROY JENKINS (vln)
'The Legend of Ai Glatson' (1978, with Andrew Cyrille, Anthony Davis)
                                                       Black Saint BSR 0022
See also Karl Berger, Carla Bley.

BUNK JOHNSON (tp)
'Bunk Johnson and His Superior Jazz Band' (1942, with George
Lewis a.o.)   Good Time Jazz M 12048

JAMES P. JOHNSON (p)
'A Flat Dream' (1939–45, with Pops Foster, Omer Simeon)
                                                        Queen-Disc Q 056
See also Bessie Smith.

J. J. JOHNSON (tb)
'The Great Kai and J. J.' (1960, with Paul Chambers, Bill Evans, Roy
Haynes, Kai Winding a.o.)   Jasmine JAS 7
'J.J.!' (1964, with big band incl Hank Jones, Thad Jones, Clark
Terry a.o.)   RCA PL 43530
See also Benny Carter, Miles Davis, Dizzy Gillespie.

PETE JOHNSON (p)
'Boogie Woogie Master' (1940–44)   MCA 1333
See also Joe Turner.

ELVIN JONES (d)
'Remembrance' (1978)   MPS 68.203
See John Coltrane, Gil Evans, Tommy Flanagan, Earl Hines, McCoy
Tyner.

HANK JONES (p)
'Bluesette' (1979)   Black & Blue 33.168
See also Cannonball Adderley, Art Farmer, Coleman Hawkins, J. J.
Johnson, Howard McGhee, Jimmy Raney, Rex Stewart, Ben Webster,
Lester Young.

JO JONES (d)
  See Count Basie, Art Blakey, Milt Buckner, Lionel Hampton, Illinois
    Jacquet, Lester Young.
PHILLY JOE JONES (d)
  See Miles Davis, Art Pepper.
QUINCY JONES (arr)
  See Milt Jackson, Dinah Washington.
THAD JONES (tp)
  'Thad Jones/Mel Lewis' (1973-4, with big band incl Pepper Adams, Billy
    Harper, Jimmy Knepper, Mel Lewis a.o.)   Reactivation JR 122
  See also Count Basie, Kenny Burrell, J. J. Johnson.

MAX KAMINSKY (tp)
  See Jack Teagarden.
STAN KENTON (p)
  'Kenton Presents' (1950, with Laurindo Almeida, Maynard Ferguson,
    Shelly Manne, Art Pepper, Bud Shank a.o.) Creative World ST 1023
BARNEY KESSEL (g)
  'The Pollwinners Exploring the Scene' (1960, with Ray Brown, Shelly
    Manne)   Contemporary S 7581
  See also Lionel Hampton, Billie Holiday, Baden Powell, Stuff Smith, Sarah
    Vaughan.
B. B. KING (vcl, g)
  'The Best of B. B. King' (1952-55)   Charly CH 30
JOHN KIRBY (b)
  '1940' (1940, with Charlie Shavers a.o.)   Jazz Anthology JA 5179
  See also Lionel Hampton, Coleman Hawkins, Fletcher Henderson,
    Chick Webb.
RAHSAAN ROLAND KIRK (saxes, fl)
  'Pre-Rahsaan' (1961-8, with Jaki Byard, Richard Davis a.o.)
                                               Prestige 68.352 (2 LP)
  'The Inflated Tear' (1968)   Atlantic ATL 50233
  See also Roy Haynes
JIMMY KNEPPER (tb)
  'Cunningbird' (1976, with Al Cohn, Dannie Richmond a.o.)
                                               SteepleChase SCS 1061
  See also Gil Evans, Thad Jones, Lee Konitz.
HANS KOLLER (ts)
  'New York City' (1979, with big band)
                                                      MPS 68.235
LEE KONITZ (as)
  'Lee Konitz and Warne Marsh' (1955, with Billy Bauer, Kenny
    Clarke, Warne Marsh, Oscar Pettiford a.o.)
                                               Atlantic ATL 50298
  'Yes, Yes, Nonet' (1979, with Jimmy Knepper a.o.)
                                               SteepleChase SCS 1119

See also Karl Berger, Miles Davis, Lennie Tristano.

VOLKER KRIEGEL (g)
'Inside: Missing Link' (1972, with Albert Mangelsdorff, Alan Skidmore,
Eberhard Weber a.o.)   MPS 88.030 (2 LP)
See also United Jazz & Rock Ensemble.

KARIN KROG (vcl)
'I Remember You...' (1980, with Warne Marsh, Red Mitchell)
Spotlite SPJ 22

GENE KRUPA (d)
'Krupa, Hampton, Wilson' (1955, with Lionel Hampton, Teddy
Wilson)   Verve 2304.482
See also Art Blakey, Benny Goodman, Lionel Hampton.

ROLF KÜHN (cl)
'Symphonic Swampfire' (1979, with Philip Catherine, N.-H. Ørsted
Pedersen a.o.)   MPS 68.216

STEVE LACY (ss)
'Evidence' (1961, with Don Cherry, Billy Higgins a.o.)
New Jazz 68.328
'Trickles' (1976, with Roswell Rudd a.o.)
Black Saint BSR 0008
See also Mal Waldron.

TOMMY LADNIER (tp)
See Sidney Bechet, Ma Rainey.

SCOTT LA FARO (b)
See Ornette Coleman, Bill Evans.

OLIVER LAKE (saxes)
'Holding Together' (1976)   Black Saint BSR 0009
See also Karl Berger, James Blood Ulmer, World Saxophone Quartet.

EDDIE LANG (g)
See Bix Beiderbecke.

YUSUF LATEEF (ts, fl, oboe)
'The Golden Flute' (1966)   Jasmine JAS 60
See also Art Blakey, Dizzy Gillespie.

LEADBELLY (vcl, g)
'Goodnight Irene, Good Morning Blues' (1939–43)
Storyville 6.23700

JEANNE LEE (vcl)
See Gunter Hampel.

GEORGE LEWIS (cl)
'The Perennial George Lewis' (1959)   Verve 2304.553
See also Bunk Johnson.

GEORGE LEWIS (tb)
'The George Lewis Solo Trombone Record' (1976)

Sackville 3012
'Homage to Charles Parker' (1979, with Anthony Davis a.o.)
Black Saint BSR 0029

See also Muhal Richard Abrams, Karl Berger, Anthony Braxton, David Murray, Sam Rivers.

JOHN LEWIS (p)

'Piano Paris 1979' (1979)   All Life AL 010

See also Miles Davis, Dizzy Gillespie, Coleman Hawkins, Modern Jazz Quartet, Charlie Parker, Lester Young.

MEADE LUX LEWIS (p)

'Tell Your Story' (1939–44)   Oldie Blues OL 2805

MEL LEWIS (d)

See Bob Brookmeyer, Thad Jones, Gerry Mulligan.

DAVE LIEBMAN (saxes, fl)

See John McLaughlin, Steve Swallow.

BOOKER LITTLE (tp)

See Eric Dolphy, Max Roach.

DIDIER LOCKWOOD (vln)

'New World' (1979, with Gordon Beck, N.-H. Ørsted Pedersen, Tony Williams)   MPS 68.237

See also Clarinet Summit.

CRIPPLE CLARENCE LOFTON (p)

See Jimmy Yancey.

LONDON JAZZ COMPOSERS ORCHESTRA (group)

'Ode' (1972, with Derek Bailey, Tony Oxley, Evan Parker, Rutherford, Trevor Watts a.o.)   Incus 6/7 (2 LP)

JIMMIE LUNCEFORD (as)

'Jimmie's Legacy' (1934–37, with big band)   MCA 1320

'Original Sessions 1942-3' (1942-3, with big band)

Jazz Anthology JA 5112

CECIL McBEE (b)

'Alternate Spaces' (1979, with Chico Freeman, Don Pullen a.o.)

India Navigation IN 1041

See also Chico Freeman, Pharaoh Sanders, Zbigniew Seifert, Wayne Shorter.

HOWARD McGHEE (tp)

'Trumpet at Tempo' (1946-7, with Ray Brown, Milt Jackson, Hank Jones, James Moody a.o.)   Spotlite SJP 131

See also Charlie Parker.

JOHN McLAUGHLIN (g)

'My Goal's Beyond' (1971, with Billy Cobham, Charlie Haden, Dave Liebman, Airto Moreira a.o.)   Elektra/Musician MUSK 52364

'The Best of the Mahavishnu Orchestra' (1971-5, with Billy Cobham a.o.)

CBS 84232

See also Carla Bley, Miles Davis.

JACKIE McLEAN (as)

'Consequence' (1965, with Billy Higgins, Lee Morgan a.o.)

Blue Note LBR 1027

'New York Calling' (1974)   SteepleChase SCS 1023
See also Charles Mingus.
CARMEN MCRAE (vcl)
  'Two for the Road' (1980, with George Shearing)
                                              Concord CJ 128
JAY MCSHANN (p)
  'The Early Bird' (1941-3, with big band incl. Charlie Parker a.o.)
                                              MCA 1338

  See also Buddy Tate.
MACHITO (perc)
  'Machito and his Salsa Big Band' (1982)   Timeless SJP 161
MAHAVISHNU ORCHESTRA (group)
  See John McLaughlin.
ALBERT MANGELSDORFF (tb)
  'Trombirds' (1972)   MPS 68.069
  'Trilogue - Live' (1976, with Alphonse Mouzon, Jaco Pastorius)
                                              MPS 68.175
  'Albert Live in Montreux' (1980, with Ronald Shannon Jackson a.o.)
                                              MPS 68.261
  See also Don Cherry, Volker Kriegel, United Jazz & Rock Ensemble.
HERBIE MANN (fl)
  'Memphis Underground' (1968, with Larry Coryell, Miroslav Vitous a.o.)
                                              Atlantic ATL 50520
SHELLY MANNE (d)
  'Songs from My Fair Lady' (1956)   MFP 50527
  See also Ella Fitzgerald, Stan Getz, Woody Herman, Stan Kenton,
    Barney Kessel, Art Pepper.
CHARLIE MARIANO (as, ss, fl, nagaswaram)
  'Helen 12 Trees' (1976, with Zbigniew Seifert a.o.)   MPS 68.112
  See also Philip Catherine, Charles Mingus, United Jazz & Rock
    Ensemble.
WARNE MARSH (ts)
  'Warne Out' (1977)   Flyright FLY 212
  See also Lee Konitz, Karin Krog, Art Pepper.
PAT METHENY (g)
  'American Garage' (1979)   ECM 1155
MEZZ MEZZROW (cl)
  See Sidney Bechet, Lionel Hampton.
BUBBER MILEY (tp)
  See Duke Ellington.
CHARLES MINGUS (b)
  'Pithecanthropus Erectus' (1956, with Jackie McLean, Mal Waldron a.o.)
                                              Atlantic 8809
  'Mingus at Antibes' (1960, with Eric Dolphy, Booker Ervin, Bud
    Powell, Dannie Richmond a.o.)   Atlantic SD 2-3001 (2 LP)
  'The Black Saint and the Sinner Lady' (1963, with Jaki Byard,

Charlie Mariano, Dannie Richmond a.o.)   Jasmine JAS 13
'Mingus at Monterey' (1964, with Jaki Byard, John Handy, Dannie
   Richmond a.o.)   Prestige 68.339 (2 LP)
See Duke Ellington, Red Norvo, Charlie Parker, Bud Powell.

RED MITCHELL (b)
   See Tommy Flanagan, Jimmy Giuffre, Jim Hall, Billie Holiday,
   Karin Krog.

ROSCOE MITCHELL (saxes)
   See Muhal Richard Abrams, Art Ensemble of Chicago.

MODERN JAZZ QUARTET (group)
   'Modern Jazz Quartet' (1952-5, with Kenny Clarke, Percy Heath,
   Milt Jackson, John Lewis)   Prestige 68.322 (2 LP)

THELONIOUS MONK (p)
   'The Genius, vols 1 and 2' (1947-52, with Art Blakey, Kenny
      Dorham, Milt Jackson, Max Roach, Lucky Thompson a.o.)
                                          Blue Note BLP 1510 & 1511
   'The Riverside Trios' (1955-6, with Art Blakey, Kenny Clarke,
      Oscar Pettiford)   Milestone 68.110 (2 LP)
   'In Person' (1959-60, with Pepper Adams, Donald Byrd, Billy
      Higgins, Phil Woods a.o.)   Milestone 68.107 (2 LP)
   See also Charlie Christian.

WES MONTGOMERY (g)
   'Movin'' (1960-62, with Paul Chambers, Johnny Griffin a.o.)
                                             Milestone 68.130 (2 LP)

TETE MONTOLIU (p)
   'I Wanna Talk About You' (1980)   SteepleChase SCS 1137
   See also Kenny Dorham, Lucky Thompson.

JAMES MOODY (ts, fl)
   See Dizzy Gillespie, Howard McGhee.

AIRTO MOREIRA (perc)
   See Cannonball Adderley, George Benson, Chick Corea, George Duke, John
   McLaughlin.

LEE MORGAN (tp)
   'Sonic Boom' (1967, with Ron Carter, Billy Higgins a.o.)
                                              Blue Note LBR 1020
   See also Art Blakey, Jackie McLean.

JELLY ROLL MORTON (p)
   'The Complete Jelly Roll Morton, vol 1/2' (1926-7, with Barney
      Bigard, Baby Dodds, Johnny Dodds, Kid Ory, Omer
      Simeon a.o.)   RCA PM 42405 (2 LP)
   'New Orleans Memories Plus Two' (1939)   London 6.24062
   See also New Orleans Rhythm Kings.

ALPHONSE MOUZON (d)
   See Albert Mangelsdorff, McCoy Tyner, Jasper van't Hof, Weather Report.

GERRY MULLIGAN (bars)
   'Mulligan/Baker' (1951-65, with Chet Baker a.o.) Prestige 68.350 (2 LP)

'On Tour' (1960, with big band incl Bob Brookmeyer, Mel Lewis,
Zoot Sims a.o.)   Verve 2304.410
See also Dave Brubeck, Miles Davis.
DAVID MURRAY (ts)
'Ming' (1980, with Anthony Davis, George Lewis, Henry Threadgill a.o.)
Black Saint BSR 0045
See also Jack DeJohnette, Sonny Murray, James Blood Ulmer, World
Saxophone Quartet.
SONNY MURRAY (d)
'Live at Moers Festival' (1979, with David Murray a.o.)
Moers Music 01054

RAY NANCE (tp, vln)
See Duke Ellington, Earl Hines.
JOE 'TRICKY SAM' NANTON (tb)
See Duke Ellington.
FATS NAVARRO (tp)
'Fat Girl' (1946–47, with Art Blakey, Kenny Clarke, Eddie Lockjaw Davis,
Kenny Dorham, Sonny Stitt a.o.)
Savoy SJL 2216 (2 LP)
See also Charlie Parker, Bud Powell.
JOE NEWMAN (tp)
See Count Basie, Lionel Hampton, Milt Jackson, Joe Turner.
NEW ORLEANS RHYTHM KINGS (group)
'NORK, vol 2' (1923, with Jelly Roll Morton, Leon Rappolo a.o.)
Classic Jazz Masters CJM 13
JAMES NEWTON (fl)
'Crystal Texts' (1978, with Anthony Davis)   Moers Music 01048
ALBERT NICHOLAS (cl)
See Louis Armstrong.
JIMMIE NOONE (cl)
'At the Apex Club' (1928, with Earl Hines a.o.)   MCA 1313
RED NORVO (vib)
'Red Norvo's Fabulous Jam Session' (1945, with Dizzy Gillespie,
Charlie Parker, Teddy Wilson a.o.)   Spotlite SPJ 127
'The Savoy Sessions' (1950–51, with Tal Farlow, Charles Mingus)
Savoy SJL 2212 (2 LP)

ANITA O'DAY (vcl)
'Sings the Winners' (1958, with big band)   Verve 2304.255
OLD AND NEW DREAMS (group)
'Old and New Dreams' (1979, with Ed Blackwell, Don Cherry,
Charlie Haden, Dewey Redman)   ECM 1154
KING OLIVER (co)
'King Oliver and his Creole Jazz Band' (1923, with Louis Armstrong, Baby
Dodds, Johnny Dodds, a.o.)   VJM VLP 49

OREGON (group)
'Oregon in Performance' (1979, with Ralph Towner, Collin Walcott a.o.)
Elektra ELK 62028 (2 LP)
NIELS-HENNING ØRSTED PEDERSEN (b)
'Jaywalkin'' (1975, with Philip Catherine, Billy Higgins a.o.)
SteepleChase SCS 1041
See also Chet Baker, Kenny Dorham, Stan Getz, Stephane Grappelli, Peter Herbolzheimer, Rolf Kühn, Didier Lockwood, Oscar Peterson, George Shearing, Toots Thielemans.
KID ORY (tb)
'Kid Ory's Creole Jazz Band' (1944-5, with Omer Simeon a.o.)
Good Time Jazz L 12022
See also Louis Armstrong, Johnny Dodds, Jelly Roll Morton.
TONY OXLEY (d, perc)
'February Papers' (1977)   Incus 18
See also London Jazz Composers Orchestra, Alan Skidmore.

CHARLIE PARKER (as)
'Bird/The Savoy Recordings' (1944-8, with Miles Davis, Dizzy Gillespie, John Lewis, Bud Powell, Max Roach a.o.)
Savoy SJL 2201 (2 LP)
'Charlie Parker on Dial, vol 5' (1945-7, with Miles Davis, Erroll Garner, Howard McGhee, Max Roach, Lucky Thompson a.o.)
Spotlite SPJ 105
'One Night at Birdland' (1950, with Art Blakey, Fats Navarro, Bud Powell a.o.)   CBS 88250 (2 LP)
'The Greatest Jazz Concert Ever' (1953, with Dizzy Gillespie, Charles Mingus, Bud Powell, Max Roach)   Prestige 68.319 (2 LP)
See also Dizzy Gillespie, Jay McShann, Red Norvo.
EVAN PARKER (ts, ss)
'Six of One' (1980)   Incus 39
See also London Jazz Composers Orchestra, Kenny Wheeler.
JOE PASS (g)
'Ira, George and Joe' (1981)   Pablo 2312.133
JACO PASTORIUS (b)
See Albert Mangelsdorff, Weather Report.
ART PEPPER (as)
'The Way It Was' (1956-60, with Paul Chambers, Philly Joe Jones, Warne Marsh a.o.)   Contemporary S 7630
'Living Legend' (1975, with Charlie Haden, Shelly Manne)
Contemporary S 7633
See also Stan Kenton.
HANNIBAL MARVIN PETERSON (tp)
'Hannibal in Berlin' (1976, with George Adams a.o.)
MPS 68.152
See also Gil Evans.

OSCAR PETERSON (p)
  'At the Stratford Shakespearean Festival' (1956, with Ray Brown,
    Herb Ellis)   Verve 2304.223
  'Tracks' (1970)   MPS 68.084
  'Nigerian Market Place' (1981, with N.-H. Ørsted Pedersen a.o.)
                                                   Pablo 2308.231
  See also Louis Armstrong, Ella Fitzgerald, Coleman Hawkins, Stuff Smith,
    Ben Webster.
OSCAR PETTIFORD (b)
  See Duke Ellington, Coleman Hawkins, Woody Herman, Milt
    Jackson, Lee Konitz, Thelonious Monk, Sonny Rollins.
JEAN-LUC PONTY (vln)
  'Open Strings' (1971, with Philip Catherine a.o.)   MPS 68.088
BADEN POWELL (g)
  'Guitar Workshop' (1967, with Jim Hall, Barney Kessel, Steve
    Swallow a.o.)   MPS 68.159
BUD POWELL (p)
  'Bud Powell, vol 1' (1947–53, with Max Roach a.o.)
                                                 Reactivation JR 112
  'The Amazing Bud Powell, vols 1 and 2' (1949–53, with Roy
    Haynes, Fats Navarro, Max Roach, Sonny Rollins a.o.)
                                         Blue Note BLP 1503 & 1504
  'Inner Fires' (1953, with Roy Haynes, Charles Mingus)
                                      Elektra/Musician MUSK 52363
  See also Charles Mingus, Fats Navarro, Charlie Parker.
CHANO POZO (perc)
  See Dizzy Gillespie.
DON PULLEN (p)
  'Warriors' (1978, with Chico Freeman a.o.)
                                            Black Saint BSR 0019
  See also George Adams, Chico Freeman, Cecil McBee.
FLORA PURIM (vcl)
  See Chick Corea, George Duke.

QUINTET OF THE HOT CLUB OF FRANCE (group)
  'Django' (1935, with Stephane Grappelli, Django Reinhardt a.o.)
                                                    CBS 52213

SUN RA (p, org, synth)
  'Strange Celestial Road' (*c* 1979)   Y Records Y 19
  See also Walt Dickerson.
MA RAINEY (vcl)
  'Ma Rainey 1923-4' (1923–4, with Tommy Ladnier a.o.) VJM VLP 81
JIMMY RANEY (g)
  'Here's That Raney Day' (1980, with Hank Jones a.o.)
                                         Black & Blue/Ahead 33.756
  See also Stan Getz.

Leon Rappolo (cl)
  See New Orleans Rhythm Kings.
Dewey Redman (ts, musette)
  See Carla Bley, Charlie Haden, Keith Jarrett, Old and New
  Dreams.
Django Reinhardt (g)
  'A Swinging Affair' (1939–44, with Stephane Grappelli a.o.)
                                              Decca MOR 530
  See also Quintet of the Hot Club of France.
Buddy Rich (d)
  'Both Sides' (1946–59, with Harry Edison, Max Roach, Phil
  Woods a.o.)   Mercury 6641 574 (2 LP)
  See also Art Blakey, Tommy Dorsey, Artie Shaw, Lester Young.
Dannie Richmond (d)
  'Dannie Richmond Plays Charles Mingus' (1980)   Timeless SJP 148
  See also George Adams, Jimmy Knepper, Charles Mingus, Bennie
  Wallace.
Sam Rivers (ts, ss, fl)
  'Essence' (1976)   Circle Records RK 2976/1
  'Contrasts' (1979, with Dave Holland, George Lewis a.o.)   ECM 1162
  See also Bobby Hutcherson.
Max Roach (d)
  'We Insist: Freedom Now Suite' (1960, with Coleman Hawkins, Booker
  Little a.o.)   Amigo AMLP 810
  'Birth and Rebirth' (1978, with Anthony Braxton)
                                        Black Saint BSR 0024
  See also Art Blakey, Clifford Brown, Benny Carter, Miles Davis, Duke
  Ellington, Thelonious Monk, Charlie Parker, Bud Powell, Buddy Rich,
  Sonny Rollins.
Perry Robinson (cl)
  'The Traveller' (*c* 1977)   Chiaroscuro CR 190
  See also Carla Bley, Clarinet Summit, Charlie Haden, Gunter
  Hampel.
Sonny Rollins (ts)
  'Saxophone Colossus and More' (with Clifford Brown, Kenny Dorham,
  Tommy Flanagan, Max Roach a.o.)   Prestige (2 LP)
  'Freedom Suite' (1957–8, with Paul Chambers, Roy Haynes, Percy
  Heath, Oscar Pettiford, Max Roach a.o.)
                                        Milestone 68.103 (2 LP)
  'Don't Stop the Carnival' (1978, with Donald Byrd, Tony Williams a.o.)
                                        Milestone 68.104 (2 LP)
  See also Clifford Brown, Bud Powell.
Jimmie Rowles (p)
  See Ray Brown, Ella Fitzgerald, Dexter Gordon, Woody Herman,
  Billie Holiday.
Roswell Rudd (tb)
  See Carla Bley, Charlie Haden, Steve Lacy, Archie Shepp.

JIMMY RUSHING (vcl)
   See Count Basie, Buck Clayton, Lester Young.
PAUL RUTHERFORD (tb)
   'Old Moers Almanac' (1976)   Moers Music 01014
   See also London Jazz Composers Orchestra.
PEE WEE RUSSELL (cl)
   See Bix Beiderbecke, Wild Bill Davison, Earl Hines, Muggsy Spanier.

PHAROAH SANDERS (ts)
   'Thembi' (1970–71, with Roy Haynes, Cecil McBee a.o.)
                                                  Jasmine JAS 53
   See also John Coltrane.
MASAHIKO SATOH (p)
   'Trinity' (1971)   Enja 2008
   See also Masahiko Togashi
ALEX VON SCHLIPPENBACH (p)
   See Globe Unity Orchestra, Manfred Schoof.
MANFRED SCHOOF (tp)
   'The Early Quintet' (1966)   FMP 0540
   See also Globe Unity Orchestra.
IRENE SCHWEIZER (p)
   See Pierre Favre.
TONY SCOTT (cl)
   'Music for Yoga Meditation and Other Joys' (*c* 1964, with Collin
      Walcott)   Verve 2304.471
ZBIGNIEW SEIFERT (vln)
   'Man of the Light' (1976, with Cecil McBee, Jasper van't Hof)
                                                  MPS 68.163
   See also Charlie Mariano.
BUD SHANK (as, fl)
   'Crystal Moments' (1979)   Concord CJ 126
   See also Laurindo Almeida, Stan Kenton.
LAKSHINARAYANA SHANKAR (vln)
   'Who's to Know' (1980)   ECM 1195
CHARLIE SHAVERS (tp)
   See Lionel Hampton, John Kirby.
ARTIE SHAW (cl)
   'The Best of Artie Shaw' (1938–41, with big band incl Billie Holiday, Buddy
      Rich a.o.)   RCA INTS 5022
WOODY SHAW (tp)
   'Master of the Art' (1982, with Bobby Hutcherson a.o.)
                                      Elektra/Musician MUSK 52402
GEORGE SHEARING (p)
   'Getting in the Swing of Things' (1979, with N.-H. Ørsted Pedersen a.o.)
                                                  MPS 68.253
   See also Carmen McRae.

ARCHIE SHEPP (ts)
'Four for Trane' (1964, with Roswell Rudd, John Tchicai a.o.)
Jasmine JAS 31
'Trouble in Mind' (1980)   SteepleChase SCS 1139
See also John Coltrane.
WAYNE SHORTER (ts)
'Etcetera' (1965, with Herbie Hancock, Cecil McBee a.o.)
Blue Note LBR 1032
See also Art Blakey, Miles Davis, Weather Report.
HORACE SILVER (p)
'Horace Silver and the Jazz Messengers' (1954–5, with Art Blakey,
Kenny Dorham a.o.)   Blue Note BLP 1518
See also Milt Jackson.
OMER SIMEON (cl)
See James P. Johnson, Jelly Roll Morton, Kid Ory.
ZOOT SIMS (ts)
'Zoot Sims' (1956)   Reactivation JR 156
See also Woody Herman, Gerry Mulligan.
ALAN SKIDMORE (ts)
'S.O.H.' (1979, with Tony Oxley a.o.)   Ego 4011
See also Volker Kriegel.
BESSIE SMITH (vcl)
'Soundtrack' (1925–9, with Louis Armstrong, Coleman Hawkins,
Fletcher Henderson, James P. Johnson a.o.)   Cicala BLJ 8025
JIMMY SMITH (org)
'Off the Top' (1982, with George Benson, Ron Carter a.o.)
Elektra/Musician MUSK 52418
See also Kenny Burrell.
STUFF SMITH (vln)
'Stuff Smith' (1957, with Ray Brown, Barney Kessell, Oscar Peterson)
Verve 2304.536
MARTIAL SOLAL (p)
'The Solosolal' (1978)   MPS 68.221
SOPRANO SUMMIT (group)
'Live at Concord '77' (1977, with Kenny Davern, Bob Wilber a.o.)
Concord CJ 52
MUGGSY SPANIER (tp)
'Memorial' (1944, with Pee Wee Russell a.o.)   Saga 6917
TOMASZ STANKO (tp)
See Edward Vesala.
JEREMY STEIG (fl)
'Music for Flute and Double Bass' (1978, with Eddie Gomez)
CMP 6ST
JOHN STEVENS (d)
'1. 2. Albert Ayler' (1971, with Trevor Watts a.o.)   Affinity AFF 81
REX STEWART (tp)
'Together 1957' (1957, with Bud Freeman, Coleman Hawkins, Hank

Jones, Cootie Williams a.o.)   Jazz Anthology JA 5201
See also Sidney Bechet, Benny Carter, Duke Ellington, Lionel Hampton,
    Fletcher Henderson.
SONNY STITT (as, ts)
    'Now!' (1963, with Hank Jones a.o.)   Jasmine JAS 25
    See also Gene Ammons, Dizzy Gillespie, Fats Navarro.
SUPERSAX (group)
    'Chasin' the Bird' (1976)   MPS 68.160
JOHN SURMAN (bs, ss, bcl, synth)
    'Upon Reflection' (1979)   ECM 1148
    See also Miroslav Vitous.
STEVE SWALLOW (b)
    'Home' (1979, with Dave Liebman a.o.)   ECM 1160
    See also Carla Bley, Gary Burton, Baden Powell.

LEW TABACKIN (ts, fl)
    See Toshiko Akiyoshi.
BUDDY TATE (ts)
    'Crazy Legs and Friday Strut' (1976, with Jay McShann)
                                                Sackville 3011
    See also Buck Clayton, Arnett Cobb, Scott Hamilton, Lester Young.
ART TATUM (p)
    'Masterpieces' (1934–44, with Edmond Hall, Joe Turner a.o.)
                                                MCA 2-4019 (2 LP)
    'Art Tatum Group Masterpieces, vol 1' (1954, with Louie Bellson,
    Benny Carter)   Pablo 2310.732
    'Art Tatum Group Masterpieces, vol 6' (1956, with Ben Webster a.o.)
                                                Pablo 2310.737
    See also Coleman Hawkins.
CECIL TAYLOR (p)
    'Air Above Mountains (Buildings Within)' (1976)   Enja 3005
    'Live in the Black Forest' (1978, with Ronald Shannon Jackson a.o.)
                                                MPS 68.220
    'Fly! Fly! Fly! Fly! Fly!' (1980)   MPS 68.263
JOHN TCHICAI (as)
    See John Coltrane, Archie Shepp.
JACK TEAGARDEN (tb)
    'Big Jack and Mighty Max' (1944, with Max Kaminsky a.o.)
                                                London 6.24060
    See also Louis Armstrong.
CLARK TERRY (tp)
    'The Happy Horns of Clark Terry' (1964, with Ben Webster, Phil
    Woods a.o.)   Jasmine JAS 28
    See also Bob Brookmeyer, Wardell Gray, J. J. Johnson.
EJE THELIN (tb)
    'Eje Thelin Group Live '76' (1976)   Caprice CAP 2007 (2 LP)
    See also Clarinet Summit, Kenny Wheeler.

TOOTS THIELEMANS (g, hca)
   'Live' (1974, with N.-H. Ørsted Pedersen a.o.)   Polydor 2489.175
   See also Bill Evans.
BARBARA THOMPSON (ts, ss, fl)
   'Paraphernalia' (1979)   MCA 1605
   See also United Jazz & Rock Ensemble.
LUCKY THOMPSON (ts, ss)
   'Body and Soul' (1970, with Tete Montoliu a.o.)   Nessa n-13
   See also Dizzy Gillespie, Milt Jackson, Thelonious Monk, Charlie
      Parker.
HENRY THREADGILL (as, ts, fl)
   See Air, David Murray.
MASAHIKO TOGASHI (d, perc)
   'Minamoto' (1980, with Masahiko Satoh)   MPS 15.581
RALPH TOWNER (g)
   'Solo Concert' (1979)   ECM 1173
   See also John Abercrombie, Oregon.
STAN TRACEY (p)
   'Hello Old Adversary' (1978-9)   Steam SJ 107
   See also Clarinet Summit.
LENNIE TRISTANO (p)
   'Requiem' (1955, with Lee Konitz a.o.)   Atlantic ATL 50245
GIANLUIGI TROVESI (cl)
   See Clarinet Summit.
JOE TURNER (vcl)
   'The Boss of the Blues' (1956, with Pete Johnson, Joe Newman,
      Frank Wess, a.o.)   Atlantic ATL 50244
   See also Art Tatum.
McCOY TYNER (p)
   'Nights of Ballads and Blues' (1963)   Jasmine JAS 35
   'Reflections' (1972-5, with Ron Carter, Bobby Hutcherson, Elvin
      Jones, Alphonse Mouzon a.o.)   Milestone M 47062 (2 LP)
   See also John Coltrane.

JAMES BLOOD ULMER (g, vcl)
   'No Wave' (1980, with Ronald Shannon Jackson, David Murray a.o.)
      Moers Music 01072
   'Are You Glad to be in America' (1980, with Ronald Shannon
      Jackson, Oliver Lake, David Murray a.o.)   Rough Trade 16
UNITED JAZZ & ROCK ENSEMBLE (group)
   'The Break Even Point' (1979, with Ian Carr, Volker Kriegel,
      Albert Mangelsdorff, Charlie Mariano, Barbara Thompson, Eberhard
      Weber, Kenny Wheeler a.o.)   Mood Records 23600

TOM VAN DER GELD (vib)
   'Out Patients' (1980)   Japo 60035
   See also Kenny Wheeler.

JASPER VAN'T HOF (p, synth)
'However' (1977, with Alphonse Mouzon)   MPS 68.181
See also Philip Catherine, Zbigniew Seifert.
NANA VASCONCELOS (perc)
'Saudades' (1979, with Egberto Gismonti)   ECM 1147
See also Don Cherry.
SARAH VAUGHAN (vcl)
'Sarah Vaughan, vol 1' (1962, with Barney Kessel a.o.)
                                          Reactivation JR 109
JOE VENUTI (vln)
'Live at Concord' (1975)   Concord CJ 30
See also Bix Beiderbecke.
EDWARD VESALA (d)
'Heavy Life' (1980, with Chico Freeman, Tomasz Stanko a.o.)
                                          Leo Records 009
See also Kenny Wheeler.
MIROSLAV VITOUS (b)
'ecm' (1980, with John Surman a.o.)   ECM 1185
See also Herbie Mann, Weather Report.

ABDUL WADUD (cello)
See Barry Altschul, Arthur Blythe.
COLLIN WALCOTT (perc, sitar)
'Cloud Dance' (1975, with John Abercrombie, Jack DeJohnette,
    Dave Holland)   ECM 1062
See also Don Cherry, Oregon, Tony Scott.
MAL WALDRON (p)
'Moods' (1978, with Terumasa Hino, Steve Lacy a.o.)
                                          Enja 3021/3 (2 LP)
See also Ron Carter, Eric Dolphy, Charles Mingus.
T-BONE WALKER (vcl, g)
'Plain Old Blues' (1946–47)   Charly CRB 1037
BENNIE WALLACE (ts)
'The Free Will' (1980, with Tommy Flanagan, Eddie Gomez, Dannie
    Richmond)   Enja 3063
FATS WALLER (p, vcl)
'Piano Solos' (1929–41)   RCA PM 43270 (2 LP)
'Ain't Misbehavin'' (1929–38)   RCA INTS 5009
DINAH WASHINGTON (vcl)
'The Swinging Miss D' (1956, with Quincy Jones big band)
                                          Mercury 6336 714
MUDDY WATERS (vcl, g)
'The Chess Masters' (1948–56)   Chess CXMD 4000 (2 LP)
TREVOR WATTS (as, ss)
See London Jazz Composers Orchestra, John Stevens.
WEATHER REPORT (group)
'Weather Report' (1971, with Alphonse Mouzon, Wayne Shorter,
    Miroslav Vitous, Joe Zawinul)   CBS 32024

'Night Passage' (1979, with Jaco Pastorius, Wayne Shorter, Joe
    Zawinul a.o.)   CBS 22134
CHICK WEBB (d)
'A Legend' (1929–36, with Benny Carter, Ella Fitzgerald, John
    Kirby a.o.)   MCA 1303
    See also Ella Fitzgerald.
EBERHARD WEBER (b)
'The Colours of Chloe' (1973)   ECM 1042
    See also Volker Kriegel, United Jazz & Rock Ensemble.
BEN WEBSTER (ts)
'Soulville' (1957, with Ray Brown, Herb Ellis, Oscar Peterson a.o.)
                                                           Verve 2304.314
'See You at the Fair' (1964, with Richard Davis, Hank Jones a.o.)
                                                           Jasmine JAS 33
    See also Don Byas, Duke Ellington, Fletcher Henderson, Billie
    Holiday, Art Tatum, Clark Terry.
DICKIE WELLS (tb)
    See Count Basie, Lester Young.
FRANK WESS (ts, fl)
    See Count Basie, Joe Turner.
MIKE WESTBROOK (p)
'The Paris Album' (1981)   Polydor 2655 008 (2 LP)
KENNY WHEELER (tp)
'Around 6' (1979, with Evan Parker, Eje Thelin, Tom van der
    Geld, Edward Vesala a.o.)   ECM 1156
    See also Globe Unity Orchestra, United Jazz & Rock Ensemble.
BOB WILBER (cl, ss)
    See Soprano Summit.
COOTIE WILLIAMS (tp)
    See Duke Ellington, Benny Goodman, Lionel Hampton, Coleman
    Hawkins, Rex Stewart.
MARY LOU WILLIAMS (p)
'The First Lady of Piano' (1955)   Jazz Anthology JA 5187
'Montreux Solo Recital' (1978)   Pablo 2308.218
TONY WILLIAMS (d)
    See Miles Davis, Herbie Hancock, Didier Lockwood, Sonny Rollins.
SONNY BOY WILLIAMSON (vcl, hca)
'Blues Roots, vol 10' (1963)   Storyville 6.23709
TEDDY WILSON (p)
'Teddy Wilson' (1956–70)   Reactivation JR 108
    See also Benny Goodman, Gene Krupa, Red Norvo, Lester Young.
KAI WINDING (tb)
'Giant Bones '80' (1980)   Sonet SNTF 834
    See also Miles Davis, J. J. Johnson.
PHIL WOODS (as)
'Chromatic Banana' (1970, with Gordon Beck a.o.)
                                                   Affinity AFF 84
'Birds of a Feather' (1981)   Antilles AN 1006

See also Benny Carter, Thelonious Monk, Buddy Rich, Clark Terry.

WORLD SAXOPHONE QUARTET (group)
'Point of No Return' (1977, with Hamiet Bluiett, Julius Hemphill, Oliver Lake, David Murray)   Moers Music 01034

YOSUKE YAMASHITA (p)
'Inner Space' (1977)   Enja 3001
JIMMY YANCEY (p)
'The Yancey/Lofton Sessions, vol 1' (1943, with Cripple Clarence Lofton)   Storyville SLP 238
LESTER YOUNG (ts)
'The Lester Young Story, vol 1' (1936-7, with Count Basie, Buck Clayton, Benny Goodman, Edmond Hall, Johnny Hodges, Billie Holiday, Jo Jones, Jimmy Rushing, Teddy Wilson a.o.)
                                                 CBS 88223 (2 LP)
'Pres and Friends' (1944, with Jo Jones, Dicky Wells a.o.)
                                                 London 6.24292
'Pres/The Complete Savoy Recordings' (1944-9, with Harry Edison, Roy Haynes, Jo Jones, Buddy Tate, Dicky Wells a.o.)
                                                 Savoy SJL 2202 (2 LP)
'Lester Swings' (1945-51, with Nat King Cole, Hank Jones, Jo Jones, John Lewis, Buddy Rich a.o.)   Verve 2610.039 (2 LP)
See also Count Basie, Benny Goodman.

JOE ZAWINUL (p, synth)
See Miles Davis, Weather Report.

INDEX

Index